The Anthology of Social Studies

Issues and Strategies for
Secondary Teachers

UPDATED EDITION

The Anthology

of Social Studies

Issues and Strategies

for Secondary Teachers

UPDATED EDITION

Roland Case

Penney Clark

Editors

Copyright 2016 Roland Case and Penney Clark
ISBN 978-0-86491-388-3

The Critical Thinking Consortium
1580 West Broadway
Vancouver, BC V6J 5K8
Fax: 604.639.6325
Tel: 604.639.6325
E-mail: mail@tc2.ca
Web: www.tc2.ca

Cover Illustration: Genie Macleod
Cover Design: Five Seventeen
Editing: Catherine Edwards
Production: M. Kathie Wraight
Photographs are used courtesy of Susan Duncan

Library and Archives Canada Cataloguing in Publication Data

Issues and strategies for secondary teachers
    The anthology of social studies : issues and strategies for secondary teachers / Roland Case, Penney Clark, editors. -- Updated edition.

Updated edition of Issues and strategies for secondary teachers, volume 2, contained in the two volume set The anthology of social studies. Includes bibliographical references and index.
ISBN 978-0-86491-388-3 (paperback)

    1. Social sciences--Study and teaching (Secondary). 2. Education, Secondary--Curricula. 3. Educational innovations. I. Case, Roland, 1951-, author, editor II. Clark, Penney, 1950-, author, editor III. Critical Thinking Consortium, issuing body IV. Title.

LB1584.I87 2015   300.71'2   C2015-907307-3

Printed in Canada
2   3   4   5   16   17   18   19

In memory of our parents
Warren and Mary Case
Hugh and Mildred Clark

Contents

Preface

We have made minor revisions in this edition to accommodate emerging changes in social studies, history and geography curricula across Canada. To this end, we have substantially redeveloped chapter 2 ("Making Sense of the Curriculum") to reflect changing outcomes and terminology, and updated the curriculum examples in chapter 23 ("Course, Unit, and Lesson Planning for Secondary Teachers"). We now refer more broadly to the goal of "thinking" (as opposed to "critical thinking") to reflect growing recognition of historical and geographical thinking. In addition, reference to the more inclusive goal of "information gathering and communication" (rather than "information gathering") recognizes the emergence of this goal as a significant student competency.

Notwithstanding these modest changes, this work is in a true sense an anthology that marries the best of theory and practice in social studies. The word "anthology" originally meant a collection of flowers. It subsequently came to refer to a collection of the "flowers" of verse and, by extension, to the "flowers" of professional and scholarly thinking. Like a bouquet, this anthology of thirty-four chapters by thirty-four teachers and teacher educators from across Canada has the diversity and richness that comes only from a multiplicity of viewpoints and experiences. Like a carefully arranged bouquet, the different perspectives—rather than competing with others in the volume—complement and accentuate the features of the other chapters. In this respect, we are especially proud of both the harmony and the diversity of ideas in this volume. Collectively, they speak of a powerful and exciting vision of social studies. As well, they blend in countless very specific, practical suggestions with important discussions of the foundational issues at the heart of social studies teaching. We believe this new book will be of even greater value as a methods text for beginning teachers in teacher education programs and as a professional resource for experienced teachers and other educators working in social studies.

In a project of this magnitude, many individuals deserve thanks for the crucial contributions they have made. We especially appreciate the authors of the works found in this anthology. We believe they are among the finest educators and teacher educators in Canadian social studies, history, and geography, and their writings reflect this expertise. In addition, we are most grateful for the support and diligence of our editorial and production team: Usha James, director of publication development; Catherine Edwards, editor; and Kathie Wraight, desktop publisher. Our thanks go out to Susan Howell and her team at Pacific Educational Press for orchestrating a smooth transfer to our new publisher.

Finally, we acknowledge the contributions of two organizations that have occupied much of our professional and academic efforts over the past number of years: The History Education Network (THEN/HiER), www.thenhier.ca, and The Critical Thinking Consortium (TC[2]), www.tc2.ca.

Roland Case
Penney Clark

PART 1 Foundations

1 The Teaching of History and Democratic Citizenship

Ken Osborne

Introduction

More than other political systems, democracy depends for its health upon the qualities of its citizens. It requires them to be knowledgeable, in the sense of possessing both general knowledge and a working knowledge of their country and the world, while also being informed about public affairs. It also requires them to be intellectually skilled, literate, able to think critically, and to handle controversy in rational, non-violent ways. No less importantly, it expects them to hold certain values, including tolerance, respect for human rights, empathy, and, of course, commitment to the principles of democracy itself. Since we are obviously not born with these qualities, we have to be taught them. Thus, education for citizenship plays an important role in democratic societies.

An effective program of citizenship education should include both analysis of public issues and direct engagement in political life, for example, through participation in election campaigns, involvement in local problems, and the like. Its focus should be on what Parker (2003) calls "enlightened political engagement" (see also Oliver and Shaver 1966; Newmann 1975; Osborne 1984). The focus of this chapter is much more restricted. It explores how history teachers can, within the constraints of existing curricula, contribute to the education of democratic citizens in a Canadian context.

The Nature and Meaning of Citizenship

CONCEPTIONS OF CITIZENSHIP

Citizenship is a notoriously vague word that means different things to different people. Its specific meaning takes its shape from the particular political and institutional context in which it is located. To some, it indicates ideological indoctrination, the preparation of loyal servants of whatever regime is in power. To others, it means instilling the disposition to abide by and to help preserve the status quo. In Canada, for example, it was the justification for sending aboriginal children to residential schools and for curtailing the linguistic and other rights of minorities.

Democratic citizenship, however, does not mean conformity or subordination, but informed and reflective participation in the affairs of one's society, consistent with democratic principles and procedures. In its contemporary form, its origins are to be found in the American and French revolutions with their insistence that "the people" have the right to govern themselves. Although historically there were many exclusions from "the people"—including women, slaves, the poor, and others—once the principle was established that the people were the only legitimate source of political authority, it became possible to argue about just who the people were. A clear distinction began to emerge between the newer concept of citizen and the older concept of subject.

This concept of the people carried a territorial connotation: the people were people of a particular sort living in a particular space, more or less united by common attributes, responsibilities, values, and aspirations. They were, or ought to be, a nation, and as a nation they considered themselves entitled to their own territorial and political unit, the nation-state. This view became nineteenth-century orthodoxy. Nationalism was entrenched more solidly than ever within this concept of citizenship. Thus arose the essential ingredients of citizenship as the word is generally understood today: first, a sense of identity with some wider community, usually defined as the nation; second, a set of rights and entitlements; third, a corresponding set of obligations; and, fourth, a commitment to the values that are seen as inseparable from citizenship in a given community.

DEMOCRATIC CITIZENSHIP AND THE STUDY OF HISTORY

At the same time, citizenship is not a static entity. Its boundaries are always being tested, sometimes expanding and sometimes shrinking. Above all, it is closely connected with struggle. What we now take for granted as democratic citizenship rights were either won by subordinate groups in a struggle against the dominant order of their day, or were yielded by the dominant order as a calculated response to a real or perceived challenge to its authority. It is a process that continues today and will persist into the future and should form a continuing theme in any history course.

From its beginnings in ancient Athens, citizenship carried a certain democratic connotation. Citizens formed a community of equals who governed themselves, though it is true that they usually comprised only a small, male, and property-owning fraction of the total society of which they were a part. By contrast, the central concepts of democratic citizenship today are its insistence that no one should be barred from citizenship because of gender, race, or class; that all citizens should be able to exercise their citizenship rights and obligations effectively; and that inequalities that frustrate this must be eliminated. To accomplish this, there is an important place for education, though education alone will not be sufficient to the task. Even so, education can at least aim to give all people the knowledge, skills, and dispositions that will enable them to exercise their rights and fulfill their obligations, and, more generally, to ensure that citizenship is not curtailed, while also taking part in the continuing debate over what it means to be a citizen in a democracy. There is an obvious role here for history.

Today, citizenship can no longer be defined in exclusively national terms. We live in an age of international problems that not only transcend national borders but are also beyond the ability of national governments to solve. The proper balance between national and global thinking and action is a matter of debate, for we are not yet at a time when we can simply give our undivided loyalty to some global authority. There can, however, be little doubt that we must think of citizenship in global as well as national terms. To speak of education for citizenship means producing citizens who can weigh their attachment to their country against their attachment to the planet and the human species (and, some would add, non-human species). Here again is an obvious role for the study of history.

More fundamentally, the attainment of democratic citizenship depends not only upon people learning how to exercise their rights and obligations, but also upon institutional change. We need to extend our conception of democracy beyond the idea of representation to that of participation, deliberation, and dialogue (see, for example, Held 1993). However, if participatory democracy is to become a reality, it will need an educational foundation. Above all, to use C.B. Macpherson's words, it will mean "a change in people's consciousness (or unconsciousness) from seeing themselves and acting as essentially consumers, to seeing themselves and acting as exerters and enjoyers of the exertion and development of their capacities" (1977, 99). Here again, there is an obvious role for education and, more specifically, for history. We could, for example, perform a useful service for our students, and for democracy generally, by teaching them about the history of citizenship, both in theory and in practice.

History, Citizenship, and Schooling

HISTORY AND THE NATION-STATE

Compulsory public schooling is the creation of the nation-state. Despite the nationalist belief that nations were the product of history or somehow created themselves, it was realized early that political ideology had to be explicitly taught and national spirit had to be created and maintained. In the words of a nineteenth-century Italian nationalist, "We have made Italy; now we must make Italians" (Hobsbawm and Ranger 1983, 267). In this process, schools were assigned a central role. For obvious reasons, the study of history was assigned a prominent role in this educational enterprise. Along with literature, and supported by a panoply of school rituals and ceremonies, the study of history was the major vehicle for the creation of national citizenship. Anything that could be shown to contribute to the building of the nation was duly commemorated and described as good. Anything that did not was either condemned or ignored as irrelevant. This meant that Canadian history, for example, was seen largely as the building of the federation, with a consequent emphasis upon central Canada. It also meant that history was seen in very Whiggish terms. History was whatever shaped and led to the present. And, as one would expect, the present was seen as a pretty desirable place to be.

History texts made it clear that nations were the work of exceptional individuals—larger-than-life explorers, heroic generals, far-sighted statesmen, intrepid pioneers. There would be an occasional reference to what might be called ordinary people, but readers were then immediately whisked off into the world of the great and famous. Thus, Canadian students learned that Confederation was the work of a handful of "fathers"; that the Canadian Pacific Railway was built by William Van Horne; that Quebec was defended by Montcalm and conquered by Wolfe. And, of course, these great men were indeed men. Women rarely appeared in the pages of these texts, and when they did, it was usually doing what was regarded as women's work, such as teaching or nursing. Working people were similarly ignored. Native people were equally invisible, and when they were described, it was usually in ethnocentric or racist terms.

HISTORY AND THE DISEMPOWERMENT OF STUDENTS

Overwhelmingly, the story of nation-building was presented precisely as story, with all the authority of narrative. The impression was created that, not only was this the way things happened, but also that they could have happened in no other way. Despite the urging of a few pedagogical innovators, no scope was allowed for historiography or interpretation. History was the story of what happened, plain and simple. From a student's viewpoint, one could not do much with a story, or at least not with stories as presented in textbooks, except to learn them and to learn from them, for the stories often carried a moral message. Even at their best, however, textbook narratives were not designed to be questioned. They were intended to entertain, to excite, and above all, to instruct. Their very form reinforced the perception that history was a body of information to be learned, a perception that was confirmed by the reduction of political education to the memorization of civics. By and large history was something before which a student stood powerless.

This disempowering view of history was reinforced by the dominant mode of teaching, which was largely examination-driven. Provincial examinations were standard practice in all provinces until the 1960s and consisted almost exclusively of questions that relied only on factual recall. In response, teachers ensured that their students were well-drilled on the material they expected to be on the examination. Obviously, there were exceptions to this. There must have been adventurous teachers such as Agnes Macphail who, in the early 1900s,

> abandoned much that she had been taught about rigid discipline and rote-learning of lessons in order to arouse her students' interest in the world around and inside of themselves. She brought newspapers into the classroom, played games, and had heart-to-heart talks with the children about what they wanted to do with their lives. She became even more unorthodox in her teaching methods as she detested the school system's emphasis on exam preparation. She persuaded her board to subscribe to a magazine and daily newspaper for her classes to study. She also brought the books of Grey County native Nellie McClung into the classroom so that older children could share her reformist and feminist ideas (Crowley 1990, 20–21).

Such teachers, however, were the exception rather than the rule. The history teaching described by Hodgetts in 1968 in schools across the country was light years removed from Macphail's imaginative practice. The bleak and depressing picture presented in *What Culture? What Heritage?* is well-known, though it is worth noting that Hodgetts himself assessed history teaching in terms of its contribution to the education of citizens. In doing so, he found it sorely wanting, producing the very opposite of the goals to which it was ostensibly committed (Hodgetts 1968).

CRITICISMS OF TRADITIONAL HISTORY

The conservative bias of history did not go unchallenged. Socialists and trade unionists attacked its class bias; agrarian radicals condemned its economic orthodoxy; feminists pointed to its gendered assumptions. Between the wars, the Women's International League for Peace and Freedom criticized textbooks and curricula for overemphasizing militarism and patriotism. The League of Nations Society called for a greater emphasis on international understanding. H.G. Wells added his powerful voice to the campaign to change history teaching, a question on which he declared himself to be a "fanatic." He argued that history teachers must take a good part of the blame for World War I, since it had resulted in large part from an excess of national and patriotic fervour on all sides, the result of the "poison called history" that had been taught in schools. Wells called instead for the abandonment of national and military history and its replacement with an emphasis on economic, cultural, and social history. He wanted history taught so that it showed the unfolding of a spirit of world community, leading in short order to the world state, and resulting in people identifying themselves not as national citizens, but as members of the human species (Wells 1939; Osborne 1991b).

Such criticisms were never more than skirmishes. Traditional history's main defences remained unbreached. During the 1960s, however, this began to change. This was the result not so much of attacks from without as disintegration from within, as history proved to have few public defenders, even among its own teachers. Admittedly, after the depressing revelations of *What Culture? What Heritage?* in 1968, there was not much to defend. Most people accepted the book's devastating criticisms of the state of history teaching in the schools. Hodgetts intended it to be the launching pad for a renewed and revived history curriculum, but instead, history found itself challenged by the new interdisciplinary subject known as Canadian Studies (Hodgetts and Gallagher 1978).

This move away from history was given some credibility by researchers who used Piagetian theory to argue that even high school students did not understand history. Some researchers flatly said that students could never understand it, since they had not reached a sufficiently sophisticated level of cognitive development (for a summary of this research, see Osborne 1975; Wineburg 2001, 28–60). Today, we have a clearer understanding of the limitations of this research, and we are more optimistic about the capacity of students to understand history (Stearns, Seixas, and Wineburg 2000; Wineburg 2001), but in the 1970s, it did not help history's cause.

The History Wars

HAS HISTORY BEEN KILLED?

Today, history finds itself under increasing pressure from courses in interdisciplinary social studies and the individual social sciences. Students still learn (or at least are taught, which is not necessarily the same thing) about the major events of Canada's past, but in the context of social studies courses rather than of history as traditionally defined. They learn about "the past," but they do not necessarily learn "history."

I have tried to explain the reasons for this shift elsewhere (Osborne 2000, 2003), but the main point is that it is presumably not coincidental that it occurred at the same time that history itself was undergoing something of a crisis (Seixas 1993). Indeed, one well-known Canadian historian, Jack Granatstein, claimed that Canadian history was dead, killed by a combination of social historians, multiculturalists, and anti-intellectual educationists, aided and abetted by the indifference of the historical profession generally. Others, such as Australia's Keith Windschuttle, added post-modernists and literary theorists to the list of history's murderers (Windschuttle 1997; Granatstein 1998; for an American example, see Schlesinger 1992).

In reality, Granatstein, Windschuttle, and others were lamenting, not so much the death of history, but rather the decline of the kind of history they favoured, essentially a chronological narrative of political and military events, placed within their social and economic context, and organized within a national, and indeed nation-building, framework. This kind of history, in fact, is far from dead, but by the 1990s, it no longer represented the cutting edge, or even the mainstream orthodoxy, of academic historical writing and research.

NEW DIRECTIONS IN HISTORY

From the 1960s onwards, historians sought new subjects to investigate and new methodologies to examine them. Social historians challenged political historians, while the more ambitious social historians aspired to write, not just social history, but an all-inclusive history of society that might even unearth the laws of social development. Labour history became working-class history as the institutional history of trade unions, labour legislation, and strikes was superseded by analyses of class formation and class struggle, and investigations of working-class culture. The history of education changed from being a celebration of social progress to an analysis of the role of schools as instruments of cultural reproduction, social control, and ideological hegemony. Feminist historians pointed out that conventional history largely ignored half the human race and totally ignored the way gender operated to shape people's behaviour and outlook. At the same time, so-called ethnic historians uncovered the past of groups who had traditionally been seen as people without a history, or at least without a history that was worth remembering. In the process, history-from-above, the history of élites and decision makers, gave way to history-from-below, the history of so-called ordinary people, who proved to be, not the victims of history, as had been commonly supposed, but active makers of history in their own right.

Today, social history has itself been to some extent superseded by a shift to cultural history and by the so-called linguistic turn. Instead of examining how the social realities of their environments shaped the people of the past, historians increasingly focus on how people's habits of mind, language, and ways of thinking shaped their understanding of the world in which they lived. The result has been an ever-increasing widening of the scope of historical writing and research, to the point that some historians now argue that history as a discipline has lost whatever coherence and cohesion it once had, so that it can no longer be considered to be a unified discipline in any real sense. At the same time, even though most historians have resisted the more provocative forms of post-modernist thinking, they have been unable to withstand post-modernism's debunking of the idea of historical objectivity. (For useful surveys of the growth of history, and the debates it has provoked, see Novick 1988; Appleby, Hunt, and Jacob 1994; Evans 1997; Iggers 1997; Shore 2002.)

HAVE HISTORY AND CITIZENSHIP BEEN FRAGMENTED?

One immediate result of this enlarging of history's scope has been to enliven the teaching of history. Teachers have at their disposal, especially as the internet has grown, an ever-increasing variety of topics, examples, anecdotes, resources, and approaches. It seems, however, that there is a price to be paid for this new richness of scene and character. The word that has been most often heard in recent years is "fragmentation." We are told that history's old narrative coherence has gone, to which some add the rider that it was always suspect anyway. The very idea of narrative has come under attack. On the one hand, scientific historians have eschewed narrative for analysis, insisting that history is not about the telling of stories but the investigation of problems and the testing of hypotheses. On the other, literary theorists have drawn attention to the artificiality of narrative, showing that history's storyline is the creation of the historian, not the revelation of the past as it actually happened.

The proliferation of historical research has raised the question of just whose version of the past is being revealed. Feminist historians, for example, have demonstrated that there was no Renaissance for women and that the French Revolution did little to advance the cause of women's rights. Historians of the First Nations have shown that the settling of the western Prairies, that celebratory textbook staple of nation-building Canadian history, was preceded by the signing of treaties, the setting aside of reserves, the institution of the pass system, and the creation of the whole array of Indian Affairs administrative practices that were designed to clear the First Nations off most of their ancestral lands and open these lands up to European exploitation. Similarly, immigration historians have revealed the ethnic and racist biases of immigration policy. If history was the story of nation-building, as it long had been in schools, it seemed that the nation had a good deal to answer for.

The result has been to call into question the traditional link between history and citizenship, at least so far as schools are concerned. More than one historian saw a clear connection between the fragmentation of history and a decline in people's sense of citizenship. Michael Bliss, for example, detected a "parallel relationship between the disintegration of Canadian history as a unified discipline on the one hand, and, on the other, the withering of a sense of community in Canada" (Bliss 1991–92, 5). For their part, political scientists drew attention to the fragmentation of Canadian citizenship, arguing that traditional conceptions of citizenship could no longer suffice: "Canadian notions of citizenship are undergoing important changes that, while they may have positive effects, require Canadians to confront traditional understandings of what it means to be a Canadian" (Lazar and McIntosh 1999, 7–8; Cairns 1995, 157–185).

HISTORY, CITIZENSHIP, AND NATION-BUILDING

From the very beginnings of compulsory public schooling in the late nineteenth and early twentieth centuries, history was taught as a nation-building subject. Textbook titles made this message clear: *Building the Canadian Nation; Canada—A Nation and How It Came To Be; From Colony to Nation*. The purpose of teaching history was to instill in the young a sense of national identity and national pride, especially in countries such as Canada, where many of the young were the children of immigrants who did not speak the languages of their new land or share its ancestral attachments. The second purpose was to teach them the personal values and political commit-

ments upon which national identity was based. In the case of Canada, this meant teaching students to value the principles of parliamentary democracy and liberal capitalism, and, before 1945 or thereabouts, attachment to the monarchy and the British Empire.

HISTORY, CITIZENSHIP, AND NATION-BUILDING: NEW QUESTIONS

But now, it appeared, the nation had a seamy side that traditional history had kept hidden. How did one square the principles of Canadian democracy with the exclusion of black, Asian, and Jewish immigrants at different times in Canada's history? With the treatment of aboriginal peoples? With the yet-to-be concluded struggles over minority rights? Was the nation, after all, simply a vehicle for legitimizing the hegemony of dominant élites? When textbooks spoke of building the Canadian nation, just whose nation were they talking about? Were history textbooks, in the words of one survey, simply "teaching prejudice" (McDiarmid and Pratt 1971)? Was history nothing more than a national myth (Francis 1997; Loewen 1996)? If old history was the story of nation-building, new history seemed to call the very idea of nationhood into question. A nation, we are told, is simply a form of "imagined community." Traditions are usually invented. Collective memory is a social construct. Heritage is an ideological and cultural imposition—that is, when it is not a purely commercial enterprise (Hobsbawm and Ranger 1983; Anderson 1991; McKay 1994; Lowenthal 1996).

The new social history called the old nation-building approach into question in another way, not so much by challenging the assumptions on which the concepts of nationhood and nationality are founded, but by the very nature of its research priorities. It was, and is, one of the standard complaints of critics of the new history that it does not take the nation as its focus of attention. In the words of one commentator, "the new research and writing in Canadian economic and social history asked implicitly whether the old paradigm of heroic nation-building was flexible enough to provide a framework for new insights. By 1970, it was clear that it was not" (Bumsted 1997, 539). To put the criticism another way, history is accused of being no longer national, or at least not as overtly national as it once was. Instead, it occupies itself with gender, race, class, region, culture, ethnicity, *mentalité*, or other such subjects, which either do not correspond to national lines, or cut across them. Working in largely unmapped territory, social historians necessarily turned to local studies. In a country as large and diverse as Canada, there was no way to write a Canadian history of the working class, for example, until the necessary local studies had been done. As a result, social history in its many forms (women's history, ethnic history, working-class history, Native history, and the rest) was not national history in the sense that political history was. It was not so much anti-national as a-national.

In the process, it disrupted the prevailing nation-building tradition in at least five ways. First, it addressed local and regional, rather than national, themes. Second, it either downplayed or ignored established historical landmarks such as the establishment of Confederation or responsible government, or went further by suggesting alternative periodizations of history. Third, it sometimes showed the national state in a negative light. Fourth, it dismissed the preoccupation of traditional history with "great men" (and the occasional woman), focussing instead on so-called ordinary people, while insisting that history was not the product of larger-than-life individuals but rather of social forces and structural trends. Fifth, by its very nature, and sometimes quite explicitly, it showed that there was an alternative version of the past to that which traditional textbooks portrayed, so that existing topics appeared in a new light, and previously unknown topics now came to the fore.

These trends should not be exaggerated. It was not so much that one version of the past replaced another, as that the new version of the past was merged with the old, at least in schools. This inevitably caused problems of inclusion and selection when it came to curriculum design and textbook writing. At the university level, it more often than not resulted in textbooks becoming larger, requiring two volumes where one had previously sufficed. It might be that the schools' move to an interdisciplinary social studies approach to the past has eased the problem of curriculum design by making it possible for them to parcel out topics among a variety of courses instead of having to pack everything into one single history course. Whatever the case, there can be little doubt that what schools teach students about the past is more comprehensive and inclusive, even if more fragmented, than it once was.

Osborne identifies four ingredients of citizenship:

- a sense of identity with a broader community;
- possession of rights and entitlements;
- recognition of accompanying obligations;
- commitment to core values.

It is widely thought that social studies and history are intended to promote citizenship. Explain what you see to be the most significant shortcomings of "traditional history"— to use Osborne's term—in promoting each of these four aspects of citizenship.

History and Citizenship

OPPOSITION TO THE NEW HISTORY: SIX CHARGES

Even so, critics have charged historians and schools alike with severing the traditional linkage between history and citizenship (Osborne 2003; for non-Canadian examples, see Nash, Crabtree, and Dunn 1997; Phillips 1998; Symcox 2002; MacIntyre and Clark 2003). In doing so, they make six broad accusations. First, they argue that history curricula no longer have a national focus, but instead emphasize regional, ethnic, or other sub-national themes. Second, they claim that history no longer tells a coherent story, having abandoned narrative for the examination of themes or issues or concepts. As a result, it is said, students are not presented with a developmentally coherent and intelligible story of the formation of the Canadian nation-state and the shaping of the Canadian people, so they lack a sense of heritage and respect for the achievements of the past. Third, critics argue that history has become "victimology," as curricula follow the example of historians and concentrate on the stories of those who have been discriminated against and exploited—not the builders of the nation, but its victims. This "black arm-band" or "compensatory" history, it is said, inevitably weakens students' sense of pride in their nation's accomplishments and thus erodes the sense of citizenship that schools were designed to create. Fourth, critics claim that curricula have responded to the imperatives of multiculturalism by transforming what should be the national story into a celebration and affirmation of distinct ethnic and cultural identities, thereby further eroding an already tenuous sense of shared nationhood. Fifth, according to the critics, history education has sacrificed content for process, so that students are no longer expected to memorize basic historical facts, but only to practise skills and feel good about themselves. Sixth, critics point to the many surveys showing how little history students remember, observing that this historical ignorance erodes the very foundations of citizenship.

THE SIX CHARGES EXAMINED

There is not space here to examine these six criticisms in detail, but most of them are open to question. Regarding the first, recent surveys of school curricula suggest that the standard topics of Canadian history (the Conquest, the War of 1812, Confederation, the settlement of the West, and so on) remain in place in school curricula, while room has been found for fuller treatment of aboriginal history, women's history, and, to a lesser extent, working-class history or people's history (Shields and Ramsay 2002; Charland and Moisan

2003). It is true that such topics are increasingly embedded in interdisciplinary social studies courses rather than in history as traditionally defined, but there is, in effect, a sort of de facto national history curriculum in place in Canadian schools. Whether it is best taught as social studies or as history is another question. My personal preference is for history, but a reasonable case can be made for either approach (Osborne 2004).

Regarding the second criticism, it is true that history curricula and textbooks no longer present the coherent narrative that was common a generation ago. Curricula are increasingly organized around themes and concepts rather than chronology, while textbooks are broken up into sidebars, short passages of text, exercises and organizers, and various other devices that, while they might increase the usefulness and attraction of the book, also sacrifice narrative line for a more segmented form of presentation. However, there is no evidence that these new approaches have had an adverse effect on students' understanding of or attitudes towards history, or, for that matter, on their sense of citizenship (Charland 2003). And the older narrative textbooks have had more than their share of critics over the years, both for what they said and for how they said it.

In the case of the third criticism, there is no evidence that history has been turned into "victimology." What has happened is that textbooks have finally begun to pay attention to those aspects of the Canadian past that have long been neglected, including the treatment of the First Nations, the history of labour, episodes of discrimination against minorities, and the like. This, however, is not to indulge in victimology, but to tell the story of the past, warts and all. We do students no favours if, in the name of a certain version of citizenship and in order to stimulate national pride, we hide from them just what their country has done, both for good and ill.

Regarding the fourth criticism, there is similarly no evidence that multicultural history has become dangerously divisive. If anything, the reverse seems to be true. The debate about possible adverse effects of multiculturalism is over what might happen rather than what is happening, over a feared future rather than an actually existing present, and to be aware of the danger is to be armed against it. This said, however, there is a trend in some history curricula to treat identity as something to be celebrated and treasured rather than to be contextualized and analyzed. For obvious reasons, minorities, who for so long have had education used against them, see in it a way of protecting their culture from the assimilative pressures of the majority. In legitimizing this tendency, however, curricula fail to take advantage of history's ability to liberate us from the confines of our culture and identity and view them from the outside, as it were. The goal of a liberal education, after all, is not to help us celebrate what we are but to learn more about what we might become, not to confirm existing horizons but to expand them. Moreover, if students are to become truly democratic citizens, they need to see how identity has been used historically as a political weapon to stigmatize outsiders and divide the world into us and them. This conflation of citizenship and identity lies behind every case of genocide and so-called ethnic cleansing known to history, and students need to understand it.

It is difficult to square the fifth criticism, that history education has sacrificed basic knowledge to nebulous slogans about meeting students' needs, with what we know about what actually happens in classrooms. Such evidence as there is does not suggest that history teaching has suddenly become overwhelmingly child-centred (Martineau 1999). Impressionistic evidence suggests that history teachers use a wider variety of teaching strategies than was once the case and generally favour what is often described as active learning, or constructivist pedagogy, to use the language of the trade, but this is far from saying that classrooms have become hotbeds of anything-goes pedagogy. If anything, the reverse is more accurate. Students still experience their share of copying notes from the overhead projector, filling in worksheets, and other such deadening routines. History teaching could certainly be more intellectually and academically rigorous, but there is a wealth of testimony to show that, in the days when factual knowledge was indisputably king of the classroom, students neither found it interesting nor remembered it for very long.

This raises the sixth criticism of history education, that many students are remarkably ignorant of even the most basic historical information. There can be little doubt that they are, not only in Canada, but also around the world. The evidence suggests that they always have been, even in the allegedly golden days of fact-based, knowledge-driven, examination-centred history teaching. It is not difficult to document a continuing series of complaints, stretching back more than a hundred years, to the effect that students do not remember most of what they were taught (see, for example, Osborne 2000; Paxton 2003).

A NEW CONCEPTION OF HISTORY AND CITIZENSHIP

It is not so much that the linkage between history education and citizenship has been abandoned, but rather that the historical research of the last thirty years has reshaped it. This new history shows so-called ordinary people struggling to take control of their lives, to redefine and extend the rights of citizenship, and to make democracy something more than the right to vote. The concept of citizenship has become more self-aware, more reflexive, and more conscious of its historical roots and political uses and abuses. The image of citizenship that emerges, implicitly or explicitly, from recent work, is not the flag-waving patriot but the informed participant in public debate and, better yet, the active participant in public affairs, committed to making democracy a reality.

THE IMPORTANCE OF HISTORY

There is an obvious role here for history education, especially in a country such as Canada, geographically enormous, regionally diverse, federally governed, officially bilingual and multicultural, some would say multinational, socially and intellectually pluralist, subject to pervasive and powerful external influences, sharing a common border and language with the world's major superpower, and constitutionally committed to democracy and human rights. In many ways Canada embodies a version of what Ignatieff calls "civic nationalism" and Habermas, "constitutional patriotism," an allegiance to civic norms rather than to ethnic or cultural heritage (Habermas 1989; Ignatieff 1994). Both concepts have been criticized for lacking the affective dimension needed for citizenship to work successfully and for ignoring their own cultural assumptions, but in a Canadian context they have much to offer. Their effective functioning, however, depends on citizens being committed to democratic principles and procedures and feeling a strong enough sense of commonality that they feel it is worth engaging with each other in the first place. In part, this must come from a sense of shared history, not in the form of one unquestioned master narrative, but as a story of debate and struggle. It follows, therefore, that history education has to introduce students to those aspects of the Canadian past, together with the multiple perspectives that both surround and arise from them, that define the country in which they are growing up to become citizens. As the political theorist Jeremy Webber puts it, "The core of any democratic community is not ethnicity or language or some catalogue of shared values. It is a commitment to a particular debate through time" (Webber 1994, 223). Citizenship in Canada, once one moves beyond the right to carry a passport and to vote, is defined in large part by an engagement in the continuing debate about the nature and future of Canada, an engagement that, if it is to be constructive and fruitful, must be historically informed.

There are, then, some obvious connections between education for democratic citizenship and the study of history. First, a knowledge of history provides the context for understanding the particular society in which we live and the world of which it is a part. Second, it helps us become aware of the range of human behaviour, both good and bad, and to that extent helps to teach us what it means to be human. Third, it provides us with a sense of context and perspective for the consideration of contemporary phenomena; it teaches us to consider the long view and makes us historically-minded, so that we are less likely to be carried away by the enthusiasms of the moment. Fourth, it provides a sense of connectedness both with what has gone before us and what will come after us; it raises our loyalties and our preoccupations from the local and the immediate to the more global and long-term. Fifth, it also connects us with the long struggle by which human beings have sought to improve the human condition, thus enabling us to become the subjects not the objects of our own existence. Sixth, it helps us cultivate that habit of mind which is best described as constructive scepticism, both by giving us a stock of knowledge against which to test what we are tempted or persuaded to believe, and by giving us the skills to distinguish a good argument from a bad one.

In short, the main advantage of history is that it enables us to think concretely and reflectively about important issues bearing on the human condition. It makes it possible for us to see the world as it is (which means understanding how it came to be that way) and to imagine the world as it might be, while also helping us think about how to get from one state of affairs to the other. As Richard Rorty (1998) put it, it socializes us, not into the country in which we actually live, but into the country we hope it might become.

None of this means that the study of history consists of mere "coverage" of subject matter. It was this examination-driven approach to history, with its determination to see that every fact was covered, whether or not it was understood, that killed students' interest in history in the first place. There is a long and complex debate among history teachers as to where best to draw the line between breadth and depth; most of us have our own answer. That there must be some appropriate combination, there can be little doubt (for some suggestions for curriculum design, see Bennett 1980; Osborne 1995; Bliss 2002).

Historical Knowledge, Historical Thinking, and Citizenship

THE NECESSITY OF KNOWLEDGE

Despite the undoubted importance of factual knowledge, recent years have seen a tendency to treat it as subordinate to the teaching of historical thinking. In part, this is a continuation of an old tradition in education, dating back at least to Socrates, that knowing-how is more important than knowing-that. It is also a manifestation of the attraction of the computer, which has led many educationists to argue that what matters is knowing how to "access" knowledge when needed, not carrying it in one's head. However, the health of democratic citizenship depends on our having knowledge in our heads, not just at our fingertips. If we are confronted with a Holocaust-denier, for example, we can hardly break off the argument while we go off to consult the internet. We have to rebut the falsehood then and there, and this requires knowledge. Orwell's *Nineteen Eighty-Four* is a chilling depiction of what can happen when people have neither independent knowledge nor any means of verifying what they are told. What makes Orwell's dystopia so frightening is not the thought police or the rat-cage torture, but the fact that the great majority of citizens never came into contact with such things precisely because their lack of knowledge conditioned them to accept whatever Big Brother's regime told them. Orwell is telling us that one of the key foundations of totalitarianism is the power to control people's knowledge of the past, and thereby to shape both their understanding of the present and their hopes for the future. Hence the party slogan: "Who controls the present, controls the past. Who controls the past, controls the future."

THE IMPORTANCE OF HISTORICAL THINKING

At the same time, factual knowledge, while crucially important, is not enough. It must be accompanied by the ability to think historically (Lee 1991; Seixas 1996; Wineburg 2001). Historical thinking, however, might be too restricted a term. In many, though certainly not all, formulations, it refers to the tools of the historian's trade, the ability to analyze a document or other source, to construct an evidence-based account, to understand the relationship between evidence and interpretation, and so on. These are certainly important abilities. But, from the perspective of democratic citizenship, they are not enough.

HISTORICAL-MINDEDNESS

We need to think in terms, not only of the skills that students need if they are to "do" history, but also of the ways in which the study of history should shape their way of looking at the world. A century ago, history educators described this as "historical-mindedness" (American Historical Association 1899). They never defined the term precisely, but we can form a pretty clear idea of what it entailed. It comprised the ability to step back from the immediate preoccupations of the present; to see things in context; to understand that things change, both for the better and the worse; to historicize the conventional wisdom of one's own times; to see the present as part of a continuum stretching from past to future; to take the long view of immediate events; to feel a sense of attachment to the past without becoming its captive; and to approach evidence and argument in a spirit of constructive scepticism. A hundred years ago, historians saw these qualities as es-

sential to citizenship in a pluralist democracy. They believed that investigating and arguing about the disputes of the past constituted a valuable preparation for citizenship by teaching students the skills and the mental outlook that would enable them to deal dispassionately with the emotion-laden issues of the present. As James Harvey Robinson put it in 1904,

> By cultivating sympathy and impartiality in dealing with the past we may hope to reach a point where we can view the present coolly and temperately. In this way, really thoughtful historical study serves to develop the very fundamental virtues of sympathy, fairness, and caution in forming our judgments (Robinson 1904, 7).

Robinson was perhaps overly optimistic, but, if nothing else, to be historically minded means being able to contextualize the pressing concerns of the present and to enlarge our understanding of what it means to be human.

The Question of Pedagogy

THE NOT-SO-HIDDEN CURRICULUM

Any approach to history that is concerned with its contribution to democratic citizenship must take pedagogy into account. The so-called hidden curriculum can be more powerful than the actual curriculum that is prescribed. For example, I once asked a grade 8 student what he was learning in his history class. He was studying the Reformation, but he told me that he was "learning to take notes from the overhead projector," which, in fact, was all that was happening in his class. In reality, he was learning a good deal more, not least the performance of a task which he did not particularly like and which he saw little point in doing, but which he knew he should do cheerfully and to an acceptable standard. In a very real sense, he was learning to be a "good" citizen, but a citizen of a specific kind.

TEACHING FOR DEMOCRATIC CITIZENSHIP

By contrast, democratic citizenship demands a pedagogy that emphasizes and exemplifies the skills and values of critical awareness, participation, involvement, and community that are central to its practice. It is exemplified in what Hodgetts called the "dialogue" approach, which characterized the best classes he observed in his national study of history teaching. It consisted of the following elements. One, students used, not one textbook, but a variety of readings containing contradictory and controversial viewpoints. Two, thanks to the work of their teachers, students were proficient in discussion techniques. Three, teachers played an important role, not as transmitters of information and taskmasters, but as organizers and guides, questioners, and catalysts. Four, classes studied a small number of topics in depth, rather than covering many more superficially, and these topics were organized as problems to be investigated. Five, while not neglecting subject-matter, teachers also emphasized intellectual skills, working with evidence, the construction and analysis of arguments, and the like. In short,

> The outstanding feature of these classes … was the almost total absence of any factual recall techniques. There was no lecturing by the teachers; no factual question-answer period to check up on what the class had remembered; the students did not read their reports aloud to each other.… Thus the entire lesson revolved around a discussion of ideas—ideas, however, that the teacher, or frequently the students themselves, insisted should be supported by relevant factual information (Hodgetts 1968, 54).

The implications of this kind of teaching strategy for the education of democratic citizens need no elaboration. It is perhaps also worth noting that this challenging teaching was not confined to so-called academic students. Hodgetts found that just over half of the classes using it were "quite average," unstreamed groupings, including some "dead-end, two-year terminals" (66).

The point is to treat history as a problem-posing subject. We should avoid teaching it retrospectively from the viewpoint of the present, where we know what happened next. Instead, we should teach it contemporaneously, through the eyes of those who lived it and could not know what happened next. Even such a standard topic as Confederation can be enlivened this way. The questions to be explored are easy enough to frame and pursue. What problems did the decision-makers of the 1860s see themselves facing? Why did they identify these, rather than something else, as problems in the first place? What courses of action were open to them? Who supported each possible choice and why? What pressures faced them? Why did they decide to do what they did? What else might they have done? Did their decision solve their problems or create new ones, or both? What were their hopes and fears? Who was excluded from the decision-making process? Substantive questions such as these should go hand-in-hand with more procedural issues: What evidence do we have and why should we believe it? What have historians had to say about what was done? What are the main interpretations, and how valid are they? How has the topic been exploited educationally and politically? This problem-posing approach can be applied to almost any topic, and allows for

endless pedagogical possibilities: role play, simulation, group work, research projects, source work, seminars, and the like.

The net effect of all this, in my experience, is to drive home to students the message that, yes, Confederation is an important event in Canadian history (otherwise people would not be arguing about it), but also that, yes, Canadians then and ever since have had different assessments and divergent interpretations of its meaning and impact. Canadians are united (or in some cases divided) as much by the debate over the event as by the event itself. In short, history teaching should combine elements of what Peter Seixas (Stearns, Seixas, and Wineburg 2000, 19–37) has described as the three approaches to teaching history. A combined approach would raise questions that challenge the "single best story" of Confederation, embrace "disciplinary" aspects of historical thinking, and introduce a "postmodern" stance by looking at how the history of Confederation has been constructed and exploited, while also making problematic the nature of history itself.

Taught in this way, history almost automatically ceases to be the static record of a dead past, a tedious recital of one-damn-thing-after-another, and becomes an initiation into a living present and an introduction to citizenship. History is transformed from a subject where students are confined to memorizing things they never knew into one where they become active investigators, thereby unlocking powers and abilities that often they do not themselves know they possess.

More than in most countries, Canada's political issues are steeped in its history: the nature of federalism; the place of Quebec in Confederation; the rights of aboriginal people; the role and power of the state; the relationship with the United States; the protection of citizens' rights; the struggle for social justice—these and many other issues reverberate through Canada's history. It does not require much imagination to see how almost any topic in Canadian, or, for that matter, any other, history can be taught so that it illuminates some aspect of contemporary citizenship. This does not mean constructing some artificial link between past and present, inventing analogies and connections that are not there, or distorting the past to serve the needs of the present. Rather, it means viewing the past in the light of men and women doing what they could to tackle the problems facing them, without any means of knowing what the future might bring. To argue that the study of history educates us for democratic citizenship is not to reduce it to applied civics and a background to current events. It is, rather, to defend its potential to illuminate the human experience. To put a slightly different spin on Croce's (1917) often-quoted observation, all history is contemporary history.

THE DEMOCRATIC CLASSROOM

Some theorists have argued that democratic citizenship education requires that classrooms must themselves operate democratically, and there is obviously some truth to this. As with most things in life, we learn democracy by doing and experiencing it, not only from reading books and listening to lectures. Some of the democratic classroom rhetoric, however, risks mistaking appearance for substance. There is nothing inherently democratic about group work or co-operative learning, for example. Everything depends on the aim the group is pursuing. Democracy is more than participation and empowerment. Fascists and racists can, and often do, feel highly empowered and participative, while also being committed to a certain vision of community. The fundamental question must always be: Once students are empowered and able to participate, what will they use their skills and powers to do? What will ensure that they use them to serve democratic principles?

A SENSE OF PURPOSE

What matters, within obvious limits, is not only the specific technique we employ, but the spirit that informs it. A good lecture at the appropriate time, for example, can stimulate students' imaginations, and help them to think critically and frame useful questions, while co-operative learning can be little more than a feel-good exercise in group work. Good teaching requires a mix of teaching strategies, tailored to the topic and the students learning it. Moreover, recent research suggests that exemplary history teachers can differ substantially in their selection of teaching strategies, ranging from the traditionally didactic to the innovatively student-centred, but nonetheless achieve similar goals, largely because what they do is anchored in a well thought-out philosophy of history and of education that they use to guide their teaching (Wineburg 2001, 155–172).

Perhaps the most important point to remember is that, if we are to teach history for democratic citizenship, we need above all to keep in mind a clear picture of what democratic citizenship entails, and conduct our classes accordingly. And changing the status of learners from their largely desk-bound, worksheet-completing, note-copying status has a lot to do with democratic citizenship. It also makes both the teaching and the learning of history more interesting, more worthwhile, and more rewarding. When taught appropriately, history can indeed fulfill its potential as the foundation of democratic citizenship.

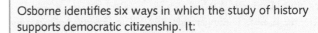

Osborne identifies six ways in which the study of history supports democratic citizenship. It:

- provides a context for understanding society;
- builds awareness of human behaviour—good and bad;
- provides a context for consideration of contemporary phenomena;
- connects the past to the present;
- connects modern audiences to the long struggle to improve the human condition;
- cultivates constructive scepticism.

These benefits will not occur without conscious effort. Think of a topic in history and list a few activities and pedagogical strategies you might employ when teaching this topic that promote each of these aspects of citizenship.

REFERENCES

American Historical Association. 1899. *The study of history in schools: A report to the American Historical Association by the Committee of Seven.* New York: Macmillan.

Anderson, B. 1991. *Imagined communities: Reflections on the origins and spread of nationalism.* Rev. ed. London: Verso.

Appleby, J., L. Hunt, and M. Jacob. 1994. *Telling the truth about history.* New York: Norton.

Bennett, P. 1980. *Rediscovering Canadian history.* Toronto: Ontario Institute for Studies in Education.

Bliss, M. 1991–92. Privatizing the mind: The sundering of Canadian history, the sundering of Canada. *Journal of Canadian Studies* 26 (4): 5–17.

———. 2002. Teaching Canadian national history. *Canadian Social Studies* 36 (2). Available from http://www.quasar.ualberta.ca/css.

Bumsted, J.M. 1997. Historical writing in English. In *The Oxford companion to Canadian literature,* 2nd ed., eds. E. Benson and W. Toye, 534–539. Toronto: Oxford University Press.

Cairns, A. 1995. *Reconfigurations: Canadian citizenship and constitutional change.* Toronto: McClelland and Stewart.

Charland, J-P. 2003. *Les élèves, l'histoire et la citoyenneté.* Sainte-Foy, QC: Les presses de l'université Laval.

Charland, J-P. and S. Moisan. 2003. *L'enseignement de l'histoire dans les écoles françaises du Canada.* Toronto: Historica.

Croce, B. 1917. *Teoria e storia della storiografia.* Bari, Gius: Laterza and Figli.

Crowley, T. 1990. *Agnes Macphail and the politics of equality.* Toronto: James Lorimer.

Evans, R.J. 1997. *In defence of history.* London: Granta.

Francis, D. 1997. *National dreams: Myth, memory and Canadian history.* Vancouver: Arsenal Pulp Press.

Granatstein, J.L. 1998. *Who killed Canadian history?* Toronto: Harper-Collins.

Habermas, J. 1989. *The structural transformation of the public sphere.* Cambridge: Polity Press.

Held, D. 1993. *Prospects of democracy: North, south, east, west.* Stanford: Stanford University Press.

Hobsbawm, E. and T. Ranger, eds. 1983. *The invention of tradition.* Cambridge: Cambridge University Press.

Hodgetts, A.B. 1968. *What culture? What heritage?* Toronto: Ontario Institute for Studies in Education.

Hodgetts, A.B. and P. Gallagher. 1978. *Teaching Canada for the 80s.* Toronto: Ontario Institute for Studies in Education.

Iggers, G. 1997. *Historiography in the twentieth century: From scientific objectivity to the postmodern challenge.* Hanover: Wesleyan University Press.

Ignatieff, M. 1994. *Blood and belonging: Journeys into the new nationalism.* New York: Farrar, Straus, and Giroux.

Lazar, H. and T. McIntosh, eds. 1999. *How Canadians connect.* Montreal: Queen's University School of Policy Studies, McGill-Queen's University Press.

Lee, P.J. 1991. Historical knowledge and the national curriculum. In *History in the national curriculum,* ed. R. Aldrich, 39–65. London: Kogan Page.

Loewen, J.W. 1996. *Lies my teacher told me: Everything you're American history textbook got wrong.* New York: Touchstone.

Lowenthal, D. 1996. *Possessed by the past: The heritage crusade and the spoils of history.* New York: Free Press.

MacIntyre, S. and A. Clark. 2003. *The history wars.* Melbourne: University of Melbourne Press.

Macpherson, C.B. 1977. *The life and times of liberal democracy.* New York: Oxford University Press.

Martineau, R. 1999. *L'histoire à l'école, matière à penser....* Montreal: L'Harmattan.

McDiarmid, G. and D. Pratt. 1971. *Teaching prejudice.* Toronto: Ontario Institute for Studies in Education.

McKay, I. 1994. *The quest of the folk: Antimodernism and cultural selection in twentieth-century Nova Scotia.* Montreal: McGill-Queen's University Press.

Nash, G.B., C. Crabtree, and R.E. Dunn. 1997. *History on trial: Culture wars and the teaching of the past.* New York: Knopf.

Newmann, F. 1975. *Education for citizen action.* Berkeley: McCutchan.

Novick, P. 1988. *That noble dream: The "objectivity question" and the American historical profession.* Cambridge: Cambridge University Press.

Oliver, D.W. and J.P. Shaver. 1966. *Teaching public issues in the high school.* Boston: Houghton Mifflin.

Osborne, K.W. 1975. Some psychological concerns for the teaching of history. *The History and Social Science Teacher* 11: 15–25.

———. 1984. *Working papers in political education.* Winnipeg: University of Manitoba Educational Monograph XII.

———. 1991a. *Teaching for democratic citizenship.* Toronto: Our Schools/Our Selves.

———. 1991b. H.G. Wells, education and catastrophe. *Journal of Educational Administration and Foundations* 62: 17–38.

———. 1995. *In defence of history: Teaching the past and the meaning of democratic citizenship.* Toronto: Our Schools/Our Selves.

———. 2000. 'Our history syllabus has us gasping'—History in Canadian schools, past, present, and future. *Canadian Historical Review* (81) 3: 404–435.

———. 2003. Teaching history in schools: A Canadian debate. *Journal of Curriculum Studies* 35 (5): 585–626.

———. 2004. History and social studies: Partners or rivals? In *Challenges and prospects for Canadian social studies,* eds. A. Sears and I. Wright, 73–89. Vancouver: Pacific Educational Press.

Parker, W. 2003. *Teaching democracy: Unity and diversity in public life.* New York: Teachers College Press.

Paxton, R.J. 2003. Don't know much about history—never did. *Phi Delta Kappan,* December: 265–273.

Phillips, R. 1998. *History teaching, nationhood and the state: A study in educational politics.* London: Cassell.

Robinson, J.H. 1904. *Readings in European history.* Vol. 1. Boston: Ginn.

Rorty, R. 1998. *Achieving our country: Leftist thought in twentieth century America.* Cambridge: Harvard University Press.

Schlesinger, A.M., Jr. 1992. *The disuniting of America: Reflections on a multicultural society.* New York: Norton.

Seixas, P. 1993. Parallel crises: history and the social studies curriculum in the U.S.A. *Journal of Curriculum Studies* 25 (3): 235–250.

———. 1996. Conceptualizing the growth of historical understanding. In *The handbook of education and human development: New models of teaching, learning, and schooling,* eds. D.R. Olson and N. Torrance, 765–783. Oxford: Blackwell.

Shields, P. and D. Ramsay. 2002. *Teaching and learning about Canadian history across Canada.* Toronto: Historica.

Shore, M. 2002. *Reading Canada's history: The contested past.* Toronto: University of Toronto Press.

Stearns, P.N., P. Seixas, and S. Wineburg. 2000. *Knowing, teaching and learning history: National and international perspectives.* New York: New York University Press.

Symcox, L. 2002. *Whose history? The struggle for national standards in American classrooms.* New York: Teachers College Press.

Webber, J. 1994. *Reimagining Canada: Language, culture, community, and the Canadian constitution.* Montreal: McGill-Queen's University Press.

Wells, H.G. 1939. The poison called history. In *Travels of a republican radical in search of hot water.* Harmondsworth: Penguin.

Windschuttle, K. 1997. *The killing of history: How literary critics and social theorists are murdering our past.* New York: Free Press.

Wineburg, S. 2001. *Historical thinking and other unnatural acts: Charting the future of teaching the past.* Philadelphia: Temple University Press.

2

Making Sense of the Curriculum

Roland Case

History, geography, and social studies teachers don't simply make up what they are to teach. Every course has a curriculum. The word curriculum—derived from the word *curricle*—refers to "the path to follow" or a course of study. Teachers must know where they are going if they are to lead students through the curriculum in a meaningful and productive way. These directives are outlined in curriculum documents that mandate what every student in a particular grade is expected to learn. For this reason they are among the most important documents a teacher needs to consider. Despite their importance, many teachers ignore or misinterpret them. Some teachers trust that covering each of the outcomes will provide a complete picture—just as joining the dots by tracing lines between each point reveals a hidden image. It is not obvious that there is a single clear picture embedded in prescribed curriculum documents—joining the dots (covering the outcomes) may not reveal any image—it may simply mean a string of activities. As a British Columbia Ministry of Education document noted:

> Curriculum is no longer "ground to be covered." Instead, curriculum evolves from the teacher's mediation between the goals of the program and the curriculum and the individual learning styles, interests, and abilities of students (1990, 25).

As an earlier British Columbia curriculum guide explained: "A curriculum is an organized statement of *intended* learning outcomes that serves as a framework for decisions about the instructional process [emphasis added]" (1988, 4). In other words, curricula are guidelines to assist teachers in developing a program of study for their own students.

Curriculum documents can help if we know how to read them. They contain more than content and skill outcomes but also elements such as goals, big ideas, rationales, and organizing strands. If we understand the role of each and how to make sense of them and appreciate how much interpretive leeway teachers have, we can take charge of the curriculum and not be enslaved to it. In other words, the challenge is as much to bring meaning to the curriculum as it is to find

meaning. It is one of the reasons why teaching is a profession requiring expertise and training. There are no recipes or instructional manuals that anyone can simply pick and follow unthinkingly. As we will see, making sense of the curriculum requires that teachers bring significant understanding of the discipline and of societal and students' needs to their reading of these documents.

Two Myths About the Curriculum

Before exploring what curriculum documents can tell us and what they leave under-determined, it may be helpful to dispel two widely held myths.

CURRICULUM DOCUMENTS ARE LARGE AND SUPERFLUOUS

One reason for overlooking the curriculum is the belief that using an authorized textbook removes the need to spend much time with curriculum documents. Textbooks that are formally authorized for use in a province must demonstrate that they address each and every curriculum outcome. While this is true of "authorized" textbooks, the same cannot be said of the countless other resources that teachers might choose to use. But even following a prescribed textbook doesn't remove the need to understand the purposes of the curriculum and to determine how best to use the resource to serve these purposes.

Consider the following example. The grade 10 history curriculum for Ontario is divided into three time periods: 1914–1929, 1929–1945, and 1945–1982 (2013B, 108-109). The same expectation related to science and technology is repeated in identical wording for each period: "identify some major developments in science and/or technology during this period and assess their significance for different groups in Canada" (112, 115, 118). A popular textbook for this course is divided into three parts to coincide with the three time periods. Each part has a section on scientific and technological developments and their impact. Let's consider how two teachers might address these outcomes using this textbook. Imagine that Mr. Smith asks his students to read each of the science and technology sections in the textbook one at a time, months apart as the class focusses in sequence on one period after another. Their question in all three cases is to determine the impact of developments at that time for each respective generation. Imagine that Ms. Chan decides to lump together her inquiry into science and technology for all three periods. She asks her students to read the three sections of the textbook at the same time. Their job is to determine the impact of the developments in science and technology with an eye to explaining why developments during some of these periods might have transformed society but not in other periods.

Both teachers are addressing the same curriculum outcomes using the same resource. One of them is following the textbook and the other is drawing upon it. In Ms. Chan's case, her students are learning more deeply about the nature and causes of the different impacts of scientific and technological developments at different times. Mr. Smith's approach is more repetitious and merely teaches about the impact without exploring why some developments might alter society and others not. Teachers like Ms. Chan are able to bring greater meaning to their subject because of their understanding of the possible reasons for teaching various outcomes and of how to best achieve these results for her students.

CURRICULUM DOCUMENTS ARE MERELY AN INVENTORY OF OUTCOMES

On the face of it, it is temping to think of curriculum outcomes or expectations as a kind of inventory of the things that must be covered to bring about the desired result. This perception is not helpful, because "covering" the specific outcomes in the curriculum doesn't lead to engaging, meaningful learning for at least four reasons.

- **Outcomes don't dictate teaching method.** Curriculum that is specified in terms of outcomes, standards or expectations describes what students should know or be able to do as a result of completing the lesson, but it doesn't indicate how teachers might involve students in learning the topic in the first place. For example, asking students to describe examples of conflict and co-operation around the beginning of the twentieth century may be a way of assessing what they have learned, but we might teach them this information by reading journals and first-hand newspaper reports that transport students back to that time period. The tendency to teach a topic by asking students to perform the task mentioned in the outcome fuels this pattern of "covering the curriculum" that students find boring.

- **Outcomes aren't organized in teachable clusters.** Specific outcomes need not be taught in the order in which they are listed, nor for that matter need they be taught individually. The pattern when "covering" the curriculum is to proceed from one outcome to the next, often in a drawn-out manner. This is what Brady (1989, 80) is referring to as an "incredible heap of miscellany." This need not be the case. For example, most of the seventeen outcomes in the Canada: A Changing Society strand of the grade 8 Ontario curriculum (plus numerous English and media studies outcomes) could be addressed through one large project—for example, inviting students to research, write, and produce a video docu-drama about Canada at the beginning of the twentieth century.

- **Outcomes don't specify priority.** Not all outcomes are of equal importance nor will they have equal value for students in a given class. Consequently, each outcome does not warrant the same amount of teaching time. In fact, a few outcomes may have great priority and deserve extended treatment, whereas others should be touched upon very quickly. The tendency when "covering" the curriculum is to teach a topic for as long as it takes to complete the selected activity—even if this means less important outcomes receive more attention than do vitally important ones.

- **Outcomes don't indicate purpose.** As previously mentioned, outcome statements don't indicate why we want students to achieve these results. If a teacher doesn't know why, it is almost certain that students won't know either. A likely result is to do things because the curriculum says so or because it's in the textbook. The lack of clear purpose is evident in the disconnected, irrelevant learning that many teachers report when asked what they remember of their own social studies classes. Isolated facts, endless colouring of maps, and tedious research reports figure strongly in their recollections. Surveys indicate that many students consider social studies their least favourite subject. The very title of a popular professional book, *If This Is Social Studies, Why Isn't It Boring?* (Steffay and Hood 1994) is a further indictment of the subject. Clearly, history, geography, and social studies have the potential to be exciting, dynamic, and thought-provoking subjects, but all too often they fail to achieve this potential. So how do we decide what we should be doing and where would we begin to look?

Figuring Out What We're Expected to Teach

Faced with the question of what to teach, a teacher might reasonably turn to the prescribed curriculum for direction. Surely all we need to do is look at the provincial documents to learn what the government expects from us. As we will see, it is not as simple as that, but it is important to know what we will find in these documents and to understand their role in developing a purposeful history, geography, or social studies program.

SPECIFIC CURRICULUM OUTCOMES

In provincial curriculum guidelines, the most specific and, one would think, most practical place to look is the lists of specific learning outcomes for a particular grade level—also called specific expectations, objectives, or standards. Let's see exactly why these outcomes do not provide a clear sense of direction and purpose. In Table 2.1 are listed typical content and skill outcomes from three curricula and sample activities that a teacher might use to address these outcomes.

In each of these examples, undertaking the suggested activity would satisfy the identified knowledge outcome and address the skill outcomes. A teacher could then confidently proceed to the next knowledge expectation in the curriculum and begin to address it.

- **Grade 8 Ontario:** a teacher might move from teaching about significant examples of conflict in Canada during this period (for example, the Boer War and the Manitoba School Crisis). From here, the teacher could move to the next curricular outcome, which involves identifying a variety of significant individuals in Canada during this period (for example, Nellie McClung, L. M. Montgomery, and Duncan Campbell Scott).
- **Grade 9 British Columbia:** a teacher might move from assessing the significance of various political, social, economic, and technological revolutions to examining the continuing effects of imperialism and colonialism on Indigenous peoples in Canada.
- **Grade 10 Alberta:** a teacher might turn from examining the impact of cultural contact between Indigenous and non-Indigenous people to investigating the foundations of globalization, including capitalism and industrialism.

These teachers might continue in a similar vein until all outcomes had been covered. But it is worth asking what has been achieved. What is the reason for wanting students to learn about conflict and co-operation one hundred years ago or the impact of imperialism on Indigenous peoples? And how do these connect with the content of the next outcomes listed in the curriculum? The effect of attempting to "cover" each outcome is to drag students through the curriculum for no apparent reason other than that the ministry curriculum guide states that topic X and skill Y must be taught. The problem is compounded when we realize that a given grade level may list many dozens of outcomes. For example, the Ontario

TABLE 2.1   SAMPLE OUTCOMES AND ACTIVITIES

ONTARIO GRADE 8 HISTORY (ONTARIO 2013A)	BRITISH COLUMBIA GRADE 9 SOCIAL STUDIES (BRITISH COLUMBIA MINISTRY OF EDUCATION 2015)	ALBERTA GRADE 10 SOCIAL STUDIES (ALBERTA EDUCATION 2007)
Specific expectation (Understanding): describe significant examples of co-operation and conflict in Canada during this period (150)	**Content standard:** [know about] political, social, economic, and technological revolutions (n.p.)	**Knowledge outcome:** examine impacts of cultural contact between Indigenous and non-Indigenous people (21)
Specific expectation (Inquiry): evaluate evidence and draw conclusions about perspectives of different groups on some significant events, developments, and/or issues that affected Canada and/or Canadians during this period (149)	**Competency standard:** assess the significance of . . . developments, and compare varying perspectives on their historical significance at particular times. . . . (n.p.)	**Skill outcome:** analyze similarities and differences among historical narratives (17)
Typical activity: Students might use sets of primary documents to draw conclusions about various conflicts and acts of co-operation from the perspectives of several groups who were involved in each.	**Typical activity:** Students might examine summaries of the various effects of the American, French, and Industrial revolutions and decide which had the greatest overall impact politically, socially, economically, and technologically.	**Typical activity:** Students might examine the immediate and long-term consequences of cultural contact between various Indigenous and non-Indigenous groups looking at identifying possible patterns in the outcomes.

grade 8 history and geography curriculum lists 54 specific expectations, and the Alberta grade 10 curriculum lists 111 specific outcomes. It is encouraging to note that the BC curriculum for grade 9 prescribes a more manageable expectation of 15 broad learning standards.

> Think back to your own experiences as a student in secondary history, geography, or social studies. Make a list of your clearest memories of these experiences—both positive and negative. Review these experiences in light of the four factors listed previously: engaging teaching methods, memorable organization, clear priorities, and a sense of purpose. To what extent can the nature of your experiences be attributed to choices your teacher made in light of these four considerations? What implications might this have for your own choices as a teacher?

GOING BEYOND SPECIFIC OUTCOMES

Ken Osborne suggests that the danger of a preoccupation with specific outcomes is that "teachers come to see themselves, or be seen by others, not as teachers of history [or social studies] but as achievers of outcomes, and history becomes little more than a sequence of outcomes to be checked off in a teacher's day-book" (2004, 4).

The antidote to this problem is a return to the question "What is our purpose?" If we know why we are teaching something, we have a better idea of its priority relative to other outcomes and we can better decide how to structure learning effectively to achieve this end.

As the highlighted text suggests, educational writers use different terms to identify the important ideas that guide teachers' interpretation of curriculum outcomes. It does not matter whether one's reason for teaching a specific outcome is characterized as a "big idea," "linchpin," "essential understanding," or "enduring understanding." What does matter is that we know why we are teaching the outcome.

Increasingly, curriculum documents provide sample "big ideas" for each grade level. For example, the suggested reason for teaching grade 8 Ontario history students about conflict and co-operation around the turn of the twentieth century is to help them understand that "Social changes that occurred at this time have had a lasting impact on Canada" (Ontario 2013A, 147). The grade 10 BC curriculum suggests that learning about various historical revolutions might help students understand that "Emerging ideas and ideologies profoundly influence societies and events" (British Columbia Ministry of Education 2015, n.p.). However, these suggested big ideas are not mandatory, and teachers are free to substitute their

IDENTIFYING THE IMPORTANT IDEAS

Big ideas

Selma Wasserman describes the reason for learning as the "big idea" that answers the questions "What is worth teaching?" and "How does what I am required to teach fit with matters of importance or consequence?" Learning experiences grounded in big ideas illuminate content in relation to "important issues and concepts" as opposed to "content that deals with acquisition of facts." Wasserman suggests that "curriculum that reflects big ideas will enrich classroom life and promote deeper and more sophisticated understanding of the world we live in" (1990, 96). Big ideas emerge from the curriculum content in the form of substantive issues that are worth knowing. In other words, identifying an overarching reason is necessary when planning for teaching. Similarly, James Duplass (2004) refers to "big ideas" as powerful, long-lasting concepts or generalizations that invite students to consider new ideas and examine their beliefs. The teacher needs to identify a relevant big idea that will resonate with students and teach towards that goal in order to create a meaningful social studies program.

Essential understandings

Lynn Erickson's strategy for identifying matters of importance is to distinguish between topic-centred (for example, memorizing facts related to the American Revolution) and idea-centred curriculum (for example, developing and sharing ideas related to the concepts of freedom and independence as a result of studying the American Revolution) (1998, 50). The focus of idea-centred curriculum is conceptual ideas and the use of facts to support understandings. Identifying what is important requires teachers to think beyond the topic and facts to the important transferable ideas or essential understandings that transcend time and culture. For example, in studying immigration, an essential understanding might be "People migrate to meet a variety of needs. Migration may lead to new opportunities or greater freedom" (52).

Linchpin ideas

Grant Wiggins and Jay McTighe present a model of curriculum design that focusses on the "linchpin" idea. A linchpin idea identifies what is worth knowing and is essential for developing understanding—"to what extent does the idea, topic or process represent a 'big idea' having enduring value beyond the classroom?" (1998, 10). Curriculum designed around linchpin ideas promotes meaningful learning rather than the acquisition of easily forgotten fragments of knowledge.

own overall desired understanding. Let's look at the range of choices that a grade 10 teacher in Alberta might have for studying the impact of globalization.

- **Economic understanding**: to learn how groups within and beyond Alberta have been affected economically by globalization. Is sustainable economic prosperity better served by opening the province to globalization or by trying to contain its progress?

- **Ethical understanding:** to appreciate the ethical implications of globalization in terms of opportunities and exploitation, wealth, and disparity. How can the economic benefits of globalization be realized without the abuses and injustices that have accompanied some past practices?
- **Personal understanding:** to understand the importance of globalizing forces in students' own lives. How have students and their communities been affected by historical globalization?
- **Historical understanding:** to understand a number of challenges facing Alberta by learning about past practices and consequences. Can we learn anything about challenges we face in the present by studying how globalization and imperialism operated in the past?

Each of these big ideas offers plausible insights for teaching the identified outcome. Some may be more interesting or relevant to students, and may be more important in the bigger scheme. Developing a coherent vision that excites and challenges students requires thoughtful consideration of how their learning will contribute to their ability to interact in and contribute to the world. Perhaps any one of these reasons would work. Does it simply depend on the direction we personally want to take our students?

Asking "why" helps us uncover important aspects of content and to situate learning experiences in a more relevant context. But how will we know which learning experience is the best one or even the one intended by the government? The answers to these questions require us to look at various elements embedded in curriculum documents that typically provide the bigger picture.

Figuring Out Why We're Teaching It

Teachers are expected to work within the guidelines provided by the provincial curriculum. This is the framework within which instructional decisions are made. It is teachers' responsibility to connect specific outcomes in meaningful ways and develop them in a context that furthers an overall vision for social studies. Identifying these connections and planning towards this purpose breathes life into the curriculum.

Three features of the curriculum are central in formulating this broader vision for teaching social studies, history, and geography. These are the general goals that the discipline promotes, the *strands* around which subject matter is organized to promote

the desired goals, and the ultimate rationale for the subject. We consider each of these elements and their role in giving purpose to our teaching. As we will see, they leave much for the teacher to fill in.

GENERAL GOALS

The goals of a course or a unit are the general educational outcomes that are to be promoted by addressing the specific outcomes. Although the precise wording differs from jurisdiction to jurisdiction (for example, they are called "Overall Expectations" in Ontario and "General Outcomes" in Alberta), their common function is to provide a more general description of what we are trying to achieve. Perhaps these goals will help in giving purpose to our teaching.

Goals are typically categorized into types. Traditionally the most widely used categories of goals were knowledge, skills, and attitudes. Despite its popularity, this categorization is confusing. Supposed "skills"—such as conducting research—require knowledge (of the strengths and key features of various information sources) and attitudes (attention to detail, curiosity). For this reason, we identify five categories of goals that are described in the adjacent highlighted text, and referred to repeatedly throughout this book. One obvious purpose in categorizing the kind of goal we are trying to achieve is that it orients us in a particular direction. For example, it is helpful to realize whether our primary goal is to promote content knowledge (understanding of certain ideas) or to foster individual action or to teach how to access information.

The extent of direction that general goals provides is evident in the Ontario grade 8 curriculum, which identifies three "overall expectations" that students should achieve by the end of the Canada 1890–1914: A Changing Society section of the course (Ontario 2013A, 152).

> **Application:** analyse key similarities and differences between Canada in 1890–1914 and in the present day, with reference to the experiences of and major challenges facing different groups and/ or individuals, and to some of the actions Canadians have taken to improve their lives.
>
> **Inquiry:** use the historical inquiry process to investigate perspectives of different groups on some significant events, developments, and/or issues that affected Canada and/or Canadians between 1890 and 1914 .
>
> **Understanding historical context:** describe various significant events, developments, and people in Canada between 1890 and 1914, and explain their impact.

As is typical of many curricula, these goals summarize in general terms what is stated in the specific outcomes. Unfortunately, they don't suggest why we would teach these outcomes. What is the point of having students learn about similarities and differences in the experiences, challenges, and reform efforts between Canada in 1890–1914 and in the present day? Do we want students to be more socially and politically active? Proud of the progress being made? Or perhaps disappointed with the recurring nature of many of our problems? We won't find the needed level of clarity of purpose from these goals.

The Alberta curriculum offers the following "General Outcome" for the cluster of specific outcomes we discussed previously:

> "Students will assess the impacts of historical globalization on Indigenous and non-Indigenous peoples" (2007, 21).

This broad outcome appears to provide a more general statement of the goal but it is not clear why we would want to further it. Are we to promote ethical appreciation of the historical implications or develop understanding of current responses to globalization? It seems that the stated goal leaves us with choices to make. These examples are instructive: general curriculum goals may sometimes suggest directions for our teaching, but they don't eliminate all the possibilities and often provide little help in understanding why we might want students to achieve this goal.

CURRICULUM STRANDS

Strands are another element commonly featured in social studies, history, and geography curriculum documents. The word "strand" refers to the parts that are bound or woven together to form the whole. There are two kinds of strands: "underlying themes," which are main threads or concepts that run throughout the curriculum, and "organizing themes," which are the categories used to sort or cluster segments of the curriculum (units within a single course or different courses within a secondary program). Both kinds of strands serve a similar purpose: they provide ways to identify the focus and organize the delivery of the curriculum.

UNDERLYING THEMES

The underlying themes highlight the continuing emphasis or the backbone of the curriculum. For example, Alberta (2007, 6–7) identifies six strands as the threads running throughout the entire K–12 curriculum:

- time, continuity, and change—essentially history;

TYPES OF SOCIAL STUDIES GOALS

Although curriculum documents and writers categorize them differently,[1] it may be helpful to organize social studies around five general goals:

- **Content knowledge.** This goal specifies the breadth and depth of understanding students should possess about their world. It includes knowledge of specific facts (for example, key figures in local community history, the capital of Canada, major current events), generalizations or theories (for example, people have many shared needs, Canada is a land of immigrants), and concepts (for example, community, democracy, fairness).
- **Thinking.** This goal refers to students' ability and inclination to assess competently what to believe and to reach defensible decisions about what and how to act. This involves acquiring the "tools" needed in reaching reasoned judgments in the range of tasks that we want students to think critically about (for example, draw reliable conclusions from historical evidence, weigh the pros and cons of various actions, decide which theory is most plausible).
- **Information gathering and communication.** This goal specifies students' abilities to identify information needs, extract information from a variety of sources (for example, textbooks, magazines, other library references, catalogues, artifacts, field trip data, community resources), and represent their findings in various forms (for example, essay, graph, chart, map, timeline, mural, model, debate, oral presentation, audiovisual media).
- **Personal and social values.** This goal refers to both personal values (for example, self-esteem, integrity, personal identity) and social values (for example, equality, respect for persons, justice, national pride, international solidarity) that are characteristic of healthy individuals, communities, nations, and, ultimately, the world.
- **Individual and collective action.** This goal refers to competence in actually solving interpersonal and societal problems (for example, dealing with siblings and fellow students, combatting school- and community-based problems, or acting on national and international concerns). It involves developing students' abilities to analyze problems in their personal lives and in society, to plan appropriate courses of action individually and in collaboration with others, to put their plans into action, and to evaluate the efficacy of their efforts.

- the land (places and people)—essentially physical and human geography;
- power, authority, and decision making—essentially politics and law;
- economics and resources—essentially economics;

- global connections—essentially global education;
- culture and community—essentially anthropology and sociology.

The curriculum specifically links three of these strands—those representing history, political science, and global education—to the outcomes that we have used as our example. These strands are described as follows:

Time, Continuity, and Change. Understanding the dynamic relationships among time, continuity and change is a cornerstone of citizenship and identity. Considering multiple perspectives on history, and contemporary issues within their historical context, enables students to understand and appreciate the social, cultural and political dimensions of the past, make meaning of the present and make decisions for the future (6).

Power, Authority, and Decision Making. Examining the concepts of power, authority, and decision making from multiple perspectives helps students consider how these concepts impact individuals, relationships, communities, and nations. It also broadens students' understanding of related issues, perspectives, and their effect on citizenship and identity. A critical examination of the distribution, exercise, and implications of power and authority is the focus of this strand. Students will examine governmental and political structures, justice and laws, fairness and equity, conflict and cooperation, decision-making processes, leadership, and governance. This examination develops a student's understanding of the individual's capacity in decision-making processes, and promotes active and responsible citizenship (7).

Global Connections. Critically examining multiple perspectives and connections among local, national and global issues develops students' understanding of citizenship and identity and the interdependent or conflicting nature of individuals, communities, societies, and nations. Exploring this interdependence broadens students' global consciousness and empathy with world conditions. Students will also acquire a better comprehension of tensions pertaining to economic relationships, sustainability, and universal human rights (7).

The many ideas raised by these three strands suggest that several of the previously identified purposes—economic, ethical, historical, and personal—may apply. It seems that here too the teacher must choose among the possibilities.

Running through the Ontario social studies, history, and geography curriculum are four underlying themes that constitute their "Citizenship education framework" (2013A, 10):

- **Active participation:** work for the common good in local, national, and global communities
- **Identity:** sense of personal identity as a member of various communities
- **Structures:** power and systems within society
- **Attributes:** character traits, values, habits of mind

But the curriculum does not specify which of these strands might apply to the early twentieth-century Canada outcomes we have been discussing. However, we might speculate that exploring the similarities and differences in the experiences, challenges, and reform efforts between Canada in 1890–1914 and the present day may be motivated by several purposes: to encourage students to be more active citizens, to help students connect with their historical and contemporary communities, or to engender understanding of the enduring power structures within Canada.

ORGANIZING THEMES

Organizing themes are the topics that subdivide a given grade level or distinguish one course focus from another. For example, there are three organizing strands for expectations in the grade 8 history and geography Ontario curriculum: application, inquiry, and understanding (historical or geographical) context. In history and geography courses at the later grades the organizing themes vary from course to course.

On the next page are two diagrams that illustrate the structure of the Ontario geography curriculum for grade 8 and the structure of the grade 8 social studies curriculum for Alberta.

PROGRAM RATIONALE

While curriculum strands suggest how the outcomes are to be divided, they don't tell us why we are teaching them. The rationale identifies the ultimate reasons for a program. In other words, a rationale for a social studies program explains the point of pursuing the goals discussed above. In this respect, the rationale is the "bottom line" of a program. In the face of uncertainty or conflicting directions, the rationale provides a basis for deciding which direction to pursue.

The tendency among some teachers is to regard discussion of the rationale for a subject as a rather abstract and irrelevant exercise. This attitude is unfortunate. Getting clear about our rationale—the reason for doing something—gives us a sense of purpose. The danger when we are unclear about

FIGURE 2.1   ONTARIO GRADE 8 GEOGRAPHY CURRICULUM

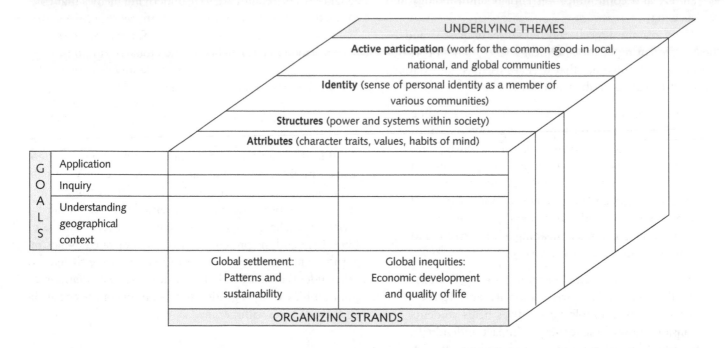

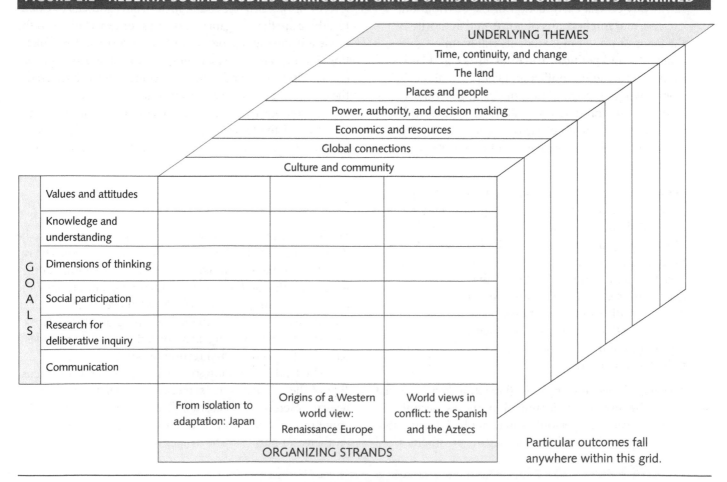

the ultimate reason for doing what we do is that we will teach a topic merely for the sake of covering it. Thus, the rationale for a subject—whether it is clearly spelled out in the curriculum or one we develop and refine individually—should serve a practical function: it should give us some sense of direction when interpreting and implementing the curriculum. This direction is especially important since, as we have tried to illustrate, curricula leave teachers considerable latitude in deciding the specifics of what will be taught and how.

Consider the following official rationales for teaching social studies in the following provinces:

- **Ontario:** "enable students to become responsible, active citizens within the diverse communities to which they belong. As well as becoming critically thoughtful and informed citizens who value an inclusive society, students will have the skills they need to solve problems and communicate ideas and decisions about significant developments, events, and issues" (2013B, 6).
- **Alberta:** enable students "to become engaged, active, informed, and responsible citizens" with an emphasis on "recognition and respect for individual and collective identity" in a diverse, pluralistic, inclusive, and democratic society and awareness of "their capacity to effect change in their communities, society and world" (2007, 1).
- **British Columbia:** "develop graduates who have the knowledge, skills, and competencies to be active, informed citizens. An informed citizen understands key historical, geographical, political, economic, and societal concepts, and how these different factors relate to and interact with each other (2015, n.p.).

All of these rationales refer to preparing citizens, but there is vagueness and variation in what this means. On first glance, the qualities of ideal citizenship are so general and open-ended—"informed" and able to "function" in a "diverse" world—that almost any kind of citizen might be implied. On closer investigation, the tone of the vision suggests some differences. The Ontario curriculum stresses an inclusive society, whereas Alberta offers a more socially active vision of the ideal citizen. The British Columbia rationale emphasizes informed decision making as a quality of citizenship. Our challenge, then, is to use these rationales to inform and give purpose to our teaching of the specific outcomes listed in these respective curricula. A more extensive discussion of the visions of citizenship embedded in social studies curricula is the focus of the next chapter, "Four Defining Purposes of Citizenship Education."

For the time being, it will be useful to consider briefly how a rationale might shape our teaching. What, for example, are the implications of the Ontario rationale for the grade 8 curriculum? How does teaching about early twentieth-century Canada foster the development of an ideal citizen? Several possibilities come to mind:

- **Values inclusion.** The study of an earlier period in Canadian history might be used to foster appreciation of the importance of ensuring that all individuals are welcomed in society and are afforded the same rights and opportunities.
- **Critically minded.** The study of conditions in previous times, especially of legally sanctioned abuses and discrimination, might be used to foster appreciation of the need for each individual to be vigilant and to develop and exercise a critical eye when formulating conclusions about contemporary issues and developments.
- **Responsible and active.** The study of Canadian history may be intended to develop students' inclination and ability to assume responsibility and exercise initiative in addressing personal and social problems.

The specific expectation for the grade 8 curriculum states: "describe significant examples of cooperation and conflict in Canada during this period" (Ontario 2013A, 150). The teaching activity offered when we first introduced this outcome was to ask students to use sets of primary documents to draw conclusions about various conflicts and acts of co-operation as seen from the perspectives of several groups who were involved in each event. We can see how adopting any of the suggested rationales listed above would add greater meaning and relevance to the activity. Students are no longer analyzing information for its own sake, but using this as an opportunity to understand how they might avoid conflict and or learn what is required to work collaboratively to solve pressing social problems. Having a purpose is not simply motivational for students; it influences what they learn from the activity. As Van Sledright notes, "How students view the purpose of engaging in topical or disciplinary study appears deeply connected to what they eventually learn and understand" (cited in Osborne 2004, 37).

Comparable examples could be developed for other curricula, but the conclusions would be the same. The stated rationales in curriculum documents indicate the kinds of purposes that we should set for our teaching, but even these leave open possibilities we must choose among.

This does not mean that we are free to do whatever we wish—we must work within the parameters set out by the curriculum even if the form and emphasis of that understanding may vary among us. As professionals, we have a responsibility to develop a program that is educationally sound and ethically defensible. In reaching decisions about the substance and shape of our social studies teaching—in refining the vision for our program—several factors are particularly relevant:

- the needs and expressed wishes of our students;
- the expectations embedded in the provincial curriculum in its stated outcomes, goals, strands, and rationale;
- the nature of social studies as a subject and the range of purposes that social studies is expected to serve;
- the expressed wishes of the local community;
- the priorities and needs of society generally;
- our own priorities and strengths as educators.

Concluding Comments

It is incumbent on us as social studies educators to explore and assess the nature and implications of each of the elements of a curriculum—rationale, strands, goals, and specific outcomes (or expectations)—when developing our social studies programs. To some extent, choices will have been dictated by the provincially prescribed curriculum, but surprisingly, most curricula require considerable teacher discretion in deciding what specifically to include and emphasize, and how to organize these items for instructional purposes.

Engaging in purposeful social studies is not an easy task—it will no doubt evolve over years of teaching and reflection. However, we can begin by thinking about our vision for social studies. If we have only the vaguest idea of what social studies is supposed to look like, how will our students learn from us?

Identify one or more specific outcomes prescribed in a social studies, history, or geography curriculum for a particular grade. Make a list of different activities you might undertake to help students meet this outcome. Review the rationale offered in the curriculum guide and formulate a particular purpose that would give meaning to the specific outcome(s) you identified and shape the activities you might ultimately select to meet the outcome. Justify your choice of rationale and teaching activity.

ACKNOWLEDGMENTS

We wish to acknowledge the assistance of Jan Nicol in preparing this chapter.

NOTE

1. Ontario identifies five overall goals: (1) concepts of disciplinary thinking; (2) evaluation of information and evidence; (3) personal and social attributes; (4) collaborative and cooperative relationships; and (5) use of technology (2013B, 6). Alberta has three categories of goals: (1) values and attitudes; (2) knowledge and understanding; and (3) skills and processes, which are subdivided into thinking, social participation, inquiry, and communication. British Columbia's most recent curriculum documents divide goals into content and three kinds of competencies: communication, thinking, and personal and social (2015).

REFERENCES

Alberta Education. 2007. *Social studies—Kindergarten to grade 12* and *Social studies 10–1*. Edmonton, AB: Author. Available online as *Social Studies 10–1* at http://education.alberta.ca/teachers/core/socialstudies/programs.aspx.

Brady, M. 1989. *What's worth teaching? Selecting, organizing and integrating knowledge*. Albany NY: State University of New York Press.

British Columbia Ministry of Education. 1988. *Social studies curriculum guide: Grades 8-11*. Victoria, BC: Author.

———. 1990. *The intermediate program: Learning in British Columbia*. Victoria, BC: Author.

———. 2015. *Building student success: BC's new curriculum—Social studies 1–9*. Available online at https://curriculum.gov.bc.ca/curriculum/social-studies/9.

Duplass, J.A. 2004. *Teaching elementary social studies: What every teacher should know*. New York: Houghton Mifflin.

Erickson, L.H. 1998. *Concept-based curriculum and instruction: Teaching beyond the facts*. Thousand Oaks, CA: Corwin Press.

Ontario. 2013A. *The Ontario curriculum—Social studies grades 1–6; History and geography grades 7 and 8 (revised)*. Toronto: Service Ontario. Available online at www.ontario.ca/edu.

Ontario. 2013B. *The Ontario curriculum—Grades 9 and 10: Canada and world studies (revised)*. Toronto: ServiceOntario. Available online at www.ontario.ca/edu.

Osborne, K. 2004. *Canadian history in the schools*. Unpublished report. Toronto: Historica Foundation.

Steffay, S. and W.J. Hood. 1994. *If this is social studies, why isn't it boring?* York, ME: Stenhouse Publishers.

Wasserman, S. 1990. *Serious players in the primary classroom*. New York: Teachers College Press.

Wiggins, G. and J. McTighe. 1998. *Understanding by design*. Alexandria, VA: Association of Supervision and Curriculum Development.

3

Four Defining Purposes of Citizenship Education

Penney Clark and Roland Case

itizenship has been recognized as the rationale or defining aim of social studies since its inception as a school subject. In 1916, the report that marked the formal introduction of social studies in the United States argued that the "conscious and constant purpose" of social studies was "the cultivation of good citizenship" (cited in Dougan 1988, 14–15). Since then citizenship has been called "the primary, overriding purpose" and the "distinctive justification" of social studies.[1] As Fitzgerald aptly describes it, again and again social studies reformers have come "reeling back to the old lamppost of citizenship training" (1979, 187). In Canada, George Tomkins claims that "the goal of 'citizenship' probably comes closer than any other to identifying the purpose that Canadians have usually believed that the social studies should serve" (1985, 15). Echoing Benjamin Barber's sentiments, Larry Booi writes that "public education is the vital vehicle for developing citizens of a democratic society and that social studies teachers have the main role to play in this regard" (2001, 22).

Unfortunately, general acceptance of citizenship education as the *raison d'être* for social studies does not provide much guidance or direction since there is little agreement as to what constitutes the ideal citizen. Citizenship is such an amorphous concept that it may be used to legitimize virtually anything in social studies (Longstreet 1985). Apparent consensus about the centrality of citizenship education is almost meaningless because of widely disparate conceptions of citizenship (Marker and Mehlinger 1992; Sears 1996), which range from nationalistic loyalty to international solidarity (Cogan and Derricott 2000).

In this chapter, we outline four interrelated rationales underlying citizenship education; each at varying times in the history of social studies has served as the defining purpose of the subject. Before looking at each of these, it is useful to explain why as social studies teachers we should care about which purpose (or mix of purposes), if any, undergirds our teaching.

A Direction for Social Studies

For many of us, decisions about what to teach in social studies will likely be informed, consciously or not, by our image of the type of person and world we hope to promote. If our model citizen is someone who is well-informed about social matters, we will devote much of our time to helping students acquire a breadth of knowledge. If our focus is the ability to make ethically sound decisions about complex issues, then we will likely engage students in investigating and discussing social issues. Perhaps our ideal citizen is someone who is committed to acting on his or her beliefs. In this case, students might undertake community enhancement projects or explore ways of living and acting in personally responsible ways. Each of these choices should, and likely will, be influenced by an implicit view of what our subject is all about.

For some of us, our conception of the "good" citizen may be so completely established that further discussion will make no difference. For others, however, exploring options may help us become more focussed and resolute in our orientation or perhaps cause us to modify our outlook in light of an appreciation of alternative purposes that might be served. If we take seriously our role as educators charged with making complex judgments about our students' well-being, then we must articulate with some clarity our ultimate educational aims. As Ken Osborne writes in *Teaching for Democratic Citizenship*:

> Good teachers possess a clear vision of education and of what it will do for their students. They are not simply technicians who take prescribed curriculum, or the textbook, and work their students through it. They incorporate the curriculum into their philosophy of education and use what it has to offer in ways that make educational sense. This involves thinking carefully about goals and about how to achieve them, and such thinking inevitably takes a teacher beyond the confines of the classroom. Educational

goals do not exist in a vacuum. They emerge from thinking about what one wants for students and for the society in which they live (1991, 119).

During the ninety-year history of social studies in North America, the four ideals listed below have traditionally been offered as "competing" rationales for citizenship education.[2] Two of the rationales identify specific *social* purposes—that is, their focus is the type of society we hope to promote through social studies—and the other two rationales serve *individual* purposes—these focus on the type of individuals that we want social studies to foster.

- **Social initiation.** This rationale posits that the primary purpose of social studies is to initiate students into society by transmitting the knowledge, abilities, and values that students will require if they are to fit into and be productive members of society.
- **Social reform.** This rationale holds that the primary purpose of social studies is to empower students with the understandings, abilities, and values necessary to improve or transform their society.
- **Personal development.** According to this rationale, the primary purpose of social studies is to help students develop fully as individuals and as social beings. Its direct purpose is neither to reform society nor to maintain

---

TABLE 3.1   FOUR "VISIONS" OF A CURRICULAR TOPIC: BUILDING THE CANADIAN PACIFIC RAILWAY

UNDERLYING GOALS

Social initiation: to promote knowledge of and pride in important events in Canadian history	**Social reform**: to encourage scepticism about the official versions of history and a concern for past injustices in Canada	**Personal development**: to nurture students' ability to work with each other and to plan and carry out self-directed studies	**Intellectual development**: to introduce students to the methods used by social scientists to inquire into the world

SAMPLE ACTIVITIES

• learn about the "glorious" saga of the CPR's construction and the impressive engineering feats that occurred • learn about famous people who were instrumental in building the railroad, including John A. Macdonald, Donald Smith, William Van Horne, and Sanford Fleming • explore the historical significance of the railroad—opening the West to European immigration, defence against American Manifest Destiny, fulfilling the Confederation promise • explore the railroad as a symbol of Canadian nationhood—the iron ribbon that binds Canada and the Last Spike at Craigellachie, BC—the linchpin joining East and West	• learn about the alternative story of the railroad's construction, including the exploitation of immigrant workers and the corruption and greed that resulted in the "Pacific Scandal" • learn about the personal sacrifices of the Asian workers who actually constructed the railroad • explore the hidden cost of its development, including the dislocation and abuse of First Nations and the demise of the buffalo • explore the myth of nationhood—for example, the symbolic Last Spike was stolen the first night	• allow students to select any aspect of the topic that interests them personally and decide on a way to represent their learning • explore potential career choices—engineers, developers, politicians—by considering the contribution each made to the railway • use co-operative activities, such as having students work together to create a mural depicting some aspect of the railway, and role-play to develop their ability to work with others	• learn about historical inquiry by developing an account of an event using primary sources • learn about geographical inquiry by plotting the demographic effects of the railway on local terrain or by planning a route using contour maps • learn about archaeological inquiry by developing an account of camp life based on artifacts recovered from a simulated "dig"

---

the status quo, but to develop each student's talents and character.

- **Intellectual development.** This rationale suggests that the primary purpose of social studies is to develop students' capacity for understanding the complex world they face by introducing them to the bodies of knowledge and forms of inquiry represented in history and the other social sciences.

Each of these camps themselves comprise variations. For example, the particulars of a social initiation rationale will vary depending on whether we are more liberal or conservative; similarly, social reformers may be radical or moderate in their outlook on social improvement. There is, as well, inevitable blurring of the lines between these camps—for example, at what point does a concern for social justice move from an accepted principle of mainstream Canadian society towards a commitment to social reform? Even pedagogical approaches overlap considerably. For example, although social initiation is typically associated with textbook-based programs, and intellectual development with engaging students in analysis of primary documents and social science research,

the reverse is not inconceivable. The point of categorizing different rationales is not to pigeonhole each of us in one camp or another, but to invite reflection about the options facing us when deciding upon our purpose—*our* ultimate reason—for teaching social studies.

The choices we are forced to make each day of our teaching lives should reflect these priorities. Although the differences are more matters of emphasis than of mutual exclusivity, in important respects the different purposes require choices among competing objectives. As illustrated by the examples in the "four visions" of the building of the Canadian Pacific Railway in Table 3.1 and the study of families in Table 3.2, the underlying rationale will significantly affect the nature and outcomes of the study.

It is likely—even desirable—that many of us will endorse aspects of all four camps. We might, for example, think that promoting a sense of responsibility for others and a recognition of the need to pull one's own weight are part of a core set of values that all citizens ought to abide by. To this extent we have some affinity for the social initiation camp. Perhaps we are concerned that many students are overly accepting of mainstream attitudes that contribute to environmental

TABLE 3.2 FOUR "VISIONS" OF A CURRICULAR TOPIC: STUDYING FAMILIES			
UNDERLYING THEMES			
Social initiation: promote students' knowledge of the role of the family and a sense of responsibility towards their family	**Social reform**: encourage sensitivity towards and support of family structures and predicaments that may not be universally accepted by students	**Personal development**: nurture students' pride in their families	**Intellectual development**: teach students how to gather and represent information used by social scientists
SAMPLE ACTIVITIES			
• learn about the important needs that families meet in society • learn about different family roles and the ways that family members work to support one another • learn about the responsibilities that each child has to contribute towards the harmonious operation of a family • learn about important celebrations that acknowledge parents' contributions (Father's Day, Mother's Day)	• explore and promote acceptance of less traditional family structures (including families with same-sex parents) and unfamiliar family practices from other cultures • learn about families who are less fortunate and what might be done to assist these families • carry out a project to help a family in need • learn how to recognize and respond when family members are acting improperly	• each child learns about his or her own family background • each child develops a treasure box representing the most powerful, positive family memories • each child plans a personal commemoration or personal act of kindness for a family member	• learn to interview family members and identify important information and ideas obtained • learn various ways of recording and presenting information and ideas (family tree, timelines, graphs, webbing) • learn how to formulate powerful questions to ask of a guest who is coming to talk about families

destruction, exploitation, inequality, and other social ills. In this case, we are espousing elements of a social reform perspective. We must also decide how best to prepare students for these civic responsibilities. If our inclination is to emphasize students' feelings, needs, values, issues, and problems, we are in effect adopting a personal development view of citizenship. This is certainly a widely held rationale for social studies, but we may nevertheless be concerned that helping students become "personally and socially fulfilled" may not do enough to prepare them to thoughtfully address the issues that they will encounter. The often quoted expression by George Santayana, "Those who do not remember the past are doomed to repeat it," suggests that students who have not studied much history will have little insight into or context for making sense of contemporary questions. Perhaps, then, preparation for civic life should focus on the knowledge and the principles of inquiry that drive history and the other social science disciplines. If this is the case, we have moved towards an intellectual development focus.

Think of a social studies unit you have taught or have seen taught. Using the "four visions" chart as a guide, identify the dominant rationale or rationales underlying this unit. Select a rationale not significantly represented in the unit and think of activities that would reflect this new rationale.

In formulating our own more specific set of purposes for social studies education, it is useful to view the four traditional camps as positions on two intersecting continua (as shown in Figure 3.1):

- **Social acceptance/social change spectrum.** Social initiation and social reform represent a range of positions on a social acceptance/social change spectrum. At one extreme, the point of citizenship education is to promote complete conformity with mainstream social norms and practices; at the other extreme, it is to promote total transformation of the social fabric. Seen in this light, the differences between the social initiation and social reform camps are matters of degree about the extent and

FIGURE 3.1 CITIZENSHIP EDUCATION MATRIX

Social studies rationales tend to be defined exclusively in terms of one of the continuums, either "social acceptance/change" or "child/subject-centred." Labelling a view as "social initiation" simply means that the dominant but by no means exclusive purpose is social acceptance. The closer the rationale is, for example, to the left of the social acceptance end of the continuum, the greater the emphasis placed on promoting the status quo. As a rationale moves towards the "social change" pole, the emphasis on the status quo diminishes until, at some point, the social reform purpose begins to dominate.

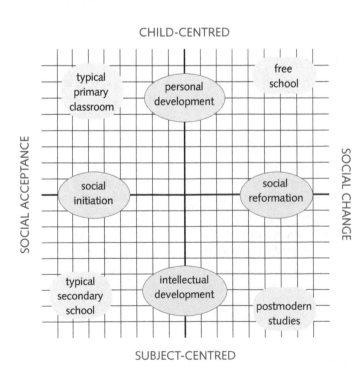

Plotting rationales within a matrix allows us to position camps in light of both sets of poles. For example, the "free school" movement in the 1960s was a radical child-centred approach to education with a strong social change mandate. Consequently, it belongs in the upper right-hand corner of the matrix. The typical secondary school program with a liberal arts emphasis is strongly subject-centred with a clear social acceptance mandate. Hence it belongs in the lower-left quadrant. Many primary classrooms would be located in the upper-left quadrant because of their child-centred, social acceptance mandate. Postmodern studies with their emphasis on making problematic the position from which scholarship is written would fall in the lower-right corner because of its critical discipline-based focus. A view of schooling in the very centre of the matrix would weight all four purposes equally: encouraging students to accept some aspects of society but to challenge others, and nurturing students' individual development in certain domains while seeking intellectual development through the disciplines.

depth that citizenship education should encourage social conformity/social transformation.

- **Subject-centred/student-centred spectrum.** Personal development and intellectual development represent a range of positions on a subject-centred/student-centred spectrum. At one extreme is a view that the best form of citizenship preparation is achieved by nurturing the whole child by focussing exclusively on his or her interests, concerns, problems, values, and so on; at the other extreme, the best form of citizenship preparation is thought to be achieved by disciplining the mind exclusively through exposure to the bodies of knowledge and forms of reasoning found in the social sciences.

Let us look at each of the traditional camps of citizenship education and consider how the differences between the camps can be explained in terms of where they fall within the matrix created by these two continua.

The Social Acceptance/ Social Change Spectrum

As indicated above, two of the traditional visions of citizenship education—social initiation and social reform—can be distinguished by the extent to which conformity with mainstream values, social practices, and world view are encouraged.

CITIZENSHIP EDUCATION AS SOCIAL INITIATION

The most common and long-standing view of the purpose of social studies, and, for that matter, of public schooling in general has been to promote a core body of beliefs and to instill the essential values and skills that are thought necessary to function in and contribute to society (Barr, Barth, and Shermis 1977, 59). The socializing role of schooling that prevailed in the 1800s was evident in the teaching of patriotism and character training, the primary components of social education at that time. Aspects of it were also evident in Canadian social studies curricula in the 1930s and 1940s, in which teachers were urged to use fables and stories about heroes (and occasionally heroines) as a means of inculcating values such as patriotism, loyalty, and courage. The "back to basics" movement of the late 1970s reinvigorated, in a very conservative voice, the call to provide all students with core knowledge and values. This tradition continues with the recent emphasis on learning the essential facts of our culture and history. J.L. Granatstein's (1998) call to teach Canada's "common cultural capital" and E.D. Hirsch's (1988) "cultural literacy" and Charles Quigley's (1991) "civic liberty" in the United

States are well-known examples of this vision. Headlines in Canadian newspapers on July 1 of each year reporting on the Dominion Institute's Canada Day History Quiz attest to continuing public interest in promoting knowledge of the basic facts of Canadian political and social history. Social initiators are likely to espouse the kinds of values (such as respect, responsibility, honesty, perseverance, optimism) advocated by the character education movement (Glaze, Hogarth, and McLean 2003) and the workplace skills of personal management, teamwork, and communication outlined in the *Employability Skills Profile* published by the Conference Board of Canada.

The social initiation rationale appears to be widely shared by social studies teachers. Jim Leming believes that in the United States, social studies teachers generally espouse a conservative version of social initiation involving "the transmission of mainstream interpretations of history and American values" (1992, 294). Linda McNeil (1986) found in an ethnographic study of teachers in six schools that a major goal was helping students maintain positive attitudes towards American institutions. In order to achieve this goal, teachers avoided content that would expose students to the injustices and inadequacies of economic and political institutions. In a survey of almost 1,800 elementary and secondary social studies teachers in British Columbia, approximately 70 per cent supported social initiation as a dominant purpose for social studies (Case 1993, 3). This compared with approximately 57 per cent who supported a social reformist role, and 38 per cent who supported intellectual development. (Respondents were not asked to comment on a personal development rationale.)

Social initiation does not necessarily require indoctrinating students into a narrow set of beliefs and values. Although nineteenth- and early twentieth-century versions of social initiation in Canada had a decidedly pro-British assimilationist bent, more recent versions embody a more multicultural, pluralistic aim (Sears 1994). An individual's perception of the prevailing, mainstream image of a good citizen may be broad-minded, including values such as an abiding respect for the rights of others and, in particular, tolerance of individual and cultural differences and freedoms. As Ken Osborne suggests, "While avoiding nationalistic chest-beating, history curricula are designed to instill in students a sense of Canadian identity, which all provinces describe as based upon respect for diversity, pluralism, and democracy" (2004, 6). Nor is social initiation inconsistent with critical thinking; but there are parameters within which this questioning is to occur—students would not be taught or encouraged to question the received interpretations of history and the foundations of the dominant world view. For example, advocates of a social initiation rationale would be less inclined to invite students to question seriously issues such as whether Confederation is something to celebrate, whether Canada is a token democracy, and under what conditions students should engage in civil disobedience. Social initiation is compatible with an active participatory citizenship; however, it would be more likely to emphasize community service projects rather than boycotts of consumer products, and voting in elections rather than political lobbying (see, for example, Alter 1997; Rappoport and Kletzien 1997).

CITIZENSHIP EDUCATION AS SOCIAL REFORM

As its name implies, social studies as social reform focusses on encouraging a better society. It posits that there is much to be improved about society and that the role of social studies is to help students acquire the understandings, abilities, and values that will launch them on this path. Although both social initiation and social reform approaches would teach students about the history and workings of our nation and the world, their dominant purposes pull in opposing directions. In the case of social initiation, the overriding point is to get students to endorse the implied world view, whereas social reformers believe the emphasis should be to prepare students to critique the existing society. And unlike the social initiation approach, where the emphasis is on getting students to participate in and contribute to the established ways of operating, the social reform approach aims to empower students to work towards a "different" society. The reform position need not imply a radical anarchistic view of social change, but by definition social reform is more controversial than the social initiation position. Jim Leming (1992) and others believe it is for this reason that social reform is espoused more often by university professors than by classroom teachers.

Social studies' closest turn towards a social reform orientation occurred in the 1970s. Jerome Bruner, earlier a proponent of an intellectual development rationale, announced in a 1971 article entitled "The Process of Education Revisited" a "moratorium" or at least a "de-emphasis" on teaching the structure of history and instead argued for teaching history in the context of the problems facing American society (21). He identified social problems such as poverty, racism, the unpopular war in Vietnam, and the extent to which schools had become "instruments of the evil forces in our society" (20) as desired foci for social studies instruction. Osborne points out that Canada, too, had a "crisis of values" at this time, with the October Crisis of 1970, new societal concerns such as sexism, the stirring of discontent among Native peoples, and a breakdown in federal/provincial relations (1984, 95). Others point to Black studies, women's studies, and third world or development studies, which have been regularly offered in Ontario

as examples of a social reform vision of social studies (van Manen and Parsons 1985, 6). More recently, some environmental education programs have raised critical consideration of local problems such as land use and conservation, as well as larger issues such as overpopulation, pollution, and resource depletion. The recent Alberta curriculum has elements of social reform in that it encourages debates around unresolved issues in Canadian identity such as the nature of federalism, the meaning of democracy, and differing conceptions of social justice (Osborne 2004, 7).

An important thread of the social reform camp is teaching students to be what Walter Werner and Ken Nixon call "critically minded"—to be inclined as a general orientation to ask hard questions about much of what we encounter (1990, 2). Students need, for example, to be taught that public media do not simply convey information but, as Neil Postman suggests, they "conceptualize" reality: "They will classify the world for us, sequence it, frame it, enlarge it, reduce it, and argue a case for what it is like" (1979, 39). The very fact that public media pay attention to or ignore an event determines what we come to see as important or worth knowing. So too with what gets taught in schools. We shape students' perceptions of what is important in school and in life by celebrating the individual efforts of famous figures (for example, Van Horne built the CPR, Cheops built the Great Pyramid) and not the collective toil of ordinary, often exploited people, or by focussing on the military outcomes of battles and not on their environmental outcomes. A social reformer would want students to be critical (in an intellectually healthy way) of the very sources and selection of information they encounter— including their teacher and their textbooks. In contrast, a social initiator, even one close to the reform camp, would want students to be more generally accepting of these sources.

Within the last thirty years, a more radical version of social reform espoused by critical theorists has appeared in the social studies literature. This version presumes that knowledge is never impartial but always represents a value position because it is constructed by people with particular values and interests (Smits 1997; Stanley 1981). Representing any knowledge as a given or as objectively true obscures its social, economic, political, and historical contexts. Social science knowledge shapes our society in conformity with some values and in opposition to others since the dominant culture within society has a major influence on the development and maintenance of social institutions. This radical form of social reform calls for "root criticism" of all knowledge in the social sciences, including critical study of gender, race, nationalistic, or social class domination of social structures and knowledge (Nelson 1985, 370). Canadian proponents of this conception include van Manen, who espouses the "emancipatory" suggestion that "a socially conscious person" ought to engage in "social criticism of all forms of hegemony including the authority of the knowledge and value orientations taught in school" (1980, 114).

A second key element in many versions of social reform is the importance attached to social action. Since the overarching goal is to improve society, students should be assisted in acquiring the abilities and the inclinations to act on their beliefs. Fred Newmann's book *Education for Citizen Action* has been influential in urging that students develop "environmental competence" (1975, 157) and engage in social action as the natural outcome of considering public issues. There has been a somewhat spotty and ambiguous inclusion of "social action" in Canadian social studies curricula. For example, the new Alberta curriculum identifies "social participation" as one of four core skills. Most of the examples refer to developing leadership skills in school and community groups, but the curriculum document does indicate that this goal "could include social action" (2006, 9). Similarly, the current social studies curriculum in British Columbia (2006, 1997) mandates action projects outside the classroom for students at several grades. However, it is ambiguous as to the rationale. It is consistent with a social initiation rationale to engage students in non-controversial forms of social participation such as cleaning up the litter around the school grounds and raising money for a local charity. A reform purpose for social action would involve students in projects that do more than perpetuate the way things are done by filling in the gaps in existing social services (Wade 2000). For example, elementary students have been involved in social reform by writing letters to the newspaper about the way baboons were caged at a Calgary zoo (Dueck, Horvath, and Zelinski 1977) and McDonald's use of styrofoam packaging (Roth 1991).

The Child-centred/Subject-centred Spectrum

Unlike the two purposes of citizenship education already discussed, which have an implied stance towards the status quo—either that the existing state of affairs is basically sound or that it is not and should be changed—the next two camps that we discuss posit no such assumption. Perpetuating or altering the social order are not their preoccupation. Rather, their concern is where to focus in identifying and developing the desired knowledge, abilities, and values. Are they found with the individual by looking to and working with the range of personal needs and everyday predicaments of students, or do they reside in the subject area, in this case in the storehouse of intellectual insight offered though the social science disciplines? The tension between these two poles was expressed by the principal of a prestigious school in India that we visited. His school and many other élite schools in India have a strong intellectual development focus. This principal implicitly acknowledged the social development emphasis of a certain rival school when he commented with a hint of criticism, "Oh yes, you can tell students from that school, they are always so well-adjusted."

CITIZENSHIP EDUCATION AS PERSONAL DEVELOPMENT

The focus of personal development is on nurturing students who are fulfilled—personally and socially. It is believed that the "good" society will follow from creating well-adjusted individuals. Important elements of this tradition are traced to John Dewey's progressivist philosophy. Osborne suggests that "Canadian progressivism spoke in terms of the growth and development of students, of meeting students' needs, of teaching the whole child, and much less of social reform or reconstruction" (1996, 42). Instead of an imposed body of knowledge or predetermined direction for social studies education, the desired understandings, abilities, and attitudes are very much those that are required to cope with and make sense of students' own lives and experiences. As Shermis explains, in this tradition "a problem is not a problem unless an individual senses it as such" (1982, 49).

The personal development rationale has had a long history. It can be seen in the 1916 report of the National Education Association Committee on Social Studies in which it was suggested that instruction be organized "not on the basis of the formal social sciences, but on the basis of concrete problems of vital importance to society and of *immediate interest to the pupil* [emphasis added]" (cited in Jenness 1990, 77). This progressive-inspired tradition came into prominence in Canada in the 1930s, a decade during which every province initiated major curricular reform. Revised provincial curricula exemplified new "child-centred" approaches, which implied correlation of subject matter to the needs and interests of the child. The emphasis was on the "whole" child who would "grow physically, emotionally and spiritually, as well as mentally" (Newland 1941, 12). Curricula were activity-oriented, with a focus on group investigation of problems or issues of interest to students; the activities were intended to promote co-operation, communication, and decision making. Social studies formed the basis of these group investigations, called "enterprises" at the elementary level in many provinces (Alberta Department of Education 1936, 288). "The social studies classroom instead of being a place where children 'learn' history, geography, and civics, is to be a real laboratory, where co-operation, initiative, originality and responsibility are developed" (Alberta Department of Education 1935, 36). At the secondary level, this approach found expression in programs referred to in different provinces as core curriculum, life adjustment curriculum, or an integration of social studies with language arts and the humanities.

In the 1960s, the values clarification movement was an important addition to the personal development orientation. Values clarification is a model for teaching values developed by Louis Raths, Merrill Harmin, and Sidney Simon (1966). It encourages students to choose their own system of values. The values clarification model has been described as "extraordinarily influential" in the development of the 1971 Alberta social studies curricula (Milburn 1976, 222).

The personal development rationale remains in evidence in contemporary social studies, especially in the elementary school. Key features of this vision include: (1) a belief that the content of what is learned is not as significant as students finding what they study personally relevant to their lives, (2) an emphasis on supporting students in pursuing their own directions and developing their own interests, (3) an emphasis on exposing students to a wide range of situations and experiences where they can work out their beliefs and develop their own positions on issues, and (4) a priority given to supporting students in feeling confident about themselves and their beliefs over challenging students to think differently or to question their values.

CITIZENSHIP EDUCATION AS INTELLECTUAL DEVELOPMENT

The definition of social studies that exemplifies the intellectual development rationale is Edgar Wesley's: "the social studies are the social sciences simplified for pedagogical purposes" (1937, 4). The defining feature of this tradition is not simply or even essentially a matter of acquiring a body of knowledge as it is mastery of the norms and methods used by scholars to gain new knowledge. It is believed that the various social science disciplines have generated the richest insights and investigative techniques for understanding our social world. Hence, developing the minds of students as social scientists and historians is thought to provide the best preparation for citizenship in a complex world. Unlike the personal development camp, intellectual development rationales see the disciplines, more than the students, providing the problems worth considering. Initiation into the academic traditions is more important than exposure to problems of immediate and personal concern, and coming to one's own conclusions is not as important as coming up with intellectually defensible conclusions.

This tradition came into its own with the publication of Jerome Bruner's slim book *The Process of Education* in 1960. Bruner referred to the "structure of the disciplines," by which he meant teaching the component parts or basic structures—the concepts, canons of reasoning, and techniques of in-

quiry—particular to each discipline. He believed that the basic ideas lying at the heart of the disciplines are simple enough for students at any level to grasp. Bruner argued that "intellectual activity anywhere is the same, whether at the frontier of knowledge or in a third-grade classroom" (14). Consequently, rather than simply presenting students with the findings of a discipline, students should take on the role of social scientist and use the inquiry techniques of the disciplines to make discoveries themselves. Before social studies was itself a subject, proponents of history education were stressing the importance of analysis of source documents for the "mental training which may be obtained from their use" (Caldwell, 1899, reported in Osborne 2003, 482). This tradition has been evident in Canada in the texts and other curriculum materials used in the late 1960s and 1970s. It also appeared in texts used for university social studies curriculum and instruction courses, such as *Teaching the Subjects in the Social Studies,* where the authors identify helping school children begin to learn the thinking patterns, or structure, of the social sciences as a major purpose of elementary social studies (Moore and Owen 1966, v). These authors explain that "a better democratic citizen [is one] who can think historically or geographically, who can think as an economist or as a political scientist, whenever these approaches are relevant to the assessment of contemporary situations" (ibid.).

A similar philosophy underlies a 1960s approach to teaching geography in the elementary school:

> the child learns, at his own level, the structure of geography and the methods used by the professional geographer. He will learn of, through use at his own level, the various subjects which contribute to the subject of geography. He will also learn through practice in the field, and later with pictures, to observe details carefully, to record these details in many ways, to analyze the data, and then to synthesize selected data to answer a problem (Social Studies Advisory Committee 1962, 139).

While the structure of the disciplines approach has been somewhat discredited,[3] the calls to promote disciplined historical and geographical understandings are as strong as they ever were. In fact, there is considerable pressure, including calls from Canadian academics (Seixas 1994, 1997; Granatstein 1998), to replace social studies with the teaching of history and geography. As Peter Seixas (1997) argues, students should approach historical accounts critically. Yet this is unlikely to happen as long as students are taught only generic critical thinking or information processing approaches. The distinct challenges of thinking within the disciplines—notions in history such as what counts as a historically significant event, the difficulties of developing historical empathy, and the bases for accepting historical claims—require discipline-specific instruction. Without a developed capacity for historical thinking, teaching about the past is little more than the "simple accretion of increasing amounts of information" (Seixas 1994, 105). According to proponents of an intellectual development rationale, since the social science disciplines are the most rigorous and insightful forms of inquiry about our social world, they represent the best tools that social studies educators can offer students in preparation for citizenship. As Osborne wrote in the context of history, "The important tasks in teaching history are to arouse in students an interest in, and even love for, the past; to give them a sense of connectedness linking the present with both the past and the future; to help them think historically; and to show them the range of human behaviour" (2000, B3).

Having a Sense of Purpose

It is evident from the foregoing discussion that the factors that influence adoption of a particular conception include deep-rooted assumptions about the role of schooling, the perceived nature of challenges facing society and students, and the teacher's personal values and theories of knowledge and learning. Because of these ideological divisions, many have despaired of arriving at a common vision for citizenship education (Marker and Mehlinger 1992, 832). Attempts to reach consensus typically result in statements of purpose that are so vague they provide no helpful direction and are of dubious educational value. For example a 1982 survey of provincial curricula by the Canadian Council of Ministers of Education concluded that the common focus is on inquiry approaches towards a goal of providing "students with the knowledge, skills, values and thought processes which will enable them to participate effectively and responsibly in the ever-changing environment of their community, their country and their world" (4). This statement could include anything imaginable and can be interpreted to apply to any of the four camps. Not only is consensus on an identifiable set of desired attributes of citizenship not currently present, the prospects of it are remote. It is no wonder that it is frequently observed that "The content of social studies is a smorgasbord of this and that from everywhere; it is as confusing and vague as is the goal of citizenship" (Barr, Barth, and Shermis 1977, 2).

In order to fill this serious gap, each of us must of necessity develop our own guiding purpose for social studies. After reading the above discussion, we may be inclined to actively promote aspects of all four rationales for citizenship education. Perhaps the most appropriate way of framing the challenge is by asking "In what respects should each of these purposes be promoted?" However, we must be care-

ful that this does not amount to unfocussed borrowing from all four camps. Vague and indiscriminate choices have produced the smorgasbord referred to above. Barr, Barth, and Shermis, later in the same book, characterize social studies in even less flattering terms, referring to complaints that the subject is "social sludge" and "social stew" and amounts to "a confusing hodge podge" (57). One reason for developing a focussed and discriminating sense of purpose is that few of the attributes of citizenship that are truly worthwhile can be nurtured quickly. Those that we are most serious about will require considerable thought and effort to bring about. Students will not, for example, develop mastery of the social science disciplines without considerable exposure to the body of knowledge and standards of reasoning in these areas. Promoting all of the purposes in a half-hearted way may mean that nothing is done very well. Besides, there is never enough time. We must inevitably establish priorities, even if these priorities change over time and depend upon the particular class we are teaching.

Table 3.3 provides a sampling of the ways in which each of the main goals in social studies might be developed, depending on the rationale. This table suggests that the range of social studies goals will be present in any given vision, but that the particular emphasis of each will vary.

In addition to our conscious choices as teachers, the influences of the hidden curriculum subtly but pervasively impose a tacit vision of citizenship on us. For example, reliance on a *single* "authoritative" text is likely to suppress key attributes of social reform and intellectual development, as will an emphasis on recall of received "accepted" facts over student-initiated interpretations of events. One way or another, consciously or unconsciously, we will likely advance a particular rationale. For all of these reasons, we should be cautious about assuming that we can do it all, or that it does not much matter which vision or collection of attributes we judge to be most defensible. It should be stressed that the choice of a dominant purpose should not be a whimsical personal preference. Rather, it requires thoughtful and professional judgment based on a number of factors including the needs, best interests, and rights of our students, their parents, and of society, more broadly.

The vague generalities common in most social studies curriculum frameworks create considerable latitude for teachers to interpret and implement their own clear sense of purpose. Many teaching activities and materials—such as use of textbooks and primary documents, analysis of issues, field trips—are common to all four camps. These standard teaching approaches may be employed in different ways depending on the ultimate purpose for teaching social studies—for example, by varying the topics debated, the amount of deference to the authority of the textbook, and the importance attached

TABLE 3.3 ILLUSTRATIVE GOALS FOR EACH RATIONALE

GOALS	SOCIAL INITIATION	SOCIAL REFORM	PERSONAL DEVELOPMENT	INTELLECTUAL DEVELOPMENT
Content knowledge	• mainstream view of history and the world • knowledge of core facts about Canada and the world • knowledge of rights and responsibilities	• alternative world views (post-colonial, feminist) • knowledge of "overlooked" facts about Canada and the world • knowledge of human rights	• self-knowledge • knowledge of personal events and background	• principal and core concepts of social sciences • broad general knowledge in each social science area • knowledge of historiography
Thinking	• framed social issues—thinking within "givens"—for example, how to better contribute to society, evaluate situations	• probing issues at the foundations of society • deconstructing media	• personal issue analysis • exploring personal viewpoints	• canons of historical reasoning and evidence • discipline-based academic issues
Information gathering and communication	• use of mainstream sources including electronic technology • established conventions for presenting information	• accessing "alternative" sources of information and viewpoints • persuasive presentations	• mainstream sources of information to meet personal information needs • exploring personal forms of expression and representation	• use of academic resources including original sources and field research • research papers and other forms of academic presentations
Personal and social values	• national pride and trust in civic institutions • honesty, loyalty, and respect for others • work ethic and assume responsibility for self	• global affiliations • abiding social and environmental conscience • sceptical attitude	• personal and cultural pride • personal integrity • individual values clarification	• academic self-confidence • intellectual curiosity and pursuit of knowledge • intellectual work ethic
Individual and collective action	• community service, school enhancement projects, and work placement • ability to work with others to solve problems	• direct political and social action (lobbying) • public advocacy and networking	• self-help and personal interest projects • personal advocacy	• field studies in academic areas • team research projects

to students' wishes. This possibility of massaging teaching objectives, activities, and resources to align with a particular purpose offers the most compelling reason for each of us to think clearly about the sort of citizen that ought to guide our social studies teaching. Every day in countless, often unconscious ways we shape students' development as members of society. If we are unclear about the direction, we will likely perpetuate the bland smorgasbord that has typified mission statements in social studies. If this is the case, we can hardly complain about a passive, unreflective, and apathetic citizenry, since we may have nurtured this "vision" by default—by failing to infuse our teaching with a coherent direction. Each of us needs a clear and reasonable rationale, even if it differs from the teacher's rationale that students encountered the year before and will encounter the year after. In fact, a diversity of well-conceived rationales may be healthy. Doing things well even if the goals differ is preferable to consistently doing things in a tepid and diluted manner. Far fewer students will be inspired or assisted by a social studies program that lacks clear focus and strong direction. To paraphrase a familiar proverb, "Where there is no vision, programs perish."

Refer back to the "Citizenship Education Matrix" on page 28. Locate the most defensible position for you on this grid by thinking of the students you currently teach or anticipate teaching, and the problems facing them and their society. Which mix of rationales would best meet these needs? Justify your position by thinking of why you would not want to be farther along each of the continua that form this grid.

NOTES

1. These comments are by Barr, Barth, and Shermis (1977) and Jenness (1990).

2. The conceptual framework for social studies developed by Robert Barr, James Barth, and Samuel Shermis (1977, 1978) has had the most impact and the greatest longevity. Their typology, which places citizenship as the ultimate goal of social studies, consists of three traditions: citizenship transmission, social studies as social science, and social studies taught as reflective inquiry. Our four-rationale framework differs from the three traditions of the Barr et al. model in three ways. Our "social initiation" is a narrower notion than their "citizenship transmission." They include any form of transmission of a world view—one which may be a mainstream view or a rather esoteric view held by a minority. For our part, we limit "social initiation" to mainstream world views and any vision of society that is different from the mainstream view as "social reform." Following Jean Fair (1977) and Brubaker, Simon, and Williams (1977), we believe that "reflective inquiry" neglects an important tradition in social studies—the child-centred, personal

fulfillment vision. We offer "personal development" to reflect this strand. Finally, following Suzanne Helburn (1977), we collapse the Barr et al. account of "reflective inquiry" with "social science" into what we call "intellectual development." Other conceptual frameworks include the five-camp model (Brubaker, Simon, and Williams 1977), seven program types (van Manen and Parsons 1985), and "elitist and activists" conceptions (Sears 1996).

3. The structure of the disciplines approach has been criticized on numerous counts (Fenton 1991; Massialas 1992; Dow 1992). Criticisms include charges that it relies overly on knowledge objectives and inquiry procedures from the social science disciplines, while ignoring the needs and interests of students and societal problems; that it uses materials that are too sophisticated for the students for whom they are intended; that it fails to involve typical teachers in material development; that it ignores the hidden curriculum of gender, social class, ethnic, and religious issues; that the logistical complexity of many of the projects is problematic; and that it fails to bridge the cultural gap between theory and the real world of teaching with its large classes, multiple preparations, and often resistant students.

REFERENCES

Alberta Department of Education. 1935. *Programme of studies for the elementary school*. Edmonton, AB: Author.

———. 1936. *Programme of studies for the elementary school*. Edmonton, AB: Author.

Alberta Learning. 2006. *Social studies—Kindergarten to grade 12*. Edmonton, AB: Author. Available online at http://www.education .gov.ab.ca/k_12/curriculum/bySubject/social/default.asp.

Alter, G. 1997. The emergence of a diverse, caring community. *Social Studies and the Young Learner* 10 (1): 6–9.

Barr, R., J.L. Barth, and S.S. Shermis. 1977. *Defining the social studies*. Arlington, VA: National Council for the Social Studies.

———. 1978. *The nature of the social studies*. Palm Springs, CA: ETC Publications.

Booi, L. 2001. Citizens or subjects? *AlbertaViews*, March/April: 28–33.

British Columbia Ministry of Education. 2006. *Social studies K to 7 integrated resource package*. Victoria, BC: Author.

British Columbia Ministry of Education, Skills and Training. 1997. *Social studies 8 to 10 integrated resource package*. Victoria, BC: Author.

Brubaker, D.L., L.H. Simon, and J.W. Williams. 1977. A conceptual framework for social studies curriculum and instruction. *Social Education* 41: 201–205.

Bruner, J. 1960. *The process of education*. Cambridge, MA: Harvard University Press.

———. 1971. The process of education revisited. *Phi Delta Kappan* 53: 18–21.

Case, R. 1993. *Summary of the 1992 social studies needs assessment*. Victoria, BC: Queen's Printer.

Cogan, J. and R. Derricott, eds. 2000. *Citizenship for the twenty-first century*. London: Kogan-Page.

Council of Ministers of Education, Canada. 1982. *Social studies: A survey of provincial curricula at the elementary and secondary levels*. Toronto: Author.

Dougan, A.M. 1988. The search for a definition of the social studies: A historical overview. *The International Journal of Social Education* 3 (3): 13–36.

Dow, P. 1992. Past as prologue: The legacy of Sputnik. *Social Studies* 83: 164–171.

Dueck, K., F. Horvath, and V. Zelinski. 1977. Bev Prifit's class takes on the Calgary zoo. *One World* 17: 7–8.

Fair, J. 1977. Comments of Jean Fair. In *Defining the social studies*, R. Barr, J.L. Barth, and S.S. Shermis, 106–109. Arlington, VA: National Council for the Social Studies.

Fenton, E. 1991. Reflections on the "new social studies." *Social Studies* 82: 84–90.

Fitzgerald, F. 1979. *America revised: History schoolbooks in the twentieth century*. Toronto: Little Brown.

Glaze, A.E., B. Hogarth, and B. McLean, eds. 2003. Can schools create citizens?: An exploration of character and citizenship education in Canadian, US, and UK schools. Special issue, *Orbit* 33 (2).

Granatstein, J.L. 1998. *Who killed Canadian history?* Toronto: Harper Collins.

Helburn, S.W. 1977. Comments of Suzanne W. Helburn. In *Defining the social studies*, R. Barr, J.L. Barth, and S.S. Shermis, 110–113. Arlington, VA: National Council for the Social Studies.

Hirsch, E.D. 1988. *Cultural literacy: What every American needs to know.* New York: Vintage.

Jenness, D. 1990. *Making sense of social studies*. Toronto: Collier Macmillan.

Leming, J.S. 1992. Ideological perspectives within the social studies profession: An empirical examination of the "two cultures" thesis. *Theory and Research in Social Education* 20 (3): 293–312.

Longstreet, W.S. 1985. Citizenship: The phantom core of social studies curriculum. *Theory and Research in Social Education* 13 (2): 21–29.

Marker, G. and H. Mehlinger. 1992. Social studies. In *Handbook of research on curriculum*, ed. P.W. Jackson, 830–851. Toronto: Maxwell Macmillan.

Massialas, B.G. 1992. The "new social studies": Retrospect and prospect. *Social Studies* 83: 120–124.

McNeil, L. 1986. *Contradictions of control: School structure and school knowledge*. New York: Routledge and Kegan Paul.

Milburn, G. 1976. The social studies curriculum in Canada: A survey of the published literature in the last decade. *Journal of Educational Thought* 10: 212–224.

Moore, E. and E.E. Owen. 1966. *Teaching the subjects in the social studies: A handbook for teachers*. Toronto: Macmillan.

Nelson, J.R. 1980. The uncomfortable relationship between moral education and citizenship instruction. In *Moral development and politics*, ed. R. Wilson and G. Schochet, 256–285. New York: Praeger.

———. 1985. New criticism and social education. *Social Education* 49: 368–371.

Newland, H.C. 1941. Report of the supervisor of schools. In *Thirty-sixth annual report of the Department of Education of the Province of Alberta*. Edmonton, AB: A. Schnitka, King's Printer.

Newmann, F.M. 1975. *Education for citizen action: Challenge for secondary curriculum*. Berkeley, CA: McCutchan.

Osborne, K. 1984. A consummation devoutly to be wished: Social studies and general curriculum theory. In *Curriculum Canada V: School subject research and curriculum/instruction theory. Proceedings of the Fifth Invitational Conference of Curriculum Research of the CSSE*, ed. D.A. Roberts and J.O. Fritz. Vancouver: Centre for the Study of Curriculum and Instruction, University of British Columbia.

———. 1991. *Teaching for democratic citizenship*. Toronto: Our Schools/Our Selves Education Foundation.

———. 1996. Education is the best national insurance: Citizenship education in Canadian schools—past and present. *Canadian and International Education* 25 (2): 31–58.

———. 2000. Who killed Granatstein's sense of history? Misguided criticisms. *National Post*, May 27.

———. 2003. Fred Morrow Fling and the source-method of teaching history. *Theory and Research in Social Education* 31 (4): 466–501.

———. 2004. *Canadian history in the schools*. A report prepared for Historica Foundation, Toronto. Available online at www.histori.ca.

Postman, N. 1979. *Teaching as a conserving activity*. New York: Delta Books.

Rappoport, A.L. and S.B. Kletzien. 1997. Kids around town: Civic education through democratic action. *Social Studies and the Young Learner* 10 (1): 14–16.

Quigley, C.N. 1991. *Civitas: A framework for civic education*. Calabasas, CA: Center for Civic Education.

Raths, L.E., M. Harmin, and S.B. Simon. 1966. *Values and teaching: Working with values in the classroom*. Columbus, OH: Charles E. Merrill.

Roth, A. 1991. Battle of the clamshell. *Report on Business Magazine*, April: 40–43, 45–47.

Sears, A. 1994. Social studies as citizenship education in English Canada: A review of research. *Theory and Research in Social Education* 22 (1): 6–43.

———. 1996. "Something different to everyone": Conceptions of citizenship and citizenship education. *Canadian and International Education* 25 (2): 1–15.

Seixas, P. 1994. A discipline adrift in an "integrated" curriculum: The problem of history in British Columbia schools. *Canadian Journal of Education* 19 (1): 99–107.

———. 1997. The place of history within social studies. In *Trends and issues in Canadian social studies*, ed. I. Wright and A. Sears, 116–129. Vancouver: Pacific Educational Press.

Shermis, S.S. 1982. A response to our critics: Reflective inquiry is not the same as social science. *Theory and Research in Social Education* 10 (1): 45–50.

Social Studies Advisory Committee, Faculty of Education, University of British Columbia. 1962. *History and geography teaching materials*. Vancouver: University of British Columbia.

Smits, H. 1997. Citizenship education in postmodern times: Posing some questions for reflection. *Canadian Social Studies* 31 (3): 126–130.

Stanley, W.B. 1981. The radical reconstructionist rationale for social education. *Theory and Research in Social Education* 8: 55–79.

Tomkins, G. 1985. The social studies in Canada. In *A Canadian social studies*, rev. ed., eds. J. Parsons, G. Milburn, and M. van Manen, 12–30. Edmonton, AB: University of Alberta.

van Manen, M. 1980. A concept of social critique. *The History and Social Science Teacher* 15: 110–114.

van Manen, M. and J. Parsons. 1985. What are the social studies? In *A Canadian social studies,* rev. ed., eds. J. Parsons, G. Milburn, and M. van Manen, 2–11. Edmonton, AB: University of Alberta.

Wade, R.C. 2000. Beyond charity: Service learning for social justice. *Social Studies and the Young Learner* 12 (4): 6–9.

Werner, W. and K. Nixon. 1990. *The media and public issues: A guide for teaching critical mindedness.* London, ON: Althouse Press.

Wesley, E.B. 1937. *Teaching social studies in high schools.* Boston: D.C. Heath.

PART 2 Ends and Means

4

Beyond Inert Facts
Teaching for Understanding in Secondary Social Studies

Roland Case

Only one in three Canadians knows who scored the winning goal that long-ago day in Moscow. Just half can place the significance of the Last Spike and almost no one knows the name of the judicial decision that gave women the right to be appointed to the Senate. These are the findings of a new poll that shows that Canadians continue to be dismally ignorant of their own history (Campbell 2000, A1).

It cannot be too strongly impressed, that Education consists not in travelling over so much intellectual ground, or the committing to memory of so many books, but in the development and cultivation of all our mental, moral, and physical powers. The learned Erasmus has long since said: "At the first it is no great matter how much, but how well you learn it" (Ryerson 1847, 56–57).

The annual release of the Dominion Institute's Canada Day quiz fuels newspaper reports, such as the first quotation above, decrying students' ignorance of national historical facts and petitioning educators to teach more Canadian history. Similar reports are made about Canadians' geographic illiteracy based on students' inability to recall basic information (Canadian Council for Geographic Education 2005). Should we be alarmed about these consistently poor results?[1] Does this necessitate spending more time on content knowledge in history and geography?

Alternatively, the problem may not be that we don't teach enough history and geography but, as suggested by the second quotation, the ways in which these subjects are taught may contribute to the forgetting of these facts. Ironically, if we stress covering more facts, we may fuel a worse problem than lack of recall of details. Consider the following editorial by a Vancouver high school student writing about his courses:

[W]e are taught in a way which focuses on the individual facts and trivia, as opposed to general understanding. This implies to the student that there's

something inherently important about the facts in isolation from their context. This is wrong thinking and bizarre. Facts are useful things, but only so far as they help you to understand the bigger picture. No one is going to quiz you in your future life about the year the Magna Carta was signed, or the nervous system of the flatworm. The reason is, of course, that nobody cares. As long as general understanding is reached, no one gives a damn about trivia. Facts come when understanding is reached. Not the other way around.

Perhaps for similar reasons, a 1943 American survey by prominent social studies educator Edgar Wesley found very little difference in the scores on a general knowledge test of American history between high school students who had studied American history and those who had not. It is also revealing that the same test was administered to a sample of adults drawn from *Who's Who in America*. The study concluded that "many well-informed, useful, successful, and even distinguished persons cannot answer 75 per cent of the items" (Wesley, cited in Barr, Barth, and Shermis 1977, 40). This last finding underscores another key conclusion: there is an important difference between "remembering" historical or geographic information—factual recall—and "understanding" these events. For example, students may not remember that the term "Last Spike" refers to the final joining of the Canadian Pacific Railway in 1885, yet they may nevertheless have some understanding of the significance and key features of this event. As historian George Wrong noted in 1924, "Education is what is left when we have forgotten most of the facts we have learned" (cited in Osborne 2000, 36). Clearly, understanding the key ideas is more complicated and more important than simple recall of dates, place names, and terminology. Unfortunately, many public reports calling for the teaching of more "content" fail to make this distinction clear.

In this chapter, I explore how we might teach social studies content in ways that foster understanding rather than mere recall of information and that stimulate student interest, not irrelevance. My reference in the title of this chapter to "inert" facts comes from Alfred North Whitehead's famous book, *The Aims of Education*, in which he suggests that "the central problem of all education" is in preventing knowledge from becoming inert (1929/67, 5). By inert, Whitehead means "ideas that are merely received into the mind without being utilized, or tested, or thrown into fresh combination" (1). Harvard educational psychologist David Perkins defines inert knowledge as "knowledge that learners retrieve to answer the quiz question, but that does not contribute to their endeavours and insights in real complex situations" (1993, 90). His colleague at Harvard, Howard Gardner, notes that "Coverage is the enemy of understanding" (cited in Antonelli 2004, 42). The paradox of "less is more" may be especially true in this respect: less direct teaching of facts may result in greater understanding of and interest in the content, which may produce increased long-term retention of information.

Calling attention to the need to see our task as engendering understanding, not transmitting information, has been a persistent theme in social studies. John Dewey wrote in his influential book, *How We Think,* that "the aim often seems to be—especially in such a subject as geography—to make the pupil what has been called a 'cyclopedia of useless information'" (cited in Hare 1994, 72). In 1960, Shirley Engle warned of a "ground-covering fetish" by which he meant the practice of "learning and holding in memory, enforced by drill, large amounts of more or less isolated descriptive material" (302). Walter Parker (1989, 41) urges that learning not be seen as "the warehousing of facts" but as the "progressive construction of understandings" and teaching not be the "telling of fact" but the leading of a construction project in which the teacher acts as a contractor—not actually building the house but contracting to students the sorts of labour that will culminate in their building of a house.

These admonitions to engage students in thinking about and with the content of the curriculum are easier said than done. Numerous challenges must be identified and overcome. This chapter focusses on teaching factual information in ways that promote understanding; in the next chapter, John Myers and I consider how to teach concepts in ways that promote conceptual understanding. By factual information, we mean beliefs about the way the world is and why it is this way. These include what in social studies are typically called "facts" and "generalizations." "Confederation occurred in 1867" and "John A. Macdonald was Canada's first prime minister" are examples of facts. "Early European exploration of North America was motivated by the desire for economic and political gain" and "Natural resources have dominated Canada's economic and social development" are examples of generalizations.[2]

Teaching for Understanding

Before examining how to teach factual knowledge in ways that increase students' understanding, it may be useful to clarify what it means to understand as opposed merely to possess (or recall) information about something. Three attributes seem especially significant:

- **Understanding implies basic comprehension of information.** Understanding a fact is not mere patter off the lips in response to a stock question. At the least, understanding implies that students can thoughtfully rephrase the answer in their own words. Richard Lederer has compiled an amusing "history" of the world gathered from students who apparently so poorly understood what was taught that they got their facts wrong. His report of students' account of ancient Rome is as follows:

  > Eventually the Romans conquered the Greeks. History calls people Romans because they never stayed in one place very long. At Roman banquets, the guest wore garlics in their hair. Julius Caesar extinguished himself on the battlefields of Gaul. The Ides of March murdered him because they thought he was going to be made king. Nero was a cruel tyranny who would torture his poor subjects by playing the fiddle to them (1987).

- **Understanding implies appreciation of significance and interconnection.** Remembering that Confederation occurred in 1867 is not the same as understanding this fact. Understanding something about Confederation requires knowing the significance of this event and how it fits into the larger historical picture. Imagine asking students: "Which is the more important event in Canada's development as a nation—Confederation or the first basketball game?" We would have little confidence that students really understand Confederation if they chose the first basketball game. This is because we would doubt that they correctly appreciated the relative magnitude of the implications of these events. Imagine also asking: "What is the relation between Canadian self-rule and Confederation?" If students could not see any connection, we again might doubt that they understood Confederation, since they seem to have little appreciation of the constellation of ideas that interconnect with the specific event or phenomenon. For this reason, amassing discreet facts adds little to understanding since it is the interrelationships that are central. Ken Osborne (2004, 4) supports this view when be observes that "It is possible, for example, for a student to master a whole list of outcomes describing the First World War, but still have no real understanding of the War as a historical phenomenon."

- **Understanding implies some grasp of the warrants for belief.** A final aspect of understanding is the need to appreciate, to some extent at least, what kind of evidence is required in deciding whether one should accept or reject a proposed statement of fact. Imagine students are told that certain statements in their textbook are thought to be false, say, that Confederation was not in 1867 or that early European exploration of North America was not motivated by the desire for economic and political gain. If students had no idea whatsoever what might count as supporting or refuting evidence for these claims, then we might wonder how well they understood what these claims signify.

Our task, if we are concerned to promote understanding, is to help students comprehend, connect, and seek justification for the information they receive. Much can be said about teaching in ways that engage students and foster understanding. In the following sections, I explore various suggestions clustered around two general themes:

- inviting students to think critically about the content;
- strategies for framing effective critical challenges.

Thinking Critically about the Content

According to Whitehead, ideas remain inert if students do not use or test them. A similar sentiment was expressed in the very first assessment of "best practice" in Canadian schools by Egerton Ryerson in his *Report on a System of Public Education for Upper Canada* (1847, 58):

> If the mind of the child when learning, remains merely passive, merely receiving knowledge as a vessel receives water which is poured into it, little good can be expected to accrue. It is as if food were introduced into the stomach which there is no room to digest or assimilate, and which will therefore be rejected from the system, or like a useless and oppressive load upon its energies.

One hundred and sixty years ago, Ryerson concluded that students must, in some fashion, "digest" the ideas they encounter—they must put the knowledge into use and assimilate or own the ideas. Answering comprehension questions after reading a text and/or taking notes while listening to the teacher are merely acts of receiving transmitted information. As Alfie Kohn reports, "Lecturing was defined by writer George Leonard as the 'best way to get information from teacher's notebook to student's notebook without touching the student's mind'" (2004, 189).

Students are digesting the content only when they think deeply about the material—that is, they begin to make reasoned judgments about or with it. As Parker notes, "Thinking is how people learn" (1988, 70). This certainly does not mean that it is inappropriate to transmit information—we must transmit information to our students. The point is that passing on information—including "covering" the Crusades and "doing" human migration—is not the heart of our task. This is merely a means to an end. Our real objective must be to support students' ability and inclination to think rigorously with and about these ideas.

The need for students to think continually about the content is crucial. It is not sufficient to "front-end load" considerable content and at a point near the end of a unit or term invite students to reflect on the ideas they have heard and read about. As Ryerson's metaphor suggests, information that has been passively acquired is not digested in a way that makes it available for future use. It ceases to be—because it never was—food for thought. For this reason we must find ongoing ways to involve students in thinking as they learn, so that they will, in fact, learn.

The most powerful way I know to help students digest what they are learning is to invite them to think critically about it using an approach I helped develop as part of The Critical Thinking Consortium.[3]

RECOGNIZING WHEN WE INVITE CRITICAL THINKING

The obvious place to begin to engage students in thinking critically is with the questions and tasks we invite them to consider. What does a question that invites critical thinking look like and how does this differ from other good questions we might ask students? We may often ask students to "think" about things, but only some of the time do we ask them to think "critically" about these things. To illustrate this difference, consider the questions in Table 4.1.

Although all three types are appropriate and valuable questions to ask of secondary students, only one type invites students to think critically.

- **Factual questions.** The questions in Column 1 ask students to recall or locate a correct answer from a source. Typically, these questions have a single correct answer. The answer already exists and the student's job is to locate it. For this reason, I sometimes refer to these as "Where's Waldo?" questions, after the children's picture book series with the same name. These books consist of sets of pictures that each contain hundreds of figures, including a funny-looking character named Waldo. Children are challenged to locate Waldo among the maze of other individuals in each picture. Although finding the correct answer can be difficult, it is not a "critical thinking" challenge because the essence of the task is to find a predetermined object, as opposed to thinking through a problem. Often questions such as "What were the main causes of World War II?" and "How does wind affect the physical landscape?" are simply "Where's Waldo" questions because the correct answer can be found in students' notes, their textbooks, the library, or in their memory. The students' task is to locate the answers in the source. Despite this limitation, these questions are useful in raising ideas to the forefront. However, if we asked only these questions, we should not presume that students have digested the information; rather, they will have simply regurgitated it.

- **Preference questions.** The questions in Column 2 invite students to share their feelings—what they like and dislike. There are no wrong answers to these questions. In that they are matters of taste. Some students might like to have been Leonardo da Vinci; others may have preferred to be Michelangelo or Raphael. Some students welcome adventure; other students do not. This type of question invites students to offer their "opinions" on matters where their answers are essentially personal preferences. Almost no answer could be said to be unacceptable. Who is to say that all students should prefer sand dunes to hoodoos or vice versa? All answers are valid.

- **Reasoned judgment questions.** Both factual and preference questions are valuable questions to ask of students—they both have a place in any teacher's repertoire. But they do not invite students' "critical" reflection. Only the questions in Column 3 invite students to think critically, because only they require students to make a judgment about which of the possible answers they might select makes the most sense or is the most

reasonable. Although there may be several (in some cases many) reasonable answers to these questions, some answers are unreasonable. For example, although plausible arguments can be made for the significance of the impact of gravity and ice erosion, it is less likely that wind erosion would be the most significant form. Questions in Column 3 ask students to go beyond locating facts and merely espousing a personal preference. When thinking critically, students are not merely reporting what they know or like. They are, in effect, offering a judgment or an assessment among possible options, determining which would be the more reasonable or justifiable choice.

The significant feature of a reasoned judgment is that we must resort to criteria. We require some basis other than our own preferences and whims for selecting one option over another. For example, in assessing the impact of various forms of erosion, it would be useful to consider the geographical scale of their impact, the permanency or historical scale of results, the visual impact, and perhaps the implications for human, animal, and plant life. These factors form the criteria for making a reasoned judgment about the most significant form of erosion.

The close relationship between the term "critical" and "criteria" is instructive. Matthew Lipman (1992) suggests that "critical" thinking is "criterial" thinking—to think critically is to think in light of or using criteria. A useful definition of critical thinking is as follows: *To think critically is essentially to assess the reasonableness of various options in light of appropriate criteria.* Notice that students may judge whether Simon Fraser, for example, was a hero on very narrow and dubious criteria, such as looks, fame, and wealth. Other criteria might include contribution to society, hardship endured, personal attributes, and respect for others. A central part of our job in helping students think critically includes inviting them to

TABLE 4.1 THREE TYPES OF QUESTIONS			
TOPIC	COLUMN 1 QUESTIONS OF FACTS	COLUMN 2 QUESTIONS OF PREFERENCE OR LIKING	COLUMN 3 QUESTIONS REQUIRING REASONED JUDGMENT
World War II	What were the main causes of World War II?	What is your favourite World War II battle?	Rank-order the causes of World War II in terms of their importance.
Renaissance	What were Machiavelli's contributions to Renaissance thinking?	If you could be any Renaissance figure you wished, who would you choose to be?	Which Renaissance figure best represents the essential features of the humanist spirit as we have defined it?
Erosion	How does wind affect the physical landscape?	What natural phenomenon created by erosion do you find the most interesting?	Which form of erosion—gravity, wind, or ice—has most significantly altered the physical landscape?

consider an appropriate set of criteria when deciding on the wisest conclusion to be derived from them.

JUDGING EFFECTIVE CRITICAL CHALLENGES

Developing effective questions or tasks that invite students to think critically is not a straightforward matter. As educators, we need to think critically about our questions. As mentioned above, if thinking critically involves thinking with criteria, we need to consider what criteria to use in judging whether a question or task is an effective critical thinking activity.

I believe an effective critical challenge will meet four criteria, which are listed in the left-hand side of Table 4.2. In the right-hand side, these criteria are applied to a question we might ask about the illustration "The 'Suburb of Happy Homes'" (Wilson, in Evenden 1995, 20), showing life in Burnaby, British Columbia in 1942.

I could, of course, ask any number of questions including Column 1, information or factual questions (for example, "How many people do you see in this picture?"), and Column 2, preference or feelings questions (for example, "Would you like to live in this time period?"). Instead, let us focus on a Column 3 question inviting reasoned judgment: "What is the month, day of the week, and time of day (within an hour) of

THE "SUBURB OF HAPPY HOMES"

Illustration by Fraser Wilson.

the scene depicted in the drawing?" Let's explore the merits of this question by considering four criteria for an effective critical challenge.

TABLE 4.2 THE BURNABY PICTURE ACTIVITY

CRITERIA FOR EFFECTIVE CRITICAL CHALLENGES	CRITERIA IN ACTION: WHAT IS THE MONTH, DAY OF THE WEEK, AND TIME OF DAY?
Clearly invite reasoned judgment among plausible alternatives It is essential that challenges pose questions or tasks that invite students to judge the reasonableness of plausible options or alternative conclusions. Since criteria give judgments rigour, the appropriate criteria should be implicit in the question. For example, when deciding which solution is the most reasonable, students might consider feasibility, effectiveness, and fairness.	Students must choose among the various months and time periods. Determining whether this requires "reasoned" judgment or mere expression of preference depends on whether we use criteria as the basis for our judgment. On what grounds might students judge whether June or January is a more reasonable suggestion for the time of year? The implicit criterion for judging the more reasonable answer is consistency with the available evidence. Students are to judge which conclusion is most consistent with the evidence in the picture (for example, the clothing worn, height of the vegetation), and with general knowledge about the world (for example, the look of plants at varying times of the year).
Are perceived as meaningful by students If students view a challenge as irrelevant and unimportant, they are unlikely to engage seriously in the activity and, over time, are likely to regard critical thinking as a boring or trivial exercise.	The challenge to decipher the time period of the scene is likely to be more engaging than the suggested Column 1 question about the number of people in the picture and the Column 2 question asking whether the students would like to live in this time period. If students had just studied about life in western Canada during the war, they might be intrigued by the invitation to apply their knowledge to solve the puzzle. Generally speaking, it is engaging to be asked a question that invites exploration, discovery, or reflection.

continued on next page

TABLE 4.2   THE BURNABY PICTURE ACTIVITY (CONT.)

CRITERIA FOR EFFECTIVE CRITICAL CHALLENGES	CRITERIA IN ACTION: WHAT IS THE MONTH AND TIME OF DAY?
Advance students' understanding of the content of the curriculum Critical thinking should not be an add-on, nor should it interrupt the pursuit of other curricular goals. Rather, challenges should involve students in thinking critically about what we want them to learn from the curriculum. In this way, they are more likely to develop an understanding of the desired curriculum outcomes.	Meeting this requirement, of course, depends on what students are supposed to be studying. By examining the picture, students are likely to learn about life in Canada during the war years. This might be one of the outcomes in the curriculum. Alternatively, if the curricular outcome deals with the differences between past and present conditions, then a more appropriate critical challenge might be to decide whether the quality of life was better for people living at the time of the drawing or in contemporary times.
Are focussed, in order to limit the background knowledge required If students are without crucial background knowledge, then the value of posing challenges may be lost. Students are likely to flounder if they lack basic information presupposed by the challenge.	The proposed challenge is relatively focussed if we compare it to related questions we might ask, for example, "What is the day of the week of the scene depicted?" Notice that the addition of this question adds further complexity, including requiring knowledge of the customs operating in Burnaby in 1942 (Would a family toil in their garden on a Sunday? Would the adults be at work on a Saturday morning? Would the children go to school?). Compare the knowledge required to determine the time of day for the scene with that required to answer the following question: What is the average annual income of this family? Clearly, this latter question would require considerably more background knowledge about the living conditions of wartime Canada.

Applying the criteria for an effective critical challenge is an important step in developing critical challenges. None of the following questions are effective invitations to think critically. For each question, decide how many of the four criteria discussed in Table 4.2 are missing to a significant extent:

- Which Canadian prime minister has served longest?
- What is your favourite period in history?
- Name three things that you noticed about this website.
- After reading this passage, identify the reasons why ozone is being depleted.

Strategies for Creating Effective Challenges

Initially, it is deceptively difficult to generate effective critical challenges. Many experienced teachers have observed that it is much like the early days of planning lessons. Our very first lesson plan took many of us days to create. Our second lesson plan was a little quicker, and, by the time we had planned our tenth lesson, we could do several in an hour. A similar pattern applies with developing critical challenges: initially it takes time and persistence to develop effective critical think-

ing questions and tasks, but eventually it can become second nature to us. In this section, I offer strategies to help you learn to develop critical challenges that satisfy each of the criteria discussed in Table 4.2.

INVITING REASONED JUDGMENT

The crucial criterion for a critical challenge is that it invites students to offer a reasoned judgment—otherwise it won't require students to think critically. Over the years, we have noted the various forms that critical challenges may take. There are at least six ways of inviting students to make reasoned judgments. Each of these ways is discussed in Table 4.3. It may help you to think of these different forms when creating your own critical challenges.

FRAMING MEANINGFUL QUESTIONS

Terrell Bell offers the following advice: "There are three things to remember about education. The first one is motivation. The second one is motivation. The third one is motivation" (source unknown). In addition to ensuring that our questions or tasks invite critical thinking, it is important they motivate students to want to learn.

TABLE 4.3 SIX WAYS TO INVITE REASONED JUDGMENT

CRITIQUE THE PIECE. One way to frame a critical challenge is to invite students to assess the merits or shortcomings of a designated entity, such as the following:

- a person (for example, a historical figure, a literary character, a contemporary leader)
- an action (for example, the proposed solution to a problem, a historical event)
- a product (for example, a passage in the textbook, a poster, an essay)
- a performance (for example, a speech, a presentation)

Sample critical challenges

- Does Canada have "responsible" government?
- Evaluate the effects of Confederation. Was it a positive or negative event for aboriginal peoples?
- Is this poster an effective visual presentation for the intended audience? (Possible criteria: catchy, convincing for the audience, clearly and concisely presented)
- On a scale ranging from great to horrible, assess what it would be like to live at this time (slave in ancient Rome, medieval serf) considering the quality of the environment, standard of living, safety, and sense of community.
- Is Simon Fraser a hero or a rogue? (Possible criteria: contribution to others, hardship endured, noble character traits, respectful of others)
- Create a report card assessing Canada's response to a pressing environmental concern (depletion of Atlantic fish stocks, climate change in the Arctic).

JUDGE THE BETTER OR BEST. Perhaps the easiest way to frame critical challenges is to invite students to judge which of two or more options (teacher-provided or student-generated) best meets the identified criteria. For example, you might ask students to determine the best solution to a problem.

Sample critical challenges

- What is the biggest (physical, daily life) difference between present conditions in Canada and conditions in another country or in a previous period in Canadian history?
- Who was the greater explorer—Vancouver or Cook?
- Which of the five suggestions is the most significant philosophical legacy of the Renaissance?
- Fresh water is an endangered commodity. Identify all the threats to safe water supplies. Which threat is the greatest concern and why? Identify possible solutions to the threat, select the most realistic and likely to be successful solution, and provide a justification for your choice.
- Should this potential recreational site be developed or left untouched?
- Would the quality of life be better sixty years ago or right now for a young person in our community (in sub-Saharan Africa)?

REWORK THE PIECE. In a third approach, students are invited to think critically as they transform a product or performance in light of new information or an assigned perspective or focus. For example, they might be asked to rewrite an account from the perspective or point of view of someone other than those in the original text—describing how a logger as opposed to an environmentalist, or a king as opposed to a peasant, would look upon relevant issues, for example. The criteria they would consider might include detailed and specific information that is consistent with the given facts and reveals the new perspective.

Sample critical challenges

- Rewrite the textbook account from another individual or group's point of view. (Possible criteria: must include same details, be believable, show significant differences)
- Given the information provided, write a letter of reference for a famous historical figure.
- Write two letters, one from the traditional perspective of First Nations peoples and one from a historical non-aboriginal perspective, about the practice of holding potlatches.
- Create a PowerPoint presentation that portrays the most significant features of an assigned time period or geographic location, as seen though the eyes of four key groups.
- Predict what might have happened if any one of the historical or geological events had turned out differently.
- Redraw the picture showing the Burnaby family scene as it would appear in the present time (or in a different period in Canada's history).

continued on next page

TABLE 4.3   SIX WAYS TO INVITE REASONED JUDGMENT (CONT.)

DECODE THE PUZZLE. Another approach to framing critical challenges invites students to use clues to solve a mystery or to explain a confusing or enigmatic situation. Asking students to use evidence from the Burnaby picture to determine the season and time is an example of decoding the puzzle.

Sample critical challenges

- Tell the story. Based on the statistics, aerial photographs, or thematic maps, develop a detailed profile of life, conditions, and events in this location.
- Using the personal qualities and characteristics as clues, identify the mystery historical figure depicted in the biography.
- Using evidence in the pictures, explain who, what, where, when, and why. (Possible criteria: based on information in the picture, uses lots of evidence to corroborate conclusions)
- Interpret the pictures and order them in their proper chronological sequence.
- Interpret the cartoonist's implicit message.
- Find out as much as you can about the region using an assigned mapping technique (scale, colour, contours).

DESIGN TO SPECS. Another effective means to frame a critical challenge is to ask students to develop a product that meets a given set of specifications or conditions. These specifications provide the criteria for judging which of the possible choices will be most effective. For example, if asked to design a rich habitat that meets the needs of an assigned animal, students would consider factors such as need for exercise, shelter, and safety to determine the specific objects to include in the habitat.

Sample critical challenges

- Write a poem about the key features in a region that represents its land and people.
- Create six questions for an end-of-unit exam that are clear, non-trivial, manageable, and require more than mere recall of information.
- Create a travelogue or itinerary to be used by an out-of-province family when planning their vacation to learn about the natural and human-made features in our province.
- Create a poster-size advertisement to discourage fellow students from smoking, effectively employing the techniques of persuasion without distorting the evidence.
- Create a detailed plan of action to address a national concern. (Possible criteria: effective, efficient, sustainable, culturally responsible)
- Write a historical narrative that accurately represents the main historical figures and events, and captures the mood of the times.

PERFORM TO SPECS. A final approach to critical challenges invites students to perform a task or undertake a course of action that meets a given set of specifications or conditions. Perform to specs is very similar to design to specs with one important difference: the focus on the latter is on the design of a product, whereas perform to specs involves acting in real time. Role-playing can be an opportunity to perform to specs if students don't simply act as they wish, but instead think carefully about which actions would be consistent with their assumed character, plausible given the context or situation, and believable.

Sample critical challenges

- Personally make a lasting contribution to (a family member, a community member, the school).
- Portray in an accurate and compelling way a mystery figure drawn for the historical period we have been studying.
- Mount a school-wide media campaign on an issue of concern to students.
- Create a tableau that accurately and clearly expresses the feelings and tensions present during the assigned historical event.
- Provide feedback to a fellow student in a manner that is constructive, respectful, clear, and honest.
- Dramatize a role play that is true to the time period, involves all the characters in a meaningful way, and captures the mood of the scene.

One of the most compelling reasons for using critical challenges as a method of teaching subject matter is the inherent appeal of being invited to think about one's own beliefs and not simply to find answers that others have produced. "The Power of Critical Challenges" is typical of many testimonials I have received about the motivational effect of inviting students to think critically.

In developing critical challenges, the following kinds of qualities in a task have greater likelihood of appealing to students:

- real-life consequences (for example, sending a letter to an actual official instead of drafting a letter to a fictional person)
- connections to present-day, topical issues
- personalized to students' lives
- tied to compelling themes (for example, justice, mystery)
- sensational details or images
- fun or engaging activities (for example, simulations)
- activities that open with an engaging hook (for example, an anecdote, role play, or a powerful example)

Another way to promote student engagement is to reduce the impediments that are likely to confound or bore students.

Following are a few suggestions:

- Strip away many of the trivial or extraneous details. For example, students need not study every major explorer or region, but perhaps only two or three representative examples.
- Minimize the kinds of tasks that student will regard as drudgery:
  - Provide manageable "inputs" (for example, avoid assigning long reading passages).
  - Limit the burden of the products that students will be required to produce without sacrificing the core understanding. For example, instead of requiring that students write an extended paragraph, ask them to summarize their arguments in note form on a chart.
- Minimize the likelihood of student frustration:
  - Keep the task focussed so students are unlikely to get bogged down. For example, if the main purpose of an activity is to develop students' ability to analyze a current issue, supply them with a few relevant background pieces rather than expecting everyone to find their own sources.
  - Ensure that students have the "tools" they will need to successfully address the task.

THE POWER OF CRITICAL CHALLENGES

Recently I was selected to be a part of the team that would be writing the Online Teacher's Guide for the new Alberta grade 7 social studies curriculum. As a part of this process, the team was given the opportunity to learn how to develop critical thinking challenges. After spending a few intensive days in Edmonton learning about critical challenges and how to create them, I decided to create one for my current junior high social studies class. These lessons were some of my most successful classes of the year. One particular lesson with my grade 8 class stood out.

I created a critical challenge on the historical figures involved with the War of 1812. We focussed on three individuals: Tecumseh, Laura Secord, and Isaac Brock. The challenge asked students to decide which of the three historical figures was the "most heroic." After creating criteria as a class for what would constitute a "hero," students were given fact sheets for the three individuals. Once the students had decided which of the three was the most heroic according to their criteria and prepared their arguments, we were to debate the heroism of the three historical figures.

I was not prepared for the lively debate that ensued. Rarely have I seen my students so engaged as they debated the heroism of Brock, Tecumseh, and Secord. My role changed quickly from teacher to referee, as I almost needed to restrain some students physically. As the bell rang, the debate raged into the hallway and on into their next class. I felt very satisfied with the lesson, as this level of engagement is rarely seen at the junior high level. However, it was not until later that night that the impact of that critical challenge really hit home.

I am the school basketball coach and that night we were playing in the city championship. It was a thrilling back-and-forth game that ended with the other team hitting a last second three-point shot to beat us. After the excitement had died down, I was in the gym cleaning up when I heard some players arguing in the hallway. I thought that some of my players were upset about the game so I went to investigate. As I opened the door, the first thing I heard was one of my players yell:

"How can you seriously say Isaac Brock was not the most heroic of the three, when he risked his own life and *died* for what he believed in?"

A smile crept across my face as I realized that the players were not arguing about the championship game they had lost only moments before, but rather, they were arguing about the topic introduced that morning in social studies. This seemingly simple critical challenge had fostered curricular understanding in a way that was perceived as meaningful and important to my students. I left the school that night as a critical challenge convert anxious to engage my students by creating more.

This story was written by Chris Good, vice-principal, École St. Gerard School, Alberta.

PROMOTING UNDERSTANDING OF THE CURRICULUM

The underlying theme of this chapter is the importance of fostering student understanding of the content of the curriculum. To do this requires making the content problematic in some way so students think critically about it, and not merely regurgitate it. Thus, a key requirement of any critical challenge is that it addresses the content we want students to understand. The examples in Table 4.4 illustrate the curricular understanding that is promoted through various critical challenges.

While developing critical challenges that help students "uncover" the curriculum takes practice, the bigger perceived obstacle is finding the time to address all of the subject matter that needs to be taught (Onosko 1989).

I want to explore this claim that inviting critical thinking means that teachers will be unable to "cover" as much of the curricular terrain as they would otherwise do if they dealt with everything in a more transmissive and less probing manner. One reason for this claim is a perception by some teachers that they are responsible for covering the entire textbook or for addressing all the main features of every era, region, or civilization mentioned in the curriculum. In a study of 1,800 social studies educators in British Columbia, one teacher wrote, "I don't have enough time to cover even 10 per cent of the textbook and other resources." Another recommended that steps be taken to "ensure that teachers do not feel that they have to 'cover' everything in the book (content) to prepare their students for their next year" (Case 1993, 6). More recently, Osborne noted that the pressure of high-stakes testing forces teachers to "cover" their courses even when they know that they need to spend more time on certain topics if students are to properly understand them (2004, 25–26).

The perceived need to cover large quantities of material may arise to some extent from a belief that our crucial task as secondary social studies teachers is to transmit information about the world. One of my objectives in this chapter is to encourage teachers to see promoting understanding as our crucial task. This would mean that we need not "get through" the textbook or "cover" every explorer or region in a unit in order to meet our responsibilities to the curriculum.

Years ago, Hilda Taba offered useful advice about balancing the quantity of information with the quality of understanding. She believed that "coverage" of topics was impossible—there was always too much to cover. Instead teachers should sample rather than survey the content. Thus, the important question for Taba was not "how many facts, but which facts we want students to think about" (Fraenkel 1992, 174). John Dewey talked of "generative knowledge"— knowledge that had rich ramifications in the lives of learners (Perkins 1993, 90). The most generative knowledge is found in powerful conceptual and factual insights that apply across many circumstances. For example, is it important that students study all the major early Canadian explorers or is it sufficient that they consider one or two explorers and come to appreciate the extent to which personal, economic, and cultural motives drove early exploration? Is it imperative that students study all the major technological inventions and their effects or is it sufficient that students come away with a few broad understandings, grounded in specific instances, of the way technology has transformed (for better and worse) almost every aspect of Canadian society? These broader insights, which span cultures and time periods, are the sorts of generative understandings that are worth emphasizing.

It is sometimes thought that devoting considerable amounts of time to in-depth studies means that students are in danger of acquiring very narrowly circumscribed understandings. There are two ways in which this shortcoming can be mitigated using a sampling approach. The notion of a geological survey of the surface of an area followed by more probing exploration at carefully selected sites is an apt metaphor for the sampling of topics. Students may receive via mini-lectures, films, or fact sheets highly condensed overviews of a period or culture, which then sets a context for more focussed case studies of particularly promising issues.

TABLE 4.4 LINKS TO CURRICULAR UNDERSTANDING

CRITICAL CHALLENGE	CURRICULAR UNDERSTANDING PROMOTED
Decode the Burnaby picture.	Learn about the customs and lifestyle within a suburban community in the 1940s.
Assess the economic, political, and social impact of the building of the CPR on European settlers, Métis, First Nations, and Asian immigrants.	Learn that certain "celebrated" events may have had significant negative results for some groups.
If you were an nineteenth-century Irish farmer intending to emigrate to Canada, which region would best meet your family's needs?	Learn about the pull factors that influenced Irish immigrants' decisions to settle in various parts of Canada.

It is also useful to consider that critical challenges need not be large-scale undertakings. Although in-depth challenges are valuable, there are many opportunities to pose "mini" challenges that take ten or so minutes to complete (for example, which of the three differences between women and men in medieval society would have the biggest impact on daily life?). Even when critical challenges are extensive, the time spent can be justified, provided many curriculum outcomes are addressed during the course of working through the challenge. The highlighted text "Bundling Curriculum Outcomes" illustrates the dozen or so outcomes in the grade 10 Alberta curriculum that would be addressed by inviting students to explore the websites of major multinational corporations such as Disney, McDonalds, Nike, and Coca Cola in the various regions of the world in which they do business, so as to draw conclusions about the impact of the global media on cultural identities.

MANAGING THE ACQUISITION OF BACKGROUND KNOWLEDGE

Students need background knowledge in order to deal competently with critical challenges. If students lack this information, and if they do not acquire it as they address the challenge, the value of posing challenges may be lost. Students are less likely to develop their ability to think critically if they are fumbling in the dark. For this reason, it is important to anticipate and manage the information required by a challenge either by narrowing the challenge or by finding effective ways to help students acquire the information.

LIMIT THE INFORMATION REQUIREMENTS

One way to limit the amount of background knowledge required is by narrowing the challenge or, as my colleague Selma Wassermann would say, "make it compact." Critical challenges must be sufficiently delimited so students need not possess encyclopedic knowledge in order to realize success.

Answering the question "Who is the greatest political leader in our country's history" is a task that could fill a book. A more focussed challenge is preferable, possibly, "Of the three historical figures we have studied, who was the greatest leader?" Similarly, completing the task "Assess the legacy of the Industrial Revolution" could fill volumes. A more focussed challenge would ask, "Based on the following two reports and your own knowledge, is the steam engine the most significant

---

BUNDLING CURRICULUM OUTCOMES[4]

Critical Challenge
To what extent do the global marketing practices in three different cultural settings of a selected multinational corporation support cultural diversity or homogenization?

Outcomes
The following grade 10 outcomes in the Alberta social studies curriculum could be addressed by this challenge.

Values
1.2 appreciate why peoples in Canada and other locations strive to promote their cultures, languages and identities in a globalizing world
1.3 appreciate how the forces of globalization shape, and are shaped by, identities and cultures

Knowledge and understanding
1.5 explore understandings, dimensions and illustrations of globalization (political, economic, social, other contemporary examples)
1.6 examine the impact of media and communications technology on diversity (universalization of pop culture, hybridization, diversification)
1.7 analyze opportunities presented by globalization to identities and cultures (acculturation, accommodation, cultural revitalization, affirmation of identity, integration)

1.8 examine challenges presented by globalization to identities and cultures (assimilation, marginalization, accommodation, integration, homogenization)

Dimensions of thinking
S.1.1 evaluate ideas and information from multiple sources
S.1.8 assemble seemingly unrelated information to support an idea or to explain an event
S.1.9 analyze current affairs from a variety of perspectives
S.2.7 develop a reasoned position that is informed by historical and contemporary evidence

Research
S.7.4 demonstrate proficiency in the use of research tools and strategies to investigate issues
S.7.11 generate new understandings of issues by using some form of technology to facilitate the process
S.7.12 record relevant data for acknowledging sources of information, and cite sources correctly

Communication
S.9.5 demonstrate discriminatory selection of electronically accessed information that is relevant to a particular topic

invention originating from the Industrial Revolution?" or, perhaps, "In the first fifty years of the Industrial Revolution, which invention most altered industry and commerce?"

PROVIDE BACKGROUND INFORMATION EFFICIENTLY

Acquiring background knowledge is obviously necessary, but teaching it often gets in the way of critical thinking. It is useful to remember that "background knowledge" is the focussed information needed to address the task at hand; this is *not* the same as "general information," which might be described as the fuller range of facts about a topic that is acquired for general interest or potential value. We often tell students more than they need to know and thereby reduce the amount of time available for them to think about the important ideas. The following list includes several strategies to teach background knowledge:

- **Don't presume that background knowledge needs to be front-end loaded.** Students can acquire necessary information as they work through the challenge and even after they have answered the challenge provisionally (for example, after students offer their considered response invite them to undertake further study to confirm whether they are right or not).
- **Deliver it economically.** One way to communicate background knowledge is to embed critical challenges in picture books. In this way, students should acquire the information they need simply by listening to or reading a story. Other mechanisms for the efficient communication of information include the following:
    - Provide point-form notes
    - Deliver short mini-lectures on the key ideas
    - Distribute teacher- or student-prepared briefing sheets
    - Use visuals to communicate information
- **Make use of students as information sources.** It is often productive to tap into the collective wisdom of the class through class and group sharing. For example, in analyzing the Burnaby picture, each student might work with a partner and then share their tentative conclusions with the entire class so that everyone has the benefit of each others' insights. Only after a common basis of background information has been developed, might students individually produce their own definitive response to the critical question. Another strategy is to divide topics among groups of students who pursue specific areas in some depth and then share their findings with the rest of the class, thereby broadening the scope of everyone's understanding.
- **Think carefully about student research.** Despite its popularity, independent library research is typically neither efficient nor reliable as a means of providing background knowledge: many students waste considerable time looking for material that does not give them all the information they need. Library research projects may be best directed to teaching students how to conduct research and not used as a means for acquiring background knowledge.
- **Where possible, frame the very acquisition of background knowledge as a critical challenge.** Find ways to chunk the acquisition of a body of knowledge into smaller bits and then frame a challenge for each segment. For example, if students were eventually to consider whether life was better now than it was sixty or more years ago, the Burnaby picture challenge could be used to teach them about life in the 1940s. In addition, students might be asked to think critically about questions they would ask of people who were alive at the time as another information-gathering strategy requiring critical thinking. The following critical challenges can be used to invite students to think critically as they acquire background information:
    - Select the five most important facts or events from the chapter.
    - Decode the contents of the picture (answer the 5Ws, who, what, where, when, and why).
    - Rank the causes or benefits in order of importance.
    - Rate the effect of a particular event or policy from the perspective of various groups.
    - Which of the provided sources offers the least reliable information?
    - Think of a powerful question and a thoughtful answer on an assigned topic.

Conclusion

The focus of this chapter is on using critical thinking as a method for teaching content knowledge. I have argued that knowledge acquisition is not a matter of transmitting bits of information, but of developing student understanding of the ideas behind the facts. Superficial coverage of information or acquisition of facts for their own sake is of marginal value—if for no other reason than it appears that much of it is forgotten almost as soon as it is taught. Our primary task is not to present students with prepackaged information for mental storage but to help them internalize, question, and utilize relevant information. I have suggested that engaging students in thinking critically about and with the content of the curriculum is most effectively accomplished through meaningful, focussed challenges for students to address.

Using a curriculum guide or learning resource as a focus, create several critical challenge questions or tasks. Endeavour to meet all of the following criteria when framing each critical challenge:

- Does it invite students to make a *reasoned judgment*?
- Is it likely to be perceived as *meaningful* by students?
- Does it *promote understanding* of curriculum content?
- Is it *focussed* to limit the amount of background knowledge?

NOTES

1. Surveys throughout the twentieth century show repeatedly that students remember very little of the history learned in schools (Osborne 2004, 35–36).

2. The word "concept" is used ambiguously in social studies by some to refer to generalizations and by others to refer to the ideas or meanings captured by words such as "justice," "table," "sustainable," and "community." We use "concept" exclusively in this latter sense.

3. For further information about The Critical Thinking Consortium, which has worked with many thousands of social studies teachers and published numerous resources, visit www.tc2.ca.

4. This example was developed by The Critical Thinking Consortium for Alberta Education as part of its online guide to support implementation of the provincial social studies curriculum. Many other critical challenges can be found on the LearnAlberta website: http://onlineguide.learnalberta.ca/.

REFERENCES

Antonelli, F. 2004. *From applied to applause.* Toronto: Ontario Secondary School Teachers' Federation, November.

Barr, R.D., J.L. Barth, and S.S. Shermis. 1977. *Defining the social studies.* Arlington, VA: National Council for the Social Studies.

Campbell, M. 2000. Our young show dismal ignorance of history. *Globe and Mail,* July 1.

Canadian Council for Geographic Education. 2005. GeoForum: About geographic education online. Available online at http://www .geoforum.ca. Accessed November 26, 2005.

Case, R. 1993. *Summary of the 1992 social studies needs assessment.* Victoria, BC: Queen's Printer.

Engle, S.H. 1960. Decision making: The heart of social studies instruction. *Social Education* 34 (8): 301–306.

Evenden, L.J., ed. 1995. *The suburb of happy homes—Burnaby: Centennial themes.* Burnaby, BC: Community Economic Development Centre and the Centre for Canadian Studies, Simon Fraser University.

Fraenkel, J.R. 1992. Hilda Taba's contributions to social education. *Social Education* 56 (3): 172–178.

Hare, W. 1994. Content and criticism: The aims of schooling. In *Papers of the annual conference of the Philosophy of Education Society of Great Britain,* ed. J. Tooley, 72–89. Oxford: New College, University of Oxford.

Kohn, A. 2004. Challenging students—and how to have more of them. *Phi Delta Kappan* 86 (3), November: 184–194.

Lederer, R. 1987. The world according to student bloopers. *Verbatim: The Language Quarterly* 13 (4). Available online at http://www .verbatimmag.com/sampler.html.

Lipman, M. 1992. Criteria and judgment in critical thinking. *Inquiry* 9 (2), May: 3–4.

Onosko, J. 1989. Comparing teachers' thinking about promoting students' thinking. *Theory and Research in Social Education* 17 (3): 174–195.

Osborne, K. 2000. Who killed Granatstein's sense of history? Misguided criticisms. *National Post,* May 27.

———. 2004. Canadian history in the schools: A report prepared for Historica Foundation, Toronto. Available online at http://www.histori.ca.

Parker, W. 1988. Thinking to learn concepts. *Social Studies* 79 (2): 70–73.

———. 1989. How to help students learn history and geography. *Educational Leadership* 47 (3): 39–43.

Perkins, D. 1993. The connected curriculum. *Educational Leadership* 51 (2): 90–91.

Ryerson, E. 1847. *Report on a system of public education for Upper Canada.* Montreal: Lovell and Gibson.

Thomas, A. 2001. We don't need no education. *The SWC Chronicle* 2 (4), June 6. (The student newspaper of Sir Winston Churchill High School, Vancouver, BC.)

Whitehead, A.N. 1929/1967. *The aims of education and other essays.* New York: Free Press.

5

Beyond Mere Definition
Teaching for Conceptual Understanding in Secondary Social Studies

John Myers and Roland Case

A few years ago, my niece (Roland's) came home with the results of an end-of-unit quiz on thirty of the most difficult concepts in social studies. The concepts included capitalism, communism, totalitarianism, liberalism, and dozens of other complex political notions. She received 96% on the quiz—the highest mark in the class. Seeking to celebrate her success and engage her in political conversation, I asked what "capitalism" meant. She immediately recited in a rather hypnotic tone a dictionary-perfect definition. I responded, "Yes, but what does it actually mean?" and my niece said she wasn't exactly sure. So I agreed that it was a difficult concept to explain and asked if she knew whether or not Canada was a capitalist country. My niece responded, "How should I know?" She was the top student in the class and she didn't really understand anything of these concepts.

Concepts are the neglected content dimension in social studies. While generally speaking we may be in danger of having an obsession with teaching factual information, we are guilty of devoting very little attention to teaching concepts. Even when concepts are taught, we often do little more than provide a definition and an example. This is unfortunate because concepts are powerful tools for making sense of our world, and memorizing definitions doesn't go very far in helping students understand their meaning. The result, to use Hilda Taba's phrase, is "the rattle of empty wagons," where students learn to parrot the labels for concepts without grasping their meaning (Parker 1988). This chapter makes a case for the importance of teaching concepts, explains what this involves, and offers teaching and assessment strategies for conceptual understanding.

The Role of Concepts

A concept is "a mental construct or category represented by a word or phrase" (Wiggins and McTighe 2005, 340). Although concepts are abstractions—meaning they are ideas—examples representing concepts do exist. For example, the concept "mountain" is a mental construct, but individual mountains do exist. Concept groupings help us organize our experiences—we can distinguish mountains from hills, and both of these from plains and valleys. Our ability to make sense of the world would be greatly impaired if we did not use concepts as organizing constructs. For example, there may be as many as 7.5 million distinguishable colours, but we can manage this diversity by grouping them into a dozen or so basic categories (Bruner 1973). In short, concepts provide the intellectual categories or lenses through which we recognize and classify the world.

A simple way to illustrate this point is to draw attention to the drawing on the following page. When asked what they see, people will typically answer "a rabbit," "a duck," "a puppet," or some other creature. These answers arise only because we possess the concepts "rabbit," "duck," and "puppet." If we were not familiar with these concepts, we would not recognize them in the drawing. Hence, the difference when looking at the drawing between seeing undefined markings and seeing representations of objects is the possession of relevant concepts. Even animals recognize and classify objects as "food" or "non-edible" and distinguish fellow animals as "prey," "mate," "predator," or "other." Concepts actually shape what we see or, as a Chinese proverb puts it, "We see what is behind our eyes." If our students do not understand, for example, the concepts "justice" and "rights," they will not see injustice in a situation where a person's rights are being violated. Similarly, Roland's niece couldn't recognize Canada as a capitalist country because she did not truly understand the concept of "capitalism."

The metaphor of concepts as intellectual lenses is especially apt in that some individuals' glasses or eyesight are not

DUCK OR RABBIT?

well focussed—they see the world in a blurred, sometimes incorrect form. The possession of rather crude concepts means that everything is reduced to vague, dichotomous categories such as "awesome" and "gross" or "fun" and "boring." Our task, then, is not solely to introduce students to new concepts in social studies, but also to refine their existing conceptual understandings so that they learn to see the world in increasingly discriminating ways. More specifically, the major focus of the secondary social studies curriculum is on helping students grasp concepts that are central to understanding economic, political, and social life (such as teaching students to distinguish "market" and "controlled" economies, to recognize when a group of people is a "nation" and when it is not, and to understand the relationship between a "human right" and a "legal right"). Because concepts organize or categorize our world, they often make most sense when paired with what they are not; we typically distinguish "observation" from "conclusion," "renewable" from "non-renewable," "capitalism" from "communism," and so on.

In addition to helping us classify and find meaning in our world, conceptual understandings are the essential building blocks for knowledge. Concepts are the basis upon which facts, theories, principles, and generalizations are constructed. Consider the following examples.

Fact: Lake Superior is the largest of the Great Lakes.
Generalization: Large bodies of water such as the Great Lakes have a moderating effect on climate.

Fact: Sir John A. Macdonald was Canada's first prime minister.
Generalization: Prime ministers are the most powerful members of their governments.

Students might memorize these statements, but they would not understand or be able to use them without knowledge of the concepts relied upon in these statements. The first pair of statements presupposes that the concepts "large," "lake," "moderating," "effect," and "climate" are understood; the second pair of statements presupposes that the concepts "prime minister," "power," "membership," and "government" are. Roland's niece might eventually learn that Canada is a capitalist country, but this fact still won't mean anything to her until she understands the concept of "capitalism." Studies going back almost a century in the area of history-learning show that emphasizing the facts at the expense of teaching the concepts impairs understanding and even retention of these facts (Wineburg 2001).

References to students' understanding or lack of understanding of a concept are potentially misleading since this may imply that concepts are either/or—either students grasp the concept or they do not. In many cases, students have an incomplete or distorted sense of a concept, which in some cases is worse than if they hadn't any conception whatsoever in the first place. For example, many students believe the opposite of "democracy" to be "communism." Since most North American students believe that democracy is a good thing, this implies that communism must be a bad thing. Communism may or may not be desirable, but it is not inherently undemocratic, as many students' misconception leads them to believe. But notice they will see communism in this light because of a conceptual confusion between economic systems (such as capitalism or communism) and political systems (democracy or dictatorship).

Challenges in Teaching Concepts

Despite their importance in helping us make sense of our world, concepts are not, generally speaking, taught effectively (Seiger-Ehrenberg 2001). Common impediments to effective conceptual teaching include:

- uncertainty over the very large number of concepts to teach, and which of those are most important to reinforce with students;
- lack of clarity about the precise distinctions between the various concepts we hope to teach (for example, How is "bias" different from "point of view"? Is the statement that "Black holes exist" or "God exists" a "fact" or an "opinion"?);
- conflation of concepts with other constructs such as facts and generalizations, and assuming that concepts can be taught the same way we teach facts;

- teaching concepts in a superficial manner by providing a definition and possibly an example or two.

Much of the rest of this chapter is devoted to suggestions on how to address these challenges.

One of the obvious difficulties is the sheer number of concepts we use in social studies. Every sentence contains concepts. Because of this, it is important to be selective. There is no point in teaching a concept merely because it is found in the curriculum or textbook. Students may already have a good grasp of the idea. For instance, most secondary students will have some understanding of "democracy" before they begin to work with it in social studies. Many students have lived in one type or another for much of their life. Rather, they need experiences to help them recognize the forms of democracy that may differ from the ones they are familiar with (distinguishing republican and parliamentary systems, direct and representative democracy, participatory and passive democracies). Our efforts should be directed towards extending understanding and correcting misperceptions of familiar concepts (the Canadian Charter of Rights and Freedoms is undemocratic) as much as introducing new concepts.

In deciding what to teach, we should introduce students to unfamiliar concepts that have significant generative potential. By "generative," we mean concepts that represent significant ideas and can be linked with other important concepts. Consider the following pairs of concepts: "plateau" and "renewable resource" or "fashion" and "culture." The first concept in each pair identifies a rather narrow notion that does not have nearly the same breadth of use as does the second concept in each pairing. Clearly, we must prioritize our teaching towards developing those concepts that will have the biggest payoff in shaping and refining students' ability to make sense of their world.

Key Features of a Concept

It is helpful, when learning to teach concepts in ways that promote student understanding, to recognize four key features of any concept (Bennett and Rolheiser 2001).

- **Concepts have a label or a name.** Even before they can speak, infants struggle to classify things with names and labels, beginning with their own name. While they will invent their own names for these groups, they will also classify objects into categories: dogs, birds, hot, painful, and so on. In fact, young children understand many sophisticated concepts long before they learn the conventional terms or labels for them. For example, long before they learn the word "discrimination," many children will understand that some individuals are picked on unfairly simply because they happen to be different. Similarly, many young students can draw conclusions from a given fact without knowing that this is called an "inference" (for example, the fact that the person waves his hand in a particular way suggests that he wants me to come towards him). As teachers, our role includes connecting students' existing conceptual understanding with the traditional words used to label these concepts. While it is helpful to know and use these labels, it is more important that students understand the meaning behind the vocabulary than for them to be able to use the words themselves.

- **Concepts are explained when examples are identified.** According to Gagné (1985, 95), concept learning refers to "putting things into a class" and being able to recognize members of that class. The American philosopher William James said: "A word is a summary of what to look for" (cited in Parker and Perez 1987, 164). Thus, recognizing the examples that fall within the concept and those that do not is at the core of understanding the concept. For instance, it would be difficult to claim that students understand the concept of "capitalism" if they cannot identify Canada as having a capitalist economy.

- **Many concepts are matters of degree.** Although some concepts are black or white—either a body of land is an island or it is not—many others are matters of degree. For example, at what point does a river become a stream? What is tall for the height of a child is not tall for a tree. If democracies take away rights of citizens during times of war or other disasters, at what point does a country cease to be a democracy and become a dictatorship instead? So-called "free market" economies are not completely without regulation, but under what conditions would an economy cease to be "free"?

- **Concepts are delineated by shared attributes.** The criteria that determine which examples belong within a conceptual category can be called attributes (also referred to as features, characteristics, or traits). For example, having three sides is an attribute of the concept "triangle"; an attribute of the concept "law" is that it regulates actions. Some attributes are absolutely necessary for inclusion. These are essential attributes (for example, we cannot refer to an object as a triangle if it doesn't have three sides; the right to vote is an essential attribute of a democratic society). Some attributes may not be shared by all examples of a concept (for example, being able to vote for political parties, while a feature of most democratic societies, is not essential, since democracies such as ancient Athens operated without a party system as do some municipal governments today).

Helping students recognize non-essential attributes deepens their understanding of a concept. Non-essential attributes include "typical" features that are often associated with the concept and may be helpful in understanding it, but are not necessarily present in all cases. For example, "mountains are (often) very high" and "mountains may have snow" are typical, but non-essential, attributes. Typical attributes of "laws" are that they often involve punishment or negative consequences if broken, and that they often prohibit or prevent action—but they may also protect or permit action. Another typical attribute of laws is that they are often written down. It may be the case that teaching students about typical features is as important as teaching them about essential features. But students must understand that a typical attribute need not always be present for the concept to apply (for example, heroes are often famous, but someone may not be famous, yet may still be a hero).

The task of identifying attributes can be challenging, especially in the case of abstract concepts. (Many social studies concepts are concrete in that they represent physical objects such as plain, plateau, archipelago, fjord, map, and globe; other concepts are abstract such as elevation, latitude, imperialism, globalization, and discrimination.)

Clarity about the attributes is key when teaching for conceptual understanding. Table 5.1 suggests key attributes for a sampling of secondary social studies concepts. Once the key essential and non-essential attributes of a concept have been identified, it is important to select from this list those items

TABLE 5.1 KEY ATTRIBUTES OF SELECTED SOCIAL STUDIES CONCEPTS	
CONCEPT	ATTRIBUTES
Bias	• an unfair preference or prejudice that colours observations or conclusions • a predisposition to praise or blame without sufficient evidence • comes in many forms: ethnocentrism, sexism, racism
Change	• all things change over time • growth is change • change is necessary for survival • change may be negative or positive • change may be gradual or dramatic
Co-operation	• co-operation does not always mean doing what you are told or that you have to "give in" • involves listening to each other in decision making • means working together for a common goal • not all "group work" is "co-operative" work
Culture	• human response to the surrounding environment • changes over time • includes many different aspects of a society (for example, language, religion, customs, laws, art, music) • is more than costumes, clothing, and food • shapes our beliefs and values in powerful ways
Human rights	• refer to things that are basic for survival or a minimal level of functioning; are not simply desirable • include both freedom from interference and entitlement to receive • apply to everyone, but the details of their application may vary from person to person
Perspective	• orients what we see and how we see things • can be physical (standing on top of or at the bottom of a hill) or mental (viewed from a teacher's, parent's, or student's perspective) • can't be avoided: everything must be viewed from some perspective • may be narrow or broad, empathetic or closed, biased or fair-minded • some perspectives are more defensible than others • we can and should be self-conscious about the perspectives we take on a given issue

about which students are most in need of instruction. It is generally unwise to attempt to teach all attributes of a concept at any one time. Instead, begin by teaching the particular attributes that students most need to understand.

Promoting Conceptual Understanding

Learning a concept involves more than simple transmission of a label or a definition. It is centrally connected with recognizing the range of application or scope of the concept. For this reason, learning to recognize whether something is or is not an example of the concept lies at the heart of conceptual understanding.

In teaching concepts that refer to concrete objects such as "maps" or "rain forest," students need to see numerous examples of the range of maps (thematic, topographic, concept) and rain forests that exist. This is also the case with concepts that refer to non-physical notions such as "bias" or "rights." For these, students require examples that highlight the particular attributes you plan to teach. For example, in teaching that "rights" can include both freedom from interference (freedom of religion, expression) and entitlement to receive (right to a lawyer, fair trial), we would include examples of each type of right.

Equally important in coming to understand a concept is knowing the limits or boundaries beyond which the concept does not apply. For this reason, non-examples are very useful in teaching. Non-examples are not simply any non-instance of the concept. Rather, they are closely related non-examples—instances that are frequently confused with the concept or are very similar but different in important respects (for example, a statutory right or a discretionary right are non-examples of a "human right").

In Table 5.2, we see examples and non-examples that might be offered to help students recognize the various at-tributes (essential and non-essential) of the concept "pencil." For example, students might be asked whether or not a pencil has to be made of wood and, if it is not, why not (it could be a mechanical pencil made of plastic or metal).

Strategies for Teaching Concepts

Considerable scholarly and professional attention has been devoted to methods for teaching concepts, most of which focus on the use of examples/non-examples. There are three general approaches offering different orientations to the use of examples and non-examples in fostering conceptual understanding:

- **concept recognition,** where the teacher identifies attributes and asks students to recognize which of the supplied items are examples and non-examples of the concept.
- **concept attainment,** where the teacher supplies items that are identified either as examples or non-examples and students must identify the attributes that distinguish the two categories.
- **concept formation,** where the teacher supplies neither identified examples and non-examples nor a list of attributes; instead, students create their own conceptual categories by sorting the items and explaining the attributes that distinguish their groupings.

Test how well you have understood some of the ideas related to the teaching of concepts. Table 5.3 contains a list of features that may or may not be necessary attributes of a mountain. For each feature, identify whether it is essential, typical, or not an attribute of a mountain. In each case, provide an example or a non-example to illustrate this feature. A sample answer for the first feature is provided.

TABLE 5.2 THE CONCEPT "PENCIL"			
ATTRIBUTES	ESSENTIAL ATTRIBUTE	NON-ESSENTIAL ATTRIBUTE	EXAMPLES AND NON-EXAMPLES
contains graphite	✓		if it did not contain graphite, but ink, it would be a pen
needs to be sharpened		✓	mechanical pencils do not need to be sharpened
made of wood		✓	mechanical pencils can be made of metal or plastic
used for writing or drawing	✓		if it wasn't, it would be a stick or pointer
has an eraser		✓	erasers are a typical but not essential attribute

TABLE 5.3 THE CONCEPT "MOUNTAIN"

FEATURES	ESSENTIAL ATTRIBUTE	TYPICAL ATTRIBUTE	NON-ESSENTIAL ATTRIBUTE	EXAMPLES AND NON-EXAMPLES
has snow on top		✓		a mountain need not have snow
is found with other mountains				
is taller than a hill				
has trees on it				
rises above its surroundings				

CONCEPT RECOGNITION

Concept recognition is the most straightforward of these approaches. It begins with the selection of the concept(s) to teach, identification of a few key attributes, and creation of a list of relevant examples/non-examples for students to consider. Students are introduced to the concept and, explicitly or implicitly, to the attributes that define the concept. Students then sort the examples and non-examples according to the identified attributes, and discuss the reasons for their choices. The teacher checks for understanding and then involves students in applying the concept in some meaningful context.

In the example found in Figure 5.1, students are asked to distinguish an opinion from a point of view (or perspective), and to recognize mental and physical points of view. In particular, two attributes were taught:

- Point of view is the location or filter that shapes our opinions, observations, and actions.
- A person's or group's point of view can be physical or mental.

The concepts might be introduced by reading an account of a car accident. Students are given sets of cards containing statements similar to those reproduced in Figure 5.1 and asked to sort them initially into two labelled piles: opinions and points of view. Subsequently, students sort the points of view pile into two kinds: physical and mental.

CONCEPT ATTAINMENT

The idea of concept attainment originates with cognitive psychologist Jerome Bruner (Bruner, Goodnow, and Austin

FIGURE 5.1 DISTINGUISHING POINT OF VIEW AND OPINION

Sort the following cards into opinions and points of view, and then sort the points of view into mental and physical.

I saw the accident while sitting as a passenger in the car that was hit.

The cost of accidents can be seen in financial and human terms.

I think the driver of the red car was speeding and didn't notice the stop sign.

My opinion of the accident is influenced by the fact that my brother was sitting as a passenger in the car that was hit.

This driver should be charged with negligence for his part in the accident.

Accidents are often very expensive.

Obviously, the driver talking on his cell phone caused the accident.

Legally, someone may be innocent of responsibility for an accident, but from an ethical standpoint they may share blame.

1967). It is a structured inquiry approach in which students are given examples and non-examples, but the particular concept is not indicated to them. In this approach, teachers select the concept they want students to attain, decide in advance on the attributes they want students to "discover," and then create or control a set of approximately ten paired examples/non-examples that will help students decipher these attributes. The examples/non-examples might be recorded as single words, phrases, actions, or images, and they may be introduced all at once to students or introduced one pair at a time as an unfolding mystery. The students' task is to ascertain which attributes explain why the examples fall into one category and the non-examples in another.

The scenario described in "Teaching about Renewable Resources" illustrates a grade 9 teacher's efforts to use a concept attainment approach to teach about renewable and non-renewable resources. The teacher begins by introducing the task and a set of ten appropriately-paired examples and non-examples. She presents the clearest contrasting pairs first and asks students to think about the differences between them. Gradually, she presents pairs representing increasingly subtle distinctions. Meanwhile, students are generating and testing their hypotheses about the attributes that distinguish the examples from the non-examples. Students who catch on to the idea are able to identify the concept and are invited to suggest their own examples, while other students continue to try to formulate the concept. A "no call-out" rule allows everyone to stay involved. At an appropriate stage, the teacher offers test examples for students to classify. These serve as initial checks for understanding. To conclude, the teacher shares the conventional labels or phrases for the concepts and helps the class reach consensus on the concepts and their defining attributes. Students discuss the changes in their thinking during the analysis of the paired examples.

The successful use of concept attainment as an unfolding mystery that students are to decipher depends on the choice and sequencing of the paired examples. The initial set of paired examples shared with the class ought to suggest several hypotheses. Midway through the set, more clearly discriminated sets of pairs should be presented to help students eliminate various hypotheses. For example, in the scenario described here, the first two pairings might suggest that

TEACHING ABOUT RENEWABLE RESOURCES

Maria Cortéz has decided that to introduce her unit on nuclear energy her grade 9 geography class needed to be clear on the nature of "renewable" and "non-renewable" resources. To make sure all students understood these concepts, she decided to use the concept attainment method. Although many of her students may have encountered these concepts in earlier grades, she wants to make sure that everyone is clear about the distinction. She makes a list of both positive "yes" and negative "no" examples of renewable resources based on her understandings of the following attribute for both natural and renewable resources:

renewable resources are natural and non-natural resources that renew or replace their supply.

She knows that the concept of renewable resources gets more complicated in the senior grades because of the influence of technologies but the grade 9s will benefit from this basic review of their understanding.

When it is time for social studies, she begins: "We are going to play a guessing game about some of the things we use. I am placing pairs of things on the board under the headings YES and NO." Ms. Cortéz puts a card with the word "water" under the YES column and another card with the word "silver" under the NO column. Then she takes a second pair of cards. She puts "paper" under the YES column and "plastic" under the NO column. Next she puts "wind" under the YES column and "gasoline" under the NO column. She then asks the class to consider the three examples under the YES column, and discuss how they are alike. "What do they have in common?"

"No call-outs, please. If you have an idea, I want you to hang onto it and see if your idea works with the next few sets of pairs." She proceeds to put "sunlight," "cotton," and "fish" under the YES column, and "oil," "salt," and "coal" in the NO column.

Now there are six cards under each column. She asks, "What idea links all the items in the YES column? If you know, can you think of a new pair of items to go in the YES and the NO columns." Several students raise their hand. At the teacher's request, Serena offers "water power" for the YES column and "polyester" for the NO column. "That's correct," replies Ms. Cortéz. "I have another pair," says Gorinder, " 'wild berries' for the YES and "crude oil" for the NO column."

Other students nod their heads in agreement. Most raise their hands when asked if they think they know the idea that links the items in the YES column. At this point, Ms. Cortéz selects a card and holds it up. "Which column does 'plastic bag' go under?" "NO." "What about 'wheat'?" "YES." "Where would 'diamonds' belong?" "NO."

The class declares that the YES examples are renewable, while the NO examples are non-renewable. Ms. Cortéz invites students to describe their thinking during the analysis of the data as a way to reconfirm the critical attributes.

"How about 'nuclear power'?" At this point, there are calls of both YES and NO. And thus an inquiry into the issues around the use of nuclear energy begins.

the YES examples are words ending in "r." The third set of pairings opposes this hypothesis. The teacher has to be clear about what to do if the ten or so pairs of examples and non-examples do not lead students to identify essential attributes, and how to deal with incorrect or partially correct hypotheses. Practice in concept attainment can help students develop skills and habits of mind useful in inquiry lessons. With experience, children become skilled at identifying relationships in the cards or specimens.

CONCEPT FORMATION

The concept formation approach evolved out of the work of social studies educator Hilda Taba (1967). In this instructional method, students begin by examining data that may be generated by the teacher or by students. Students are encouraged to explore ways of classifying or sorting the data and attach descriptive labels to their groupings. Working individually, or better yet, in teams, students might use a mind map.[1] Students are helped to form their own understanding of a concept by linking the examples to the labels and by explaining their reasoning. Finally, students apply their understanding of the concept or concepts by predicting consequences, explaining unfamiliar phenomena, or hypothesizing and testing their hypotheses.

Consider the use of concept formation to explore the concept of identity. The teacher might provide students with definitions, excerpts from personal statements, provocative images, and other artifacts that suggest particular identities (hockey uniforms, flags, corporate logos). After examining the items, the teacher invites students to look for ways of grouping them (for example, "What things belong together?"). Students might arrange items by identifying feelings associated with identity (such as pride, sense of belonging, and competition); others might focus on sources of identity (for example, peer pressure, advertising, family values) and kinds of identity (for example, cultural, family, national, regional). The teacher might prompt students with questions such as:

- How are these categories different from or similar to ...?
- What does this tell us about ...?
- What are some of the advantages and disadvantages of identity?

Each group would be asked to explain its rationale for the classification system. Drawing attention to the different ways in which students classify is an important purpose of the activity. At some point, the teacher should ask students to assign labels or names to grouped items (for example, "personal identity," "national identity," "loss of identity").

In another class on ecozones (areas of the country which can be identified by their general living [biotic] and non-living [abiotic] characteristics), the teacher provides students with sets of photographs of various regions of Canada (prairie, montane cordillera, southern Arctic, etc.). Working in groups, students sort the photographs into categories and distinguish among the categories. Students then explore the differences and similarities and conduct further research on the conditions for people living in each ecozone.

Concept formation provides students with an opportunity to explore ideas by making connections and seeing relationships between items. This method can help students develop and refine their ability to recall and discriminate among key ideas, to see commonalities and identify relationships, to formulate concepts and generalizations, to explain how they have organized data, and to present evidence to support the way in which they have organized the data.

In concept formation, students often develop the data set and even if the teacher provides the data, it is the class that establishes the classification system. This means that the concepts are identified by the students. These may or may not match the teacher's specific intentions. The strength of this approach is its open-ended opportunity for students to explore their own connections.

CHOOSING AMONG THE APPROACHES

A decision about which of the three approaches to use depends partly on the nature of the concept to be taught. Concept recognition and concept attainment are best used with concepts that have clearly defined attributes. Most concrete concepts such as "island" have one clear set of attributes that define examples (that is, either it is completely surrounded by water or it is not). Many concepts in social studies are of this type (for example, democracy, secondary industry, hypothesis, fact, assimilation), as are most concrete concepts found in geography and economics. Other concepts are "relational"—best defined when compared to other concepts (for example, an aluminum can might be considered as waste when thrown out as garbage, but would not be if it were recycled). Examples of this class of concept include "strong," "deep," "opposite," and "pollution." Relational concepts can also be taught using concept recognition or concept attainment when the pairs represent examples at opposing ends of a continuum (such as comparing free and controlled economies). If a concept has an "or" in its definition, it likely has two or more sets of alternative attributes (for example, a citizen can be either a native-born or a naturalized member of a state). Such concepts as "symbolism," "equality," "justice," "controversial," and many abstract concepts in history are of this kind. Concept formation may work best with such concepts. Table 5.4 contains examples of concept teaching using a continuum of real to abstract sources and activities.

TABLE 5.4   A CONTINUUM OF LEARNING EXPERIENCES FROM REAL TO ABSTRACT

	REAL EVENTS AND ACTUAL OBJECTS	PHYSICAL REPRESENTATIONS AND ROLE PLAYS	VISUAL REPRESENTATIONS	VERBAL REPRESENTATIONS
Sources	On-location sites and actions; genuine artifacts	Replicas or simulations	Photographs, drawings, and videos	Stories and words
Samples of teaching the concepts "delta" and "co-operation"	• during a field trip, visit a river delta • take part in classroom activities where students are allowed to work together and where they must work alone	• make a papier mâché model of delta • role-play situations where students are co-operative and where they are not	• examine photographs or videos of delta formation • look at pictures depicting people both co-operating with each other and not co-operating	• read textual description of the creation and features of a delta • read accounts and discuss situations where students are co-operative and where they are not

OTHER STRATEGIES

Although the use of example/non-example pairs is the most powerful means to help students understand concepts, other strategies are potentially useful complementary strategies. These strategies include the following.

- **Provide an opportunity to "experience" the concept.** Whether it is concrete or abstract, it is important for students to "experience" a concept. The need for tangible first-hand experience is especially acute when introducing a new concept. With concrete concepts, these experiences may be provided by using actual physical objects or pictures, rather than merely referring to examples. In the case of abstract concepts, it is often more difficult, but even more necessary, to provide students with opportunities to "experience" key attributes of the concept. In teaching about "co-operation," for example, we might involve students in simulated situations where they work at odds with each other's goals, side by side in parallel, and in interdependent ways. It may be useful to examine Table 5.4, which represents a continuum from real to abstract. Where feasible, start as far as possible to the left of the chart in providing students with opportunities to experience a concept.
- **Provide or generate a definition.** Although on their own definitions do not capture all the attributes of a concept, providing or having students create a definition (especially if they have explored examples and non-examples) contributes to their conceptual understanding.
- **Explore the etymology of the word that represents the concept.** Etymology explores the linguistic origins of a word and its formation and development through time.

Sometimes a word's origins provide a clue identifying an essential attribute of the concept. For example, the origin of the concept word "perspective" is the Latin word that refers to an optical instrument for viewing objects.

- **Compare derivative words.** Derivative words are words that come from the same stem as the concept under investigation. It is interesting, for example, to compare the notion of a periscope with the concept of perspective. A periscope is a physical device for viewing objects from under water, whereas a perspective is a more general reference to any viewpoint from which observations are made.
- **Examine synonyms and antonyms.** Often synonyms and antonyms are helpful, because students may be more familiar with these other words and their understanding of the concept under investigation can be reinforced.

Table 5.5 summarizes the strategies mentioned above and their specific applications to the teaching of the concept of "perspectives." All five strategies would rarely be used at any one time.

Assessing Conceptual Understanding

Numerous strategies can be used to assess how well students have understood a concept.

- **Recognize instances of the concept.** Provide students with original examples and non-examples and ask whether they are instances of the concept. Are the following examples of perspective?

TABLE 5.5 OTHER STRATEGIES

TEACHING IDEAS	"PERSPECTIVE"
Experiential introduction	<ul><li>Show footage of an incident (hockey game/J.F. Kennedy shooting) taken from two or more camera angles.</li><li>Have students describe objects from different physical locations (for example, crawl under the desk, stand to one side).</li><li>Ask students to look through textbooks or magazines to detect the implicit view of women.</li><li>Offer documents of a specific event in early Canadian history from British, French, and First Nations viewpoints.</li><li>Arrange for students to compare editorials on the same issue from different newspapers or letters to the editor from the same newspaper.</li></ul>
Definition	<ul><li>a mental or physical outlook or point of view</li></ul>
Etymology	<ul><li>science of optics</li><li>an optical instrument for looking through or viewing objects</li></ul>
Derivative words	<ul><li>perception</li><li>periscope</li><li>keeping things "in perspective"</li></ul>
Synonyms or antonyms	<ul><li>point of view</li><li>vantage point</li><li>orientation</li></ul>

- Viewing the Rocky Mountains from the air.
- Comparing Christian and Islamic approaches to the afterlife.
- The wrong political party won the last election.
- I don't like it when people run in the school hallway.
- **Generate examples.** Ask students to provide their own original examples of the concept:
  - Give two examples of ways of looking at the benefits of gun control.
  - Offer two perspectives on the significance of the political elections in Iraq.
- **Explain specific attributes.** Ask students to address questions about specific attributes:
  - Is it possible not to bring a perspective to any particular observation?
  - Are all perspectives equally warranted?
- **Distinguish similar concepts.** Ask students to distinguish non-examples from examples:
  - Explain in your own words the difference between an informed and an uninformed perspective. Give examples of each.
  - Explain in your own words the difference between a perspective and a judgment. Give an example of each.
- **Apply the concept.** Ask students to apply the concept in an assignment:

- Compare the view of the Parliament Buildings from the air and from the street.
- Write two letters to the editor on an issue of concern to you. One letter should look at the issue from a personal perspective and the other from a broader societal point of view.

The rubric in Figure 5.2 invites students to self-assess their ability to recognize examples of a concept, explain why a particular suggestion may or may not be an example of the concept, and provide their own examples in varying situations.

Identify an abstract concept that is not discussed in this chapter, but that is central to social studies at a particular grade level. Identify at least three important attributes and develop a set of between six and eight paired examples/ non-examples that you might use in a concept recognition or concept attainment lesson to teach these attributes.

FIGURE 5.2   SELF-ASSESSING STUDENTS' CONCEPTUAL UNDERSTANDING

	SOPHISTICATED UNDERSTANDING	GOOD UNDERSTANDING	BASIC UNDERSTANDING	LACK OF UNDERSTANDING
Recognizes examples of the concept	I can easily identify examples of the concept, even in the case of complex or difficult situations.	I can identify most examples of the concept, but I have trouble with some of the more complex or difficult examples.	I can identify obvious examples of the concept, but I am confused by the complex or difficult examples.	I struggle to identify what are supposed to be very simple examples of the concept.
Explains why the concept does or does not apply	I can easily explain when a suggestion is or is not an example of the concept, even in complex or difficult situations.	I can explain in most cases when a suggestion is or is not an example of the concept, but I have trouble explaining some of the more complex or difficult examples.	I can explain in obvious cases why a suggestion is or is not an example of the concept, but I have trouble explaining the complex or difficult examples.	I struggle to explain what are supposed to be very simple examples of the concept.
Provides own examples of the concept	I can think of my own examples of the concept, even in complex situations.	I can think of my own examples of the concept in most situations, but I have trouble thinking of examples in some of the more complex or difficult cases.	I can think of my own examples some of the time, but I have trouble thinking of examples in complex or difficult cases.	I struggle to think of examples in what are supposed to be very simple situations.

Conclusion

The focus of this chapter is on teaching concepts in ways that foster understanding. We have argued that conceptual knowledge is not a matter of transmitting bits of vocabulary to students. Rote acquisition of definitions is not worthwhile—students can't use the concepts and they will have difficulty making sense of any factual information that relies on these concepts. In promoting conceptual understanding, we have emphasized the importance of identifying key attributes for selected concepts and teaching these largely through the use of examples and non-examples. Providing opportunities to "experience" concepts is also valuable, especially for new concepts. Our goal should be to teach important concepts using strategies powerful enough to make them meaningful, memorable, and usable.

NOTE

1. Mind maps and other visual tools such as Venn diagrams can be used to help students explore concepts, and for teachers to assess student understanding. For ideas and resources on using visual tools such as mind maps, concept maps, and other graphic organizers, see Bennett and Rolheiser (2001) and McEwan and Myers (2002).

REFERENCES

Bennett, B. and C. Rolheiser. 2001. *Beyond Monet: The artful science of instructional integration.* Toronto: Bookstation.

Bruner, J.S. 1973. *Going beyond the information given.* New York: Norton.

Bruner, J., J.J. Goodnow, and G.A. Austin. 1967. *A study of thinking.* New York: Science Editions.

Gagné, R.M. 1985. *The conditions of learning and theory of instruction*, 4th ed. New York: Holt, Rinehart and Winston.

McEwan, S. and J. Myers. 2002. Graphic organizers: Visual tools for learning. *Orbit* 32 (4). Available online at http://www.oise .utoronto.ca/orbit.

Parker, W. 1988. Thinking to learn concepts. *Social Studies* 79 (2): 70–73.

Parker, W. and S.A. Perez. 1987. Beyond the rattle of empty wagons. *Social Education* 51 (3): 164–166.

Seiger-Ehrenberg, S. 2001. Concept development. In *Developing minds: A resource book for teaching thinking*, 3rd ed., ed. A.L. Costa, 437–441. Alexandria, VA: Association for Supervision and Curriculum Development.

Taba, H. 1967. *Teacher's handbook for elementary social studies.* Palo Alto, CA: Addison-Wesley.

Wiggins, G. and J. McTighe. 2005. *Understanding by design*, expanded 2nd ed. Alexandria, VA: Association for Supervision and Curriculum Development.

Wineburg, S. 2001. *Historical thinking and other unnatural acts: Charting the future of teaching the past.* Philadelphia: Temple University Press.

6

Enriched by Teaching Aboriginal Content

Lynn Newbery, Cathy Morgan, and Christine Eide

What We Learned

We are three West Coast educators whose combined teaching experience represents about eighty years in the classroom as elementary and secondary teachers and as faculty associates at Simon Fraser University working with student teachers. We are not aboriginal; however, we arrived at places in our teaching careers where we became passionately committed to seeking out aboriginal content and incorporating it into our curricula. We share some of our stories, called "Beginnings" here. We share the lessons we learned. We learned to handle racism and stereotyping, to infuse the provincial curriculum with aboriginal content, to become co-learners with our students, and to discover and appreciate the richness of local sites for learning, and the magic of traditional stories. We share the ways in which we have changed. Underlying our work is the belief that our students have achieved a fuller understanding of the Canadian story, a broader knowledge and understanding of aboriginal experiences and cultures, and a deeper

BEGINNINGS #1: LYNN

I was fortunate. As a young teacher, I learned three valuable lessons: the importance of confronting racism and stereotyping, how to infuse the curriculum with aboriginal content, and that there were rewards to becoming a co-learner with my students. This is how it happened.

In the mid-sixties I moved to a British Columbia coastal community from Toronto, where I had taught social studies and English for four years. A teacher shortage in the community of Alert Bay led to my agreeing to teach half days. The assignment included grade 7 social studies—Canadian history, beginning with the explorers. A few days before school started, I was given a textbook that seemed ancient. I knew my class contained about 60 per cent aboriginal students. I was also aware of problems of racism that existed in this small but vibrant fishing community. As I examined the textbook, I was dismayed to find words like "savage" and "uncivilized" used to describe Native people. My impulse was to hide the book, because I was afraid that I could not protect my Native students if other students chose to use this language to make fun of them. My alternative plan for social studies was to focus the year's work on traditional ways of life on the coast. I was ignorant of First Nations culture or history (I realized how deficient my education, which included a degree in modern history from the University of Toronto, had been), any sense

of what I could or should do, or how to go about it. This was probably a good thing. In my naive state, I saw no barriers.

And so began a year of exciting learning for us. We were all teachers and we were all learners. I plunged into reading each night from books I gathered; the students brought their learning and knowledge from home. Together, we shared a rich experience. The non-Native students joined in the project, working with their Native friends and researching in the library. We ended the year by travelling in a fishing boat to the mouth of a river where the students engaged in a "dig" in an old abandoned village midden. It was a year that changed me as a teacher.

I discovered that it was a positive experience to become a co-learner with my students and explore with them the tasks of seeking resources and organizing and sharing knowledge. I learned about First Nations culture on the coast, which was reviving after a hundred years of repression. I began to learn about the history of First Nations because this community had been subjected to the brutal application of the anti-potlatch laws enacted by the Canadian government. I learned that with my increased knowledge I could infuse provincial curriculum with aboriginal content. Since then I have learned that all subjects can be infused with aboriginal content. I also learned that I didn't need to hide biased textbooks but that I could use them to help students deal with racism and stereotyping.

connection to our land. We direct our stories and learning to non-Native teachers who have not travelled this road in the hope that our experiences will encourage you to discover and share with your students the richness of teaching aboriginal content.

Confront Racism, Bias, and Stereotyping

Students are exposed to bias against aboriginal people in print, music, and film, and in real day-to-day situations. We can help them identify, name, and combat this by introducing them to the concepts of racism, bias, and stereotyping; by building awareness and understanding of these problems; and by providing positive role models. I have outlined some ideas about how to accomplish these goals in the highlighted text below. Many more ideas can be found in a number of

professional resources (see, for example, British Columbia Ministry of Education 1998, 2000; Manitoba Education and Youth 2003; McCue and Associates 2000a, 2000b; Sawyer and Green 1990; Sawyer and Lundeberg 1993; Sawyer and Napoleon 1991).

Become a Co-learner with Students

The Canadian history we learned in high schools and universities often omitted aboriginal peoples. As noted by the Royal Commission on Aboriginal Peoples, "From the Commission's first days, we have been reminded repeatedly of the limited understanding of aboriginal issues among non-aboriginal Canadians and of the obstacles this presents to achieving reconciliation and a new relationship" (1996, volume 5, 92). Yet we live with this story today even if we do not know the

STARTING POINTS FOR CONFRONTING RACISM

Teach the concepts

- Work on the vocabulary: bias, opinion, viewpoint, prejudice, discrimination, stereotyping, racism. (See chapter 5 in this volume for suggestions on how to introduce these concepts.) Discuss prejudices students have encountered as young people ("you are too young"), as males or females, or as members of ethnic and religious groups.

- Expose older students to the use and inadequacy of the common stereotypical references to Native peoples—"noble savage," "silent hunter," "drunken Indian." For an exposé of Native stereotypes in Canadian culture, read *The Imaginary Indian* by Daniel Francis (1992).

Promote awareness of the problems

- Collect pictures that show people of various ages, gender, and ethnicity. Number each picture and post them around the classroom. Distribute a questionnaire containing questions about people in various contexts, for example, "If you were lost in a strange city, which person would you feel most comfortable approaching for help?" Ask students to respond to each question by selecting one of the numbered pictures. Use students' answers to explore stereotypical assumptions and to discuss the problems of systemic discrimination.

- Pose problems that touch upon discrimination. Ask students, for example, to imagine they live in a lovely three-bedroom house but the family is being transferred for a year and the house must be rented. Who will they rent it to? Create applications from a variety of people (for example, three nurses who work in the local hospital; two East Indian male university students; a First Nations family—the dad works for the hydro company and the

mom looks after three young children; a Caucasian bank executive whose wife is a social worker with no children). Distribute the applications to groups of students for review. Each group is to select the applicant to whom they would rent the house. Debrief by having a student from each group explain the reasons for their choice and for their reservations about the other applicants.

- Look at First Nations names used for cars and sports teams (for example, Braves, Pontiac, Chieftains, Cadillac) and the use of the "tomahawk chop" by sports fans.

- Examine your textbook for examples of bias or stereotyping.

Provide powerful role models

- Arrange for older students to watch movies that offer powerful portrayals of aboriginal perspectives. Notable examples include *Whale Rider* (New Zealand), *Rabbit-Proof Fence* (Australia), *Atanarjuat* (Canada), *Powwow Highway* (American with Canadian actor Gary Farmer), and *Smoke Signals* (produced completely by aboriginal people and featuring two Canadian actors in the lead roles).

- Introduce students to aboriginal role models. Most aboriginal groups have produced excellent poster series featuring actors (Adam Beach, Gary Farmer), writers (Thomas King, Eden Robinson, Tomson Highway), doctors, judges, musicians, lawyers, prominent educators, and politicians who have achieved national prominence. Historical figures to introduce include Tom Longboat, Alwyn Morris, Lady Amelia Douglas, Pauline Johnson, and Joseph Brant.

- Watch the National Aboriginal Achievement Awards each spring on CBC television.

BEGINNINGS #2: CATHY

I arrived in a small northern community in 1971 to teach primary grades, without much background knowledge about the isolated rural area. As a member of the dominant culture, it never occurred to me while I attended public school in the 1950s and '60s that aboriginal people were not represented in the curriculum (except in stereotypical ways such as "Ii" for Indian and "Ee" for Eskimo on the alphabet chart).

I wanted to know more about the local Gitxsan culture in my area, but it was not a topic discussed by the parents of the children in my classroom. I sought books about the local community to familiarize myself with the stories and history of local First Nations groups. I began to make posters and big books that incorporated First Nations material in pattern books such as Bill Martin's *Brown Bear, Brown Bear, What Do You See?* which I adapted to *Eagle, Eagle, What Do You See?* I began to involve children in writing captions for their own stories rather than reading from readers that depicted an urban circus story in which all the faces in the crowd were white.

In those early stages, I tried to adapt materials myself without consulting the Native community. Now I seek resources that have been locally developed or approved by Elders or by First Nations Education Committees. I try to find an aboriginal resource person to bring into the class. I recall a quote about the importance of sharing the community's history with my students: "Without history, a society shares no common memory of where it has been, of what its core values are, or of what decisions of the past account for present circumstances" (National Centre for History in the Schools, cited in Bredekamp and Rosegrant 1995, 116).

I understand that history began here long before Europeans arrived so I take my students to visit the First Nations historic sites in the community. I am learning to build lessons that connect students to these sites and to the traditional stories of their aboriginal ancestors. After visiting a local site, students simulated a midden dig in the classroom to think critically about how the various animal bones may have been used in the diet of the original inhabitants of the site. We learned about the prevalence of rabbit bones and understood why some aboriginal inhabitants were called "People of the Rabbit." Building my knowledge of First Nations history and cultures has taken some work, but I learned that I did not have to invent everything and that many resources were available.

I learned to handle my fear of being "politically incorrect." This concern can be simply illustrated by considering the confusion that arises over nomenclature. What terms should be used? What are the distinctions between "First Nations," "indigenous peoples," "aboriginal," "Native," and "Indian"? When considering a specific group of people should we speak of a house, a clan, a tribe, or a nation? And then there are the proper names of specific groups. Many of those names have changed in the last twenty years as First Nations have reclaimed their traditional names. The language groups can also cause confusion. For example, the Gitxsan (formerly spelled Gitksan) language is part of the Tsimshian language group but the Gitxsan cannot be called Tsimshian since that name applies to the First Nation that lives in another area of the West Coast.

It takes a bit of effort to learn the proper terms. I accepted that I was a learner and that I will make mistakes. As I learned, my knowledge deepened. As my knowledge increased, the danger of being trivial lessened. I learned to seek out the human resources living in nearby communities, to seek out the conferences that offered First Nations presenters and themes, and to have the confidence to ask questions. I am also learning to hear quieter voices, to listen before speaking, and to seek the wisdom of the Elders. My classroom was enriched with new learning, new resources, and new strategies, and my classroom became a better place to be.

---

story. A Gitxsan elder, Marie Wilson, talked about being surrounded by her ancestors whenever she spoke. The Gitxsan have a saying, "We walk on the breath of our grandfathers." The past is alive around us and even though people may not know the events of history, they live with the attitudes and emotions and consequences engendered by past events.

My appreciation for the experiences of aboriginal peoples in this country has grown as I learned about the Indian Act, the denial of the right to vote for aboriginals in the late nineteenth century, the return of the right to vote in the late 1950s and early 1960s, the fight for aboriginal fishing rights, the denial of language and culture (especially as acted out in residential schools), and the loss of the land. Blaming people for their difficulties is easy to do. Understanding the causes of the difficulties requires learning on our part. Many excellent resources on aboriginal history and culture are available for educators and students wishing to learn more (for example, Campbell et al. 2003; Carlson 1997; Kainai Board of Education et al. 2004, 2005a, 2005b; Manitoba Education and Youth 2003).

I invite all of us to leave behind any need to be "the classroom expert" for our students and, instead, acknowledge that we too are constantly learning about aboriginal peoples. The key is to participate in this shared inquiry with enthusiasm, respect, and commitment. The Nova Scotia teachers' guide for the Mi'kmaq history and culture course expresses this well:

> [T]he nature of instructional leadership provided by non-Native teachers will necessarily be different. They will actively share in the learning process with their students. In their attitudes and behaviours they will demonstrate their interest in the history of the

Mi'kmaq people, their respect for Mi'kmaq culture and spirituality, and their commitment to open-minded dialogue between the inheritors of different cultures (cited in Pohl, 2003).

▌▌

Identify various outcomes or topics in the social studies curriculum for your grade level that provide opportunities to incorporate aboriginal history, culture, and issues. In each case, briefly describe how this might be done in a way that increases understanding both of the curricular topic and of aboriginal people.

Infuse Aboriginal Content

The goal of building understanding and admiration for the resilience of aboriginal peoples everywhere in Canada will not be advanced simply by creating a designated course or unit. We should look for opportunities to infuse aboriginal points of view and issues throughout the social studies curriculum and beyond. Suggestions for integrating aboriginal discussions into the study of traditional topics in social studies, current events, and other curricular subjects are found in the highlighted text below.

INTEGRATING ABORIGINAL CONTENT

Embed into traditional social studies topics
There are many opportunities to infuse aboriginal content into the topics normally addressed in social studies. Below are a few examples:

- **War of 1812.** The War of 1812 provides an opportunity to explore the concept of great leaders by studying the visions, activities, successes, and failures of three prominent aboriginal leaders of the time—Joseph Brant, Tecumseh, and Pontiac.
- **Confederation.** This classic event in Canadian history is often studied from French and English perspectives and from the colonial points of view. It would be interesting to explore Métis and First Nations reactions.
- **Human rights.** International instances of human rights abuse can be supplemented with examples of the Canadian government's treatment of aboriginal peoples (for example, the removal of the right to vote, and to meet to discuss land claims, to hire lawyers, or to raise monies to pursue land claims; and the setting up of residential schools for Native children and banning these children from speaking their own languages).
- **Forts and military.** Elementary students enjoy the study of forts, weapons, and knights. First Nations had forts, weapons, armour, rigorous warrior training, and systems of defence and battle tactics.

Infuse aboriginal concerns into current event discussions
Aboriginal perspectives can enrich the study of current events as suggested by the following examples:

- **Catastrophic diseases.** Germ warfare and smallpox epidemics were not new in the twentieth century. Aboriginal peoples suffered the ravages of disease after contact with Europeans. Smallpox epidemics in British Columbia in 1862 reduced the population of Haida Gwaii from about ten thousand to five hundred in a very short period of time. Germ warfare was first used in North America by General Amherst in 1763 when he distributed smallpox-infected blankets to the Mi'kmaq.

- **Repatriation of cultural treasures.** The plundering of cultural artifacts by the Nazis, the destruction of antiquities by the Taliban, and the looting of museums in Iraq can be connected to the experiences of First Nations peoples whose art and bones linger on in many museums and private collections around the world, or whose totems and masks were destroyed in huge bonfires in British Columbia. Recently the Field Museum in Chicago returned the bones of 150 Haida to Haida Gwaii.
- **Arranged marriages.** First Nations had marriages arranged for controlling property rights and status, and as a method of selecting and training chiefs.

Integrate with other subjects
Aboriginal content can be integrated with other subject areas. The following ideas are drawn from *Shared Learnings* (British Columbia Ministry of Education 1998):

- **Physical Education.** Invite elementary students to research and learn a traditional aboriginal game or dance to teach to the class.
- **Science.** Investigate traditional uses of plants by aboriginal peoples, traditional ceremonies for honouring the animals and conservation practices, and stories that teach children how to respect plants and animals. Instead of studying simple machines in the context of pyramid-building in ancient Egypt, focus on West Coast First Nations practices that allowed them to raise huge cedar beams for building their large communal houses.
- **Mathematics.** Graph aboriginal information. For example, bar graphs can be used to illustrate the population of aboriginal peoples in each province and territory.
- **Health.** Discuss with students the ideas of balance and symmetry, and their importance in aboriginal life (that is, for a healthy life, the mind, body, and spirit must be in balance). Explore the implications of these qualities for students' own well-being.

Access Resources: Materials and People

There are many excellent resources developed by aboriginal educators, writers, artists, and filmmakers. This list identifies some of them.

- The seven-video series *First Nations: The Circle Unbroken* (National Film Board) is an excellent resource covering a range of important topics. It is designed for high school students and contains lesson ideas. Historical footage of aboriginal people in traditional settings can be found on the National Film Board website at www.nfb.ca (go to "Educational Resources" and click on "Documentary Lens").
- Curriculum materials developed by school districts and government agencies. Lists of materials can be obtained by contacting almost any school district or provincial ministry of education.
- The Royal Commission on Aboriginal Peoples is available online at www.ainc-inac.gc.ca/ch/rcap/sg/sgmm _e.html.
- Contact Indian and Northern Affairs Canada to locate teaching resources. There is a separate listing for each province in the blue pages. Or call Info Canada, 1-888-O-Canada (622-6232) or go to www.ainc-inac.gc.ca.
- Contact your local friendship centre. Publications by the Ministry of Indian Affairs and Northern Development provide contact information for hundreds of aboriginal cultural centres and friendship centres across Canada (McCue and Associates 2000a, 54–67; 2000b, 60–73). Use the yellow pages in the phone book and check listings under "aboriginal."
- Use the internet to find resources. Some useful sites include:
  - Aboriginal Rights Coalition of BC at arcbc.tripod.com
  - Links to aboriginal resources at www.bloorstreet.com/300block/aborl.htm
  - BC Archives at www.bcarchives.gov.bc.ca/index.htm
  - Aboriginal Resources and Services of the Library and Archives of Canada at www.collectionscanada.ca/Aboriginal/index_e.html
- Visit your public library and your school library. You might be surprised at the collections there.
- Speak to someone at your local community college or university to locate human resources. First Nations courses are increasingly available across the country.
- Tune into the Aboriginal Peoples Television Network (APTN).
- Visit the reserve or friendship centre closest to your school on June 21, National Aboriginal Day.
- Make connections with educators, historians, traditional teachers, and chiefs on the nearest reserve. These people are valuable resources who can help secure guests for your classroom, suggest learning resources, and answer questions about protocols.

Explore Local Sites

No matter where you live in Canada, you are living on someone's traditional territory. The sites are beneath your feet and local aboriginal people can tell you about them. In many places the rocks themselves explicitly point to stories. Here are some points of interest, to name just a few:

- mysterious stone faces at the end of the Baie Verte Peninsula, Newfoundland;
- hundreds of petroglyphs at Bella Coola, British Columbia;
- petroglyphs outside Peterborough, Ontario;
- Dreamer's Rock, Manitoulin Island, Ontario, where visions were sought;
- Siwash Rock in Vancouver, British Columbia.

Sometimes these sites are in the news because of government decisions with regard to the land. Students can discuss the ethics of turning burial grounds into garbage dumps, paving them over for parking lots, or making golf courses over them (an issue in the Oka Crisis in 1990). Teachers have used government decisions to increase sensitivity in students to First Nations concerns and at the same time to practise critical thinking skills and debating techniques.

Teach Local Aboriginal History

The land where we live had ten thousand years of stories embedded in the rocks prior to the arrival of Europeans and a few hundred years of stories since. Until we appreciate what the land means to aboriginal peoples, we will not be able to comprehend the issues surrounding land claims. We should make an effort to seek out the stories of the land where we live. We can learn the stories that are told on the totem poles and in the traditional and the more recent stories. Even something as simple as learning the local aboriginal place names can enrich our knowledge of where we live. Even where the land is paved over, as it is in our major cities, the stories still exist. Finding them can build a sense of belonging and commitment to the land for all students. Imagine being in Wanuskewin Heritage Park in Saskatoon and thinking about the thousands of years that the nomadic tribes of the plains gathered there. Several pre-contact sites have been identified in this place whose Cree name is loosely translated as "living in harmony." People who are aware of the events and stories of the place they are in find their experiences are enriched by their knowledge.

As teachers, we can help our students experience this rich connection to the land. We can do this by seeking the local history of an area. I have learned to ask the following questions wherever I am:

- Who were the original people who lived here? Do their descendents still make it their home today?
- How can we learn about the culture of the local aboriginal people?
- What are the aboriginal names for places here and what do the names mean?
- What stories and oral histories are part of the local aboriginal people's culture?
- Where can we obtain information regarding the history and the stories of this place?
- Who might be able to share these with us and what is the protocol in using this information with our students?
- How can we have all of our students share in this local knowledge?
- What pictures can I find of this area in local, provincial, and national archives?

Teach Aboriginal Stories

Traditional stories are a fundamental part of aboriginal cultures. As Thomas King wrote, "The truth about stories is that that's all we are" (2003, 2). They are the truth on which cultures are built and land is claimed. The stories contain everything of importance—who the people are, how they came to be, how they obtained their crests and territories, what the events of their histories and everyday lives were, what the lessons are that they want to teach their young. Title to land is invested in the stories that are sung and told. Until we try to appreciate the stories, we will never understand land claims. This point is illustrated by the following incident:

> One of the Gitxsan elders asked government officials at a land claims meeting, "If this is your land where are your stories?" He spoke in English, but then he moved into Gitxsan and told a story. All of a sudden everyone understood … how stories give meaning and value to the places we call home; how they bring us close to the world we live in by taking us into a world of words; how they hold us together and at the same time keep us apart" (Chamberlin 2004, 1).

I have learned much from aboriginal teaching stories. One example in our area is the story "The Mountain Goats of

Temlaham." In this story, young boys are mistreating a young goat. They pay no attention to the voices of their Elders warning them that the whole community will suffer from their lack of respect to the kid. The kid is rescued by one boy who defies the rest. The mountain goat people then invite the boys' people to a feast up on the mountain. When everyone is there feasting, the mountain shakes and tumbles and the people are killed except for the one exceptional boy who had saved the kid that was being mistreated. The mountain that rumbled and fell is now called Roche des Boules: "mountain of the tumbling rocks"—and every once in a while, even today, we hear the rockfalls. It reminds us of the need to be respectful of nature. The equality of all life—human, animal, and plant— is clear and all life is to be respected and treated well.

There are a number of ways to help students appreciate and understand traditional aboriginal stories:

- Expose students to a large selection of the stories, including many local ones. A Ministry of Indian Affairs and Northern Development (2000) publication lists a wide selection of children's literature about aboriginal peoples. Collections of traditional stories can be found at www.hanksville.org/storytellers/alfa.html.
- Provide models for the class of the various types of stories: creation stories, humorous stories, everyday stories, teaching stories, trickster stories, transformation stories, and stories containing the oral histories.
- Form literature circles in which four to five students can share a story they have read and analyze it as to type, purpose, what it reveals about values and beliefs, and about aboriginal world view.

- Ask students to choose the story they like best as a group and present it using the oral traditions to the class.

Conclusions

The three of us were fortunate that our lives took us into areas where First Nations cultures were strong. Most teachers do not have this opportunity, but our experiences have led us to believe that important benefits are available to all Canadian teachers who make an effort to learn about and include aboriginal content wherever we teach to whomever we teach. However, as the cartoon implies, this is unlikely to happen if we remain on the narrow, mainstream culture road.

Some of us began our journey taking very small steps—a lesson here or there, perhaps a guest speaker, perhaps a craft or art approach. Eventually we graduated to integrated units

THE ROAD LESS TRAVELLED

Cartoon by Erica Ball. Courtesy of the artist.

in social studies and language arts. Others of us plunged in, planning an entire year with an aboriginal emphasis. Regardless of where we began, we have arrived at the same place—committed to incorporating aboriginal content into the mainstream of our teaching. It has been a wonderfully enriching journey. We invite the reader also to choose this less-travelled road and find the richness there.

Research the aboriginal history of your immediate area and locate notable sites nearby. Look for sources of information including people, publications, and educational facilities (museums, libraries, cultural centres) that might assist you in planning and delivering an engaging study of this history.

REFERENCES

Bredekamp, S. and T. Rosegrant, eds. 1995. *Reaching potentials: Transforming early childhood curriculum and assessment*, vol. 2. Washington, DC: National Association for the Education of Young Children.

British Columbia Ministry of Education. 1998. *Shared learnings: Integrating BC aboriginal content K–10*. Victoria: Author.

———. 2000. *BC First Nations studies 12: Integrated resource package 2000*. Victoria: Author. Available online at http://www.bced.gov.bc.ca/irp/irp_ss.htm.

Campbell, K., C. Menzies, and B. Peacock. 2003. *BC First Nations Studies*. Victoria: British Columbia Ministry of Education.

Carlson, C.T., ed. 1997. *You are asked to witness: The Sto:lo in Canada's Pacific coast history*. Chilliwack, BC: The Sto:lo Heritage Trust.

Chamberlin, J.E. 2004. *If this is your land, where are your stories? Finding common ground*. Mississauga, ON: Knopf Canada.

Francis, D. 1992. *The imaginary Indian: The image of the Indian in Canadian culture*. Vancouver: Arsenal Pulp Press.

Kainai Board of Education et al. 2004. *Aboriginal perspectives (Aboriginal Studies 10)*. Edmonton: Duval House.

———. 2005a. *Aboriginal perspectives (Aboriginal Studies 20)*. Edmonton: Duval House.

———. 2005b. *Aboriginal perspectives (Aboriginal Studies 30)*. Edmonton: Duval House.

King, T. 2003. *The truth about stories*. Toronto: House of Anansi Press.

Manitoba Education and Youth. 2003. *Integrating aboriginal perspectives into curricula*. Winnipeg: Author. Available online at http://www.edu.gov.mb.ca?ks4/docs/policy/abpersp/index.htm.

McCue, H. and Associates. 2000a. *The learning circle: Classroom activities on First Nations in Canada (ages 8 to 11)*. Ottawa: Ministry of Indian Affairs and Northern Development.

———. 2000b. *The learning circle: Classroom activities on First Nations in Canada (ages 12 to 14)*. Ottawa: Ministry of Indian Affairs and Northern Development.

Ministry of Indian Affairs and Northern Development. 2000. *An aboriginal book list for children*. Ottawa: Author.

Pohl, A. 2003. Handling aboriginal curriculum studies appropriately. Coalition for the Advancement of Aboriginal Studies, Faculty of Education, York University, Toronto. Available online at http://www.edu.yorku.ca:8080/~caas/AbStudies.html.

Royal Commission on Aboriginal Peoples. 1996. *Final report of the Royal Commission on Aboriginal Peoples*. 5 vols. Ottawa: Queen's Printer. Available online at http://www.ainc-inac.gc.ca/ch/rcap/sg/sgmm_e.html.

Sawyer, D. and H. Green. 1990. *The NESA activities handbook for Native and multicultural classrooms*, vol. 1. Vancouver: Tillacum Library.

Sawyer, D. and W. Lundeberg. 1993. *The NESA activities handbook for Native and multicultural classrooms*, vol. 3. Vancouver: Tillacum Library.

Sawyer, D. and A. Napoleon. 1991. *The NESA activities handbook for Native and multicultural classrooms*, vol. 2. Vancouver: Tillacum Library.

7

Teaching the Tools to Think Critically

Roland Case and LeRoi Daniels

Neither the hand nor the mind alone would amount to much without aids and tools to perfect them.
—Francis Bacon, *Novum Organum* (1620)

The idea of critical thinking is not new. For decades—no, for centuries—it has been recognized as an important educational goal by practitioners and theorists alike. Curriculum documents and learning resources in all subjects and at every level of schooling recommend that students be taught to think critically. Despite this long-standing expectation, the extent of critical thinking and the manner in which it is taught are disheartening. Many studies document the preoccupation with transmission of information and rote application of "skills," and how little class time is devoted to thinking. The depressing irony is that critical thinking is much valued and yet inadequately addressed. Or, as Walter Parker (1991, 234) puts it, the teaching of thinking remains "more wish than practice."[1]

Numerous factors contribute to this situation. One enduring reason is the dilemma of how to get students to think for themselves and simultaneously teach the subject matter we want them to learn. This tension is captured in the so-called division between the teaching of "content" and "process." Confusion surrounding how to integrate these seemingly competing goals has led to opposing camps, with some educational theorists urging a focus on content, while others espouse an emphasis on general skills. The former are preoccupied with covering the subject matter of the curriculum, the latter with teaching mental operations. This division is educationally bankrupt since it is based on a false dichotomy: thinking without content is vacuous, and content acquired without thought is mindless and inert. As Richard Paul (1993, 277) notes, "one gains knowledge only through thinking."

The problem of transmitting information without getting students to think is that students frequently adopt ideas without understanding them. Research suggests, for example, that a large proportion of university students who have passed examinations in physics are unable to provide credible explanations for simple real-world problems, such as which of two balls, one heavier than the other, would hit the floor first when dropped (Mackenzie 1988). In explaining this anomaly, teacher-author Richard Feynman concludes: "After a lot of investigation, I finally figured out that the students had memorized everything, but that they didn't know what anything meant" (cited in Mackenzie 1988, 61).

Even educators who endeavour to engage their students in thinking critically about the content of the curriculum are often hampered by vagueness about what that would involve for the students they teach. Without a clear understanding of what is involved in critical thinking, we are likely to adopt a superficial approach, have significant gaps in our treatment, or proceed in an ineffectual if not counterproductive manner.

Profile of Exemplary Critical Thinkers

A useful general strategy to assist in unpacking vague or confusing notions is to consider actual examples of the concept—both positive examples (what it looks like when it is demonstrably present) and negative examples (what it looks like when it is demonstrably absent). We use this strategy in our professional development workshops to help educators refine their understanding of critical thinking. We invite workshop participants to think of individuals whom they deem exemplary critical thinkers and to identify the attributes or traits these individuals exhibit that distinguish them as such.

In the highlighted text is a list of attributes exhibited by exemplary critical thinkers. What can we learn from this list about the nature of critical thinking? You will notice that the list is divided into five parts. We have created these divisions to better reveal the diverse attributes reflected in our collective ideas about what makes a good critical thinker.

Before examining a representative sample of the responses we receive, take a moment to think of an exemplary critical thinker you know and list several qualities that make this person such a good thinker.

TYPICAL ATTRIBUTES OF EXEMPLARY CRITICAL THINKERS

Part I

- are open to new ideas
- persist, have staying power, while thinking through a problem
- have empathy; can appreciate others' points of view
- have the courage of their convictions and aren't afraid to take an unpopular stand
- question ideas; don't accept everything at face value
- don't jump to conclusions
- are flexible and willing to change tactics
- don't take themselves too seriously—can laugh at themselves
- are willing to live with ambiguity; don't require black-or-white answers
- welcome challenges

Part II

- restate a problem in unambiguous language or in graphic form
- confirm understanding by restating in their own words
- ask questions to probe for more information
- examine issues from varying perspectives
- look for connections between what is already known and what is new
- test ideas using a "reality check"
- focus on one thing at a time, breaking complex challenges into manageable bits
- consider the assumptions presupposed by a position
- look for possible counter-arguments or negative consequences

Part III

- have extensive general knowledge; are experienced; are well-read
- are knowledgeable about the specific topic

Part IV

- recognize common informal fallacies (for example, "straw person," "slippery slope," ad hominem arguments, hasty generalizations)

Part V

- recognize arguments that are well supported
- value clarity and specificity

ATTITUDES OR HABITS OF MIND

Part I of the list contains more items than any of the other parts. The inference is that the salient qualities of critical thinkers are most frequently of this first type. But what is the common feature of this set of qualities? It may be somewhat surprising to realize that they are attitudes. This suggests that an individual's attitudes—or, to use the term that we prefer, habits of mind—are key constituents of good critical thinking. People who are, for example, closed to new ideas or inflexible in their thinking are seriously impaired in their ability to arrive at justifiable resolutions.

Recognizing the role of attitudes in critical thinking challenges a popular perception that critical thinking is a skill or set of skills. This perception is unfortunate since no amount of "skill" will overcome the limitations of closed-minded prejudicial thinking. The case of people who deny the Holocaust illustrates this point. Such individuals may be clever, have extensive knowledge of the events, be able to marshal persuasive arguments, and possess many other qualities on our list of attributes. Despite considerable critical thinking ability, however, these individuals are fundamentally mistaken in their belief that the Holocaust did not happen because, in many cases, their racial prejudices prevent them from impartially considering the evidence. Open-mindedness is but one habit of mind needed by critical thinkers. The tendency of some people to leap to conclusions underlies yet another crucial mental habit of a good thinker: the inclination to deliberate—to think before acting. As we will illustrate, successful critical thinking is significantly (but by no means exclusively) a matter of attitude.

THINKING STRATEGIES

The qualities listed in Part II are most closely aligned with what are loosely called skills, although for clarity we refer to them as thinking strategies. In addition to possessing certain attitudes, good critical thinkers use a variety of tactics or supports to work their way through the challenges they face. These strategies may be very elaborate, such as following a comprehensive decision-making model that begins with identifying the issue, then considering the consequences, researching each option, and so on. Alternatively, we may employ focussed strategies when addressing a specific task (for example, gaining clarity about a problem by restating it in one's own words, asking others for clarification, or representing the problem graphically). There are literally thousands of strategies—in the form of procedures, models, graphic organizers, and other types of heuristics—that guide individuals in working through challenges. Because critical thinking typically has been labelled a skill, such attributes have received considerable attention by teachers. But the strong association of critical thinking with skills has often meant that the other attributes of good thinking have been overlooked.

BACKGROUND KNOWLEDGE

Looking at Part III of the list of attributes of exemplary critical thinkers, we see that critical thinking involves more than strategies and attitudes; it also requires background knowledge. Many of us are incapable of thinking very critically about certain difficult topics, for example, nuclear physics or baroque art—not because we lack appropriate habits of mind or thinking strategies, but because we are largely ignorant of these subjects. Obviously, students cannot think critically about a topic they know little or nothing about. Yet this fact is overlooked if we treat critical thinking as a set of general skills that can be applied regardless of context.

Consider the example of teaching students the so-called operation of analysis. A generic strategies approach expects students to learn to analyze any object or event, without reference to the need for knowledge of the topic. Without adequate background knowledge, students must, of necessity, guess or speculate blindly. We cannot effectively teach students the process of analyzing, say, a poem for its metre, rhyme, and symbolism in the same way as they would analyze a historical document for its authenticity. Although both forms of analysis share a few strategies (such as isolating each discrete part and reading between the lines), successful completion of the task is determined, in large measure, by possession of the relevant background knowledge in poetry or history. Students won't be able to make sense of a historical document if they know little of the events mentioned in the document or of the general climate of the times.

In this respect, the "generic" approach to critical thinking is not only ineffective but potentially counterproductive since it may reinforce an undesirable habit of mind—that of being prone to making hasty or uninformed judgments. Our alternative conception—at least the picture emerging from the first three parts of our list of attributes—suggests that "analysis" requires a variable array of at least three types of attributes. Depending on the context, good thinkers will possess suitable habits of mind (such as an inclination to attend to detail and refrain from jumping to a conclusion), as well as relevant background knowledge in the field under investigation, and appropriate thinking strategies (such as isolating each discrete part and listing the features of each).

CONCEPTUAL KNOWLEDGE

There is another relevant type of knowledge—conceptual knowledge or knowledge of vocabulary. Although this is not frequently cited as a key attribute of critical thinkers, it is reflected in Part IV of our list of attributes: avoidance of fallacies.

Teachers of young students or students who are not native speakers of the language of instruction have long recognized the importance of concepts. For example, we teach students key vocabulary before reading a story in language arts and explain concepts in science or social studies before analyzing physical or social phenomena. What has not been so widely appreciated is the need to teach the vocabulary of thinking. Students cannot enter deeply into conversations about their thinking if they do not have the words to identify or recognize key distinctions. For example, if students cannot distinguish evidence from a conclusion or do not know what a reason is, they are less likely to provide sound justifications for their opinions.

Knowledge of a seemingly simple distinction between, for example, the concepts "what I like" and "what is worthwhile" is key to students' ability to think critically. When asked to determine the better dietary choice—hamburger or salad—many students, especially younger ones, will select what they like to eat. They do not think about the relative merits of each option but merely report their preference. Critical reflection occurs only when students have the conceptual lens to distinguish between considering what is worthwhile, such as what would be a good dietary choice (nutritious, environmentally sound, easy to prepare, tasty, widely available, inexpensive)—and what is likable, merely a pleasing personal choice. Conceptual distinctions such as "what I like" and "what is worthwhile," "evidence" and "conclusion," or "cause" and "effect" allow us to see important features of good thinking, without which we are left in a conceptual haze. Knowledge of the vocabulary of critical thinking is another of the underacknowledged attributes of good thinkers.

CRITERIA

The final, and possibly least acknowledged, set of attributes of exemplary critical thinkers is reflected in Part V of our list. Attributes such as concern for well-supported arguments and for clear, unambiguous statements refer to commitments to applying relevant criteria when thinking critically. As we suggested above, when thinking critically we are not merely espousing a personal opinion or belief. We are, in effect, offering a judgment or an assessment of the worth or reasonableness of some idea, product, or action. We can see why this is so by imagining a poor critical thinker.

A typical profile of the quintessential non-critical thinker is likely someone who simply accepts at face value everything he or she is told, or typically rushes to conclusions without deliberation. The missing ingredient is the individual's lack of any assessment or judgment as to whether or not the ideas or conclusions are sensible. Or, putting it positively, thinking critically requires that individuals assess the reasonableness of the alternatives before them. And assessments inevitably are done on the basis of criteria. For example, in deciding whether or not a particular movie is good, typically we will have reasons for our assessment. It may simply be that the movie made us laugh—in which case, our criterion for good movies is the amount of humour. Alternatively we may have a more elaborate set of criteria: we might feel that the movie had a poignant message, that the visual effects were breathtaking, and that the actors were engaging. These reasons reveal additional implicit criteria for our assessment of the movie (such as the significance of the message, the quality of the cinematography, and the believability of the acting). To think critically is essentially to engage in deliberations with the intention of making a judgment based on appropriate criteria. Notice that students may judge movies on quite narrow and dubious criteria, such as the amount of adventure and violence. Our job in helping students think more critically about movies includes encouraging them to care about a wider and, arguably, more adequate, set of criteria. For this reason, an important category of critical thinking tool is awareness of and concern for the relevant "criteria for judgment."

The close relationship between the term "critical" thinking and "criteria" is instructive. Matthew Lipman (1988) suggests that the word "critical" should be seen as a synonym for "criterial"—that to think critically is to think in light of, or using, criteria. To put it another way, the grounding on criteria is what gives our judgments rigour. When thinking critically about a movie, we are not asserting a personal preference ("It's good because I like it") or reaching a conclusion based on a dubious set of considerations ("It's good because it contains lots of bloodshed"). Rather, we are offering a reasoned assessment of the merits of the movie, a judgment based on an ample set of relevant criteria. An important critical thinking objective is to help students identify and appreciate relevant criteria for judging diverse endeavours across the curriculum, from what makes for an appropriate classroom pet, or a sound solution to a social problem, to the qualities of a good argumentative essay or an effective visual display.

The "Tools" Conception in a Nutshell

Summarizing the points made thus far, we believe that the basic building blocks of thinking are not usefully cast in terms of generic skills or mental operations. We do not learn to analyze, interpret, evaluate, predict, and so on and then simply apply these "processes" to a particular situation. Extrapolating from our discussion of the five types of attributes possessed by exemplary critical thinkers, we suggest that promoting critical thinking among our students is largely a matter of helping them to develop mastery of an increasingly broader repertoire of five types of intellectual resources.

We offer the notion of intellectual resources or "tools" to explain the development of good thinking. The ability to think critically develops over time as individuals acquire more of the tools of good thinking. The metaphor of intellectual tools is preferable to that of mental operations because we cannot teach students to be good analyzers or predictors per se; students can learn to analyze or predict in specific contexts only by acquiring the diverse tools required in that context. Students will not become better at predicting weather, earthquakes, or story endings unless they acquire the relevant information, learn to attend to detail, and develop other tools required for thoughtful completion of these tasks. Notice, too, that there is no "process" of predicting that is discrete from "content": we cannot (thoughtfully) predict weather without knowledge of meteorology.

It is also significant that our categories draw support from within the diverse body of literature on thinking. We have come across schools of thinking that focus separately on each of the five categories we identify. More specifically, in the critical thinking as background knowledge camp, we find advocates such as John McPeck (1981), E.D. Hirsch (1988), and Daniel Willingham (2007) arguing that sound thinking is best served by promoting student mastery of the discipline's subject matter. David Perkins and his associates (1993) believe that the central ingredients of good thinking are thinking dispositions—what we call habits of mind. Similarly, Harvey Siegel (1988) suggests that these are the most important features of a critical thinker, while Stephen Norris and Robert Ennis (1989) list dispositions as one of two categories of essential ingredients of critical thinking. Prominent among advocates of the centrality of criteria for judgment (also called intellectual standards) are Matthew Lipman (1988) and Richard Paul (1988). The informal logic school of thinking stresses two categories from among our tools: those criteria for judgment reflected in the formal and informal rules of logic (for example, the rules of class, conditional, probabilistic reasoning) and what we refer to as critical thinking vocabulary—concepts such as argument, validity, credibility, truth, soundness, induction, deduction, and various informal fallacies. The final category of tool—thinking strategies—is arguably the most widely espoused. Much of the literature on promoting thinking skills is a matter of teaching strategies for carrying out various operations (see, for example, Glaser 1984). The fact that collectively the different camps espouse all of our categories of tools is grounds for believing that our conception represents a more complete synthesis of the range of critical thinking attributes than is otherwise found.

It should be obvious that nurturing critical thinking is a long-term evolutionary goal. The ability to think critically develops gradually as students expand upon and enrich their pool of intellectual resources or tools. It requires incremental, collective effort; no one teacher can do it quickly or on her own. Clearly we must take the long view. The work of promoting critical thinking is a K–16 (kindergarten to university) challenge. But each of us is responsible for doing his or her part in promoting the tools that will help students to reason carefully and effectively in the range of endeavours addressed in the various subject areas.

Based on scholarly research and professional work with thousands of teachers, we are convinced that developing the tools for thought requires teacher effort at every level in the educational system in marshalling a four-pronged approach. The four prongs are represented graphically in Figure 7.1.

CREATE A CRITICAL COMMUNITY

Critical thinking cannot be learned independently of the broader forces operating within the classroom and the school. Consequently, it is essential to foster "critical" communities in which teachers and students interact in mutually supportive ways to nurture critical reflection. The point of forming a critical community is to create an environment, or climate, that embodies and reinforces the tools of thought. This is especially significant for acquisition of the desired habits of mind that are likely to develop only if they are modelled and continuously supported. Building a community of thinkers is also instrumental in countering a tendency to view thinking as a solitary enterprise. Although we want students to be independent-minded and to make up their own minds, we should not expect them to do so entirely on their own. There is a key difference between thinking for oneself and thinking by oneself. Good critical thinkers regularly engage in dialogue with others to broaden their knowledge, test their ideas, and secure alternative perspectives. Learning to contribute to and make use of other people's wisdom can only be learned through participation in a critical community. Further discussion of this dimension of critical thinking is found in chapter 8, "Supporting a Community of Critical Thinkers."

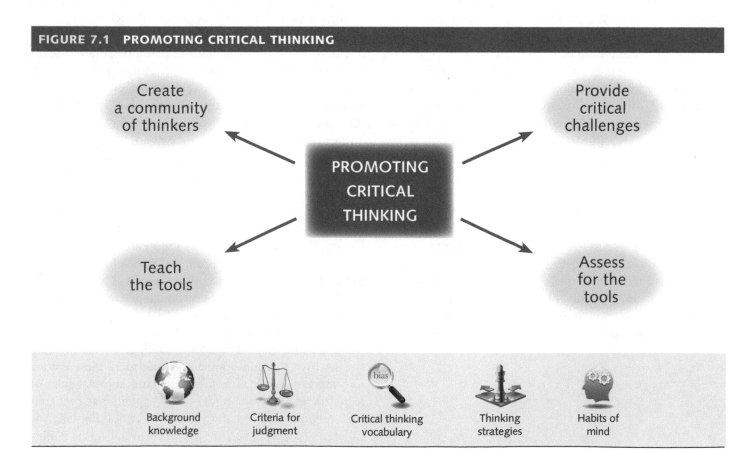

FIGURE 7.1 PROMOTING CRITICAL THINKING

PROVIDE CRITICAL CHALLENGES

The contextual nature of the tools means they are best learned within the context of a curriculum-embedded challenge that students may think through. Students need abundant occasions to employ the tools as they work through meaningful "problematic" situations. If a situation is not problematic (that is, there is only one plausible option or a correct answer is obvious), then it does not call for critical thinking—it is not a critical challenge. Further discussion of this dimension of critical thinking is found in chapter 4, "Beyond Inert Facts."

TEACH FOR THE TOOLS

Students require "enabling instruction" in the tools if they are to develop as critical thinkers. In relevant contexts, students should be introduced to the range of tools required for the tasks. The ability to think critically develops over a lifetime by acquiring and refining the vast repertoire of tools that an expert would draw on in responding to problematic situations. As we have seen, there are five kinds of tools:

- **Background knowledge.** Critical thinkers possess relevant information about a topic that is required for thoughtful reflection.
- **Criteria for judgment.** Critical thinkers understand the appropriate criteria or grounds for deciding which is the most sensible or defensible response to the challenge before them.
- **Critical thinking vocabulary.** Critical thinkers possess the concepts and distinctions that facilitate thinking critically. Although the other tools also refer to concepts, "critical thinking vocabulary" refers to concepts that are not included in any of the other tools and that address distinctions foundational to thinking critically about thinking—for example, the difference between "conclusion" and "premise," or "cause" and "effect."
- **Thinking strategies.** Critical thinkers are fluent in the repertoire of procedures, heuristics, organizing devices, and models that may be useful when thinking through a critical challenge.
- **Habits of mind.** Critical thinkers possess a wide range of the values and attitudes of a careful and conscientious thinker.

ASSESS FOR THE TOOLS

It is not sufficient merely to teach the tools. Because assessment influences what is learned, we must also assess for critical thinking. Teachers signal to students what is and is not important by assigning marks to some assignments and not to others and by "weighting" parts of assignments with different values. If student mastery of the tools is not assessed, not only are students (and teachers) left in the dark about their growth, but they are also implicitly encouraged to believe that critical thinking is unimportant.

The "Tools" of the Trade

Growth as a critical thinker depends ultimately on developing understanding and competent use of five types of intellectual resources or tools. As we have stressed, students' ability to undertake any task thoughtfully depends on the range of tools they have for that particular task. The value of conceiving critical thinking as the competent use of contextually relevant tools is best seen in examples of individuals attempting to think through particular challenges.

THE TOOLS IN ACTION

Our first example, Table 7.1, is adapted from work by our colleague Jerrold Coombs (Bailin et al. 1999). It illustrates the varied range of tools brought into play when thinking critically about an environmental issue. Specifically, it describes a hypothetical student's deliberations over what stance to take on a compromise proposal to develop and conserve various areas of a mature (or old-growth) forest. The tools she employs at each step of her deliberations are identified to reveal the adequacy of our model in accounting for the diverse elements of sound thinking.

In this example, the young woman's possession of an array of diverse tools empowers her to reach a critically thoughtful decision. It is important to note that critical thinking does not require reaching a single "correct" answer. An equally thoughtful person might reach a different position on this controversial issue. What would make both their conclusions critically thoughtful is the extent to which their deliberations reflect the use of the intellectual tools characteristic of a careful and conscientious thinker.

Also noteworthy is the observation that critical thinking is a matter of degree; an individual's sophistication and ability as a thinker is related to the range and level of mastery of the tools. All of us, including young children, think critically to some extent in some circumstances at least. That is to say, all of us possess and use some of the tools for thought. Equally true is the claim that all of us can improve our ability to think critically. We can do so both by deepening our grasp of the tools with which we currently have some familiarity and by acquiring additional tools.

TABLE 7.1 THINKING CRITICALLY ABOUT LOGGING OLD-GROWTH FORESTS

Outlined in the left-hand column below is a hypothetical response by a young woman to this issue: Should she endorse or reject the government's plan to permit logging in some areas of a forest and to designate other areas as a wilderness park? The tools embedded in her critically thoughtful response are indicated in the right-hand column.

SCENARIO	CRITICAL THINKING TOOL
The young woman has read a number of arguments for and against the government's plan that have appeared in the local newspaper. The arguments are presented roughly as follows:	
Anti-Development Side Environmentalists claim that the government has sold out to the forestry industry and unions. Some of them claim that they cannot afford to lose any more old-growth forest. They point out that forests are needed to prevent the buildup of carbon monoxide that causes global warming, that the forests are home to many species that are increasingly endangered by reductions to their habitat, and that old-growth forests enrich the aesthetic quality of life in the area. Some persons feel so strongly about the need to preserve old-growth forests that they have publicly announced that they have "spiked" (driven long nails into) many trees in the area and plan to recruit volunteers to spike many more.	**Background knowledge:** knowledge of the arguments made by the proponents of the anti-development side
Pro-Development Side Supporters of the government plan argue that the forestry industry needs to log at least part of the area and other old-growth forests if it is to continue to provide jobs for people, supply lumber to build houses, and contribute to government revenues. They claim that the land set aside for the park and for limited logging will be more than enough to maintain the aesthetic beauty of the area and to preserve the animal life there. They also argue that, since the logged areas will be replanted, there will not, in the long run, be any reduction in forested land in the area.	**Background knowledge:** knowledge of the arguments made by the proponents of the pro-development side
Several of the young woman's friends have joined demonstrations protesting against the government's decision to permit logging. The young woman checks her immediate impulse to rush out and join her friends because she wants to be sure that she is doing it for the right reasons, not simply for fear of disappointing her friends.	**Habits of mind:** open-mindedness and independent-mindedness
The young woman considers whether the consequences of stopping to deliberate about the best thing to do would likely be worse than acting without further deliberation. She decides that there is sufficient time for more careful deliberation before acting.	**Criteria for judgment:** extended deliberation is not always desirable
She attempts to understand clearly all the reasons for supporting the government's decision and those for protesting and trying to change that decision.	**Criteria for judgment:** possession of an adequate body of evidence
In doing this, she considers whether the claims of the government, the forestry industry, and environmentalists about the likely consequences of the government's policy should be believed.	**Habits of mind:** an inquiring or "critical" attitude
She knows that all of these groups have access to experts in economics and ecology, but also that they stand to gain by misrepresenting the facts about the likely consequences.	**Criteria for judgment:** concern for reliability of authorities
She also considers how adequate the newspaper accounts of reasons for and against the government's decision are likely to be.	**Criteria for judgment:** attention to the accuracy and unbiased nature of information sources
She is also aware that the emotionally charged language and other fallacious forms of persuasion used in the newspaper reports could influence her to adopt views not supported by good reasons. She makes a point of watching for and dismissing these fallacies.	**Critical thinking vocabulary:** can recognize informal fallacies

TABLE 7.1   THINKING CRITICALLY ABOUT LOGGING OLD-GROWTH FORESTS (CONT.)

SCENARIO	CRITICAL THINKING TOOL
She considers whether she has any assumptions or preconceptions that would prevent her from making an unbiased assessment of reasons for this case.	**Habits of mind:** fair-mindedness
She decides her attachment to environmentalism and lack of contact with persons whose livelihood depends on logging may lead her to undervalue economic reasons for permitting logging.	**Habits of mind:** open-mindedness
Consequently, she decides to talk to forestry workers to get a more sympathetic understanding of their point of view.	**Criteria for judgment:** concern for a broadly grounded inquiry **Thinking strategy:** seeks counsel from a variety of parties in a dispute
She is aware that there may be other options open to her besides simply accepting the government's decision or joining protest marches. She tries to think of other plausible courses of action that would produce more desirable consequences.	**Thinking strategy:** looks for multiple possible options
Because she is aware that others may already have thought of plausible alternative courses of action, she seeks out knowledgeable people to discuss with them what they think ought to be done and why.	**Thinking strategy:** confers with recognized experts
In the course of the discussions, she often asks for clarification of the terms other people use and gives examples of what she means by various terms she uses to make them clear to others.	**Thinking strategy:** check for clarity and shared meanings of terms by asking for and providing examples
Having identified the likely consequences of each of the courses of action that seem plausible, she considers whether any of the courses of action involves treating others unjustly or otherwise acting immorally.	**Criteria for judgment:** concern that her decision does not unnecessarily harm others or treat them unfairly
She decides to rule out the option of joining the tree-spiking expeditions, because she has good reason to believe that this course of action could cause serious injury to persons working in the lumber industry and would subject her to criminal prosecution.	**Criteria for judgment:** seek to make an impartial judgment that would be acceptable even if the person were one of the other parties who may be adversely affected by the action
Accordingly she tries to imagine what it would be like to be a lumber mill worker facing the choice of not working or risking serious injury. She decides it would be morally wrong to subject them to such risk if there are other options available for adequately preserving forests.	**Thinking strategy:** test the fairness of moral judgments by sensitively imagining oneself in the predicament of others
Having ruled out those options that she has good reason to regard as immoral, she considers which of the remaining courses of action would produce the best consequences overall—which, that is, would most fully realize the things she values without producing unacceptable negative consequences.	**Habits of mind:** commitment to decide on rational grounds
Having made a tentative decision about which course of action is best, she decides to discuss it with others (including those who might have reached a different decision), explaining her reasoning and inviting counter-arguments.	**Thinking strategy:** talk through one's thinking on an issue, inviting others to poke holes in the reasoning
She wants to be sure she hasn't overlooked any important considerations or failed to appreciate the significance of any of the likely consequences for other things she values.	**Habits of mind:** intellectual work ethic
Lacking any good reasons for changing her decision, she proceeds to act on it.	**Habits of mind:** commitment to act on the basis of reasoned judgment

TEACHING THE TOOLS

As illustrated by the young woman in our hypothetical scenario, any given intellectual task will require a range of tools for thinking critically. An important function of the tools approach is to help teachers identify what students need to be taught in order to undertake a given task in a critically thoughtful manner. To illustrate the instructional value of our model, we examine two cases in which students are taught the tools they need to ask thoughtful questions. We begin with a scenario in which primary students are taught to think critically about developing "powerful" questions.

In "Developing Powerful Questions," Tami systematically aided her primary students to construct questions thoughtfully by teaching four tools. Notice that teaching the tools is not the same as giving students the answers or doing the thinking for them. Tami did not give students questions they might ask; rather she helped them develop the intellectual resources to complete the task thoughtfully for themselves. Not only was the students' ability to pose powerful questions aided by the tools their teacher helped them acquire,

but their understanding of the subject matter—in this case, the significance of Remembrance Day—was enhanced by the experience.

We can appreciate the contextual nature of teaching the tools—and by implication the limitations of generic thinking models—by contrasting the tools Tami developed with those developed by a junior high school teacher as she helped students think critically about questions for an end-of-unit test in social studies, described in "Developing Examination Questions."

We can see the contextual nature of the tools involved in posing effective questions by contrasting the two situations. The required background knowledge in one case was knowledge of World War II; in the other, it was knowledge of the Civil War period in seventeenth-century England. Karen's sample "question frames" offered a thinking strategy—a strategy that complements brainstorming—to help students generate questions. Karen's articulation of the criteria (different from the criteria offered in the primary class) focussed students' thinking on the features of good examination questions.

DEVELOPING POWERFUL QUESTIONS[2]

As part of their social studies curriculum, Tami McDiarmid's kindergarten to grade 3 class was to learn about the significance of Remembrance Day (November 11). In fostering appreciation of this event, Tami invited her students to think of questions they might ask a classroom guest who was to speak about his World War II experiences. Left to their own devices, many students would likely have asked rather trivial or irrelevant questions. Tami sought to support her students in thinking critically about the questions they might ask by focussing their attention on four tools: some critical thinking vocabulary, criteria for judgment, a thinking strategy, and background knowledge.

A few days prior to the visit, Tami reintroduced key vocabulary by reminding her students that they had talked previously about two kinds of questions: "weak" questions and "powerful" ones. Armed with this distinction, the class discussed what powerful questions "look like or sound like"—or, to use our terminology, they discussed the criteria for judging powerful questions. Tami recorded on chart paper the following student-generated criteria:

Powerful questions ...

- give you lots of information
- are specific to the person or situation
- are open-ended; can't be answered by yes or no
- may be unexpected
- are usually not easy to answer.

Next, Tami made use of a thinking strategy—that of brainstorming—that her students had already learned to

use. Brainstorming does not invoke critical thinking, but it is a useful strategy to help with the generation of ideas. While brainstorming, individuals are discouraged from making judgments about the proffered ideas; the point is simply to come up with as many ideas as possible. The critical thinking began in earnest when students, working in pairs, began to assess the brainstormed questions. Using the agreed-upon criteria as their guide, students discussed whether their proposed questions were likely to elicit lots of information, were obvious or predictable, and so on. Some "weak" questions were rejected; others were modified to make them more powerful.

Tami had developed a fourth tool—that of relevant background knowledge—during the three weeks preceding the guest's visit by reading and discussing various children's stories involving the war. Without the knowledge acquired from these stories, many students would have been incapable of asking a thoughtful question.

Here are a sampling of the student-generated questions asked of the World War II veteran:

- Where did you live during the war?
- Were there any women in World War II? If so, what were their jobs?
- What started the fighting?
- Why was Canada involved?
- What was your safe place?
- Why did you fight in the war?
- Do you remember some of your friends from the war?
- Which countries did you fight over?

DEVELOPING EXAMINATION QUESTIONS[3]

Karen Barnett, a junior high humanities teacher, borrowed an idea from a fellow teacher, Bob Friend. Rather than simply assigning exam questions, she had her students create an end-of-unit quiz consisting of six questions and an answer key focussed on their study of seventeenth-century England. Students were informed that their test would be drawn exclusively from their questions. To support her students in completing this task, Karen provided them with three tools: background knowledge, criteria for judgment, and a thinking strategy.

The required background knowledge—knowledge of the focus of the questions—was acquired by reading the relevant chapter in their textbook and by undertaking a variety of related assignments. When framing their six questions, students were instructed to consider four criteria. Questions:

- must be clear so that fellow students will understand what is required;
- should address a non-trivial aspect of the contents of the chapter;
- can be answered within a half page (or twenty minutes); and
- must require more than mere recall of information.

Karen further supported her students' efforts by offering a thinking strategy—the use of "question frames"—to help generate questions that went beyond mere recall of information. More specifically, students were invited to frame questions using prompts such as the following:

- Compare ... with ...
- What conclusions can be drawn from ...
- Decide whether ... was correct when ...
- Predict what would have happen if ...
- What was the effect of ...
- Decide which choice you would make if ...

A list of the best student-generated questions was distributed to the class well before the test. The following questions were submitted by one of the students in Karen's class:

1. Compare the ideas of Thomas Hobbes and John Locke on government.
2. Do you think Cromwell was correct in chopping off the king's head, and what advantage did government gain over royalty because of this?
3. What were the effects of the civil war on the monarchy and the peasantry?
4. If you were the king, how would you handle the pressures of government and the people?
5. Compare the power of the government in the early 1600s to the power it has today.
6. What do you think would have happened if the people hadn't rebelled against the king?

Significantly, teaching students to think critically about the questions they posed contributed to their understanding of the subject matter. The criteria that Karen set, notably that students ask non-trivial questions, required them to think about what was important about the historical period. So too did her inclusion of student-generated test questions. Since these questions went beyond mere recall of information, studying for the test required that other students think about the issues raised. Karen insists that had she posed the very questions her students produced, she would have been bombarded with complaints: "How do expect us to know this? You never told us the answers to this!" Instead, not only did students take seriously the assignment to create the questions (in some cases reading the textbook for the first time), but they were also more motivated to study for the test since the questions were posed by their peers.

This last point—the motivational value of critical thinking—is important. Although not all students will welcome opportunities to think critically, more often than not students prefer to think about matters than to regurgitate facts or apply undigested ideas. This is especially true when the issues or topics students are asked to think critically about are meaningful to them.

ASSESSING THE TOOLS

Thus far we have focussed on teaching the tools. Another useful feature of the tools approach is the parallel between instruction and assessment. Assessment is a major obstacle for many teachers in their efforts to promote critical thinking. If there is no single correct answer to look for in student responses, knowing what to assess is often difficult. As our last two examples illustrate, students might pose any of a nearly infinite number of effective questions. Does this mean that virtually any question is acceptable? If not, on what basis should we assess these questions?

The topic of assessing critical thinking is discussed more extensively in the final three chapters of this book. Let us say here simply that the key consideration is not whether we agree or disagree with the conclusions students reach but instead assess the quality of the thinking that supports their answers. In assessing critical thinking, we should look for evidence that shows that students' answers embody the relevant tools competently. Assessing students on the complete range of tools that a particular task requires may be unrealistic. A more appropriate approach is to assess only those tools that students were expressly expected to employ in the task before them. In other words, we should endeavour to assess the tools that the students were instructed to use. Returning to the two examples of teaching students to pose effective questions, let us see what this looks like in practice.

ASSESSING THINKING ABOUT POWERFUL QUESTIONS

In learning to pose powerful questions to the war veteran, the primary students were expressly taught four tools, all of them potentially forming the criteria for assessing students' thinking. Notice our use of criteria in two contexts: we talk about assessment criteria and criteria for judgment. Assessment criteria are the grounds for assessing students' work and, in the area of critical thinking, we recommend using all five tools as sources of assessment criteria. The tool we refer to as criteria for judgment is but one of the criteria that may be used to assess critical thinking.

The actual questions could be evaluated on two criteria: judgment and background knowledge about World War II. We could assess the former by seeing how well the question each student posed met the agreed-on criteria. (Alternatively, students might be asked to explain how their question satisfies each criterion). Students' questions could be used to assess background knowledge by looking to see whether or not any question reveals factual errors. The teacher could circulate among the groups, assessing use of the brainstorming strategy by observing whether students readily volunteered questions and accepted all suggestions without criticism. Students' understanding of the conceptual distinction between weak and powerful questions could be assessed by providing sample questions and asking students to identify which are weak and which powerful.

ASSESSING THINKING ABOUT TEST QUESTIONS

In the second example, students were provided with three tools to support their thinking about examination questions: a range of criteria for determining effective test questions, the "question frame" strategy for generating questions, and background knowledge on the historical period. The student-generated questions could be assessed on all three grounds: how well they satisfied the stipulated criteria for judgment, the extent to which the questions represent a variety of question frames, and on the knowledge of the period implied by the questions asked. (A more appropriate source for assessing students' background knowledge would be the answer key that was to accompany each student's six questions.)

Since the focus of the second example was on posing test questions, we made no mention of the tools needed to help students think critically about their answer key (and, by implication, about their answers on the actual end-of-unit quiz). It would be instructive to briefly consider what these tools might be. Obviously, there is no definitive list of tools that teaches students to answer exam questions thoughtfully. Often the identified tools depend on the teacher's priorities

for the assignment, the perceived needs of the students, and the demands of the curriculum. Consequently, our suggestions are just that. We do think, however, that there will be considerable agreement on the sorts of tools that we would recognize as being appropriate.

A useful place to begin thinking about which tools to assess is to imagine a weak student response to a sample question (poor responses are often more revealing). Using the question, "What do you think would have happened if the people hadn't rebelled against the king?", consider the following obviously flawed answer: "If the people hadn't rebelled they would have quickly forgotten their troubles and gone back to watching television."

What relevant tools appear to be absent in this answer? The historical error of assuming the existence of television in the seventeenth century comes immediately to mind. That is, the background knowledge is incomplete. The bald assertion that the citizenry would quickly forget their problems is vague, somewhat implausible, and is not supported with any evidence. These deficits suggest gaps in understanding the criteria for judging a thoughtful response.

The historical error about watching television might suggest stressing the need for students to read the chapter carefully. In addressing the gaps in criteria for judgment, we might explore with students the importance of a detailed (or specific) answer and whether it is plausible and amply supported by evidence (or reasons). The specification of these three criteria for judgment might raise the need to teach critical thinking vocabulary: all students would not know the difference between plausible and actual outcomes. (An outcome need not be actual, or even likely, for it to be plausible.) We might also try to nurture an empathetic habit of mind. Empathy, and in this particular case historical empathy, involves an appreciation of how others in different situations and contexts might feel. If students were inclined to put themselves, metaphorically speaking, into the heads and hearts of those living in the seventeenth century, their answers to the questions might be more detailed and plausible. In casting about for thinking strategies to help students construct a thoughtful answer we might recommend a "template" for their answers. Perhaps students might employ a three-point outline:

1. briefly summarize the position taken;
2. elaborate on what is meant or implied by the position; and
3. offer several pieces of evidence to justify the position.

We might imagine other hypothetical student answers, including ideal answers to help us elaborate on and refine our list of requisite tools. For example, our imagined exemplary answers might include refutation of possible objections to the stated position, or suggested alternative positions and evaluations of the relative merits of each. If we thought these were reasonable and appropriate expectations, we might introduce additional tools, including teaching the concepts of "argument" and "counter-argument" and revising the suggested three-point outline to add a new step:

4. anticipate possible objections to their position and provide a counter-argument for each.

Needless to say there are other possibilities for tools to teach and, in turn, to assess. The point to appreciate is how varied the tools, and how much better students' answers will likely be, if they have been taught to use some of these tools.

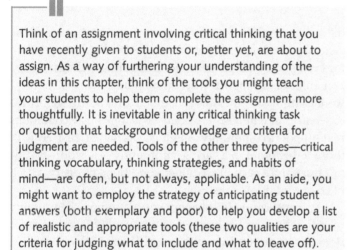

Think of an assignment involving critical thinking that you have recently given to students or, better yet, are about to assign. As a way of furthering your understanding of the ideas in this chapter, think of the tools you might teach your students to help them complete the assignment more thoughtfully. It is inevitable in any critical thinking task or question that background knowledge and criteria for judgment are needed. Tools of the other three types—critical thinking vocabulary, thinking strategies, and habits of mind—are often, but not always, applicable. As an aide, you might want to employ the strategy of anticipating student answers (both exemplary and poor) to help you develop a list of realistic and appropriate tools (these two qualities are your criteria for judging what to include and what to leave off).

NOTES

1. The widely cited study of one thousand American classrooms by John Goodlad (2004) concluded that from the early grades school-based activities and environments condition students to reproduce what they are taught, not to use and evaluate information. Fred Newmann's (1991, 324) research on sixteen schools observed that most instruction "follows a pattern of teachers transmitting information to students who are expected to reproduce it." Sandra McKee (1988) found in her study of high school teachers that four per cent of classroom time was devoted to reasoning and an average of only 1.6 student-posed questions per class.
2. This example is based on a lesson described in McDiarmid, Manzo, and Musselle (2007, 115–119).
3. Based on personal communication with Karen Barnett.

REFERENCES

Bailin, S., R. Case, J. Coombs, and L. Daniels. 1999. Conceptualizing critical thinking. *Journal of Curriculum Studies* 31 (3): 285–302.

Glaser, R. 1984. Education and thinking: The role of knowledge. *American Psychologist* 39 (2): 93–104.

Goodlad, J. 2004. *A place called school: Twentieth anniversary edition.* Whitby, ON: McGraw-Hill.

Hirsch, E.D. 1988. *Cultural literacy: What every American needs to know.* New York: Vintage Books.

Lipman, M. 1988. Critical thinking: What can it be? *Educational Leadership* 45: 38–43.

Mackenzie, J. 1988. Authority. *Journal of Philosophy of Education* 22 (1): 57–65.

McDiarmid, T., R. Manzo, and T. Musselle. 2007. *Critical challenges for primary students.* Rev. ed. Vancouver: The Critical Thinking Consortium.

McKee, S.J. 1988. Impediments to implementing critical thinking. *Social Education* 52 (6): 444–446.

McPeck, J. 1981. *Critical thinking and education.* New York: St. Martins.

Newmann, F.M. 1991. Promoting higher order thinking in social studies: Overview of a study of 16 high school departments. *Theory and Research in Social Education* 19 (4): 324–340.

Norris, S.P. and R.H. Ennis. 1989. *Evaluating critical thinking.* Pacific Grove, CA: Midwest Publications.

Parker, W. 1991. Achieving thinking and decision making objectives in social studies. In *Handbook of research on social studies teaching and learning,* ed. J. Shaver, 345–356. Toronto: Collier Macmillan.

Paul, R.W. 1988. *What, then, is critical thinking?* Rohnert Park, CA: Center for Critical Thinking and Moral Critique.

———. 1993. The critical connection: Higher order thinking that unifies curriculum, instruction, and learning. In *Critical thinking: How to prepare students for a rapidly changing world,* R. Paul, 273–289. Santa Rosa, CA: Foundation for Critical Thinking.

Perkins, D.N., E. Jay, and S. Tishman. 1993. Beyond abilities: A dispositional theory of thinking. *Merrill–Palmer Quarterly* 39 (1): 1–21.

Siegel, H. 1988. *Educating reason: Rationality, critical thinking, and education.* New York: Routledge.

Willingham, D.T. 2007. Critical thinking: Why is it so hard to teach? *American Educator,* Summer: 8–19.

8 Supporting a Community of Critical Thinkers

Roland Case and Philip Balcaen

Critical thinking does not develop in a vacuum and lasting gains cannot be expected from isolated efforts. Nurturing critical thinking requires establishing on-going practices and structures that reinforce thoughtful reflection in our classrooms and schools. As Barbara Rogoff suggests, this requires more than "piecemeal incorporation of innovative techniques into an otherwise inconsistent fabric" of traditional teaching and learning (1994, 214). This chapter discusses what it means to support, and what is involved in supporting, a community of critical thinkers.

The Nature of Classroom as Community

Over the past two decades it has become popular to talk about a particular classroom atmosphere in terms of a community. This is an especially attractive metaphor for the kind of atmosphere that is conducive to critical thinking. Various writers identify four principles that define a group of individuals as a community (Lipman 1991; Newmann 1990):

- Participants are "committed to a common goal" that gives them unity.
- Participants do not work in isolation, but "interact in collaborative pursuit" of their goal (in other words, communication is key to a community).
- Participants "agree on the general procedures" to follow.
- Participants assume "individual responsibility"—each individual is responsible for contributing to the common goal.

Of course, there are many variations of classrooms as communities. These classrooms are variously referred to as caring communities, learning communities, communities of learners, and communities of inquiry. The underlying commonality is the commitment to creating a community atmosphere within the classroom; the qualifier indicates subtle differences in the particular common goal and some of the general procedures that are followed. A "caring" community, for example, would give primacy to creating feelings of trust and emotional support, whereas a community of "inquiry" would emphasize the shared pursuit of knowledge. These differences in emphasis are relatively subtle—the conditions that support a community of inquiry overlap extensively with those to be found in a caring community—as students cannot learn from each other under conditions of distrust, lack of co-operation, and disrespect.

We must emphasize that our conception of a community of critical thinkers has more in common with the other variations of community than there are differences. For example, a critical community presupposes a deep and abiding concern for each other's feelings and ideas, and in this respect must be, to a significant extent, a caring community. The common feature—the notion of a classroom as a community—is central to understanding the kind of atmosphere recreated in a critical community or, for that matter, in other types of classroom communities.

Distinguishing "Traditional" and "Community" Classrooms

It may be helpful in getting further inside the notion of a classroom as community to distinguish it from other kinds of classroom atmospheres. In an illuminating article, Rogoff (1994) distinguishes a classroom community from teacher-run and student-run classrooms. She argues that teacher- and student-run classrooms exist at opposite ends of a spectrum, whereas classrooms as communities are in a different category altogether. Studies suggest that traditional teacher-directed classes may not create an atmosphere conducive to student thoughtfulness (Newmann 1991, 330). Goodlad's study of more than a thousand schools in the United States noted that despite the rhetoric of promoting creativity, individual flexibility, and independent thinking, the practice in many schools was quite different: "From the beginning, students experience school and classroom environments that condition them in precisely opposite behaviours—seeking 'right' answers, conforming, and reproducing the known" (2004, 291).

Many have thought that the alternative to a teacher-run classroom is a student-run classroom. Rogoff argues that this is not the case. Neither teacher-run nor student-run classrooms support thinking as well as a classroom as community does. This last comment is potentially confusing because a classroom community is often referred to as a student-centred classroom. Consequently, it will be useful to distinguish teacher- and student-run classrooms and then to contrast these with the notion of community-based classrooms. While doing this, we will explain the key advantages of the community approach. Key differences between teacher- and student-run classrooms are summarized in Table 8.1.

Rogoff suggests that on the spectrum of teacher- and student-run classrooms any diminution of teacher control directly increases student control. In the area of decision making in the extreme teacher-run class, the teacher makes all the rules, determines what is studied, sets the schedule for the class, and so on. The student's role is passive, merely to comply with the teacher's dictates. Conversely, in a student-run classroom, in order not to inhibit students' creativity and initiative, teachers assume a laissez-faire or "hands-off" approach. In the most extreme version, individual students are left to decide for themselves what to study, when, and how. Teaching and learning in a teacher-run classroom is largely through direct instruction in the accepted beliefs and ways of proceeding. In a student-run classroom, there is no direct instruction, no telling, no "right or wrong" answer, and no correct way of doing anything (Richardson 2003). Consequently, the teacher's role is largely to encourage students as they individually make their own sense of the material they engage with.

The dominant values of the teacher-run classroom are control and student replication of received beliefs and correct ways of acting. This point was vividly espoused by prominent nineteenth-century American educator William Torrey Harris when he commented that "the first requisite of the school is order: each pupil must be taught to conform his behaviour to a general standard, just like the running of the trains" (cited in Barell 1991, 29). In a student-run classroom, the dominant values are a permissive atmosphere to nurture the free expression of ideas and actions. Apart from rare notable experiments such as the "free" schools movement in the 1960s and 1970s, student-run classrooms, in any pure form, have not operated extensively. However, some proponents of such movements as student-centred education, values clarification, discovery learning, whole language, and teaching for creativity seem to espouse a student-run philosophy within certain areas of the curriculum. For example, one elementary science teacher who had recently been introduced to "constructivist learning" but had developed a misconceived idea about it was reported to state, "Constructivism has taught me I do not need to know any science in order to teach it. I will simply allow my students to figure things out for themselves, for I know there is no right answer" (MacKinnon and Scarff-Seatter 1997, 53).

Clearly, choosing either a completely teacher-run class or a completely student-run class seems extreme. Teacher-run classes reinforce conformity and discourage individual thoughtfulness, whereas student-run classes abandon standards and preclude developing shared understandings. This seems to suggest the need to find a middle ground between these extremes. Herein lies the value of Rogoff's comparison of these two types of classroom structures. The middle ground between these poles—a classroom that is partly teacher-run and partly student-run—might be seen to imply that some of the time the teacher would initiate, direct, and control and at other times students would. When it was the teacher's turn

TABLE 8.1 TEACHER- AND STUDENT-RUN CLASSROOMS

	TEACHER-RUN CLASSROOM	STUDENT-RUN CLASSROOM
Decision making	teacher initiates and dictates; students react and comply	students initiate and decide for themselves; teacher responds and permits
Principles of teaching and learning	teacher transmits received knowledge and practices; students absorb and adopt	students construct their own understandings and ways of doing things; teacher encourages but doesn't "interfere" in student learning
Teaching practices	teacher-directed instruction (for example, show and tell, repetition, drill and correction)	student-directed learning (for example, self-discovery, unaided exploration, hit and miss)
Dominant values	compliance and replication	permissiveness and individual expression

to decide, students would be expected to comply, and conversely when it was the students' turn to decide, the teacher would stand back and permit—so, too, in the teaching and learning dimension. In those topics where a right way or a correct answer was required, the teacher would transmit the received knowledge and students would accept it; in other areas, where no received answer was expected, students would freely discover and individually conclude for themselves. Any compromise between these polar philosophies is a matter of determining when students are free to decide by themselves and when they must do as they are asked, and, by extension, when teachers are to assume a laissez-faire role and when they are to "call the shots."

THE THIRD WAY: CLASSROOM AS COMMUNITY

Rogoff invites us to see the classroom as community as a qualitatively different option to any position on the teacher/student–run continuum. It is not a matter of deciding whether the teacher or the student is "in charge." Rather it requires col-

ROLAND'S ATTEMPT AT A COMMUNITY OF THINKERS

After years of talking about the classroom factors that promote student thoughtfulness, I decided to "walk the talk" and try to implement them in my methods course for pre-service social studies teachers. My typical routine would have been to open the first class with a talk about my expectations for the course supplemented with a detailed written syllabus outlining the topics and required readings for each week, and the precise nature of the assignments including their length, format, and due day (including, in some cases, the precise hour by which they were to be handed in). Instead, I said surprisingly little beyond welcoming students to the class and almost immediately invited them into a set of activities to help design the course contents.

We began by sharing in small groups and then as a class our most memorable (both positive and negative) experiences as students in elementary and secondary social studies. Students then examined two documents—the provincial curriculum and a recent Ministry of Education report on the state of social studies teaching. The students' task was to identify key elements of effective social studies teaching and the challenges these presented to prospective teachers. Finally, I offered my own critique of the "good, the bad, and the ugly" of social studies.

Working in groups, students identified the most important areas or topics they would need to master if they were to teach the prescribed curriculum in a manner that realized the successes and avoided the pitfalls they had identified in their personal experiences, the published documents, and my observations. As well, they were to suggest in general terms the kinds of activities, readings, assignments, and resources that might help them to achieve these ends. We compiled a collective list of these objectives and strategies and I indicated that I would return the following week with a proposed outline of our course of study that represented my best attempt to accommodate their recommendations. I warned that some of their suggestions may not be feasible given my limitations, realistic given the constraints we faced, or consistent with university policy (I did have to assign grades). I indicated that I might add a few topics of my own that past experience had taught me were valuable for beginning teachers, but that I would provide a rationale for these additions. Also, I

announced that the next few classes would address topics that I had prepared in advance since I would need time to make the necessary preparations.

The "extra" preparations that I had to make were quite minimal since the kinds of topics and activities the students had identified were remarkably similar to those that I would have included anyway. The students and I were "on the same page" so to speak because, in the past, I had designed my course trying to answer the very questions I had put to them, and the documents and comments I presented to them informed (oriented) their thinking in directions that I thought desirable.

There were various other strategies that I implemented in my efforts to create a "critical" community. Three of these were especially significant:

- During the second class, we discussed and affirmed that my proposed course outline captured the spirit and many of the specifics of their recommendations. I then suggested that there were two kinds of questions that students could ask of teachers: "Tell me what to do and say" and "Help me advance my thinking and actions." I announced that for the first three weeks of class students were allowed to ask either kind of question, but that after that date, I would respond only to "Help me advance my thinking" questions. I offered examples of the first kind of question that students might pose if they wanted more information about the first assignment for the course (for example, How long does it have to be? Must it be typed? Should we offer our own opinion? What kind of answer are you looking for? Do we have to cite our sources?). I then inquired what these questions might look like if they were reframed as questions that wouldn't simply dictate what to do but would assist students in furthering their own thinking on these issues. Initially, several students offered what essentially were more specific restatements of the first kind of question (for example, Can it be less than five pages? Is it okay if I don't type it?). The class grew silent as they realized they were hard pressed to frame a question that satisfied the new requirements. I offered an example:

"I see the first assignment is worth only 10 per cent of the final grade, that it has two parts, and you have not asked us to access outside sources. Given that the assignment is largely a personal reflection and I do write in a rather concise manner, I think I could do a competent job in about three pages. Does this seem reasonable to you?"

We practised reframing other questions around the first assignment and almost immediately students began (with limited success) to attempt "Help me advance my thinking" questions. My typical response to their partial efforts was "Well, what do you think?" followed by, "Why do you think that?" This promoted students to think through the topic so they could eventually frame the second kind of question. But more often than not, by then students realized that they had actually worked out their own thoughtful answer and, with a few exceptions, didn't need me to affirm it.

- Every class (they were three-hour sessions), we arranged our chairs in a circle and spent approximately thirty minutes discussing emergent concerns, offering news and updates, and listening to students present on an assigned "mini-topic" that we had wanted to look at but didn't have time to devote a full class to. My role was to moderate the conversation and listen. Wherever possible, I returned the week following with an action that took up one or more of the ideas discussed in the previous week. In this way, I signalled to students by my actions that their opinions mattered.

- Students were expected to self- and peer-assess the major assignments using detailed rubrics that I had carefully developed and which the class had reviewed and, when necessary, modified. It was difficult initially to get students to use the descriptors as the basis for their assessments. Either the students hadn't really internalized these criteria or they ignored them, preferring to assign the rating they hoped to get. This was especially problematic when

students were invited to assign marks. Things improved after much practice and with the addition of a rubric in which I evaluated students on their ability to self- and peer assess in a criterion-based, fair-minded manner. The result, as those who have been able to get their students to use a rubric effectively will attest, was a significant shift away from the teacher as the sole arbiter of standards to a shared responsibility with students.

The result of my various efforts was the most satisfying teaching experience of my career. Students acquired a much deeper understanding and competence than I had previously seen. Students reported they worked much harder in the course and found it very satisfying (this is not the same as enjoying the course, as many students agonized over tasks that pushed the boundaries of their teaching). Most felt that they had not simply acquired ideas and strategies from the course, but that it had changed them as teachers.

I can't close this story without noting that I tried to replicate these conditions in the next course I taught with much less satisfying results. Although many of these students reported similar results, one-third of the students did not. I was so dissatisfied with this group's performance in the course that I felt compelled to withhold their grades until they had redone the major assignment. I suspect the disappointing results with this group were because of things I had neglected or done differently and their modest level of commitment to the course and to teaching. They likely lacked a defining element of a community—namely a genuine commitment to a common goal: instead of caring about advancing their professional learning, they seemed more interested in getting through the course. The moral of this epilogue is not to undermine the power of creating a community of thinkers— in the first course and for the majority of students in the second course, the results were superior. However, I offer this cautionary note to remind us that, despite the value of this approach, there are no quick fixes or universal remedies in education.

laborative participation and decision making—a community effort—involving differentiated roles and responsibilities. Before looking at these elements, consider the description in the highlighted text of Roland's efforts at creating a community of learners in his own university teaching.

The principles of a classroom as community, which to some extent are embodied in this example, can be summarized in Table 8.2.

Decision making in a community is not an "either/or" proposition; rather, it is a shared responsibility. Notice that Roland and the students negotiated the course contents. Similarly, the regular implementation of ideas emerging from the weekly circles signalled to the students that their voices were being heard. According to some researchers, students'

sense of being able to influence their learning, as opposed to relying exclusively on someone else—typically a teacher— to direct them, is a significant factor in encouraging students to think for themselves (Barell 1991, 71; Resnick 1989, 9). In a classroom as community, teaching and learning are collaborative—the teacher does not tell students what to think, and, conversely, students are not free to think whatever they happen to feel like. The teacher's role is to frame the tasks, actively mentor students, and support students in developing the "tools" they need in order to reach thoughtful conclusions. For their part, students must work within the negotiated structures and shared norms as they engage seriously with the subject matter. Norm-guided participation and collaboration among all community members are the dominant values.

TABLE 8.2 CLASSROOM AS COMMUNITY

Decision making	teacher and students negotiate mutually acceptable decisions within established parameters
Principles of teaching and learning	teacher orients, mentors, and monitors while students engage rigorously with the subject matter in concert with others
Teaching practices	teacher teaches the "tools" to enable students to reach thoughtful responses to structured but open-ended tasks
Dominant values	norm-guided participation and collaboration

The picture of a classroom as a community may sound idealistic. So how would one systematically undertake to nurture such an environment in an elementary or secondary classroom? Before looking at specific strategies to support a community of critical thinkers, we want to offer a few thoughts on the importance of carefully scrutinizing our existing practices to ensure their consistency with our overarching goal.

The Role of the Hidden Curriculum

The need to look closely at our practices arises not simply because we may miss out on opportunities to support critical thinking. The situation is more disturbing: many classroom practices actually undermine thinking. A particularly important dimension of classroom climate is what is loosely called the "hidden curriculum." The term "hidden" is thought by some to be misleading in that it suggests a conscious but covert attempt to teach contrary to the formal or official curriculum. Many believe that the so-called hidden curriculum is largely unintentional—that many of us do not deliberately send mixed messages to our students, but in large part we are unaware of the messages that our students draw from their classroom experiences. These unintended messages often have a more significant effect on student learning than do our deliberate efforts. This point was affirmed by studies of various educational programs to promote respect for others (Daniels and Case 1992). For the most part, specific programs and activities intended to increase respect for others had a marginal impact; the determining factor was the climate within the classroom. What mattered was whether or not teachers provided a safe forum for student dialogue, solicited and valued student opinions, and otherwise acted in ways that modelled respect for the feelings and ideas of others.

Even a commonplace activity such as teacher talk may have an unintended message for students. For example, studies of the factors that influence students' willingness to contribute to class discussions suggest that teachers commonly monopolize the talk. Not only does this reduce the opportunities for students to contribute, it creates the impression in students' minds that their opinions don't really matter (Hess 2004, 152). One study suggested that 80 per cent of students would talk less in class if they felt their opinions weren't valued.

Consider the implications of the hidden curriculum in the context of the traditional classroom debate. The objective for each team in this activity is to prove that the other side is without merit by refuting, belittling, or ignoring opposing arguments. There is a tacit prohibition against changing one's mind partway through the debate. Crossing to the other side is akin to politicians switching party allegiance—both are seen as betrayals. Increasingly, teachers are replacing this adversarial format with more open-ended discussions in which students are encouraged to see the merits of all sides and to recast binary options as polar positions along a continuum. To facilitate this approach, class discussions may be configured in a U-shape. Students with polar views (either strongly agreeing or strongly disagreeing with the proposition) seat themselves at either tip of the "U"; students with mixed opinions sit at appropriate spots along the rounded part. At varying stages in the discussion students are encouraged to move along the spectrum as their intellectual positions on the issue change. In this way, less dogmatic attitudes are encouraged: the implicit messages of the traditional debate—black or white, fixed opinions with the objective of winning the argument—are supplanted by different messages of the U-shaped discussion, the value of provisionally held positions as one tries to figure out the most defensible personal stance from a continuum of options.

The lesson to be learned from these examples is that nurturing a classroom community of thinkers is an orientation that pervades all of our actions. Not only must we be proactive in introducing elements that will support thinking, we should be vigilant in identifying and altering habits that may undermine our efforts.

Strategies for Building Community

Each of us can build and sustain communities of thinkers in our classrooms by working on five fronts:

- setting appropriate classroom expectations;
- implementing appropriate classroom routines and activities;
- personally modelling the attributes of a good critical thinker;
- shaping the communicative interactions within the class to encourage thinking; and
- developing the tools students need to participate in a reflective community.

Before exploring specific strategies in each of these areas, we offer an account in highlighted text of Philip's efforts at creating a virtual community of learners among his students.

Classroom Expectations

The expectations we set for our students influence the tone of our classrooms. One of the significant factors in Roland's attempt to create a community was the kind of questions students were expected to ask. Typically, at the outset of each year we devote considerable time to establishing behavioural expectations (for example, students are expected to be punctual, keep the classroom clean, treat each other respectfully). It is worth considering the following kinds of classroom expectations that support thinking:

- Students are expected to make up their own minds—not simply take someone's word for things.
- Students and teacher are expected as a matter of course to provide reasons or examples in support of their observations, conclusions, and behaviour.
- Students and teacher are expected to seriously consider other perspectives on an issue and alternative approaches to a problem before reaching a firm conclusion.
- All persons are to be treated respectfully by everyone, even if their ideas seem wrong or silly.

- It is not simply permissible but expected that students will disagree with one another; however, differences of opinions must never be directed personally as attacks on the person.
- It is not acceptable merely to criticize and complain—the pros of a position should always be examined as should possible solutions to problems.
- The insincere use of critical techniques to show off or to be contrary is not tolerated (this does not mean that there is no place for well-intentioned devil's advocacy).

Classroom Routines and Activities

A community of thinkers is supported by building into the daily classroom operation various routines and activities that habituate students to particular frames of mind. The weekly discussion in Roland's class provided an ongoing mechanism by which students could air their concerns and influence the direction of the course. The following list includes some of the routines that support a critical community:

- Using the vocabulary of critical thinking as a matter of course in classroom discussion (for example, "What can you infer from this picture about the individual's mood or feelings?" "What assumptions are you making?").
- Consistently assigning tasks, including those that are for marks, that contain a non-trivial commitment to thinking critically.
- Involving students in scrutinizing accounts, textbooks, news articles and reports, and other "reputable" sources of information for bias, stereotyping, overgeneralization, and inaccuracy.
- Regularly soliciting student ideas and suggestions and (when appropriate) using them in setting assignments, establishing rules for the class, and establishing criteria for evaluation.
- Praising thoughtfully supported, insightful, or empathetic responses (even if flawed) over merely correctly recalled responses.
- Inviting students regularly to explore and defend positions from particular points of view, especially from perspectives that are not personally held by them.
- Involving students regularly in identifying and defending criteria to evaluate their classroom behaviour and work, and then applying these criteria to themselves and their peers.
- Providing students with adequate time to reflect on their learning and to think about their answers before being asked to respond.

PHILIP'S ATTEMPT AT A VIRTUAL COMMUNITY OF THINKERS

For several years I have been using various online technologies with pre- and in-service teachers to support the teaching of thinking. Initially, my approach was to rely on electronic technologies as convenient tools to communicate with students between class periods. I began with e-mail exchanges to monitor concerns and address student questions. Later, I used a dialogue forum (FirstClass) to post logistical information about the course and provide a forum for students to discuss the syllabus and other practical matters. Both these approaches afforded some benefit; notably all of us (including me) arrived to the face-to-face sessions better informed about each other's views and questions.

Recently, I have begun creating more authentic virtual learning communities that do more than act as peripheral technical support to the face-to-face sessions. I now use Knowledge Forum (KF) software (discussed in Scardamalia and Bereiter 1991) to support "knowledge building" where my students actively collaborate to develop the content of the discussions—the topics and resources we will consider—and how we will operate and be assessed. This software provides the architecture through which forum participants structure the discussion and collectively construct emergent understandings. It has played a significant role in nurturing communities of thinkers.

I have tried to support these virtual communities by acting on the five fronts discussed above:

- **Setting appropriate expectations**. At the outset, all of us agree on general expectations. These expectations include that participants take seriously the topic being discussed, attend to responses made by others, and contribute to the building of a positive virtual community. In one group, participants began to add their expectations as they identified a negative tone in some notes. As a consequence, the group developed a code of etiquette for our deliberations. These included expectations that we would always acknowledge contributions made within a note before offering contrary points of view, and that we would focus on the ideas while avoiding any personal criticism.

- **Implementing appropriate routines.** The most fundamental routines involve making frequent contributions to the forum: we post regular messages (usually one per week) intended to "advance understanding of the topic" and respond to several messages (usually two per week). Building on the KF framework we routinely provide structural clues to help everyone keep up with the discussions. These include the following:

  - creating informative and engaging titles for each note (for example, Kohn trashes standardized testing: Does he make sense?);
  - mentioning the question we are addressing (for example, What assumptions is Alfie Kohn making? Or, Do cell phones have a constructive role to play in the classroom?);
  - identifying "keywords" in our notes (for example, inference, bias, conclusion, opinion) to help others search and organize the database;
  - making explicit references to other participants' notes (for example, X says "...," but I think ..., because ...);
  - embedding outside sources, including internet links, graphics, and video clips.

- **Personal modelling of critical thinking attributes**. I try as best I can to model sound thinking and respectful discussion in my own notes. To encourage student use of the features of the software, I make a point of using various "scaffolding" labels ("An Alternative Point of View," "My Conclusion," or "Flaws in the Argument") to identify the kind of contribution I am making to the discussion. Such declarations help participants identify the thinking concepts in play.

- **Communicative interactions**. The structure and deliberative pace of online communication within a virtual community provide rich opportunities to ask probing questions and offer thoughtful responses. The KF software is particularly effective at helping participants move beyond merely offering observations and opinions to the weighing of multiple options and the seeking of informed consensus on topics. I have found these virtual interactions have transferred to more thoughtful face-to-face discussions in the classroom.

- **Tools for a reflective community**. Success is unlikely if a majority of participants lack the skills needed to contribute to a virtual community. I have found it imperative to teach participants both how to use the software to build community and the thinking tools needed to contribute.

While I am generally pleased with the results, every group has not been entirely successful in building a virtual critical community. One explanation for the less successful cases is participant unwillingness to use technology to support their work together. Another factor is the vulnerability felt by some participants over "publishing" their thoughts within the virtual environment. This sense of vulnerability requires careful attention during face-to-face encounters and assurances, supported with actions, that participants will be treated with the thoughtful consideration they deserve.

Teacher Modelling

Albert Schweitzer is reported to have noted, "Example is not the main thing in influencing others, it's the only thing" (reported in Norman 1989, 27). This principle applies to critical thinking. If we want our students to be good critical thinkers we must model these attributes ourselves in the kinds of ways suggested below:

- Don't be dogmatic and don't always have an answer. Live with ambiguity—be satisfied with tentative conclusions until full review of complex issues can be carried out.
- Sincerely attempt to base all comments and decisions on careful and fair-minded consideration of all sides.
- Be willing (if asked) to provide "good" reasons for your decisions and actions (this does not mean that the lesson must be interrupted every time a student asks for a justification).
- Be careful to avoid making gross generalizations and stereotypical comments about individuals and groups, and seek to expose stereotypes in books, pictures, films, and other learning resources.
- Be willing to change your mind or alter your plans when good reasons are presented.
- Regularly acknowledge the existence of different positions on an issue (for example, looking at events from different cultural, gender, and class perspectives).
- Don't be cynical—adopt, instead, a realistic but questioning attitude towards the world.

Communicative Interactions

The "talk" that goes on within a classroom exerts a powerful influence on the atmosphere. Classroom communication can be divided into three categories:

- whole class discussions on a common topic;
- teacher interactions with individual students; and
- communication among students.

WHOLE CLASS DISCUSSIONS

Teachers can support a community of thinkers by attending to their communicative interactions with the class as a whole. Diane Hess (2004, 152) has identified four impediments to successful classroom discussions:

- a tendency for teachers to talk too much;
- "discussion" questions that don't invite discussion;
- lack of focus and depth in student contributions; and
- unequal participation by students (some students monopolize discussions and others are marginalized).

The obvious solution to teacher dominance of class discussions is to remind ourselves constantly that most of the talk should come from our students. It may also help to avoid signalling to students our own opinions on the issue under discussion. Instead, we might raise questions or offer statements that invite disagreement, not end it.

Another significant determinant of student participation in whole class discussion is the nature of the questions asked. If the questions are essentially matters of factual knowledge (for example, What was urban life like one hundred years ago?) or personal preference (for example, Would you have liked to have lived then?), there is little real opportunity for students to engage each other in genuine debate. In the case of factual questions, either students remember (or can guess) the answers or they don't know the answer and therefore have little to offer. Disagreements typically hinge on factual details (for example, Did they or did they not have cars?). There is relatively little to discuss other than to assert an answer. Preference questions are difficult to debate since they are largely matters of personal inclination (for example, You would like to live without electricity and I wouldn't). The most productive kind of questions for classroom discussions are ones that we have referred to in chapter 4 as critical challenges. These are questions that do not have a pre-specified right answer. To respond to them, students must render their own judgments based on relevant factors (for example, Considering social, physical, and mental health, was the quality of life for the average young person better now or a hundred years ago?). Such questions leave lots of room for debate, especially if students are well prepared for the discussion.

On the point of student preparedness for class discussions, the following strategies intended to support reluctant discussants contain useful advice to increase the likelihood that all students are ready for a discussion (Wilen 2004, 53):

- Base classroom discussions on a common text that students have read or an experience they have shared.
- Invite students to think about the topic beforehand and to write down a few questions they might have.
- Provide students with an opportunity to review information or to gather their thoughts prior to discussing the topic as a class.
- Divide students into pairs to develop questions and to prepare and rehearse a few points they might offer.

Teacher questioning is a key aspect of classroom discussion. Although there are no hard and fast rules for the kind and order of questions to ask, it does make sense to consider a general sequence when trying to engage students in group discussion. In the following questioning pattern, a discussion is initiated by asking one student to state and support a position and, if necessary, to clarify the position or the supporting reasons. Other students are invited to offer their positions and supporting reasons, and then to respond to those who disagree with them. Finally, the teacher might draw attention to unrecognized information or add provocative clues to stimulate further discussion. The objectives in asking these questions are to help students articulate their beliefs, extend their thinking, and engage with others. The questions listed below illustrate non-intimidating ways of framing each kind of prompt:

Invite a judgment and a reason or two
- What is your conclusion and what causes you to think this?
- Can you tell me what you think about the issue and a reason why?

Seek greater clarity (only if judgment or reason is unclear)
- That's interesting; can you give me an example?
- Can you help me understanding what you're saying? Is your point "this" or "this"?

Solicit other students' judgments and reasons
- Does anyone have a different opinion? Why or why not?
- Who has the same opinion, but for different reasons?

Invite students to respond to each other's comments
- What might you say to those who don't agree with your position?
- Some have mentioned [a reason]; does everyone agree that this is a convincing reason?

Add new information or provide clues to push students' thinking
- No one has mentioned [piece of information]. Would this make a difference to your thinking?
- Do you think it is important that [new piece of information]?

INTERACTIONS WITH INDIVIDUAL STUDENTS

In addition to whole group communications, a community of thinkers is also affected by teacher interactions with individual students. There is a delicate trade-off when responding to student questions. On one hand, answering their questions helps them learn; on the other hand, knowing that the teacher will provide the answer may discourage students from thinking for themselves. The difficulty that students in Roland's university methods class had in framing a question that advanced their own thinking illustrates the concern when students are freely given the answers. Although there are many occasions when student questions should be answered di-

rectly, it is worth considering ways of encouraging students to answer their own questions:

- Turn the question back on the student or onto others in the class (for example, Well, what do you think? What is your best guess as to the answer? How would you respond?).
- Prompt students with clues or hints or present an example or new situation that might help them see their response as problematic (for example, Have you considered…?).
- Suggest tentative answers, including those that many students would see as flawed (for example, Well I'm wondering if it could be…? I'm not sure, some people might think…).

INTERACTIONS AMONG STUDENTS

There is much that could be said about helping students learn to communicate respectfully and thoughtfully with each other. The area we will touch upon is peer feedback, which is one of the important occasions for inter-student communication involving critical thinking. When asked to offer peer feedback, students are in effect thinking critically about another's work—they are offering assessments based on identifiable criteria (for example, I think your work is interesting and well organized). The following suggestions may help to guide students during feedback sessions:

- Emphasize peer feedback as an invitation to see the positives, not just the negatives.
- Begin by critiquing the work of those not in the class, and before asking students to put their work on the line, have the class critique something you have done (for example, an essay you wrote as a student, a class presentation you made). When it is time for peer critique, start with group assignments so the responsibility is shared among several students.
- In the early days of peer critique, do not allow negative comments—only allow remarks on positive features. A good indication of the time to make the transition to concerns/areas to consider is when students voluntarily ask each other to identify what is missing from or could be improved with their work.
- Model and set a few simple guidelines for peer critique: perhaps insist that each student start with two (or more) positive comments before offering a (single) concern, and that negative comments be phrased in the form of a query (for example, "I'm unclear why you did it this way. Could you explain what you had in mind?").
- Ensure that the early instances of peer feedback are low-risk, relatively easy to perform, and have an obvious benefit.

Tools for Community Participation

Just as students need instruction in how to function as citizens in society, so too do they need to be taught how to be effective contributors to a classroom community of thinkers. The classic image of the isolated thinker is a misleading one; we should not expect to be able to think through all of our "problems" by ourselves. Rather, we should actively develop, supplement, and test our ideas in conjunction with others—put our heads together. Many students may be unwilling or unable to contribute to and benefit from collaborative reflection. Perhaps they do not listen very well, or they cannot accept any form of criticism, or they do not know how to monitor what they say, or they have no confidence in their ability to contribute to the discussion. Students need these tools if they are to participate as effective members in a community of thinkers. Some of the key tools[1] are suggested below:

Background knowledge
- knowledge that individuals may see things in significantly different ways;
- knowledge of how individuals are likely to react in various situations.

Criteria for judgment
- consider whether their comments are relevant to the discussion (on topic);
- consider whether their comments will be clear to everyone.

Critical thinking vocabulary
- unanimous, consensus, minority positions.

Thinking strategies
- group-management strategies such as taking turns, assigning co-operative roles, active listening, and keeping a speaker's list;
- strategies for critiquing in a non-threatening manner including putting the comment in the form of a question, preceding a comment with a caveat, or preceding a comment with positive remarks;
- strategies for presenting information in group settings include limiting comments to a few points, speaking from notes, and connecting remarks to a previous speaker's comments.

Habits of mind
- independent-minded—willingness to make up one's own mind;
- sensitivity to others—attention to the feelings of others;
- self-monitoring—attention to how one's actions are affecting the group.

Review the list of strategies for each of the five fronts:

- Setting appropriate classroom expectations.
- Implementing appropriate classroom routines and activities.
- Personally modelling the attributes of a good critical thinker.
- Shaping the communicative interactions within the class to encourage reflection.
- Developing the tools for student participation in a reflective community.

Select one or two strategies from the list that you think would be realistic and most effective to implement in your teaching situation.

Conclusion

In this chapter we have argued how important it is to attend to the atmosphere that pervades a classroom, particularly as it relates to student thinking. Building on the metaphor of classroom as community, we distinguished classrooms in which students are partners in the decision-making process from those that are typically referred to as teacher- or student-run classrooms. The core features of a classroom community include a commitment to a shared purpose, agreed-on procedures, and joint responsibility. Using examples from our own university-based teaching, we illustrated various ways in which teachers might nurture a community of thinkers in their own classrooms.

NOTE

1. The tools referred to in this list are explained in chapter 7, "Teaching the Tools to Think Critically" by Roland Case and LeRoi Daniels.

REFERENCES

Barell, J. 1991. *Teaching for thoughtfulness: Classroom strategies to enhance intellectual development.* New York: Longman.

Daniels, L. and R. Case. 1992. *Charter literacy and the administration of justice in Canada.* Ottawa: Department of Justice, June.

Goodlad, J. 2004. *A place called school: Twentieth anniversary edition.* Whitby, ON: McGraw-Hill.

Hess, D.E. 2004. Discussion in social studies: Is it worth the trouble? *Social Education* 68 (2): 151–155.

Lipman, M. 1991. *Thinking in education.* Cambridge: Cambridge University Press.

MacKinnon, A. and C. Scarff-Seatter. 1997. Constructivism: Contradictions and confusions in teacher education. In *Constructivist teacher education: Building new understandings,* ed. V. Richardson, 38–56. London: Falmer.

Newmann, F.W. 1990. Higher order thinking in teaching social studies: A rationale for the assessment of classroom thoughtfulness. *Journal of Curriculum Studies* 22 (1): 41–56.

———. 1991. Promoting higher order thinking in social studies: Overview of a study of 16 high school departments. *Theory and Research in Social Education* 19 (4): 324–340.

Norman, P. 1989. *The self-directed learning contract: A guide for learners and teachers.* Burnaby, BC: Faculty of Education, Simon Fraser University.

Resnick, L.B., ed. 1989. *Knowing, learning and instruction: Essays in honor of Robert Glaser.* Hillsdale, NJ: Lawrence Erlbaum.

Richardson, V. 2003. Constructivist pedagogy. *Teachers College Record* 105 (9): 1623–1640.

Rogoff, B. 1994. Developing understanding of the idea of communities of learners. *Mind, Culture, and Activity* 1 (4): 209–229.

Scardamalia, M. and C. Bereiter. 1991. Higher levels of agency for children in knowledge building: A challenge for the design of new knowledge media. *The Journal of the Learning Sciences* 1: 37–68.

Wilen, W.W. 2004. Encouraging reticent students' participation in classroom discussions. *Social Education* 68 (1): 51–56.

9

Portals to Understanding
Embedding Historical Thinking in the Curriculum

Mike Denos

Some of my most meaningful teaching moments have happened when I least expected them. One such event occurred on a May afternoon in my sun-drenched portable while teaching a History 12 class on the Falklands War. The students had been discussing why such a minor, seemingly low priority possession would cause a major conflict. I suggested in passing that unpopular regimes, such as the Argentinean *junta,* may be tempted to manufacture conflict to stir up nationalist sentiments and rally political support. I mentioned that many suspected the Greek military dictatorship of attempting to prop up its faltering regime by initiating a crisis on Cyprus in 1974. At this point, a young man, who I will call Peter, jumped out of his seat and yelled, "That's a complete misrepresentation of history!"

Peter was of Greek heritage and he felt that I had unjustifiably maligned his people, culture, and past. His contributions in class to that point had been almost non-existent. His dramatic reaction to my comment was one more validation of my belief that all students, many of whom profess to have no interest in history, can be drawn into a historical discussion if we can find a way to tap into their interests or sensitivities.

In responding to Peter, I asked how he knew my statement was a "complete misrepresentation of history." He said that all one had to do was look at the facts. I asked the class if that was all we really had to do, look at the facts. Did the facts really speak for themselves? Well, no, several students responded. They pointed out that there were facts, and then there were other facts; it was a matter of which facts you selected and how you used them that determined your version of an event. And so we were off.

We discussed how we would get to the truth about the Greek junta's motivations regarding Cyprus. Students arrived at a four-step approach:

- Gather all relevant and credible primary and secondary documents we could on the event.
- Based on those sources, establish which of those events and which sequence of events we could all agree were most factual and accurate.

- Based on that agreed-upon sequence of events, construct the most plausible arguments or explanations for the crisis, and determine who was most responsible for provoking it.
- As a group or individually, decide which explanation best withstood critical scrutiny.

Over the next couple of days, that is exactly what we did. Although we never fully resolved the question—certainly not to Peter's satisfaction—the exercise transformed my students. Instead of wanting to learn just enough history to pass the provincial exam, they became a group eager to learn, to discuss, and to try to *understand* history.

This transformation highlighted two inadequacies that characterize history taught strictly as an informational account:

- Students cannot properly understand history unless they know what is involved in thinking deeply and critically about it.
- Inviting students to think about history is more likely to engage them in the subject matter.

Students' ability to grasp both the nature of the discipline we call history and the content they learn in history class is impaired if they do not see history as consisting of accounts that must be constructed, interpreted, and assessed. In other words, neither the *subject* nor the *subject matter* of history can be properly understood without engaging in historical thinking.

From that moment forward, I approached the history curriculum as a series of questions and issues to be argued about and understood rather than as a sequence of causal events to be catalogued and recounted. I came to appreciate more fully the difference between knowing history and understanding history. As well, I realized that while it was possible to know a great deal about something without understanding it, it was not possible to understand it without knowing a great deal about it.

The Problem

My challenge was figuring out how to structure my classes to emphasize historical understanding, while at the same time covering the required content. It is exciting and rewarding to explore a particular event in depth, but in most public schools, teachers cannot teach their entire course in this manner and still meet the content expectations. All high school teachers face the pressure of curriculum coverage, especially in courses that have government examinations. Teachers fear, quite reasonably, that if they teach for depth, they will be unable to meet the requirements for breadth.

In addition, teachers recognize that "covering" the curriculum is necessary to provide the basic broad knowledge of history that students need to effectively think historically. We should not expect students to think critically about an event in a historical vacuum. It is not possible to think effectively about a historical problem or issue if one has no knowledge of its context.

Eventually I concluded that resolving these seemingly contradictory pursuits of breadth and depth would depend on my approach. Many of us front-end load the required "factual historical knowledge" and then assign students end-of-chapter questions using that knowledge. I now believe that we can accommodate critical thinking and enhance subject matter retention with only slight modifications to this approach. These involve changing the way we frame questions and where we pose them in the learning sequence, and giving greater responsibility to students for assessing and understanding historical conclusions. This means building our units and lessons around questions that require reasoned judgment based on an examination of relevant materials, and formulating questions that require students to learn and apply skills of historical analysis. By embedding the need to think historically into the process of acquiring historical knowledge, we can bridge the tension between providing the required content (breadth) and promoting historical thinking (depth).

Research versus Inquiry Questions

Modifying the way we frame questions seems simple but is the most elusive of the modifications I propose. Many times we frame questions that look as though they require reasoned judgment when actually, they merely require research. Furthermore, not all critical inquiry questions invite historical thinking. Thus, we need to learn to frame questions that require genuine inquiry into issues that are central to the discipline of history.

The first task in learning to design questions that re-quire critical inquiry is to distinguish between "research" and "inquiry." Although these terms are sometimes used synonymously, there is an important distinction to be drawn.[1] Conducting research is typically a matter of finding factual information on a topic or "re-searching" the ideas and facts that others have uncovered. The professional historian, of course, goes beyond researching secondary sources and pursues what is often called "original research," and what I refer to as "critical inquiry." The term "original research" indicates that a study is intended to produce new knowledge and not simply reproduce what others already know, usually resulting from a fresh examination of primary sources. While it is neither realistic nor beneficial to expect students to do much "original historical research" with their limited backgrounds, students do need to appreciate and experience history as a genuine inquiry where their task is not merely to find out what others know (they must, of course, do this as well), but also to reach their own conclusions using this information. Even if others already know the answer, in a genuine inquiry, the students' task is to reach their own conclusions and not simply summarize the conclusions offered by others. *A critical inquiry requires that students make reasoned judgments, based on criteria, to formulate their own justifiable conclusions.*

The examples in Table 9.1 illustrate the difference between "re-search" questions (those involving mere factual retrieval) and inquiry questions (requiring reasoned judgment). The questions in both columns are good questions, but only the inquiry questions in the right-hand column invite students to make reasoned judgments. The research questions require students to make choices to some extent, but they do not demand justification for those choices. In responding to the first research question, students could simply list five factors that led to the decision of the colonies to join Confederation and summarize information from the textbook explaining why each was a contributing factor. Ranking the factors requires a reasoned defence of the prioritization based on criteria for assessing causal connections. Similar distinctions hold true for the other pairs of questions. Research questions can be, and often are, reduced to fixed answers. Inquiry questions require interpretation and justification with no set answer; the quality of the answer depends largely on students' abilities to marshal compelling evidence that supports their conclusions. They must, of course, base their conclusions on accurate historical facts.

It is also useful to reconsider where we place our questions in the sequence of learning. Rather than completing a lesson or unit with an inquiry question, we can begin the study with the question and a discussion of the criteria needed to answer it. This helps students focus on what to consider as they learn about an event and examine relevant materials. The highlighted text, "The Impact of Islam," illustrates this shift

TABLE 9.1 DISTINGUISHING RESEARCH FROM INQUIRY

RE-SEARCH QUESTIONS AND TASKS	INQUIRY QUESTIONS AND TASKS
List five factors that led to the decision of colonies to join in Confederation.	Rank in order of importance the five identified factors leading to the decision of colonies to join in Confederation.
Describe John A. Macdonald's contributions as a leader.	Was John A. Macdonald a great leader?
Compare life in New France with life in the American colonies.	What was the biggest difference between life in New France and in the American colonies?
Why were Japanese Canadians interned during World War II?	Based on the evidence provided, were the authorities justified in interning Japanese Canadians during World War II?

from front-end loading information and then asking critical thinking questions to embedding historical thinking in the acquisition of information.

Student Responsibility for Understanding

Placing greater responsibility on students for assessing information and constructing their understanding of history requires teachers to have some faith in students' ability and their willingness to complete assigned tasks. We may need to help students develop the necessary work ethic and critical habits of mind. This might best be accomplished in small doses at first, so that students become comfortable making, and being accountable for defending, their own judgments. However, becoming accustomed to taking on more responsibility for their learning is only the beginning. Students also require sufficient context and background information to think effectively. This often requires that the teacher select and provide pertinent sources, rather than setting students free on the internet or in a library to do research. In the name of efficiency, it is probably best to emphasize analysis of teacher-provided materials over student gathering of materials.

THE IMPACT OF ISLAM

Danny, a student teacher who I was observing, was teaching a Social Studies 8 class on the effects of Islam on the lives and culture of Arab peoples and of those who converted to Islam as a result of conquest. He arranged for the class to read aloud two short sections from their textbook that described the life of early nomadic Arab cultures and the spread and influence of Islam throughout Arabia, Africa, and into Spain. Danny stopped the reading at various places to elaborate on the text and then wrote significant points on an overhead for students to copy in their notebooks. At the end of the thirty-minute lecture/discussion, Danny assigned the following questions:

What was life and society like for the Arabs living in the Arabian Peninsula before Islam? List five or six points.

The Arabs conquered an empire stretching from _____ to _____.

When the Arabs conquered a certain area, what did they bring with them that would have an effect on the people around them? One example is Islamic faith. What are two other examples?

In our post-conference meeting on the lesson, I spoke with Danny about embedding his questions in his teaching. Instead of reading the text without a clear focus, I suggested that he create a chart with two columns on the board. He might label the columns "Arab Peoples Before Islam" and "Influences of Islam (on Arab and Conquered Peoples)." I suggested that he then ask students to read the first section of the text and identify five significant facts about Arab life and society before Islam. He might instruct students to rank their facts in order of significance, and to be prepared to defend their ranking. Once the students had read the materials, the class could break into groups and create group rankings. Then the class as a whole could devise rankings. The same process could take place for the second section of reading based on the question, "What effects did Islam have on Arab peoples and on those they conquered?" After the two lists have been compiled, he might invite students to write a paragraph on the following: *Based on your lists comparing pre-Islamic life and the effects of Islam on Arab and conquered peoples, identify those features in Islam that were most responsible for the social changes that took place after Arab conquests.* (This was the unspoken overarching challenge of the lesson.)

In the revised lesson, students cover the same material but with two differences: they would be engaged in using the content they were expected to learn, and they would assess its significance as they learned it.

Promoting Historical Thinking

Framing questions that promote critical thinking will likely enhance a student's understanding of history. However, historical thinking is more than simply thinking critically. Historical thinking affects students' very understanding of the discipline. The need to think historically in order to understand the discipline arises because history inevitably consists of partial accounts constructed for specific purposes. No single account can present all that is known. Historians must be selective in the topics they focus on and the details they mention (for example, stressing daily life over political events; famous peoples over ordinary citizens; World War I and II, but not the Crimean and Korean wars). In addition, all accounts must be viewed from within a perspective (for example, Canadian history might be written from pan-Canadian, French-Canadian, First Nations, immigrant, or American perspectives).

Furthermore, as new social, economic, and political issues arise, we often revise our conclusions about the past. I was taught in school that Christopher Columbus *discovered* America; yet this is no longer seen as the "truth." In this sense,

"revisionist" history is the only history there is. Though it is about the past, historical knowledge is also shaped by conditions and priorities in the present. Recently the environment, religious conflict, and gender issues have acquired greater prominence in the curriculum. Current textbooks differ in content from those in use twenty years ago, and even more than those written fifty years ago. Ten years from now, other issues will arise and our narratives about and historical understanding of the past will change with them. Unless students are taught to recognize and explore the factors that influence what gets represented as history, and to understand that there can never be *the* history of an event or a period, they will not understand the nature of the subject. In this respect, the history class must be a place where students both learn the content of history and learn to question the interpretations they encounter.

Fortunately, in recent years, considerable work has been done on examining the nature of historical thinking and identifying aspects or concepts that serve as portals into historical understanding. Most prominent in the development of these concepts is the work of Peter Seixas (Seixas and Peck 2004, Seixas 2006), who has identified six concepts that serve as ways to begin to explore historical events.

HISTORICAL SIGNIFICANCE

Behind the selection of what and who should be remembered, researched, taught, and learned is the issue of historical significance. Questions of significance are foundational to thinking about history, because historians cannot include all that has happened in the past and students are required to learn about and appreciate the most important events. But what is important, historically speaking? How do we decide whether a historical event is significant for everybody or just for some people? Whose history is it? For Canadians, Remembrance Day is a significant holiday. To Americans, the eleventh hour of the eleventh day of the eleventh month is not as significant a milestone. Instead, Americans celebrate Memorial Day, a similar holiday remembering their war dead on the last Monday in May. The reason the two allied nations remember their war dead on different days lies in the significance each nation attaches to the end of World War I. Thinking about significance helps students learn how decisions about what to report and study in history are made, and to recognize that these decisions are open to ongoing review.

Historical thinking questions built around the concept of significance include:

- Why was the Indian Act of 1876 such a significant event in aboriginal and government relations? Is it still a significant factor in the lives of First Nations peoples in Canada? Why or why not?

- Which of the early explorers of Canada are the most historically significant?
- Which was the more significant event in the history of Canadian self-rule: passage of the Statute of Westminster in 1929 or repatriation of the Canadian Constitution in 1982?

The highlighted text, "Criteria for Assessing Significance," suggests three broad criteria that can help students judge the historical significance of an event or person. Applying these criteria to the dropping of the first atomic bomb, we can see why this event is so significant: it was especially prominent at the time; the magnitude, scope, and impact of its consequences were immense; and Hiroshima is remembered to this day, and has assumed iconic status.

EVIDENCE AND INTERPRETATION

The concept of evidence is concerned with the validation, interpretation, and use of primary and secondary sources of historical information in the construction of history and historical argument. The central questions of evidence and interpretation are "How do we know what happened?" and "Which version of events should we believe?" These questions invite students to examine primary documents for authenticity and reliability, and secondary sources for accuracy, bias, and plausibility. The goal of examining evidence is to learn how to use both primary and secondary sources to construct and assess credible accounts of the past.

As illustrated in the following examples, questions about evidence often invite students to weigh the evidence supporting a particular conclusion or to draw their own conclusions based on available evidence:

- Identify the biases in the following two textbook accounts. Explain which statement offers the more plausible explanation of who was most responsible for construction of the Canadian Pacific Railway. Support your argument with evidence.

> The railway was built chiefly on the backs of Chinese coolie labour, using land obtained for almost nothing from the Indians and capital raised for the most part in Britain (Francis 1997, 15).

> William Van Horne [was] a 38-year-old general manager of a smaller railway in the American Midwest. Van Horne was the ideal choice. He was intelligent and dedicated and the word "cannot" did not exist in his vocabulary. He would spend the next four years driving him-

---

CRITERIA FOR ASSESSING SIGNIFICANCE

- **Prominence at the time.** To what extent was the event/person/trend important at the time of its occurrence?
- **Consequences.**
  - *Magnitude.* What was the magnitude of the impact? Did it result in major changes?
  - *Scope.* What was the scope of the impact? Did it affect a few people in a limited area or a broad range of people in a large area?
  - *Depth of impact.* What was the lasting nature of the impact? Were its effects short-lived? Were there consequences that affected subsequent events/people/trends?
- **Historical prominence.**
  - *Remembered.* Is it widely remembered and memorialized in popular culture and professional history? Does it have an iconic status?
  - *Revealing:* Does it tell us something crucial about the time? Is it emblematic of a condition or period of history?

---

self and his employees unmercifully until the CPR was completed (Cranny, Garvis, Moles, and Seney 1999, 188).

- Examine the two recruitment and propaganda posters from World War II. Answer the following questions, supporting your conclusions with evidence based on your observations:
  - What do the posters have in common?
  - What type of person (for example, age, gender, social class, and ethnicity) was wanted in the air force?
  - What emotions were used to motivate people during the war?
  - How were women targeted differently than men?
  - What inadvertent messages do they relate about attitudes in Canadian society in 1939?

Canadian War Poster Collection, Rare Books and Special Collections, McGill University Library

Library and Archives Canada, Acc. No. 1983-30-148

CONTINUITY AND CHANGE

Continuity and change help us place ourselves in time and help us understand the historical journey leading to our present condition. Students need to investigate what has changed or stayed the same over periods in history if they are to comprehend their own time. Not only are the subtleties of change and continuity difficult to distinguish, our conceptions of each are dependent upon life experiences and world view. For example, a student who has come from a country where profound change has taken place in a short period of time will view change differently than a student from a more stable environment.

Historians use the concepts of continuity and change to organize time in several ways:

- chronology: to sequence events in order of their occurrence to help us organize our understanding;
- periodization: to create periods as a way of differentiating segments of time (for example, the Roaring 20s, the Dirty 30s);
- progress and decline: to evaluate improvement or regression over time.

Questions involving continuity and change include the following:

- Who had more independence and freedom—a 16-year-old in Toronto in 1900 or a 16-year-old in Toronto in 2000? Is the life of a 16-year-old today an example of progress or decline? Support your arguments with evidence.
- In what major ways did the 1960s in North America alter a woman's social role from her role in the 1950s? In what major ways did a woman's role remain the same?
- If an economic disaster similar to the depression that took hold of North America in the 1930s were to occur today, would governments be able to respond differently and more successfully than they did in the 1930s? Why or why not?

CAUSE AND CONSEQUENCE

The concepts of cause and consequence ask the questions: "Who or what brought about the event?" and "What were its consequences?" It is important not to oversimplify these concepts. There is rarely a singular cause for or consequence of an event. Causes are multiple and layered, and can stem from long-held beliefs, individual leadership, long-term social conditions, and institutional structures, as well as short-term actions and events (for example, no single cause can, or should, be identified as responsible for the fall of Rome).

Furthermore, causes have both intended and unintended consequences that may, in turn, bring about further events.

Questions that invite consideration of cause and consequence include the following:

- Identify and explain which of the following factors were causes or consequences of the Great Depression and which were simply antecedent and subsequent events.
    - the stock market crash of 1929
    - the "Dust Bowl" in the prairies in the 1930s
    - overproduction as the industrial capacity of the US and Canada exceeded demand
    - economic nationalism and tariffs
    - international debt
    - unemployment
    - World War II
- Why didn't Hitler and the Nazis win World War II?
- Many scholars argue that the Treaty of Versailles was a major cause of World War II. Yet the treaty was meant to prevent another war. What elements of the treaty had a direct causal relationship to World War II, and which had unintended consequences that led to the war?

HISTORICAL PERSPECTIVE-TAKING

The concept of historical perspective-taking addresses these questions: How did the people of the time perceive an event? How did it reflect their values? What was it really like to live in this period? How were their values and perceptions similar to and different from our own?

The opposite of historical perspective-taking is presentism, the imposition of a contemporary perspective when interpreting events in the past. Asking students to imagine how they would feel if they were a particular historical person is more likely to undermine historical perspective-taking than it is to advance it. Students are inclined to apply modern lenses that distort the past and what it meant for the people living at the time. Coming to grips with the idea that "reality" was different for other people in other times is both one of the most fascinating and challenging tasks in history. At the most basic level, this means students should not presume that the words used in historical documents mean the same to the people who wrote them as they do to us who read them now. And it certainly requires that students, when drawing conclusions about the past, become informed about and remain conscious of the values, beliefs, and customs of the time. Rather than asking students to project how they would feel if they were a historical person, we want to ask students to imagine how a person must have thought and felt, as a product of his or her time.

Questions of historical perspective-taking typically include asking students to explain or anticipate how people in an identified time might have felt and thought:

- Provide students with several documents by someone from another time (for example, selected excerpts from *Roughing It in the Bush* by Susanna Moodie) and ask students to try to explain the author's perspective. Invite students to focus their attention on interpreting the prevailing social environment.
- Ask students to write a letter or diary entry or create a drawing or poster from the perspective of an assigned historical person. Provide students with sources on the broader social norms and beliefs that underlie the person's perspective to help them acquire the historical context for the perspective they are expected to adopt.

THE MORAL DIMENSION

The moral dimension invites students to assess the ethical appropriateness of past events in light of our present values and with a consideration of the norms and conditions operating at the time of the events.

Moral judgments require a suspension of judgment, until that person, group, or event is put fully into context. Dropping an atomic bomb on a civilian population hardly seems justifiable in any circumstance, but if one does not examine the context in which it was first dropped, the moral discussion will be skewed and the judgment pre-determined. Before one renders a fair judgment, it is important to understand the values upon which actions took place were based.

Questions inviting moral judgment include the following:

- Should the Canadian government have apologized for the *Komogata Maru* incident and offered monetary compensation to the direct descendants of those who were turned away or to the Indo-Canadian community?
- Argue for or against the following statement:

  The decision to drop the atomic bomb on Hiroshima was justified given the context of the times.

Using Portal Concepts in Unit Planning

Collectively, these six concepts serve as entry points or portals into an examination of history. They give the students a leg-hold—a secure place to begin an investigation. I like to compare thinking about a historical event to solving a crossword puzzle. One could start a crossword puzzle in a linear fashion solving the word for "one down" or "one across" and then work onwards in sequence from there, just as one might start chronologically analyzing the first incident in a major historical event. One can also (and most commonly) solve a crossword puzzle by going to the clues most readily understood and working outward from what has been most accessible to putting the whole puzzle together. In the same way, one does not need to use these concepts in a linear order, but rather, one can pick the concepts that most readily lead to an initial exploration of a historical event and work outwards to include other concepts as they apply to the question being explored. As well, one can look at several aspects at once and construct a convergence for a complete narrative.

Every unit needs a "big idea" that serves as scaffolding upon which to build the unit. Planning each unit starts with the questions: "What is important for the students to understand about this event, person, or period?" and "Why is it important for them to understand it?" From those two questions, the teacher should be able to formulate an overarching question on which to build his or her unit. The concepts for historical thinking can be very useful in formulating these overarching questions, and also in creating other questions that support the overarching question. The key is to frame questions that require students to offer an assessment based on certain criteria. An overarching question that does not require meeting criteria upon which the answer can be assessed is really only asking for opinion. The value of this set of concepts in developing these questions and activities is suggested by the examples on Confederation found in Table 9.2.[2] Any of the suggested questions could serve as the overarching question for a unit.

My own preference in planning the Confederation unit would be to test the validity of the commonly accepted myth that without the vision of John A. Macdonald, there would be no Canada. It's not that myths are totally misleading, since they often embody elements of the truth or at least the spirit of the truth. We need mythical stories to build our initial understandings of the past in part because students respond to and grasp stories more quickly than historical case studies and primary sources. Challenging such stories can also be a very effective way to promote understanding. As Ken Osborne (2000, n.p.) points out: "stories can raise questions as easily as they impose answers. They can be open-ended and multi-perspective. They can even be used as vehicles of their own deconstruction. Above all, they are a wonderful way of making abstract ideas intelligibly concrete, of combining the cognitive with the affective." Examining myth not only starts with what the students know, but it also encourages historical thinking by challenging widely-held assumptions. Given that notion, several questions could be formulated as an overarching question:

- Would Canada have become a nation in 1867 without the leadership of John A. Macdonald?
- Who or what was the most important cause in the founding of the Canadian Confederation? (This is a rewording of the Cause and Consequence question.)

If one of these questions became the unit focus, then the questions formulated for historical significance and cause and consequence would be used as supporting questions to build towards this end. On the other hand, my overarching question might be: "Did the original terms of Confederation set up an inevitable rift between English and French Canadi-

ans?" In addressing this overarching question, I would probably focus on the concepts of evidence, continuity and change, and historical perspective.

Another way to use these concepts as portals is to begin with an overarching question and then generate questions from it using the concepts as prompts. This approach is illustrated in the unit questions on Canada's role in World War I outline in Figure 9.1. The war itself is often said to have defined Canada as a nation, and certain events from World War I, such as Vimy Ridge, have assumed iconic status. It almost goes unchallenged that World War I was the birthing place of the modern Canadian nation. Yet was it? With this

TABLE 9.2	DEVELOPING QUESTIONS AND ACTIVITIES ABOUT CONFEDERATION	
	QUESTIONS	ACTIVITIES
Historical significance	What was the most significant event that led to Confederation?	In groups, decide the five most important events that led to Confederation. Select one as the most important. What was the most significant event that led to Confederation?
Evidence and interpretation	Using the original terms upon which each province agreed to Confederation, and researching editorials and speeches of the times, which province got the best deal out of joining Canada?	Choose one of the four original provinces as your province. Based on evidence from your research, prepare an editorial showing how your province (or another province) got the best deal out of joining Canada. Using the original terms upon which each province agreed to join Confederation, and researching editorials and speeches of the times, which province got the best deal out of joining Canada?
Continuity and change	What were three major ways the colonies of British North America changed after Confederation, and what were three major ways they remained the same?	Choose one of the four original provinces of Canada and identify the major changes that took place after Confederation in that province and the things that remained the same. Report your findings to the class. As a class, decide for all the provinces on the three major commonalities and differences. What were three major ways the colonies of British North America changed after Confederation, and what were three major ways they remained the same?
Cause and consequence	Who or what was most responsible for Confederation?	Using the supplied primary and secondary documents, write a one-page essay that supports your choice for which person or factor was most responsible for Confederation. Who or what was most responsible for Confederation?
Historical perspective-taking	What was the most critical way the view of Confederation differed between English-speaking and French-speaking Canadians?	With a partner, and using the supplied primary and secondary documents, create a short play that identifies the critical difference in how English and French Canadians viewed their new confederation. What was the most critical way the view of Confederation differed between English-speaking and French-speaking Canadians?
Moral judgment	Were the fathers of Confederation motivated primarily by nationalism or by greed? Were the fathers of Confederation heroic visionaries or largely fearful of an American takeover of British North America?	Using all you have learned in this unit, prepare a debate on one of these topics. Were the fathers of Confederation motivated primarily by nationalism or by greed? Were the fathers of Confederation heroic visionaries or largely fearful of an American takeover of British North America?

in mind, I might pose the overarching question for a unit on World War I:

- Was Canada's role in World War I most responsible for its development as an independent nation in the twentieth century?

The other portal concepts can be explored to plan the unit on World War I. Students would answer each of the satellite questions before using what they learned in their earlier explorations to complete a summative activity that addressed the overarching question.

One final observation must be made. All the suggested questions require that students assess the possible answers in

FIGURE 9.1   OVERARCHING QUESTION AND SUPPORTING QUESTIONS

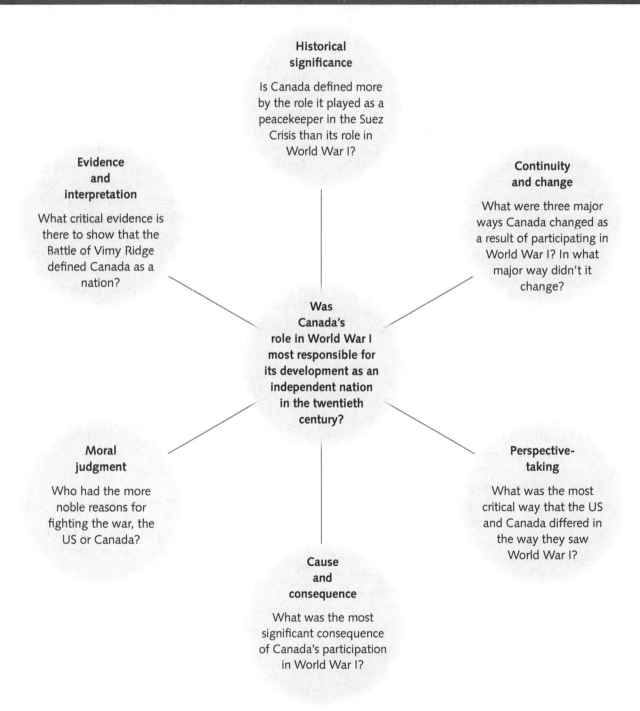

Historical significance

Is Canada defined more by the role it played as a peacekeeper in the Suez Crisis than its role in World War I?

Evidence and interpretation

What critical evidence is there to show that the Battle of Vimy Ridge defined Canada as a nation?

Continuity and change

What were three major ways Canada changed as a result of participating in World War I? In what major way didn't it change?

Was Canada's role in World War I most responsible for its development as an independent nation in the twentieth century?

Moral judgment

Who had the more noble reasons for fighting the war, the US or Canada?

Perspective-taking

What was the most critical way that the US and Canada differed in the way they saw World War I?

Cause and consequence

What was the most significant consequence of Canada's participation in World War I?

light of agreed-upon criteria. Students cannot thoughtfully answer a question such as, "Who had the more noble reasons for fighting World War I, the US or Canada?" without identifying those qualities that define a "noble" war, including the following:

- Was it fought for the betterment of all people, not just for national interest?
- Was fought to protect an ideal (for example, democracy) and not primarily to gain money, land, and colonies.

Collectively, the students and teacher need to agree upon the criteria before answering the question.

Challenges for Teachers

No doubt there will be a learning curve for many when trying to use the six concepts effectively. Teaching about historical thinking presents challenges and may require adjustments to our teaching. Below are some of the significant approaches used to teach using these concepts:

- **Make history problematic.** Teachers will need to present historical information in the context of exploring genuine questions and issues. (The students might generate some of these with teacher guidance.)
- **Assemble multiple resources.** Teaching historical thinking requires that students have access to a variety of primary and secondary sources that reflect a multiplicity of perspectives on the topics they explore. In the interest of efficient use of class time, this will often necessitate that the teacher selectively provide these sources. This will, of course, add to preparation time.
- **Accept alternative interpretations.** Teachers must be willing to put aside their preferred historical interpretations and welcome differing perspectives and understandings presented by students.
- **Teach the tools.** Students must understand the concepts and criteria that underpin their ability to think historically and have regular opportunities to apply them as they make sense of and use the historical information they acquire.
- **Shift the focus in assessment.** When evaluating student work, the notion of looking for the right answer must be exchanged for a search for well-justified or well thought-out explanations.

In short, teaching students to think historically will require additional effort, openness, and student independence. The objective of this chapter is to help meet these challenges by suggesting in practical ways how the six concepts can be used to deepen students' thinking and understanding about the past.

Conclusion

Under the pressure to cover the curriculum, history teachers often teach by "mentioning." This harkens back to the old notion that students are empty vessels to be filled with knowledge. Although "teaching by mentioning" is very efficient from the teacher's point of view, it is not a very effective way for students to learn. Study after study has shown that retention is highest when engagement with the content comes about through doing and thinking rather than listening and seeing. By using the six concepts, students can learn by thinking historically about the content they confront. Making our courses problem-centred rather than front-loading knowledge with a critical thinking follow-up will both increase retention of historical content and help students understand the discipline of history. With some alterations in our instructional approach, we can change students' notion of history from a story to be remembered to a story to be critically and thoughtfully appreciated and analyzed. It may even lead to a moment in your class when a student stands up and says, "I think I have a more credible interpretation of that event" rather than saying, "That's a complete misrepresentation of history." When that happens, you can pat yourself on the back and know that your students are learning history in your class rather than being taught it.

Select a topic from the curriculum involving some aspect of history. Use at least three of the historical thinking concepts discussed in this chapter to help you identify several activities to help students think about this topic in historically meaningful ways.

ACKNOWLEDGMENT

I wish to acknowledge the great extent to which this chapter borrows from the published work of Peter Seixas and from my discussions with him. The ideas for this chapter are developed more fully in Denos and Case (2006).

NOTES

1. The distinction between "research" and "inquiry" was introduced to me by Roland Case in a lecture on historical thinking made to the BC Social Studies Teachers Association in October 2006.
2. Some of the ideas for this unit are drawn from a powerful simulation on Confederation by Buium and Thompson (1998).

REFERENCES

Buium, G. and J. Thompson. 1998. *Critical Challenges in Law and Government: Re-enacting Confederation—A Simulation.* Vancouver: The Critical Thinking Consortium.

Cranny, M., G. Jarvis, G. Moles, and B. Seney. 1999. *Horizons: Canada Moves West.* Scarborough, ON: Pearson Education Canada.

Denos, M. and R. Case. 2006. *Teaching About Historical Thinking.* Vancouver: The Critical Thinking Consortium.

Francis, D. 1997. *National Dreams: Myth, Memory and Canadian History.* Vancouver: Arsenal Pulp Press.

Osborne, K. 2000. History as storytelling. *Canadian Social Studies* 35 (1). Available online at http://www.quasar.ualberta.ca/css/CSS_35_1/voices_from_the_past.htm.

Seixas, P. 2006. Benchmarks for historical thinking: A framework for assessment in Canada. Unpublished paper. Vancouver: Centre for the Study of Historical Consciousness, University of British Columbia. Available online at www.historybenchmarks.ca.

Seixas, P. and C. Peck. 2004. Teaching Historical Thinking. In *Challenges and Prospects for Canadian Social Studies*, eds. A. Sears and I. Wright, 109–117. Vancouver: Pacific Educational Press.

10

Portals to Geographical Thinking

Kamilla Bahbahani and Roland Case

We believe that an important way to meet the challenges of effective geography instruction is by problematizing geography. While there are many examples of innovative and engaging instruction in the discipline, geography has unique characteristics and a history that often lead to more traditional instructional methods. This traditional approach, in general, has not fulfilled the promise of the discipline to engage students in active learning about the world around them. We begin by looking at the challenges to effective geography instruction, and the need to invite secondary students to think critically about the geography curriculum. We then discuss and provide illustrative examples of six concepts that we refer to as "portals" that can be used to engage students in thinking geographically.

The Challenges of Geography Teaching

Geography is a wide-ranging subject, addressing issues from natural physical processes to urbanization, from protection of the environment to economic disparities. It offers insight into the most pressing issues of the day: global warming, migration and settlement, environmental degradation and conservation, and international aid and development. As a discipline, it has both strong historical roots and exciting new research in many spheres. And if this were not enough, geography also connects us with diverse corners of our increasingly interdependent world, providing insights into how our neighbours on the planet live, and why they make the choices they do.

Despite these strengths, geography struggles to find a prominent and engaging place in the high school curriculum. In part, this is because geography is usually folded into general social studies education, and few teachers are trained specifically in geography. As a result, geography is often reduced to factual knowledge and basic skills: students memorize imports, exports, and capital cities; colour in maps; and

decipher contour lines. Geography instruction often breaks down into a series of discrete, disconnected lessons.

Taught in this manner, geography becomes largely a matter of learning factual information about the human and physical environment. Answers to the questions posed already exist in textbooks. As a result, students have few occasions to question or problematize the subject matter. This approach does not encourage students to see geography as a body of conclusions that must be constructed, interpreted, and assessed, or as an opportunity for problem solving that has relevance to their lives and the world around them.

Instead of embracing geography as a stimulating subject, many students are bored by it. The challenge is not simply to find ways to make geography more relevant to students. It is, more importantly, a matter of making the study of geography more intellectually active. If students remain passive recipients of geographical facts instead of inquirers into the dynamic nature of geography, they are less likely to be engaged. Involving students in thinking geographically is more likely to excite students because it is inherently more appealing to be invited to draw original conclusions about challenging situations than simply to find answers that others have produced.

Current Attention to Thinking in Geography

The most notable attempts to identify the key concepts in geography education are the National Geography Standards (NGS) of the Geography Education Standards Project (1994) developed for American teachers, and their counterpart, Canadian Geography Standards (Semple 2001). These standards provide a useful organizing framework for the vast subject matter of geography. As the authors of the American standards explain, they are benchmarks that "specify the essential subject matter, skills, and perspectives that all students should have" (Geography Education Standards Project 1994, 9).

However, these standards do not provide much direction for inviting students to inquire into geography. They do not require that students interrogate the concepts, evaluate the validity of claims, assess the relative merits of different accounts of similar phenomena, or extrapolate from the given information to consider its implications in new situations. In other words, their focus is more on the key knowledge outcomes of geography than on knowledge-building and geographical thinking.

Despite its educational value, geographical thinking is not particularly well represented in curriculum documents. For example, the "geographical thinking" outcomes of the Alberta social studies curriculum for grade 8 are largely limited to interpreting and constructing maps and using multimedia applications and technologies, such as Geographic Information Systems (GIS) software, to prepare graphs and maps (Alberta Education 2007, 6). In the Ontario grade 8 geography curriculum, the expectations for map and graphic skills involve creating and interpreting maps, graphs, and population pyramids (Ontario Ministry of Education 2004, 75). These activities do not explicitly elicit analysis of the values inherent in representations and interpretations. Similarly, in the Canadian Geography Standards, we find the following description for sample learning activities for map, globe, and atlas use for grades 9 to 12:

> Develop maps, tables, graphs, charts, and diagrams to depict the geographical implications of current world events (for example, maps showing changing political boundaries and tables showing the distribution of refugees from areas affected by natural disasters) (Semple 2001, 46).

While students will learn to represent concepts in graphical form, they are not necessarily engaged in critical analysis of the content represented, or assessing the importance or soundness of the data represented.

Geography as Critical Inquiry

Students can learn to see the study of geography as a genuine inquiry where their task is not merely to find out what others know (they must, of course, also do this) but to reach conclusions and solve problems using the available information. Even if others already know the answer, in a genuine inquiry, students' task is to make their own assessments and not simply locate the conclusions offered by others. Students will learn to think geographically if they are regularly invited to make reasoned judgments about the most justifiable conclusions or interpretations emerging from the material presented to them.

The difference between factual questions that expect students to *find* an answer and critical inquiry questions that invite students to *reason through* the material is illustrated by Table 10.1. In the left-hand column are the six essential elements of geography identified in the Canadian Geography Standards (Semple 2001). The second column lists one of the learning objectives associated with each essential element. The third column describes a learning activity suggested in the Canadian Geography Standards to teach each of the identified outcomes. The last column suggests how teachers might use one or more of the portal concepts to address these sample objectives though a critical inquiry—either a task, question, or problem requiring that students reason with and about the information.

Each of the critical inquiries listed in Table 10.1 problematizes the content described in the learning outcome. They convert the factual content of geography into an issue for analysis or a problem to be resolved. The benefits of such an approach, we believe, are heightened student engagement, deeper levels of understanding, and increased ability to apply geographical ideas beyond the textbook. Ultimately, this approach turns students into geographers—or at least, gets them thinking more like geographers.

Study each of the paired examples in Table 10.1. Try to identify the key difference between each paired example in terms of expected student thinking. Discuss whether or not the critical inquiries are likely to have the results suggested by the authors—heightened student engagement, deeper levels of understanding of the learning outcomes, and increased ability to apply geographic ideas beyond the textbook.

In the rest of this chapter, we discuss six "portal" concepts for geographical thinking that can help teachers regularly problematize the curriculum. A portal is a beckoning entry-way—a channel into the heart of new territory. Portals to geographical thinking are entrances through which students are asked to think about geography and geographical content. The concepts we introduce here build on the work of Peter Seixas in historical thinking (Denos and Case 2006; Seixas and Peck 2004). We propose this parallel framework to better understand how to engage students in thinking critically within the discipline of geography—in other words, to help students learn to think geographically.

TABLE 10.1   FROM INFORMATION GATHERING TO CRITICAL INQUIRY

	BROAD LEARNING OBJECTIVE	SAMPLE LEARNING ACTIVITIES	CRITICAL INQUIRIES
The world in spatial terms—location	Apply concepts and models of spatial organization to make decisions (grades 9–12).	Explain the recent shift in retail shopping from original CBDs (central business districts) or suburban shopping centres to retail parks such as Bayer's Lake Park as part of the multiple nuclei model of development.	Rank order the three most significant changes brought on by retail suburbanization of the central business district.
Places and regions	Evaluate how humans interact with physical environments to form places (grades 9–12).	Explain why places have specific physical and human characteristics in different parts of the world (for example, the effects of climate, tectonic processes, settlement and migration patterns, site and situation components).	Which of the UNESCO heritage designations in Canada represents the most notable example of the interaction of humans with the environment.
Physical systems	Describe how physical processes affect different regions of the Canada and the world (grades 9–12).	Explain how extreme physical events affect human settlements in different regions (for example, the destructive effects of hurricanes in the Caribbean basin and the eastern United States, the ice storms in eastern Canada, and earthquakes in Turkey, Japan, and Nicaragua).	Based on the data provided about the destructive effects of an extreme physical event in several places (for example, hurricanes in the Caribbean Basin and the eastern United States, or earthquakes in Turkey, Japan, and Nicaragua) develop an in-depth profile of each place.
Human systems	Describe the structure of different populations using key demographic concepts (grades 6–8).	Compare Canada and an economically less developed country using natural increase, crude birth rate, crude death rate, and infant mortality.	Based on a comparison of natural increase, crude birth rate, crude death rate, and infant mortality rate in Canada and a selected less-developed country, identify the biggest differences for the provision of education, health care, housing, and water between the two countries.
Environment and society	Describe how humans prepare for natural hazards. (grades 6–8).	Explain the ways humans prepare for natural hazards (for example, earthquakes, floods, tornadoes, snow storms).	What are the biggest differences between Canada's preparedness for three common natural hazards with those of selected countries prone to similar hazards?
Uses of geography	Analyze the ways in which physical and human features have influenced the evolution of significant historic events and movements (grades 9–12).	Examine the historical and geographical forces responsible for the industrial revolution in England in the late eighteenth and early nineteenth centuries (for example, the availability of resources, capital, labour, markets, technology).	Humans or nature? Create an annotated pie chart rating the relative influence of geographical and historical forces on the advent of the industrial revolution in England in the late eighteenth and early nineteenth centuries.

Geographical Importance

What can we conclude about the importance of various geographical features or aspects that make them worthy of examination and attention? Teachers can involve students in considering geographical importance through critical inquiries such as these:

- For an assigned region, rank order the three most significant industries in terms of their political, social, environmental, and economic importance.
- You have been commissioned by the local chamber of commerce to produce a map to entice senior citizens to move to your area. What are the five most important types of features to include and the two most important categories to leave off?

Questions of importance are foundational to thinking about geography. They involve making judgments about relative significance or value of a particular location or phenomenon. The need to think about geographical importance arises because inevitably we need to prioritize or highlight certain aspects over others. For example, we frequently want to determine the most important industries or products in a region or identify the most notable features to highlight in a tourist brochure or on a regional map. As Wolforth explains, "We do not see Iran, Indo-China or Israel 'as they are' rather how others have chosen to present them to us" (1985, 79). Students must learn to recognize and explore the factors that influence what gets represented (is deemed important) and omitted (is deemed less important). Only then will they appreciate the selective nature of geographical information and understand why there can never be a single geography of a place or region. As Werner (2000, 197) explains "A travel account, for example, describes much more than a 'place'; it also implicates the traveler's interests, curiosities, priorities, sensibilities, fears, longings, and stereotypes, which in turn tell us about the writer's cultural and political milieu, and his or her assumptions regarding the expectations of audiences."

National Geographic magazine, for example, was well-known in the past for representing the exotic and primitive aspects of many cultural groups. Why were these features profiled and not others? Similar questions can be asked about the choice of what to represent in maps. Maps and map reading are possibly the most common element in geography instruction, and the feature most people remember when looking back on their geography classes. No map can present all that is known—geographers must be selective in the topics to address and the details to omit. Like statistics, maps can be made to say just about anything. The purpose of a map drives the choice of what features are important to include. Consider the difference between presenting the parks and cultural features of a region versus the incidence of crime and traffic accidents. As suggested by the example in the highlighted text, comparing different maps of an area can provide a window on mapmakers' decisions about geographical importance.

The controversy between the Mercator and Peters projections illustrates the inevitability of decisions about representing what is important, geographically speaking, and how these influence our understanding. How do we decide whether a geographical feature is significant? Thinking about importance helps students learn the decisions that geographers must make about what to report and study in geography and to recognize that the very nature of geographical representation is open to critique.

Evidence and Interpretation

How adequately does the geographical evidence justify the interpretations offered, and what interpretations might plausibly be made from the evidence provided? Teachers can involve students in considering evidence and interpretation through critical inquiries such as these:

- Determine what the maps of North America drawn by early European explorers reveal about their beliefs and world view.

JUDGING IMPORTANCE FROM MAPS

In this activity, students are presented with four maps of the same city (Smithers, British Columbia). In exploring the implied importance attributed to various features, students might undertake the following tasks:

- draw inferences about the map-makers' purposes (for example, to attract people to local business; to make Smithers seem like an accessible location);
- determine what information was excluded and included (for example, excluded the location of similar businesses;

excluded or included streets either to ease navigation or to make the city appear larger; included natural amenities and sports facilities in the area);
- identify possible biases of the map-makers (for example, exaggerated the relative size of the city in the region);
- discuss the impressions these maps would create about the city (for example, that Smithers is a small town, or that Smithers is located in a mountainous region).

continued on next page

MAP 1

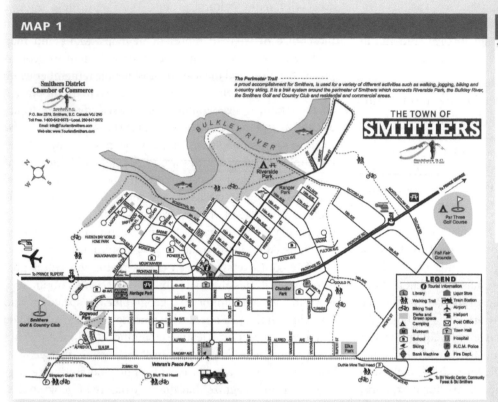

Source: Tourism Smithers

MAP 2

Source: Sandra Smith, Spark Design

MAP 3

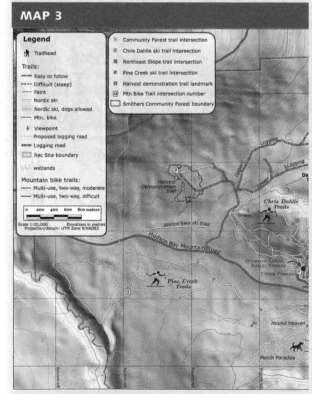

Source: Tourism Smithers

MAP 4

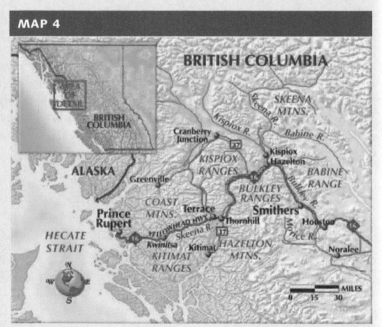

Source: Bill Tipton, Compart Maps

- Assess the evidence for global warming on a scale from highly speculative to completely convincing.

The concepts of evidence and interpretation are concerned with the reliability, validation, and use of various primary sources (for example, surveys, maps, GIS, counts, aerial photos, geologic surveys, satellite images, architectural and city plans, interviews) and secondary sources of geographical information. Interest in these notions emerged with the "new geography" espoused by educators such as James Fairgrieve in Britain and Neville Scarfe in Canada in the mid-1900s. In the new geography, students were to "learn how people live in other countries by investigating the evidence of maps, illustrations, statistics, travellers' tales and other direct sources of information" (Wolforth 1985, 71). This portal invites students to scrutinize the information found in various kinds of sources, and to think carefully about the interpretations made of the available evidence.

It is useful to distinguish geographical evidence from geographical information—information becomes evidence only when it is examined in the context of conclusions to be drawn or assessed. Issues of evidence invite questions such as: How do we know what a place is really like? What can we legitimately conclude from the data? Are the conclusions plausible?

Patterns and Trends

What can we conclude from the variations and distribution of geographical phenomena over time and space? Teachers can involve students in considering patterns and trends through critical inquiries such as these:

- What different patterns might you notice about changing climate if you used the following temporal scales: geologic time (10,000 years), historic time (200 years), recent history (last 10 years), or current events (last month)?
- Based on immigration trends, develop a population profile for Canada in 2050.

The concepts of patterns and trends are significant notions in geography. They undergird geographers' attempts to look for constancy and change in spatial arrangements over periods and across regions and places. They include efforts to develop models (such as the idea of hinterland) to explain and predict patterns. Geographers explore constancy and change to understand the driving forces that maintain or shift patterns across space and time. Understanding these driving forces assists them to extrapolate so as to predict constancy and change into the future, in light of changing conditions, for varied regions. The focus of these investigations spans a multitude of topics, including regional disparity, patterns of resource use, communications and road networks, innovation diffusion, species and ecosystem change, and cultural differences within and between groups. These pattern generalizations can be viewed at different scales of time (geologic, historic) and space (global, regional, local).

The purpose of this portal is not to describe the models and present the generalizations, but to invite students to develop models themselves, or to use existing models to draw new insights and fresh conclusions about the nature of regions and driving phenomena for constancy and change. For example, students might study historical trends related to resource exploration, extraction, and depletion in various regions to help predict the likely pattern over the next twenty years for various resource development projects (for example, oil sands or wind energy).

Interactions

How do particular human and environmental factors and events influence each other? Students can be invited to consider interactions through critical inquiries such as these:

- Rank order the impact of the following on desertification in the southwestern United States: diversion of major rivers, expanding population, industrial agriculture, climate change, fuel prices, and recreational and lifestyle patterns.
- If Vancouver was an American city, how might its social and economic development have been different?

Humans, the natural environment, and the built environment continuously interact across space and time in complex ways. Underlying the notion of interactions is the dynamic of mutually reinforcing physical and human factors that shape the world and which, in turn, are shaped by it. Questions of interactions must go beyond listing the ways in which a group or place has been influenced by various climatic, economic, and geographical factors. Rather, we want to encourage students to identify and rate for themselves the influences that have shaped the world, and to extrapolate from knowledge of interacting forces how the world might have been otherwise and what we might expect in the future. Understanding of the reciprocal, cyclic nature of many of these interactions encourages students to probe for complex understandings of system functioning.

The interactions of various natural and human factors are illustrated in the highlighted text, "Predicting Immigration Patterns." For instance, as students examine data correlating immigration levels with economic and political hardship, they can begin to see the cyclical influence of financial and civil factors on people's decisions to emigrate. Students can appreciate the reciprocal nature of some factors as they note the attraction that prospective immigrants have towards communities inhabited by individuals with cultural, linguistic, and racial backgrounds similar to their own. Deliberations about which location to choose for the immigrants profiled in the activity in the highlighted text illustrates how the interaction of various factors influence a decision.

PREDICTING IMMIGRATION PATTERNS

Invite students to use demographic statistics from Statistics Canada databases and other sources of information to draw conclusions about the economic, political, social, and geographic factors that attract potential immigrants to various Canadian regions. Students can record their evidence and conclusions for each region on a chart similar to the one depicted below. Based on these findings, students draw conclusions about the likely appeal of each region for potential immigrants. Referring to profiles of representative immigrants to Canada such as the two following examples (adapted from Misfeldt and Case 2002, 113), students might identify factors that would influence these people's decisions about where to relocate, and determine which region is most likely to attract each potential immigrant.

> **Wai Wing Li** is a Hong Kong Chinese who has done very well in the manufacturing trade over the past twenty years. Since China has repossessed Hong Kong, he wants to move to Canada to more freely pursue business opportunities. He hopes to be free to run his company as profitably as possible. His children were educated in Canadian private schools and both now attend university in Canada. Li is in his 40s and wishes to invest his money in new business ventures in Canada, preferably in shipping and transportation. While his English is passable, Li feels he may need to rely on the skills of the employees he hires for communication.

> **Katiana Jean** currently lives in Haiti and wants to immigrate to Canada to improve her standard of living. She is 20 years old and unmarried. Katiana has completed high school and is fluent in French and speaks a little English. She has a strong work record, is in good health, and has a little money saved. She is hoping to find a community where she will be able to meet other people who have migrated from Haiti.

Finally, students might gauge the plausibility of their conclusions about the likely destination for each profiled immigrant by comparing their results with actual immigration patterns.

IDENTIFYING FACTORS AFFECTING IMMIGRATION

Region _____

FACTORS	SUPPORTING EVIDENCE (FACT)	IMPACT ON DECISION (INFERENCE)
Economic	• • •	
Political	• • •	
Social	• • •	
Geographic	• • •	

A Sense of Place

What are the social, cultural, and physical features and identities that characterize a place? Teachers can involve students in taking on the perspective of a place through critical inquiries such as these:

- What would be the three biggest differences in lifestyle for middle-class Chinese-speaking teenagers living in Kowloon (Hong Kong) and Richmond (British Columbia)?
- From the collection of internet photographs of your assigned regions, select the five most representative images and the five most atypical images. Explain your choices and describe the difference in perceptions derived from the two sets of images.

Everything is situated in a particular physical milieu. Locations are unique clusters of influences that give rise to a particular sense of place. These locations can vary in size, from a sense of what makes your town or city special to broader characteristics that might define a continent such as Europe. An important part of the "regions" focus in geography beginning early last century was that

> areas of the earth's surface are to be studied in terms of the particular character resulting from the phenomena, interrelated to each other and to the earth, which fill the areas (Hartshorne 1939, 57, cited in Wolforth 1985, 71).

Developing this spatial perspective requires understanding the social, cultural, and physical features and identities that characterize a place. Without a sensitive understanding of the realities of place, students may unintentionally develop mistaken or "foreign" impressions of the experiences and characteristics of other places. We see this with the Romanization of many parts of the world by early explorers and subsequent travellers who imposed their own culture and language onto those regions they inhabited, and interpreted those regions and language through their own culture. As suggested by the highlighted example of a tea plantation in the Kerala region of India, taking on the perspective of a place requires more than acquiring the geographical facts about a place—it requires developing a tangible sense of what it means to "inhabit" the space.

Geographical Value Judgments

How desirable are the practices and outcomes associated with particular geographical actions and events? Teachers can involve students in offering and assessing geographicalal value judgments through critical inquiries such as these:

- What would be the most effective and responsible ways to combat rising sea levels in small Pacific Island nations?
- Negotiate a consensus proposal acceptable to key stakeholder groups (local citizens, oil and gas companies, the provincial government, the federal government, environmental organizations) for developing the Alberta oil sands. Prepare proposals for development of the tar sands based on assigned positions, and meet with other stakeholder groups to reach consensus on a win-win solution.

Value (norm-based or normative) judgments in geography arise in the context of drawing conclusions about desired actions and effects. Other portal concepts invite students to inquire into the ways things are and the reasons they occur. The role of value judgments is to engage students in considering what should happen or whether what has happened is desirable. Interest among geographers in making value judgments arose in what is sometimes referred to as welfare geography: "evaluating different spatial arrangements in terms of the extent to which they contribute to or detract from human welfare" (Wolforth 1985, 77).

Geographical value judgments can be offered through various lenses—including economic, environmental, cultural, political, and ethical—and from various groups' perspectives. For example, the highlighted text, "Responding to Natural Disasters," describes an activity inviting students to explore the range of economic, environmental, and social factors that planners must consider when assessing various long-term responses to the Indonesian earthquake of December 2004.

Overlapping Inquiries

There is, of course, considerable overlap between these six concepts. For example, questions of evidence and interpretation may arise in the context of uncovering the interactions among phenomena or investigating a particular sense of place.

The sample lesson found in chapter 25 illustrates how the six portals can be used as multiple entry-ways into the same topic. In this lesson, students reflect on changes in the Nlaka'pamux world view as a result of initial contact with Europeans in the early 1800s in British Columbia. Students learn about the earlier Nlaka'pamux world view by studying a map attributed to this group prior to the arrival of Europeans. They then learn about the changes brought about by contact and try to imagine a map drawn by a Nlaka'pamux map-maker seventy years after the fact.

Depending on the portal used, students can be invited to examine many aspects of aboriginal-European contact:

IMAGINING A SENSE OF PLACE

Invite students to describe the experience of living and working on a tea plantation in the Munnar district of Kerala, India, based on the photographs presented here. Help students explore the unique sense of this place using the following prompts:

- What is the standard of living in this area? What is the quality of life in this area?
- What is the basis of the local economy?
- What is the climate?
- What is the terrain?
- How connected is this place with the rest of the world?
- What types of activities would people typically engage in on a daily basis?

- What can you infer about the local inhabitants' world view—their views about what is important, their relationships to others and to the environments, the purpose of life?

RESPONDING TO NATURAL DISASTERS

Invite students to examine possible long-term responses to the earthquake and ensuing tsunami that struck Indonesia in December 2004. Their job is to tease out the implications of four options and the likely consequences for each intervention. They are to recommend an approach that will significantly reduce damage from any future tsunami in the region and be economically, environmentally, and socially justifiable.

Scenario 1: No major investment by the government; focus on reliance on external aid from foreign governments, international agencies, and international non-governmental organizations.

Scenario 2: Development of a tsunami alert system in the region.

Scenario 3: Relocation of affected populations to new areas.

Scenario 4: Development of new building codes and flood management systems.

- **Geographical importance.** Based on the Nlaka'pamux map, what seem to be the most important aspects of their surroundings? How does this differ from what European map-makers of the time saw as important to include in their maps?

- **Evidence and interpretation.** What conclusions can you infer from the Nlaka'pamux map about their world view?

- **Patterns and trends.** Based on what has been included in the map, and your knowledge of the impact of colonialism on aboriginal peoples, what would have changed over the seventy years and what would have remained relatively constant?

- **Interactions.** Which aspects of European influence (trade, disease, religion, power) most affected the Nlaka'pamux way of life? What features of the Nlaka'pamux way of life had an impact on European explorers and early settlers?

- **Sense of place.** What are the main features of place depicted by this map? What would it have been like to live there before contact?

- **Geographical value judgment.** Based on the nature and ramifications of European interactions with the Nlaka'pamux, what is a responsible response to present-day aboriginal land claims and calls for linguistic and cultural autonomy and support?

As can be seen, while each portal offers students a different way of problematizing aboriginal-European contact, they all work together to draw students more deeply into the topic.

Concluding Thoughts

Geographical instruction has enormous potential to activate students intellectually and socially. Through its attention to humans' place in the world and current social and environmental issues, geography can create aware citizens with the knowledge and ability to take action for positive social change. However, geography as a vehicle for change is dependent on its ability to arouse critical awareness in students. The portals described above offer a vehicle for students to inquire critically into important issues facing society; to develop complex, contextualized, and grounded understandings of issues; and to see the many dimensions of problems, from understanding the varied sources of available data to awareness of the moral implications of knowledge and actions. We hope these portals assist teachers in approaching the fertile content of geography in ways that create meaningful and enjoyable classroom experiences, and enhance student learning.

Select a topic from the curriculum involving some aspect of geography. Use at least three of the portal concepts to identify several activities that would help students think about this topic in geographically meaningful ways.

ACKNOWLEDGMENTS

We are grateful to Stan Garrod, whose unpublished article "Learning to think like a geographer" has informed our writing of this chapter.

We also want to thank Bob Sharpe, Associate Dean of Arts at Wilfred Laurier University, for his thoughtful comments on our work.

REFERENCES

Alberta Education. 2007. *Social studies: Kindergarten to grade 12*. Edmonton: Alberta Education.

Denos, M. and R. Case. 2006. *Teaching about historical thinking*. Vancouver: The Critical Thinking Consortium.

Geography Education Standards Project. 1994. *Geography for life: The national geography standards*. Washington, DC: National Geographic Society Committee on Research and Exploration. Available online at: http://ncge.net/publications/tutorial/standards/.

Misfeldt, C. and R. Case, eds. 2002. *Immigration in 20th century Canada*. Vancouver: The Critical Thinking Consortium.

National Council for Geographic Education. 1994. *National Geography Standards*. Available online at http://www.ncge.org/standards/.

Ontario Ministry of Education. 2004. *Ontario curriculum: History and geography, grades 7 and 8.* (Revised). Toronto: Author. Available online at http://www.edu.gov.on.ca/eng/curriculum/elementary/sstudies.html.

Seixas, P. and C. Peck. 2004. Teaching historical thinking. In *Challenges and prospects for Canadian social studie*s, eds. A. Sears and I. Wright, 109–117. Vancouver: Pacific Educational Press.

Semple, S. 2001. *Canadian national standards for geography: A standards-based guide to K–12 geography.* Vanier, ON: The Royal Canadian Geographical Society. Available online at: http://www.ccge.org/ccge/english/Pro_development/programs_geoStandards.asp.

Werner, W. 2000. Reading authorship into texts. *Theory and Research in Social Education* 28 (2): 193–219.

Wolforth, J. 1985. Geography in social science education. In *A Canadian social studies,* ed. J. Parsons, G. Milburn, and M. von Manen, 70–82. Edmonton: Faculty of Education, University of Alberta.

11

Teaching a "Critical" History

Avner Segall

Introduction

In 1492, Columbus discovered America. Or so most students learned (and some continue to learn) in schools throughout North America and the world. This statement is no longer accepted at face value, and this "discovery" is no longer celebrated as the glorified event we were once made to believe it was. This arises because questions have been raised about the very term *discovery* (how can someone discover a place already inhabited by others?) and its devastating effects on those already living in the newly "discovered" place. Significantly, these questions have not emanated from new historical knowledge about Columbus' landing and its after-effects. Rather, such questions have surfaced because of new lenses used to examine old historical knowledge. In other words, changes in how we view the past may not be the result of new information but may emerge instead from new theoretical frameworks used to re-examine existing information. Some have termed this re-visionist history—a way to look at history again (to re-view and re-vise it) and thus use it differently, ask different questions of it, come to new understandings about it: about what history is; about how and why we have used and have been used by it; about how we could think of and with it differently. New intellectual fields generated in the latter part of the twentieth century are responsible both for this shift in *what* history elevates to prominence and in the ways in which it does so as a discipline.

Indeed, since the early 1980s, developments in historiography, intellectual history, and philosophy of history—both influencing and influenced by postmodernism, poststructuralism, feminism, and postcolonial theory[1]—have attempted to redefine the boundaries of history, of historical accounts, of what counts as "historical," and of how (and what) history counts. Scholars have raised significant questions regarding historians' claims to knowing the past. [2] Putting many of history's taken-for-granted procedures and assumptions about knowledge and knowing into question, they have challenged the classical notions of objectivity, reality, and truth. Scrutinizing traditional history as an unmediated, picture-perfect presentation of the past "as it was," they have advocated a heightened awareness of history's creative functions, thus returning the historian from the supposedly objective sidelines to the very centre of what could, at best, be defined as interpretive history making—partial, subjective, and always partisan. Exploring history as a set of conventions designed to discipline knowledge and knowing in particular ways, these scholars have both highlighted and questioned the politics and ideologies embedded in, and the consequences of, the production of history as a disciplinary practice: What counts as history? Whose history counts? And what and who are advantaged and/or disadvantaged by the kind of accounts we currently consider as *history*?

Building upon such critical challenges to history and applying them to the teaching of history, this chapter engages with what it might mean to teach history that is no longer an accumulation of dates and facts about the past as it actually was, but rather a study of how the past is represented as (and represented in) history. That is, a process of educating which is both the study and practice of interpretation (Scott 1996), where the investigation of interpretation—whether it be historians' interpretations or those given to the past by textbook authors, curriculum documents, teachers, or students—itself becomes an important component in the process of teaching and learning history.

Despite the reluctance by many historians and history educators to embrace these challenges, the issues summoned into the discussion in, on, and about history can no longer be avoided in the study of history, especially considering the responsibility history education has towards enabling students to critically engage the world. How should educators respond responsibly to those challenges? Indeed, what are the implications (and complications) of such challenges for the educational endeavour? How might they allow us to think differently about what we currently do in history classrooms as well as conceive ways of engaging history differently? In other words, how might they help us re-think not only what we teach but how we teach.

Consider a topic such as "Westward Expansion." The terminology (language) used while considering this topic explicitly and implicitly positions students to reach certain conclusions. What assumptions are inherent in the term "Westward Expansion"? Whose perspectives are provided, whose are silenced, whose ignored? What issues frame our investigation? What alternative issues could frame it otherwise? Instead of using "Westward Expansion," which implies continental integrity and manifest destiny, not to mention a West that was supposedly closed (an odd notion for those already inhabiting it), what if we use terms such as "Eastern Invasion," "European Aggression," or simply "Colonialism"? What do these alternative terms suggest, open up, instigate that the term currently used does not? What, for example, might it mean to teach an entire unit on "opening" the Canadian or American West from a First Nations' perspective rather than simply (and in the best cases) include it as an aside? What does the very idea of not considering such an option tell us about ourselves as teachers—our affiliations, assumptions, and world views? What might it tell us about where we are located and what agendas we both consciously and unconsciously promote in classrooms?

And what, to bring in another issue, if we imagined teaching that or any other unit not only through a different perspective but using different genres, alternative ways of knowing? How would teaching and learning be otherwise (or would it?) if we used a novel or a film such as *Dances with Wolves*, instead of a textbook? Will we simply be studying history using other means or does our use of these "other" means do violence to history as we have learned to see it? Are we compromising historical accuracy when we replace facts with what is considered fiction? Indeed, to what degree and in what ways are history and story separate and separable entities? Or does the separation between the two have more to do with how we have come to think about history than with what it is historians actually do?

History: Transparent Record or Constructed Story?

Questions about the relationship between "truth" and "fiction" in historical representations are not new; they have underpinned the discipline of history since the days of Herodotus—the "father of history"—and his immediate successor, Thucydides. While Herodotus tended towards overt fiction, Thucydides attempted the construction of realistic, documentary accounts. However, even Thucydides' own version of what he defined as a realistic, documentary history is not devoid of embellishments and fiction. Describing the Peloponnesian War, Thucydides provides speeches that, in his own words, are "given in the language in which, *it seemed to me*, the several speakers *would* express...the sentiments *most befitting* the occasion" (Thucydides 1972, 47–48, cf. Hamilton 1996, 10; my emphasis). The difficulty of distinguishing between *record* and *story*, between fact, theory, and fiction in historical texts, and discussions of the appropriate degrees to which historians negotiate the probable from the possible as they give meaning to the past, do not seem surprising in the context of ancient Greece. "Memory—Mnemosyne—after all, was the mother of the Muses, and the leading muse, Clio, presided over history" (Hamilton 1996, 9).

Even as late as the early nineteenth century, the division between history and story, between historian, poet, and philosopher, and between art and science was blurred. Some of the most notable historians, such as Michelet, Ranke, and Tocqueville, were considered historians as a result of what they wrote about, not as a result of their method. Insofar as their method alone was concerned, they could have been just as easily described as artists or philosophers. The same can be said of "novelists" like Balzac, of "philosophers" like Hegel and Marx, and of "poets" like Heine and Lamartine (White 1978, 42). Indeed, Hegel, Balzac, Nietzsche, and Tocqueville all rejected the idea of the historian's "innocent eye," and stressed the active, inventive aspect of historians' "inquiry" (54). The legitimacy of historians crossing disciplinary boundaries very much ended in the second half of the nineteenth century as history increasingly estranged itself from art and philosophy and affiliated itself with "science" (50). Breaking with philosophy, literature, and theory, and increasingly tying their scholarly commitments to science, history increasingly separated theory from story and fact from fiction, and divorced writers from the world they inscribed. Knowledge was predefined, rational, and absolute, and was "out there" waiting to be discovered, accurately, through the adequate application of the "scientific method." Facts became a priority, serving the double role of evidence and guarantor. Historians did not stand between the text and the past but, rather, properly employing the historical method, illuminated the past and represented it "as it was." This, as Southgate (1996) explains, implied

that there is a past reality or truth, waiting to be discovered and described. The historian just has to clear away the darkness and confusion, behind which that past sometimes regrettably takes refuge, so that it can be seen in all its proper light and clarity. Admittedly, there may be complications, and certain precautions have to be taken: data must be approached without prejudices; facts must be clearly differentiated from opinion; evidence must be accepted only from impartial witnesses, and duly subjected to critical analysis; objectivity must be maintained, with any personal prejudices properly suppressed; and the record subsequently written must be scrupulously accurate. But given a properly professional approach, it should be possible to learn and then convey the truth of what is out there waiting to be discovered as the past (12).

Regarding history as a window to the past rather than a story about it highlighted historians' new role as scientists and researchers, not writers and interpreters. As such, reality and interpretation were considered separate and separable entities, where the legitimacy of a historical account rested upon its faithfulness to a past that lay outside of or pre-existed interpretation. By expunging the author's presence from the text—eliminating the first person (the "I") as narrator—history seemed not only objective and true but also to tell itself (Scott 1996).

History Through a Critical Eye/I

Following the emergence of postmodernism, poststructuralism, feminism, and postcolonialism in the late twentieth century, all areas of intellectual life have been rendered problematic. Exploring science not as a neutral enterprise but as a socially constructed endeavour that promotes particular ways of thinking, seeing, and being means that concepts such as "facts," "reality," "objectivity," and "truth" no longer seem as unproblematic as they once did (Southgate 1996, x). As science lost its innocence, so did the idealized version of history affiliated with it. What became of interest was not history's ability to provide an objective and faithful record—a clear window to the past—but its made-up quality and the politics of construction surrounding that "making."

THE CONSTRUCTED NATURE OF HISTORY

With language no longer considered a "mirror'" reflecting a separate reality but an inherent constituent of that reality (that is, creating the world it puts forward rather than merely describing one that pre-exists description), various scholars suggested that history take a more reflexive look at its operations and do so in a manner that shows self-consciousness of its own creations (Berkhofer 1995, 8). Exposing what Leitch (1986) called the "made up" quality of knowledge, such scholars have challenged history's existing, unproblematized discourses and practices, "spotlighting the politics of historical methodology, the politics of the viewpoint from which history is seen and told, and the politics of the discipline as a professional community" (Berkhofer 1995, 8). Scrutinizing the notion of the "real," these critical scholars invite both historians and history educators to explore history not simply as a record of the past, more or less faithful to the facts, or even as an interpretation answerable to the evidence. Rather, they ask us to see history as something created, made by historians and that such "making" inevitably and unavoidably promotes some ways of thinking about the world and its people rather than others. In doing so, they challenge us to consider history as a literary form, similar (even if not identical) to other kinds of creative writing (Samuel 1992, 220–221).

This is because although traditional history—the kind most often found in schools—proclaims itself *the* story of the past, the past and history are not one and the same. As Seixas (1993, 307) points out, history is, and thus can only be considered as, a discourse—a way of speaking—about the past, a story constructed to make meaning (of the past) both in and from a particular present. Arguing that history is always both already more and less than the past itself, Lowenthal (1985) proclaims—borrowing L.P. Hartley's phrase—that the past is "a foreign country" never fully accessible to the historian or to the student of history. The very process of constructing the (unknowable) past, claims Lowenthal, demands creative changes to make it convincible and intelligible: "history conflates, compresses, exaggerates; unique moments of the past stand out, uniformities and minutiae fade away" (214).

As such, neither the past nor history tell themselves. Writing the past is a deliberate process—a "selection, ordering, and evaluation of past events, experiences, and processes" (Kaye 1991, 71). Always positioned to tell a particular story from a particular time, place, and perspective, historians story the past in ways that promote certain understandings and interpretations over others. Meanings given to the past are never objective or neutral, for such meanings are not in the past but are given to it by outsiders (Jenkins 1991). Consequently, any historical narrative is simultaneously "a representation that is an interpretation and an interpretation that passes for an explanation" (White 1978, 51). It is, then, "not the case that a fact is one thing and its interpretation another." Rather, a fact is presented where and how it is within the historical narrative in order to sanction the interpretation to which it is meant to contribute. And the interpretation derives its credibility from the order and manner in which facts are presented within it. (White 1978, 107). Facts serve a narrative; they do not organize themselves into that narrative all on their own.

Since the only way we can access the past is through stories about it, and since historians do not find stories in the past but form the past into stories (White 1978), the literary, even fictive—in the sense of it being made rather than made up—quality of history is central. While historians may use methodologies and discourses different from those used by writers of fiction to emplot their (his)stories, they nevertheless employ discursive practices and devices, conventions, and modes of narration similar to those utilized by writers of literature. The difference between history and fiction, in which "fiction is conceived as the imaginable and history as the actual," states White (1978, 98), must give way to the recognition that such differences "are matters of degree rather than of kind" (78). For the differences held between history and literature result not as much from the actual practices of those producing them but from claims made about such practices. It is not simply that historians write real things and writers of fiction do not but, rather, that history "purports to tell only the real things and to refer only to a real, not imagined, world" (Berkhofer 1995, 68).

The author suggests how historical accounts such as the "discovery" of America and western expansion might change if viewed through different eyes. Select a significant historical person, event, or period in the curriculum and locate a textbook account of this topic. See if you can identify the following "angles" from which this account is written:

- purpose(s) in writing (for example, celebrate, condemn, explain, cast doubts)
- dominant lens of inquiry (for example, economic, political, environmental, social)
- dominant cultural or national perspective(s) (for example, British, Canadian, American, First Nations)
- represented voices (for example, male/female; owners/ workers; wealthy/poor; leaders/followers; residents/ newcomers; winners/losers)

Imagine alternative angles for each of these four categories and sketch out in note form the key features and changes in language that might be included in a "revisionist" account of this topic.

IMPLICATIONS FOR HISTORY EDUCATION

What might such a view imply for the study of history in schools? Does it make for a more meaningful history or does it complicate it to the degree that it becomes impossible, if not irrelevant? As I will explain in the remainder of this chapter, I believe the former (for a view of the latter, see Seixas 2000). That is because, as others, I believe that claiming that historical reality is produced by the procedures and mechanisms of the discipline and pointing to the various ways in which it achieves its authority, is not a denial of the seriousness or the usefulness of the enterprise called history. Nor

does this "plunge us into the abyss" (Scott 1996) or, as some traditionalists have claimed, put history in "mortal danger" (Jenkins 1995, 25). Instead, it elevates the study of history to a higher level of reflexivity and agency by reconciling history with its own name and making visible that the production of meaning is human—constructed by people—and subject to change over time as do the perspectives of historians who construct it (Scott 1996). Often, these changes are not because new evidence has emerged but, as illustrated by the discussion of Columbus' discovery of America, because the lenses—the questions, perspectives, values—with which historians view old evidence undergo change.

Lowenthal's (1985) insistence that the past is a "foreign country" poses a problem for traditional history education: If that foreign country is never fully knowable, why bother studying it? But the essence of history and its education, as the chapter thus far has proposed, is, of course, not about full access to the past. If the past is indeed a foreign country, what we need to explore in history classrooms is who issues the visas to get there? Who designs the itineraries? Who takes the snapshot (Fulbrook 2002, 175) upon arrival, writes back the postcards? And what do those reveal not only about the place itself but also about those reporting back to us as well as about the kind of meanings we make out of those "postcards" as we engage them in history classrooms?

Teaching and Learning History with a Critical Eye/I

In *A philosophy of history in fragments*, Heller (1993) claims that people "are thrown into a World, but only by having been thrown into History do they have a world" (33). The issue, therefore, is not whether one has a past but how one "gets thrown" into history to claim a world. Or, as Yerushalmi (1982) has put it, what kind of past, and whose past, shall we have in order to do the "claiming"? These questions lead to other, more immediate questions for educators: What kind of history do we wish to have our students "thrown in"? And what kind of "claiming" do we desire? Our choice is between a self-reflexive history that is aware of its contingency and recognizes its pedagogical nature, and a history that acts as though it simply tells the facts as they are. The decision facing us is between a history in which students are receivers of knowledge or one in which they are its producers as they critically examine knowledge for the assumptions, world views, and values it promotes. In short, our choice is between history education that provides students with *what* to think or one that encourages them *to* think.

History encountered in schools today, however, is predominantly of the first kind. It is still, by and large, focussed on memorization and recitation of disconnected, discrete facts, names, and dates. While students may, at times, be asked to do more—to critically engage with what texts say (for example, compare two accounts regarding the origins of World War I)—they are rarely asked to examine what texts do (for example, how the particular information provided/ ignored and the ways in which the story is told invite readers to explore the topic from a particular perspective and thus generate particular conclusions). Questioning, of that or any other sort, is impeded, since textbooks, currently the major source of knowledge in history classrooms, are often written as if their authors do not exist, as if interpretation had nothing to do with the words on the page (Seixas 1994), as if they simply transcribe a given truth (Schrag 1967). This results, as Wineburg (1991, 501) illustrates, in students believing that textbooks merely report the facts, simply convey what happened, and learn that history is a closed story about the past.

Engaging history as straight information, as objective and true, Hvolbek (1991) explains, we advance students' estrangement from it. By not inviting students to question history and to read against its grain, students are left with the notion that the historical narrative is non-negotiable. And when history is accepted as uncontestable truth and an end in itself, conversation is over. As educators, we cannot afford to consider history education simply as a place where existing, and from a variety of viewpoints highly contentious, truths are simply re-stated and reinforced. What we should be promoting instead is history education in which such truths are made to face students' critical responses, ones in which those truths are made to assume a historical responsibility for how they have positioned us all to think about the world and its people (Felman 1982, Said 1978). Such a response-ability, Willinsky (1998) offers, entails an examination of "what has been lost and what has been brought forward as *history*" (134), as well as a reconsideration of "how the past remains present in the way we tend to see the world" (244). Willinsky believes that students have the right to see what history has made of them, and how it has rendered the world both sensible and possible, even if (and as) this knowledge might complicate and implicate their education. Thus engaging history with a critical eye/I is not only about adding what or who has gone missing in the story of the past, but about a way of interrogating their exclusion when (and even as) we include them. Willinsky illustrates this point using the example of China:

> When the world-history textbook terminates the timeline of Chinese history in the sixteenth century …the problem is not simply that it thereby misses the reality or truth of China…. What is required of teachers here is an explanation of the textbook's suspension of Chinese history that would increase the intelligibility of the West's project with history and

its teaching…. Good teachers have long found supplementary works on China to cover what's missing from the traditional program. But it also needs to be made apparent to students that such exclusion is not simply an oversight but a feature of how the disciplines of geography, history, science, language, and literature have gone about dividing the world after the Age of Empire (250).

The educative value teachers can develop in relation to history is quite different if they begin from the conviction that we must give meaning to history (for example, asking what and who does history advance, gloss over, silence, ignore?) rather than find meaning and direction in it (Roth 1995, 143). Teaching history in this manner entails having students explore texts (and history-as-text) as subjective constructions needing to be actively read; where students are made to consider that between the "facts" and the text(books) lie "analysis, interpretation, and narration…shaped by values, skills, questions, and understandings of a particular teller" (Holt 1990, 17). This opens up new pedagogical opportunities that force attention onto the text of history (how it has been constructed and how it constructs both readings and readers), not simply through it onto its content (Kellner 1989, 4). Such a focus allows educators to use texts to ask different questions about knowledge, about our relationship to the past, present, and future. This pedagogical approach invites students to inquire into not only what historical accounts say about the past but also, and simultaneously, how such accounts come to have meaning. That is, how they use language, codes, and conventions to convey their meaning and to make readers believe (in) it. In this regard, Werner (2000) offers a set of important questions that can be adapted to guide such an examination of almost any historical text:

- What and whose story is this text attempting to convey?
- What and whose interests does it advance and/or marginalize?
- What might the text tell us about the assumptions, commitments, and values of its author, of the time/society in which s/he wrote, as well as those the author assumed of his/her intended readers?
- Is (and in what ways is) the author speaking about/for/ to/with those s/he is portraying (and what textual devices are used to do so)?
- What reading position (political, social, cultural perspective) does the text invite you, its reader, to assume?
- How does the text accomplish that positioning (what textual devices or conventions does it recruit)?
- How might this text be read by a member of a marginalized group (for example, a woman, a working-class person, an African American, a First Nations person)?

- What is this text silent about? Whose voices are marginalized, excluded? How might including that which the text is presently silent about and the voices currently excluded change the "story"?

Using such questions to acknowledge that history is constructed not by (or for) itself but by some one for some (other) body and in order to promote particular understandings by that some (other) body, opens it up to questions of its production: How is the "real" produced and maintained? This allows students to examine under what conditions and through what means they have been positioned to know as history legitimizes some perspectives, stories, and ways of storying while relegating others to the periphery. How one stories the past, as much as who stories it and for what (and whose) purpose, therefore, becomes inseparable from the knowledge being produced and the opportunities such knowledge allows other—different—interpretations to be cultivated. Exploring these issues allows for an examination of the lack of innocence in language by looking at the textual staging of knowledge (Lather 1992, 120). It also invites students to recognize the extent to which language practices articulate, objectify, and rationalize social reality, as well as the extent to which those with the power to "name the world" are able to dominate its meaning (Knoblauch and Brannon 1993, 23).

Examples where such an examination might take place abound: The most obvious might be how terms such as "terrorist" and "freedom fighter" are ascribed to the same person(s) by those standing on opposite sides of a conflict. A terrorist in the eyes of the Bush administration is viewed as a freedom fighter by those supporting acts of violence against the US. But these terms aren't only used by those on opposite sides of a conflict; both may be used by one side as political consequences change. The Taliban in Afghanistan, for example, were considered freedom fighters by the US as long as they fought the former Soviet Union in the 1980s yet are considered terrorists (or at least a regime supporting terrorism) following September 11. Defining them as such was part of justifying the US war in Afghanistan; after all, it is (and would only be acceptable by the public as) a "war on terrorism," not a "war on freedom fighters." In other words, terms are not stable; they shift with the changing political landscapes that give them meaning. It is the relationship between those shifts, rather than the meanings of words in and of themselves, that ought to be explored.

The idea that how we define something/someone positions others to act towards it/them in particular ways is not confined to politics. It is inherent in any medium that intends to teach us about the world, including the history textbook: how might we be positioned to engage with US history if we are invited to think of the internal war that took place in that country in the mid-1800s as the Civil War, the War Between the States, or the War of Northern Aggression? Each of these terms positions students to engage with the topic differently, to assume different loyalties, to conceive of its causes and ramifications differently. Similarly terms such as "First" and "Third" World or "developed," "developing," and "undeveloped" (or underdeveloped) countries direct students to give particular meaning to the world and its people. Yet such terms are not natural or neutral, nor are they terms coined by those living in "underdeveloped" countries. Rather, they were conceived by the rich industrial nations in the West as ways to divide the world to their own advantage (after all, whose sense of "development" or lack thereof underlies these terms?). And what do terms such as the "Far East," "Middle East," or "Near East" (not in vogue recently) mean? Far from where? The middle of what? Since those living in China or Japan presumably see themselves, as most people do, living at the centre rather than in some far away, remote region, the question remains who has had the power to ascribe distance to others while putting themselves at the centre of the world and thus as *central* to and in it?

The power to name the world is not restricted to its manifestations through words. Maps have played, and continue to play, an integral part in this process. Maps—very often Mercator projections—used in many classrooms normally depict the world from a perspective that gives prominence to the northern hemisphere (where such maps are most often produced). Maps also serve more immediate purposes that advance larger political and ideological goals. A case in point are recent maps of the Middle East (that term again!) used by the US media as well as in schools whereby, post-9/11, maps of the region now include countries as far east at Pakistan. To what degree is this "expansion" of the region a result of geographical, historical, social, cultural, political, or economic shifts in the region itself that require a re-thinking of its boundaries? Or is this "expansion" (to my knowledge, found only in the US) the result of a desire to link 9/11 and the US response to it to the already prevailing notion that terrorism and the Middle East are synonymous. If the Middle East breeds terrorism, then its boundaries need to be expanded to where terrorists reside. It also might help explain the otherwise problematic relationship between seeking to capture terrorists in Afghanistan and the war in Iraq.

But meaning remains contested not only when different words are used; it is so more often than not even when similar words are used. Take, for example, the War of 1812, whose results are portrayed quite differently in Canadian and US textbooks. Textbooks south of the forty-ninth parallel normally depict the US as the victor while those north of the border, in line with traditional Canadian notions of "fairness" and "that it's not only about winning" often depict both sides as winning some aspects of the war while losing others. And do the Battle of the Plains of Abraham and its ramifications have a similar meaning for all Canadians or might those in Quebec consider the event differently than those in English-speaking Canada? That is, even if the outcome of an event is depicted similarly in textbooks across Canada, are the meanings ascribed to it the same? And how have such different meanings contributed over time to Canadians' understandings of what Canada means (and should mean) as it attempts to bring its various constituent groups together or keep them apart? While the ways in which different meanings are ascribed to similar events and processes might be investigated, it is also important to explore how, in spite of these differences, particular renditions of the world—past, present, and future—prevail; and how is the persistence of such stories, that benefit some at the expense of others, related to the idea that those with the power to name the world come to determine its meaning? Why do such differences exist and how are they related to the idea that those with the power to name the world come to define its meaning?

Reconsidering History Through a Critical Eye/I

When students are invited to explore meaning and its construction in such a fashion, new questions could be asked about what history currently is and is not, as well as what it can and cannot be; about why we learn about the past; about how we use that knowledge and how we have been used by it (Rosenstone 1995). Such a focus, however, requires educators to pose different questions in history classrooms. Primarily, it requires a shift from asking students "What is true?" to an exploration of "What is truth, for whom, and why?" Instead of asking whether a text accurately reflects the past, we need to ask: accurate according to what conventional and methodological practices, whose discourse, whose standards, whose past? As we problematize various historical textualizations (the textbook, a novel, a film) and make judgments about them and the world, we ought to ask: Why and how do different media, different texts, different genres produce different truths about a common past? Why do different audiences believe different truths? Comparing a textbook rendition of, for example, the Kennedy assassination with its depiction in a Hollywood movie or comparing the coverage of a recent historical event in a newspaper article, a magazine piece, or a television newscast, we ought to have students examine what makes some media, some narratives, some conventions more convincing in their storying of the past. Readings that compare how various communities make meaning of the same

past and question the authority and conventions of different interpretive communities to tell the past helps students see texts presented in the history classroom not simply as ways to describe the world, but as instruments crafted to achieve specific social and political ends (Wineburg 1991).

While such a pedagogical approach emphasizes the need to provide students with tools to critically read and re-write historical texts as well as historicize all texts they encounter both inside and outside of school, it does not necessarily advocate that learning the (events of the) past is insignificant. Indeed, a critical approach to history education does not entail, as Zammito (1993) suggests, "ceasing to 'do' history and restricting oneself to thinking about [its constructedness]" (806). Rather, the juxtaposition of those two terms—"doing" history and "thinking" about what underlies that doing—as separate methodologies becomes problematic. As White (1978) points out, doing history already requires theories about what to investigate in the past, how to go about conducting that investigation, and how to make meaning of that investigation and justify one's representation of it to others. While some may argue that students should be devoting their time to learning what happened in the past rather than attempt to scrutinize what historians have tried to make of it, that separation too is untenable. For historians can only know the past in the form of text alone. In other words, historians "read" texts in order to "write" new ones. Consequently, history education does not engage the "real" past but interpretations of the past in the form of texts—a textbook, an article, an artifact, a primary or secondary document, a poem, a poster, a video, and so on. So it is not that engaging with the textuality of (and in) history is an extension activity one does after facts are known. Rather, it is the only way in which facts can be presented in the first place.

Engaging the inevitability and partiality of inscription and how language and author(ity/ship) become factors of truth, we begin to see how history inevitably and unavoidably constructs and conditions knowledge. Once the realism of history and its authority are broken down, it becomes evident that history could have been and could still be other than what it is (Southgate 1996, 54). This illustrates to students that there is choice in history. And choice not only means that history is not inherited but constructed (out of a variety of possibilities). It also implies that history and, more importantly, its uses, can be changed, not only by historians but also by students of history. Such changes, however, are constructed through the meanings students do and can bring to their readings of historical sources. As much of the literature in critical literacy/cultural studies illustrates (Ellsworth 1990, Fiske 1989, Giroux and Simon 1989, Lankshear et al. 1997, Luke 1995), meaning does not reside in the text. Meaning is negotiated between reader and text depending on the authorial invitations for reading (the language the author uses as well as how he or she structures the story) as well as the kind of lenses each reader brings to his/her reading. Meaning, as Buckingham (1993) explains, does not lie in a text to be passively accepted. It is actively produced by readers based upon their ability to critically engage the instructions and invitations given by the text in conjunction with the meanings and interpretive strategies students bring to their interaction with text. Learning, in both cases, entails questioning and evaluating knowledge, the discourses that frame such knowledge, and the power to legitimate knowledge as unquestioned currency in determining the stories societies believe and live by.

To engage history not only with a critical eye towards what is provided as history but also to do so with a critical "I" requires that students are invited to critically explore who they are as readers and what kind of lenses they bring to their interactions with historical texts in order to produce the kind of meanings they ultimately produce. In other words, students should be made to consider how they have been influenced by history, experience, language, and culture to read the world in particular ways and how such positionings help determine what and how they understand of/in the world. The intent is not on determinism—this is my past hence I read and can only read this way. Rather, the intent is to help students see a multiplicity of locations and to recognize that they have choices in how they read. What becomes important in thinking this way in history education is that there is no meaning without a reader and that each reader makes different meaning. What this means is that part of the focus should be how and why different readings are generated rather than have one student provide a "correct" answer and then move on. The idea is not necessarily to generate a correct answer (though sometimes that is what is required), but to explore the range of readings, compare them, investigate them, and learn from them just as much, if not more, than from the meaning intended by the author of the text.

We want to help students see that knowledge and the structures through which knowledge is produced and perceived are not fixed or static but human constructions that have been discursively won and therefore could (and should) be critically evaluated and reconfigured. This, in turn, encourages students to actively produce their own meanings rather than accepting institutionalized meanings as givens. It also allows them, to borrow from Postman and Weingartner (1969), to "begin seeing things not as *they* [texts] are but as *we* [readers] are" (95).

Conclusion

Under the cloak of objectivity, truth, and realism one currently finds in many history classrooms, there lies a world of creativity, construction, invention, and selection. History is active, not passive; its study ought to be the same. It must involve contestation, deconstruction, and action, not passivity, blind acceptance, and retention. The purpose of studying history, then, is not making the strange in the past familiar but making the familiar ways in which we have come to know the past strange. It is not about constructing a coherent, linear historical narrative about the past but, rather, about blasting history open, rupturing its silences, highlighting its detours, and questioning its limits while, at the same time, pursuing its newly opened possibilities (Giroux 1996, 51).

To arrive at that, we must create pedagogical environments in which history—its uses and implications—are called into question; a space in which what is taken for granted in the "doing" and learning history are exposed as custom and then unsettled by a shift into the elsewhere of the possible. How we engage history in classrooms determines the kind of questions students can (and hopefully will) ask of history, of society, of their own education, of themselves. While history, as a discipline, might look back to the past to construct its texts, its stories, its narratives, its discourse, the kinds of questions it asks (and does not ask) are all embedded in the political, economic, social, cultural, and intellectual milieu of its present. To study history is thus to address both elements of the historical enterprise as well as to ask how those elements play out in the educational endeavour in which history is engaged. If we care "how the past means" (Rosenstone 1995, 10), what we need are pedagogical structures that will make the construction of the past as important as, and an inherent part of, the very past which has supposedly given rise to meaning in the first place. To activate such structures, teachers and students must first imagine a history education that no longer simply explores the past for what it was but begins seeing history for what it is, for how it could be otherwise.

Though history education purports to inform students primarily about the past, it has as much, if not more, to do with the present and the future. For it is from a present that we construct pasts and upon which we create futures. The educational value in studying history is, thus, not only the study of the past itself, for "its own sake," but also the understanding such a study might provide as to which particular pasts and ways of "storying" the past we have chosen to call our own, and how those choices have positioned us to act (or not act) in the world.

The author stresses the value of interrogating the forms of representation in history—the choice of words and the use of textual and non-textual sources. Select a particular topic in the textbook that is represented through verbal and visual means. Photocopy the page(s) and prepare annotations on the range of choices apparent in this account (for example, use of the word "pioneer"—someone who prepares the way—instead of "intruder," selection of photographs that are quaint, pleasant, or representative of a particular perspective). Prepare an alternative page(s) that is still consistent with the historical record but makes different choices about how to re-present this topic.

ACKNOWLEDGEMENT

A different—longer, more theoretical—version of this chapter first appeared in *Theory and Research in Social Education* in 1999.

NOTES

1. It is impossible to provide a brief explanation of postmodernism, poststructuralism, or postcolonialism in a way that does justice to these terms. That is because all three are multivariant—that is, there are many manifestations of each and they are best considered in the plural (for example, as postmodernisms). While I will attempt an explanation, it is advisable for those unfamiliar with these terms to refer to a dictionary of philosophy (such as Oxford is), of social thought, or of cultural and critical theory. You may even start with popular publications such as "Postmodernism [or any of the other terms] for Beginners."

    Postmodernism exhibits scepticism towards and/or a rejection of the grand narratives (the meta-stories) that underlie modernism (a project of the Enlightenment), their belief in universalism, truth, and progress, and the social order they maintain. Postmodernism denies the possibility of acquiring "true" knowledge about/in the world. Rather, it claims that what we know is always tentative and constructed. Wishing to disrupt the idea that knowledge comes from nowhere, postmodernism explores knowledge as local and tentative, always reflecting and advancing particular interests. For readings in postmodernism, see David Harvey, *The condition of postmodernity* (1989); Linda Hutcheon, *A poetics of postmodernism* (1988); Jean-François Lyotard, *The postmodern condition* (1984).

    Poststructuralism calls for a critical examination of the relations between individuals and social structures and the role of that relation in the construction of meaning, identity, and subjectivity. It rejects structuralism's belief that meanings are inherent in structures (of language, society). Instead, poststructuralism explores the interaction between structures and human agency, examining not only how structures work to invite particular meanings but also how and why people accept, negotiate, ignore, or reject those invitations within the power/knowledge nexus. Believing there is no access to "reality" outside of language (that is, reality is always constructed by and understood through language), poststructuralism focusses on the centrality of language/discourse in the organization of human experience and the complex ways in which individual human subjects come to understand themselves and/in the world. To read further in poststructuralism, see Michel Foucault, *The archaeology of knowledge* (1972), *The order of things* (1973), *Discipline and punish* (1977), and *Power/knowledge* (1980); Jacques Derrida, *Writing and difference* (1978), *Of grammatology* (1997).

    Postcolonialism/postcolonial theory problematizes the Western humanistic assumptions underlying colonialism and the meta-narratives upon which it was based. As a critical theoretical/political movement generated in response and resistance to colonialism, postcolonialism seeks to revisit, remember, and interrogate the social, political, and cultural practices of colonialism and their ramifications. For readings in postcolonialism, see Homi Bhabha, *The location of culture* (1984); Gayatri Chakravorty Spivak, *The postcolonial critic* (1990) and *A critique of postcolonial reason* (1999); Edward Said, *Orientalism* (1978), *Culture and imperialism* (1994), and *Out of place* (1999).

2. See, for example, Hayden White (1973, 1978), Dominic LaCapra (1985, 1994), Joan Wallach Scott (1988, 1996), Robert Berkhofer (1995), and F. R. Ankersmit (1983, 1994).

REFERENCES

Ankersmit, F.R. 1983. *Narrative logic: A semantic analysis of the historian's language.* The Hague, Netherlands: Martinus Nijhoff.

———. 1994. *History and tropology: The rise and fall of metaphor.* Berkeley, CA: University of California Press.

Bhabha, H. 1994. *The location of culture.* London and New York: Routledge.

Berkhofer, R.F., Jr. 1993. Demystifying historical authority: Critical textual analysis in the classroom. In *History anew: Innovations in the teaching of history today*, ed. R. Blackey, 21–28. Long Beach, CA: California State University Press.

———. 1995. *Beyond the great story: History as text and discourse.* Cambridge, MA: Harvard University Press.

Buckingham, D. 1993. *Children talking television: The making of television literacy.* London: Falmer Press.

Derrida, J. 1978. *Writing and difference.* Chicago: University of Chicago Press.

Derrida, J. 1997. *Of grammatology.* Baltimore: Johns Hopkins University Press.

Ellsworth, E. 1990. Educational film against critical pedagogy. In *The ideology of images in educational media: Hidden curriculum in the classroom*, eds. E. Ellsworth and M.H. Whatley, 55–67. New York: Teachers College Press.

Felman, S. 1982. Psychoanalysis and education: Teaching terminable and interminable. In *The pedagogical imperative*, ed. B. Johnson, 21–44. New Haven: Yale University Press.

Fiske, J. 1989. *Understanding popular culture*. London: Routledge.

Foucault, M. 1972. *The archaeology of knowledge*. New York: Pantheon Books.

———. 1973. *The order of things*. New York: Vintage Books.

———. 1977. *Discipline and punish: The birth of a prison*. New York: Pantheon Books.

———. 1980. *Power/knowledge*. New York: Pantheon Books.

Fulbrook, M. 2002. *Historical theory*. London: Routledge.

Giroux, H.A. 1996. Is there a place for cultural studies in colleges of education? In *Counternarratives: Cultural studies and critical pedagogies in postmodern spaces*, ed. H.A. Giroux, C. Lankshear, P. McLaren, and M. Peters, 41–58. London: Routledge.

Giroux, H.A. and R.I. Simon. 1989. Popular culture as pedagogy of pleasure and meaning. In *Popular culture: Schooling and everyday life*, ed. H.A. Giroux and R.I. Simon, 1–29. New York: Bergin and Garvey.

Hamilton, P. 1996. *Historicism: The new critical idiom*. London: Routledge.

Harvey, D. 1989. *The condition of postmodernity*. Oxford: Blackwell.

Heller, A. 1993. *A philosophy of history in fragments*. Oxford: Blackwell.

Holt, T. 1990. *Thinking historically: Narrative, imagination, and understanding*. New York: College Entrance Examination Board.

Hutcheon, L. 1988. *A poetics of postmodernism: History, theory, fiction*. London: Routledge.

Hvolbek, R.H. 1993. History and humanities: Teaching as destructive of certainty. In *History anew: Innovations in the teaching of history today*, ed. R. Blackey, 3–9. Long Beach, CA: California State University Press.

Jenkins, K. 1995. *On* What is history? *From Carr and Elton to Rorty and White*. London: Routledge.

Jenkins, K. 1991. *Re-thinking history*. London: Routledge.

Kaye, H. 1991. *The powers of the past: Reflections on the crisis and the promise of history*. Hemel Hempstead, UK: Harvester Wheatsheaf.

Kellner, H. 1989. *Language and historical representation: Getting the story crooked*. Madison, WI: University of Madison Press.

Knoblauch, C.H. and L. Brannon. 1993. *Critical teaching and the idea of literacy*. Portsmouth, NH: Boynton/Cook Publishers.

LaCapra, D. 1985. *History and criticism*. Ithaca, NY: Cornell University Press.

———. 1994. Canons, texts, and contexts. In *Learning history in America*, ed. L. Kramer, D. Reid, and W.L. Barney, 120–138. Minneapolis: University of Minnesota Press.

Lankshear, C., J.P. Gee, M. Knobel, and C. Searle. 1997. *Changing literacies*. Buckingham, UK: Open University Press.

Lather, P. 1992. Post-critical pedagogies: A feminist reading. In *Feminism and critical pedagogy*, eds. C. Luke and J. Gore, 120–137. London: Routledge.

Leitch, V. 1986. Deconstruction and pedagogy. In *Theory in the classroom*, ed. C. Nelson, 45–56. Urbana, IL: University of Illinois Press.

Lowenthal, D. 1985. *The past is a foreign country*. New York: Cambridge University Press.

Luke, A. 1995. Text and discourse in education: An introduction to critical discourse analysis. *Review of Research in Education* 21: 3–48.

Lyotard, J.F. 1984. *The postmodern condition: A report on knowledge*. Minneapolis: University of Minnesota Press.

Postman, N. and C. Weingartner. 1969. *Teaching as a subversive activity*. New York: Delacorte Press.

Rosenstone, R.A. 1995. *Visions of the past: The challenge of film to our idea of history*. Cambridge, MA: Harvard University Press.

Roth, M.S. 1995. *The ironist's cage: Memory, trauma, and the construction of history*. New York: Columbia University Press.

Said, E. 1978. *Orientalism*. New York: Pantheon Books.

———. 1994. *Culture and imperialism*. New York: Vintage Books.

———. 1999. *Out of place*. New York: Knopf.

Samuel, R. 1992. Reading the signs II. *History Workshop Journal* 33: 220–251.

Schrag, P. 1967. Voices in the classroom: The emasculated voice of the textbook. *Saturday Review* 21, January: 74.

Scott, J.W. 1988. *Gender and the politics of history*. New York: Columbia University Press.

———. 1996. After history? Paper presented at the History and the Limits of Interpretation Symposium, Rice University, TX. March 15–17. Available online at http://www.ruf.rice.edu/~culture/papers/Scott.html.

Seixas, P. 1993a. The community of inquiry as a basis for knowledge and learning: The case of history. *American Educational Research Journal* 30 (2): 305–324.

———. 1994. When psychologists discuss historical thinking: A historian's perspective. *Educational Psychologist* 29 (2): 107–109.

———. 2000. Schweigen! Die kinder! Or, does postmodern history have a place in schools. In *Knowing, teaching, and leaning history*, eds. P. Stearns, P. Seixas, and S. Wineburg, 19–37. New York: New York University Press.

Southgate, B. 1996. *History: What and why? Ancient, modern, and postmodern perspectives*. London: Routledge.

Spivak, G.C. 1990. *The postcolonial critic*. London: Routledge.

———. 1999. *A critique of postcolonial reason*. Cambridge, MA: Harvard University Press.

Thucydides. 1972. *History of the Peloponnesian War*. Trans. R. Warner. Harmondsworth, UK: Penguin.

Werner, W. 2000. Reading authorship into texts. *Theory and Research in Social Education* 28 (2): 193–219.

White, H. 1973. *Metahistory*. Baltimore, MD: John Hopkins University Press.

———. 1978. *Tropics of discourse: Essays in cultural criticism*. Baltimore, MD: Johns Hopkins University Press.

Willinsky, J. 1998. *Learning to divide the world: Education at empire's end*. Minneapolis: University of Minnesota Press.

Wineburg, S.S. 1991. On the reading of historical texts: Notes on the breach between school and academy. *American Educational Research Journal* 28 (3): 495–519.

Yerushalmi, Y.H. 1982. *Zakhor: Jewish history and Jewish memory*. Seattle, WA: University of Washington Press.

Zammito, J.H. 1993. Are we being theoretical yet? The new historicism, the new philosophy of history, and "practicing historians." *Journal of Modern History* 65 (4): 783–814.

12

Escaping the Typical Report Trap
Teaching Secondary Students to Conduct Research

Penney Clark

Consider this scenario: We assign a research report on some topic—a political leader perhaps, or Canada's role in World War II, or economic aid to developing countries. Students head for the library and select from the shelf or the world wide web the first three sources they find. They copy or download the first paragraph from the first source, the second paragraph from the second source, and so on until their report meets the required word count. Come presentation time, students troop one by one to the front of the class to read their reports in low, monotonous voices. It seems that they understand little of the content since they can't answer questions based on the information they've just presented. And judging from the largely irrelevant questions from other students, the rest of the class wasn't listening or simply didn't understand the presentation.

What can we do to avoid this disappointing, yet all-too-common, scenario? Perhaps the place to begin our escape from this largely fruitless, time-consuming trap is to clarify why we engage students in conducting research and preparing reports in the first place. Is it primarily so students can learn about political leaders, World War II, or economic development? No, because while acquiring information may be one of our objectives, there are faster, more efficient ways to achieve this end. Surely the more important purpose is to develop students' ability to conduct research independently, to synthesize that research in meaningful ways, and to clearly communicate their findings to others. As the above scenario suggests, many so-called research projects may do little to help students develop these abilities.

In this chapter, I present a seven-step model for helping secondary students learn how to carry out and present research. The key to success is to devote as much, or more, attention to the process of conducting research as to the final product, a report. Teacher and teacher-librarian guidance along the way is crucial. We should not send students unaided

to the library, assignment in hand, and expect them to present a well-written, original, and thoroughly researched report on the due date. The complex task of conducting and reporting on research can be interesting and educationally useful if we implement strategies that actually teach students how to complete the various tasks involved in a research project:

- select and focus a topic;
- formulate guiding questions;
- identify relevant information sources;
- extract information from sources;
- record and organize information;
- synthesize information into an effective presentation format;
- assess and revise at each stage of the project.

Select and Focus a Topic

Any successful research project begins with thoughtful selection of a topic and the narrowing of that topic to manageable proportions.

SELECT A TOPIC

Three interrelated considerations are relevant when choosing a topic:

- **Curricular importance.** Student research provides an opportunity to develop a richer understanding of curriculum content than would be achieved by using a single resource or textbook, because it can involve a variety of resources and perspectives. But since research is time-consuming, topics should be selected carefully for their relevance to the broader goals of the curriculum. This may mean research questions set by the teacher that demand more than mere information summaries. Such questions can encourage students to draw conclusions from their research and defend a position.

- **Availability of resources.** The choice of topic depends to some extent on the resources available. Teacher-librarians can be a great help in locating resources with diverse perspectives and rich detail. They will often place materials on reserve so they are available to students when needed. If school resources are limited, teacher-librarians can also assist by borrowing outside resources on a short-term basis.

- **Student interest.** Research projects provide opportunities for students to explore individual interests. They can have powerful motivational value if students care about the topic. The teacher can stimulate interest in topics by raising provocative questions that students might expect to encounter. Allowing students a say in selecting topics is another way to increase interest. This can be as simple as providing students with a list of curriculum-related topics from which they can choose.

FOCUS THE TOPIC

Research projects are unmanageable if the scope is too grand or vague. Since students often have trouble zeroing in on a topic, they may need assistance in articulating the scope of their research. Before directing students to choose their own topic, model with the entire class the focussing strategy illustrated by the following example.

Begin with a broad general theme, such as "European exploration and colonization of North America" and, as a class, brainstorm a list of categories within this theme. The list might include:

- famous explorers and their contributions
- technology used for exploration
- colonization of New France
- the fur trade

Then select one of these categories and generate a list of more specific topics that fall within its scope. For instance, narrower topics under the heading "fur trade" might include:

- fur forts
- trade routes
- daily life of a voyageur
- role of women in the fur trade
- beaver hats and fur fashion
- aboriginal and European exchanges
- the Hudson's Bay Company

These narrower topics then become the focus for individual research projects. After modelling this procedure with the entire class on a topic unconnected to the theme(s) of the actual research project, invite students, individually or in small groups, to undertake a similar process when selecting their own topics. Students may want to consult with friends and family and scan the textbook or other resources for help in generating a list of categories and topics. Before allowing students to proceed with their research, check that their topic choices are not too broad.

Formulate Guiding Questions

Inviting students to frame questions they will endeavour to answer through their research is often helpful in providing even greater focus and purpose. When generating guiding questions that will have meaning for the students, start with what they already know about their topic and then move to what is unknown.

START WITH WHAT STUDENTS KNOW

Students are often pleased to discover that they already know quite a bit about a topic. Getting them to record this information at the outset encourages them to connect it with the information they acquire during their research. One caution: some of the information that students already "know" may be incorrect—but it can be recorded anyway. Then, as they gather new information, students can check the accuracy of their original claims.

As demonstrated in Figure 12.1, webbing is a way to generate and record what is already known. Ask students to think of everything they can that links to the keywords or ideas contained in their topic. Webbing encourages the free flow of ideas since students make any links that come to mind, rather than fitting information into predetermined slots.

MOVE TO THE UNKNOWN

Once students have reviewed what they already know about a topic, they can turn their attention to what more they would like to know. If students are interested in a topic, there will be many questions. Listing and then organizing these can help students target the most important and interesting aspects of the topic.

One strategy is to list student questions about a topic on chart paper, and then cut up the paper so that each question is on a separate piece. Either as a whole class or in smaller groups, students can sort the questions into categories and develop a single, more general question for each one. As Table 12.1 shows, the topic of the Hudson's Bay Company might

FIGURE 12.1   WEB OF PRIOR INFORMATION

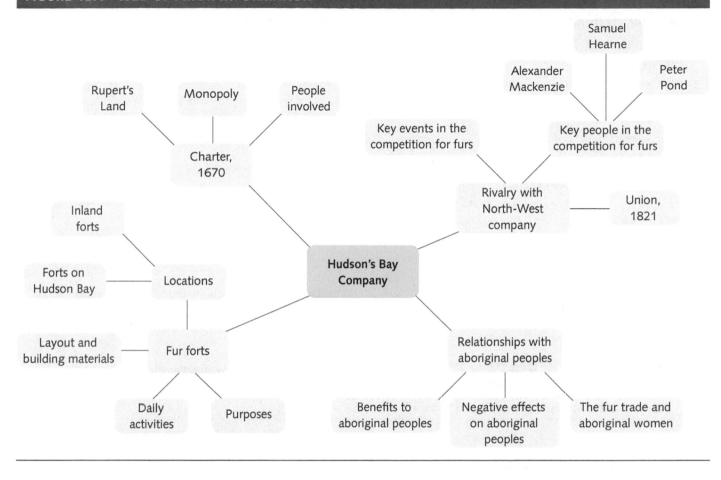

elicit fifteen specific questions that could be grouped under four general questions.

Armed with a few general questions (that summarize the many specific ones they have), students are better able to use information sources effectively. With a clear focus for reading, students have less difficulty separating relevant from less relevant information. Otherwise, they will often assume that if the author considered it important enough to mention, it must be important enough to include in their notes. With questions in mind, students can scan for answers, rather than reading every word and constantly wondering what they should be looking for.

Identify Relevant Information Sources

A third step in conducting research is to help students learn how to identify possible sources of information and then select the most relevant and reliable sources. Identifying information sources is an area where the teacher-librarian can be of particular assistance, both in making appropriate resources available and in helping students locate the most useful ones.

IDENTIFY POSSIBLE SOURCES

The possibilities for information sources are infinite. It may be useful, before students begin their research, to brainstorm specific options as a group. If this is not feasible because individual projects are too varied, encourage students to brainstorm individual lists. Information sources can include print, people, and places, audiovisual materials, computer resources, and the internet.

- **Print texts.** These include encyclopedias and other reference books, magazines, almanacs, non-fiction trade books, literature, and newspaper clipping files, which can all be found in school and public libraries. Printed information can also be found in certain types of material that are not meant to be long-lasting. Many such items are not found in libraries because they are frequently updated and therefore not saved. Examples include

TABLE 12.1 STUDENT QUESTIONS ABOUT THE HUDSON'S BAY COMPANY

BRAINSTORMED QUESTIONS	GENERAL QUESTIONS
• How was the Hudson's Bay Company different than the North-West Company? • Why were the Hudson's Bay Company and the North-West Company rivals? • Who won the rivalry? • What were the results of this rivalry?	What were the chief turning points in the rivalry between the Hudson's Bay Company and the North-West Company?
• What roles did aboriginal women play in the fur trade? • What roles did aboriginal men play in the fur trade? • How did the lives of aboriginal peoples change as a result of the fur trade? • Were there aboriginal people who were not involved in the fur trade?	Was the fur trade ultimately beneficial or detrimental to aboriginal peoples?
• Who formed the Hudson's Bay Company? • Why was it formed? • Where was it formed?	What circumstances caused the founding of the Husdon's Bay Company?
• Who obtained the furs? • How did the furs get to the fur forts? • For what commodities were furs traded? • What was the day-to-day operation of a fur fort like?	How did the Hudson's Bay Company fur-trading system operate?

pamphlets and bulletins published by advocacy groups such as environmental organizations, government departments, and agencies such as tourist bureaus and travel agencies. (See chapter 26, "Bringing the Outside In," for use of these kinds of print resources.)

- **People and places.** Parents, businesses, professional and lobby groups, and community organizations such as local historical societies and ethnic group associations can all be sources of guest speakers or interviewees. Places might include historic sites, museums, government agencies, and various kinds of resource centres. These can be particularly useful information sources for less capable readers. (See chapter 26, "Bringing the Outside In," for suggestions on interviewing people, hosting guest speakers, and conducting field trips.)

- **Visual and audiovisual sources.** These include pictures, drawings, graphs, slides, posters, videotapes, DVDs, and CD-ROMs. (See chapter 28, "Training the Eye of the Beholder," for use of visual and audiovisual materials as information sources.)

- **Electronic information sources.** The internet, electronic databases, and other computer-related materials have become increasingly useful for conducting research. It is crucial, however, that students learn how to use search engines and similar tools to manage these sources and assess their credibility. (See chapter 14, "Integrating Computer Technologies into Secondary Social Studies," for a discussion of locating and selecting appropriate electronic information sources.)

SELECT RELEVANT AND RELIABLE SOURCES

Once students have generated a list of possible information sources, encourage them to think about which sources seem the most promising. Initially, it might be useful to suggest possible information needs (for example, a few facts about Peter Pond or the routes taken by Alexander Mackenzie) and ask students to identify the most promising source or sources from a list of possibilities (for example, an online encyclopedia, Google maps, historical atlas of Canada).

Figure 12.2 is adapted from a chart that teacher-librarian Elizabeth Smith and teacher Rachelle Beaulieu used to help students at Shaughnessy Elementary School in Vancouver evaluate the suitability of various information sources on early Canadian explorers. In groups, students researched an assigned person or topic using the common sources listed on Figure 12.2. While doing this, students assessed the quality of the content and ease of use of each source and offer reasons

FIGURE 12.2 EVALUATING RESOURCES ON CANADIAN EXPLORERS

3 = Very good   2 = So-so   1 = Poor

	Detailed (depth of info)	Up to date (currency)	Information from various perspectives	Easy to locate relevant sections	Easy to understand	Other:	TOTAL	RANK
Canadian Encyclopedia Online	3 2 1	3 2 1	3 2 1	3 2 1	3 2 1	3 2 1		
Canadian Encyclopedia **Print Edition**	3 2 1	3 2 1	3 2 1	3 2 1	3 2 1	3 2 1		
World Book **Print Edition**	3 2 1	3 2 1	3 2 1	3 2 1	3 2 1	3 2 1		
Ebsco Magazine **Search Tool**	3 2 1	3 2 1	3 2 1	3 2 1	3 2 1	3 2 1		
Internet source #1:	3 2 1	3 2 1	3 2 1	3 2 1	3 2 1	3 2 1		
Internet source #2:	3 2 1	3 2 1	3 2 1	3 2 1	3 2 1	3 2 1		
Internet source #3:	3 2 1	3 2 1	3 2 1	3 2 1	3 2 1	3 2 1		
Other:	3 2 1	3 2 1	3 2 1	3 2 1	3 2 1	3 2 1		

for their ratings. After totalling the scores and rank-ordering the sources, each group reported its findings to the rest of the class.

Select a topic in the social studies curriculum and locate three relevant print or electronic information sources suitable for students at this grade level. Plan an activity with student-ready materials to teach students how to judge which of these sources is the most appropriate for the assigned topic.

Extract Information from Sources

The next step in conducting research is to extract the desired information from the source. To do so effectively and efficiently, students need to use such tools as tables of contents, indices, keywords, and search engines competently. It should not be assumed that all students are adept at using these information retrieval tools, especially within electronic resources.

This is yet another step in which the teacher-librarian can be of assistance. Some teachers and teacher-librarians team-teach research skills. Preparation work is cut in half when the teacher and teacher-librarian each prepare a lesson on a specific skill (for example, using a table of contents or an index, or navigating a website) and teach that lesson to half the class and then to the other half.

Record and Organize Information

The next step—learning to record and organize information in a form that will be helpful in completing a report—requires specific teaching. Four strategies for helping students record and organize information are described below: partner talk, guiding question folders, note-taking columns, and data charts.

PARTNER TALK

Partner talk is a strategy for organizing information that relies heavily on extended discussion prior to any written recording. Before beginning to write their reports, individual students explain to a partner what they already know or have found out. This approach can be used whether students in each pair have different topics or the same one.

Here is one way to organize a partner talk, developed by Ann McIntyre, who was a teacher-librarian in Edmonton public schools:

- Students work in pairs. Each partner tells the other what he or she already knows about the topic, and explains what they have found out about each of the guiding questions. The partners also ask each other questions.
- Individually, partners find a resource book and read relevant sections.
- Partners return and relate the new information they found.
- Partners question each other to find out what additional information is required.
- Partners turn to the resources used previously, or to new ones, to answer these additional questions.
- Partners share answers. Repeat previous steps until all needed information has been gathered.
- Students prepare their reports.

GUIDING QUESTION FOLDERS

Students write each of their general questions at the top of a separate sheet of paper. They create an additional final sheet with the title "Bibliography." All sheets are kept in a folder. As students conduct research, they record information with relevant page numbers on the appropriate sheet, always remembering to record the source on the bibliography page, indicating the title, author, date and place of publication, and the publisher's name. When students write their first draft, the needed information is organized for them.

NOTE-TAKING COLUMNS

Note-taking columns are made by taking sheets of paper and drawing a line down the middle of each one. Write each guiding question on a separate sheet, as in the guiding question folder strategy. Students use the left-hand column to jot down information from the reference source. An alternative way to use the left-hand column is for students to paste a photocopy or printout of every text they are referencing. If necessary, they may use the back, or make their own form. Then they underline or highlight sentences directly in the photocopied or printed text. Stress that they are to focus only on information that pertains to their research question. In the right-hand column, students restate the information in their own words. This increases the likelihood that they will understand what the notes mean. Emphasize that their notes should be clear and understandable (so they can remember the important information) and expressed in point form so that the notes are not too long. Student note-taking can be assessed using the rubric reproduced in Figure 12.3. Afterwards, students can cut the notes in the right-hand column into strips and use them to create an outline for their report. To reduce the likelihood of plagiarism, compare the ideas (underlined or recorded) in the left-hand column of the sheets with the student's final report in order to ascertain how closely these sources match the final product.

DATA CHARTS

Data charts are an effective format for recording information for three reasons: the limited space requires students to record information in point form; the framework encourages use of several information sources; and the listing of only a few questions or topics focusses students on the major issues. Until everyone is comfortable with the format, it is advisable to use data charts as a class rather than having students use them individually. Group practice runs should focus on topics unrelated to the topics students will explore for their individual projects.

The steps involved in class use of data charts are illustrated in Figure 12.4 and are listed as follows:

- Prepare a blank data chart on an overhead transparency and individual charts for every student. Ask students to record information on their individual sheets when the information is recorded on the overhead.
- Identify and record a title for the research topic.
- Generate numerous questions. Invite students to discuss which of these questions are the most important or interesting. List four or five major questions in the first column.
- In the second column, record what students already know in response to each question.

FIGURE 12.3   ASSESSING STUDENTS' NOTES

	WELL-DEVELOPED 5	COMPETENT 3	UNDERDEVELOPED 1
Relevant ideas in left-hand column	Almost all relevant ideas and no irrelevant ideas are highlighted or listed.	Many relevant ideas and several irrelevant ideas are highlighted or listed.	Very few relevant ideas and many irrelevant ideas are highlighted or listed.
Clear and understandable notes	Almost all the relevant ideas and no irrelevant ideas are highlighted or listed.	Approximately half of the notes are expressed clearly and with enough detail to be understandable.	Very few of the notes would make sense to someone reading them.
Brief and in point form	All of the notes are written in very brief phrases.	Approximately half of the notes could be shortened without any loss of meaning.	Almost all of the notes are too long.
In student's own words	Everywhere appropriate, notes are in the student's own words.	Approximately half of the notes are copied exactly from the text.	Almost all of the notes are copied exactly from the text.

FIGURE 12.4   DATA CHART: GEOGRAPHY OF CHINA

OUR GENERAL QUESTIONS	WHAT WE ALREADY KNOW	SOURCE:	SOURCE:	SOURCE:
1. What are the most significant physical features of the assigned region? Summary statement:				
2. What are the most significant political features of the assigned region? Summary statement:				
3. What are the most significant cultural features of the assigned region? Summary statement:				
4. What are the most significant economic features of the assigned region? Summary statement:				

- Provide students with the titles of two or three brief sources that they will use as information sources. So that students do not become bogged down in any one source, choose brief ones. Pictures are useful not only because they are compact, but also because they demonstrate to students the variety of possible information sources. Record the titles at the top of the remaining columns.
- Read or show the first source to students. Invite students to share information from this source that answers any of the questions in column one. Decide as a class on the best and briefest response to each question. Record each response in point form.
- Repeat this procedure with all other sources.
- Working together as a class, develop a summary response statement for each question.

Synthesize and Present Information

The most common methods of synthesizing and presenting research information are written reports and oral presentations.

STRATEGIES FOR WRITTEN REPORTS

- **Explain to a colleague.** Ask students to explain their topics to other students, using their notes as a guide, prior to drafting a written report. This lets them practise expanding their notes into sentences and sequencing their information logically. In addition, questions asked by other students may indicate information gaps that need to be addressed. (This approach is similar to partner talk except that students work from notes. Partner talk is oral until the final step.)
- **Draft without notes.** It can be useful to have students write the first draft of the report without reference to their notes. This encourages students to think carefully about what they are writing and helps them to make the report their own. They can return to their notes for their second draft.
- **Selective efforts.** Polished written reports require several drafts, each of which must be edited. It may not be necessary, however, to take every report through to final polished product. One option is to allow each student to choose from among the reports assigned over the given year which one will receive the extra effort. These are the ones that will receive a professional-looking laminated cover and be displayed publicly.
- **Writing from a point of view.** Students can represent what they have learned from their research from a particular point of view. It is more interesting for

ESSAY FORMAT

Essays are often the format of choice in secondary school social studies classes. The following outline provides a useful approach to helping students develop an essay:

Proposed title: _____

I. Opening paragraph/Introduction
(background, focus/problem, research question, possible interpretations, thesis)

_____

_____

_____

Thesis statement: _____

II. Body

   A. Topic sentence: _____

   1._____

   2._____

   3._____

   4._____

   5._____

Concluding sentence/lead-in to next paragraph:

_____

   A. Topic sentence: _____

   1._____

   2._____

   3._____

   4._____

   5._____

Concluding sentence/lead-in to next paragraph:

_____

Continue for the desired number of paragraphs.

III. Concluding Paragraph
(thesis restated, first subtopic, second subtopic, third...etc., concluding statement)

_____

_____

_____

Social studies teacher Elizabeth Bancroft of Coquitlam, BC, uses this format as a way to help students organize their thinking prior to the final stage of essay writing.

students to write—and for the teacher to read—a letter from a settler on the Prairies to relatives in the Ukraine than a straightforward description of life on a prairie homestead. Similarly, a child's day-to-day journal of a hypothetical visit to contemporary China may be more engaging than a summary of historic sites, industries, and cultures.

This type of writing is often referred to as RAFT writing—Role, Audience, Format, Topic. Students write in role (for example, from the point of view of a political leader, immigrant, inventor, or famous person in history) to a particular audience (to newspaper readers, a relative, prospective employers, or television viewers) using a particular format (newspaper editorial, poem, letter, journal entry, telephone conversation, or rap song) on a certain topic.

The depth of understanding of the subject need not be diminished when students use an unusual format. In fact, the opposite is more likely. For instance, it would be more challenging for students to write entries in Sir John A. Macdonald's journal during the Pacific Scandal crisis than a straightforward account of the crisis. To write entries in Macdonald's journal, students must add to their knowledge of events an understanding of how Macdonald would feel about them, how he saw his role, and how he viewed the role of others.

Offer students opportunities to display their reports in prominent locations. The teacher-librarian can help in this regard since the school library is an appropriate place for public displays of student work.

STRATEGIES FOR ORAL REPORTS

- **Using visual aids.** Visual aids help make presentations more interesting to an audience. Students who are not aural learners may have difficulty listening for any length of time to an oral presentation. Visuals also provide memory cues to guide the oral delivery. Visual aids help presenters feel more at ease; they will know that the eyes of the audience will be directed elsewhere for at least part of the presentation. In addition, pointing to a picture or map gives presenters something to do with their hands, thus reducing nervousness.
- **Synthesizing another student's report.** To encourage students to listen carefully when others are presenting their reports, it is useful to ask students to take notes. One approach is to ask each student to use his or her notes to write a summary of another student's report.

There is no rule that says oral reports must be made by a student standing in front of a group of thirty others. There are alternatives to the whole class presentation:

- **Rotating presentations.** Locate speakers at different spots around the room and arrange for small groups of students to rotate from one speaker to the next. It is not essential that every student hears every other student's presentation. This approach has several advantages over the whole class/one-speaker-at-a-time method. First, it is far less intimidating for a student speaker to make a presentation to a small group than to the entire class. Second, the speaker has the opportunity to repeat the speech several times, gaining confidence and improving delivery with each presentation. Third, members of the audience may be more attentive in this format because they are not forced to sit in one place for long periods. Also, they have more opportunity to ask questions because there are fewer questioners.
- **Co-operative group presentations.** In this approach, a group of students works together to make the presentation, each focussing on a particular aspect of the topic. One student might serve as a moderator, introducing the topic and panellists, calling on questioners, and keeping things running smoothly. This approach is helpful to the speakers. They can assist one another with difficult questions and the burden of response does not fall on a single individual. In addition, students have an opportunity to develop group participation skills such as co-operating with and listening to others and taking responsibility for contributing to discussions. Students, however, should not simply be thrust into a co-operative project without being helped to develop the tools needed for effective co-operation. These include the willingness and ability to listen carefully to others in the group, await one's turn to speak, and share materials. (See chapter 22, "Co-operative Learning in Secondary Classrooms," for skill-building strategies.)

ALTERNATIVE REPORTING FORMATS

There are many alternatives to formal oral and written reports. A number of alternatives are listed below. Any of these can be approached in various ways. For instance, a timeline may consist entirely of words, it may be illustrated, or it may be presented "live." Pat Shields (1996) suggests that in a "living timeline" format, students prepare role plays using costumes and props to suggest historical figures, either real or fictional, whom they have researched. The role plays are presented in chronological order so viewers can see how perspectives have changed over time.

The depth of understanding of the subject need not be diminished when students use an unusual format. In fact, it must often be greater in order to make the writing ring true. For instance, it would be more challenging for students to write entries in Sir John A. Macdonald's journal during the Pacific Scandal crisis than a straightforward account of the crisis. It is one thing to simply describe events and quite another to present them from the perspective of one of the key players. To write entries in Macdonald's journal, students must add to their knowledge of events an understanding of how Macdonald would feel about them, how he saw his role, and how he viewed the role of others.

Alternative reporting ideas

role play	journal or diary
model	mobile
photo essay	advertisement
mural	game
cartoon	bulletin board display
panel discussion	collection
debate	chart
newspaper	play
film strip	letter
videotape	audiotape
story	poem
map	diorama
scrapbook	slides
collage	demonstration
illustrated timeline	song
position paper	field trip (student-planned)
TV or radio quiz show	computer program
banquet	poster
itinerary for imaginary trip	crossword puzzle
résumé	simulated interview
review	learning centre
annotated bibliography	skit
poster	

Assess Student Research

It is misleading to place assessment at the end of this model, since assessment should not be viewed as the last step in a research project, but rather as an ongoing part of the entire process. Three strategies for effective assessment of student research projects are:

- to generate and share assessment criteria prior to completion of any assignment;
- to assess research procedures in addition to products;
- to include self- and peer assessment.

SET CRITERIA BEFOREHAND

Set out, or better yet, negotiate the assessment criteria at the very outset or at an early stage of the research project. This way, there are fewer surprises. Assessment is less menacing for students if they know how their work will be assessed and if they have had some say in establishing the basis for assessment. Encourage students to use the criteria to assess their own work before presenting it for teacher assessment. For example, the criteria listed below could be discussed with students when preparing an oral presentation or a written report.

Criteria for assessing an oral or written report

Content
- is accurate
- covers major points
- is sufficiently detailed
- is interesting

Organization
- begins with an effective introduction
- is arranged in logical sequence
- has an effective closure

Presentation (oral)
- is easily heard
- is delivered while looking at audience
- is delivered with an expressive speaking voice

Presentation (written)
- is clearly written
- uses correct spelling and punctuation
- uses descriptive language

Visual aids
- effectively illustrate key points
- are clear
- are visually appealing

ASSESS PROCEDURE AND PRODUCT

All aspects of the research process can and should be assessed, starting with students' ability to focus their topics and frame guiding questions, through the effective use of data charts, to the quality of the final written, oral, and visual products. Assessing along the way makes the task less onerous for the teacher and provides students with ongoing feedback, which reduces the likelihood that mistakes made early on in the process will scuttle the entire project. A form such as the "Research Project Feedback" illustrated in Figure 12.5 could be used for ongoing teacher notes on each student's progress through the research project.

INCLUDE SELF- AND PEER ASSESSMENT

Self-assessment and peer assessment should be part of every research project because they provide students with additional, more immediate feedback than a teacher alone can provide. Students must learn how to provide constructive feedback to others; this in itself is a valuable learning experi- ence. Students need to think about and learn ways to make comments in a positive and sensitive manner (for instance, precede any concerns with several positive features, put forth concerns in the form of a query or issue to think about). Figure 12.6 is an example of a joint assessment sheet that can be used by students and teachers to assess a poster presentation.

FIGURE 12.5   RESEARCH PROJECT FEEDBACK

Topic: _____   Name: _____

SKILLS	COMMENTS
Topic ☐ is worth pursuing; ☐ is narrow enough to be manageable.	
Guiding Questions ☐ are relevant to topic; ☐ adequately summarize specific questions.	
Information Sources ☐ are relevant to topic; ☐ provide reliable information.	
Extracting Information ☐ uses appropriate locator aids (for example, index, table of contents, guide words, computerized directory to library resources).	
Recording and Organizing Information ☐ notes are brief; ☐ notes are well organized; ☐ notes cover important points related to topic; ☐ notes are drawn from several sources; ☐ notes are expressed in student's own words.	
Presenting Information ☐ written drafts have been carefully edited and corrected; ☐ presentations are appropriate for audience and topic; ☐ visuals are thoughtfully designed and constructed; ☐ written and oral reports are thoughtfully sequenced; ☐ reporting (in any form) clearly and accurately presents the collected information.	

FIGURE 12.6   SELF- AND TEACHER ASSESSMENT OF A POSTER

	TEACHER RATING				SELF RATING			
	Definitely	Mostly	Partly	Not at all	Definitely	Mostly	Partly	Not at all
Important content/ message								
Clear content/ message								
Well laid-out/ designed								
Visually appealing								

Parting Comment

Throughout this chapter, I have pointed to the value of making maximum use of teacher-librarians. They can be helpful in many ways, including identifying appropriate resources in the school resource centre, obtaining other materials from outside sources, designing activities that require resource centre support, instructing students in skills needed to work through the research process, and providing a public venue for displaying finished reports.

Research projects are more time-consuming than simply supplying students with information. How should we decide when a topic is best addressed through student research? Examine the topics for a specific grade in the social studies curriculum. Decide which and how many of these topics over the course of the school year might best be addressed in a research project. Would you structure each research assignment in a similar manner? If not, how might you alter them to best achieve the information-gathering and reporting outcomes in the curriculum?

REFERENCES

Shields, P. 1996. Experiencing and learning through simulations and projects. *Canadian Social Studies* 30 (3): 142–143.

13

Infusing a Spirit of Critical Inquiry

Garfield Gini-Newman and Laura Gini-Newman

From Piaget to the present, educational research suggests that students learn best when actively engaged: arithmetic is mastered through the use of manipulatives, science through experimentation, and physical education through participation in athletics. So how do we engage students in the study of far-off lands or long-ago events? The answer, we believe, lies in critical inquiry. Teachers can engage students in learning about social studies by involving them in shaping questions that guide their study, giving them ownership over the directions of these investigations, and requiring them to analyze critically rather than merely retrieve information. In these ways, we shift classrooms from places where teachers "cover" the curriculum to places where students "uncover" the curriculum.

This uncovering of the curriculum occurs only when students investigate questions that have a clear, worthwhile purpose and present problems or challenges that they perceive as meaningful. We use the term "critical" inquiry to mean inquiry that is not essentially the retrieval of information but rather a process of reaching conclusions, making decisions, and solving problems. Of course, some students may enjoy gathering information, but all students' depth of learning and sense of engagement are greatly enhanced when tasks require them to think critically at each step of the way. This point is illustrated by the typical research-project scenario described in the highlighted text, "Researching a Topic."

If we expect students to become critical thinkers and problem solvers, then we must challenge them to solve problems and embark on personally relevant journeys of inquiry. This outcome is unlikely if students are fed mounds of information with little opportunity to pose their own questions or to thoughtfully re-examine their emerging conclusions. Even well planned, interesting, and colourful lessons can fail to involve students in thinking meaningfully about the ideas. Active involvement requires that students digest and make personal sense of the ideas, not simply to listen and recite or to read and record.

Building motivation to learn is an important reason for encouraging critical inquiry (McGaugh 2003). Linking social studies to issues meaningful to students is crucial if we

RESEARCHING A TOPIC

Students in grade 2 are asked to select any topic they wish, provided it deals with animals, and to prepare a short presentation supported by a display board summarizing their research. Samantha chooses cats. On the day of the presentation, she relays to her classmates the information she has found. Soon her classmates begin to ask questions. "Do you have a cat?" asks one student. "No," replies Samantha. "Do you want to have a cat?" asks another classmate. "No," replies Samantha. "Do you like cats?" asks another. "No!" Samantha exclaims, becoming somewhat frustrated by the questions. "Why is there a dog on your display?" comes a final question. "Let's move on to the next presentation," the teacher interjects.

What went wrong with this task? The absence of purposeful inquiry made Samantha select a topic and prepare a report without needing to think critically about the choices she was making or the significance of the information she was gathering. Had she been supported in asking a more purposeful question and processing the information critically, she might have selected a topic of genuine interest to her that would have led her to think more deeply about her findings. Samantha could have been asked, for example, to consider what kind of pet would make the best addition to her family. She then could have generated criteria for a suitable choice, including personal preference, cost to purchase and maintain, amount of care needed, habitat requirements, and diet. Using these criteria, she might then have researched several animals before making her choice. What's more, she would need to reach a conclusion and explain her thinking. Clearly, in this scenario Samantha would have been more involved, cognitively and emotionally, in her inquiry.

expect to engage them (McMahon and Portelli 2004; Armstrong and McMahon 2002). Where there is no engagement, students do not pay attention and consequently are unlikely to learn. Engagement is more likely when our curriculum is built around meaningful questions (including ones formulated by students themselves), stimulating challenges, and relevant projects. In a classroom of critical inquiry, unsolved problems, intriguing mysteries, and purposeful questions are used to excite students to learn.

While recognizing the need to challenge students, teachers also must provide the necessary scaffolding for student success such as building on prior learning, providing concrete experiences, and arranging many opportunities for students to engage in focussed dialogue with their peers. This helps anchor students' learning and develop the knowledge and skills they need to direct their research, analyze their findings, and draw their own conclusions. Creating a safe environment where risk-taking is encouraged and students are not being marked down for their mistakes is also important. Students should be allowed to "fail forward" by having opportunities to practise, revise, edit, and polish their work before submitting it for marking.

In this chapter, we explore five dynamic elements of critical inquiry and suggest teaching strategies for creating a classroom built around it.

The Dynamics of Critical Inquiry

Critical inquiry is an attempt to infuse a spirit of exploration throughout the curriculum. At its heart is a provocative question or challenge that arises out of the interplay of asking, investigating, reflecting, creating, and sharing. With these multiple entry points, teachers are better able to tailor instruction to meet the varied needs of their learners. For example, students may respond to a challenge first by reflecting on what they know, sharing initial thoughts and ideas with peers, and then carrying out an investigation. Others may choose to investigate, share their preliminary findings, reflect on what they know and do not know, and then return to further investigation. Similarly, once students have completed their investigation, opportunities to share and reflect are integral parts of any creative process. Figure 13.1 outlines the dynamic nature of critical inquiry.

FIGURE 13.1   DYNAMIC ELEMENTS OF CRITICAL INQUIRY

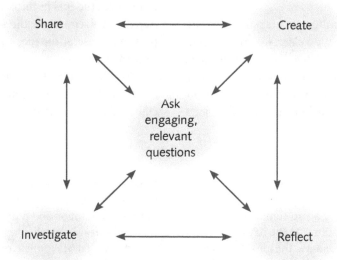

Ask: Inquiry begins with meaningful questions that are connected to the world around us, build on prior knowledge, and excite curiosity.

Create: The invitation to create a product or other representation of learning provides an opportunity to link new ideas with prior knowledge. This coalescence of ideas leads to the generation of additional thoughts and theories.

Reflect: Reflection on the path taken and the conclusions formed is an integral part of the dynamics of inquiry as it assists in the consolidation of learning. Reflection may lead to revisions in the investigation, affirm conclusions, or open new lines of inquiry.

Investigate: Investigation puts curiosity into action. As they gather information, students are likely to refine or redirect their questions, clarify ideas, and begin to make connections.

Share: Sharing with others the product of their journey of inquiry allows students to refine their ideas and reflect on how they arrived at this point.

Asking Questions

As suggested by the scenario described earlier in this chapter, students are too often detached from their research projects, a situation which usually guarantees that learning will be limited and of little lasting value. Framing effective inquiry questions is an important first step in any research.

Building on prior knowledge and asking questions of broad significance are vital to the success of social studies curricula. Students are more likely to become engaged if they are working from a question of more universal than particular importance. Also, the open-ended nature of the questions asked is crucial to the success of an inquiry-based classroom. Questions that send students to textbooks and other sources seeking the "correct answer" or that encourage them merely to prepare lists for their response do little to develop critical thinking or create genuine interest in social studies. Consider, for example, this question: "When and why did each province and territory join Confederation?" The question requires students to locate information and prepare a list of dates and reasons. When revised to read "Considering the interests and needs of your assigned province or territory, would you have supported entry into Confederation at the time each joined?", the question is more thought-provoking and exposes the historical reality that not everyone supported Confederation.

INQUIRY QUESTIONS AS UNIT ORGANIZERS

A powerful and engaging method of curriculum development is to build the entire year around provocative questions that challenge students to explore and apply their learning. When a course has a central inquiry question at its heart, it assists students in looking for the "big ideas" or the "enduring understandings," to use the term of Grant Wiggins and Jay McTighe (1998). Overarching questions reduce the likelihood of students bogging down in the details of history and geography. A provocative inquiry question provides them with a central reference point to reflect on as the year unfolds. Such central questions serve as excellent summative assessment questions. For example, a central question such as "Is Canada a country we can be proud of?" provides a focus for

SAMPLE "BIG" INQUIRY QUESTIONS

Rules and Responsibilities
- What are the three most important rules you must follow each day, at home, at school, and in your community? How might your day change if there were no rules and no one had any responsibilities?
- What are the biggest differences between the rules and responsibilities in your life and those that your parents, grandparents, or teachers had to follow?

The Medieval World
- When people of the future study us, they will learn that tall office buildings and huge stadiums were built in most cities. When we study the medieval world we see that cathedrals and castles were often the most important buildings. What can we learn about a society by its buildings?
- Would you like the opportunity to live in medieval Europe if you could be taken back in time? Would you change your mind if you found out you would be a peasant? A member of the clergy? Nobility? Who had a better life in medieval Europe, men or women?

Early Civilizations
- In some areas such as Egypt, China, and India, early civilizations developed along river valleys. In other areas such as Mexico, Chile, and Japan, they did not. How important was the role of geography in shaping early civilizations?
- How should we measure the greatness of past civilizations? Which of the early civilizations did the best job at meeting the needs of the people who lived in them?

Twentieth-Century Canadian History
- At the beginning of the twentieth century, Prime Minister Sir Wilfrid Laurier commented that "as the nineteenth century belonged to Canada, so shall the twentieth century belong to Canada." If Laurier were alive today, would he believe that his words have come true or would he be disappointed?
- More elusive than the sasquatch is the search for Canadian identity. Have the events of the past century forged a unique Canadian identity and how have those events defined who we are as a country?

World History
- The historian E.H. Carr and others of the liberal tradition portray history as a steady march forward. In stark contrast, Felipe Fernández-Armesto claims that the very thought of history as progress is Eurocentric and repugnant, that history merely lurches chaotically from event to event. Do the trends of the past five hundred years offer more support for Carr's view of steady historical progress or for Fernández-Armesto's view of random chaos?
- What effect would it have on our textbooks if we changed how we measure the greatness of past civilizations (for example, lasting monuments they have built, size of the empire they established, degree to which they extended basic rights to all who lived in their society, respect for the environment)? What are the hallmarks of a truly great civilization? Which past civilization best embodies these attributes?

learning about the history of the country. Around this central question, more specific critical inquiry ones addressing particular aspects of the curriculum might be framed:

- Was the deportation of the Acadians justifiable?
- Were French Canadians treated fairly and respectfully following the Conquest of New France?
- Have Canada's aboriginal people been treated with dignity and respect?
- Does Canada act more responsibly towards the environment today than it did in the past?
- Have science and technology improved the lives of all Canadians?

EFFECTIVE QUESTIONS FOR CRITICAL INQUIRY

Not all questions are created equal. As illustrated in Table 13.1, care must be taken to distinguish between questions of factual recall, questions of preference, and questions of critical inquiry. While each have value when used correctly, inappropriate use can become a barrier in meeting the intended learning objectives. If critical thinking is considered an integral part of a social studies program, then questions of critical inquiry are vital to the program's success.

Factual recall questions that have a single correct answer or a limited range of responses are useful as checks for understanding. When the purpose is to assess students' comprehension of key facts and processes, narrowly focussed questions are useful; but if the purpose of posing a question is to prompt student thinking, then open-ended questions of critical inquiry are necessary. Critical inquiry questions require thoughtful consideration of evidence gathered against a set of criteria. Although answers will often vary, a question such as "What is your favourite flavour of ice cream?" is not an inquiry question but rather one of preference. A question such as this does not build on human curiosity; it does not require investigation, the convergence of new learning with prior understandings, or the application of criteria. (For more about

framing questions that invite critical thinking, see chapter 4, "Beyond Inert Facts: Teaching for Understanding in Secondary Social Studies.")

SUPPORTING STUDENTS IN ASKING QUESTIONS

Equally important to the quality of questions posed by teachers is the students' own ability to ask powerful questions. In genuine critical inquiry, provocative questions, which form the basis of the inquiry, should emanate from students as well as the teacher. Yet all too often, students are unaccustomed to or ill-equipped for asking critical questions. Beginning in the primary grades, students are presented with research projects that often follow a similar process: students select a research topic, reflect on what they already know about the topic, consider what more they would like to know about it, and, following their research, summarize what they have learned. The intent of this type of exercise is commendable, though it often has a glaring flaw: rarely are students taught how to frame meaningful critical inquiry questions. As a result, their questions are typically limited to factual retrieval. Consequently, there is often little purpose to their research and no expectation that students will draw conclusions, merely that they will gather information.

If students are to become effective critical thinkers, they must learn to ask as well as respond to powerful questions. Throughout the school year, teachers should encourage students to ask critical inquiry questions on important issues, including events in the news and issues related to their school and community. Explicit teaching of the three types of questions, accompanied by opportunities to practise answering them, are vital if students are to move from questions of factual recall to critical inquiry questions. Teachers may wish to consider beginning a unit with factual recall questions and invite students to work in small groups to tweak the questions into critical inquiry questions. For example, students might move from considering "What three challenges did aboriginal peoples encounter during this period?" (factual retrieval)

TABLE 13.1 THREE TYPES OF QUESTIONS		
FACTUAL RETRIEVAL	**PERSONAL PREFERENCE**	**CRITICAL INQUIRY**
Ask students to locate information.	Ask students to express a personal opinion or preference.	Ask students to reach a conclusion or solve a problem.
<ul><li>Answers are often "right there."</li><li>Answers have a single correct answer.</li><li>Useful in assessing comprehension of key facts.</li></ul>	<ul><li>Answers are not grounded in careful reasoning, but invite an emotional or "gut" response.</li><li>There are no wrong answers; it depends entirely on how each person feels towards the topic.</li></ul>	<ul><li>Answers require thoughtful consideration of evidence in light of a set of relevant factors or criteria.</li><li>Typically open-ended and there are often several reasonable answers.</li></ul>

to "What was the most significant challenge that aboriginal peoples encountered during this period?" (critical inquiry). Students could also review questions from a chapter in their textbook and group the questions into the three types, then suggest rewording of several of the factual recall questions so that they become questions of critical inquiry. Activities such as these support students in learning to frame effective questions while deepening their understanding of the subject matter and developing their capacity for critical thinking.

Throughout the process, encourage students to sustain their focus on critical inquiry by continuous self-monitoring and reflection on the quality and relevance of their questions. This helps to create self-directed, self-motivated students as their research empowers their thinking, leading to the creation of new knowledge rather than merely inviting regurgitation and organization of a body of information culled from other sources.

> Assemble a list of five research questions or topics (either think of ones you have completed, look in a teacher resource, or ask students to suggest examples). Critique their effectiveness in light of the criteria discussed in this chapter (are open-ended, have broad significance, require thoughtful consideration). Keeping the same general topics, reframe each of these research projects into a more engaging critical inquiry.

Reflecting on Ideas and Strategies

Metacognition is a vital part of learning. Throughout an inquiry, students should be encouraged to take time to reflect on how the new information they uncover either challenges or affirms their beliefs, and to consider the validity of their conclusions in light of the evidence. Also important is self-reflection about the choices students make in conducting their research. Careful reflection occurs as students consider the nature of the questions they pose, assess the sources they are using, generate the criteria for guiding their decision making or judgments, weigh the evidence gathered in light of these criteria, consider the process by which they arrived at their conclusions and the validity of their conclusions, and finally, consider how purpose and audience will inform the presentation of their conclusions.

Instead of simply noting similarities and differences between people, places, or things (for example, in one community people make houses out of wood and in another, they make houses of ice), invite young students to reflect on the significance of the differences they notice. On their own or

as a class, students might record or draw the features being compared (for example, types of houses, modes of travel, health conditions). Students would offer an assessment of the amount of difference between each of the compared features (for example, the houses are nearly the same, contain some differences, or are very different), and explain their thinking. After comparing individual features, students might offer an overall assessment of the degree of difference between the communities, then share their summary conclusions with the class.

Earlier we saw how provocative questions can be an effective means to frame a unit of study. These same questions can be used at the beginning of a unit to prompt student reflection on their prior knowledge and beliefs. Posing questions as an anticipation guide (see Figure 13.2 for an example) can be useful for raising important questions and garnering a sense of students' prior knowledge and attitudes before delving into a unit of study. Anticipation guides are generally used as a literacy strategy to prepare students to read a piece of text. Adapted, they become an excellent framework for a unit and a diagnostic activity. After responding to the anticipation guide questions, the teacher might debrief with students and explain that these are the essential questions for the unit. In fact, the questions can became focus questions for individual lessons and serve as the basis for an end-of-unit assessment.

Investigation

Being engaged by provocative questions primes the pump for learning, but providing support to meet the varying students' needs is vital if all students are to experience success. Before setting students free to conduct research, teachers need to lay some foundations. One such support are graphic organizers that can help students structure and make sense of the information they uncover in their investigations.

A teacher presentation road map can be a useful tool to help students learn from short lectures. Essentially, the road map "chunks" the teacher's presentation into meaningful pieces much like the outlines that are often put on the board before a talk begins. When using a road map, encourage students to record three or four key points in each box. Remembering that students can only pay attention for 10 to 15 minutes before needing to process what they have taken in, teachers should employ a think/pair/share strategy after addressing a couple of points on their presentation road map. This allows students to review what they have heard, share and support one another, and consolidate their learning by explaining their notes to their peers.

Another strategy to support students is collaborative note-taking (see Figure 13.3). Collaborative note-taking

FIGURE 13.2   ANTICIPATION GUIDE

Circle the answer that best describes your opinion.

1. Considering the causes of the War of 1812, it is difficult to assign blame to one country.

Strongly agree   Agree   Don't know   Disagree   Strongly disagree

My explanation:

2. There were several heroic figures in the War of 1812.

Strongly agree   Agree   Don't know   Disagree   Strongly disagree

My explanation:

3. The outcome of the war was determined by several key battles.

Strongly agree   Agree   Don't know   Disagree   Strongly disagree

My explanation:

4. Considering the causes and outcome of the War of 1812, Canada was the winner of the war.

Strongly agree   Agree   Don't know   Disagree   Strongly disagree

My explanation:

---

encourages students to make point-form notes from a reading or during a presentation and then exchange notes with a peer. Each student reviews a fellow student's notes, adds information that was missed, and asks reflective questions. Afterwards, students jointly discuss and make notes on how the noted information connects with their world or with the central question(s) of the unit.

Students most often encounter Venn diagrams in mathematics classes. But consider their power when they are used to invite students to draw conclusions about the relationships between people, places, and things. For example, students might be asked to determine which of the Venn diagrams in Figure 13.4 best represents the relationship between the role of women in ancient Egypt and in contemporary Canadian society. In responding to this question, students would search a variety of sources including textbooks and websites, in order to locate words, phrases, or visuals that they can place within each circle to support their conclusion. It would be helpful for students to explain their conclusions in small groups and to adjust their findings based on the discussion.

Students need to search broadly for evidence and to consider multiple perspectives. To do this, they should consult a variety of sources to gather as many views as possible. They should be encouraged to gather information from various textual and non-textual sources (books and magazines, electronic sources, field visits to museums and other sites, visuals, interviews). They need to be taught how to read various text forms including a wide range of primary source material. Teachers should explicitly teach students how to read and decode visual text forms such as cartoons, artworks, and maps. (See other chapters in this volume for strategies on promoting these forms of information literacy.)

FIGURE 13.3 COLLABORATIVE NOTE-TAKING

Reflective questions:	My point-form notes on key facts, terms, ideas, and concepts:	Fellow students' additional notes:
	•	•
	•	•
Reflective questions:	•	•
	•	•
	•	•
Reflective questions:	•	•
	•	•
	•	•

Connections with other topics or the contemporary world:

FIGURE 13.4 COMPARING THE ROLE OF WOMEN IN ANCIENT EGYPT AND CONTEMPORARY CANADA

  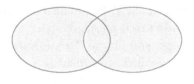

This graphic suggests that the role women played in the two societies was completely different and that there was no overlap or continuity.

This graphic suggests that the role of women expanded from ancient times (centre) so that by the present day in Canada, women were continuing to fulfill all the roles they had in ancient Egypt and had added several more roles.

This graphic suggests that while there were some roles they played in both societies, there were also roles unique to each society.

Sharing of Ideas

The opportunity to seek assistance, receive feedback, and hear responses from peers, parents, and teachers is a vital part of critical inquiry. As the previous examples suggest, graphic representations of ideas and conclusions are excellent vehicles enabling students to share their thoughts and conclusions prior to completing a summative task. Similarly, various forms of in-class debate and discussion, such as the "Academic Controversy" strategy described in the highlighted text, provide a forum for the exchange of ideas that, when combined with reflection, extend student learning and challenge students' thinking. Infusing opportunities to share through inquiry provides students with feedback that will enrich their understanding of the curriculum.

Creating

Students' opportunities to create new knowledge through the fusion of prior knowledge and current learning are largely dependent on the nature of the tasks assigned by teachers. Tasks that are narrowly focussed on recall of pre-determined information preclude critical inquiry and present fewer opportunities for students to take ownership over their learning. Conversely, assessment tasks that invite students to engage in critical inquiry tend to encourage students to apply their learning in ways meaningful and relevant to the learner.

In effective classrooms, assessment drives instruction. Knowing what students are to achieve and how they will demonstrate it should be the basis on which daily instruction is planned. Differentiated assessment ensures that students with varying learning styles, interests, and aptitudes are given opportunities to demonstrate their learning. The key to differentiated assessment is establishing clear targets and not confusing methods with targets. For example, assessment targets might include student understanding of the "big ideas and concepts" being studied and the abilities to conduct research, think critically, and communicate their findings and conclusions effectively, considering purpose and audience. If these were the assessment targets (or objectives), then a variety of methods might be used to assess student learning. Students could write a report, prepare a visual essay, create a bulletin board display with relevant images and captions, or deliver an oral presentation. Encouraging students to select the best method to demonstrate their learning is yet another way to shift the focus of learning from teacher- to student-directed learning.

Assessment tasks can further student learning and not simply measure it; when clear targets are provided from the outset and when students receive frequent feedback, they

ACADEMIC CONTROVERSY

Academic controversy is a strategy created by David and Roger Johnson (described in Bennett and Rolheiser 2001) that establishes small co-operative groups of four to six students to explore both sides of a designated issue. Each group is divided into A and B teams. The controversy is then identified in the positive (for example, "Canada should work with the United States to provide direct and indirect military aid to eradicate terrorism"). The A students prepare the "pro" side and the B students prepare the "con." Once students have prepared their opening arguments, each team shares its ideas with the opposing students. To encourage students to present ideas concisely, each team is allowed no more than ninety seconds. While each team presents its points, the opposing team practises active listening and takes notes. There should be no interruptions. Once both sides have presented their views, the A and B teams each gather to plan a rebuttal. In planning their rebuttal, they should consider the flaws in the opposing team's arguments. Each team has approximately sixty to ninety seconds to present its response. Once both sides have presented their rebuttal, the teams switch sides and repeat the process. The final step in the academic controversy, after students have presented opening points and rebuttals from both sides of the issue, is to hold a round robin. During the round robin, students explain where they stand on the issue individually.

then have opportunities to improve their work through revision, editing, and polishing. Throughout these tasks, students need appropriate scaffolding to ensure success and to encourage them to reflect on what they are learning (Earl 2003). At some time this may require allowing students to "fail forward." Learning from their mistakes can often provide powerful and lasting learning. But to have the confidence to fail forward, students need to know that their teacher is available to support them as needed and that failed attempts will not affect their final grade negatively. This requires that teachers embrace the concept of "assessment as learning" and provide feedback and guidance without grading students on the process of learning. Of course, at some point, students will need to demonstrate their learning through some kind of performance; and teachers do need to grade students on performances.

The authentic assessment task described in the highlighted text "The Great Sandcastles/Snow Sculptures Competition," which is built around critical inquiry, challenges students to create and explain a replica of an ancient landmark.

THE GREAT SANDCASTLES/SNOW SCULPTURES COMPETITION[1]

The Challenge

Throughout the ages, people have created lasting landmarks. From the Great Pyramids of Egypt to the Great Wall of China, from the soaring cathedrals of medieval Europe to the grace and perfection of the Parthenon, architecture tells us much about the people who created the buildings.

The Great Sand Castle/Snow Sculpture Competition invites you to build an accurate scale model of an ancient site at a local beach or in the snow. To prepare for the challenge, you will need to find books with pictures and information about the site and the society that constructed the architecture. You will need to look carefully at the pictures and take research notes. Once you are familiar with the structure, its purpose, and the sponsoring society, you should prepare a detailed plan including a sketch, required tools, and any extra materials needed to construct the model out of sand or snow. You are also to prepare an informative viewers' guide in the form of a brochure that provides details of the original structure and explains why this structure best represents the early civilization from which it came. Information you might include in the brochure:

- Who built it?
- What was its purpose?
- Where was it built?
- When was it built?
- How was it built?
- Why is it an important site?

In meeting this challenge, you will work in groups of three to complete the steps outlined below.

Each Student's Responsibilities

- Prepare a bibliography of between four and seven sources.
- Prepare two to three pages of research notes and gather four or five visuals related to the society and the structure.
- Prepare a sketch of the structure.
- Write a 250- to 300-word summary explaining the purpose of the structure, its method of construction, and how the structure was reflective of various aspects of the society that built it, including:
  - the influence of religion on the social and/or political structure of the society;
  - social divisions within the society; and
  - the relationship between those in positions of authority and the general population.
- Actively participate in the construction of the scale model.
- Be able to explain the structure, its purpose and its relationship to the civilization which built it to observers.

Each Group's Responsibilities

- Establish deadlines for each of the steps relative to the date established by the teacher for the building of the structure.
- Assign responsibility to individuals for preparing the final sketch and gathering the tools and materials needed (one student), and preparing a viewer's guide (two students) and produce a group agreement which clearly lists the agreed due dates and individual responsibilities.
- Collaboratively scan sources to select a suitable structure.
- Prepare a detailed plan for the construction of the scale model drawing on the sketches and notes of group members.
- Gather necessary tools and resources in preparation for the construction of the model.
- Construct the scale model in sand or snow.

Concluding Comments

Organizing the social studies curriculum around critical inquiry ensures a focus on key curricular ideas and concepts while allowing students to explore topics and issues of personal interest and relevance. In addition to engaging students, critical inquiry contributes to their cognitive development by challenging them to make decisions, solve problems, and draw connections. The ability to conduct focussed research and to analyze critically are crucial life skills.

There is no question that the most efficient means to "cover" an over-built curriculum is to teach from a teacher-focussed, lectured-based approach. Teaching students the skills they need to be successful takes time. Putting the proper scaffolding in place to assist them in meeting the expectations of the curriculum requires time spent on teaching critical thinking skills. And so the age-old debate rages on. Should teachers take the time to teach effectively or make sure they cover the entire curriculum? On closer inspection, however, it is evident that this debate exists only when curriculum is viewed through the eyes of the teacher. When viewed through the eyes of the learner, can there really be any debate? Should we quickly cover curriculum knowing that little of what is taught is retained beyond the final exam, or should we develop students' ability to learn independently and to think critically about the world around them, thus preparing them for the challenges they will face for a lifetime? Perhaps we need to consider the success of our classes based on what students retain in the years to come rather than on ephemeral results of tests.

> Think back to a research project you were asked to undertake in social studies. Using ideas discussed in the five elements of critical inquiry (ask, create, reflect, investigate, and share) suggest revisions to your original research project that would make it more personally engaging and educationally worthwhile.

NOTE

1. Details of the Great Sand Castles/Snow Sculptures Competition can be found in Newman (2001).

REFERENCES

Armstrong, D. and B. McMahon. 2002. Engaged pedagogy: Valuing the strengths of students on the margins. *Journal of Thought*, Spring.

Bennett, B. and C. Rolheiser. 2001. *Beyond Monet: The artful science of instructional integration.* Toronto: Bookation.

Earl, L. 2003. *Assessment as learning: Using classroom assessment to maximize student learning.* Los Angeles: Corwin Press.

McGaugh, J.L. 2003. *Memory and emotion.* London: Weidenfield and Nicolson.

McMahon, B. and J. Portelli. 2004. Engagement for what? Beyond popular discourses of student engagement. *Leadership and Policy in Schools* 3 (1): 59–76.

Newman, G. 2001. *Echoes from the past: Teacher's resource.* Toronto: McGraw-Hill Ryerson.

Wiggins, G. and J. McTighe. 1998. *Understanding by design.* Alexandria, VA: Association for Supervision and Curriculum Development.

14 Integrating Computer Technologies into Secondary Social Studies

Susan Gibson

Electronic information has assumed a new importance in schools. Teachers are under increasing pressure to ensure student mastery of the technological skills required in an information-based society. According to Leu, "The internet is entering classrooms at a rate faster than books, newspapers, magazines, movies, overhead projectors, television or even telephones" (2000, 425). This move to computerize has significant implications for social studies educators. Although computers are commonplace in most Canadian schools, many questions remain regarding their use in supporting and enhancing student learning. This chapter explores ideas and resources for making effective use of computers as a tool to support students in constructing knowledge in secondary social studies. More specifically, I address five areas:

- using the internet to access information;
- using the internet to organize and synthesize information;
- using computers to represent constructed knowledge;
- using computers as problem-solving tools; and
- using computers to facilitate communication and collaboration.

Before doing this, I want to briefly discuss what we know about the most effective uses of computers and the benefits they provide.

Educational Uses and Benefits

Over a decade of research indicates that the most effective uses of computers are in information processing and to enhance productivity in student completion of tasks. Software that allows students to apply new learnings as they work on projects—including databases, spreadsheets, multimedia, e-mail, and network search engines—show the most potential (Jona-

ssen 1996). This is especially true when computer resources are used to support authentic tasks; when they facilitate visualization, analysis, and problem solving; and when they offer opportunities for feedback and revision (Means 2001). Computer resources used in these ways have the potential to develop intellectual skills of inquiry, reasoning, problem solving, decision making, and critical and creative thinking (Adams and Burns 1999; Boethel and Dimock 1999). An inquiry approach to learning with computers places less emphasis on acquiring and presenting information and more on constructing knowledge, making meaning, drawing on personal life experiences, and taking responsibility for one's learning. The most meaningful learning experiences with technology are those that are active, co-operative, constructive, intentional, and authentic (Jonassen, Howland, Moore, and Marra 2003).

The benefits of using computer tools such as the internet in these ways include the following:

- providing quicker and easier access to more extensive and current information in a variety of forms (graphs, pictures, text) and through a variety of modalities (auditory, visual), all of which increase students' motivation to further explore ideas;
- providing opportunities to research independently and explore more varied, real-world topics in greater depth at the learner's own pace, which puts more control over the learning into the hands of students, increases active engagement in their learning, and creates greater feelings of empowerment;
- enabling students to represent their learning in a variety of ways through the creation of original and innovative work that can be shared with a global audience;
- allowing students from different cultural or linguistic backgrounds with limited English proficiency to learn through the visual aspect of the information available

and providing opportunities to use computers to improve their written and spoken abilities;

- providing assistive technologies for students with disabilities, including voice recognition systems, speech synthesizers, talking books, Braille display, image magnifiers and specially designed keyboards that give visual, aural, and tactile support and allow students to be more in control of their own learning experiences.

There is a wide variety of computer-related tools to facilitate students' inquiry and knowledge construction. Internet websites are useful resources for various stages of inquiry, including accessing information, organizing information, and representing results. The remainder of this chapter looks at specific examples of how to design meaningful computer-based learning experiences around inquiry, problem solving, communication, and collaboration. All of these uses treat students as active creators and shapers of their own knowledge who are able and willing to think for themselves (Boyer and Semrau 1995).

Using the Internet to Access Information

The internet is a valuable resource for supporting students in search of information related to an inquiry. The greatest advantage of the internet is that students have access to an abundance of up-to-date information from a variety of perspectives. Locating useful and accurate information can be a struggle, however. The profusion of things to access via the internet can easily sidetrack students, leading to a great deal of time off task. Information gathering can easily become a mindless exercise in which quantity overrides quality. This sort of information-gathering exercise does little to promote deeper thinking and understanding. There is also a danger that students will stumble on inappropriate sites, despite the use of Net Nanny and other protective software. Consequently, students need to become critical thinkers who can determine for themselves what makes a website inaccurate or inappropriate.

Because of the glut of information students are exposed to, they need to learn the skills to become information managers. This includes the acquisition of critical information literacy skills—skills that can be enhanced by the use of computer technologies. According to Todd, Lamb, and McNicholas (1992), information literacy is the ability to use information purposefully and effectively. It involves the process of defining the tasks for which information is needed, locating appropriate sources of information to meet needs, selecting and recording relevant information from sources, understanding

and appreciating information from several sources, being able to combine and organize information effectively for best application, presenting the information learned in an appropriate way, and evaluating the outcomes in terms of task requirements and increases in knowledge.

Critical literacy skills must be carefully taught and monitored to ensure students are developing proficiency in their use. Adolescents need to be instructed and have opportunities to practise examining critically and making appropriate informed, ethical choices. They must be taught to recognize that each website represents a particular viewpoint and that it is important to examine several points of view on any issue. Figure 14.1 from Case (2003) shows some of the questions that students can be taught to ask about the sites that they are accessing.

It is also important to address concerns about plagiarism and copyright involving the internet. The website of the Media Awareness Network (www.media-awareness.ca) is an excellent Canadian source for ideas about developing critical literacy and for information on plagiarism and copyright. Students also need to be taught how to distinguish fact from opinion.

There are countless controlled educational sites that deal with social studies topics. The highlighted text "Controlled Educational Sites" describes three kinds of these sites: scavenger and treasure hunts, virtual field trips, and virtual museums.

Select a topic from the curriculum or from a student textbook. Search the internet to locate possible sources that students might access, or consult resources prepared in an abridged form. Develop an activity in which students are not simply finding information at these sites but also using the information to reach a conclusion on some issue.

Using the Internet to Organize and Synthesize Information

In addition to learning to locate and evaluate information on the world wide web, students' inquiry and knowledge construction can be supported with web-based tools for synthesizing and organizing. Databases such as the Statistics Canada database featured in the highlighted text are useful for integrating information from a variety of sources, stimulating critical thinking, visualizing complex historical relationships, and developing conceptual understanding (Ehman and Glenn 1991). Databases can be structured by the teacher or left open-ended so students can select the information they wish to represent and then design the database to represent that information. The spreadsheet is another tool that

FIGURE 14.1   ASSESSING THE CREDIBILITY OF INTERNET SITES

Name of site: _____

As a source of ideas on: _____

	REASONS FOR CONFIDENCE		REASONS FOR DOUBTING	
	Evidence from site	Implications for believability	Evidence from site	Implications for believability
Authorship What do we know about the creators of the site that might affect the believability of its contents?				
Sponsorship What do we know about the individual(s) or group(s) who sponsored the site that might affect the believability of its contents?				
Sources of ideas What do we know about how information in the site was obtained and verified that might affect the believability of its contents?				
Indicators of care Does the site's presentation style, tone, and format provide clues about the believability of its contents?				

CONTROLLED EDUCATIONAL SITES

Scavenger Hunts and Treasure Hunts

Scavenger hunt and treasure hunt websites are good places to start doing web activities with students to get them used to accessing information, moving round different websites, and reading to locate specific information. These sites often provide a specific challenge to students in the form of questions or clues that they need to use in order to find the answers on the websites provided. For an example, at Adventures of Cyberbee (www.cyberbee.com/sshunt.html), there are a number of hunts that students can be involved in related to social studies topics. On one hunt, they can follow Harold, a Holocaust survivor, on his journey as he tells his survival story through interactive maps, photos, text excerpts, audio clips, and e-mail exchanges. Students are challenged to discover what was contained in the suitcase Harold mistakenly took back to his hiding place and how it saved his life (available at www.remember.org/harold/map.html).

Virtual Field Trips

Virtual field trips can be used to support student inquiry and knowledge construction because they allow students to travel through time and space to places that would otherwise be out of reach. Often these tours provide images and text describing the particular site being toured. These visuals give students important contextual information that helps personalize their study of a country from afar. The Global Trek site (teacher.scholastic.com/activities/globaltrek/index.htm) allows students to travel to different countries, meet people from those countries, and keep a travel journal of their experiences. The Virtual Tourist website (www.virtualtourist.com/vt) provides virtual trips to any country in the world by simply highlighting the chosen country on a world map. Teachers can also design their own virtual field trips using sites like TramLine (www.field-trips.org) or the Global SchoolNet Foundation site (gsh.lightspan.com/project/fieldtrips/index.html).

continued on next page

Virtual Museums

Students can access the collections of a number of virtual museums as a part of their inquiry. Through these sites, students are able to get involved in further authentic tasks such as analyzing primary documents and engaging in the processes that historians use (Bass and Rosenzweig 1999). The Canadian Broadcasting Corporation site (archives.cbc.ca) contains clips from radio and television stories about people, conflict and war, disasters and tragedies, arts and entertainment, politics and economy, life and society, science and technology, and sports. The site also has a teacher section that includes educational materials and activity ideas for using the resources provided on the website. Web-based news services can also be used to help students develop critical awareness of current events (see for example www.newsworld.cbc.ca/flashback, www.mycanadiannews.com, and www.newspapers.com).

Canada's Digital Collection (www.collections.ic.gc.ca) is another recommended website that provides artifacts representing Canadian history, culture, aboriginal communities, and Canadian landscapes. One section called "Wings Over Alberta" contains stories about Alberta's role in World War II. There is also a component to this website that has students engaged in submitting proposals to create their own web pages about some aspect of Canadian history. At another site, The Memory Project (www.thememoryproject.com), students can share stories of Canada's military heritage using the personal artifacts and oral histories of actual veterans. At the War Museum (www.warmuseum.ca/cwm/overtop/index_e.html), students can engage in an interactive story about life in the trenches during World War I. At a site like "A Time for Peace" (members.tripod.com/flash.d/remembrance/a-time-for-peace.html), students can submit questions to veterans.

Two other web-based Canadian museum collections that social studies teachers should find useful are the Canadian Museum of Civilization (www.civilizations.ca) and the Virtual Museum of New France (www.civilization.ca/vmnf/vmnfe.asp).

STATISTICS CANADA DATABASES

Some databases, such as those developed by Statistics Canada, are available online (www.statcan.ca/english/edu/power/toc/contents.htm). The benefit of using an online resource is that it tends to be kept up to date. This site is designed primarily for teachers, and contains examples and grade-appropriate exercises on how to read, use, and create a variety of tools to organize data. The Statistics Canada site also offers activities that engage students in using historical census data. In one of these activities (www.statcan.ca/english/kits/jtalon1.htm), students are provided with access to the census data from 1665 and 1666, and are challenged to use this data to take on the role of Jean Talon as he tries to convince the King of France to take a greater interest in New France. In another activity, they can use the census information of 1861 to conduct an analysis of the shipbuilding industry in colonial Nova Scotia (www.statcan.ca/english/kits/ship/ship1.htm). The latest addition to the site is a 24-hour population clock that shows instant estimates of a country's population that can be used to track trends and do global comparisons (www.statcan.ca/english/edu/clock/population.htm).

can be used to store, organize, and analyze data. Most word-processing programs have built-in spreadsheet and database applications that make these tools easily accessible for teachers and students. For example, a site like Zoomerang (www.zoomerang.com) allows students to design, conduct, and interpret the results of online surveys.

Visual organizers are another set of tools that can be used to organize information. For example, Inspiration (www.inspiration.com) is a concept-mapping tool that can be used in the early stages of research to brainstorm ideas and check on students' understanding of a topic or concept. "By uncovering students' individual understandings, teachers can determine the influence of students' prior knowledge and further their education through new experience" (Adams and Burns 1999, 25). Graphic organizers can also be accessed at the Graphic Organizer website (www.graphic.org).

Using Computers to Represent Constructed Knowledge

The internet can be useful for representing the results of an inquiry. Students can create and post their own work on web pages. Not only does this add authenticity and relevance to their learning, but it also allows students to become designers and publishers rather then simply users of information (Staley 2000).

The highlighted text, "Mr. Smith's 'Ancient' Web Pages," tells of Mr. Smith's experiences in helping his grade 11 class create web pages and PowerPoint presentations to demonstrate what they had learned about ancient civilizations.

STUDENT WEB PAGE PUBLISHING

Some websites provide publishing opportunities based on activities undertaken through the site. At the Global School House site, for example, there is a component called "International Schools Cyberfair" (www.gsn.org/cf) where students are encouraged to conduct research in their local

MR. SMITH'S "ANCIENT" WEBPAGES

Mr. Smith's grade 11 class is working on a unit about ancient civilizations using an inquiry-based, problem-solving approach supported by the internet and a selection of computer software (World History Illustrated: Rome, Microsoft Encarta, Ancient Lands). The title of the unit is Rome: The Ultimate Empire? There are a series of activities that the students can select from and agree to complete under contract with the teacher. All students are required to create a web page for the unit that becomes the home page for all of the work completed over the duration of the unit. Students can select from a list of tasks. They record their selections on a contract, which is co-signed by the teacher. All of the tasks present students with a scenario that contains a problem to be solved. For example, one task challenges students to take on the role of an aide to Emperor Marcus Aurelius and help him to come up with a plan to save the empire from ruin. Another has students prepare a report to Emperor Commodus on whether or not the spread of Christianity poses a threat to Rome's imperial power. The report is to be in the form of a PowerPoint presentation. The number of words on each slide is restricted in order to promote attention to key ideas and the synthesis of information. A third activity challenges students to create a web museum that highlights the five most important achievements or contributions of Roman civilization. Another has students developing a web-based "Hall of Imperial Roman Fame and Shame" that presents their picks of famous and infamous Romans. As a part of their research for each of these tasks, the students have to locate appropriate websites, evaluate those sites, and select the most appropriate and relevant information; they can analyze the information and pick out the main ideas, then apply the information in order to complete the assignments. Students can choose to work co-operatively or independently, and can choose to combine and extend the project to varying degrees. They are also encouraged to engage in reflection throughout the learning process.

Mr. Smith likes this inquiry-based approach to social studies because "it has all of the elements of meaningful learning with technology." The unit activities emphasize the skills of information literacy, searching techniques such as using search engines and Boolean logic, as well as problem solving while students attempt to find the needed information to address the problem. The internet provides students with an opportunity to work with information in different ways, at different speeds, and at different times, and they can go back over the information as often as they need to for clarification. An added benefit of using the internet is that "the students had to do the research and the thinking." All of these possibilities increased the students' ability to make learning connections. According to Mr. Smith, "Another advantage of using the internet and the software in this way is that different perspectives on the issues are available rather than relying on one textbook." He feels also that the students take more responsibility for their learning and have increased pride in their work. The weaker, non-academic students get "a good feeling about learning." Finally, Mr. Smith thinks that "the problem-based approach leads to a shift from focussing on the content to focussing on skill development, which provides lifelong benefits for students."

communities, then post the findings on the Global School House website to be shared with classrooms around the world. The "Doors to Diplomacy" page at the same site (www .globalschoolhouse.org/doors) challenges middle school and high school students around the world to produce web projects that teach others about the importance of international affairs and diplomacy.

Digital video technology lets students both communicate and express themselves through media. These visual capabilities have made it easier for students to record video documentaries to be included as a part of their web pages. Also, multimedia student authoring programs like Hyperstudio provide students with the opportunity to experience a multi-sensory learning environment since they can create their own interactive multimedia presentations. They can use graphics, video, animation, and sound to meet their differing learning needs. Slide shows can be created in ClarisWorks, KidPix, Microsoft PowerPoint, Adobe Persuasion, or Corel Presentations. Using computers for product-oriented projects such as designing multimedia presentations can be highly motivating for students. Students learn not only how to organize information for their presentation using these tools, but also how to create their own representations of their knowledge about a topic, which increases their ability to express their individuality and their unique perspectives (Boethel and Dimock 1999).

Using Computers as Problem-Solving Tools

Although the majority of school-related work on the world wide web is directed to searching for information on a topic, it has great potential as a motivating force in social studies by engaging students in simulations and WebQuests. Simulations can be powerful tools for making abstract content and complex ideas more accessible to learners (Goldman, Cole, and Syer 1999; Schacter and Fagnano 1999). "Utilizing computer modelling as a visualization [can be] a powerful bridge between experience and abstraction" (Dede 2000, 172). Participatory simulation software can also help students "develop a sense of empathy for the subject and jettison contemporary assumptions and values to understand an event as it really was" (Staley 2000, 9). Providing students with such alternative ways to learn, including both verbal and non-verbal ways, can be of help to those with mild learning disorders (Shields and Behrmann 2000).

Careful selection is important to an effective social studies program if simulation software is being used. Before deciding on a software program, familiarize yourself with its contents, as you would with any other resource. Consider the level of interactivity the software promotes. Software that has a drill-and-practise format tends to have the purpose of transmitting information and then ascertaining student recall of that information through lower-level questioning and built-in right-answer tests. Some software programs cover only a very narrow slice of a topic and at times deal with content that is outside the curriculum.

A popular web-based activity for developing problem-solving skills is a WebQuest. A WebQuest is a specially designed website that engages students in a task or inquiry to solve a problem using web-based resources (Dodge 1996). Most of the resources used for the inquiry are other websites that have been vetted and linked directly to the WebQuest site. Through a WebQuest, students can actively explore issues from a number of different viewpoints, find answers, and reach moral and ethical decisions about real contemporary world problems. A WebQuest can help to develop critical and creative thinking, and problem-solving and decision-making skills. WebQuests can easily be tailored for diverse needs in the classroom.

A WebQuest is typically divided into five sections (see the samples on the next page). The first part of the WebQuest lays out the task or the problem to be investigated. Students are then assigned roles or provided with differing perspectives on the issue or problem being investigated. Working either independently or in groups, they explore the issue or problem under guidance and in a manner that is meaningful to them. Students access the information provided, analyze it, synthesize and evaluate it, then transform it in some way to demonstrate their understanding of the particular view that they are to take in response to the problem being investigated. They then share their findings with the whole class. The teacher acts as a facilitator, checking to see that students understand the role they are to take, and that they are on task. The highlighted text, "Mrs. Woods' WebQuests on Confederation," describes how Mrs. Woods, a grade 8 teacher, used a WebQuest in her teaching about Confederation.

COMPUTER-BASED SIMULATIONS

The Tom Snyder series Decisions Decisions 5.0 (ddonline. tomsnyder.com/issues/animaltesting/intro.cfm) helps to promote higher level thinking and decision-making skills as it engages students in collaboratively and interactively investigating issues such as animal testing. Expert advisors help students to examine the issue from a number of different perspectives before they vote on an action. Another site, The Stock Market Game Program (www.SMG2000.org) develops students' understanding of economic concepts as they engage in a simulated stock market scenario.

Other selections from the Tom Snyder Productions catalogue can help teach students geographic skills. Geography Search engages students in a simulated ocean voyage where they learn about latitude, longitude, the earth's rotation, and weather and wind patterns. The Inspirer Geography Series has students collaboratively investigate issues related to geography in countries around the world. Further opportunities for authentic learning can be built into a unit on developing geographical skills through a site like the Geographic Information System (www.esri.com), which allows students to create and manipulate layers of maps so they can collect detailed information about a place. Two other websites that provide opportunities for map creation are the Canadian Geographic Map Maker (www .canadiangeographic.ca/mapping/newmain.html) and the Atlas of Canada (www.atlas.gc.ca/site/english/index.html). Other examples of simulations can be found at www .simulations.com.

The next generation of virtual reality educational software, including simulated gaming environments, holds much promise for allowing more direct interaction and collaboration for users as they test viable, situation-based solutions to problems in virtual environments. As an example, a website that uses a Multiuser Virtual Environment Experiential Simulator (MUVEES) to immerse students in a simulated city of the 1880s in order to examine health concerns can be viewed at www.virtual.gmu.edu. Microworlds and virtual reality simulators are beginning to grow in popularity as ways to engage students in simplified three-dimensional versions of real-life scenarios for testing hypotheses (www.microworlds.com).

Using Computers to Facilitate Communication and Collaboration

Computer technologies can be helpful in developing communication and collaborative skills. Students are fascinated by the possibilities of electronic communication for exchanging ideas about topics of mutual interest with other students and adults in different parts of the world. Collaboration among learners within and beyond the classroom walls can be en-

WEB-BASED HISTORICAL ARTIFACTS

The McCord Museum offers a free online "history laboratory" in which images and objects from 1840–1945 are given a central role (www.mccord-museum.qc.ca). This laboratory draws upon the Keys to History resource, a database of 110,000 images of artifacts that was developed in collaboration with seven other Canadian museums. This fully bilingual web resource provides tools that allow students to access information, organize and synthesize facts, and share knowledge. They are invited to analyze primary documents and engage in the process that historians or museologists use. Thematic tours (via video, images, and text) provide insights into major events in Canadian history and aspects of daily life that shaped the Canadian experience.

Observation, quizzes, and role-playing games include placing objects in their proper context; recreating period dress; discovering the identity of unusual objects; locating the odd man out in period settings; finding the link between two historical figures; and Mind your Manners!, a game that explores the Victorian period and the Roaring Twenties.

Another creative tool on the McCord Museum site is the Web Folder, which allows users to create their own visual presentation based on images from the collections with added comments, personal images, and hyperlinks. Using this tool, students carry out an inquiry and can integrate resources from elsewhere. The Web Folder presentations are saved on the server, where they can then be printed, saved on the user's computer, or presented to their class.

These resources and tools were developed for secondary schools. A pedagogical guide entitled ClioClic offers two types of activities: documenting a political cartoon, an object, or a historical photograph; or conducting an investigation into a historical event or fact. For these investigations, ClioClic invites students to reflect on different themes (such as child labour) and take on various roles. In order to help students conduct a more in-depth research, ClioClic provides additional historical resources, such as excerpts from history books, writings from various historians, a summary of the period covered, and links to other relevant sites.

MRS. WOODS' WEBQUESTS ON CONFEDERATION

Mrs. Woods wanted to use the web in a way that would develop and apply her grade 8 students' critical and creative thinking, problem-solving, and decision-making skills. She chose a WebQuest because she felt that it would provide an active, integrated, and connected approach to learning social studies. Through the WebQuest, her students "have a challenge presented to them and they have to find a way of coming up with a solution." One of the teachers at her school developed a WebQuest for the Fathers of Confederation (www.edu.pe.ca/vrcs/grade8/projects/confed.html). For that project, each student was to play the role of biographer and choose a Father of Confederation to research. Tasks included responding to pre-established questions by researching either in books, in non-print media, or on the internet. The final project included the development of a website with appropriate links. Each student then had to present his or her individual project to the class. The role of the class was to provide feedback. These web pages were then posted on the school website. Students in other classes and in successive

grades were encouraged to use these student sites as sources of information for their research projects. She liked that the use of the internet was less directed and more engaging and empowering for students. She felt that through its use students become more knowledgeable, more worldly, and more proficient about finding information, as well as more co-operative. She would like to see students use the internet to post their own work and not simply to retrieve information presented by others. Mrs. Wood felt that such an application-type approach to concepts and ideas that normally were addressed only through knowledge-type strategies benefitted her students because they were "using whatever media or tools they had available to demonstrate that they know that content. I think that approach helps address different learning strategies and different learning styles that students have." Students were encouraged to showcase their research by creating web pages in the areas of research they had done.

hanced through the use of computers. Information gathered in this fashion is viewed by students as being more connected to "real" local, national, and global issues. Interactive web-based collaborative projects are an excellent way to engage students in projects with other students and experts from around the world. Some research contends that gender bias pervades computer technologies and makes computers less friendly for girls; however, electronic participation has been found to be more gender-equitable and can counteract male dominance (Linn 1999). As well, providing opportunities for collaborative activity through the use of technology has been shown to heighten girls' interest in computing (Butler 2000).

Communication tools such as e-mail, listservs, bulletin boards, newsgroups, and chat groups build on students' desire to communicate and share their understandings. Computer networking also allows students to communicate and collaborate with content experts and fellow students around the globe. Online conversations through e-mail can prompt reflection and help students think about their ideas and how best to articulate those ideas so that they are clear to others. Such conversations also encourage self-checking for understanding and identification of inaccuracies in one's own expressed ideas, which can lead to rethinking and reframing of former ideas.

According to a report from SchoolNet (Industry Canada 2002, 1–2) the benefits of a telecollaborative approach to learning include:

- placing students in a position where they can discover the world and share the results of their experiences;
- involving learners in new roles as active participants, creative interpreters of the world, and experienced collaborators; and
- providing for a greater range of learning by doing and constructing content.

Through the use of electronic communication, students are able to speak for themselves. Online chat allows more than one student to "talk" at the same time. As well, a world wide web opportunity like e-mates gives students an opportunity to interact with a real audience without the inhibiting factor of peer pressure (Richards 2000). It "frees the child with special needs from fear of being stigmatized as well as enabling them to network with other children to share feelings about having a disability" (Shields and Behrmann 2000, 13). E-mail and threaded discussions can "act as a conduit rather than an impediment to conversation" (Richards 2000, 4).

There is great potential for computer technologies to help develop effective citizens, since students gain first-hand knowledge of other cultures through online learning communities. Such increased exposure to first-hand information could potentially overcome students' insular views of the world. Some scholars suggest that broader exposure to other cultures through increased internet access can spread democratic ideals internationally and help stem the growth of potentially incendiary nationalism (Githiora-Updike 2000, 63). Staley (2000, 9) calls online discussions "a type of democratic performance."

The highlighted text "Mr. Chang's Telecollaboration Project" is the story of one teacher who engaged in a telecollaborative project to enhance his students' learning about environmental issues. Other examples can be found in "Connected Learning Projects."

Making Do With Limited Computers

Before closing I would like to discuss the possibilities for making maximum use of computing if a computer lab is not available and you have only one computer in your classroom. One

MR. CHANG'S TELECOLLABORATION PROJECT

A group of junior high students from various classrooms across the country were brought together through the use of video-conferencing to discuss environmental issues with a focus on the Kyoto Protocol. Also in attendance were provincial and federal Ministers of the Environment. The students discussed the issues with federal and provincial representatives and then came up with a plan of action for the schools to take. Mr. Chang, one of the teachers involved, described his observations of this activity:

There's layers of communication that you can see evidenced when students are video-conferencing that are different than talking amongst their friends. It is far more public speaking than talking to your teacher in class, answering questions and answers. There's a change in the dynamic when confronted with a whole series of strangers that you have to communicate with. Students come to realize that "These eyes are beyond just my peer group." They now have a world audience and they're concerned about their impression that they leave that audience with. This leads them to consider the audience more perhaps than they would in a closed, thirty-student classroom.

Another thing that Mr. Chang reflected on was the opportunities that video-conferencing provided for expanding students' understanding of others.

It really does sink that concept home, that you're talking to other audiences who may have other cultural values or religious values that you have to be sensitized to when you're making your presentations. So when we're talking to Finland, of course, the hour and the time frame forces us to recognize that something's dramatically different. So already they're sensitized to people who are living under different situations and different value systems that they need to take into consideration. Sometimes there are real eye openers, because all of a sudden they realize, for example, that the people in Edmonton don't really care about the cod in Newfoundland, and we've had that discussion a couple of times with one of our schools out in St. John's. So what strikes interest and what's of value to the students is quite dramatically different, even as we go across our nation.

CONNECTED LEARNING PROJECTS

One form of telecollaborative project involves students in interactive, online expeditions. Numerous websites are available for students to "accompany" real-life participants as they undertake actual adventures. The Global Schoolhouse (www.gsn.org) provides opportunities for students to engage with adventurers as they travel around the world. Through daily updates on the web and through conversational discussion boards, students can ask questions of the adventurers and keep in touch with the latest discoveries as the journeys unfold. There are also opportunities to plan an individualized online expedition and to find worldwide partners who may wish to partner up with other classes for an adventure. The Globallearn (www.globalearn.com) website also offers online expeditions twice a year where teams of explorers go to different parts of the world to document local environments and ways of life. These explorers post journals, research logs, and photos each day to the website. Classes can send messages to the explorers, and teachers can customize their study of the expedition to meet students' needs and interests by choosing materials and activities that are suited to their students' learning styles. *National Geographic* also provides online expeditions (www.nationalgeographic.com/explorer).

Webcams are another technology that help to connect students globally as they get to view what is happening live somewhere in the world. One educational webcam site, A Bird's Eye View of Webcams, has a "Moments in History" section that provides students with present day images of the locations of past events (www.abirdseyeviewof.com/Historywie.html) as well as a wide variety of other viewing locations.

idea is to set the computer up as a learning station where students work in groups on certain aspects of research projects that require access to the internet. Rotate each group through the computer station so that everyone has access to internet resources at some point in the inquiry. Only one computer is needed if you have a projection device to allow you to share simulations and WebQuests with the entire class. In the case of a WebQuest, the home page of the site can be projected onto a screen at the front of the class and the teacher can walk the class through each step. When students are divided into task groups, the materials can be printed off for each group and the remainder of the WebQuest can be completed without accessing the computer, or with rotating access to the one classroom computer by each group. You can also use educational software or internet sites from the front of the classroom to anchor learning or guide a discussion. (See www.teachnet.com/how-to/organization/onecompclass040799.html for other ideas about using one or a few computers in the classroom).

Concluding Remarks

The main focus of this chapter is the efficient and effective integration of computers into the curriculum and specifically the use of the internet to help students construct knowledge. I believe that the most effective uses of computer technologies are those that foster meaningful learning by engaging learners in authentic, inquiry-oriented learning experiences that recognize the active role of the learner in constructing meaning about the world. A number of internet-based tools provide support for students throughout their inquiry. These tools—

including virtual museums and field trips, spreadsheets and databases, concept-mapping tools, and simulations—have the potential, if used in meaningful ways, to develop students' ability to think critically and creatively, solve problems, make sound decisions, and collaborate with one another.

> Select a topic from the curriculum or from a student textbook. Using electronic resources mentioned in this chapter or located elsewhere, develop an activity in which students use computers not to gather information but to solve problems or organize and synthesize ideas. Plan how you will help students undertake this knowledge-construction task using a computer.

NOTE

1. The teacher stories provided in this chapter are based on actual classroom examples collected as part of a three-year study supported by the Social Sciences and Humanities Research Council on internet use in Canadian schools. The teachers and their schools have been given pseudonyms to guarantee anonymity.

REFERENCES

Adams, S. and M. Burns. 1999. *Connecting student learning and technology*. Southwest Austin, TX: Educational Development Laboratory.

Bass, R. and R. Rosenzweig. 1999. Rewriting the history and social studies classroom: Needs, frameworks, dangers, and proposals. *Journal of Education* 181 (3): 41–61.

Boethel, M. and V. Dimock. 1999. *Constructing knowledge with technology: A review of the literature.* Southwest Austin, TX: Educational Development Laboratory.

Boyer, B. and P. Semrau. 1995. A constructivist approach to social studies: Integrating technology. *Social Studies and the Young Learner* 7(3): 14–16.

Butler, D. 2000. Gender, girls, and computer technology: What's the status now? *Clearing House* 73 (4), March/April: 225–229.

Case, R. 2003. Making critical thinking an integral part of electronic research. *School Libraries in Canada* 22 (4): 13–16.

Dede, C. 2000. A new century demands new ways of learning. In *Digital classroom: How technology is changing the way we teach and learn,* ed. D.T. Gordon, 171–174. Cambridge, MA: Harvard Education Letter.

Dodge, B. 1996. Active learning on the web. Available online at http://edweb.sdsu.edu/people/bdodge/active/ActiveLearningk-12.html.

Ehman, L. and A. Glenn. 1991. Interactive technology in the social studies. In *Handbook of research in social studies teaching and learning,* ed. J.P. Shaver, 513–522. New York: Macmillan.

Githiora-Updike, W. 2000. The global schoolhouse. In *Digital classroom: How technology is changing the way we teach and learn,* ed. D.T. Gordon, 60–66. Cambridge, MA: Harvard Education Letter.

Goldman, S., K. Cole, and C. Syer. 1999, July 12–13. *The technology/content dilemma. Evaluating the effectiveness of technology proceedings.* Washington, DC: Eric Document No. ED452821.

Industry Canada. 2002. A study of grassroots projects: Online project-based collaborative learning. Available online at http://www.schoolnet.ca/alasource/e/resources/toolkit/tele/index.asp.

Jonassen, D. 1996. *Computers in the classroom: Mindtools for critical thinking.* Englewood Cliffs, NJ: Prentice Hall.

Jonassen, D., J. Howland, J. Moore, and M. Marra. 2003. *Learning to solve problems with technology.* Upper Saddle River, NJ: Merrill Prentice Hall.

Leu, D. 2000. Exploring literacy on the internet. *The Reading Teacher* 53 (5), February: 424–429.

Linn, E. 1999. Gender equity and computer technology. *Equity Coalition* V, Fall.

Means, B. 2001. Technology use in tomorrow's schools. *Educational Leadership* 58 (4): 57–61.

Richards, G.A. 2000. Why use computer technology? *English Journal* 90 (2), November: 38–41.

Schacter, J. and C. Fagnano. 1999. Does computer technology improve student learning and achievement? How, when, and under what conditions? *Journal of Educational Computing Research* 20 (4): 329–343.

Shields, M.K. and R.E. Behrman. 2000. Children and computer technology: analysis and recommendations. *Future of Children* 10 (2), Fall–Winter: 4–30.

Staley, D.J. 2000. Technology, authentic performance, and history education. *International Journal of Social Education* 15 (1): 1–12.

Todd, R., L. Lamb, and C. McNicholas. 1992. The power of information literacy: Unity of education and resources for the 21st century. Paper presented at the annual meeting of the International Association of School Librarianship, Belfast, North Ireland.

15 Reading Comprehension Strategies in Social Studies

Paul Neufeld

Historical Neglect

The importance of teaching reading comprehension strategies in social studies should be obvious. Since social studies is, after all, a text-laden subject, being able to read and comprehend texts effectively is crucial for success. Despite research confirming that students can effectively be taught strategies for improving their reading comprehension (National Reading Panel 2000), such instruction rarely occurs (Durkin 1978/79, Pressley 2002a).

Before World War I, little thought was directed towards teaching students how better to comprehend what they were reading. Reading instruction consisted of oral reading practice, the hallmarks of which were accurate and fluent recognition and pronunciation of words. In the decade after the war, the emphasis shifted from improving oral reading towards gaining meaning from text. For the next forty years, reading comprehension instruction consisted largely of students answering teacher-presented questions about specific selections (Pearson and Dole 1987). Dolores Durkin, after observing more than ten thousand minutes of instruction in her landmark study of reading and social studies instruction, concluded that giving, completing, and checking assignments consumed a large part of the teaching periods and that no actual instruction in how to comprehend was taking place (1978/79, 481). Despite the importance of reading in social studies and other subjects, and a growing body of research suggesting the efficacy of teaching students how to comprehend, more than two decades after Durkin's famous study, researchers continue to document the limited extent to which such instruction actually occurs (Pressley 2002b).

In this chapter, I present the basic principles and introductory tools required to teach reading comprehension in social studies. In the process, I hope to communicate why reading comprehension instruction should not be viewed as the exclusive domain of English/language arts but instead has an important place in social studies. I begin by defining reading comprehension and outlining the role of thinking in reading comprehension. The bulk of the chapter looks at specific reading comprehension strategies and offers a framework for developing self-regulated student use of a repertoire of these strategies.

Reading Comprehension as Thinking

Comprehension is defined here as constructing a reasonable understanding of a text. Three principles underlie this deceptively simple definition: 1) comprehending a text requires active, intentional thinking through which a reader constructs meaning (Alexander and Jetton 2000); 2) varying interpretations of texts are to be expected because of differences in people's background knowledge and experiences; and 3) not all interpretations of a given text can be considered valid (Pressley 2002b). Clearly, comprehension is a function both of what the reader brings to the text (for example, his or her background knowledge of the topic) and the ideas conveyed through the words themselves. Thus, two students reading the same historical account may reach differing impressions about some aspects of the text. If both readers have comprehended the text, however, the essence they extract from the story should be similar (Pressley 2002b).

Comprehending a written text is a multifaceted undertaking, requiring both automatic and intentional thinking. Readers must engage in thinking at the word level (for example, decoding of words, accessing one's memory of word meanings) and at what has been called the above-word level. Thinking at the above-word level consists of the purposeful use of procedural or "how-to" strategies when attempting to comprehend a text (Alexander and Judy 1988). Although my focus in this chapter is solely on developing above-word-level strategies, other challenges to reading comprehension must not be overlooked. These include attending to the reader's general knowledge of the world and specific knowledge of the particular topic; knowledge of relevant vocabulary; the ability to activate such knowledge; and competence in word-level processes such as decoding and fluency (that is, the ability to read at an appropriate rate and with expression). Difficulties in any of these areas may render above-word-level strategies unavailable to the reader. Consequently, comprehension-strategy instruction should complement, not replace, various long-standing practices such as providing vocabulary instruction and building students' background knowledge prior to having them read.

A substantial body of research supports the value of teaching students to use question asking and answering to support their efforts to comprehend what they read (Rosenshine, Meister, and Chapman 1996). Question asking and answering can be viewed as the foundation for all the other strategies. In other words, the process of asking and then answering questions of oneself and of the text activates the other strategies. What differs from one to the next is the type of questions one asks. Developing the ability to ask and answer questions of oneself and the text before, during, and after reading is an essential part of becoming a strategic reader. The ultimate goal is for question asking and answering to become a habit—a natural and pervasive part of a student's reading routine.

Without guidance, many students will not spontaneously generate and use effective question asking and answering strategies. These students will benefit from explicit instruction in a few well-researched strategies, and ongoing guidance in learning to select, activate, and use the strategies without direct prompting from others (Pressley 1998). The strategies described below can be applied regardless of the kind and length of the text—whether one is reading whole books, research articles, chapters within books, or passages within chapters.

Reading Comprehension Strategies

Researchers have identified many individual reading comprehension strategies that are both teachable and useful. These strategies can be clustered into two groups: pre-reading strategies, and during- and after-reading strategies (Schuder 1993).

PRE-READING STRATEGIES

As the name suggests, these strategies help students comprehend texts by involving them in thinking about the text before they actually start to read it. Four of these strategies are discussed below.

- **Clarify a purpose for reading.** A simple but important first step is to encourage students to think consciously about the crucial question: why they are about to read a particular text. Some common reasons for reading social studies texts are to prepare for a class discussion, study for a test, or gather important information for completing a task such as writing a paper. Questions for students to ask include:
  - Why am I reading this text?
  - How should my purpose affect the way I read the text?
- **Overview the text.** Overviewing involves quickly surveying the text before reading it. The intent is to develop an overall sense of the text, determine its relevance to the purpose for reading, and identify sections that are particularly relevant to the purpose. Implementing this strategy involves considering the title and major headings, reading the introduction and conclusion, and examining text support features such as tables and graphs, with the purpose of answering questions such as the following:
  - What does this text appear to be about?
  - What major topics are covered in the text?
  - What text structure(s) does the author use to present the information? (for example, enumeration, time order, compare and contrast, cause and effect, problem/solution)
- **Activate prior knowledge.** Having developed a general sense of the content and organization during the overviewing process, readers can invoke knowledge they already possess that may be relevant to the text. Prior knowledge provides a mental connection linking ideas in the text with the reader's existing knowledge of the topic and the world. This practice has been shown to improve both recall and comprehension (Anderson and Pearson 1984). At this point, typical questions for students to ask and answer include:
  - What do I already know or think I know about this topic?
  - How does what I already know about this topic relate to this particular text?
- **Make predictions about the text.** Students can learn to make predictions about a text by drawing on answers produced using the overview strategy and by drawing on prior knowledge of the topic (Pressley 2002b). For instance, after scanning an article on the history of the Olympics, a student might forecast that the text will provide information about sports such as wrestling that were popular in ancient Greece. Such predictions can then be used as hypotheses to test as the student is reading. A typical prediction question for students to ask and answer is:
  - I think this text is going to be about …

> Before reading any further, review the questions to ask and answer when overviewing a text. Apply this strategy to the rest of the chapter and then read the chapter to test how well you were able to develop an overall sense of this part and to identify particularly relevant sections.

DURING- AND AFTER-READING STRATEGIES

According to Pressley and Wharton-McDonald (1997), students should learn to use strategies while reading a given text and after they finish reading it, as well as use strategic thinking before beginning. Strategies applied during these phases are intended to help students: 1) understand and remember what they have read; and 2) monitor their comprehension and remedy misunderstandings when breakdowns in comprehension occur. As was the case with pre-reading strategies, readers' ability and inclination to ask and answer questions of the text, and of themselves, drives the use of any particular strategy. Three types of strategies are addressed.

- **Analyze text structure.** The term "text structure" refers to the organizational logic of a text. It identifies the form in which information is organized for presentation. Most texts are written using relatively few organizational structures—enumeration, time order, compare and contrast, cause and effect, problem/solution, and description (see Table 15.1, "Common Text Structures"). As shown in Table 15.2, adapted from categories proposed by Vacca and Vacca (1999), each of these text structures, with the exception of description, is typically associated with a set of keywords that readers can use to identify the particular structure or structures.

Helping students identify organizational structure facilitates their comprehension (Taylor and Beach 1984). For instance, recognizing that a particular text compares and contrasts the leadership styles of former prime ministers provides a framework for understanding the information presented. Not surprisingly, once students learn to identify organizational structures, they can apply this strategy when overviewing texts before reading them. Key questions for students to ask are:

TABLE 15.1 COMMON TEXT STRUCTURES		
TEXT STRUCTURE	**EXPLANATION**	**VISUAL REPRESENTATION**
Enumeration	Lists items or ideas that follow in order (for example, stages in the passage of legislation, instructions for building an igloo).	
Time order	Lists a sequence of events in time (for example, the daily schedule of a pioneer, major events in the history of a civilization).	
Compare and contrast	Highlights similarities and differences between two or more things or events (for example, comparing life in nineteenth and twenty-first century Canada, differences between capitalism and communism).	
Cause and effect	Shows how events (causes) lead to other events (effects) (for example, causes of poverty, escalation of violence in a dispute).	
Problem/solution	Shows the development of a problem and one or more solutions (for example, dealing with pollution or traffic congestion).	
Description	Presents the main features of a person, event, object, or scene (for example, conditions for new immigrants, daily life in a community).	

TABLE 15.2   USEFUL WORD CLUES

	ENUMERATION	TIME ORDER	COMPARE AND CONTRAST	CAUSE AND EFFECT	PROBLEM/ SOLUTION
Keywords	to begin with first secondly next then finally most important also in fact for instance for example	on (date) not long after now as before after when following	however but as well as on the other hand not only … but also either … or while although unless similarly yet	because since therefore consequently as a result this led to so that nevertheless accordingly if … then thus	

- Do I see any keywords associated with specific text structures?
- What text structures are used to present the information? (for example, enumeration, time order, compare and contrast, cause and effect, problem/ solution)

- **Summarize the text.** Another strategy is to teach students to summarize coherently and briefly what they have read. Creating well-developed summaries is difficult. To support this task, students are advised to ask and answer questions such as "What organizational structure(s) does the author use to present the information?", "What is the gist of the text?", and "What are the author's main points?".

  - *Oral summaries.* Duke and Pearson (2002) recommend the use of oral summaries for "on-the-fly" comprehension checking that involve pausing momentarily after reading a section and checking comprehension by constructing a brief oral summary of what has just been read.

  - *Visual summaries.* Visual summaries include visual organizers such as semantic webs and Venn diagrams, strategies that are not typically regarded as summarizing tools. Vacca and Vacca (1999) point out that visual organizers provide graphic representations of both important information and the structure of knowledge contained in the text. Visual organizers also depict how these ideas relate to one another. Keep in mind that constructing appropriate organizers requires that readers be able to identify the organizational structure of a text. For instance, as suggested in Table 15.1, a Venn diagram or matrix can be used to summarize and compare and contrast text structure, but neither can be used to summa-

rize a cause and effect or problem/solution organizational structure. There are many commercially produced instructional packages to teach about visual organizers. Such products, however, may not be necessary and may in fact get in the way of students' learning to use visual summaries effectively on their own. The power of visual organizers is realized only when students learn to construct them to accurately represent the particular texts they are reading—something mass-produced visual organizers can seldom accomplish. Most importantly, students find it liberating to create their own tools.

- *Written summaries.* Teaching students to write summaries in complete or partial sentences is another useful strategy. A common approach, as suggested below, is to teach students rules to apply when constructing written summaries (McNeil and Donant 1982):

  1. Delete unnecessary material (for example, delete interesting details that are not germane to the topic at hand).
  2. Delete redundant material (for example, delete repetitious statements made in the text).
  3. Select a word to replace a list of items (for example, replace "beans, flour, sugar, and dried fish" with "food").
  4. Select a word to replace the individual parts of an action (for example, replace a long description of explorers crossing a mountain pass with "the explorers crossed the mountain pass").
  5. Select a topic sentence (that is, one that captures the main idea or gist of a paragraph or passage).
  6. Create a topic sentence if one is not available.

- **Monitor comprehension.** As with previous comprehen-

FIGURE 15.1   DOCUMENTING THE DETAILS

One way to introduce students to the 5W questions is to use a chart in which the reader provides evidence from the text to support a response to each question.

	READER'S RESPONSE	EVIDENCE FROM THE TEXT
WHO are the main actors in the text?		
WHAT have they been doing?		
WHERE did the actions take place?		
WHEN did the actions take place?		
WHY have they done these actions?		
Questions I have:		

sion strategies, the ability to ask and answer questions is essential for clarifying, comprehending, and correcting misunderstandings. Baker (1985) points out that many readers, particularly younger ones or poor ones, are unable to monitor their understanding while reading. Examples from the seemingly endless number and type of questions that students could ask to assist in monitoring are:

- Is what I just read clear to me? Do I "get it?"
- Can I answer who, what, when, where, why questions about the text?
- What about the text is still fuzzy or unclear?
- **Use fix-up strategies.** Following the identification of a breakdown in comprehension, students must know to clarify the failure and apply "fix-up" strategies to remedy the situation. Two questions to help remediate a breakdown in comprehension are:

- Given my purpose for reading, how important is it that I clearly understand this portion of the text?
- What strategies could I use to help me better understand what I'm reading?
  - Re-read part or all of the text.
  - Look ahead in the text.
  - Relate the information in the text to what the reader already knows about the topic.
  - Examine other resources on this topic (for example, books, web pages, videotapes).
  - Consult someone who might resolve my confusion (for example, student, teacher, parent).

Review each of the text structures outlined in Table 15.1 and decide which one (or ones) are evident in this chapter.

Instruction in the Strategies

Thus far I have discussed strategies that will help students become better at comprehending what they read. Next I focus on how to teach these strategies. Two phases for teaching reading comprehension strategies are described below: explicit instruction in individual strategies (Roehler and Duffy 1984) and teaching for self-regulated use (Collins-Block and Pressley 2002). The move from explicit instruction to teaching for self-regulated strategy use is not entirely sequential. Instead, there is considerable movement back and forth between the two phases. Students are more likely to master independent self-regulated use of a given strategy if it is taught and learned in a meaningful context that directly applies to the course material they are expected to read (Gambrell, Kapinus, and Wilson 1987). This is accomplished by using actual content area materials during both phases of the process.

EXPLICIT INSTRUCTION OF INDIVIDUAL STRATEGIES

This initial phase of instruction focusses on helping students become competent users of the specific comprehension strategies discussed above. I recommend a four-step framework in which the teacher explicitly teaches the strategy to be learned, rather than simply presenting it, hoping that students "catch on."

- **Introduction.** A first step is to introduce the strategy by explaining what it is and why it is useful. This can be done by offering a simple description and/or definition of the strategy (Baumann and Schmitt 1986). Next, ask students what, if anything, they already know about the strategy, provide a rationale for learning the strategy, and offer evidence of how it can improve their reading comprehension.
- **Modelling.** An effective way to teach students how to use a strategy is to show how it works (Dansereau 1987). Generally speaking, reading and learning processes are covert thinking activities that students seldom get to view in others. As students look on, teachers are advised to demonstrate while thinking aloud and explain their thought processes while using the strategy.
- **Guided practice.** Guided practice involves providing students with numerous opportunities to use a strategy in an environment where support and feedback are readily available. In this step, the teacher and students together share responsibility for implementing a comprehension strategy. For example, after modelling several examples of identifying organizational structure(s), highlight several relevant words in a new passage and ask students to

identify the text structure. Gradually release to students the responsibility for executing the strategy through a progression, starting with the whole class then proceeding towards small-group and individual guided practice. The transition from teacher-directed to student-directed execution with extensive practice in a supportive environment is essential for developing independent use of a strategy (Pearson and Dole 1987). Perhaps the biggest and most crippling deficiency in prevailing approaches to teaching reading comprehension strategies is the failure to provide numerous opportunities for supported practice.

- **Independent practice.** In the final stage, independent practice, students assume full responsibility for using the strategy (Baumann and Ballard 1987). Teacher monitoring and feedback are important, however, to ensure correct use of the strategy and to build student confidence. To reduce the likelihood of a pattern of failure, it is wise after the first few instances of independent practice to discuss students' responses along with their methods of reasoning (Pearson and Dole 1987).

The highlighted text "Teaching a Comprehension Strategy in Action" provides an example of explicit instruction in a reading comprehension strategy using this framework.

TEACH FOR SELF-REGULATED USE

The goal of teaching reading comprehension is to foster student mastery of a growing repertoire of individual strategies in a self-regulated fashion. The challenge in becoming an independent strategic reader is not simply a matter of acquiring knowledge of various strategies, but also of knowing exactly when, given the specific purpose and text, to employ particular strategies (Malone and Mastropieri 1992, 278). When assisting students in learning when and where to use each strategy, it is helpful to review why such strategies are useful and to provide multiple opportunities to practise them using actual course content (Gersten and Carnine 1986).

Teaching for self-regulated use should begin as soon as students understand what the particular strategy is and how it works. In practice, then, the two phases are more nearly parallel than sequential, with the teacher providing instruction in when and where to use different strategies as the opportunity arises. For instance, a teacher might model a previously taught strategy while introducing students to text structures. Nonetheless, as students acquire increasingly larger repertoires of strategies, there is a natural progression from explicit instruction of individual strategies towards instruction on the coordinated and self-regulated use of multiple strategies.

If students are to become competent strategic readers,

TEACHING A COMPREHENSION STRATEGY IN ACTION

The scene is Mr. Carling's Canadian history class. Mr. Carling has a well-deserved reputation as an excellent teacher who works tirelessly to instill a passion for history and learning. To this end, in addition to having a strong focus on content, his classes are directed towards helping students become more effective learners. It is late September and Mr. Carling is eager to start helping his students learn how to better comprehend the history texts they will be reading through the year. He has chosen to begin with teaching them to overview a text before reading it.

Introduction

Sitting on the table at the front of the class, Mr. Carling addresses the students: "Okay, today I'm going to introduce a strategy, a thinking tool if you like, that will help you become a better reader of your social studies textbooks, and other information books, for that matter. With time and practice, this tool will, if you choose to use it, help you better comprehend what you read in this course and in other courses. The strategy is called overviewing.

"Does anyone have an idea what I mean by overviewing?" A few students raise their hands and take a stab at answering his question. Mr. Carling points to Kevin who says, "This is just a guess but I'm thinking it might be when you skim over what you're supposed to read before you actually read it." Marcy jumps in and adds, "Yeah, I think it means looking over the chapter and trying to figure out what it's about before you actually read it." Nodding in agreement, Mr. Carling says, "You're certainly on the right track." He then adds clarity to the informal definitions provided by the students. "Overviewing," he says, "involves reading through the title, introduction, major headings, and conclusion of a chapter or book prior to reading it in an effort to get a rough idea of what the text is about. Often people will also have a look at things like pictures and graphs as they overview a chapter.

"Now, I hope you're thinking to yourself, 'Why would I want or need to do that? Why wouldn't I just start reading?' Well, the answer to those excellent questions is that because doing so will help you better understand and remember the information in the chapter. In a minute, I'm going to show you how and why this is the case."

Modelling

Mr. Carling jumps down from his perch on the table and says, "Okay, now I'm going to show you how this strategy works. I'm going to demonstrate it for you. As I'm doing this, I want you to pay very close attention to what I am saying. I'm going to share the way I'm thinking with you so that you can think in the same way when it's your turn to do an overview." He then asks students to take out their textbooks and open to page 84, the chapter on the War of 1812. Once the students are settled, he models overviewing for them.

"The title of the chapter is 'The War of 1812.' All right, I'm thinking things are looking pretty straightforward then. It seems obvious that I'm going to be learning about the War of 1812 when I read this chapter, now doesn't it?" Next, Mr. Carling reads the introduction to the chapter, pausing to reflect on what he has read after he finishes. "Hmm, that refreshes my memory a bit, I'm remembering now hearing somewhere that the War of 1812 was between Canadians and Americans. I'm now going to read through the headings and see if I can get a big picture of where the author is going with this chapter. I want to identify the major topics."

He then flips through the chapter pausing to read each of the major headings aloud and then to "think out loud" about how they relate to one another and what he knows or thinks he knows already. In addition, he looks over various illustrations and text boxes that provide interesting tidbits about the war. After reading aloud the first few lines of one text box, he pauses and says as if to himself, "That's kind of interesting. I didn't know Laura Secord was a real person. Okay, but I need to be careful here; as interesting as that blurb is I don't think it's crucial at the moment. Remember, I'm trying to get a broad sense of what the chapter is about." When Mr. Carling reaches the end of the chapter he reads the chapter summary and then says, "All right, I think I've got a pretty good idea of what this chapter is about. Based on my overview, I'm quite sure, pretty much certain in fact, that I'm going to be learning about the War of 1812, which was a war between Canada and the States, and it looks to me as if we won."

Once he has completed his overview, he discusses the processes he went through. He asks the students if they agree with his assessment and asks them to provide him with reasons for their positions. For instance, when Isabella jumps in and says, "Yes, I totally agree with you," he asks her to explain why she agrees. Isabella says, "Oh that's easy, because the title is 'The War of 1812.'"

After they've spent some time discussing the content of the overview, Mr. Carling says, "Now I want you to think about the thinking I did and the questions I asked and answered as I conducted my overview of the chapter. Can you help me generate a list of things I did?" With guidance from Mr. Carling, the students generate the following to-do list and list of questions to ask and answer for conducting an overview, which he writes on the chalkboard:

Overviewing to-do list:
- Read the title.
- Read the introduction.
- Read the major headings.
- Look at the pictures and other extras (be careful not to get sidetracked).
- Read the conclusion.

Questions to ask and answer when overviewing:
- What does the chapter appear to be about?

continued on next page

- What are some of the major topics?
- Do I know anything about this already?
- How can I use this to help me get ready to read?
- After reading: Was I right?

Finally, after going over a few key vocabulary terms and engaging in an informal discussion with the students centred around what they think they know about the War of 1812, Mr. Carling assigns the chapter for students to read.

Guided practice

After a day working through a series of activities associated with the introductory chapter on the War of 1812, Mr. Carling revisits the overviewing strategy with students. He begins by reminding them about the strategy and his modelling of it. Through discussion, he elicits from the students the goal of the strategy and the major steps involved. Then he tells them that today they will have an opportunity to implement the strategy of overviewing as a class as they prepare for another reading on the War of 1812. After handing out the reading, Mr. Carling asks if anyone can suggest how they might start. Anton answers, "Yeah, we could read the title and talk to ourselves about it like you did the other day." Mr. Carling laughs and says, "Okay, so what would you say to yourself, Anton?" Anton replies, "I'd read the title, 'The War in Upper Canada,' and then I'd say to myself, 'It looks like this is going to be about the part of the war that took place in Upper Canada, wherever that is." Mr. Carling says, "Anton has got us off to a good start. Can someone suggest what we might do next?" Carlos suggests they should be able to get an even better idea about the chapter by reading the introduction.

After reading the introduction aloud and eliciting student thoughts on what it tells them about the chapter, Mr. Carling and the students read the headings and the conclusion, working through the overviewing process together as they go. An important aspect of the guidance provided by Mr. Carling is his continual requests of students to provide the reasoning behind their statements. He wants to be sure that students are not simply randomly guessing about the content, but offering informed guesses based on the text and their background knowledge. When they have completed their overview, students read the text.

The process described above occurs repeatedly over the next few weeks. Each time Mr. Carling assigns a new chapter, he and the students overview it before reading. As the class grows more proficient at this strategy he withdraws from the process, allowing students to take increasing responsibility for its implementation. Moreover, there is a corresponding shift in grouping structures used for the practice sessions, from whole class modelling and practice to small group and ultimately individual practice.

Independent practice

- As students develop fluency with overviewing, Mr. Carling provides opportunities to practice this strategy independently as they seek to learn from texts they are reading for assignment purposes. He has already introduced them to making predictions about what they are about to read, and students are adding this technique to their repertoire of reading comprehension strategies.

they require many opportunities to discuss the texts they read (Pressley et al. 1992). While discussing the content of the texts is important, such discussions should also extend to the process students engaged in while trying to comprehend the text. These discussions should take place in small groups where students discuss both their understandings of the text and the strategies they used to construct those understandings. In the beginning, students will need considerable teacher input, but as they become more capable, the teacher should gradually withdraw his or her support. Teacher support should focus on prompting students to be active readers by asking them to think about the kinds of strategies they should use (Pressley 2002b). For instance, following reading, a teacher might ask students what kinds of strategies would help them retain the important information from the text and why they would use these strategies. After students implement such strategies, the teacher might ask them to share the information and critique the strategies they used to help retain it. Without making these discussions teacher-centred, the teacher should participate by sharing the understandings he or she constructs and by modelling the strategies used to construct them.

Conclusion

Achieving success in social studies requires that students be able to comprehend the texts of the discipline. Unfortunately, many students struggle to read such texts and learn from them if they are not provided with instruction in how to do so. Moreover, despite research supporting its effectiveness, instruction in how to comprehend is not a feature of many social studies classes. It is my hope that this discussion will help social studies teachers make comprehension instruction a meaningful component of the instruction they provide.

I offer five principles to keep in mind while planning and providing this instruction:

- Remember, the purpose of comprehension instruction is to help students better comprehend challenging texts. Comprehension strategies are a means to this end, not an end in themselves.
- Teach a few comprehension strategies well rather than teaching many strategies poorly.
- Provide many opportunities for students to practise the strategies they are learning for real purposes.

- Help students learn to adapt comprehension strategies to their needs, individual preferences, and the text at hand, instead of using them in a lockstep fashion.
- Be patient. It may take several years to become an effective teacher of reading comprehension.

REFERENCES

Alexander, P.A. and T.L. Jetton. 2000. Learning from text: A multidimensional and developmental perspective. In *Handbook of reading research,* vol. III, ed. M.L. Kamil, P.B. Mosenthal, P.D. Pearson, and R. Barr, 285–310. Mahwah, NJ: Lawrence Erlbaum.

Alexander, P.A. and J.E. Judy. 1988. The interaction of domain-specific and strategic knowledge in academic performance. *Review of Educational Research* 58: 375–404.

Anderson, R.C. and P.D. Pearson. 1984. A schema-theoretic view of basic processes in reading. In *Handbook of reading research,* ed. P.D. Pearson, 255–291. New York: Longman.

Baker, L. 1985. How do we know when we don't understand? Standards for evaluating text comprehension. In *Metacognition, cognition, and human performance,* ed. D.L. Forrest-Pressley, G.E. MacKinnon, and T.G. Waller, 155–206. New York: Academic Press.

Baumann, J.F. and P.Q. Ballard. 1987. A two-step model for promoting independence in comprehension. *Journal of Reading* 30: 608–612.

Baumann, J.F. and M.C. Schmitt. 1986. The what, why, how, and when of comprehension instruction. *The Reading Teacher* 39: 640–646.

Collins-Block, C. and M. Pressley, eds. 2002. *Comprehension instruction: Research-based best practices.* New York: Guilford Press.

Dansereau, D.F. 1987. Transfer from cooperative to individual studying. *Journal of Reading* 30: 614–619.

Duke, N. and P.D. Pearson. 2002. Effective practices for developing reading comprehension. In *What research has to say about reading instruction,* 3rd ed., eds. A. Farstrup and J. Samuels, 205–242. Newark, DE: International Reading Association.

Durkin, D. 1978/79. What classroom observations reveal about reading comprehension. *Reading Research Quarterly* 14: 481–533.

Gambrell, L.B., B.A. Kapinus, and R.M. Wilson. 1987. Using mental imagery and summarization to achieve independence in comprehension. *The Journal of Reading* 30: 638–642.

Gersten, R. and D. Carnine. 1986. Direct instruction in reading comprehension. *Educational Leadership* 43: 70–78.

Malone, L.D. and M.A. Mastropieri. 1992. Reading comprehension instruction: Summarization and self-monitoring training for students with learning disabilities. *Exceptional Children* 58: 270–279.

McNeil, J. and L. Donant. 1982. Summarization strategy for improving reading comprehension. In *New inquiries in reading research and instruction,* ed. J.A. Niles and L.A. Harris, 215–219. Rochester, NY: National Reading Conference.

National Reading Panel. 2000. *Teaching children to read: An evidence-based assessment of the scientific research literature on reading and its implications for reading instruction: Reports of the subgroups.* Washington, DC: National Institute of Child Health and Development.

Pearson, P.D. and J.A. Dole. 1987. Explicit comprehension instruction: A review of research and a new conceptualization of instruction. *Elementary School Journal* 88: 151–165.

Pressley, M. 1998. *Reading instruction that works: The case for balanced teaching.* New York: Guilford Press.

———. 2002a. Comprehension strategies instruction: A turn-of-the-century status report. In *Comprehension instruction: Research-based best practices,* ed. C.C. Block and M. Pressley, 11–27. New York: Guilford Press.

———. 2002b. *Reading instruction that works: The case for balanced teaching* (2nd ed.). New York: Guilford Press.

Pressley, M., P. El-Dinary, I. Gaskins, T. Schuder, J.L. Bergman, J. Almasi, and R. Brown. 1992. Beyond direct explanation: Transactional strategies instruction of reading comprehension strategies. *Elementary School Journal* 92: 513–555.

Pressley, M. and R. Wharton-McDonald. 1997. Skilled comprehension instruction and its development through instruction. *School Psychology Review* 26: 448–466.

Roehler, L.R. and G.G. Duffy. 1984. Direct explanation of comprehension processes. In *Comprehension instruction: Perspectives and suggestions,* ed. G.G. Duffy, L.R. Roehler, and J. Mason, 265–280. New York: Longman.

Rosenshine, B., C. Meister, and S. Chapman. 1996. Teaching students to generate questions: A review of the intervention studies. *Review of Educational Research* 66: 181–221.

Schuder, T. 1993. The genesis of transactional strategies instruction in a reading program for at-risk students. *Elementary School Journal* 94: 183–200.

Scott, D., C. Falk, and J. Kierstead. 2002. *Legacies of ancient Egypt.* Richmond, BC: The Critical Thinking Consortium.

Taylor, B.M. and R.W. Beach. 1984. The effect of text structure instruction on middle-grade students' comprehension and production of expository text. *Reading Research Quarterly* 19: 134–146.

Vacca, R.T. and J.L. Vacca. 1999. *Content area reading: Literacy and learning across the curriculum,* 6th ed. New York: Longman.

16

Nurturing Personal and Social Values

Roland Case

The teaching of values is one of the most important yet deeply controversial goals in social studies. Many believe that becoming educated is not simply, or even essentially, a matter of acquiring a body of knowledge, but that the nurturing of personal and social values that will guide our decisions and actions in just and productive ways is equally important. By personal values I mean those that individuals hold about themselves, such as self-esteem, integrity, personal responsibility for one's actions, and pride in one's work. Social values refer to the values that we hold about others and about society generally, including national pride, commitment to justice, respect for law, respect for the environment, and a co-operative and empathetic attitude. Many people see social studies in particular as providing an important opportunity to promote the fundamental values that society requires of its citizens. But despite the central role of values education, which is often referred to as character education (Burrett and Rusnak 1993; Glaze, Hogarth, and McLean 2003), in citizenship, there is considerable controversy about it.[1] The dominant historical objections to the teaching of values in schools revolve around three issues:

- **Should we nurture values?** Should values be taught in school, or should schools be value-free?
- **Which values to nurture and who decides?** Which values are to be promoted in schools? Who selects and defines these values, and on what basis?
- **How should values be nurtured?** What methods can and should teachers use to promote values in a manner that respects the rights of students and parents?

In this chapter, I deal mainly with the last question by exploring three overlapping approaches to promoting personal and social values. But before doing so, I offer a few remarks about the other two questions.

Should We Nurture Values?

In some respects, the question whether teachers should teach values in school is moot. Schools cannot be value-free and teachers cannot avoid promoting values. The fact that we praise children for being honest, thoughtful, and punctual signals the embedded values in our schools. Every time we permit or prohibit certain behaviour, we implicitly promote certain values over others: school rules against fighting or throwing rocks, for example, attest to how we value individual well-being and the protection of property. Such rules inevitably affect the values that students develop.

Whether educators want to or not, inevitably, through either the explicit curriculum or the "hidden curriculum"—the implicit norms and values that are promoted, often unintentionally, through the way we run our schools and conduct our classes—we influence student values and attitudes. For example, if we mark students' work for neatness or praise them for asking probing questions, we are encouraging them to act in particular ways; if we do not reinforce neatness or an inquiring attitude, we implicitly tell students that these behaviours are not valued. Such is the case with everything we do (or do not do) in school. The only real choice teachers have about promoting values is whether their influence will be largely hidden and inadvertent or explicit and systematic.

In an interesting article, Daniel Duke (1978) illustrates how schools may affect students' attitudes in unintended and undesirable ways. He suggests that many students may develop a cynical attitude towards our legal system because of common school practices. We can appreciate the hidden lessons schools teach students about the fairness of our system of laws by contrasting the espoused civic ideals with the regulatory practices that actually operate in many schools. Duke concludes that it is difficult for students to develop respect for law and principled behaviour if their experiences in school, which is the first and most extensive public institution young citizens encounter, consistently reinforce the opposite. Table

16.1 contrasts the rhetoric about the rule of law with the practices that Duke saw actually operating in many schools.

Ultimately, decisions about values issues—including whether schools should intentionally teach values—should be subjected to rational scrutiny. Teachers must thoughtfully assess the pros and cons before making their decision. Table 16.2 lists competing reasons for and against the intentional teaching of values in schools. It is interesting to note that, at least according to this list, the majority of objections to teaching values intentionally are not against the idea *per se*, but are concerns about which values to promote and how to do so responsibly. These are the issues to which I now turn.

TABLE 16.1   WHAT SCHOOLS "TEACH" ABOUT OUR LEGAL SYSTEM

WE TELL STUDENTS...	YET, OFTEN IN SCHOOLS...
• that we live in a society based on democratic principles	• school rules tend to be determined by those least subject to their application
• that all people are to be treated equally before the law	• many teachers fail to enforce school rules consistently
• that the punishment should be reasonable and that it should fit the crime	• the consequences for disobeying school rules frequently lack logical relationships to the offences; for example, the punishment for skipping classes is often suspension from school
• that society is committed to safeguarding the rights of individuals against abuse by the state	• students have few options if they disagree with a claim brought against them by school authorities
• that no one is above the law	• teachers frequently fail to model the rule-governed behaviour they expect of their students

TABLE 16.2   SHOULD SCHOOLS INTENTIONALLY PROMOTE VALUES?

REASONS FOR	REASONS AGAINST
• Teaching about values is part of the school's mandate. Official rationales for public education typically refer to the need to develop the values of productive citizenship. For example, the Ontario Ministry of Education (2004, 2) identifies the need to "develop attitudes that will motivate them [students] to use their knowledge and skills in a responsible manner." Alberta Learning (2003, 2) lists a number of values and attitudes that are necessary for active and responsible citizens, including respecting the dignity and equality of all human beings, social compassion, fairness, justice, honouring and valuing the traditions and symbols that are the expressions of Canadian identity, and valuing lifelong learning.	• Values promoted in schools may conflict with those shared by individual parents, local communities, or society more generally.
• Teaching values is a precondition for many other objectives in the curriculum: knowledge and skills cannot be developed without accompanying value components. For example, students will learn little if they do not have self-esteem, curiosity, and open-mindedness. Students will be unable to work co-operatively unless they have some respect for the feelings of others, are willing to play by the rules, and so on.	• Students may be indoctrinated into accepting values that are essentially individual in nature (that is, teachers may fail to respect individual students' freedom of conscience or right to their personal inclinations).
• Many important values need attention, and schools have a significant, perhaps unique, opportunity to make a difference. If racism and discrimination are promoted within some families, how will these undesirable—and in some cases illegal—values be countered if not by the educational system?	• Despite their best intentions, it is feared that schools will do a poor job of promoting values (for example, instead of teaching about equality, schools may unintentionally promote condescending attitudes towards various cultural or racial groups).
	• Values often raise extremely sensitive issues that may profoundly upset students.
	• Because values may be controversial, actively promoting them may, in certain circumstances, present a professional risk for the teacher (for example, the teacher may become embroiled in a controversy).

Which Values to Nurture?

There are no simple answers for determining which values to promote intentionally in schools. Nevertheless, it is useful to consider the degree of consensus about the value (although this is by no means the only criterion, it is a promising starting point). On one end of the spectrum are values (especially very general values) that are widely acknowledged as acceptable or even highly desirable attributes of citizens. Honesty, pride in one's work, concern for the well-being of others, and respect for the property of others are examples of values that would likely have broad public support. A justification for including these values in the public education curriculum derives from the notion of *in loco parentis*—the notion that schools must, to some extent, take up the role and act on behalf of parents. Promoting certain values can be seen as an extension of the type of upbringing that reasonable parents would wish for their children. As was suggested in the 1931 Hadow report: "What a wise and good parent would desire for his [or her] children, a national educational system must desire for all children" (cited in Cassidy, 1994).

The kinds of personal and social values listed below seem indispensable for healthy human existence and would likely be broadly supported. No doubt some may object to these suggestions or insist on adding other essential values. This list is drawn largely from the values advocated fifty years ago by a social studies curriculum committee, cited by Ralph Tyler in his classic book on curriculum design (1969, 92–93). Promoting these values, at least in general terms, is unlikely to conflict with broadly held parental or community values, although from time to time individual parents and community members may not share them. This "consensus" list may serve as the starting point for identifying the values to be nurtured in schools.

Personal values
- acceptance of self; realization of one's own worth
- integrity, honesty, and frankness with self
- sense of hopefulness about the future
- willingness to seek adventure; sense of mission
- desire to make a productive contribution to society
- love of truth, however disconcerting
- respect for work well done
- appreciation of beauty in art and the environment
- pride in family and ethnic background
- personal hygiene and health
- self-discipline and self-direction
- independent-mindedness (the courage of one's convictions).

Social values
- respect for the dignity and worth of every human being
- commitment to equal opportunity for all
- tolerance and kindness
- desire for justice for all
- acceptance of social responsibility
- commitment to free thought, expression, and worship
- commitment to peaceful resolution of problems
- respect for privacy
- national pride
- environmental stewardship
- fair-mindedness
- concern for well-being of animals
- respect for the rule of law.

At the other end of the spectrum are personal and social values that are profoundly controversial, particularly positions or attitudes on specific issues such as abortion, same-sex parenting, affirmative action, and capital punishment. In these cases, since society generally is sharply divided, teachers should assume that there may not be a single most acceptable position; well-informed, thoughtful people may not share the same values. In such cases, if the issue is to be raised (and it may be that in many communities some value questions are too controversial to be raised in school), the objective should not be to promote a specific position, but rather to encourage students to the extent feasible to make up their own minds after thoughtful consideration. The teachers' responsibility would be to act in a respectful and fair manner, seeking to instill appreciation of the need for sensitivity when dealing with divisive issues and to facilitate students' gathering and assessing information pro and con before deciding for themselves. A fair manner may not mean that teachers devote identical attention to all sides. If students are already well aware of one side, it may be necessary to spend more effort helping them to see other sides. However, it should be clear that teachers are not favouring a side because it reflects their own position, but rather to ensure that students see all important viewpoints. Because students may be unduly influenced by their teachers, it is important to consider under what conditions teachers should withhold their own personal positions from students.

Many values are largely matters of personal inclination, such as the dictates of religious conscience, life choices, political affiliations, and personal aspiration. In schools that are committed to cultural and political pluralism, it is inappropriate to espouse or favour the values of one religious or political ideology over those of others. Consequently, it would be inappropriate, for example, to act as former US vice-president George H.W. Bush advised when he encouraged schools to teach about the law so as to "combat criticism of our representative government" (reported in American Bar

Association 1982, 1). As Ken Osborne notes, "a well-informed, democratic and interested citizen need not be supportive of government policies" (1982, 59). Since in these matters there is no agreed-upon "correct" set of values (nor should there be), the teacher's role is to encourage students to explore and clarify these values for themselves. Although teachers should not presume which conclusions students will reach about these values, there may be considerable merit in providing them with opportunities to examine their own belief systems.

Teachers' concerns about indoctrinating or imposing personal beliefs may be reduced by resolving to encourage students to make up their own minds about values on which there is little agreement, and by communicating this commitment to parents, which may help alleviate suspicion and opposition. Yet some issues divide communities deeply, and taking the open-minded view may not satisfy everyone. Our dilemma is, on the one hand, a responsibility to develop students' ability to engage with and resolve value issues in non-violent, thoughtful ways, and on the other, a responsibility to respect, within limits, the parents' right to raise their children as they see fit. Ultimately, these decisions are matters of professional judgment—of deciding what is most defensible in light of the needs and rights of the individuals and groups whom educators have a responsibility to serve. The more contested or individualistic the value, the more sensitive and vigilant teachers must be about empowering students to make up their own minds thoughtfully, and about parents' right to be informed about and direct their children's education.

Merely because some values may be inappropriate in schools and others, if addressed at all, must be handled with extreme sensitivity, does not mean that there are values about which consensus among reasonable people cannot be reached. I believe there are many such personal and social values that are essential components of any social studies curriculum. And there may be many others that, if taught appropriately, have a legitimate place in public education.

> Take a moment to think of the five most important values— social or personal—that you would want to nurture in your classroom. Consider why you think these are so important. What might you do to reinforce and model these values in your teaching?

What Methods Should Be Used?

So much has been written on teaching about values that it is difficult to get a handle on this field. For our purposes, I believe it useful to focus on three broad approaches:

- creating classroom and school environments that reinforce desired values;
- facilitating direct "emotive" experiences that evoke desired sensitivities;
- engaging students in thoughtful deliberation about their values.

Although they will be discussed separately, these approaches overlap and should be mutually supportive.

CREATING REINFORCING ENVIRONMENTS

Values do not develop in a vacuum. In fact, they are more likely to be nurtured by the subtle yet pervasive influences operating within a social environment than they are by short-lived instructional techniques. The literature on the hidden curriculum attests to the power of environmental conditions in supporting or inhibiting the acquisition of attitudes. For example, the tone or atmosphere in a classroom is overwhelmingly cited as a primary factor in developing social attitudes (Leming 1991, Patrick and Hoge 1991). Studies reported by Judith Torney-Purta (1983) indicate that the particular content of the curriculum is less influential in developing students' political attitudes than is establishing a classroom climate where students feel free and have opportunities to express their opinions. Teacher behaviour is especially important in signalling to students what really counts. Teachers who are open-minded are more likely to foster these attributes in their students. Similarly, teachers who sincerely demonstrate their empathy for others are more likely to nurture empathetic tendencies in their students. There may be no more effective way of promoting values than by sincerely and consistently communicating to students through our actions that certain values matter. Examples of teacher behaviour, expectations, and activities that reinforce concern for others are suggested below:

Student expectations and activities

- A code of rules or principles of behaviour towards fellow students is clearly articulated and closely enforced.
- Verbal or physical abuse of students by students is as unacceptable as verbal or physical abuse of teachers by students.
- Good deeds by students are acknowledged.
- Students are frequently engaged in role reversals where they are asked to think of how others might feel in various situations.
- Students are frequently asked to express why they care or do not care about events or people that may seem remote from their lives.

- Students are invited to participate in projects in which they do something positive for others.

Teacher modelling

- The teacher refrains from put-downs and sarcasm, and is always conscious of treating students (and colleagues) with the utmost respect and deference.
- The teacher is willing to admit error, either publicly or privately, and attempts to redress the action if he or she treats a student unfairly.
- The teacher will often undertake random acts of kindness.
- The teacher is seen by students as a caring person with compassion for their concerns and difficulties.

FACILITATING DIRECT EXPERIENCES

A second approach to nurturing personal and social values is to provide opportunities for students to "feel" the effect of caring for such values. Unlike a reinforcing environment, whose goal is to habituate students gradually to particular frames of mind, direct experiences provide students with opportunities to encounter for themselves, vividly and emphatically, the power and merit of certain ways of being. Often these experiences will open students' minds and hearts to perspectives they would otherwise miss or downplay. There are at least three types of direct experiences that nurture values: vicarious, simulated, and first-hand.

- **Vicarious experiences.** To live vicariously is to encounter life through the experiences of another. Film and literature—both fiction and non-fiction—are especially effective in this regard. Vicarious experiences allow students to live the lives of others and in doing so to ex-

perience the power of feeling and caring about matters that may otherwise be foreign or remote. Susan Inman, a teacher at Windermere Secondary School in Vancouver, uses a National Film Board video, *Where the Spirit Lives*, to enhance student sensitivity to the feelings and concerns of First Nations individuals. Prior to viewing this moving film about the plight and courage of First Nations students in residential schools, several of her students had shown indifference, perhaps even callousness, to First Nations people. The video personalized—put a profoundly human face to—what were previously stereotypical images. I remember as an elementary student being moved profoundly by a historical novel about the Jesuit martyr, Isaac Jogues. Although I have since tempered my feelings towards these missionaries, I have never lost my sense of admiration for individuals who are so committed to a principle that they are willing to endure great hardship and sacrifice. At the primary level, children's stories provide powerful vehicles to invite the young to consider important values. The highlighted text, "Values-Based Stories for Primary Children," illustrates a few of the many thousands of stories that can serve this purpose. (See chapter 29 in this volume for more ideas on the use of literature in social studies.)

- **Simulated and role-play experiences.** Drama, role play, and other simulations allow students to adopt and act out the predicaments of others. One of the most famous examples of a simulated experience was described in the award-winning documentary *The Eye of the Storm* (Peters 1987). In an effort to help her grade 3 students appreciate the consequences of bigotry, Jane Elliott began, without announcing she was going to do so, to discriminate against the blue-eyed children in her class, and the

VALUES-BASED STORIES FOR PRIMARY CHILDREN

Students are introduced to the unfairness of inequitable sharing of jobs through *Piggybook* by Anthony Browne (1986). It describes a mother who does all the household chores until she leaves home for a short time and the rest of the family learns to recognize their selfish behaviour. After discussing the unfairness of this situation, students list jobs done at home and develop criteria for assigning responsibility for them in their own family or in an imaginary family. Students are invited to decide on a new job they will undertake at home or at school. A week or so after assuming their new tasks, students report on their experiences and receive a note of appreciation for their efforts.

Students explore the idea of doing more than they are expected to do through *The Gardener* by Sarah Stewart (1997). In this story, a young girl undertakes a project to cheer up her sombre uncle. Using events from the story, students

learn to distinguish acts of kindness from jobs that people have a responsibility to carry out. Students then discuss and apply the criteria for an act of kindness before choosing and implementing an appropriate action for a family or community member. When the kind actions are completed, students discuss their contributions to the happiness of others.

The story *Fly Away Home* by Eve Bunting (1991) tells how a homeless boy is given hope after seeing a trapped bird find its freedom. It is the anchor for a lesson on developing empathy for homeless people, exploring ways in which students might help them. Students listen to the story, then compare their own lives to that of the main character. After discussing the difficulties that homeless people experience, students select three helpful items that they personally would recommend giving to a shelter.[2]

next day discriminated against the brown-eyed children. Students were moved by the unfairness of this contact with prejudice. In a follow-up documentary, *A Class Divided*, filmed almost fifteen years after the simulation, the students in Elliot's class described the profound influence the earlier experience had in shaping their values.

- **First-hand experiences.** Powerful, evocative experiences need not be second-hand. Students can encounter value-nurturing situations in real-life contexts through guest speakers, field trips, exchanges, pen pals, and social-action projects. A skilled guest speaker can do much to change student attitudes. Certainly many of my own stereotypical attitudes towards ethnic and racial groups were exploded when I first encountered articulate and impassioned individuals from these groups. Social-action projects can also be important value-nurturing experiences. As Mary-Wynne Ashford reports in her article "Youth Actions for the Planet" (1995), involvement in environmental and humanitarian projects can counter the global hopelessness prevalent among many students.

To illustrate the power of role-play experiences, imagine the effects of the activity "The Eporuvians Come to Call," described in the highlighted text, in helping students empathize with what others may feel about perceived inequities. A 1986 Australian Broadcasting Corporation film entitled *Babakiueria*—a phonetic spelling of "barbecue area"—offers a similar reversal of perspective with aboriginal explorers discovering a group of white inhabitants in a campground.

Experiences such as these—whether brought about vicariously, through simulation, or in first-hand encounters—help to evoke students' sensitivities to important values. The point is not to manipulate students into a particular perspective, but to ensure that students who may be self-absorbed will experience other predicaments and feelings.

THE EPORUVIANS COME TO CALL[3]

The following three scenarios are intended to evoke empathy for the historical treatment of First Nations people. The teacher reads an imaginary scene and allows students time to reflect (and write) about their thoughts before proceeding to the next scene.

Scene 1: You're playing in your backyard when a group of odd-looking men dressed in strange clothes walks into your yard. They look dirty and hungry, and are shouting and gesturing in a strange language. They try hard to communicate with you, but you can't understand them. You can tell, though, that what they are saying is important.

Not knowing what else to do, and because they look hungry, you invite them into your house and give them some cake and tea. Soon you are able to communicate with them using hand signals and gestures. You still don't know what they want, but you begin to understand that they are from a far away land called Eporue. They really like your town and they want to stay.

- How would you feel? Scared? Flattered? Angry? Friendly? Annoyed? Curious? Excited?
- What would you do? Would you help them out? Ask them to leave?

Scene 2: Imagine that you welcome the Eporuvians. After all, you want to be helpful, and they seem so lost. You let them stay in your house, and you keep feeding them. You show them around the town and introduce them to your friends. You begin to notice, however, that they have a disagreeable habit of taking your things. All in all, they don't seem too considerate. You begin to wonder whether making friends with them was such a good idea after all. You also start to wonder if these house guests will ever leave.

After a while, you begin to realize that they want to keep living in your house and taking your things. In fact, they think that they own the place—and the land it's on, too. They stick the Eporuvian flag in the ground, and claim your yard for their leader.

- What would you do? Organize your friends to drive them out? Try to reason with them? Trick them into leaving? Give up and be friends?
- How would you feel? Scared? Angry? Puzzled? Disappointed?

Scene 3: By now, they don't bother talking to you much anymore, except when they want something from you. They bring their relatives, and lots of other Eporuvians, to live in your town. Eventually, they tell you and your family to leave, and give you a broken-down shack to live in, with no yard, no running water, and lots of other people crowded into it (who have all been forced off their land as well).

You never get your land back. For two hundred years, the story of how the Eporuvians forced you off your land is handed down. You tell your children, who tell their children, and so on, for ten generations.

- How will your descendants feel about the Eporuvians? Would you call them heroes or villains?
- If you were a descendant of the Eporuvians, how would you feel about what happened? Would you feel any responsibility to extend friendship to these people?

PROMOTING THOUGHTFUL DELIBERATION

The third approach to values education encourages students to think about their attitudes. On its own, it will rarely be sufficient in itself, and perhaps may not be the best first step in promoting such change. But we are in danger of manipulating and indoctrinating students if at some point we do not encourage them to reflect on the implications and significance of their values. Eventually, students must thoughtfully make up their own minds. Generally speaking, the deliberative approach to attitude development has two strands:

- **values clarification**, wherein the objective is to help students clarify the values they hold and the implications of these values for other aspects of their lives; and
- **values analysis**, which proposes a more critical examination of student values and in which students assess the adequacy of the reasoning behind their value stances.

VALUES CLARIFICATION

Louis Raths, Merrill Harmin, and Sidney Simon (1966) are the best-known proponents of the values clarification approach, although many others have espoused it and it is widely evident in current educational practice. Its underlying premise is that individuals experience dissonance as a result of their being unclear, confused, or uncommitted to their values. Since values are seen to be an intensely personal and emotional matter, the teacher's role is to help students overcome this dissonance by inviting them to clarify and affirm their own values. This approach identifies three features of a sincerely held value:

- **choosing**: individuals must choose their values by considering the implications of a range of alternatives, without pressure or influence from others;
- **prizing**: once chosen, individuals should be happy with the choice and be willing to publicly affirm the value;
- **acting**: individuals should act consistently to reaffirm and strengthen their commitment to the value.

The teacher's primary responsibility is to encourage students to clarify their own values for themselves. Teachers facilitate this process by organizing activities that stimulate students to think about their values, and by providing occasions for students to publicly affirm, celebrate, and act on them. This was very much the approach followed in the previously mentioned use of literature to invite young students to consider what action, if any, they would like to adopt in response to a situation described in the story (for example, unfair allocation of tasks, people in need). In helping students clarify, teachers might ask questions that invite students to identify their values, to think about the personal meaning and implications, and to consider the consistency of their words and deeds through the use of clarifying questions such as the following:

- Is this something you value?
- How did you feel when it happened?
- What are some good things about it?
- Have you thought much about it?
- Where does this idea lead? What are its consequences?
- Do you do anything about it?
- Is what you have just said consistent with … [a previous action or comment]?

Other clarifying activities include inviting students to rank-order alternatives or locate values on a continuum and to reflect on and discuss provocative statements, problems, or issues posed by the teacher. Concurrent with activities to clarify values would be opportunities to publicly affirm and act on them. A classic values clarification activity, described in "A Personal Coat of Arms," is to create a personal coat of arms in which students symbolically represent and share their most cherished values.

VALUES ANALYSIS

Unlike the values clarification approach where the focus is on students personally clarifying their choices through reflection and action, the focus of values analysis is on students critically examining their value assumptions and reasoning. This latter approach holds that on their own students may not always see the gaps or inadequacies in their thinking and that students actually may hold discriminatory or prejudicial attitudes. As long as students are consistent and willing to act on them, the values clarification approach would find these values acceptable. Values analysis holds that some values may be unreasonable and that even if students sincerely hold them, they should be helped to seeing the position's limitations. This is especially important with social or ethical values: those we hold towards others. The similarities between the values analysis and values clarification approaches should not be overlooked. Both respect the importance of students making up their own minds after thoughtful consideration. The main difference is that the values analysis approach wants to teach students to think critically about their values, especially their ethical values. These values are seen to be far less private a matter than is presumed by the values clarification approach.

The Association for Values Education and Research (AVER) that used to operate at the University of British Columbia was a prominent advocate of the values analysis approach. AVER's work provides a structure to help teachers and students reflect on their values more critically. The AVER

A PERSONAL COAT OF ARMS

A popular values clarification project is to have students create a personal coat of arms that symbolically represents the values that each holds dear. The project integrates well with social studies units on knights and chivalry, First Nations peoples, patriotism and nationalism, cultural heritage, personal growth, and self-esteem. The undertaking can be more or less ambitious, but since the purpose is to help students identify and celebrate their own values, there is merit in taking the time to ensure that the project fosters self-discovery and personal pride.

- **Creating context.** Introduce the project by drawing attention to the historical and contemporary uses of coats of arms and heraldry (for example, First Nations, medieval and contemporary nobility, national flags, university and family crests). Explain that many citizens treat their national flag with great reverence because it is a symbol of their homeland. They may be outraged when people burn or trample on the flag. Soldiers carry the flag into battle as a symbol of what they are fighting to protect. Desecrating a flag or other personal crest shows disrespect or scorn for that person or group's cherished values. Ask students to consider for a moment the values they would fight to promote or protect.
- **Identifying the values.** Depending on the time available and student level, the crest may contain one or two panels only, although a crest will usually contain between four and six panels, each representing a different value. An outline of a coat of arms such as the sample represented here may be provided to students, either as a working copy (that is, as a prototype for a poster-size design that they will eventually create) or as the final copy. Typically, the teacher establishes the number of panels and the themes. The following are common themes for panels:

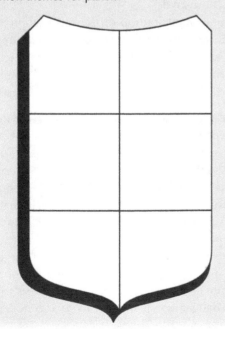

- most cherished family characteristic or event
- most cherished ethnic/cultural characteristic or event
- most cherished national characteristic or event
- most cherished personal character trait(s)
- most cherished character trait(s) sought in one's friends
- most significant personal accomplishment(s) to date
- personal motto or guiding principle
- most significant personal aspiration(s)
- most significant contribution(s) one could make to one's friends or family
- most significant contribution(s) one could make to the world at large
- what one would hope to be remembered by—one's epitaph.

Selection of the themes should be guided by the specific goals of the project. For example, if increased cross-cultural awareness is an objective, then the first and second values on the above list would be especially relevant.

- **Exploring the values.** Once the themes have been established, students should then be assisted to explore thoughtfully what this means for them personally. Again, depending on the specific themes, students might be assigned one or more of the following tasks:
  - interview a relative about his or her family or ethnic background;
  - read about individuals who exhibit character traits that they admire;
  - as a class, brainstorm a list of character traits or life goals, and rank-order their priorities;
  - think about what they would do if they had one year to live and were guaranteed success in whatever they attempted;
  - discuss with others who know them well what is seen to be their strengths and ambitions.
- **Representing one's values.** Although words may be appropriate in some panels (for example, a personal motto or epitaph), a coat of arms' impact lies in its symbolic representation. Depending on student level, simple drawings, photographs, or magazine illustrations on regular-sized paper may suffice. Alternatively, students might be asked to create a shield-sized poster.

  Regardless of size, the effect is more powerful if students spend time exploring different types of symbols, including corporate logos (for example, the Nike "swish" represents the wing of the goddess Victory, and victory in Italian is *nike*) and national flags and crests (the dramatic rising sun in the Imperial Japanese flag, the olive branches of peace caressing the globe in the United Nations flag). It is especially valuable to point out the symbolism in each design (a dove symbolizes peace, lions symbolize courage). The significance of particular colours may also be explored

continued on next page

approach (1978, 1991) is based on a reconstruction of the logic of value reasoning into three elements:

- **the value judgment:** a statement about what the person judges to be desirable or undesirable or what ought, or ought not, to be (for example, "School is horrible" or "School should be illegal");

- **the factual evidence to support the judgment:** a descriptive or factual statement of what actually is, was, or is likely to be, which is seen to be relevant to the judgment taken ("I have to work very hard in school");

- **the implied or underlying value principle:** the more general value position that the person has accepted implicitly by virtue of the factual reason offered ("Situations that force people to work very hard are horrible—or ought to be made illegal").

When students offer and defend a position on a value issue (for example, whether it is wrong to tell a white lie, or whether Canada should accept more immigrants), their reasoning can be reconstructed using these elements into deductive arguments, consisting of a major premise (the implied value principle), a minor premise (the factual evidence), and a conclusion (the value judgment). For example, a student might offer the following judgment on the desirability of increased immigration quotas: "It's stupid for the Canadian government to increase immigration levels." When asked to provide factual evidence to support this conclusion, the student might respond: "The more new immigrants we accept, the more current residents are out of work." The implied value principle that the student must accept if the reasoning is to be valid is that "The Canadian government should not adopt policies that cause unemployment among Canadian residents." This reasoning can be roughly translated into the following syllogism:

Major premise (implied value principle)	The government should not adopt polices that cause unemployment among Canadian residents.
Minor premise (factual evidence)	Increasing immigration quotas causes unemployment among Canadian residents.
Conclusion (value judgment)	Therefore, the government should not increase immigration quotas.

The point of reconstructing value reasoning in this way is to provide teachers with three points at which to help students think critically about their views. Students can be taught to query whether or not: (1) the major premise (implied value principle) is acceptable, (2) the minor premise (factual evidence) is factually true, and (3) the conclusion (value judgment) follows from the premises, especially when all of the reasons are considered.

The unique contribution of the AVER approach is the tests or challenges that students and teachers can apply in assessing the acceptability of the implied value principle. University of British Columbia professor Jerrold Coombs (1980) has identified four ways to challenge our principles:

- **Consistency with other basic values.** An obvious test of the acceptability of an implied principle is whether or not it is consistent with other more basic tenets in one's own value system. It would not be justifiable to accept a principle that is inconsistent with one's fundamental values. For example, if I believe it wrong to discriminate against people on the basis of race, then I would be inconsistent in accepting a principle that suggested that white immigrants be given priority. Similarly, if I believe that the lives of people ought to be placed above money, then I would not be consistent if I rejected refugees whose lives were in danger merely in order to save tax dollars.

- **Consequences for everyone involved.** A second way to evaluate the acceptability of implied principle is to assess the consequences of adopting it for all of the people likely to be affected, especially those likely to be the most significantly affected. Students should take on these others' perspectives and ask: "How would I feel if I were in someone else's shoes? Would I judge the principle to be fair from that perspective?" If I would find it unfair to accept the implied principle if I were in someone else's position, then that is a reason for not finding the principle acceptable. Even young children use this test when they ask, "How would you like it if I did that to you?"
- **Consequences in other relevant situations.** A third way to test an implied principle is to consider the consequences in other similar situations. If using the implied principle in these situations would be undesirable, then this is a reason for rejecting or at least modifying it. Consider, for example, the implied principle that it is always wrong to tell a lie. It would be appropriate to imagine situations where telling a lie might be justified. Suppose I were living in Nazi Germany during World War II. Would I consider it wrong to lie to soldiers who asked if there were any Jewish people living in my house? If I think I am justified in lying in this situation then I should modify my implied principle to something like "It is wrong to lie unless it is to protect someone's life." It would then be useful to imagine situations that were not a matter of saving a life but in which I would still consider lying acceptable. The point of the test is to explore other situations where the same principle might apply to determine if I can accept the consequences of adopting the principle in these situations. If not, then the principle needs to be modified or rejected.
- **Consequences for repeated instances.** A final way to test the acceptability of an implied principle is by supposing that repeated instances of a situation were to occur. If the consequences of repeated applications are unacceptable, with no rational way to justify allowing only some instances of the act, then fairness requires preventing everyone from acting in that way. For example, although it may not be particularly undesirable for one person to walk across grass in a park or to throw a cigarette butt on the ground, the effect of everyone doing it is ruined grass or horrible litter. The philosopher Marcus Singer (1958, 162) refers to this as the generalization argument: "If the consequences of everyone's acting in a certain way would be undesirable, then no one has the right to act in that way without a reason or justification."

Each test would need to be explained to students, perhaps introduced one at a time. Students need to learn when a test is likely to be relevant, perhaps by having students apply a particular test to a list of principles that has been supplied to them.[4]

To illustrate how the AVER approach can help students think more critically about their value positions, the highlighted text, "Reasoning About Canada's Immigration Quotas," outlines a six-step model for values analysis applied to the issue of Canada's immigration quotas.

As I hope this discussion of the AVER approach indicates, there is need to teach students how to think critically about their values. Although there are multiple approaches to values education—classroom environment, direct experiences, and values clarification—teachers ultimately must encourage students to reflect critically on their values, especially on their social or ethical values: those pertaining to how others are to be treated.

Concluding Remarks

I want to close this chapter on values education with a plea for two virtues: sensitivity and perseverance. Although we should be sensitive to our students in all that we do, there is particular need for caution when dealing with values. Not only are values rife with controversy, they are deeply tied to students' feelings. We have a special responsibility to enter into this domain with the greatest of sensitivity for our students.

The consequences of a failure in this regard were demonstrated to me while visiting a high school in New York City several years ago. I had been invited to observe a lesson where an abbreviated version of the personal coat of arms activity described earlier was introduced. The teacher opened the lesson by sharing a personal coat of arms he had made. It was sketched in pencil on a regular sheet of paper and, consequently, was not readily visible to students. He explained to the class the four panels on his coat of arms, and assigned students to develop their own. The values they were to represent were an aspect from their cultural background, their favourite food, their favourite activity, and the epitaph they would like for their headstone. Their coats of arms were to be photocopied so that he could hand them out. Students were given only a few minutes to think about and sketch a symbol to represent each value. A male student asked if he could complete the activity at home, but he was told to finish it before the end of class. He then volunteered to come back after school to complete the assignment, whereupon the teacher suggested that if he just got down to work immediately he would be finished in no time. With fifteen minutes remaining in the period, the teacher randomly divided the class into groups of four. Students were to explain their coat of arms to the other three members of their group. In one group, I noticed the sole

REASONING ABOUT CANADA'S IMMIGRATION QUOTAS

- **Identify and clarify the issue under discussion.** Before getting too far into a topic, students need to be precise about the issue. For example, is the dispute over the criteria for selecting new immigrants or the size of annual quotas of immigrants allowed into Canada? Students need to understand that Canada sets quotas for three classes of immigrants: (1) refugees who are fleeing political oppression or desperate conditions; (2) family immigrants who are applying to be reunited with their relatives; and (3) independent immigrants who have no political or family claims (many of whom are wealthy applicants willing to invest in Canadian businesses).

- **Generate possible factual reasons, pro and con.** Once an issue is clarified, students should consider the reasons, pro and con. It is important that the reasons be framed as factual or description statements (that is, what actually is, was, or is likely to happen). Individually or as a class, students may list pro reasons down one column and con reasons down the other column, as illustrated below. Issue: Should Canada increase its immigrant quotas for:
  - refugees?
  - family class immigrants?
  - independent immigrants?

PRO	CON
<ul><li>many immigrants may be in desperate economic need</li><li>many immigrants may need protection from war and political persecution</li><li>increased immigration adds to the population size of Canada</li><li>increased immigration results in enriched lives and lifestyle for many new immigrants</li><li>many immigrants bring talents and human resources that benefit Canada</li><li>immigrants provide a pool of workers to fill low paid jobs that may otherwise go unfilled</li><li>increased immigration helps to unite separated families</li><li>increased immigration adds to Canada's cultural diversity.</li></ul>	<ul><li>many Canadians may feel invaded by more immigrants</li><li>many immigrants take advantage of the system</li><li>immigrants drain money away from other Canadians through increased need for social programs</li><li>increased immigration leads to overcrowding in some areas</li><li>increased immigration drives down the minimum wage</li><li>increased immigration discourages integration of ethnic groups into mainstream society</li><li>increased immigration fuels racial/ethnic tensions</li><li>increased immigration leads to higher housing prices</li><li>increased immigration will lead to the European culture becoming a minority in Canada</li><li>increased immigration will lead to the white race becoming a minority in Canada.</li></ul>

- **Investigate the accuracy of the factual claims offered.** Students should be discouraged from accepting at face value the factual reasons they offer. Often, students will have little evidence for their beliefs and, in some cases, their beliefs may be inaccurate or only partly true. For example, it is not obvious that increasing immigration drains money away from current residents. One of the government's motives for increased immigration is providing a larger consumer base of support for domestic industries and businesses. As well, Canada saves money if it accepts immigrants who have already been trained as, say, medical doctors or computer analysts, rather than educate candidates domestically. After seeking evidence students should, where appropriate, modify or reject suggested reasons. For example, the claim that immigrants drain money may be found to be clearly false in the case of independent immigrants, or the suggestion that increased immigration leads to higher house prices may be false in the case of refugees.

- **Test the acceptability of each implied principle.** With each factual reason that is thought to be true, students should be helped to identify the implied value principle by reconstructing the logic of their reasoning into a deductive argument. For example, the principle implied by the argument that many Canadians may feel invaded by increased immigration goes something like this: "The government should not adopt policies that cause Canadian residents to feel a sense of invasion." Students would then apply to each of the implied values one or more of the principle tests discussed earlier. Principles found to be unacceptable should be modified or rejected. Three of the tests are useful in assessing the acceptability of the above-mentioned principle:

  - *Consequences for everyone involved.* Students should endeavour to put themselves in the position of someone whose parents live in another country but who cannot immigrate because other Canadian residents feel somewhat invaded. Or put themselves in the position of someone who is in danger of being tortured in their home country if their application for refugee status is rejected simply because some Canadian residents may feel invaded. Would students still think it fair to accept this principle if they were in these peoples' predicaments? If not, then the principle should be modified or rejected.

- *Consequences in other relevant situations.* Students should endeavour to think of a different government policy they support, but that many people might find invasive. Perhaps the issue is mandatory seat belts. Would students be willing to give up on the policy merely because many Canadians resent having to wear seat belts? If not, then they do not accept the principle that merely because people feel invaded, policies should be scrapped.
- *Consequences for repeated instances.* Students should consider the consequences if every government policy were to be scrapped because many people feel invaded. Would governments be able to act at all if this principle was accepted? There are few, if any, policies, including limits on gun control, smoke-free areas, and anti-discrimination laws, that would not threaten some group. The consequence of the implied principle, if accepted, might be that governments could never implement any policy.

- **Weigh all remaining (valid) reasons, pro and con.** After eliminating the reasons that are unwarranted because of unacceptable implied principles, the next step is to assess the collective weight of the remaining reasons. This involves deciding the importance of the values underlying each one (the implied principles) and the extent to which each position affects these values. For example, students must consider whether a relatively modest loss of economic benefit to current residents should be given priority over the life-and-death protection afforded political refugees whose lives may be in danger.
- **Present and defend a judgment on the issue.** Finally, students should determine their own stand on the issue. This may be a simple for-or-against position, but more often it will be a qualified stance. For example, students might decide that immigration quotas should be increased in some areas and decreased in other areas, or that quotas should be increased across the board, provided immigration fraud is reduced. Students would be expected to demonstrate how their position is the stronger alternative and how it accommodates the valid concerns of the opposing perspective.

female student being ignored by the three male students in her group. She sat the entire time with her coat of arms in her slightly outstretched arms, waiting to be invited by the others to explain her cherished values.

This values lesson was not sensitively handled. The young woman's self-esteem was damaged that day. The male student who wanted to take his coat of arms home to do a proper job learned that "getting it done" was the main thing. And the personal pride of everyone in the class was diminished by having their values treated in such a slapdash fashion and trivialized by such banal questions.

And now a point about perseverance. In talking about the slow pace of significant educational change, Ralph Tyler likens teachers' efforts to the effect of dripping water upon a stone: "In a day or week or a month there is no appreciable change in the stone, but over a period of years definite erosion is noted. Correspondingly, by the cumulation of educational experiences profound changes are brought about in the learner" (1969, 83). Clearly we must take the long view on nurturing personal and social values. It requires incremental, collective effort—no one teacher can do it quickly or on his or her own. Each of us is responsible for doing our small part to promote the values that will guide students in thinking and acting as responsible human beings and citizens. Arguably, there is no goal more important than this for social studies educators.

Think back to one of the five most important values that you identified earlier. Make a list of possible activities or resources that you might use to nurture each value. Be sure to think of ideas for each of the three kinds of approaches described in this chapter: creating reinforcing environments, facilitating direct experiences, and promoting thoughtful deliberation.

NOTES

1. Alfie Kohn (1997) draws attention to the fundamental ambiguity in the term "character education." In its broad interpretation, character-building refers to any attempt to help children develop desired traits. In its narrow sense, it refers to an approach to inculcating a work ethic and other socially conservative values using exhortations to behave, extrinsic rewards, and other forms of moral training.
2. Lessons can be found in Abbott, Case, and Nicol (2003).
3. The Eporuvian role play was developed by Anne Hill, an elementary teacher in Terrace, British Columbia.
4. Teaching activities for introducing principle-testing are described more fully in the AVER teaching materials (1978, 1991).

REFERENCES

Abbott, M., R. Case, and J. Nicol. 2003. *I can make a difference.* Richmond, BC: The Critical Thinking Consortium.

Alberta Learning. 2003. *Social studies—Kindergarten to grade 12* (validation draft). Edmonton, AB: Author. Available online at http://www.education.gov.ab.ca/k_12/curriculum/bySubject/.

American Bar Association. 1982. What's happening in law-related education? *LRE Report* 3 (3): 1–6.

Ashford, M-W. 1995. Youth actions for the planet. In *Thinking globally about social studies education,* ed. R. Fowler and I. Wright, 75–90. Vancouver: Research and Development in Global Studies, University of British Columbia.

Association for Values Education and Research. 1978. *Prejudice.* Toronto: OISE Press.

———. 1991. *Peace: In pursuit of security, prosperity, and social justice.* Toronto: OISE Press.

Browne, A. 1986. *Piggybook.* New York: Alfred A. Knopf.

Bunting, E. 1991. *Fly Away Home.* New York: Clarion Books.

Burrett, K. and T. Rusnak. 1993. *Integrated character education.* (Fastback #351). Bloomington, IN: Phi Delta Kappa Educational Foundation.

Cassidy, W. 1994. An examination of caring and compassion in social studies education. Unpublished paper. Burnaby, BC: Simon Fraser University.

Coombs, J.R. 1980. Validating moral judgments by principle testing. In *Practical dimensions of moral education,* ed. D. Cochrane and M. Manley-Casimir, 30–55. New York: Praeger.

Duke, D.L. 1978. Looking at the school as a rule-governed organization. *Journal of Research and Development in Education* 11 (4): 116–126.

Glaze, A.E., B. Hogarth, and B. McLean, eds. 2003. Can schools create citizens?: An exploration of character and citizenship education in Canadian, US and UK schools (special theme issue). *Orbit* 33 (2).

Kohn, A. 1997. How not to teach values: A critical look at character education. *Phi Delta Kappan.* Available online at http://www.alfiekohn.org/articles.htm#education.

Leming, J.S. 1991. Teacher characteristics and social education. In *Handbook on research on social studies teaching and learning,* ed. J. Shaver, 222–236. New York: Macmillan.

Ontario Ministry of Education. 2004. *The Ontario curriculum—Social studies grades 1–6—History and geography grades 7 and 8 (revised).* Toronto: Queen's Printer. Available online at http://www.edu.gov.on.ca.

Osborne, K. 1982. Civics, citizenship and politics: Political education in the schools. *Teacher Education* 20, 58–72.

Patrick, J.J. and J.D. Hoge. 1991. Teaching government, civics and law. In *Handbook on research on social studies teaching and learning* , ed. J. Shaver, 427–436. New York: Macmillan.

Peters, W. 1987. *A class divided: Then and now.* New Haven, CT: Yale University Press.

Raths, L.E., M. Harmin, and S.B. Simon. 1966. *Values and teaching: Working with values in the classroom.* Columbus, OH: Merrill.

Singer, M.G. 1958. Moral rules and principles. In *Essays in moral philosophy,* ed. A.I. Meldon, 160–197. Seattle: University of Washington Press.

Stewart, S. 1997. *The Gardener.* Vancouver: Douglas and McIntyre.

Torney-Purta, J. 1983. Psychological perspectives on enhancing civic education through the education of teachers. *Journal of Teacher Education* 34: 3–34.

Tyler, R. 1969. *Basic principles of curriculum and instruction.* Chicago: University of Chicago Press.

17 Embedding Global and Multicultural Perspectives

Roland Case, Özlem Sensoy, and Michael Ling

Much has been written about the importance of helping students understand the multicultural, globally connected world in which they live. Responding to this challenge should not, we believe, focus on teaching facts about various cultures and countries. Rather, our goal is better directed towards helping students view the world—and the events and people within it—in a different light. As Louis Perinbaum (1989, 25) observes, global education is a way of looking at the world more than it is the accumulation of information. The same can be said for multicultural education. This characterization is often discussed in terms of developing multicultural and global perspectives.

Before explaining what we mean by multicultural and global perspectives, we would like to clarify the difference between global education and multicultural education. These terms overlap to a great extent. Perhaps it is most helpful to view multicultural education as a subset of global education because the cultural dimensions of our global reality are one aspect—albeit a very significant part—of a wider set of political, economic, and social dimensions. It might be suggested that this characterization is potentially misleading since multiculturalism, especially in a country like Canada, is not simply a matter of international interests. Rather, multiculturalism is very much a part of our national reality and identity. However, even in this respect, Canadian multiculturalism cannot be separated from its global connections. Events such as the "war on terror," trade relations with China or the United States, and outsourcing of jobs to India, all have impact on cultural relations within Canada. The difference then is largely a matter of emphasis: the "content" of multicultural education is the national and international contexts of culture and cultural relations, whereas global education attends to a broader set of topics that include global development and trade, human rights, the environment, and culture.

What is a Global/Multicultural Perspective?

A perspective implies a "point of view"—a vantage point from which, or a lens through which, observations occur, and an "object" of attention—an event, thing, person, place, or state of affairs that is the focus of the observations. Thus an economic perspective (the point of view) would consider the financial costs and benefits of a proposed action (the object). Similarly, an ethical perspective would look at the morality of an action. A global/multicultural perspective refers to a point of view or set of lenses for viewing people, places, and things around the world. These perspectives consist of two elements—a substantive and a perceptual dimension.

- The **substantive dimension** refers to the "object" of focus within a global/multicultural perspective. These are the world events, states of affairs, places, and things that global and multicultural educators want students to understand. The substantive dimension is concerned with fostering knowledge about the people, beliefs, and customs beyond students' own cultural group and country, and knowledge of events, places, and issues beyond the local and immediate.

- The **perceptual dimension** refers to the "point of view" or lens of a global/multicultural perspective. These are the habits of mind, values, or attitudes from which we want students to perceive the world and the plurality of cultures within it. The perceptual dimension, reflected in spatial metaphors such as narrow or broad, ethnocentric or cosmopolitan, and parochial or far-reaching, describes a mindset or outlook—a capacity to see the "whole picture" with its complexity and diversity. Nurturing the perceptual dimension of a global/multicultural perspective requires developing the mental lenses through which the local and international world is to be understood in more holistic, interrelated, and complex ways.

An attempt to explain global and multicultural education requires articulating both the range of phenomena to be explored (the substantive dimension) and the desired lenses through which this examination is to occur (the perceptual dimension). Before elaborating on this two-dimensional account, let us consider why we should care about nurturing global/multicultural perspectives.

Why a Global/Multicultural Perspective?

The aim in prompting global/multicultural perspectives is to expand and enrich students' views of the world so they are not ethnocentric, stereotypical, or otherwise limited by a narrow or distorted point of view. Unless students recognize that their particular lenses are not universally shared and see the need to adopt multiple and far-reaching perspectives, many students are likely to view the world predominantly through their own cultural lenses, lenses shaped narrowly by their own interests, location, and experiences.

Research on freehand maps drawn by students from different nations illustrates the importance of helping students perceive the world in diverse and encompassing ways. In a classic study, Thomas Saarinen (1973) compared sketch maps of the world created by high school students from four cities: Calgary (Canada), Helsinki (Finland), Makeni (Sierra Leone), and Tucson (USA). These sketches, which provide metaphorical pictures of students' images of their world, suggest how students' understandings are mediated by the lenses through which they view things. As might be expected, most students depicted their home country and home continent with a high degree of accuracy and detail, often locating them in the centre of their map. This positioning of themselves at the centre of the world is symbolic of their socialization and outlook. Typically, more distant continents were relegated to the "outer reaches" of the page and often reduced to vague blotches far smaller than their actual land masses warranted. These depictions symbolize the reduced levels of awareness of and significance attached to "foreign" regions.

Curiously, some international features such as Hawaii, the British Isles, and the "boot" of Italy were exaggerated or rendered with unusual precision. For varying reasons, these "distant" features had particular significance for the mapmakers—perhaps the students had visited the place, had relatives living there, or had read about some event or place associated with that country.

Instruction in school may unintentionally reinforce students' parochial or distorted world views by focussing on quaint and superficial aspects and further estrange cultural groups by fostering a "we/they" dualism. For example, many curriculum materials promote what might be called a "food–costumes–customs" approach to the study of cultures. However, learning about ethnic dishes and "strange" holiday practices is unlikely to promote an enlightened perspective on the lives and concerns of people in these "foreign" cultures (Zachariah 1989). Well-intentioned attempts to interest elementary students in other cultures by featuring the exotic and exceptional elements of these cultures may make these people more "alien" to some students. By attending to the bizarre, and to some extent trivial, cultural dimensions, we may actually reinforce stereotypical perceptions (Schuncke 1984, 249).

Other distortions are also commonplace. For example, students may regard Africa and South America as primitive frontiers if their exposure to these continents is entirely in the context of subsistence living, genocide, drug runners, and deforestation. Many students are often surprised to learn of the existence of well-educated, affluent people living in modern African cities because the media-based representations they often see are restricted to jungles and rural villages. Similarly, when poverty is discussed, students are likely to regard people in these situations with condescending paternalism unless students are also shown instances of initiative and self-sufficiency. Unfortunately, until quite recently, treatment of Africa, South America, and the Middle East in Canadian social studies curricula focussed predominantly on ancient (and now fallen) civilizations (Case 1989, 6) and the curriculum in at least one province referred to the study of "primitive" cultures (British Columbia Ministry of Education 1983, 40).

These types of lingering ethnocentric and stereotypical perceptions will not be resolved simply by teaching more about the world—merely having more information may not advance students' understanding—because much of what we notice and the interpretations we make depend upon the lenses through which we filter this raw data. Approaching a study with a parochial attitude is likely to confirm, not dispel, stereotypes and prejudices. We must attend directly to the perceptual lenses that colour students' sense-making.

What Comprises the Substantive Dimension?

As indicated earlier, the substantive dimension refers to the range of global/multicultural topics—world events, states of affairs, places, and things—about which students should be informed. Many writers have offered accounts of what we refer to as the substantive dimension of global/multicultural education. Kniep (1986), Hanvey (1976), and Banks (2004) are among the most widely cited. Kniep and Hanvey, for example, identify five topics that form the main objects of global study. Interestingly, the focus of the first topic is multiculturalism.

- **Universal and cultural values and practices.** Hanvey uses the term "cross-culture awareness" to refer to knowledge and respect for the diversity of ideas and practices to be found in human societies around the world. Kniep emphasizes the importance of teaching about both commonality and diversity: teaching about universal human values that transcend group identity (for example, equality, justice, liberty) and about diverse cultural values that define group membership and contribute to differing world views (for example, values related to aesthetics, lifestyle, or the environment).
- **Global interconnections.** Kniep talks of "global systems" and Hanvey speaks of "global dynamics" to describe knowledge of the workings—the key features and mechanisms—of the interactive economic, political, ecological, social, and technological systems operating worldwide.
- **Present worldwide concerns and conditions.** Both writers identify the need to know about current and emerging global issues and problems—Hanvey calls it "state of the planet awareness." These persistent, transnational issues, which span peace and security, economic development, environmental, and human rights concerns, include population growth, migration, poverty, natural resource use, science and technology, health, and international and intranational conflict.
- **Origins and past patterns of worldwide affairs.** Kniep stresses the importance of "global history"—seeing the historical evolution and roots of universal and diverse human values, of contemporary global systems, and of prevailing global issues and problems.
- **Alternative future directions in worldwide affairs.** Hanvey stresses the importance of "knowledge of alternatives"—also called "awareness of human choices"—learning of alternatives to the ways in which the world is currently run, including alternatives to unrestrained economic growth, current foreign aid and technical assistance policies, and consumption patterns.

Although the substantive and perceptual dimensions intertwine, this list of topics identifies the content that these prominent global educators see as the main focus for global education. In essence, they believe that students need to know that people across the world share some values and differ in others, that events and forces in the world interconnect in powerful ways, that the world is facing a number of serious issues with deep historical roots, and that humankind has the potential and, indeed, the obligation to alter the existing ways of "doing business."

An important concern in global, and, obviously in multicultural education, is the teaching about cultures. As was discussed earlier, there are many pitfalls, in part because of a stereotypical view of the notion of a "culture."

Contrary to the way in which it is often taught, culture is not a unified, fixed entity. In fact, culture is not a "thing" at all, but rather the name we give to the set of beliefs, values, behaviour, and ways of living that any community of people expresses. Culture is created by people collectively as a way of adapting to social and environmental circumstances. Therefore, as circumstances change, so does culture. One indication of the malleability of culture is the way that many peoples of the world have very quickly responded to and have made use of new technological innovations. The Inuit, for example, were incorrectly thought by many in the 1930s and '40s to live a static, unchanging existence. The snowmobile, however, was very quickly incorporated into Inuit culture and some would now suggest it has become essential to the Inuit way of life. We have to look no farther than the introduction into contemporary Western culture of cars or telephones during our grandparents' lives, television during our parents' lives, and computers into many of our own lives, to see how new inventions become so much a part of the cultural landscape that one often wonders how people ever did without them. They become so integral to our day-to-day existence that they seem almost invisible—a "natural" feature of our existence. We don't notice them as unique or novel in any way; they are just "there" in our lives.

It is important to appreciate that a culture should always be made sense of relative to the circumstances in which it was created and now exists. Material technologies (for example, costumes, food, housing) are not in and of themselves culture; they are simply physical objects that may reveal much about a group when we look closely at how they are used by a particular people. What is important to recognize is that "artifacts," and other material or cultural expressions, including words, manners, and gestures, are not just arbitrary "things" in our worlds. Rather, they embody sets of ideas about how members belonging to a particular cultural group perceive, relate to, and act in the world.

Ironically, we are often unable to see our own cultural responses and yet we are often excessively conscious of the practices of others. The case of able-bodiedness illustrates this "blindness" (left-handedness is another example). Those of us who are able-bodied may go about the entire day, perhaps even weeks and months, without thinking about our ability to access public space. This blindness is called *privilege*. Such privilege (able-bodied) causes us to "not see" that public space is not universally accessible. We overlook how our environment (for example, restaurants, schools, parks, and transportation systems) accommodates "our" bodies as the norm. Only when we encounter those whose bodies are socially defined as outside the norm of the able-bodied do we notice "their" differences. This blindness is also illustrated in many aspects of social life. For example, many English-speaking Canadians would say that American and British English speakers *have* accents but that Canadians do not. Similarly, other groups are said to *have* cultural practices but "we don't."

These examples illustrate the importance of attending to the role of cultural traditions in shaping our behaviour, identities, environments, and assumptions, and to the fact that when we are part of the dominant group, our culture is the invisible norm against which other cultures are measured. Put another way, a culture provides an invisible screen or a lens through which participants interpret and respond to the world, a so-called world view. Why do I feel it is inappropriate for me to burp loudly after a meal in a restaurant, yet this may be entirely appropriate in another context? Such are the ways society, by way of culture, orients our views so that we may respond to "other views" with resistance or even hostility. Put this way, it becomes easier to see that any cultural expression should be seen as a particular response to social and environmental circumstances.

It is also important to recognize that often there is a *dominant* cultural tradition that has greater access to opportunity and power. For example, the dominant religious tradition in Canada is the Christian tradition. This historical fact has resulted in the dominance in "our" nation of Christian practices (such as Easter and Christmas) and institutionalization of these celebrations through state-sanctioned holidays. Although many other faith communities are celebrated for the diversity they bring to Canadian culture, these groups are not afforded comparable institutional recognition of their cultural practices. Of course, institutional holidays in Japan, India, Iran, and other countries will reflect the traditions of the dominant groups in these nations.

▌▌

Examine the text and pictures dealing with cultural groups found in various textbooks and other teaching resources. What portrait of these cultures is depicted? To what extent are superficial or unusual aspects profiled? Is there greater emphasis on differences or similarities between these groups and students' cultural roots?

What Comprises the Perceptual Dimension?

A major—possibly the key—challenge in developing a global/multicultural perspective is to transform a parochial perspec-

tive (that is, making sense of the world from a superficial, narrow, or ethnocentric point of view) to a broad-minded multi-perspective (that is, making sense of the world from varied and "enlightened" points of view). There is little value in promoting knowledge of alternative future directions, for example, if students are going to immediately dismiss these ideas because they don't suit students' immediate and possibly narrow interests—hence the need to help students see things from a more "global" and "culturally diverse" perspective. To better appreciate both what this involves and how to promote it, we characterize the perceptual dimension in terms of three lenses, or habits of mind: open-mindedness, full-mindedness, and fair-mindedness.[1]

OPEN-MINDEDNESS

Open-mindedness refers to a willingness to consider new ideas and alternative ways of looking at people, places, and events. Its opposite is closed-mindedness—the unwillingness to explore other ways of looking at things or the inability to see things as others might. Nurturing open-mindedness involves encouraging two traits:

- **Recognizing differences in points of view.** Students must realize that individuals and groups do not always see the world, or explain events that occur in it, in the same way, thus it is necessary to develop the ability to see things from differing viewpoints.
- **Entertaining various points of view.** Students need to accept the right of others to hold points of view that differ from their own and to be willing to and able to consider varying perspectives—including diverse cultural points of view.

Open-mindedness is *the* crucial feature of the perceptual dimension. It identifies an openness to things that are unfamiliar or even strange to us. It involves more than understanding that people have different opinions on an issue—for example, some people are in favour of mandatory use of seat belts and others oppose mandatory use. It involves what Hanvey (1976, 4–5) refers to as "perspective consciousness"—an awareness that individuals and groups have world views or "cognitive maps" that are not universally shared by others and may be shaped by factors that we are unaware of and unable to control. Young students may need particular help in appreciating that there may be more ways to see an event than their own. Multiple points of view involves looking at issues from different disciplinary perspectives (for example, seeing the economic, environmental, and political implications of a position) and also from different personal and cultural perspectives.

In introducing point of view, it may be useful to encourage students to view and describe concrete objects from different physical locations (for example, the look of a pencil or a classroom from the front, back, and sides). Stories also provide opportunities for students to take on a role and describe events and feelings from different characters' perspectives. It is also useful to invite students to attend to shifts in their own perspectives when new information is added to a circumstance. Discuss, for example, how a person might feel if they saw another student sitting alone eating lunch in the cafeteria. Suppose the person moved farther into the cafeteria and noticed that the solitary student was his or her younger sibling. How might this information affect the person's perception of the scene? Or what if the person him- or herself is the one sitting alone eating lunch? Each piece of information may create an internal shift affecting both feelings and the description of the event.

Encourage students to approach the study of other cultures from the point of view of an insider in that culture. Another strategy—a twist on the mental maps activity discussed earlier—is to invite students to draw mental maps from designated perspectives—say, from the point of view of someone living in their hometown, and then from the perspective of a group that students have been studying in class (Johnson 1997). Students would be encouraged to depict on their maps the characteristics of the world that would be most relevant to the people from whom the perspective is being taken—for example, Europe might be prominent on a map if many local immigrants had come from Europe, or Japan might be prominent if imported cars were popular.

When comparing cultural points of view, it is important to remind students of the heterogeneity within any group. Although "Europeans" or "Japanese" as a group might share some traits, not all members within the group necessarily share points of view on all (or even most) things. A useful analogy can be drawn with being a student in twelfth grade. As a group, twelfth-graders share experiences such as writing provincial examinations; however, it is simultaneously true that within this group there are very distinct points of view.

Students may be open-minded with regard to some issues and not others, often depending on the degree of personal investment or familiarity with the points of view. For example, we are less likely to be open-minded when self-interest or deeply held values are at stake. The difficulty in seeing the other side was confirmed during a workshop one of us offered for teachers in India. We asked participants to entertain possible reasons why a political group that had killed fourteen innocent people the day before may have acted in a principled manner. Many of the teachers were able to undertake this exercise in perspective-taking; others seemed unwilling and incapable of doing so. Although we personally might believe that killing fourteen bystanders was not justi-fied, unless we seriously consider the reasons for this group's actions, we should worry that we have reached an ethnocentric, closed-minded conclusion.

Teacher modelling is also an important way to encourage student open-mindedness (Torney-Purta 1983, 33). Modelling open-mindedness requires that teachers consistently and sincerely attempt to base their classroom comments and decisions on careful consideration of all sides, and to show a willingness to change their mind or alter their plans whenever good reasons are presented.

FULL-MINDEDNESS

Full-mindedness refers to the inclination to make up one's mind on the basis of adequate understanding of the whole story. Its opposite is simple-mindedness—a penchant for leaping to conclusions or settling for simplistic or incomplete explanations. Promoting full-mindedness includes helping students develop the following traits:

- **Anticipating complexity.** The inclination to look beyond simplistic accounts of complex issues, and to look for ramifications and interconnections and to see phenomena as part of a constellation of interrelated factors.
- **Recognizing stereotyping.** The ability to identify and dismiss portrayals of people or cultures that are superficial generalizations or objectifications that portray cultures or countries as quaint, eccentric, or objects of curiosity.
- **Suspending judgment when warranted.** A willingness when dealing with complex matters to withhold coming to a firm conclusion until varying viewpoints, and the evidence for them, have been considered.

Anticipation of complexity involves fostering student scepticism of explanations that fail to consider with sufficient imagination the range of interacting factors and consequences of most global events; it is a call to resist seeing events in the world as isolated and localized. Although it is inevitable, and often desirable, that global/cultural issues be simplified somewhat, it is important to discourage superficial or naive views (that is, black-and-white accounts and definitive lists of the causes of events). If students are not alerted to, or if they refuse to accept, the messy reality of many of our enduring global predicaments, they will be satisfied with crude and simplistic responses to problems. Simplified solutions, however, are unlikely to succeed—world famine will not be resolved by producing more food (we already produce enough food to feed everyone) and we will not eliminate poverty merely by creating more jobs (many people considered to be below the poverty line are fully employed or are not capable of working). Unless students anticipate the ramifications of a course of action, they are less likely to advocate proposals that adequately accommodate the interconnected nature of many global situations. A case in point is the Green Revolution, which failed to accommodate the social, psychological, financial, and agricultural implications of abandoning supposedly unsophisticated farming practices.

One of the most important implications of anticipating complexity is that any cultural practice should always be considered in the context in which it is expressed. In other words, we need to be sensitive to the situation in which cultural values and beliefs are expressed instead of simply leaping to conclusions. Historical, political, and social factors influence the expression of "culture." For example, Madonna's version of pop-culture dance may have been controversial in the mid-1980s, early in the development of music-video culture. In today's context, a similar dance style may well be viewed as "normal" in this genre.

Cultural stereotyping is the tendency to see individuals and societies in simple, superficial, and often negative ways. To avoid this requires an awareness of the breadth and depth

BELIEVE IT OR NOT

Students are introduced to and invited to react to the "unusual" practices of an unidentified group (the Inuit). It is anticipated that some students may initially find these actions "odd" or "unusual." The objective is to encourage students to respond more respectfully to situations that initially seem "foreign" by helping them see the rashness of their initial impressions.

WHAT DO YOU THINK OF A GROUP THAT ...	
Their behaviour	Your initial reaction
• once lived in snow houses in winter	
• plays soccer at midnight	
• used moss diapers for their babies	
• softened animal skin by chewing it	
• made sleds out of frozen fish	
• made sails for their boats from animal intestines	

After recording their initial reactions, students learn about the reasons for each practice (below are suggested advantages of two of these practices) and are invited to reconsider their initial impressions. In this way, students are helped to appreciate the resourcefulness of the Inuit and that the lifestyle of other cultures may seem unusual at first glance, but once they understand why people live a certain way, the actions are generally perceived to be thoughtful.

RATIONALE/ADVANTAGES FOR SELECTED INUIT PRACTICES	
Behaviour	Rationale
moss diapers	• moss is widely available • moss can be stored in the winter • moss diapers are free, absorbent, and soft • moss diapers are environmentally friendly (moss is biodegradable) • moss can be packaged tightly and is lightweight for travel
sails made of intestines	• intestines are strong (they won't rip easily) • intestines are lightweight (they will not slow down the boat and can be transported easily) • intestines are easy to sew together • intestines are available any time animals are killed • the sails are environmentally efficient (parts of animals that may not be eaten or otherwise be used are used)

of cultural practices. The activity in the highlighted text may help elementary students appreciate the sophisticated wisdom behind seemingly "silly" practices.

Educators can discourage simple-mindedness by stressing the rationale for practices but also by attending to the interrelated factors involved in most events and the inevitability of ramifications for most actions. For example, solutions to global population problems should be discussed in the context of competing social and religious pressures, such as parents' reliance on their children to supplement family incomes and to provide for old-age security, deep-rooted religious beliefs and cultural values, and state-mandated rules regarding family size (such as China's one-child policy). Young students can be introduced to the complexity of events by having them trace the myriad consequences of a single action (for example, the effects of an environmental change) or the range of factors that have influenced an event (for example, all the people and countries that contributed to the breakfast eaten that morning). Fostering student appreciation of complexity may require replacing superficial exploration of many topics with fewer, but more in-depth, case studies. In general, teachers who model an appreciation of the complexity of most issues are likely to promote student acquisition of this attribute (Newmann 1991, 330).

Recognition of stereotyping refers to developing students' ability to identify the inadequacy of accounts of people, cultures, or nations that are limited to a narrow range of characteristics (that is, important features of the group are ignored) or that depict little or no diversity within them (that is, differences within the group are ignored). Unlike the previously discussed element of complexity, which focusses on explaining events with appropriate intricacy, resisting stereotyping involves describing groups of people with sufficient diversity. For example, during the Cold War period especially, the tendency in the West was to talk about Eastern Europe as if it were a single entity. Similarly, the crude treatment of African culture in many social studies textbooks fails to do justice to the fundamental differences among African cultures and to their richness (Beckett and Darling 1988, 2–3). As was mentioned earlier, stereotyping occurs when educators, however well-intentioned, focus on the quaint or exotic features of a culture. For example, curriculum resources regularly stereotype Egypt as a museum or curiosity piece—as the land of pyramids and sphinxes.

In addition to cultural stereotyping, a particularly relevant form of stereotyping is the inclination to focus on "we/they" dualisms. Casting issues as "our" cultural group against "other" cultures is stereotyping whenever it disguises the shared values that underlie supposedly competing interests. This tendency, sometimes called "essentializing" group characteristics, attributes to all members of a group a limited set of qualities. Similarly, dualisms among international sectors (for example, north-south, east-west, developed-developing countries) involve stereotyping whenever the interests of all countries in a bloc are reduced to the interests of the bloc and set in opposition to the interests of other blocs. The problem with these dualisms are their tendencies to ignore the cross-boundary similarities and shared interests in many issues and problems (for example, Eastern Europeans are likely as concerned about cancer as are North Americans) and to polarize camps on issues when divisions are not warranted (for example, ending the nuclear arms race was a goal shared by people on both sides of the Iron Curtain). Of course, we can go to the opposite extreme by exaggerating the extent to which one group's interests are shared by all nations and peoples.

Recognizing stereotypes is important because unflattering stereotypes of people, cultures, or nations are often deliberately encouraged. For example, creating hostile stereotypical images of people from an opposing country is sometimes used to fuel distrust or hatred against them (Silverstein 1989). Even in situations where the motives are benign, the effects of stereotyping are often undesirable. The eugenics movement in Western Canada and in many American states is an example of the disastrous effects of well-intended stereotyping. The so-called science of eugenics called into question the "fitness" of certain groups to have and raise children. Based primarily on unflattering stereotypes about people with mild disabilities, aboriginal peoples, and those of Eastern European origin, members of these groups, considered to be "feeble-minded" or to have loose morals, were evaluated by boards that had the power to sterilize those deemed to be socially undesirable. This occurred in North America during the same time in which similar claims about the superiority of certain races were the popular ideology in Western Europe.

As this example illustrates, condescending and paternalistic attitudes towards people from various cultures may be a function partly of our stereotypical images of these people (Werner, Connors, Aoki, and Dahlie 1977, 33). Building students' resistance to stereotypical accounts decreases their inclination to dehumanize or marginalize groups, because students see these groups as having a full range of human attributes. In other words, we should try to inoculate students against accepting portrayals of members of other cultural groups "as cardboard characters in a stilted puppet play" (Zachariah 1989, 51). On a positive note, we can develop students' resistance to stereotyping by increasing their appreciation of the similarities and shared interests among cultures, and by combatting tendencies to paint issues in black-and-white terms.

The previously mentioned strategies for promoting an appreciation of complexity are appropriate for encouraging appreciation of global/cultural diversity: gross generalizations about people and nations should be discouraged, and examples of differences within cultural and national groups should be provided. Although more extensive study of fewer cultures or nations may be preferred to the relatively superficial study of many peoples, we must guard against stereotypical impressions encouraged when a heterogeneous entity, say Africa or aboriginal peoples, is considered exclusively in the context of one sample, say Nigeria or Haiti. As a general rule, we should avoid presenting only the dominant images of a country or people—that is, avoid dealing exclusively with the poverty in Africa and with the civility in Japan.

Being open-minded also implies having a tendency to suspend making firm judgments when evidence is inconclusive or when a thorough examination of the issue has not been carried out. As the Scottish philosopher David Hume observed, a wise person proportions his or her belief to the evidence. Teachers can encourage full-mindedness in their students by not always having the answer and by being comfortable with uncertainty—that is, being satisfied with tentative conclusions until a full review of complex issues can be carried out.

FAIR-MINDEDNESS

Fair-mindedness refers to the inclination to give a fair hearing to alternative points of view—to judge matters on the basis of their own merits, and not simply in terms of our own interests and preferences. Its opposites are bias and self-absorption. Promoting fair-mindedness includes encouraging a willingness and ability to:

- **empathize with others:** to place oneself in the role or predicament of others or at least to imagine issues from the perspectives of other persons or groups;
- **overcome bias:** to resist imposing the interests or perspective of one's own group over those of other countries or peoples.

The ability to empathize does not imply that we must agree with the positions taken by others or be supportive in all cases—it requires solely that we try to understand in a vivid way what others think and how they feel. Empathy is not the same as open-mindedness, although the two are related. Empathy presupposes an openness to ways different from our own, but it goes farther than openness, in that empathy requires that we "feel" the other person's predicament. The need to promote empathy arises because merely learning more about other people or countries may not increase students' appreciation of what other people's lives are really like. However, the inclination to empathize with others is not identical with promoting unqualified acceptance of others—

a sensitive exposure to certain practices may legitimately redouble students' sense of another's oddness or unreasonableness. Thus, promoting empathy is not tantamount to encouraging moral relativism—students may still judge that certain practices are undesirable or unappealing. However, as the common expression suggests, we shouldn't criticize another until we have walked in that person's shoes.

Bias refers to an unwarranted or unfair preference for one's own interests or affiliations. It was reflected in contrasting descriptions of British and Iraqi actions provided by the British press at the height of the Persian Gulf War in 1991. More specifically, British forces were described as "cautious" and "loyal," and Iraqi troops as "cowardly" and "blindly obedient"; British sorties were "first strikes" and "pre-emptive" while Iraqi initiatives were "sneak missile attacks" and "without provocation" (*The Guardian* 1991). And more recently, in the reporting in the aftermath of Hurricane Katrina in New Orleans, black residents were said to be "looting," while white residents were merely "finding" provisions (Yahoo!News 2005). These accounts are prejudiced even if we all agree that Iraq deserved condemnation for provoking the war and that the residents were looting, because otherwise identical actions were judged differently merely because of which side performed them.

There are three forms of bias that are particularly relevant for multicultural and global education:

- **Ethnocentrism.** This refers to the view that one's own cultural group is superior to all others. It is not necessarily ethnocentric to prefer most features of North American life to customs and practices in other cultures; rather, it is ethnocentric to judge them better simply because they are our ways. Unless students are able to see the merits of other cultures, the study of other cultures will simply fuel the belief that "our ways are the best and the others are inferior." As Jenness (1990, 412) remarked in his extensive review of social studies, some educators are concerned that "the world studies program may well turn out to be a fatter photo album, ethnocentrically selected and arranged." In North America, for example, people typically bathe once a day, which is considered sufficient to maintain a socially acceptable measure of cleanliness. From a Japanese perspective, however, bathing merely once a day may be regarded as very unclean. Either perspective, seen from an ethnocentric point of view, would regard the other as inappropriate—either deficient or excessive cleanliness—missing the point that these behaviours are socially defined responses (or adaptations) to particular conditions.
- **National fanaticism.** This refers to a refusal to assess policies and events involving our own country impar-

tially or to recognize that, on some occasions, national best interests, as opposed to the interests of other countries or people, should not be paramount.

- **Presentism.** This refers to a preoccupation with the interests and well-being of current generations to the exclusion of the interests of persons yet to be born into the world. In other words, the felt urgency of our immediate needs and desires may preclude our fair-minded consideration of others' future needs. Concern with this form of bias underlies much criticism about our inadequate sensitivity to the long-term environmental consequences of national policies and consumer decisions.

To encourage fair-mindedness, students should regularly be expected to explore and defend positions from different points of view, especially from perspectives that are not personally held by them. For students who have difficulty in being fair-minded, teachers may try "challenging" their thinking in non-threatening ways by presenting opposing reasons and by looking for inconsistencies in their attitudes. More likely, however, reasoning with students will not be sufficient. Students may benefit from exposure to evocative situations where they can "feel" for themselves the power and merit of other perspectives. There are at least three sources of these sorts of visceral experiences:

- **Vicarious experiences** where students come to live the lives of others through films and stories. There are many collections of films and stories about various countries and cultures; many of these have been written or produced by people from other cultures.

- **Simulated experiences** where students act out through role play or another type of simulation activity the predicament of others.
- **First-hand experiences** where students encounter in "real-life" meaningful contexts—through field trips, classroom guests, exchanges, pen pals, social action projects—the points of view of others.

The highlighted simulation, "What's Fair," is intended to help students develop empathy for those who may be living in poverty. Experiences such as these—whether brought about by reading a story, participating in a simulation, or experiencing things first-hand—help to evoke students' sensitivities to points of view that they might otherwise downplay or ignore.

Conclusion

Our four objectives in writing this chapter have been to:

- illustrate the importance of helping students approach the study of their world from a more "global" and "diverse" perspective;
- explain five main areas of the substantive—or content—dimension of this perspective;
- explain three key traits of the perceptual—or attitudinal—dimension;
- suggest ways in which the perceptual dimension may be nurtured—through direct instruction, teacher modelling, and "experiential" activities.

WHAT'S FAIR?

At the start of the day, randomly distribute a coloured card to each student upon entering the class—in a class of thirty students have three gold cards (or ten per cent of the class), nine silver cards (thirty per cent), twelve green cards (forty per cent), and six white cards (twenty per cent). Offer no comment about the card, but at the break and/or at lunch time, distribute food according to the following schedule:

	SNACK	LUNCH
Gold card	21 Smarties (or raisins)	sandwich, milk, apple, and a cookie
Silver card	9 Smarties (or raisins)	sandwich
Green card	4 Smarties (or raisins)	plain slice of bread
White card	1 Smartie (or raisin)	crust of bread

It will take little time for students to erupt into complaints about unfairness. Debrief the activity by noting the parallel between, on the one hand, the unfairness of students getting more goodies than others merely because they happened to get a particular card when they came into the room and, on the other hand, the unfairness of people having greater wealth than others merely because they happened to be born in a particular country or social class. To avoid anxiety and resentment, it is wise to end the activity by equalizing the distribution of goods among students. If students who have more resist, this too is significant and worth exploring in class: why might those with wealth or power resist policies that may potentially take away their advantage?

Although our focus is social studies, it is apparent that promoting a global/multicultural perspective should not be limited exclusively to this subject, nor should it be an occasional add-on that occurs within a designated unit. Rather, efforts to promote a global perspective can and should be embedded in much of what we do each day.

Locate the teaching instructions in a resource dealing with a specific cultural group. Look for evidence suggesting how the suggested activities support or undermine the following elements of a multicultural/global perspective:

- **Open-mindedness:** a willingness to entertain new ideas and alternative ways of looking at people, places, and events. It requires:
  - recognizing differences in points of view, and
  - entertaining various points of view.
- **Full-mindedness**: the inclination to make up one's mind on the basis of adequate understanding of the whole story. It requires:
  - anticipating complexity,
  - recognizing stereotyping, and
  - suspending judgment when warranted.
- **Fair-mindedness:** the inclination to give a fair hearing to alternative points of view—to judge matters on the basis of their own merits, and not simply in terms of our own interests and preferences. It requires:
  - empathizing with others, and
  - overcoming bias.

Design one or more activities to enhance a multicultural/global perspective on the featured cultural group.

NOTE

1. In an earlier article, Case (1993) identified five interrelated elements of the perceptual dimension (open-mindedness, anticipation of complexity, resistance to stereotyping, inclination to empathize, and non-chauvinism). In a 1995 article intended for elementary students, these traits were collapsed into three more general categories: open-mindedness, full-mindedness, and fair-mindedness.

REFERENCES

Banks, J.A., ed. 2004. *Diversity and citizenship education: Global perspectives.* San Francisco: Jossey-Bass.

Beckett, K. and L. Darling. 1988. The view of the world portrayed in social studies textbooks. Occasional paper #13. *Explorations in Development/Global Education.* Vancouver: Research and Development in Global Studies, University of British Columbia.

British Columbia Ministry of Education. 1983. *Social studies curriculum guide: Grade 1–grade 7.* Victoria, BC: Author.

Case, R. 1989. Global perspective or tunnel vision? The mandated view of the world in Canadian social studies curricula. Occasional paper #23. *Explorations in Development/Global Education.* Vancouver: Research and Development in Global Studies, University of British Columbia.

———. 1993. Key elements of a global perspective. *Social Education* 57 (6): 318–325.

———. 1995. Nurturing a global perspective in elementary students. In *Thinking Globally about Social Studies Education,* ed. R. Fowler and I. Wright, 19–34. Vancouver: Research and Development in Global Studies, University of British Columbia.

The Guardian. 1991. Mad dogs and englishmen. February 22.

Hanvey, R.G. 1976. *An attainable global perspective.* New York: Global Perspectives in Education.

Jenness, D. 1990. *Making sense of social studies.* New York: Macmillan.

Johnson, C. 1997. Expressing a global perspective: Experiences in a Mexican classroom. Unpublished paper.

Kniep, W.M. 1986. Defining a global education by its content. *Social Education* 50: 437–446.

Newmann, F.M. 1991. Promoting higher order thinking in social studies: Overview of a study of 16 high school departments. *Theory and Research in Social Education* 19: 324–340.

Perinbaum, L. 1989. A new frontier for teachers. *Alberta Teachers' Association Magazine* 69: 23–25.

Saarinen, T.F. 1973. Student views of the world. In *Images and environment: Cognitive mapping and spatial behavior,* ed. R.M. Downs and D. Stea, 148–161. Chicago: Aldine Publishing.

Schuncke, G.M. 1984. Global awareness and younger children: Beginning the process. *Social Studies* 75: 248–251.

Silverstein, B. 1989. Enemy images: The psychology of US attitudes and cognitions regarding the Soviet Union. *American Psychologist* 44 (6): 903–913.

Social Studies and the Young Learner. 1994. Special theme: Global perspective in a new world, March/April.

Stewig, J.W. 1992. Using children's books as a bridge to other cultures. *The Social Studies* 83 (1): 36–40.

Torney-Purta, J.V. 1983. Psychological perspectives on enhancing civic education through education of teachers. *Journal of Teacher Education* 34: 30–34.

Werner, W., B. Connors, T. Aoki, and J. Dahlie. 1977. *Whose culture? Whose heritage? Ethnicity within Canadian social studies curricula.* Vancouver: Centre for the Study of Curriculum and Instruction, University of British Columbia.

Willms, J. 1992. The children next door: Bringing the global neighbourhood into the classroom. *Orbit* 23 (1): 14–16.

Yahoo!News. 2005. As discussed at http://www.media-awareness.ca/english/resources/educational/teachable_moments/katrina_2_photo.cfm.

Zachariah, M. 1989. Linking global education with multicultural education. *Alberta Teachers' Association Magazine* 69: 48–51.

18

Teaching for Hope

Walt Werner

One cannot live in this media-rich culture without feeling some unease about the future. Weekly we encounter disturbing images of urgent proportions. A litany of enormous challenges—including poverty and famine, human rights abuses and repression, desertification and ecological stress, social chaos, and international debts—confronts our increasingly interdependent world. After Lebanon, Cambodia, and Ireland came Ethiopia, Sudan, Bosnia, and Rwanda [then Iraq, Afghanistan, and Darfur—Ed.], and we have come to expect that a list of similar place names will continue. Systemic interactions among diverse problems are overwhelming in their complexity and ambiguity, and this leads to uncertainties. According to the Club of Rome,

> Never in the course of history has humankind been faced with so many threats and dangers ... the causes and consequences of which form an inextricable maze.... Individuals feel helpless, caught, as it were, between the rise of previously unknown perils on the one hand, and an incapacity to answer the complex problems in time and to attack the roots of evil, not just its consequences, on the other hand (King and Schneider 1991, 127–128).

Even though this barrage of bad news leaves us psychologically fatigued, we still need to rationalize the realities of what we see and hear, because no matter what our politics, we want a better future (Kennedy 1993; Roche 1993).

For children, though, pictures of a broken world speak directly to their own future. Implied is their tomorrow. Whether this realization occurs in a dramatic moment of insight or slowly awakens as a vague awareness, the consequence can be uncertainty about the future or, even worse, some loss of hope.

Classrooms are unwitting partners in this loss. It begins when youth encounter texts and images that imply a deeply problematic future. Through classroom projects, video and print resources, and discussions of current events, students glean bits of information from which they construct their personal views, often of a crisis-ridden and confusing world created by adults who seem unwilling or unable to change it. "Youngsters piece together these fragments in a jumbled patchwork of mixed perceptions that make them anxious," observed Van Ornum (1984, 16). "The world is not safe. If adults are scared and helpless, what chance do kids have?" When unchecked, these feelings lead over time to insecurity or cynicism about the prospects for individual and collective futures.

Such outcomes, however, are educationally unacceptable because schools are in the business of strengthening realistic hope in the future. Let me illustrate with an event from a grade 10 social studies class. Groups were organized around research projects related to a number of global issues. I thought they were learning well to sort through controversial problems when a young woman quietly informed me that she would rather drop out of her study group and do an individual project on cowry shells. When asked what social or economic issues were represented by these natural artifacts, she replied that she was not aware of any issues nor was she interested. She simply wanted to study the shells, as she said, "because they're beautiful." I suddenly realized that here was a sixteen-year-old whose sense of future was threatened. The cumulative effect of my "ambulance chasing" pedagogy was a sense of helplessness, a feeling that the range and complexity of issues were too difficult to understand, let alone solve. My focus on problems left her with a deepening uncertainty.

Anyone who is a teacher is necessarily an optimist. Our working with young people represents a commitment to the future. We are teaching for hope. But what does it mean to have hope? Many years ago, Philip Phenix reminded educators that "Hope is the mainspring of human existence." This is no idle slogan, for, as he explained, "conscious life is a continual projection into the future.... Without hope, there is no incentive for learning, for the impulse to learn presupposed confidence in the possibility of improving one's existence"

(1974, 123). Essential to hope is a knowledgeable and reflective confidence in the future and a willingness to engage it. The future, whether one's own or that of a larger group, is seen as open, having possibilities, rather than foreclosed or predetermined. This belief entails confidence that current problems and worrisome trends can be addressed in response to care and effort, that good planning and strategic action taken today can have significant consequences. In short, hope expresses itself as a "Yes" to tomorrow.

How can youth's sense of hope for the future be strengthened through classrooms? Part of the answer lies in the important roles that emotion, information, vision, and efficacy have in young people's coming to understand the problems and complexities of their larger world. Through a teacher's sensitive use of these four avenues, hope can be encouraged during discussions about global issues.

Select two current crises that are widely reported in the news. Arrange to discuss these crises with three or four students. Ask them what they feel about each crisis, what they know about them, whether they see the possibility of positive resolutions, and whether there is anything the students can do to help bring about a solution. Summarize their responses and draw several conclusions about the levels of hopefulness these students express.

Emotion

Honest treatment of subject matter, whether in the humanities or sciences, will at times give rise to emotionally loaded concerns and questions about the future. For decades, educators have known that harm to learning does not necessarily come from material that evokes emotion (Jones 1970, 69–86). Any learning that is memorable and important is also emotion-full. Expressions of feeling—such as surprise, anger, wonder, uncertainty, awe, consternation, commitment—engage the interest and imagination of students, extend their involvement with the subject matter, and imbue the curriculum with the kind of personal significance that impels rather than hinders learning.

There is an emotion, however, that is not a friend of learning: anxious students do not perform well. Anxiety about the future rests on feelings of helplessness and isolation in the face of threatening prospects (Jones 1970). And when children are unwilling to talk freely about topics that engender this sense of aloneness and hopelessness, their uninformed imaginations give rise to misperceptions of issues that can further reinforce anxiety (Stackhouse 1991).

How can the study of global problems and issues help youth feel less anxious about the future, less helpless about the prospects for change, and less alone in their imaginations? That students feel threatened by questions about the future needs to be dealt with rather than avoided. Classroom discussions, when sensitively directed by the teacher, can counter anxiety. For example:

- Watch for *signs of anxiety*, and seek ways to ameliorate this feeling and to promote a sense of community and efficacy. Indicators of a loss of hope can be varied. For example, off-hand comments or jokes during conversations about world problems may indicate fear, confusion, resignation, or anger; these refusals to discuss issues seriously may be masking deeper ambivalences. Expressions of apathy or lack of interest—such as protesting the topic, disengagement from discussion, or incomplete or poorly done projects—may also be attempts to protect oneself.

- Take seriously *the sentiments* about anxiety or hopelessness that children express during discussions of current events and issues. Help them articulate the reasons for these attitudes, and where appropriate, provide counterexamples and new information that challenges narrow or unsubstantiated beliefs.

- Focus discussions not only on the informational content of issues, but also on their *emotional content*. How do students feel about the issue? Emotions have to be shared—listened to and discussed—in order to be understood and harnessed for learning. As concerns are expressed, children realize that they are not alone in their imaginations about the future; there are broader communities of concern embracing people around the earth.

Information

Shielding children from global problems cannot be a solution to preserving their sense of hope. Purging the curriculum of topics that raise concerns for young people, or focussing discussion only on "safe" areas, are not options except for making classrooms more sterile places. As Van Ornum suggests, "Today's young people, for better or worse, are savvy and cynical. Old before their time, they know a dodge when they see one" (1984, 3). They already know from television that many people lead wretched lives because of environmental degradation, armed conflicts, and poverty, and that some adults are not hopeful about change (Kaplan 1994). But if children hear little acknowledgement of these realities, they conclude that educators either do not care or are not being honest; neither case instills confidence in learning about global issues. The perceived dark side of the world calls for information rather than silence.

Thoughtful discussion of information is essential, though, because a source of hopelessness can be misinformation, misunderstood information, or a lack of information about the nature and extent of a problem. Any defensible belief in the future has to include, among other things, an adequate knowledge—a realistic understanding and honest appraisal—of what the situation is. Herein lies a responsibility of educators to ensure that students have accurate and balanced input when discussing global issues, and to check whether the inferences drawn from classroom conversations and other texts are reasonable. Sketchy or inaccurate "facts," as well as hearsay, casual comments, and a neglect of context, can lead to unwarranted conclusions, overgeneralizations, or false impressions of what the future might be like (Jickling 1994).

If we want students to develop a reasoned hope in the future, then during classroom discussions:

- probe for *inferences* that children hold about the future. Are these inferences warranted by the best information at hand? Could their conclusions lead to unfounded fears or unrealistic expectations? Uninformed or misinformed fears and confidences both constitute naiveté.
- provide greater awareness of the broad range of *institutions* dedicated to gathering and disseminating reliable information about issues, and of the many groups that use this information to lobby governments for new policies or changed laws. This research and development work is premised on a strong confidence in the future.

Emphasis in the classroom upon inert information—often packaged as worksheets and end-of-chapter questions—only provides youth with disconnected "facts" about the state of their world. Unless meaningful connections among these isolated bits and pieces are forged, the picture of the larger world may make little sense beyond a bewildering array of problems. Hope falters when the content learned by students does not lead to better understanding.

Vision

Hope cannot rest only upon an understanding of what is or will be the case (information), but also upon imagined alternatives and how these may be achieved (vision). "Where there is no vision," says an ancient proverb, "people perish." It is not enough to want a "better world" without articulating what this might mean: What are one's priorities for an improved world, and how could they be achieved? Alternative futures are defined as we "name" them through goals, plans, and policies. Problem solving calls for a willingness to project outcomes and to choose from among competing scenarios. Rich imagination is the stuff of hope. But imagination with-

ers whenever young people are treated as less than mindful agents through unimaginative pedagogy.

Children's hope is strengthened as their imaginations are engaged in understanding and "making" their world:

- Introduce *visionary concepts* that define alternatives for the future. Some examples are "sustainable environment," "respect for the rule of international law," "the commons," and "human rights." That these concepts may be controversial does not disqualify them from classrooms, but highlights the fact that they represent important values for envisioning the future.
- Discuss why the world community has forged institutions that embody and implement *collective visions* for the future. Examples include the world court and international law, as well as the many other agencies and covenants of the United Nations (Department of Foreign Affairs and International Trade, 1994).
- Give students opportunities to define and share *personal visions* for the future. Imagination is clarified and enlarged as it is challenged in a context of alternatives (Boulding 1995; Korten 1995). Not only do the visual and performing arts offer multiple modes for expressing doubts and hopes about the future, but also through "writing and sharing stories, creating images, and participating in role plays, we can simulate events as though we are already in the future. Our objective in such visualizations is not to predict the future, but to perceive potential futures in the here-and-now and to conceptualize what it will take to get there from here" (Bryant 1995, 40). Visions can be created and shared through various avenues, including poetry, music, drama, dance, story, drawing, and painting.

Hope is never fostered when students' own creative envisioning of desirable futures is disallowed, when information about the world is treated as a given to be received rather than re-imagined. Youth need to theorize about possibilities.

Efficacy

A concern that youth express when they begin to recognize the extent of world problems is why adults are not solving them. This query is not about more information on specific government policies and projects, but more deeply about how the world of adults works. It is an attempt to understand the kind of world in which they live: Is it a world in which adults do not care about problems that occur elsewhere? where adults do not know what to do? or where adults care more about present interests than consequences for the future? Some of children's deepest fears about abandonment are here tapped (Hevesi 1990). They seek assurances that adults can be trusted to protect the new generation's future. No wonder they become apprehensive.

Our goal is to encourage the development of those abilities and dispositions that allow young people to engage in appropriate personal, social, and political action. Hope is indistinguishable from a belief that individuals and groups influence and shape their futures through action. A strong sense of personal efficacy is a driving force behind any achievement. Without it, there is little open-mindedness to new ideas, willingness to reflect on one's own plans, or motivation and confidence in becoming proactive. To paraphrase Saul Alinsky, "There can be no darker or more devastating tragedy than the death of people's faith in themselves and in their power to direct their future. Denial of the opportunity for participation is the denial of human dignity…." Students need to understand why they are not powerless to make a contribution at some level.

Fostering efficacy is not an add-on to studies of global issues, but should be part and parcel of the ongoing discussions:

- Focus on the worldwide extent of *agencies, partnerships,* and *networks* engaged in problem solving. Young people are not aware of the range of groups—whether governments, international institutions, non-governmental organizations, grassroots community initiatives, or the private sector—committed to action and what they are doing. The important understanding here is that the difficulties facing our interdependent globe are being worked on by many people in various ways.

- Infuse *good news stories* about the successes that individuals, groups, and institutions are having in their actions. Elicit examples of actions that have been and are being taken to solve problems. Valuable experience and skills have been gained over the past decades, and considerable progress was achieved in areas such as health, agriculture, and social justice (Canadian International Development Agency 1987). The purpose for introducing positive examples is to provide a balanced and honest, not utopian, view of the gains that are made locally and internationally.

- Encourage discussion of *personal actions* that could be taken at home and in the school or community. The complexity of issues and problems does not preclude consideration of meaningful action: What can I personally do? Is there collective action that we should plan? Depending upon the age and circumstances of students, activities may involve letter-writing, changing one's consumer habits, attending a seminar for further information, joining the work of a community organization, or forming a school club. Appropriate action is not only a

way to apply what is learned, but also a means for understanding issues better and strengthening efficacy.

Curricula and classrooms are largely organized around and for passivity. Often students are taught political incapacity rather than efficacy through the large amounts of inert knowledge they are given. They learn inadvertently that "doing school work" is not meant to be "real work" that has any direct impact on (or even relevance for) larger issues. This is why discussions about efficacy are so important for undercutting learned helplessness.

Conclusion

Classroom discussions of global issues may increase student anxieties about the future. This is why educators need to reflect on the roles that emotion, information, vision, and efficacy may have in shaping young people's beliefs about their tomorrow. I am not advocating that we put a light and happy face on the world. Youth already have a sense of dark crises on the horizon, but these realities need not imply despair. Hope requires a careful understanding of issues, and the development of reasoned visions and a realistic sense of efficacy. It is then that the sobering images on TV screens and the problems they imply can be seen with possibility.

Let me conclude with a personal anecdote. Late one night I heard my son, who was in grade 1 at the time, call from his room. I turned on the light and noticed that he had been crying. "When I grow up," he announced, "there will be no more wilderness." Whatever he meant by "wilderness" was not as important at this point as his expression of a threatened personal future. This loss of hope had started earlier in the day during a classroom discussion about stresses on ecosystems around the world, followed that evening by a television documentary on the loss of wilderness in western Canada. Because he lacked adequate information and the necessary conceptual tools to appraise the issues, what little understanding he gained from these two events led to a confused and anxious inference about his own future. I assured him that, although wilderness was indeed under serious threat in places, many groups of concerned people just like him were working to protect ecosystems through new policies and laws, and that there were things that he and I could do as well. Over the next few days, we sought new information, shared our visions, and explored ways to enhance efficacy.

> Think of a contemporary local, national, or international issue or problem that you would want to explore with students. Use the author's four key ideas of emotion, information, vision, and efficacy to develop a list of a dozen activities or discussion points that you could use to build hope in students as they explore the issue.

ACKNOWLEDGMENT

This chapter appeared originally in 1995 in *Thinking globally about social studies,* ed. R. Fowler and I. Wright, 57–60. Vancouver: Research and Development in Global Studies, University of British Columbia.

REFERENCES

Boulding, E. 1995. Why imagine the future? *Context: A Journal of Hope, Sustainability, and Change* 40: 50.

Bryant, B. 1995. Rehearsing the future. *Context: A Journal of Hope, Sustainability, and Change* 40: 39–50.

Canadian International Development Agency. 1987. *Sharing our future: Canadian international development assistance.* Hull: Minister of Supply and Services Canada.

Department of Foreign Affairs and International Trade. 1994. *Canadian reference guide to the United Nations.* Hull: Minister of Supply and Services Canada.

Hevesi, D. 1990. NY children feel both fearful, guilty about the homeless. *Globe and Mail,* May 22.

Jickling, B. 1994. Studying sustainable development: Problems and possibilities. *Canadian Journal of Education* 19 (3): 231–240.

Jones, R. 1970. *Fantasy and feeling in education.* New York: Harper Colophon Books.

Kaplan, R. 1994. The coming anarchy. *Atlantic Monthly,* February: 44–76.

Kennedy, P. 1993. *Preparing for the twenty-first century.* New York: Random House.

King, A. and B. Schneider. 1991. *The first global revolution: A report by the Council of the Club of Rome.* New York: Pantheon.

Korten, D. 1995. A new day's coming in. *Context: A Journal of Hope, Sustainability, and Change* 40: 14–18.

Phenix, P. 1974. Transcendence and the curriculum. In E. Eisner and E. Vallence, eds., *Conflicting conceptions of curriculum* (117–132). Berkeley, CA: McCutchan.

Roche, D. 1993. The new world order: Justice in international relations. *Global Education* 1 (1): 31–38.

Stackhouse, J. 1991. There's method in the misery. *Globe and Mail,* October 18.

Van Ornum, W. 1984. *Talking to children about nuclear war.* New York: Continuum.

19 Law-Related Education for Citizenship and for Life

Wanda Cassidy and Margaret Ferguson

"Hey, Jo, your essay comes straight from the internet!"

"Did you see the big fight in the hallway after school?"

"Someone stole my wallet during P.E. class."

"Hector is such a bully!"

"It's just not fair that Zoe is always picked on just 'cause she's different."

"Did you hear that Marcus was expelled again? This time he can't come back!"

"Hey, someone is spreading lies about me on MSN!"

"The police dog is back, sniffing lockers!"

Every day in secondary schools, teachers and students face issues and dilemmas that are related to law. These issues may not be immediately identified as legal; however, the law has much to say about how we treat others, privacy, fair decision making, being respected and heard, and making sure that rules are applied fairly to all. As the opening comments suggest, students learn implicitly about law every day through policies and practices at school, and how these are developed and implemented.

The secondary social studies curriculum also provides many opportunities for students to learn about law. In British Columbia, for example, social studies traditionally has been seen as encompassing the disciplines of history, geography, law, and economics (Bognar, Cassidy, and Clarke 1997). Law-related topics or themes are found at each grade level of the social studies curriculum across Canada. Topics at the secondary level include: the founding of Canada; disputes over boundaries, language, and issues of exploration; settlement of the West; land issues and First Nations peoples; immigration, human rights, and multiculturalism; the environment; government, citizenship, and the Charter of Rights

and Freedoms; differences between forms of government and the meaning of democracy; and Canada and its place in the world, conflict, international agreements, and trade. Several provinces also offer a senior elective solely or substantially devoted to law. In British Columbia, for example, students have the option of taking Law 12, or Civics 11, which includes a law component.

Yet secondary social studies teachers sometimes feel uncomfortable teaching the law dimension of the curriculum. Some feel unqualified to teach law, since their university degree is in history, geography, or another social science discipline. Many are unaware of the resources and services that exist to support the teaching of law (Kuehn, Yates, and Mainville 1995). Some feel that the curriculum is already overloaded, and therefore they prefer to skirt over those areas they know less about. In this chapter, we address the important role law plays in the social studies curriculum, argue for a broad approach to teaching law-related content that all social studies teachers can master, and suggest useful instructional strategies and classroom resources.

What Is Law-Related Education?

The term "law-related education" or LRE was coined over thirty years ago to describe the kind of education about law that is appropriate for students in publicly funded schools. There is a tendency to think that studying law means learning the body of rules and procedures that lawyers acquire in law school or that adults learn in a piecemeal fashion as they proceed through life. This is not the recommended approach for schools: most classroom teachers are ill-equipped to disseminate such information and the technical aspects of law are not the most appropriate law-related content to teach in public schools. For this reason, the term "law-related education" was coined to distinguish teaching about law in schools from teaching laws to lawyers and other legal professionals.

Rather than transmitting technical information about laws, LRE is more centrally concerned with promoting student understanding of the role that law plays in society and in their personal lives. Certainly, specific laws are studied from time to time, but the emphasis is on understanding why we have laws, the sources of law, legal institutions and structures, and other aspects of the foundations of law. The content of LRE is the ideas or concepts underlying the legal system—notions such as rights, responsibilities, authority, justice, and equality. LRE examines the values or beliefs embodied in our law, such as respect for property and human life. LRE involves developing basic citizenship attributes—such as critical thinking and conflict resolution—to help students participate effectively in a legally regulated world, and to effect change when the rules no longer reflect the kind of community we want. LRE encourages active learning and uses community resources to gain a realistic look at the legal system in operation. Important LRE objectives include reducing cynicism and encouraging students to understand the limitations of law, and assume some responsibility for making the system responsive to people's needs.

LRE seeks to develop critically aware and socially responsible citizens who are willing and able to make a positive difference in their neighbourhood, community, and nation. These aims are intertwined with the goals of social studies education more broadly: preparing young people for citizenship, developing student's abilities to think critically about issues, and encouraging students to take action to make the world a better place (Marker and Mehlinger 1992, Newmann 1989). Law professor Hugh Kindred captures the value of law-related education in furthering social studies goals:

> In a participatory democracy, it is vital that students learn about their rights and duties as citizens. Knowledge of the institutions that control the society is a prerequisite to intelligent democratic action.... In addition, it is important that students know not only their civic responsibilities, but also their freedoms of action within the Canadian system of government. The measure of good citizenship is not inculcated conformity, but a healthy respect for the rights of others as well as one's own, and an allegiance to orderly processes, even in diversity. The character of law encourages such critical, yet constructive attitudes. Consequently its study will develop them in students, the next generation of Canadian citizen (1979, 534).

As well, there is a profoundly practical reason for learning about the law. LRE is basic to survival in a world where law is pervasive. We marry, have families, travel, conduct business, worship, and even die according to law. Our written laws proliferate at a staggering rate. The federal government has enacted hundreds, if not thousands, of statutes and every province has approximately five hundred statutes in place. Thousands of regulations appended to these statutes contain the procedural "nuts and bolts" that affect how we act. Add municipal bylaws to this list and it is easy to appreciate that the long arm of the law reaches into almost every aspect of our lives. Without some appreciation of the nature and scope of this influence, students' ability to function in society is impaired. Furthermore, ignorance of the law is not considered a justifiable excuse when a law is not followed.

Efforts to infuse LRE are typically organized around three approaches (Starr 1989):

- **conceptual:** focussing on the core concepts and principles in law;
- **practical:** stressing the day-to-day implications of law;
- **participatory:** involving students in the application of law-related procedures.

Most programs in Canadian social studies classes combine elements of all three approaches, depending on curriculum expectations, grade level, and teacher and student needs and interests. We suggest there should be a fourth approach, which considers the informal or "hidden" curriculum of school policies and practices (Jackson 1990; Jackson, Boostrom, and Hansen 1993).

The Conceptual Approach

The conceptual approach examines central legal ideas such as liberty, justice, and equality—concepts that form the bedrock of a democratic society and which are lauded in school. Students have strong notions about what is right or fair, and are intrigued by dilemmas that present opportunities to examine issues of power, authority, privacy, responsibility, and property. This approach to LRE focusses on broad principles and concepts, and emphasizes critical thinking.

One way to address concepts is through a case study. Cases can either be real (for example, historical events, actual court cases, or current events), or taken from literature or built around imagined dilemmas. In each instance, students must identify which facts are important to the case, wrestle with the key issues, weigh the arguments, and come to a reasoned decision that is justified according to the evidence. There is no "pat" or "right" answer in a case study. Rather, the case study is a process whereby students hone important social studies skills such as separating relevant from irrelevant facts, synthesizing the issues into one key problem or question needing resolution, articulating the different perspectives and arguments, coming to a reasoned decision, and justifying the decision with logical and persuasive reasons (Bognar et al., 1997). The case study method follows a similar format to the inquiry model of problem solving (Joyce and Weil, 1996), an approach sometimes cited in social studies curriculum documents (Bognar et al., 1997): outline the facts; identify the key issue(s); discuss the main arguments; make a decision; and justify the decision with reasons. The highlighted text, "Case Study Method," suggests a five-step structure for a case study.

There are many opportunities in the social studies curriculum to address legal concepts. For example, in order to understand the roles, rights, and responsibilities of a citizen in a democracy, students need to understand the role law plays in our society, why laws are needed, how an outdated law might be changed, legitimate processes for citizenship involvement, and what penalties are appropriate if the public peace and well-being is jeopardized. The study of government and politics is not complete without an examination of the rule of law, the responsibilities of different levels of government, the role of the judiciary, and the importance of the Charter of Rights and Freedoms. The topic of immigration, for example, should address the historical treatment of certain minority groups, how legislation has changed over time, current multicultural policies and human rights legislation, beliefs about inclusion and diversity, and how these are reflected in policies and practices. The highlighted text, "Introducing Rights and Freedoms," describes an activity to help students think about the range of rights that Canadians enjoy.

The Practical Approach

The focus of the practical approach is law's impact on the daily lives and decisions of Canadians. At the secondary

CASE STUDY METHOD

- **Find the facts:** Who is involved? What happened? What is the complaint or charge? What facts are important? Which facts are irrelevant?
- **Frame the issues:** Identify the key issue and pose it as a question (for example, Should logging be restricted in the habitat occupied by the Spirit Bear? Was Louis Riel guilty of treason? Should Ocean Oil Tanker Inc. pay for the damage caused by their oil spill?).
- **Discuss the arguments:** An issue always gives rise to two or more points of view. What are the arguments for and against? Which arguments are most persuasive? Why?
- **Reach a decision:** After students wrestle with the case and reach a decision, the court decision may be discussed, a historical event replayed, or the story's ending communicated.
- **Examine the reasoning:** Students should back up their decision with reasons. In a real case, judges often disagree with each other. In appeal cases involving more than one judge, one judge writes the majority decision, and other judges may write minority opinions. Students may be invited to do the same.

school level, topics typically include youth justice issues, school attendance, family disputes, leaving home, renting an apartment, working, and buying a car and other goods. Young people may not be aware that the law has an impact on their lives on a daily basis.

A simple activity to convey the role law plays in one's life is to ask students to list all the things they did on one day, from the time they got out of bed until bedtime. Students begin to see that law regulates what goes into the toothpaste they use, the way beds are constructed, home building materials, what is written on their breakfast cereal boxes, the type

INTRODUCING RIGHTS AND FREEDOMS

- As a class, discuss the notion of a "right" and a "freedom."
- In groups, brainstorm all the rights and all the freedoms you think we have as Canadians. Record each suggestion on a strip of paper.
- Working in your group, categorize these rights and freedoms, and put a label on each category.
- Students share their categories with another group and discuss similarities and differences.
- Returning to their groups, students make changes to their list of categories and prepare a final list of rights and freedoms on chart paper.
- Each group shares its ideas with the full class.
- Teacher discusses students' ideas, and leads them to analyze their suggestions.

- Teacher hands out the annotated version of the Canadian Charter of Rights and Freedoms and discusses with class the similarities and differences between their versions and the Canadian document.
- Teacher asks students questions such as: Should rights and freedoms be written down in a charter? Are there values and beliefs that Canadians share that are not recorded in the charter? How does Canada's Charter of Rights and Freedoms differ from the Bill of Rights in the United States? What should be the relationship between the courts and the legislators? Should the charter override government decisions?
- Each student then chooses one right or freedom, or a bigger conceptual question to address in a research project.

of fabric in their clothes, how parents can treat them, where they can ride their bike or drive their car, school hours, what can be said in school textbooks, what they can or cannot say or do to a fellow student, the air they breathe, the movies they see, and the CDs they listen to.

Another activity is based on the daily newspaper. Ask groups of students to identify any article, an advertisement, or a section from the newspaper that relates to law. Initially, students may find a few obvious examples, such as a crime committed, a lawsuit, or a police matter. However, with guidance, students will come to see that almost every part of the newspaper is connected to law—including the sports pages, advertisements, the classified section, the comics, the entertainment section, and most headlined articles. As the highlighted text "Law in Our Everyday Lives" suggests, law regulates and shapes almost everything we do on a daily basis.

Appreciating the practical implications of rights contained in documents such as the United Nations Convention on the Rights of the Child or the Canadian Charter of Rights and Freedoms requires that students understand that human rights exist to protect the most basic of human needs. Students learn the importance of these entitlements by examining the consequences that follow when these rights are not respected. Using Figure 19.1 (adapted from Nicol and Kirk 2004), students might consider the point along a continuum from total absence to complete luxury at which meeting this basic need becomes a right. Students would decide this by considering the implications, on the one hand, of not meeting the need for a person's well-being and, on the other hand,

of placing an unfair burden on the rest of society who would have a responsibility to see that this right is respected. The articulation of this point can be used to generate a statement of rights (for example, every child has a right to enough food so that…), which can be posted to a class charter, and eventually compared with the UN Convention on the Rights of the Child or the Canadian Charter of Rights and Freedoms.

> ■
>
> Select an important legal principle (such as equality, justice, personal responsibility, or the rule of law) and develop one or more activities to help students better understand the concept and to nurture their appreciation of its importance as a personal and social value.

The Participatory Approach

Many LRE advocates stress a participatory approach to learning in which students engage directly with legal resources in the community and with real or realistic law-related problems. Judges, lawyers, legislators, human rights advocates, environmentalists, and others are invited into the classroom, and students interact with local law-related agencies. Courthouses are open to the public, and many courts (with prior permission) will allow classes to view a trial in session or conduct their own mock trial in a spare courtroom. Many law-related agencies are willing to share their knowledge with

LAW IN OUR EVERYDAY LIVES

- **Name.** Laws specify the surname a child can take. Everyone's name is registered on a legal document, the birth certificate. There is a legal procedure to follow for changing one's name.
- **Address.** Do students live in a village, city, or town? This designation is determined by law. Zoning laws specify the type of dwellings that can be built in an area. The procedures for numbering homes and naming streets in municipalities are regulated by law.
- **School.** Laws require children to attend school, and these laws set the number of hours of instruction per day and per year. The law requires property owners to pay taxes to support schools and sets out the rights and responsibilities of teachers and principals.
- **Pets.** Municipalities have laws that affect the type of pet one can have, and whether or not a pet requires a licence and a leash on public property. Cruelty to animals can be a criminal offence.
- **Family.** Laws specify how marriage must take place, how people come to assume rights and responsibilities as a

mother or father, under what conditions divorce can occur, how adoptions occur, who is entitled to inherit property when a family member dies, and so on.
- **Food.** Laws regulate the handling and packaging of food, specify what foods can be imported and exported, and spell out what businesses must do before they can sell food.
- **Transportation.** Drivers and owners of vehicles have many laws to obey—licensing, insurance, and traffic laws. The use of bicycles, scooters, and skateboards is also regulated by laws.
- **Contracts.** Any time goods are bought or sold, we are entering into a contract. Consumer protection laws ensure that contracts are fair.
- **Money.** Laws establish what currency is legal tender in a country.
- **Businesses.** The formation and operation of businesses are governed by law, including the rights and responsibilities of employers and employees.

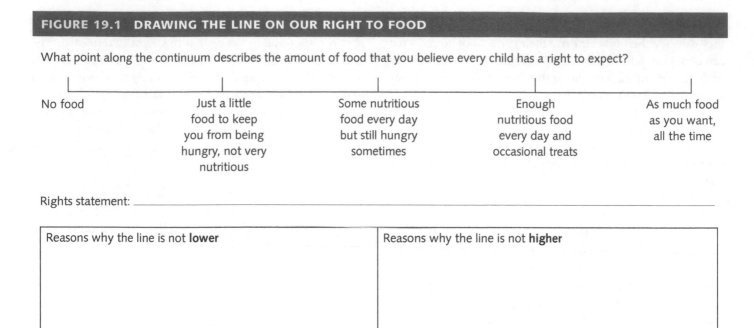

FIGURE 19.1 DRAWING THE LINE ON OUR RIGHT TO FOOD

What point along the continuum describes the amount of food that you believe every child has a right to expect?

No food	Just a little food to keep you from being hungry, not very nutritious	Some nutritious food every day but still hungry sometimes	Enough nutritious food every day and occasional treats	As much food as you want, all the time

Rights statement: _____

Reasons why the line is not **lower**	Reasons why the line is not **higher**

students (for example, immigrant services societies, Native friendship centres, human rights groups, mediation services, media watch groups, internet regulators, consumer protection agencies, animal rights groups, or multicultural groups). See the additional resources at the end of this chapter for contact information on public legal education agencies that have a mandate to support teachers in various provinces and territories.

The participatory approach stresses that students learn about law by experiencing legal processes and decision making in ways that simulate real life. This means that mock trials and role plays based on legal procedures are central to LRE pedagogy. Simple simulations or role plays may be developed based on neighbourhood or school issues, historical events, or stories from literature.

Mock trials, which involve more formal enactment of legal procedures than do role plays, have been used in social studies classes to address historical and current events (Hawkins and Barnett 2000, Hou and Hou 1984, Norton 1992). In a mock trial, students put a character on trial and then enact the trial playing the roles of the accused, the witnesses, court personnel, and the media. Mock trials have been conducted informally in-class or conducted with costumes and props in a local courthouse or other public place with actual members of the judiciary or legal professionals presiding. Classes have retried Louis Riel; examined a gold rush murder case tried by the infamous hanging judge, Matthew Baillie Begbie; re-enacted interesting cases like the man who killed his mother-in-law and used sleepwalking as a defence; and put such fairy-tale characters on trial as Goldilocks, Han-

sel and Gretel, Peter Pan, and Alice in Wonderland. Current events also provide engaging scenarios that can be used as the basis for mock trials.

Historical events provide an excellent source of material for mock trials or role play about law-related issues. History is full of examples of good and bad leadership, of people who display responsible or irresponsible behaviour, and of decisions that involve freedom, equality, justice, or privacy. History examines how people (or countries) solve conflict and the consequences of actions taken. It is not difficult to create a mock trial from a historical event, or from a current event.

The Moot Appeal

Teachers may also chose the moot appeal as a way to address a topic or theme in the social studies curriculum. In a real appeal court case, the legal issues that surfaced in a trial are re-examined by a panel of five to nine judges. The facts of the case are not re-visited; rather, the focus is on whether the trial judge made an error in law. An appeal involves the lawyers for the appellant (the party appealing the case), lawyers for the respondent (the party defending the trial court decision), and the justices of the appeal court. Cases appealed to the Supreme Court of Canada are often good choices for a moot appeal with students, as the issues are controversial, topical, and precedent-setting.[2] Recent Supreme Court decisions involve funding for autistic children and same-sex marriages.

An example of a historical case that raised the issue of

ORGANIZING A MOCK TRIAL

There are three phases to a trial: the preparatory phase, the trial itself, and the post-trial discussion. The phases for a criminal mock trial are outlined below.

Preparatory phase

- Decide on the story or event for the trial, or choose one of the scripted or packaged mock trials available.[1]
- Help students understand the criminal charge, the facts of the case, and the key issues.
- Review basic information with students about the justice system (adversarial model, need for impartial decision, role of court personnel, innocent until proven guilty, concept of intent, reasonable doubt).
- Assign (or allow students to choose) their roles: the accused, witnesses, Crown prosecutors, defence lawyers, court clerk, court reporter, sheriffs, and media (court artist, newspaper reporters, television journalists). A lawyer or school principal should be asked to play the role of judge.
- Divide students into four small groups that will each prepare their case:
  - Crown prosecution and their witnesses;
  - defence lawyers, the accused, and their witnesses;
  - court personnel; and
  - the media.
  If following a script, emphasize that the case should be presented without notes as much as possible. For more complex trials involving role cards instead of a script, emphasize the development of arguments, writing good questions to be asked in court, and presenting one's evidence as convincingly as possible.
- Invite students to prepare costumes that represent their role.

Enacting the trial

- If the trial is conducted in the school gymnasium, library, or classroom, design the room to model a real courtroom, as illustrated in Figure 19.2 (adapted from Cassidy and Yates 2005).
- Once the trial begins, it should continue without interruption until the jury reaches a decision and the sentence is rendered (if guilty), or the accused is set free (if not guilty). The teacher's role is to take notes and comment following the trial, not to guide or interrupt the trial.
- A criminal trial follows this procedure:
  - Sheriff calls the court to order.
  - Lawyers introduce themselves.
  - Court clerk reads out the charge(s).
  - Accused pleads "guilty" or "not guilty" to charge(s).
  - Prosecution makes an opening statement saying what they hope to prove and listing the witnesses it plans to call.
  - Prosecution calls the first witness to the stand.
  - Defence cross-examines the witness.
  - (Repeat until all of the prosecution witnesses have been called.)
  - Defence makes opening statement, and lists the witnesses it plans to call.
  - Defence calls the first witness.
  - Prosecution cross-examines the witness.
  - (Repeat until all of the defence witnesses have been called.)
  - Defence makes closing argument to the jury.
  - Prosecution makes closing argument to the jury.
  - Judge speaks to the jury to encourage it to make a careful and impartial decision.
  - Jury in private discusses the charge(s) and determines whether the accused is guilty or not guilty of each charge.
  - Court clerk asks the jury foreperson to read out the verdict.
  - Judge sentences the accused if guilt is found on one or more charges.
  - If an acquittal results, the accused is free to go.

Post-trial discussion

- Immediately after the trial, debrief with students, allowing them to share their feelings and thoughts about the trial, and to come out of role.
- With the full class listening/contributing, address each group:
  Jury: What evidence was most convincing? Which characters were most believable? Why did they decide the case as they did?
  Lawyers: Which arguments were most persuasive? Would you change your presentation in any way?
  Witnesses: What did you experience being in the witness box? Did any aspects of the trial surprise you?
  Court personnel: Why is the role of court clerk and court reporter important? Did the sheriff feel any differently about the role after donning a costume?
  Media: What parts of this trial are you going to write about or present to classmates? What role does the media play in real court cases?
  Whole class: What did you learn about the law and court system as a result of participating in this trial?
- The days following the trial provide other opportunities for reflection, or more in-depth investigation of aspects of the justice system and conceptual issues such as the advantages and disadvantages of the adversarial model, whether judgment by peers in a jury system is the best method of determining guilt, whether there are better ways to resolve disputes than through the courts, and so on.

FIGURE 19.2 COURTROOM LAYOUT

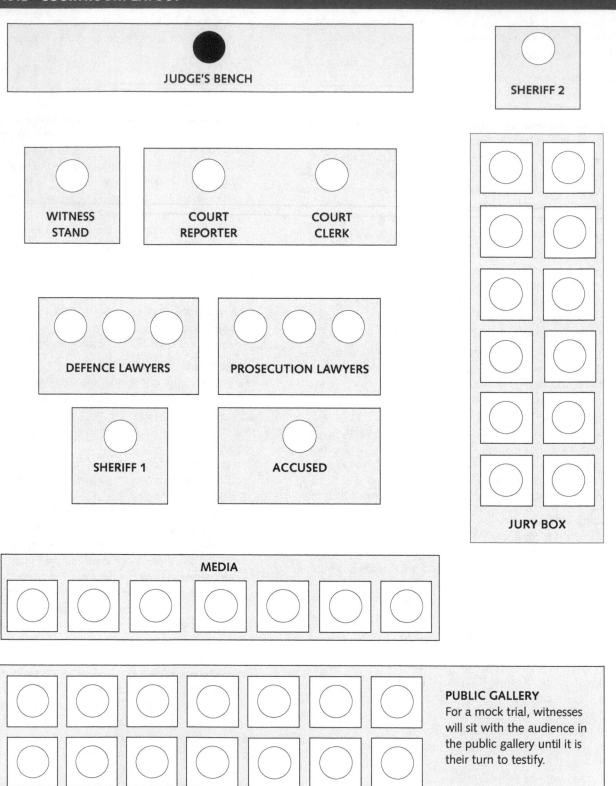

JUDGE'S BENCH

SHERIFF 2

WITNESS STAND

COURT REPORTER

COURT CLERK

DEFENCE LAWYERS

PROSECUTION LAWYERS

SHERIFF 1

ACCUSED

JURY BOX

MEDIA

PUBLIC GALLERY
For a mock trial, witnesses will sit with the audience in the public gallery until it is their turn to testify.

political interference in administrative decision-making and the rule of law is the case of *Roncarelli vs. Duplessis*. This incident, described in the highlighted text, involved the premier of Quebec at the time, Mr. Duplessis, and a prominent restaurateur, Mr. Roncarelli.

Alternative Dispute Resolution

Often there are better ways to solve disputes than by resorting to the courts. The court process is expensive, time-consuming, and often results in people becoming estranged or feeling as if a decision is being forced on them by a third party. More and more, people are resorting to alternative dispute resolution procedures to resolve difficulties. One such method is mediation. In mediation, parties work together with the help of a third party to come to a mutually agreeable decision. This involves give and take, with each side letting go of certain demands or moderating others in order to come to an agreement. This procedure may be simulated in class, and students will learn listening and negotiating skills in the process.

The justice circle is another law-related strategy that may be used in the classroom to resolve a conflict, to address a topic in the curriculum, or to hone particular skills. Justice circles are based on the First Nations' Sentencing Circle concept, where the goal is to bring healing to the victim and to the community, and to restore (rather than punish) the offender. The justice circle provides an opportunity for everyone who has been affected by an offence to be given a chance to speak. Through this process of listening, sharing, and discovery, an equitable and fair solution is reached. This process encompasses important social studies objectives, such as listening to one another, working towards the common good of all, co-operative learning, questioning, appreciating another's point of view, analyzing the issues, appreciating diversity, and community participation.

The Informal Curriculum

Teachers would be remiss if they focussed exclusively on the formal curriculum of social studies education, yet failed to

RONCARELLI VS. DUPLESSIS

The setting was Montreal in 1946. Many Quebecers were Roman Catholic and the Church played a dominant role in the social and political life of the province. The Jehovah's Witnesses were a small sect that objected to organized religion, and were opposed to the Roman Catholic Church because of the power it wielded and because it co-operated with Hitler in Germany to suppress the sect. The Jehovah's Witnesses were distributing their literature in Quebec, and some of it was critical of Catholicism. Many districts passed by-laws preventing the distribution of their literature without police permission. The Witnesses continued to sell their magazines and this resulted in demonstrations and some violent attacks against them. Some members of the sect were arrested, and while charges were usually dropped, those arrested either had to provide bail or spend time in jail. Mr. Roncarelli was a member of the sect, but did not distribute literature, and only paid the bail for several of the Witnesses in jail.

On December 4, 1946, Premier Duplessis instructed the chairperson of the Liquor Commission, Mr. Archambault, to order the police to raid the restaurant owned by Mr. Roncarelli. The police descended on the popular restaurant, confiscated all the wine on the premises, and demanded the liquor licence. The police then searched the premises for five hours looking for Jehovah's Witnesses literature, but found none. When a reporter called the premier's office to find out what was going on, the premier replied that Roncarelli was a "mass supplier of bails," which, he claimed, was a "provocation of public order... and definitely contrary to the aims of justice."

Mr. Roncarelli had not broken any liquor laws, nor had he run his restaurant improperly. But because of the withdrawal of the liquor licence, Mr. Roncarelli had to close the restaurant he had run for 34 years. He could not find other employment and became bankrupt. In 1951, Mr. Roncarelli sued Mr. Duplessis in civil court for $118,741 for loss of his business and possible profits. The Quebec superior court awarded him only $8,123.53 to cover the loss of the liquor seized and loss of profits from the date of the seizure to the date when his liquor licence would have expired. Roncarelli appealed the decision and Duplessis filed a counter-appeal in the Quebec Court of Queen's Bench. The case was heard in 1956 and Duplessis was found not liable. Roncarelli then appealed to the Supreme Court of Canada.

The Supreme Court restored the Quebec Superior Court decision and raised the award to $33,123.53 plus interest, equalling $45,000. The judgment, however, did not come down until 1959, almost thirteen years after the raid. The court determined that the removal of the liquor licence was meant to cause financial loss so that Roncarelli could no longer post bail for Jehovah's Witnesses. Bail, however, is a human right. Moreover the court ruled that no government official was above the law; the rule of law was paramount and fundamental to our constitution.

MEDIATION: SKATEBOARDING IN THE NEIGHBOURHOOD

Several local teenagers like to skateboard in their neighbourhood, which has a lot of cul-de-sacs. Almost every evening, especially in the summertime, teens are on the streets with their skateboards. Some of the neighbours are tired of the noise and want the teens to go elsewhere. The parents of the teens are happy that they are close to home and don't want them to leave. Besides, they say, it is a free country, and kids should have the same right to use the sidewalks and streets as the adults. They also point out that some of the adults in the neighbourhood make noise with their lawn mowers and leaf blowers. In order to solve the impasse, one of the neighbours, who is a mediator by profession, has offered to help resolve the problem, provided that both parties agree to talk openly and frankly and come to a mutually agreeable solution.

The class can either be divided into three sub-groups: the skateboarders/parents; the neighbours who have complained; and the mediators, or the class can be divided into triads, with one student playing the role of the skateboarder, one the neighbour, and one the mediator. A role of the mediator is to encourage both sides to present their case, to ask questions, to compromise, and to help the parties reach a mutually agreeable solution.

JUSTICE CIRCLE ACTIVITY: VANDALIZING THE PLAYGROUND

One warm evening in May, three fifteen-year-old friends, Tom, Harj, and Jenny, decide to hang out at the playground of their old elementary school. The teens swing high on swings that are too small for them and they damage the seats. They jump on the ends of the teeter-totters until one of them breaks in the middle. They jump on the bouncing equipment until it is damaged. Then they dump out the garbage from the garbage cans. After this frenzied activity, they realize the damage they've done, and feel badly. Each runs home, hoping that no one can connect them with the mess that has been left in the schoolyard.

The next morning, the damage is discovered first by the children and then by the school principal, who calls the police. When the police interview the neighbours, some report that they saw the teenagers playing on the grounds the previous night and one of them recognizes all three. The police go to the teens' homes to question them about the vandalism. At first, each denies knowing anything about the playground, but after much questioning, the truth comes out and each youth admits contributing to the damage.

The police take into account that the teenagers are young and that this is their first offence. They go to the principal of the elementary school to consult with her about what action to take. Because the teens had been students at the school a few years earlier, the principal thinks that the school should play a role in determining what happens to them. The principal decides that a justice circle would be an appropriate mechanism to deal with the offenders and the damage they've done.

Activity Guidelines
- **Becoming familiar with the case:** As a class, discuss the case and talk about what might have motivated the teens to do what they did. Talk about the amount of damage done and how each player might feel about the episode.
- **Assign roles:** Each student should assume and develop a role: as one of the teens, the teens' parents, the school administrators, playground supervisors, some of the elementary students, the elementary school counsellor, former and current teachers of the youths, others who know the teens. The goal of the justice circle is to do what is best for all players, considering society's interests and what is in the best interests of the offenders.

Justice Circle procedure:
- Arrange the chairs in a circle, with the teacher acting as judge and facilitator.
- Use a talking stick to ensure that only one person talks at a time.
- Each person has two minutes to give his/her character's point of view.
- The victims (elementary school staff and students) speak first.
- The offenders and their parents and representatives speak next, followed by others.
- After everyone has spoken, the judge summarizes what has been said, and then asks for suggestions from each side as to what should be an appropriate resolution, including any compensation.
- The judge tries to find common ground. The group then votes on whether they can accept the recommended resolution, or makes further recommendations until everyone is satisfied with the outcome.

Debriefing
After the circle is dissolved, the following questions may be asked:
- Is this method of dealing with the problem fair to all parties involved?
- Would this resolution process hurt or help the community to heal from the effects of an offence?
- Would this process help an offender? Do you think that he or she would commit another similar offence?
- What are the negative and positive aspects of this way of deciding justice matters?

consider the law-related implications of the informal or "hidden" curriculum. What we do in the classroom—what is modelled and practised—has a powerful effect on students' learning (Jackson 1990; Jackson, Boostrom, and Hansen 1993; Noddings 1992). Establishing working principles for the classroom and a few rules to support these principles helps to model for students the ideals of thoughtful law-making and citizen involvement. These conditions for a "democratic" classroom can be nurtured at the beginning of the school year by considering and, if appropriate, inviting students to consider the following kinds of questions:

- What are the shared values and beliefs that will form the basis of the classroom community?
- Will these values be reflected in classroom rules or procedures?
- Will students' views be solicited?
- How will these values and beliefs be demonstrated? Will there be rules, and what will the rules say?
- Will students have input into the rules?
- How will the teachers deal with challenges to the rules?
- How will rules be enforced and who will judge whether a rule has been broken?
- Will the consequences for the breach of a rule be fair and flexible so that the context of the offence is considered?
- Is there a need to clarify or modify the rules as situations develop? How will this be done?
- How does one measure the fairness or appropriateness of a rule? (Should all students find the rules acceptable, or is it sufficient that the majority agree?)
- Should all students consent, or is it sufficient that the majority agree?
- How will the teacher encourage co-operation and fairness among students?
- Will the teacher promote success for each student and welcome diversity in the classroom?
- How will he/she build community and respect among students? How will conflict be resolved?
- Will students be given the right to be heard, and recourse if they take issue with a decision?

The way decisions are made, and the input given to students, teaches important principles of human rights, law-making, and citizen involvement. Teachers who espouse democratic principles should endeavour to involve students in decisions affecting them and to model and practise those principles held dear. The informal curriculum has a powerful effect on children's learning (Jackson, Boostrom, and Hansen 1993; Noddings 1992).

Another major source of everyday law has to do with the concept of justice or fairness. Teachers frequently deal with questions about "what's fair." Adjudicating disagreements and managing conflict afford opportunities for law-related education, because resolving disputes is a major function of law. Many schools have peer mediation programs where students involved in conflict learn to solve their differences without the intervention of teachers, helped by trained student mediators.

The growing interest in social responsibility and in restorative justice is also compatible with law-related education, particularly if the programs developed are respectful of individuals, give credence to due process, allow for diversity and reasonable dissent, seek to be just and fair, and work towards the common good of all (Whitley 2002). It is also important that the whole school community, not just the social studies teacher, be involved in these initiatives, working together to model and practise the values of responsibility or restoration, rather than expecting only the students to comply (Epstein 1999). Approaches that engage all stakeholders and become embedded in school culture have a far greater impact on learning than programs that merely articulate the goals but do little to implement them.

Conclusion

The law dimension is an essential part of an adequate social studies education. The kind of education in law we advocate is not that of mini lawyers-in-training, but rather sensitizing students to the role that law plays in their lives and in a democratic society. We have illustrated a range of opportunities and strategies for incorporating law-related topics into the formal and informal curriculum. No single approach to LRE is required—you are encouraged to start small with an approach that best suits your purposes and resources. By doing this, you will join elementary teachers across North America who are advancing students' awareness of legal concepts and procedures and empowering them to be effective and responsible members of their classroom, school, and neighbourhood communities.

Create a list of approximately ten basic principles embedded in our formal justice system (for example, the right to be heard, to be presumed innocent until proven guilty, freedom of expression, freedom of conscience). Develop a detailed plan for classroom operations that would model these values in ways that are appropriate and realistic for students at the grade level you teach.

NOTES

1. For a list of trials, see the Law Courts Education Society of British Columbia website or consult www.acjnet.org/teacher/ and www.lawconnection.ca.
2. Supreme Court of Canada decisions can be accessed through a link from www.lawconnection.ca or from www.acjnet.org.

REFERENCES

Bognar, C., W. Cassidy, and P. Clarke. 1997. *Social studies in British Columbia: Results of the 1996 Provincial Learning Assessment.* Victoria, BC: Province of British Columbia.

Cassidy, W. and R. Yates, eds. 2005. *Once upon a crime: Using stories, simulations and mock trials to explore justice and citizenship in elementary school.* Calgary: Detselig.

Epstein, J. 1999. Creating school, family, and community partnerships. In *Contemporary issues in curriculum,* 2nd ed., eds. A. Ornstein and L.S. Behar-Horenstein, 422–441. Boston: Allyn and Bacon.

Hawkins, S. and Judge C.C. Barnett. 2000. Series of advanced mock trials. Vancouver: Law Courts Education Society of B.C.

Hou, C. and C. Hou. 1984. *The Riel rebellion: A biographical approach.* Vancouver: Moody's Lookout Press.

Jackson, P.W. 1990. *Life in classrooms.* New York: Teachers College Press.

Jackson, P.W., R. Boostrom, and D. Hansen. 1993. *The moral life of schools.* San Francisco: Jossey-Bass.

Joyce, B. and M. Weil. 1996. *Models of teaching.* 5th ed. Boston: Allyn and Bacon.

Kindred, H. 1979. Legal education in Canadian schools? *Dalhousie Law Journal* 5 (2): 534–542.

Kuehn, S., R. Yates, and R. Mainville. 1995. *Law-related education survey.* Report produced for the Department of Justice Canada. Ottawa: Government of Canada.

Marker, G. and H. Mehlinger. 1992. Social studies. In *Handbook of research on curriculum,* ed. P.W. Jackson. New York: Macmillan.

Newmann, F.M. 1989. *Education for citizen action: Challenge for secondary curriculum.* Berkeley, CA: McCutchan.

Nicol, J. and D. Kirk. 2004. *Caring for young people's rights.* Richmond, BC: The Critical Thinking Consortium.

Noddings, N. 1992. *The challenge to care in schools: An alternate approach to education.* New York: Teachers College Press.

Norton, J. 1992. The state v. the big bad wolf: A study of the justice system in the elementary school. *Social Studies and the Young Learner* 5 (1): 5–9.

Starr, I. 1989. The law studies movement: A brief look at the past, the present and the future. In *Law vs. learning: Examination for discovery,* ed. W. Crawford, 11–15. Toronto: Canadian Law Information Council.

Whitley, C. 2002. Building citizenship, democracy and a community of learners within a context of a restorative justice model. Unpublished master's project. Burnaby, BC: Simon Fraser University.

PUBLIC LEGAL EDUCATION AGENCIES IN CANADA

There are a number of organizations and resources available to teachers who wish to enhance the program they offer in law-related education.

Alberta
Centre for Public Legal Education Alberta
800, 10050 – 112 Street
Edmonton, AB T5K 2J1
Tel: 780-451-8764
Fax: 780-451-2341
http://www.cplea.ca/

British Columbia
Centre for Education, Law and Society
Simon Fraser University
13450 – 102 Avenue
5th floor Galleria – Room 5288
Surrey, BC V3T 0A3
Tel: 604-268-7840
http://cels.sfu.ca
http://www.lawconnection.ca

Justice Education Society of BC
260–800 Hornby Street
Vancouver, BC V6Z 2C5
Tel: 604-660-9870
http://www.lces.ca
http://www.justiceeducation.ca/

Legal Services Society
400–510 Burrard Street
Vancouver, BC V6C 3A8
Tel: 604-601-6000
http://www.lss.bc.ca

People's Law School
150–900 Howe Street
Vancouver, BC V6Z 2M4
Tel: 604-331-5400
http://www.publiclegaled.bc.ca

Manitoba
Community Legal Education Association
205–414 Graham Avenue
Winnipeg, MB   R3C 0L8
Tel: 204-943-2382
http://www.communitylegal.mb.ca

New Brunswick
Public Legal Education and Information Service of New Brunswick
P.O. Box 6000
Fredericton, NB   E3B 5H1
Tel: 506-453-5369
http://www.legal-info-legale.nb.ca

Newfoundland
Public Legal Information of Newfoundland
Suite 227, 31 Peet Street, Tara Place
St. John's, NL   A1B 3W8
Tel: 709-722-2643
http://www.publiclegalinfo.com

Northwest Territories
Law Society of the Northwest Territories
4th Floor, Diamond Plaza
5204 50th Avenue
Yellowknife, NT   X1A 1E2
Mailing Address (Canada Post):
PO Box 1298, STN Main
Yellowknife, NT   X1A 2N9
http://www.lawsociety.nt.ca

Nova Scotia
The Legal Information Society of Nova Scotia
5523 B Young Street
Halifax, NS   B3K 1Z7
Tel: 902-454-2198
http://www.legalinfo.org

Ontario
Community Legal Education Ontario
180 Dundas Street West, Suite 506
Toronto, ON   M5G 1Z8
Tel: 416-408-4420
http://www.cleo.on.ca

Justice for Children and Youth
Canadian Foundation for Children, Youth and the Law
415 Yonge Street, Suite 1203
Toronto, ON   M5B 2E7
Tel: 416-920-1633
http://www.jfcy.org

Prince Edward Island
Community Legal Information Association of Prince Edward Island
Royalty Centre, Room 111
40 Enman Crescent
Charlottetown, PE   C1E 1E6
Tel: 902-892-0853
http://www.cliapei.ca/

Québec
Barreau du Québec
445 boulevard Saint Laurent, S215
Montréal, QC   H2Y 3T8
Tel: 514-954-3400
http://www.barreau.qc.ca/?Langue=en

Commission des Services Juridiques
2, Complexe Desjardins
Tour de l'Est, Bureau # 1404
Montréal, QC   H5B 1B3
Tel: 514-873-3562
http://www.csj.qc.ca

Gouvernement du Québec
Ministère de la Justice
1200 route de l'Eglise, 6ième étage
Sainte-Foy, QC   G1V 4M1
Tel: 418-643-5140
http://www.justice.gouv.qc.ca/English/accueil.asp

Saskatchewan
Public Legal Education Association of Saskatchewan
500–333 25th Street East
Saskatoon, SK   S7K 0L4
Tel: 306-653-1868
http://www.plea.org

Yukon
Yukon Public Legal Education Association
2131 2nd Avenue (Tutshi Building), Suite 102
Whitehorse, YK   Y1A 1C3
Tel: 867-668-5297
http://www.yplea.com

20

Give Peace a Chance

Susan Hargraves and Mary-Wynne Ashford

In a world where war is fought on-screen in our living rooms and nail scissors are confiscated as potential weapons of terror at airports, students arrive in our classrooms already "well-schooled" in the business of war and violence. They bring knowledge, beliefs, fears, and attitudes that reflect what they have learned from television and movies, including misperceptions and biases. Although there are exceptions, few people would deny the pervasive sense of cynicism and hopelessness that currently prevails in the face of domestic and international conflict and tension. Teachers are not exempt from this malaise. How do we approach questions of violence and non-violence in the social studies classroom without furthering the belief that war is inevitable and that we are powerless to bring about peace? How do we begin to teach without first confronting the heavy emotional cloud that often produces psychological numbness and closed-mindedness? And should we?

Individual educators and groups have struggled to find answers to these questions and in the process have developed a pedagogy of peace education. There is a core set of principles, guidelines, and practices intended to infuse peace education into the curriculum in ways that avoid desensitizing students and inducing cynicism. In this chapter, we present many of these ideas in the context of a six-step framework for teaching for peace and illustrate each step with classroom activities and examples. Before doing this, we look at the history and mandate for peace education.

Evolution of Peace Education

In the early 1980s, a rapidly growing peace movement gained the attention of many North American educators. Working independently and in groups, both with and without school district support, teachers began to raise the issue of nuclear war and its prevention in their classrooms. This movement grew out of a sense of urgency, fuelled by the belief that nuclear war was imminent. The *Bulletin of the Atomic Scientists* regularly published a picture of a clock indicating how close the world was to nuclear war. During this period, the clock reached "two minutes to midnight." The movement also grew out of a sense of increasing alarm, as young people all over the world reported fear and hopelessness regarding their future. An almost evangelical fervour marked much of the resulting classroom activity. Not surprisingly, so did controversy.

While peace education became a popular movement in the early 1980s, it had originated with the establishment of the United Nations at the end of World War II. The preamble to the charter of UNESCO (United Nations Educational, Social and Cultural Organization) states the goal of peace education at this time: "since wars begin in the minds of men [sic], it is in the minds of men that the foundations of peace must be constructed." Initially, the purpose of peace education was to prevent conventional war and, as we mentioned above, by the early 1980s the focus had shifted to preventing nuclear war. Peace education has further evolved from a preoccupation with preventing war to the promotion of a "culture of peace." "The Hague Agenda for Peace and Justice in the 21st Century," the document arising out of the Hague Appeal for Peace Conference and presented to the UN, contains the following statement:

> A culture of peace will be achieved when citizens of the world understand global problems, have the skills to resolve conflicts and struggle for justice non-violently, live by international standards of human rights and equity, appreciate cultural diversity, and respect the Earth and each other. Such learning can only be achieved with systematic education for peace (Hague Appeal for Peace 2000, 6).

Peace education now takes many forms: conflict resolution, global education, development education, environmental education, education for liberation and empowerment, social justice education, anti-bullying, and more.

Peace education includes developing knowledge about armed conflicts and the roots of violence and aggression in its various forms. Violence includes overt acts resulting from unresolved conflict as well as the more subtle forms inherent in the structures of a relationship or of a society that are known as "systemic violence." At the heart of this concept is the interrelationship of violence, aggression, inequity, and injustice, which is characterized by conflict and operates at any level from the personal and local to the national and global. This description is familiar to most social studies teachers.

Conflict resolution and peer mediation have became increasingly central to the peace education curriculum. This emphasis was largely the result of increased youth violence, as well as a recognition that peace begins with each of us. That is to say, we cannot imagine or expect peace on the world stage if we do not practise it in our own lives. By learning and applying the attitudes and skills of peaceful resolution of differences, students can learn two important lessons: conflict need not result in violence and injury, and, more importantly, there is hope for peace in the world.

Groups and agencies dedicated to the causes of peace and justice have become more skilled and effective in preventing, limiting, and containing armed violence though effective conflict-resolution strategies. Because conflicts tend to be cyclical, even the work of healing after the violence contributes to the prevention of violence in the future. One thinks of the work of the Truth and Reconciliation Commission first used in South Africa in this regard.

What is less well known is the proliferation of non-governmental organizations (NGOs) and their members working both at the UN and in the field, often in unspeakable conditions, risking their lives to broker peace. Along with inter-governmental and international agencies, these groups are using proven and effective strategies of conflict-resolution. Peace building strategies include:

> early warning; protection of human rights; promotion of democracy; support to indigenous dispute resolution; stakeholder dialogue; election monitoring; community mediation; bridge-building; confidence-building and security measures; civilian peace monitoring; violence containment; economic and technical assistance; arms embargoes; economic sanctions; peace-keeping; reconciliation measures; restorative justice and humanitarian diplomacy (Mathews 2001, 8).

In addition, the last ten years has witnessed an exponential growth in the role of civil society. Largely at the invitation of the UN, civil society organizations (CSOs) are engaged in discussions with government officials at all levels about all manner of global issues. This has created a kind of multi-layered diplomacy, where change is occurring from the top down and the bottom up. Members of CSOs are pressing governments to take strong positions at the UN and in other forums to build strong support for international law, limit the arms trade, and secure human rights in all corners of the globe. With evidence of such public support, governments are better able to take actions.

Since the events of September 11, 2001 at the World Trade Center in New York, another shift has occurred in the peace education movement. War no longer seems quite so remote nor so removed from North American lives. It has become very personal. Previously, the major casualties of war were soldiers; now, the overwhelming majority are civilians. No longer are wars fought on designated battlefields; targets are now found in schools and shopping malls' not simply in global "hot spots" but across North America and Europe. There is no "safe distance" from the violence. In terms of resolving conflict, the stakes have become a lot higher. Peace education certainly still includes global issues of war prevention, but it must extend also to personal experience in resolving conflict and overcoming the threat of violence. To paraphrase Gloria Steinem, "the political has become the personal."

Engaging Students in Peace Issues

The biggest challenge for peace educators is to capture the hearts and minds of young people in ways that will have positive consequences beyond the classroom. Unfortunately, social studies curricula typically fail to create impassioned citizens, committed to taking on the responsibilities of participating as active citizens. More often than not, students become cynical and apathetic about social issues. So what does it take to reach students at the level of deep engagement that leads to action? We believe most teachers can answer this question by reflecting on those peak experiences when the class is electrified and a powerful exchange has taken place. All teachers have had these moments. In fact, they may be what keep us in such a demanding profession. We need to ask ourselves what it is about those moments that has produced such engagement and be prepared for answers that may surprise us. The highlighted text describes an example from our own teaching experience of heightened student engagement.

Why is it that this story and countless others connect so powerfully with youth? Egan (1979) suggests that universal themes such as these captured in stories are especially well-suited to the developmental stages of young people. Specifically, he suggests that youth between the ages of 9 and 15 typically are interested in romantic, idealistic themes that explore binary opposites: war/peace, good/evil, and so on. These stories are set in exotic places and times far removed from the present. In later adolescence, students move into a "philosophic" phase where they look to grand schema to make sense

HOLOCAUST EDUCATION CENTRE'S SUITCASE PROJECT

In cities throughout the world, Holocaust education centres have created projects designed for schools to help educate about the Holocaust. Most of these use a powerful travelling exhibit, the "suitcase project." This involves the loan to schools of small suitcases that are actual artifacts collected from the Nazi death camps. On the outside is painted in white the name of the owner and their date of birth. These are suitcases in which children sent to the death camps carried all their personal belongings. With true Nazi efficiency, these were collected and stored, providing tangible evidence of lives that were terminated, and for which often nothing else remains.

While reading *The Diary of Anne Frank* with a grade 8 class, I received one of these suitcases to supplement the teaching and learning. It is not possible to adequately express the change that occurred as students who already knew about the personal fears and struggle of one family came face to face with the suitcase. A shift occurred, and the reality suddenly came home.

This profound shift among students is not limited to my experience. A CBC (2001) documentary and a subsequent book by Karen Levine (2001), both called *Hana's Suitcase*, captured the impact of one such suitcase on students in Japan. As they watch to see what is revealed as the suitcase is opened, the look on the faces of those young Japanese students is unmistakable. Though far removed in space and time, the message is "brought home" to students.

How are we to understand this phenomenon? We believe the power of this lesson stems from a compelling narrative. The story of Auschwitz and other death camps is one of the most compelling of the last century. It readily evokes big questions that are universal and timeless. The small brown suitcase with the hand-painted letters is the vehicle that makes all of that tangible and real for students. It creates the felt presence of a real child and her suffering in all its atrocity and injustice.

of the world: particular instances are brought together in a whole that provides a single explanation. Egan contends that if we want to engage learners fully, we must present information in terms that fit these stages of intellectual development. And then we need to search out those vehicles, such as *Hana's Suitcase*, that have the power to "bring it home" to our students. Only then will they be ready to engage in meaningful actions.

In developing an alternative approach to combat youth cynicism and apathy, we have drawn ideas and strategies from a number of sources. Many of these have been developed and refined in classrooms. The framework we propose encourages teachers to shift from a textbook-based social studies program towards one organized around active experiences designed to engage students' emotions and challenge their thinking. We believe the following six-step approach to issues addresses the unique challenges of engaging students in peace education:

1. choose a compelling narrative;
2. set up a dilemma;
3. explore the issues;
4. present alternative solutions;
5. take a stand;
6. undertake action.

CHOOSE A COMPELLING NARRATIVE

Stories are powerful starting points for meaningful learning because of their potential to make a deep impression. Everyone loves a good story. It may be a story read aloud, a video segment, a graphic novel, a speaker, or another narrative form. The key word is "compelling." Stories often bring those rare moments where you can hear a pin drop—and they often leave a lasting memory. In telling stories of peace-making, we can begin to deliver the message that armed violence is not inevitable and, far from being the ultimate solution, war is the ultimate failure. Telling stories of war and peace through the experiences of individuals brings us back to the real impact of war, which is so often lost in language like "casualties" and "collateral damage." When war is humanized, it loses much of its glamour. In telling the whole story of war and peace, we bring much-needed balance back into the social studies curriculum and begin to replace despair with optimism.

The following criteria are important when choosing compelling narratives:

- **Engage the emotions.** As has already been observed, students come to issues of conflict with a strong emotional component. They may be actively fearful and anxious, or they may be psychologically numb and fatigued. Either way, students need a safe way to approach and open up to the ideas and possibilities you will present. A story allows that safe distance because it is easier to contemplate the perils of a stranger than your own.
- **Address "big questions" in the human drama.** Young people are often interested in fundamental questions about life. They are preoccupied with the relevance of things they are learning. We risk losing students in trivial detail unless we frame ideas in terms that reflect the deepest yearnings of the human spirit: What gives life meaning? What is worth dying for? Is violence ever

justified? What constitutes freedom? Is equality for all, or only an elite?

- **Set up a dynamic tension of "binary opposites."** Adolescents are often accused of being dramatic. Perhaps they are, but if they shape events in life and death terms, that is because that is how they see them. Kieran Egan (1979) suggests this is a natural way of viewing the world for children and young adolescents, roughly aged 8 to 15, although older children and adults can also be engaged by dichotomous themes such as good and evil, justice and injustice, war and peace, and so on. By setting up these opposite extremes, students are able to clarify and understand issues in ways that make sense to them. This is not to say that, as teachers, we should encourage students to see the world in black and white terms. Rather, binary opposites are a starting point to meet students where they are and allow them entry. From there, we can help complicate their thinking and lead them into the "gray zones."

- **Invite identification with a situation or character, often heroic.** For many adolescents, if it isn't about them, then they are not interested: "They look at the world as they would a mirror, to see themselves" (Egan 1979). The role of the story is to help students associate the character or the cause with themselves. When we introduce students to people who show great personal strength in their commitment to justice, human rights, and non-violence, we are offering new heroes for their consideration. Heroes need not be world leaders, but may be ordinary people taking extraordinary actions—and many of them are young. It is our job to choose the story well, so that such a link is made with a heroic figure or noble cause. This is not "heroic" in the superhero sense, but rather the triumph of the insignificant or common person against formidable odds. Some examples are people who have won the Nobel Peace Prize but whose names are scarcely known. For example, Rigoberta Mench is a Guatemalan peasant woman who stood up against terrible injustice at great risk to herself. The inspiring stories of many who have been awarded the Nobel Peace Prize, including those imprisoned for demanding human rights in their countries, showcase the strength of the human spirit.

- **Draw students into the key concepts of grade level curriculum.** Curriculum guides specify many relevant themes to cover in peace education: first contact between aboriginal groups and Europeans, colonialism, imperialism, revolution, exploration, trade, settlement, industrialization, evolution of responsible government, the growth of democracy, immigration, and so on. Despite themes as exciting as these, often we find uncompelling stories—if we tell any stories at all. It may be that we look to the obvious, telling a story set in the time and place we are studying. Instead, we should look to find exciting stories that engender interest in the broader themes, even if far removed from the particular context specified in the curriculum. For example, when studying colonialism in Canada we might begin with the movie *Rabbit Proof Fence*. While this feature film is set in the Australian outback, it presents a powerful account of residential schools and governemnt attempts to assimilate aboriginal people. Not only does the film capture young people's attention, it leads to many questions. From those questions, we can draw students into the Canadian experience with its particular differences.

Identify three or four topics or concepts in the social studies curriculum that provide an opportunity to explore issues related to peace education. For each topic, identify two or more narratives drawn from news stories, literary selections, or films that could be used to engage students in the issue. Focus on stories that capture the underlying theme powerfully, if not the particulars of the topic.

SET UP A DILEMMA

Once students have made heartfelt connections with a topic through an introductory narrative, the next step is to draw out a larger dilemma. We might do this in the form of a key question: Can justice be achieved without violence? Do nuclear weapons provide security or threaten peace? How do you rid a country of a dictator without going to war? How could genocide in Rwanda have been prevented? These questions help students see the issues underlying the event or situation. The compelling narrative sets the context, engaging the hearts and minds of the learners. Posing the dilemma raises the issue that students are to focus upon.

For example, we might explore the concept of colonialism through binary opposites such as freedom/oppression, equality/inequality, justice/injustice, or conflict/peace. I have used a case study (Wasserman et al. 1991) about Donald Marshall to explore colonialism in Canada. Marshall is a Micmac man who was wrongly imprisoned for eleven years for a murder he did not commit. I introduced his story using a National Film Board movie called *Justice Denied* (Cowan 1989). In it, students see a restless teen with whom it is easy to identify. The key question I chose was, How is this possible in Canada? What should be done about it? It is a "big question" in that it leads to an investigation of the rule of law and its unequal application to aboriginal Canadians in Nova Scotia. It outlines clearly the unsavory residue of colonialism still active within this country. It touched a chord within my students. They have felt similarly misunderstood and mistreated. It is a powerful learning vehicle that lays the foundation for an understanding of systemic violence and it's attendant cycle of retribution—key ideas in understanding the dynamic tensions in the world today. Perhaps most importantly, this example also provides hope for the future by demonstrating how liberal democracies have mechanisms of self-correction and that in Canada, ordinary citizens—marginalized ones, in this instance—can ultimately achieve justice.

EXPLORE THE ISSUES

Helping students explore the issues raised by the dilemma involves teaching them to identify, entertain, and compare the varying embedded perspectives. The point of an initial examination of the issue is to identify key players and their positions. Once identified, encourage students to unearth the assumptions, biases, beliefs, and values that underpin these positions. There are many ways to do this. We might ask questions such as, What experiences or interests does this group or individual have that has brought them to this position? What do they stand to gain or lose in the resolution of this problem? Or use the adage of journalists, "Follow the money" to find what is behind a crisis.

In his well-known work on global education, Hanvey (1987) speaks of "perspective-consciousness" as an "awareness that each of us has a worldview or 'cognitive map' that is not universally shared by others and may be shaped by fac-tors we are unaware of and unable to control" (85). It is this awareness that forms the foundation of all conflict resolution. How do we enhance students' awareness that the way they see the world may be different from how others see it, and that does not necessarily make one wrong? Furthermore, is it developmentally appropriate, or even possible, for teenagers to do so? Or, stated another way, isn't it appropriate for teenagers to be egocentric? What role does empathy play in developing this mind-set? In order to be aware of others' perspectives, is it necessary to stand in their shoes? While we may start out placing ourselves at the centre of the universe, it is both possible and desirable to move beyond that view and to do so early in life. In conflict situations, much of the tension is generated by an inability to appreciate another point of view. Conversely, resolution is greatly facilitated when disputants can understand that there is more than one perspective on a given issue. This paves the way for more than one "right" answer. Developing perspective-consciousness requires building empathy, suspending judgment (the ability to listen to a contrary point of view in an accepting, not dismissive frame of mind), and good communication (particularly listening and questioning).

When using story, student research into an issue does not need to result in a typical report or essay. Stories invite role-play. As students take on characters and begin to see through their eyes, they enter the narrative and it becomes their own. This is illustrated in the highlighted discussion of a role play involving the Donald Marshall case.

THE CASE OF DONALD MARSHALL JR.

In the Donald Marshall example discussed earlier, I used a role-play strategy that included appointing my students members of the Royal Commission of the province of Nova Scotia, charged with the same task as the actual commission: "to determine how one individual could be the victim of a miscarriage of justice, and to get to the bottom of why that miscarriage occurred" (Wasserman et al. 1991). This established a powerful purpose for learning.

To do this, students watched *Justice Denied* (Cowan 1989) in order to collect facts about events and characters. They used a two-column retrieval sheet with the headings facts on one side and questions on the other. We kept a running record of their questions on charts around the room (Why is Donald so aggressive? Was this self-defence? Why isn't the sergeant listening to the witnesses? Why are people lying?).

After collecting this information, students were assigned either an individual (Donald, his friends, witnesses, the main detective) or a group (the local police, the lawyers, the RCMP, the jury). Their task was to create a profile, including key values and assumptions, of an assigned character or group. Further data was provided by newspaper accounts and a case summary. The group findings were presented to the whole class, and during this time, reference was made to the questions on the charts.

In the end, we compared student findings with those of the original Royal Commission. In exquisite detail, the commission's report outlined bias and discrimination at all levels, just as the students had done. It added, "the tragedy of the failure of the justice system is compounded by evidence that this miscarriage of justice could and should have been prevented, or at least corrected quickly, if those involved in the system had carried out their duties in a professional and/or competent manner. That they did not is due in part to the fact that Donald Marshall Jr. is a Native."

It is important to stress the eventual correction and redress. Although the Nova Scotia criminal justice system was riddled with racism causing unspeakable injustices against innocent people, Canada is committed to the principle of rule of law. This commitment is one of the true strengths of a democratic society: failures will occur, but when they do, they will be corrected eventually.

As students learn to identify perspectives, they can begin to move out of dichotomous thinking by identifying several positions on a given issue. Without assistance from the teacher, an adolescent's tendency may be to think in black and white polarizing terms. The objective is to introduce students to shades of gray. A good rule of thumb is to find three to five positions on a given issue. For example, the initial polar positions on international intervention against a government that is perpetrating violence against its citizens may be something like either "Sovereign nations must solve their own problems" or "The international community has a moral duty to intervene." Through discussion, other positions emerge: "Carefully targeted economic sanctions can be used to apply pressure to change," or "An independent international agency such as the UN needs to assess the situation and make recommendations," or "Fight fire with fire: use assassins and spies to bring about necessary changes." Through considering and studying several perspectives, problem-solvers are able to find the best solutions.[1]

Various activities to nurture students' perspective-taking abilities are described in the highlighted text, "Perspective-Taking Activities."

PRESENT ALTERNATIVE SOLUTIONS

In generating solutions, the most important requirement is a clear understanding of the problem from the various perspectives of the people who own it. And the critical part in that understanding is identification of the interests underlying their positions.

As stated earlier, the enormous growth in the involvement of civil society and its effectiveness in doing the work of peace on the frontlines around the world since 2000 is due in large measure to the growing sophistication in the use of conflict-resolution strategies. Chief among these is the identification of the interests beneath a given position. In their seminal work, *Getting to Yes: Negotiating Agreement Without Giving In*, Fisher and Ury (1981) define these terms clearly with several examples. In the simplest terms, imagine two sisters fighting over an orange. The girls' raised voices exasperate their mother who jumps in to solve the conflict. She cuts the orange in half and gives one half to each of the sisters, thereby solving the problem, right? Wrong! The "position" of each sister was that they wanted the orange. Had anyone taken the time to talk and listen, they would have learned that one wanted the rind—all of it—to bake a cake,

PERSPECTIVE-TAKING ACTIVITIES

Frame of reference activity

Frame of Reference is an activity that helps students graphically set issues and individuals in context (Hyerle 1991). As illustrated, invite student to draw a circle in the centre of a piece of paper. Inside the circle ask students to write a name, concept, or issue they wish to learn more about. They then draw another circle around the first, making it large enough to record information. In the larger circle, students record all the factual data they can about the word in the centre. For example, if the centre contains "suicide-bombers," the outer circle would contain details that answer the questions: Who? What? Where? When? How? Next, students frame the circles within a rectangle close to the edges of the page. Within this frame, students record the answer to the question: Why? as they detail the beliefs, experiences, and values that make up the frame of reference of a suicide-bomber.

This frame can also be used to detect assumptions in one's own perspective. For example, invite students to place a controversial historical event or contemporary issue in the centre—September 11th, the war in Iraq, North Korea's sale of nuclear weapons technology, space weapons programs. In the concentric circle, ask students to write everything they know and believe about it. Within the outer frame, they write what it is about them that has led them to their beliefs. In other words, through what lens do they view this issue?

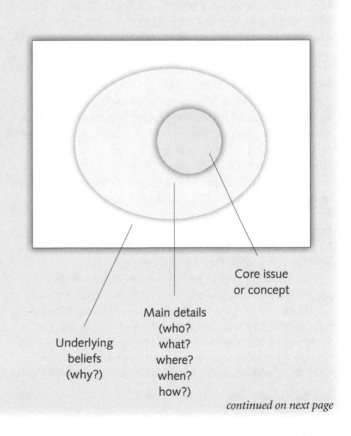

Core issue or concept

Main details (who? what? where? when? how?)

Underlying beliefs (why?)

continued on next page

Retelling the story

An effective activity, enjoyed by students of all ages, is to retell a familiar story, usually a folk or fairy tale, from a different point of view. While this may seem an appropriate elementary activity, secondary students enjoy and benefit from it too. A published example of this is *The True Story of the Three Little Pigs* by A. Wolf as told by John Scieczka (1989) in which the wolf tells quite a different story from the familiar one. Students can rewrite other familiar stories, changing them as required by the shift in point of view. This activity also works well as a role play or drama. Older students can apply this strategy beyond literature to factual accounts of news and historical events. Develop a grid such as the one illustrated below to classify how various individuals might view an event or issue differently.

Perspectives	Key Events		

Adversarial roles

Inviting adversaries to role play each other is an effective strategy used in teaching conflict resolution. If emotions are running high, this is best done by separating students and working with each independently. This technique has proven very effective in breaking conflict deadlocks. Students are most successful using this technique when they have had prior experience role playing conflict scenarios that do not involve them personally. Students are more likely to acquire the basic skill if removed from the emotional heat of a real conflict. Begin by generating a list of typical conflicts (for example, someone takes another student's book without asking, a student is excluded by former friends) or inviting students to anonymously prepare their own list of typical conflicts at home or school. Select a simple two-person conflict. In pairs, ask students to take a role and play it. After two or three minutes, announce "Switch roles" and ask students to take on the role of the other character. The goal is not necessarily to resolve the conflict, but to experience the change in perspective that accompanies a changed role. Debrief the experience by discussing how students felt taking on the role of their adversary and what they learned from it.

This technique works well also in helping students appreciate the complexity of a controversial issue. Instead of taking on one role, ask students to assume many different roles related to the same issue. This can be done using a co-operative learning model with a jig-saw format. Students become "experts" in a certain point of view, present their case, then assume another, somewhat contrary point of view.

The believing game

A powerful tool for developing perspective created by Educators for Social Responsibility is called "The Believing Game" (Elbow 1983). This has been used extensively with secondary students, but it can be adapted for younger students. It is not, however, an introductory level activity. It should be preceded by experience in identifying one's own, then others' points of view. The typical process for playing the game is to have a representative (real or role played) present an unpopular view to a class, such as banning the eating of meat or advocating nuclear war. Prior to this, students outline their contrary belief by making a list of twenty reasons for eating meat or eliminating nuclear weapons, for example. Students are asked temporarily to suspend their beliefs and embrace the speaker's ideas. They do this by silencing any disagreement "inside their heads" and by asking questions that would help them accept this different point of view. Examples of these questions might be: "Tell me more about how you came to that decision/belief" or "Help me understand why you believe x" or "Can you tell me more about your experiences or background that have led you to this conclusion?" As this questioning continues, students "affirm" those parts of the belief that they can now accept. For example, they might say something like, "I can accept that having a strong disincentive for using nuclear weapons is necessary to keeping peace." At the same time, they may be silencing internal voices of disbelief, such as, "But using nuclear weapons as a disincentive may lead to accidental nuclear war." A technique for silencing voices of doubt is to have students imagine doubts as logs floating down a river; when doubts appear, let them float by. Little by little, the class identifies what they are able to "believe."

After the presentation and question-answer sessions are concluded, the experience is debriefed in two parts. The first part debriefs the process by asking questions such as, "What was that like for you?" or "What was difficult for you?" or "What surprised you in that experience?" A key question at this point is to ask how students' thinking has changed as a result of this activity. It is important to note that this process can cause anxiety for students, because it asks them to move outside the security of familiar and comfortable beliefs. The more deeply held the belief, the greater the potential for anxiety. Sensitive debriefing of the process is essential.

The second part of the debriefing is equally important. This is the place where students now disagree with what they have heard. It is helpful if the class has previously articulated their contrary beliefs in some detail before beginning "The Believing Game." At this point, the list of reasons that students had generated initially would be reviewed and changes made. If the "game" has been successful, students will want to modify their reasons. This does not necessarily mean that they will have completely changed their minds and adopted the opposing point of view. They may have shifted positions to a middle ground. Or they may have identified new reasons for holding the positions they do. Whatever position they choose should be based on a deeper appreciation of the competing tensions in the issue.

while the other wanted the juice—all of it—to make icing. With half each, neither got what they wanted.

In conflict resolution language, this was a lose-lose solution, or compromise. If the real "interests" had been identified, a win-win solution would have been easy: one sister would have taken the rind and the other sister, the inside. When one knows the interests, or reasons behind a position, new solutions may present themselves. This is true whether the conflict involves siblings fighting over a limited resource, union negotiators at the bargaining table, multinational companies seeking off-shore drilling rights, warring factions on the brink of civil war, or ethnic groups heading towards genocide. When conflicts harden into positions, violence is seldom far behind. Unearthing interests and finding common ground can often avert estrangement or bloodshed.

This is sometimes described as creating a bigger pie. Instead of starting with a fixed resource where "some for you means less for me," look for ways to expand the options. For example, the World Bank helped break a deadlock in the dispute between India and Pakistan over the waters of the Indus River by offering to fund new irrigation projects, storage dams, and other initiatives of mutual benefit to both countries. Their identification of shared interests and a previously unconsidered means to achieve them led to agreement. In the previous example of the orange, the identification of different interests created an expanded option. Positional bargaining tends to reduce options for solution. Interest-based bargaining coupled with creative thinking leads to new and often unimagined solutions.

TAKE A STAND

If we do all that is described above we will have done an excellent job of promoting understanding of issues at a deep level. We will in all likelihood also have helped students understand themselves better and develop more complex problem-solving techniques. But we should not stop at this point. If we do so repeatedly, we communicate to students that it is sufficient to know "about" an issue, but not necessary to do anything about it. Unwittingly, we discourage engagement in civic affairs and foster a learned apathy.

On the other hand, we do not want students to leap from understanding to action. As an intermediate step we may want to encourage students in the crucial action of declaring themselves publicly on a given issue. With adolescents, this must be a carefully crafted exercise. Students need a great deal of practice in taking a stand, especially in front of their peers. Many are inclined to take a passive or non-committal stance. The two activities in the highlighted text, "Activities for Taking a Stand," describe how we can help students learn to take a stand in ways that are comfortable and natural to them.

ACTIVITIES FOR TAKING A STAND

Human graph

The Human Graph is an excellent technique for breaking the passivity habit (Bellanca and Fogarty 1990). It is also known as Taking a Stand. Place a line of masking tape from one end of the classroom to the other, or post signs around the room that say "Strongly Agree" at one end and "Strongly Disagree" at the other. Identify the mid-point or neutral place in the middle. Students are then asked to "take a stand" on a given statement (for example, the driving age should be reduced to 14 or high school students should receive a minimum wage from parents). Students can discuss their reasons for the stand they have taken. Class activities are then conducted that give students new information on the topic. The graph is repeated and students are encouraged to reconsider their stand, based on the new information received. Teachers can facilitate student movement by speaking personally about how their thinking and beliefs have changed over time (for example, "I used to think thirty was old, but now forty seems young"). Emphasize the importance of staying open to receive new information, and to the possibility that beliefs may ultimately be proven wrong.

Declaring a position

Post signs around the room that represent various positions on a given topic. For example, the following positions might be offered when discussing the role of arms in promoting national security:

- A Star Wars II missile defence system is essential to creating security.
- Only total unilateral disarmament will promote security.
- Every nation needs an arsenal of weapons that act as a deterrent to war.
- Weapons of mass destruction need to be limited to the responsible nations.
- Nations should give up individual defence systems in favour of international bodies charged with protecting their interests.

Invite students to stand beside the statement that most clearly represents their view on the topic. In their self-identified group, they brainstorm reasons for their choice, which they then present to the class. Offers students the opportunity to change positions. In classrooms where peer pressure is impossible to ignore, allow students the opportunity to indicate any change in position by anonymous ballot.

UNDERTAKE ACTION

Action is an essential, though often overlooked, part of teaching citizenship. Teachers can prepare students for social action by creating a tone of participation and activity within the classroom. Students become well-practiced at declaring their views, making choices based on them, and acting to carry them out.

Student projects may take the form of direct social action—hands-on work to fill a need. This might include a roadside clean-up or collecting socks to be distributed to the homeless. Projects may take the form of indirect social action, where students seek to influence opinion by holding educational forums, by letter-writing or other forms of lobbying. Projects may be part of a course or though an extra-curricular club. Students may initiate their own actions with the support of a key teacher, or students may become involved with the myriad of agencies and groups working to help children in unsafe and exploitative situations, such as initiatives to rid the world of land mines or stop the recruiting of child soldiers. Some classes have chosen to write as pen-pals to let children in other countries know they are not alone or forgotten. Others have chosen to raise funds to help agencies do their work. The highlighted text, "Hana's Suitcase in Japan," describes the actions of one class in Japan in response to its encounter with Hana's suitcase.

Various advocacy groups are associated with most justice/human rights issues. Examples include the Association in Defence of the Wrongfully Convicted or the Innocence Project, which lobbies on behalf of prisoners believed to be innocent. Amnesty International has a similar mandate and a more global focus. Groups like these often have speakers or educational packages that provide information about their efforts. Teachers should confirm that the operating mandates of advocacy groups conform to district and school guidelines. Students can also choose to work outside of school with groups that ignite their interest.

We suggest the following guidelines when involving students in effective action.

- Students participate in generating ideas for action.
- Students choose their action from a range of options, including the choice not to act. Some students are reluctant, but if we work with them to expand options so that they find an action that is comfortable for them, we may reduce the likelihood of them sinking into apathy.
- Actions taken should achieve results more often than not. In dealing with immense problems, such as nuclear disarmament, it may be advisable to assess the success of the action in terms of the immediate goal, such as getting a letter to the editor published or a benefit dance organized, rather than in terms of the long-term goal.

HANA'S SUITCASE IN JAPAN

When students in Japan were first introduced to Hana's suitcase by their teacher, they had many questions. Mainly they wanted to know more about Hana. They wrote letters to find records about her. With much persistence in the face of many obstacles, not only were Hana's records found, but drawings she had produced in the ghetto had also been saved. Photocopies of these were sent for the students to view. These gave them an idea of the kind of child Hana was, and made them hungry for more information. The students also wanted others to know what they were learning and began to produce a monthly newsletter full of drawings, poems, and stories that was sent to schools worldwide. This led to an exhibition called, "The Holocaust Seen Through Children's Eyes." Visitors shared the students' curiosity, wondering also, "Who was Hana?" "What happened to her?" The teacher decided to go to the Czech Republic and the detention camp where Hana had been interned to find out. The full story of the remarkable events that followed are recorded in the book, *Hana's Suitcase*. In brief, the teacher not only discovered records of Hana, she learned that Hana had an older brother who survived the Holocaust and was living in Toronto. Imagine his surprise when he received a letter from a teacher in Tokyo about his sister. Although he was 72 years old by then, George Brady travelled to Tokyo to meet that teacher and her students. The meeting led to a worldwide tour of the exhibition that has now been seen by over 52,000 people. Mr. Brady and the Japanese teacher have travelled together to deliver the students' messages. This project illustrates not only the tremendous dedication and commitment of the teacher, but also the power that student messages can have.

- Actions taken are based on understanding and information. Everyone is included and every position is treated with thoughtful respect. Encourage students to reconsider their positions in light of any new information.
- There is an element of mutuality in acts of altruism. Mutual benefit may be the most controversial and difficult suggestion to implement. What we mean is that the action must not be entirely one-sided, that as students give, they also receive. The aim is to purge the action of any element of "do-goodism," with its inherent sense of superiority. It is better if students experience a choice to make the world a better place for someone as a choice to make it better for themselves as well. Examples include a buddy-program between seniors and adolescents, where each helps the other. Students complete chores, while the seniors provide an audience for student essays, help with homework, or share home baking. Both benefit beyond the immediate cross-generational relationships and the breaking down of stereotypes.

- Actions taken must neither indoctrinate nor serve the teacher's personal agenda.
- Evaluate actions for course credit, because they are part of the curriculum.

Margaret Mead said, "Never doubt that a small group of thoughtful, committed people can change the world. Indeed, it is the only thing that ever has." We would like to paraphrase by saying "never doubt that a small group of thoughtful, committed *youth* can change the world. Indeed, it has often been the only thing that has." In recent years two remarkable examples come to mind.

In Czechoslovakia, the revolution that brought totalitarianism to an end began with high-school students, apprentices, and other adolescents. They took to the streets to demand a freedom they had never known, while their cynical parents cowered at home, "internally colonized by the totalitarian system, people who had lost the sense that there was a way out" (Havel 1990, n.p.). When locking their children up proved ineffective, parents began marching with them in the streets out of fear for their children's safety. Fear turned to enthusiasm as the "children evoked from their parents their better selves" (Havel 1990). In a few short weeks without resorting to violence, the "Velvet Revolution" brought freedom to Czechoslovakia. We might well ask: "where did these young people who never knew another system find their desire for truth, their love of free thought, their political ideas, their civic courage and civic prudence? How did their parents—the very generation that had been considered as lost—come to join them? How is it possible that so many people knew immediately what to do, without advice or instruction?" (Havel 1990).

How is it that this story was repeated ten years later in Serbia, where a generation of youth armed with impetuousness, spray paint, and slogans took to the streets to overthrow Slobodan Milosevic? Without organization and hierarchy they spread like termites, eating away at the established order. They managed to "shake their parents and grandparents out of their lethargy. Adults started feeling ashamed of their apathy" (Chiclet 2001). Where bombs failed, non-violent strategies succeeded. Where adults were paralyzed in despair, youth found the vision and courage to overthrow a dictator.

Conclusion

If social studies education in Canada has failed to produce active citizens with creative vision and relentless passion, the fault lies not in the nature of young people today. It may suggested that lack of social engagement among Canadian youth is partly because life is relatively easy for many and they ex-

perience few of the fundamental challenges confronted by youth in the previous examples. If this explanation were true, we would expect to hear stories of youth optimism and contentment. Such is not the case. Could it be that here, as in other places, cynicism, despair, and apathy contaminate our outlook and thereby influence our children?

Whatever conclusions we draw to the questions posed above, several things are clear. If we are to successfully prepare students for the challenges they face as global citizens in the twenty-first century, we must first reach behind their façade of indifference and apathy. We must give them reasons to care and information about how to translate that caring into effective action. More than that, we must work with them to become active, engaged citizens of this world, capable of making a difference. Above all else, we need to provide students with experiences that demonstrate that hope is justified and optimism well-founded. As teachers, we can make all the difference.

> Select a topic from the social studies curriculum that provides an opportunity to explore an issue related to peace education. Think of at least three possible social action projects—both direct and indirect—that would deepen students' understanding of the curricular topic, be feasible to carry out, and help them feel more empowered as citizens.

NOTE

1. After the failure of the world to stop the genocide in Rwanda, and the mixed results of intervention by NATO in Kosovo, the former Secretary-General of the UN, Kofi Annan, challenged nations to examine the question of when, if ever, it was appropriate for one state to intervene militarily in another state for humanitarian purposes. Canada took up the challenge and struck a distinguished international commission to respond to the questions and to create guidelines and criteria for such interventions if they were found to be appropriate. The report of this commission is a valuable resource for teachers because it concludes that sovereignty is accorded to nations that protect all their citizens. If a nation is unwilling or unable to protect all its citizens, that responsibility falls to the international community; that is, the right of national sovereignty is trumped by the human rights of the citizens. The result is "The Responsibility to Protect: Report of the International Commission on Intervention and State Sovereignty" (Evans et al. 2001). The guidelines in the report make an excellent basis for discussion of questions such as "How do we get rid of a dictator?" and "Is it acceptable to bomb a country for humanitarian reasons?"

REFERENCES

Bellanca, J. and R. Fogarty. 1990. *Blueprint for thinking in the cooperative classroom*. Arlington Heights, IL: Skylight.

Chiclet, C. 2001. Otpor: The youths who booted Milosevic. *The Courier UNESCO*, March. Available online at http://www.unesco.org/courier/2001_03/uk/droits.htm.

Cowan, P., director, and A. Symansky, producer. 1989. *Justice denied*. National Film Board of Canada.

Egan, K. 1979. *Educational development*. New York: Oxford University Press.

Elbow, P. 1983. Critical thinking is not enough. The Reninger Lecture, University of Northern Iowa, Cedar Falls, IA, April.

Evans, G., et al. 2001. *The responsibility to protect: Report of the International Commission on Intervention and State Sovereignty*. Ottawa: The International Development Research Centre. Available online at http://www.iciss.ca/report-en.asp.

Fisher, R. and W. Ury. 1981. *Getting to yes, negotiating agreement without giving in*. New York: Penguin.

Hague Appeal for Peace. 2000. *The Hague Agenda for Peace and Justice in the 21st Century*. New York: Author. Available online at http://www.haguepeace.org/index.php?action=resources.

Hanvey, R.G. 1987. An attainable global perspective. In *Next steps in global education: A handbook for curriculum development*, ed. W.M. Kniep, 83–109. New York: American Forum.

Havel, V. 1990. *A contaminated moral environment*. Presidential address broadcast to the people of Czechoslovakia, January 1. Available in part online at http://www.renewamerica.us/forum/?date=060514&a=2&message=15.

Hyerle, D. 1991. Visual tools for mapping minds. In *Developing minds: Programs for teaching thinking*, ed. Arthur L. Costa, 401–407. Arlington, VA: Association for Supervision and Curriculum Development. Available online at http://www.thinkingfoundation.org/research/journal_articles/journal_articles.html.

Levine, K. 2001. *Hana's suitcase: A true story*. Toronto: Second Story Press.

———, producer. Hana's suitcase. *The Sunday Edition*, CBC, January 21, 2001.

Mathews, D. 2001. *War prevention works: 50 stories of people resolving conflict*. London: Oxford Research Group.

Scieczka, J. 1989. *The true story of the three little pigs* by A. Wolf. New York: Scholastic.

Wasserman, S., L. Bickerton, R. Chambers, G. Dart, S. Fukui, J. Gluska, B. McNeil, and P. Odermatt. 1991. *Cases for teaching in the secondary school*. Coquitlam, BC: CaseWorks Press.

21

All Talk and No Action?
The Place of Social Action in Secondary Social Studies

Penney Clark

It is generally agreed that the preparation of citizens is the raison d'être of social studies. However, establishing that citizenship education is the ultimate purpose of social studies doesn't tell us very much. The crucial question to address is to determine exactly what the qualities of a good citizen are. Is it sufficient that students are capable of informed debate on social issues? Or does effective citizenship also require developing the will and the ability to "act" to address local, national, and global problems?

Prominent Canadian (Osborne 1982) and American educators (Newmann 1975, Goodlad 2004) have long argued that students should be taught not solely to discuss social issues but also to act on them. This attention to social action is apparent in recent provincial curricula. For example, the Alberta curriculum states that the role of social studies is to help students "become active and responsible citizens, engaged in the democratic process and aware of their capacity to effect change in their community, society and world" (Alberta Education 2007, 1). The "Social Participation" outcomes for most grades in this curriculum include expectations that students will contribute to the well-being of their school and the broader community (Alberta Education 2007, 18). In British Columbia, a significant part of the grade 11 civics curriculum is devoted to social action (British Columbia Ministry of Education 2005, 23).

Of course, it is not enough simply to ask students to undertake a project. If they are to succeed in this endeavour and learn about active citizenship, they need to be taught how to plan and implement action projects responsibly. This chapter focusses on developing these abilities by discussing various examples of social action undertaken by secondary students and by presenting a framework to guide teachers in selecting and conducting social action projects.[1]

Types of Social Action

A useful starting point is to identify the different categories of social action that students might undertake. One classification views social action projects along a continuum extending from, at one end, "direct action" (directly addressing a problem oneself) to, at the other end, "indirect action" (influencing, or using as intermediaries, those who hold power and who are in a position to effect change). Both direct and indirect action can occur at local, provincial, national, or global levels.

INDIRECT ACTION

An example of indirect local action is lobbying school or community authorities to change an undesirable rule or policy. The highlighted text, "In Our Own Backyard," describes a project in which grade 10 students investigated options for a local park, and then made recommendations to the Parks Board, parents, and other members of the community (Case et al. 2004).

An example of indirect global action is fundraising in order to send money to a relief organization such as UNICEF (United Nations International Children's Emergency Fund). Another example is the World Vision 30 Hour Famine. Participants raise funds for various projects through sponsorships and then go without food for 30 hours. Usually, there are a number of school sponsored events during this time in order to keep participants' minds off the state of their stomachs. (Experiencing a feeling of hunger can be worthwhile in itself.) These are indirect actions because, although students know they are helping in a general sense, there is no direct contact with the people they are helping, and they have no control over how the funds they raise are administered. There is also no opportunity to observe specific results of their actions.

IN OUR OWN BACKYARD

The Parks Board in an urban community developed a questionnaire in order to obtain community responses about priorities for use of a local park. The board expressed a particular interest in hearing from young people. The park was home to over 170 species of birds, amphibians, reptiles, and mammals, housed an art gallery and a museum, and accommodated activities such as hiking and boating. The grade 10 teacher in the school across the street decided to try to interest her students in getting involved in this process.

The class began by identifying existing park uses in relation to community needs, and sharing ideas about what should be done. They identified the "problem" as how to make their views known in a way that could influence public opinion on appropriate park uses.

The students began their investigation with a walk through the park, trying to view what they saw through the eyes of the various users. They decided to use the questionnaire developed by the Parks Board to express their views. In addition, they decided to set up booths during Environmental Week at the school as a means of communicating their ideas to other students, parents, and members of the broader community.

The students decided to set up on-site data collecting stations throughout the park. Data collection methods would include taking photographs, obtaining maps, and maintaining individual journals to record research information, questions, and reflections. The students also decided to invite guest speakers to their class, including a representative from the Fish and Wildlife Department, in order to deepen their understanding of the park environment.

The students gathered information using the methods they had planned. They hypothesized what the consequences of increased activities on vegetation and wildlife habitat would be. They also identified the priorities of various stakeholders: homeowners wanted views and property values maintained, families wanted recreation areas for children, and arts patrons wanted increased musical presentations. The students began to be aware of how complex decisions related to land use are.

They identified a variety of park use options such as picnic space, encouraging native vegetation, and increasing the number of trails. They began to ask questions such as: What would be the best balance among the diversity of needs? What options would have lasting positive change?

The students then completed the Parks Board questionnaire. The Parks Board was very appreciative, pointing out how difficult it had been in the past to get input from the youths. The students said that as a result of their efforts they felt more confident about themselves, became better-informed citizens, knew more about how to be involved in their community, learned research and problem-solving skills, and were better able to listen to other people's perspectives and question their own. The Parks Board acted on the students' suggestion that the natural state of the park be maintained as much as possible. The new management plan focussed on improving water quality in the park and enhancing the habitat for local animals and birds.

DIRECT ACTION

Examples of direct local action include cleaning up the school grounds or a local park, visiting the elderly at a senior citizen's home, or caring for animals at a local wildlife habitat. In the highlighted text, "Sleuthing Students Make a Difference," University of British Columbia instructor Bill Willson describes how students learned about the environmental damage that can be caused by improper disposal of building products, the importance of governmental regulations in this regard, and the power of the media.

Travelling to another country and engaging in a building project there is an example of direct global action. This sort of project, although relatively common at the senior secondary level, involves only a very limited number of students at a time. However, there are forms of direct social action at the global level that can be carried out from home. An example of such a project involved a grade 9-10 mechanics class in Prince George, British Columbia, that constructed twelve hand-operated pumps for a rural development project in northern Kenya (Scoten 1988). Students were pro-vided with both general and specific information about East Africa. For example, women in rural Kenya spend an average of four hours a day gathering water from sources that are most often contaminated. After the pumps were sent to Kenya through a development agency, the class received a video that showed their pumps being assembled, and later a photograph of a Kenyan villager drawing clear water from a well with the aid of the first installed pump. Students contributed to the outcome without actually travelling to Kenya.

Another example of direct action at the global level is "Project Love." This project is sponsored by CODE (Canadian Organization for Development through Education), an organization that promotes literacy and education in the developing world. Students assemble Project Love kits, which hold basic school supplies such as a pencil, eraser, notebook, and ruler packed in a reusable plastic bag, and send them to developing countries. Students raise funds to help cover the cost of the supplies and shipping. In the past, the kits have been sent to Belize, Guyana, Ethiopia, and Tanzania, among other countries.

SLEUTHING STUDENTS MAKE A DIFFERENCE

One of the most successful social action experiences I have been involved with started in the student parking lot of the secondary school where I taught social studies. One weekend, several truckloads of construction waste were dumped at the side of the student parking area, a pristine park-like setting.

My first block on Monday afternoon was a grade 11 social studies class that switched places with a science class for the next period. The science teacher and I often combined our blocks in order to conduct joint field trips and explore common themes.

The day after the mess was discovered, the two classes went to the site of the crime and were asked to form questions about the situation. These questions were used as the basis of a mini-unit. The sixty-four students decided that they would like to do three things: find out who had created the mess and get the culprit to clean it up or face charges; research what harm the various paints, drywall, and other construction materials could do to the environment and what laws governed the disposal of such materials; and finally, develop an environmental awareness program for the students at the school.

Our social studies and science periods were combined over the next ten afternoons, and students worked through their action plan in eight groups of eight. The parking lot site of investigation expanded to include the school and municipal library, the Port Moody City Hall, various office telephones, internet websites and technical classes in the school. In the process, students contacted civil servants at all three levels of government, contractors, district staff responsible for grounds, administrators, recycling companies, and the media, as well as neighbours, teachers, and students in their community.

The results were spectacular. The objectives of both courses were met, and the students were carrying us along in the wake of their self-directed research. We were amazed by their maturity and the levels of skill they had. They worked independently and eagerly to conduct a highly effective research project that far exceeded our greatest expectations. Our students became experts in basic environmental knowledge regarding common building products and government regulations. Their sleuthing exposed the development site (which was about twenty kilometres from the school) and the contractor responsible for the dump. When the contractor refused to negotiate with the students, the media was contacted.

Student representatives presented their evidence to the local media, leading to coverage of the story in both the evening newscasts, and later in three newspapers. Needless to say, this caught the full attention of the contractor, who quickly got in touch with the school. He met with both our administration and our students and an agreement was reached to clean up the mess, which turned out to have been created by one of his subcontractors.

The log books, reports, posters, and videos on the specifics of environmental damage caused by building products were masterfully designed. The quality of the research into government regulations regarding waste and how and where various waste could be recycled or disposed was remarkable. But it was the maturity, pride, and sense of empowerment we saw in our students that was the real reward. The keen interest of our student citizens was successfully united with the achievement of social studies and science objectives in a way that was of benefit to the larger community in which they lived.

Bill Willson
Sessional Instructor, University of British Columbia

"Adopting" a child from a developing country is another example of direct action, to the extent that students have direct involvement and a degree of control from the initial planning and fundraising through to the end results. They have personal information about the "adoptee" and are aware of the family's living circumstances. In addition, students normally have personal contact in the form of letters and photographs. They know how the money they raise is to be used, can see its effects, and can send additional money or goods if they wish.

A final example of direct global action involved a group of students from three school districts near Victoria, BC ("BC Students Team Up" 1996, p. 5). These students raised $5,000 to help build a school in a Kenyan village as a way of commemorating the 1994 Commonwealth Games, which took place in Victoria. They gathered information by communicating with a Canadian development worker in Kenya and interviewing Kenyan athletes who attended the games. Fundraising efforts included a benefit concert.

Framework for Social Action Projects

There are many things to consider when guiding students through a social action project. Below is a framework identifying six tasks. Depending on the project, not all will be required, and teachers may be able to move quickly through other steps.

Laying the groundwork

1. *Preplan for the project*

   What factors might a teacher consider before formally deciding to undertake a social action project? At this preliminary phase, a teacher should select a suitable focus for the project and secure advice and approval from key parties.

2. *Introduce the idea to students*
   How might undertaking a social action project be presented to students? The teacher might consider how to connect this project to students' interests and to topics in the curriculum.

Guiding students through the project

3. *Clarify the problem*
   What is the problem in need of attention? Students gather information and articulate a clear statement of the problem.

4. *Agree on a sound solution*
   What are the different ways in which the problem could be solved and which is the most promising solution? Students assess the relative merits of alternative solutions, and decide upon the best option.

5. *Plan an effective course of action*
   How will the proposed solution be put into effect? Students consider specific challenges, resources, and strategies in developing an action plan.

6. *Implement and evaluate the action*
   Is the planned action working? Students manage progress of the project and debrief the experience.

The rest of this chapter is devoted to unpacking the specific considerations involved in each of these tasks.

Task 1: Preplan for the Project

The preliminary planning for a project has two parts: selecting a suitable focus and securing the advice and approval of key participants.

SELECT A SUITABLE PROJECT FOCUS

Five questions are useful to consider when selecting and shaping the focus for a project:

- Is it relevant for my students?
- Is it appropriate for my school and community?
- Does it grow out of and support the curriculum?
- Are there adequate resources?
- Is it worth the effort?

STUDENT RELEVANCE

There is little point in attempting a project if students do not support it. Rahima Wade (1995) found, when working with a grade 4 class in a suburban American school over the course of a school year, that unless students saw a meaningful or enjoyable connection between a social action project and their own lives, they had little interest in further involvement. For example, Wade tried to interest students in fundraising to purchase a goat for a poor family in Haiti. Although most students voted in favour of participating in the project, only three students came to an out-of-school meeting to plan a course of action. Wade abandoned the project, concluding that it was too far removed from the students' own interests and life experiences.

Lewis describes how her upper elementary students from a low-income area became excited about school because of a social action project. As she says, "it was not an imaginary situation or a case study in a textbook—it existed in their neighborhood" (1991, 47). She describes how engagement in social action made the curriculum relevant for these students:

> Children anxiously await answers to letters, and track legislation. No one knows for sure what will happen next. When the Jackson children sat in the Utah Legislature watching the votes for their hazardous waste fund flash on the wall, they exhibited as much enthusiasm as if they had been counting points on the scoreboard at a basketball game (49).

We should not presume that students will always be enthusiastic about the same projects that would interest adults (Wade, 1995). For example, in the context of creating a class Bill of Rights, students in a grade 4 class decided to write letters to their principal requesting permission to chew gum and wear hats in class. Most adults would not consider these issues to be of great importance, but the grade 4 students felt differently and decided to act on their concerns. Students' sense of empowerment can result only when they take ownership of, and feel enthusiasm about, a project. Of course, all students need not participate in a particular project, nor should those who do not wish to become involved prevent others from having the opportunity to do so. To the extent possible, we should allow for alternative routes for students who are not committed to the selected project or who want to pursue an alternative course of action.

APPROPRIATENESS FOR THE COMMUNITY

It would be inappropriate for a teacher to encourage students to engage in a project that violates the values of the community. The uproar caused by such an action may negate students' feeling of efficacy and make them unwilling to engage in future projects. When assessing a project's suitability in light of the cultural, religious, political, and economic characteristics of the school and community, we might ask ourselves the following questions:

- Does it respect the belief systems and cultural values of students and parents, as well as local histories and sensitivities?
- Would it lead to unproductive conflict or stress? A project that is appropriate in one school may create unproductive controversy in another. Although controversy will be part of any project related to sensitive issues, it may be wise to modify a project's focus if there is potential for unproductive conflict.

CURRICULUM MATCH

Social action projects have the potential to promote many curricular outcomes, including the skills needed to organize information, write proposals and reports, deliver public presentations, co-operate with others to achieve a shared goal, listen thoughtfully to the ideas and opinions of others, construct a compelling argument, and interact effectively with adults. Content knowledge is also promoted through social action projects. For instance, academic peer-tutoring projects in reading and math have been shown to positively affect achievement scores for both tutors and their pupils (Hedin 1987).

ADEQUATE RESOURCES

Facilities, materials, time, knowledge, and abilities are needed to complete a project successfully. The following questions are worth considering in this regard:

- Do students have the background experience, prior knowledge, and developmental maturity for grappling with the concepts, complexities, and implications of this action? Can they be expected to acquire what they are missing or can "outside experts"—parents and community members—make up for any shortfalls in expertise?
- Can parents be counted on to provide assistance and any materials that may be needed? If outside activities are involved, will adequate supervision and transportation be available?
- Is the project do-able within the available time? Success often depends upon having sufficient time. Would holidays interrupt the project? How will it fit with the time demands of other school events?

WORTHWHILE

Social action projects may require students and teachers to spend considerable in-class and out-of-school time on the project. Thus, it is important that the benefits warrant the effort. In addition to achieving curriculum outcomes, an important measure of the success of a social action project is its impact on student empowerment. Involvement in social action projects contributes to student assertiveness and self-esteem (Kohn 1990). Students who work in projects where they see that they have made a difference feel valued and involved (Yaeger and Patterson 1996). Fifteen-year-old Gabrielle Reed worked at an orphanage in Thailand for a week playing with HIV-positive babies and taking older children on excursions in the community. On her return, she described her trip as "completely life changing" (Duane 2004, 43).

Although there is much discussion of empowerment in educational literature (Apple 1982; Giroux 1988), few have studied it in the context of empowering students in classrooms. Rahima Wade (1995) is an exception. She spent most of a school year in a grade 4 classroom and assisted students in a number of social action projects. She concluded that student ownership of a project is central to the development of a sense of empowerment. Students must see a connection between the activity and their own interests. Other critical factors were the teacher's willingness to relinquish some control of classroom decision-making, and the teacher's actions in fostering empowerment, such as providing choices and including time in the school day for student-initiated projects. Wade cautions that these findings do not necessarily indicate that students will become socially proactive adults. As she points out, this depends on a number of factors, such as family influences and other experiences, students' own personalities and interests, and whether there are additional school opportunities to hone students' social action skills.

An important criterion for determining whether a social action project is worth the effort is if it contributes to a sense of student empowerment.

SECURE SUPPORT FROM KEY PARTIES

It is always a good idea to secure community and administrative support for any proposed project. Social action projects are more public, and may be more controversial, than other school activities, and some people may consider it inappropriate for students to be involved in social action projects during the school day. More often than not, potential criticisms can be avoided by keeping parents and the school administration informed about the project.

Clearing the project beforehand with the school administration by pointing out the congruence of project objectives with the curriculum will help if there is any negative parental or public reactions (Kreisberg 1993). Informing parents by letter of the proposed activities allows them to air concerns and helps to garner their support. This is preferable to explaining after the fact if some controversy emerges. It can also be helpful to have parents and others participate in planning discussions or serving as panel members when different perspectives on the issues are presented.

The author recommends five factors to consider when selecting a social action project:

- relevance for students
- appropriateness for the school and community
- curriculum match
- available resources
- whether it is worthwhile

Identify four or five possible projects that have been recommended for students to undertake at your grade level and use these criteria to assess each option. Identify and justify your selection of the one or two most promising options.

Task 2: Introduce the Idea to Students

Some social action projects arise from students' interests and concerns. Most projects arise from curriculum units already taking place in the classroom. The project is a natural outcome of the learning. Even history units can lead to social action. For instance, students who have learned about treaty agreements that were made with Canada's aboriginal peoples in the past may wish to investigate current land claims issues and make their opinions known in a public forum. An example of a social action project that grew from a history unit is described in the highlighted text, "Staking a Claim for History."

If a project does not naturally arise from student concerns or from the curriculum, it would be important to stimulate student interest through a guest speaker who has personal experience with the issue, a newspaper article, a news clip or documentary film, or a field trip to the site of the controversy.

Task 3: Clarify the Problem

An important part of learning to participate in social action is developing the ability to clearly identify the problem to be solved. Two useful strategies are to involve students in researching the problem and then in exploring its complexities.

STAKING A CLAIM FOR HISTORY

For twenty-five years, Charles Hou, a secondary social studies teacher in Burnaby, British Columbia, has taken groups of between sixty and eighty students on a week-long hike along the Harrison-Lillooet portion of the gold rush trail to the Cariboo. Students get a taste of what it was like to be a miner travelling to the Cariboo to seek gold. When this trail was threatened by a mining company, students produced a calendar of photographs of their trip to publicize the historical importance of the route. They demonstrated on the front steps of the provincial legislature and gave a calendar to each member of the Legislative Assembly. They also made presentations to local historical societies. As part of their lobbying efforts, the class invited the BC Gold Commissioner to explain to them how to make a claim. They then garnered publicity by actually staking a claim on a part of the trail, while a newspaper reporter and photographer recorded the event. As a result of the students' efforts, the BC government designated the route a heritage trail, making the official announcement to the media in the school cafeteria. Students achieved the result they were working towards and brought the past into the present.

GATHER INFORMATION

Students need to collect information about a problem just as they would with any other research project, and they may need assistance with this research. This can involve helping students to frame clear questions, determine their information needs, and develop strategies for gathering the necessary information. See chapter 12, "Escaping the Typical Report Trap," for specific teaching suggestions.

RECOGNIZE COMPLEXITY

Successful projects depend on students recognizing the complexity of the problem under investigation, and appreciating the various perspectives that are held, and that there may be multiple contributing causes. The difficulties that emerge when this is not done are illustrated by an incident involving a grade 1 girl who came home from school and accused her logger father of being a murderer because his tree-cutting was eventually going to kill everyone. The little girl had been read a story at school about British Columbia's Carmanah Valley and environmentalists' efforts to save the old-growth trees there. Officials in the IWA-Canada (International Woodworkers of America) local were concerned about what they saw as an unbalanced treatment of logging and took the issue up with the local school board (Rees and Fraser 1992). This child should have been reminded that she used wood in various ways every day of her life. She needed to understand that loggers do not simply "murder" trees, but chop them down in order to meet very real human needs. Even at six years old, a child can begin to appreciate the complexity of environmental issues, and that their solutions are more often a matter of balance than of taking an either-or position. Teachers have a responsibility to see that students are well-informed about opposing views.

In another situation, after observing student volunteers at community food programs for three years, one researcher concluded that an understanding of the underlying problems was not promoted through these experiences (Willison 1994). When asked why they thought people went to the programs to obtain meals, students responded that clients were "hungry, homeless, excessive users of drugs and alcohol, unemployed, sick, uneducated, and do not want to work. On some occasions, students responded that the clients 'did not have any self-respect'" (89). These exclusively negative stereotypes were reinforced by a teacher who made comments such as, "See how much sugar these people take, they need sugar because of drug addictions" (88). Willison points out that these stereotypical notions were true for only a portion of the food program clients. Many were actually employed, but their income was insufficient to meet their needs. Student preparation for this project should have included an examination of the underlying conditions of poverty and the history of local food provision programs.

Advocates for total banishment of child labour in Third World countries have been cautioned by UNICEF about the complexity of the issues involved. Child factory workers in developing countries may be the sole support of their families. If all child labour were banned, these families might starve, and these children might be forced to turn to more oppressive sources of income, such as prostitution. Many aid workers advocate working instead to improve children's working conditions, and provide health care and educational programs, rather than outright banning of child labour (Vincent 1996). A UNICEF report recommends that governments focus on increasing educational opportunities, enforcing labour laws, and addressing social problems such as caste and ethnic divisions that exacerbate the problem (Stackhouse 1996). Clearly social action is complex, and unintended consequences must be considered carefully.

Task 4: Agree on a Sound Solution

The next stage after defining a problem is to agree on a solution. While it is impossible for students to anticipate all the consequences of their proposed action, they should carefully examine possibilities and likely courses of action under various circumstances. Careful consideration of an action proj-

ect was evident when a grade 8 class considered "adopting" a child in Africa (Ashford 1995). After carefully considering this plan, class members realized that the project was not as desirable as it had initially seemed. It was a long-term project that could not be continued when students left grade 8, and there was no guarantee that the incoming grade 8 class would be willing to carry on with the commitment.

Students need to be well informed about the potential impact of various action options. Students in Toronto were highly successful in their efforts to have fast-food giant McDonald's change from its Styrofoam clamshell packaging to paper (Roth 1991). However, scientific experts, as well as environmentalists, have since argued that McDonald's has caused more harm than good by this move. For example, James Guillet (1990), professor of chemistry at the University of Toronto, states that his own twenty-five years of research, as well as other scientific studies, simply did not support students' claim that when the foam disintegrates, it produces a chemical that has been associated with a breakdown of the earth's ozone layer. As well, the volume of trees that are needed to provide the new paper packaging and the magnitude of pollution produced through paper production may be worse environmentally than the plastics previously used. Guillet concludes with the following caution:

> Environmental problems are extraordinarily complex. There is no magic solution to pollution. What we must do to minimize environmental damage is to make informed and intelligent choices. Media-supported campaigns such as this make great television, but they also exploit the natural altruism of young children and do little to inform the public. Children's crusades should have no place in the formulation of public policy (1990, D7).

Students in Surrey, British Columbia, sent letters to the *Vancouver Sun* (June 25, 1996) expressing concern about the exploitation of Indonesian factory workers who make Nike products. These students were justifiably angry at Nike for paying their workers wages of $2.20 a day, while at the same time paying basketball superstar Michael Jordan $20 million a year to represent the company. Many of the students called for a boycott of Nike products. These students thought it worthwhile to take the time to write letters in order to publicly air their concerns. They may well have chosen the best action under the circumstances. However, they would have had confidence in their decision only if they had carefully investigated the situation before reaching their conclusion. For instance, did they consider the possibility that driving up wages in Indonesia might result in Nike moving its factories to another country where labour costs are lower? Did they anticipate that other large corporations considering options for locating their factories might also avoid Indonesia? What alternatives to a boycott of Nike did they consider? Perhaps it would be more desirable to encourage all companies or countries in the region to establish minimum-wage laws. Perhaps as more large corporations build factories in Indonesia they will compete for the labour that is available and wages will rise. Canadian businessman Subhash Khanna, who imports clothing from South Asia, argues, "If you don't do business with Third World countries you will increase their poverty and have more kids dying of hunger" (cited in Vincent 1996, 50). It is important that students consider potential consequences before reaching a decision.

Figure 21.1 is intended to help students explore the implications of each proposed solution for one or more groups who may be affected by the proposed actions.

Task 5: Plan an Effective Course of Action

After deciding on a solution, the next task is to develop a plan to put the solution into effect. The purpose of an action plan is to guide students in implementing the project. The quality of the plan depends largely on the thoroughness of students' deliberations. Use of a simple task analysis chart such as Figure 21.2 can support students in identifying the many steps to be taken, the resources required to complete each step, and the people responsible.

While planning a course of action, invite students to reflect on the soundness of their proposals by considering the following criteria:

- **Clear.** Are the goals and tasks of the plan clear to us?
- **Effective.** Are the proposed strategies likely to lead to the desired solution? What might some other effects of these strategies be (i.e., unintended consequences)?
- **Respectful.** Does the proposed strategy respect the feelings of all sides? Have we judged how the strategies will affect people? Does it respect the rights and legitimate interests of those who might be affected?
- **Realistic.** Is the plan do-able given our time and available resources? How much class time is realistically available to devote to the project? How much outside help will be necessary?
- **Comprehensive** What did we have to leave out of the plan? Does it contain and sequence the important tasks necessary for successful implementation?

Task 6: Implement and Evaluate the Action

By this stage, students should have a good sense of their project and what needs to be done next. Now the teacher's task is to help students bring the project to a successful conclusion. Wade (1995) found that students responded enthusi-

---

FIGURE 21.1 CONSEQUENCES FOR STAKEHOLDERS

Stakeholder group: _____

Identify the anticipated consequences for each proposed solution and indicate for an assigned stakeholder group or for various stakeholders whether the results are likely to be very negative (-2), very positive (+2), or somewhere in between.

OPTIONS	ANTICIPATED CONSEQUENCES	
		-2 -1 0 +1 +2
		-2 -1 0 +1 +2
		-2 -1 0 +1 +2

FIGURE 21.2   ACTION PLAN

ACTIONS TO BE TAKEN	RESOURCES REQUIRED	WHO WILL BE RESPONSIBLE

astically to projects where they were closely supervised and assisted by their teacher or another adult. Students did not carry through on projects where they were left to their own devices. For instance, a group of students planned to write letters to American soldiers in Saudi Arabia after one student suggested the plan, but no one followed through. However, most students were enthusiastic about and participated in a project initiated, organized, and supervised by Wade in which students made puppets to send to India to teach villagers to make a simple solution for curing diarrhea, a common killer of children.

As students work through their project, and after its completion, encourage them to assess their decisions and actions in light of their own opinions, the opinions of other students, the responses of those who were affected by the action project, and both short- and long-term consequences. Figure 21.3 suggests questions to ask students as they debrief their experiences.

There is a risk that students will feel that, in spite of all their efforts, they were ultimately unsuccessful in achieving their goals. Lewis (1991) gives a description of the discouragement one boy might feel early on in his project:

Successful phone calling is a simple place to begin. Students often fail at this initial step. For example, Joe may get access to use the school phones (which might require a notarized letter from his parent). He dials the main number for the Department of Transportation seeking information on the placement of a street light near the school. It takes four transfers before he reaches the correct party who can help him. Ms. So-and-So says she will mail some information to Joe and asks for the school address.

Joe panics. Although he can instantly recall all the states in the NFL, he doesn't know the school address. He asks Ms. So-and-So to wait, then runs into the secretary's office to find out the address. Seven people are lined up at the secretary's desk. By the time Joe gets the address and returns to the phone, Ms. So-and-So has hung up. Joe can't remember how to get through to her again and gives up. His first attempt to become involved in citizenship, and he stubs his toe and loses interest (48).

Two ways to reduce the likelihood of perceived failure are to prepare students to carry out the steps necessary to

FIGURE 21.3 REFLECTING ON OUR PROJECT

Identify two ways in which you think this action project was successful.

List three factors that helped and three factors that hindered the success of the project.

HELPING FACTORS	HINDERING FACTORS
•	•
•	•
•	•

What might you and your fellow students have done differently to make the project more successful?

Identify the most important thing you have learned from this project about planning and conducting social action.

---

complete the project and to encourage students to define "success" very broadly. Suggestions for developing the necessary competencies have been discussed throughout this chapter. In terms of students' definition of success, this need not mean that the intended change is achieved. It can simply mean that students develop a sense of efficacy by actively participating in the process to affect change, even if, ultimately, that change does not occur. If students feel proud that they acted on their convictions, they are likely to want to engage in more such projects. Students should also be reminded that even though no immediate positive consequences stemmed from their social action, desirable changes may yet occur over the long term. (See "Teaching for Hope" in this volume for a discussion of the importance of nurturing student hopefulness and for factors that affect this goal.)

Conclusion

There is no doubt that engaging in social action involves uncertainties. It can place both teachers and students in situations where they are unfamiliar with the circumstances and unsure how to proceed. Social action can be much more visible, and also more controversial, than other social studies activities, and may invite criticism from outside sources. Nevertheless, there are significant benefits. Prominent among these is a sense of empowerment, possession of which increases the likelihood that students will become active citizens in their adult lives. In the final analysis, it is difficult to conceive of social studies as citizenship education without the possibility of social action. The "cost" of a social studies program that is all talk and no action is the preparation of citizens who are unqualified and unwilling to work to improve their community, their nation, or their world.

The author stresses the need to prepare students with the knowledge and abilities required to complete the social action project they have embarked upon. Identify a suitable project for students at your grade level and plan mini-lessons on how you would teach two or three of the most important social action competencies required by this task.

NOTE

1. This chapter draws heavily on the framework and ideas in *Active Citizenship: Student Action Projects* (Case et al. 2004), a teaching resource designed to develop students' abilities to think through each step of a social action project.

REFERENCES

Alberta Education. 2007. *Social studies, Grade 9*. Edmonton, AB: Author. Available online at http://www.education.gov.ab.ca/k_12/curriculum/bySubject/social/default.asp.

Apple, M. 1982. *Education and power*. Boston: Routledge & Kegan Paul.

Ashford, M-W. 1995. Youth actions for the planet. In *Thinking globally about social studies education*, eds. R. Fowler and I. Wright, 75–90. Vancouver: Research and Development in Global Studies, University of British Columbia.

BC students team up to build school in Kenyan village. 1996. *BC Education News*, April: 5.

British Columbia Ministry of Education. 2005. *Civic Studies 11: Integrated resource package 2005*. Victoria, BC: Author. Available online at http://www.bced.gov.bc.ca/irp/irp_ss.htm.

Canadian Organization for Development through Education (CODE). "Project Love." *Canadian International Development Agency: Youth Zone*. Available online at: http://www.acdi-cida.gc.ca/CIDAWEB/acdicida.nsf/En/REN-218125424-PTX.

Case, R., C. Falk, N. Smith, and W. Werner. 2004. *Active citizenship: Student action projects*. Richmond, BC: The Critical Thinking Consortium.

Duane, R. 2004. Student spreads kindness. *North Shore News*, June 13.

Giroux, H.A. 1988. *Schooling and the struggle for public life*. Minneapolis: University of Minnesota Press.

Goodlad, J. 2004. *A place called school: Twentieth anniversary edition*. Whitby, ON: McGraw-Hill.

Guillet, J. 1990. Kids' crusades bad idea. Letter to the editor, *Globe and Mail*, December 1.

Hedin, D. 1987. Students as teachers: A tool for improving school climate and productivity. *Social Policy* 17: 42–47.

Kohn, A. 1990. *The brighter side of human nature: Altruism and empathy in everyday life*. New York: Basic Books.

Kreisberg, S. 1993. Educating for democracy and community: Toward the transformation of power in our schools. In *Promising practices in teaching social responsibility*, eds. S. Berman and P. La Farge, 218–235. Albany, NY: State University of New York Press.

Lewis, B.A. 1991. Today's kids care about social action. *Educational Leadership* 49 (1): 47–49.

Newmann, F. 1975. *Education for citizen action*. Berkeley, CA: McCutchan.

Osborne, K. 1982. *The teaching of politics: Some suggestions for teachers*. Toronto: Canada Studies Foundation.

"Project Love." *Canadian International Development Agency: Youth Zone*. Available online at: http://www.acdi-cida.gc.ca/CIDAWEB/acdicida.nsf/En/REN-218125424-PTX.

Rees, A. and K. Fraser. 1992. Book turns 6-year-old against her father. *The Province*, February 20.

Roth, A. 1991. Battle of the clamshell. *Report on Business Magazine*, April.

Scoten, J. 1988. Integrating development education into industrial arts: A pilot project. In *Explorations in development/global education*, eds. W. Werner and R. Case. Vancouver: Centre for the Study of Curriculum and Instruction, Faculty of Education, University of British Columbia.

Stackhouse, J. 1996. Hazardous child labour increasing. *Globe and Mail*, December 12.

Vancouver Sun. 1996. Air Jordan comes in for a crash landing with Surrey students. Letters to the Editor, June 25.

Vincent, I. 1996. The most powerful 13-year-old in the world. *Saturday Night*, November.

Wade, R.C. 1995. Encouraging student initiative in a fourth-grade classroom. *Elementary School Journal* 95 (1): 339–354.

Willison, S. 1994. When students volunteer to feed the hungry: Some considerations for educators. *Social Education* 85 (2): 88–90.

Yaeger, E.A. and M.J. Patterson. 1996. Teacher-directed social action in a middle school classroom. *Social Studies and the Young Learner* 8 (4): 29–31.

SUPPLEMENTARY READINGS

Association for Supervision and Curriculum Development. 1990. *Educational Leadership* 48. This issue is devoted to the theme of social responsibility.

Baydock, E., P. Francis, K. Osborne, and B. Semotok. 1984. *Politics is simply a public affair*. Toronto: The Canada Studies Foundation.

Berman, S. 1990. Educating for social responsibility. *Educational Leadership* 48 (2): 75–80.

Berman, S. and P. La Farge, eds. 1993. *Promising practices in teaching social responsibility*. Albany, NY: State University of New York Press.

Botting, D., K. Botting, K. Osborne, J. Seymour, and R. Swyston. 1986. *Politics and you*. Scarborough, ON: Nelson.

Chamberlin, C. 1985. Knowlege + commitment = action. In *A Canadian social studies*, rev. ed., eds. J. Parsons, G. Milburn, and M. Van Manen, 231–248. Edmonton, AB: Faculty of Education, University of Alberta.

Chamberlin, C., B. Connors, and B. Massey. 1983. Project Athens: Can schools teach active citizenship? *One World* 22 (2): 33–39.

Clarke, P. 1999. Smoking salmon for social justice. *Teacher: Newsmagazine of the BC Teachers' Federation* 11 (5): 13.

Conrad, D. 1991. School-community participation for social studies. In *Handbook of research on social studies teaching and learning*, ed. J.P. Shaver, 540–548. New York: MacMillan.

Conrad, D. and D. Hedin. 1991. School-based community service: What we know from research and theory. *Phi Delta Kappan* 72 (10): 743–749.

Engle, S. and A. Ochoa. 1988. *Education for democratic citizenship*. New York: Teachers College Press.

Hartmann, T. 2000. Peace cranes. *Teacher: Newsmagazine of the BC Teachers' Federation* 12 (7): 4.

Kielburger, M. and C. Kielburger. 2002. *Take action! A guide to active citizenship*. Toronto: Gage Learning.

Lyman, K. 1995. "AIDS—You can die from it." Teaching young children about a difficult subject. *Rethinking Schools* 10 (2): 14–15.

Van Scotter, R. 1994. What young people think about school and society. *Educational Leadership* 52 (3): 72–78.

Wade, R.C. 1994. Community service-learning: Commitment through active citizenship. *Social Studies and the Young Learner* 6 (3): 1–4.

———. 1996. Prosocial studies. *Social Studies and the Young Learner* 8 (4): 18–20.

Wade, R.C. and D.W. Saxe. 1996. Community service-learning in the social studies: Historical roots, empirical evidence, critical issues. *Theory and Research in Social Education* 24 (4): 331–359.

Werner, W. 1999. Selecting "hot" topics for classrooms. *Canadian Social Studies* 33 (4): 110–113.

22 Co-operative Learning in Secondary Classrooms

Tom Morton

In the 1980s, co-operative learning marched—sometimes with considerable fanfare—to the centre stage of accepted educational practice. Researchers and practitioners alike applauded co-operative learning for its power to improve academic achievement, especially among students who had traditionally not done well in school, and for its potential to enhance interpersonal relations, especially among ethnic groups and between handicapped and able students.

Since then, many teachers have embraced co-operative learning. Many others, however, have run up against the common barriers to implementing a new practice, and abandoned the approach in favour of more traditional group work or whole-class instruction. In speaking of the United States, Seymour Sarason (1995, 84) suggests rather bluntly that what passes frequently for co-operative learning is a charade and often a misnomer for traditional group work. Although research on the current situation in Canada is sparse, the reality of co-operative learning, especially in secondary schools, may be less like a mainstage performance than a fringe festival play—creative, exciting, but marginal. This situation arises partly because of a failure to appreciate that co-operation is not merely a teaching technique but a fundamental commitment to a set of core values.

Morton Deutsch (1949) coined the term "co-operative learning" sixty years ago, but the idea of group learning has been around for a longer time. At the beginning of the twentieth century, John Dewey recommended that students work together on problems that had relevance to their lives. However, the barriers to effective group work are long-standing and deeply rooted, often extending to the very core of teaching beliefs. Dewey wrote of his attempt to buy work tables for his elementary school. He could not find anything other than individual desks. Finally, a salesperson identified the problem: "I am afraid we do not have what you want. You want something at which the children may work. These are all for listening!" (1916). Similar practical and philosophical barriers impede effective implementation of co-operative learning.

This chapter seeks to clarify key elements of effective co-operative learning, and to suggest ways to implement co-operative approaches in social studies. I begin by offering three reasons why co-operative learning should play an important role in our subject and then explore three challenges to its implementation. I then introduce two of the best known approaches to co-operative learning—the Learning Together model, developed by brothers David and Roger Johnson with help from their sister, Edythe Holubec, and the Structural Approach, first developed by Spencer Kagan and recently revised with help from his wife, Laurie, his son, Miguel, and many associates. I explore the principles behind each approach, offer sample lessons, and distinguish these models from each other and from traditional group work and direct instruction.

Why Co-operative Learning in Social Studies?

Co-operative learning is an approach to teaching in which students work together in small groups that are carefully designed to be cohesive or positively interdependent. At the same time, group members are individually accountable for their own learning and for contributing to the group's learning. This approach to learning can contribute to the goals of social studies in at least three ways:

- **Academic achievement.** Considerable research suggests that co-operative learning, properly implemented, promotes academic achievement—in the case of social studies, the acquisition of a body of knowledge in the social science disciplines and the ability to investigate and communicate these ideas. Two notable reviews, a meta-analysis of 475 research studies (Johnson and Johnson 1989) and a similar review with stricter selection criteria of 60 studies (Slavin 1989), concluded that co-operative learning produced moderately large gains in achievement when compared to control conditions.

- **Constructivist learning.** There is considerable cognitive research suggesting that learners must "construct" knowledge if it is to be internalized and integrated with other background beliefs. Co-operative learning facilitates the transaction or construction of ideas. One of the more effective ways of making personal sense of ideas is to explain them to others. Perhaps this contemporary approach was expressed earliest by the Roman philosopher Seneca when he said, "Qui docet, discit," meaning whoever teaches, learns (also translated: when you teach, you learn twice) (Stone 2005, 95).

- **Citizenship values and attitudes.** Co-operative learning promotes the values and dispositions of a responsible citizen. Well-planned co-operative lessons offer students opportunities to express themselves and reflect on their civic competence—the abilities and values of citizenship (Myers 2003a, 2003b). Since its early years, co-operative learning has been closely linked with promoting mutual respect and liking, regardless of differences of intellectual ability, ethnicity, race, handicapping conditions, social class, or gender. It does this by encouraging students to appreciate their own background and those of others, and by fostering commitment to a set of foundational values including respect for civic responsibilities, freedom of expression, fairness, and equality.

Challenges to Co-operative Learning

A prominent researcher, Robert Slavin, warned educators during the rise to popularity of co-operative learning in the 1980s that it was being "oversold and under-trained." At the time, many teachers were encouraged to implement an approach to teaching that they may have inadequately understood and that possibly was at odds with their beliefs and practices. If co-operative learning is to be more than the charade that Sarasan describes, we must recognize and commit ourselves to several basic principles.

NEED FOR TEACHER COMMITMENT AND STUDY

One of the preconditions for co-operative learning is recognition of the commitment and study required to implement it competently. Co-operative learning is not merely a technique to vary the usual instructional bill of fare. An occasional group task or a lesson or two on co-operation in the midst of business as usual will not create a learning community and improve interpersonal relations. As David and Roger Johnson (1992, 45) note: "Simply placing students in groups and telling them to work together does not in and of itself result in co-operative efforts—or positive effects on students."

Teachers must anticipate that implementing co-operative learning will create problems and raise questions: What do I do about students who resist being in the same group? What about the quiet students? What about the group that doesn't get down to work, finishes early, or talks too loudly? Most of us will need help in resolving these problems and, over time, forging a learning community from what may be very diverse and reluctant learners. Help may come from a co-operative support group formed by teachers themselves—much like the ones in which we expect students to participate— or through independent self-study or outside help from a school board consultant or support teacher. (Contact information for co-operative learning groups is listed at the end of this chapter.)

ALIGN CLASSROOM PRACTICES AND VALUES

The basic values of co-operative learning, such as collaboration, equality, and inclusion, may conflict with teaching philosophies, curriculum content, and classroom organization. Because of these conflicts, some teachers may be reluctant to extend co-operative learning beyond a few token lessons. One source of value conflict is the importance in co-operative learning given to social or interpersonal goals. Most co-operative models teach interpersonal skills and encourage group self-reflection, both to help students for academic purposes and for their own sake. In contrast, the norms in some classrooms, more in secondary schools than elementary, affirm that learning means academic learning only. Social goals may not merely be downplayed, they may be actively suppressed by factors such as the way seating is arranged into rows so as to minimize student interaction and maximize teacher control.

As well, co-operative learning may conflict with deeply held beliefs about individualism and competition. In a co-operative classroom, common watchwords are "Two heads are better than one" and "You have a right to ask any group member for help and you have a duty to help anyone who asks." Students sit facing each other, they know the names of their classmates, and they may ask for a chance to study together before a test or have a partner for a project. Teachers who believe strongly in individual learning and competition may be uncomfortable with this kind of classroom.

Even if students are not separated from each other in the classroom, they are often pitted against each other. We send enduring messages that fellow students are potential barriers to success whenever we grade by the curve, display only the best papers on the wall, sort children into winners and losers in spelling bees, and encourage students during a teacher-led discussion to compete to get the answer quickly. In his book *No Contest: The Case Against Competition*, Alfie Kohn (1992) summarizes the research on the effects of these sorts of classroom practices when compared with co-operation. He found that competition is associated with less generosity, less inclination to trust, less willingness to see other viewpoints, and poorer communication.

Co-operative learning will never be more than a fringe methodology or a charade unless the practices and embedded values operating within our classrooms support co-operation. We must recognize that almost everything we do or say in our classes may influence co-operation (Sapon-Shevin and Schniedewind 1992).

BUILD STUDENT SKILLS AND HABITS OF CO-OPERATION

If co-operative learning is to be effective, we need to include considerable instruction and student reflection on interpersonal skills and attitudes. When problems occur, such as a conflict or a reluctant participant, students and the teacher should discuss them. One motto of the Johnsons' has been "Turn problems back to the group to solve," and they insist that co-operative groups put their academic tasks to one side and address personal problems first. By teaching social skills and establishing the habit of reflection on group dynamics, students can recognize that they have the power to make co-operation work.

Describing the essence of co-operative learning can be like "The Six Blind Men of Hindustan," the old poem about the blind men who touch various parts of the elephant—the leg, the trunk, the tusk—and declare the animal to be just like a tree, a snake, a spear, and so on. By one account, there are more than twenty co-operative learning models (Myers 1991). In this chapter, I explore two of the more popular models: the Johnsons' Learning Together model and the Kagans' Structural Approach. My purpose is to show the key ingredients involved in co-operative learning, identify the ways in which it differs from traditional group work, and give some useful ideas for implementing either of these models.

The Learning Together Model

ELEMENTS OF THE LEARNING TOGETHER MODEL

The Johnsons' model offers one of the best-known explanations of the principles of co-operative pedagogy (Johnson, Johnson, and Holubec 1998). According to their model, five elements are essential for effective co-operation:

- **Establish positive interdependence.** Group work will be co-operative only if there is positive interdependence: group members must believe that their success depends on the success of others or, as the Johnsons say, "We sink or swim together." Positive interdependence can be seen as both an element of lesson design and as a spirit of mutual helpfulness. Teachers might create positive interdependence by asking small groups to come up with a single product or to share a limited number of resources such as one instruction sheet, paper, felt pen, glue stick, or pair of scissors. Planning for positive interdependence is especially important in the early months of the school year, when students may not have developed the skills or motivation to co-operate.

- **Require individual accountability.** Individual accountability can be incorporated into lesson planning and, over time, can stimulate students to contribute to the group effort and to value such contributions. On the one hand, when students know that they are accountable for their own learning and for helping the group learn, both group productivity and individual achievement are enhanced. On the other hand, resentment is likely if some members are not pulling their own weight. When some students hitchhike on the efforts of others, hard-working group members may lessen their effort to avoid being "suckers." To encourage individual accountability, we might require each student to be ready to explain the contents of a common product or assign each student a specific section of a shared product.

- **Encourage face-to-face interaction.** Co-operative learning requires face-to-face interaction where the conversation helps students advance their own thinking on the matter before them. This element is often referred to as "purposeful talk" and it emphasizes the role of talk in thinking. To achieve a high level of academic achievement, students must meet in groups to discuss and refine their thinking. To achieve a feeling of caring and commitment, students must encourage and help each other. Sitting together, but working independently and occasionally copying each other's notes, is not interaction.

- **Teach interpersonal or social skills.** Social skills refer to behaviours such as sharing, listening, and encouraging that enable a group to work together. Students do not necessarily know how to behave co-operatively. In the first few weeks of co-operative work, we may have to teach what might simply be called "good classroom manners," for example, students move quickly and quietly to groups, use a person's name, talk in quiet voices, stay with the group, avoid wandering around, and sit so that they face each other. In classes with many impetuous students, it may be several months before we can introduce more advanced social skills such as encouraging participation or active listening. The timing and particulars may differ, but the need to teach rather than assume social skills is crucial.

- **Allow for processing.** Students require the time and procedures to analyze whether their group is functioning and their individual mastery of the requisite social skills. Research suggests that academic achievement is greater when co-operative groups reflect on their process. It is advisable to devote regularly between five and fifteen minutes of group time for students to write about or discuss group interactions. The participation pie activity described in Figure 22.1 is one strategy for facilitating reflection about group interactions.

Planning an effective Learning Together lesson may take considerable time to master. The suggested sequence of steps outlined in the highlighted text, "Planning a Learning Together Lesson," is one way we can attend to key considerations in implementing co-operative learning.

DETERMINING GROUP COMPOSITION

As one can see by examining the list in the highlighted section, there are a number of operational details besides the five elements; group composition, especially, needs prior consideration. Group size should be small, ranging from two to five students, and the groups should be mixed according to academic level, ethnicity, gender, and socio-economic status. Compatibility is another ingredient in the mix. Considerable research and teacher experience suggest that heterogeneous groups enhance class cohesiveness, inter-group relations, and academic achievement for all students.

However, when unaccustomed to co-operative learning, students typically want to choose their own group members, mainly friends who are often similar to themselves. Consequently, there may be tension when teachers choose groups. To lessen this tension, spend some time explaining the reasons for mixed groups along the lines of the following:

PLANNING A LEARNING TOGETHER LESSON

Specify lesson objectives
- academic content
- social skills

Decide about operational details
- group size
- assignment to groups
- room arrangement
- materials
- student roles

Introduce the lesson
- explain the academic task
- structure positive interdependence
- create individual accountability
- explain expected use of social skills
- set criteria for success

Monitor students
- look for evidence of the expected social skills (by student or teacher observation)
- provide opportunities for processing

Evaluate
- academic achievement
- group functioning

- Social studies class is where we learn how to be good citizens and part of that is learning to work with others who may be different from us but with whom we share this classroom and this planet.
- Often we work better with those who are not our friends, because there is less social talk about sports or movies and the like.

FIGURE 22.1 PARTICIPATION PIE

Divide the pie to illustrate how much each member of your group participated in the task. Write down their names in the appropriate section. Below give reasons why you divided up the pie as you did and suggest things you might do to improve the co-operative sharing of the group.

Reasons:
Ideas for improvement:

- Each student will probably work with everyone in the class at some point during the year.
- You don't have to like your teammates; you only have to work with them.
- When we play sports, go to church, temple, or synagogue, join a trade union, or are born into a family, we are in a team, so why not in the classroom?
- Especially for a highly diverse class: There are lots of different people in this classroom and in our neighbourhoods, but in this country, we say that this is a good thing and that we should respect each other and learn to work together.
- Especially for older students: Learning to work with others is key for a successful career; when hired for a job, we do not choose our fellow employees and we certainly do not choose the customers. Business research suggests that people who get fired from their first jobs do so because they can't get along with their boss and their co-workers.

Some students may still disagree with you, but they will know that you have a clear plan and purpose for your groupings.

Although most experienced practitioners argue strongly in favour of teacher-selected teams, during the early part of the year when we are unfamiliar with our students or for a break at any time of the year, random choice is recommended. There are several enjoyable, creative ways to do this such as counting off the names of famous figures, counting off in a foreign language, distributing playing cards with the common cards sitting together, or lining up according to birth date without talking—a challenge—and then grouping students next to each other. As a class develops into a learning community, one that is inclusive by habit, students may be able to choose their own heterogeneous groups.

MAKEOVER LESSON BASED ON LEARNING TOGETHER

The significance of the Johnsons' Learning Together model can be seen by contrasting its five elements and key decisions with traditional group work. In the example described in Figure 22.2, students are asked to use a study sheet using the PAID strategy to analyze a primary document that, in this case, is a pair of political cartoons with contrasting views of women's attempts to gain the right to vote early in this century. Let us explore how the analysis of the cartoons through traditional group work might differ from a co-operative group approach.

PREPARATION

If this were traditional group work, as stated above, students might select their own groups. Most students would choose their friends, meaning that most of the groups would be of the same gender, ethnicity, class, and status level. The group size might vary from two to twenty. With such homogeneous groups, few of the social goals of co-operation would be realized and probably neither would the academic goals in some groups. In contrast, the Learning Together teacher will carefully select groups to include a high achiever, a low achiever, and one or two middle-level achievers for a group of three or four. In addition, the teacher would consider gender, ethnicity, and general compatibility.

Students also need to be comfortable with a number of routines such as seating arrangement—what the Johnsons call "eye to eye and knee to knee"—and some kind of quiet signal to indicate the time to stop group work and pay attention to the teacher. Often, the success of a lesson depends on these and other small lesson details.

POSITIVE INDEPENDENCE AND INDIVIDUAL ACCOUNTABILITY

The Learning Together teacher would next set the interdependence. Each group might have goal interdependence, the common goal of completing the PAID form for analyzing political cartoons. There could also be resource interdependence if each group has a single set of handouts to share and role interdependence if there are different, complementary roles such as those described in the Co-operative roles instructions in Figure 22.2. Individual accountability exists if the teacher randomly asks students to explain their answer. The roles also give special responsibilities to each student.

If this were traditional group work, there would be little positive interdependence or individual accountability. All students would have their own set of handouts and the groups would be instructed to complete the PAID questions and share their answers. Even if the teacher instructs them to share, without structured interdependence there would be little impetus for students to co-operate; and if they did share answers, they would have little motivation to refine and develop them. In addition, without individual accountability, some students would say and do little and might merely copy the work of others.

SOCIAL SKILLS

In traditional group work, social skills are often omitted entirely or are superficially addressed by general admonitions such as "I want you to listen." In the Learning Together model, the teacher discusses why listening is a good idea and teaches specific strategies, for example, by asking "What kinds of things would you be likely to say if you were listening care-

FIGURE 22.2 CO-OPERATIVE CARTOON ANALYSIS

PAID strategy instructions

Discuss and write out an answer to the following questions for each cartoon. All group members should agree with the answers and be ready to explain them.

P = Point of view. What is the point of view expressed in the cartoon? What message is being communicated?

A = Assumption. What assumptions does the cartoonist make about his or her subject? What values or value judgments are apparent?

I = Information. What relevant information about the topic do you already know? Does the information support the cartoonist's point of view? Does the cartoon's message seem to make sense based on your own experiences?

D = Device. What cartooning devices does the cartoonist use (for example, light and dark, line, size, caricature, symbols, exaggeration, composition, and stereotyping)?

Co-operative roles instructions

Before discussing your ideas to the questions, divide the following roles among group members. Each person must fulfill a role as the group answers the questions:

- **Checker:** confirms that everyone in the group agrees with each decision and can explain the reasons for it.
- **Recorder:** writes down the group's questions and reads them back to the group to confirm the wording.
- **Encourager:** invites individual members who may be silent to share their ideas and encourages the group if it gets bogged down.
- **Gatekeeper:** ensures a balanced discussion by politely asking students who might be talking too much to give others a turn.

fully to someone? What would you look like as you were listening carefully?" The teacher might record responses on a poster or ask three or four students to role-play positive and negative examples. To understand the importance of social skills and to be able to use them well are major learning objectives for the Johnsons.

PROCESSING

At some point, co-operative groups will be asked to reflect on how well they worked together so they might improve their social skills, resolve any group problems, or simply celebrate their success. This reflection may be done in various ways: students might keep a journal, the teacher could make observations and report on them to the class, the group could discuss what they did well and identify areas for improvement, or individuals might complete a self-reflection form such as the Pair Reflections described in Figure 22.3. Typically, in traditional group work, student reflection at the end would be solely about the content of the lesson.

Select a lesson, preferably one you have planned. Using the example of the remake of the cartoon analysis lesson into a co-operative lesson as a guide, modify the activities of your selected lesson so that it has the five elements of effective co-operative learning suggested by Johnson and Johnson.

The Structural Approach

Another popular co-operative learning model, the Structural Approach, includes similar elements to the Johnsons' but with a few key differences. The Johnsons' approach focusses on the elements of co-operative learning so that teachers can develop lessons embodying these principles. The Kagans and their associates instead provide planned lesson structures that have the co-operative elements built into them. At first look, their repertoire of co-operative structures or lesson formats may appear to be a "cookbook," but each structure has a solid co-operative foundation and is suitable to different teaching situations.

The Kagans define structures as content-free ways to organize social interaction within the classroom. The structures are the "how" of instruction, while the lesson content is the "what." The more than 150 structures in the Kagan model may seem daunting. However, there is no need to use all or even most of the structures. In fact, the Kagans advocate teaching students one structure a month. The large repertoire provides flexibility in choosing co-operative procedures for a specific topic or learning objective.

Structures can be as simple and brief as Think-Pair-Share, which can take mere minutes to complete. In the Think-Pair-Share structure, the teacher poses a problem or a question and individually the students think, write, or draw an answer, then one person shares ideas with his or her partner for a measured time—between twenty to sixty seconds depending on the activity—while the partner listens and offers feedback. The two students then switch roles: the next person shares his

FIGURE 22.3   PAIR REFLECTIONS

Name: _____   Name of partner: _____

	Never				Always
I made certain my partner and I both understood the material we were studying.	1	2	3	4	5
I listened to the contributions of my partner.	1	2	3	4	5
I felt that my partner listened to me.	1	2	3	4	5
We stayed on task.	1	2	3	4	5

List two adjectives that describe how you feel about your work together:

1. _____

2. _____

or her ideas while the other person listens. The teacher then asks students to share their ideas with the entire class.

A structure can also be as involved as Co-op Co-op, which is a structure for group research projects that has ten steps and involves considerable student autonomy. With this structure, students form groups with others who share an interest in a topic, research an aspect of that topic, then pool their knowledge to prepare a class presentation. Co-op Co-op may take a full semester to complete. Additional Kagan structures are described in the highlighted text, "Co-operative Structures Appropriate for Secondary Students."

Each Kagan structure incorporates the same positive

CO-OPERATIVE STRUCTURES APPROPRIATE FOR SECONDARY STUDENTS

- **Numbered Heads Together.** Students number off within their teams. The teacher asks a question that has multiple answers or a complex answer and the teams discuss possible responses. The teacher calls a number and the student with that number from each group explains his or her group's answer.

- **Corners.** The teacher poses a question, statement, or issue and offers four or so possible responses each assigned to a corner of the room. Students move to the corner that best represents their choice and pair up to explain the reasons for their choice. The teacher then begins a whole-class instruction and calls on students to explain their choices. This activity is most effective if students are then asked to paraphrase the reasoning of students from other corners.

- **RoundRobin and RoundTable.** The teacher poses a question that has multiple answers. In RoundRobin, students take turns giving an answer or idea orally. In RoundTable, students write down or construct answers in turn or simultaneously on a single sheet of paper. For social studies, this might include listing main ideas from the text, details from a picture, or recollections from a field trip or video.

- **Values Line.** Students are given a values issue and then order themselves in a line according to their opinions on the question. Next they fold the line to talk to a partner about the reasons for their choice. Before they offer their opinions, they must paraphrase what their partner has said.

- **Timed-Pair-Share.** This is a very versatile approach that is a more carefully structured form of Think-Pair-Share, where students turn to a partner and talk about something. The teacher poses a question to the students who are in pairs. The students then think by themselves or write or draw an answer to the question. Then one of the students shares his or her thoughts for a measured time—twenty seconds to two minutes—while the other student listens. The students then switch roles. Almost any thought-provoking question a teacher would normally ask of a whole class could become Timed-Think-Pair-Share: after looking at a picture or listening to a story, the teacher could ask, "What does this tell us about...?"

- **Review.** Students could write down everything they remember and then share, or they could do an oral review, answering the question: What have we learned from reading this story or newspaper article? Other possible questions could include:
  - A question asking for a reason why something happened.
  - A question asking for a prediction.
  - A question that asks students to reflect on how they think. For example, what steps do we need to follow when we interview someone about their work? What should we be thinking about when we try to help someone?

- **Placemat.** This begins with a similar approach to RoundTable. Teams of two to four students are given a large sheet of paper divided into sections according to the number of students in the group with a square or circle in the middle. Students are given a question and they write or draw their answer in one of the sections. The steps include:
  - Assign students a topic or question that requires reflection, for example, what students know about the city, Canada, the government, or some controversial issue.
  - Each student writes down or draws what he or she knows or thinks in his or her own space, leaving the centre blank.
  - Students take turns sharing their thoughts with the group or rotate the paper to view each other's responses. Optionally, they may place a star beside the most important idea each of the other students has written.
  - As a group, students combine their ideas to write their best answer or a consensus answer in the central section of the placemat.

- **Team Web.** Each team is given a large sheet of paper and each student a different coloured pen. Students are asked to construct a web about a topic of study. Optionally, the teacher may provide all or some of the sub-topics and ask students to provide a detailed explanation and identify connecting links. The key to this exercise is the coloured pens: each student must contribute to the web and write in a different colour, thus making individual accountability easy to monitor.

- **Carousel Sharing.** One person from each team stays at the team's workplace to be a spokesperson for their topic. The other team members rotate from spokesperson to spokesperson learning as much as they can about a topic, which they must understand in order to complete a task. After the carousel, each rotating group of students provides feedback to their own spokesperson about what they learned from the other teams' spokespeople.

interaction and individual accountability as the Johnsons do, but the Kagans suggest two alternative principles: "equal participation" (the use of strategies such as taking turns that promote the broad involvement of all students) and "simultaneous interaction" (as many students as possible contribute at the same time). The acronym for the Kagans' principles is PIES: positive interdependence, individual accountability, equal participation, and simultaneous interaction.

There is also a different emphasis from the Learning Together approach on social skills. In an article contrasting the two approaches, Kagan (2001) agrees with the value of social skills, but argues that there is no need to take extra time to teach them and process their use when they are embedded in the structure. For example, a social skill such as active listening is integral in Corners and encouraging participation is important in RoundTable.

MAKEOVER LESSON USING THE STRUCTURAL APPROACH

To better understand a structure and its four principles, let us contrast direct instruction of a class studying a video with co-operative instruction using the Kagans' model. A typical form of direct instruction using a video might appropriately be labelled the "Whole Class View-Question-Answer" approach. It has three parts:

- the teacher shows the video;
- students complete worksheets or answer questions individually during or after the showing;
- when the assignments are completed, the teacher calls on students one by one for their answers to the questions.

In this approach, during the showing of the video, there is little interaction among students or with the teacher, at least if the class is orderly. If a section of the video is confusing or complex, students get little or no help until the end. The question and answer session is intended to help all students learn, but in many classes it may be competitive if students are vying for the teacher's attention with cries of "Me! Me!" and hands jabbing the air. Student-to-student interaction is competitive when strong students triumph, while those who are not quick with the answer or not aggressive enough to win the teacher's attention lose.

This approach is quite different from a co-operatively structured activity that uses the steps of Pairs View (Morton, 1996) described in the highlighted text.

The Pairs View strategy illustrates the four key principles of the Kagans' approach:

- **positive interdependence.** Pairs View has both role interdependence, because students have complementary and alternating roles, and goal independence because

PAIRS VIEW

- The teacher pairs students A and B and explains to the pairs that they have a common goal: to generate a list for each partner that contains the metaphors in the video used to describe Canada.
- The teacher shows the video and stops it every five to ten minutes or after a noteworthy metaphor.
- When the video is stopped for the first time, A tells B what he or she identified as a metaphor and what it means. B listens and then helps as needed.
- Both A and B take notes.
- After the explanation and notes are completed, the video is turned on again.
- After a suitable period, the pause is repeated but with B identifying the metaphors.
- The cycle repeats and the roles reverse with every pause until the video is finished.
- With the whole class, the teacher randomly calls on different As and Bs to explain the main ideas or answers.

students have the common goal of each completing a set of notes.

- **individual accountability.** In Pairs View, students are accountable in three ways: their roles require them to explain to each other what they have learned, each is to have a set of notes, and they are accountable because anyone can be called upon to respond to questions on the video.
- **equal participation.** Learning teams can deteriorate quickly if one person dominates or someone else withdraws. In Pairs View, the requirement that each person take turns talking ensures involvement of both partners.
- **simultaneous interaction.** In the final stage of the traditional approach, Whole Class View-Question-Answer, only the teacher or one student at a time talks about the video. The rest sit idle. At each pause of Pairs View, however, half of the class is talking simultaneously.

Comparing Learning Together and the Structural Approach

There need not be any differences in a lesson taught following the Johnsons' model or Kagans'. The key difference between them is in the planning steps before the lesson is taught. Nonetheless, because of the different emphases of these two models, dissimilar lessons may result.

Let us imagine that we are planning a lesson on interpreting graphs. Following the planning steps of the Learning Together model outlined earlier, we would begin by deciding on the lesson objectives, group size, and selection procedure, then consider how to create interdependence. We might choose goal interdependence (for example, a single list of answers) or resource interdependence (for example, each group member has a different graph). We would then consider individual accountability such as each student taking turns writing an answer or being ready to respond to the teacher's question. The next decision would be on a social skill: checking for understanding or taking turns seem appropriate here. Throughout the lesson, we would monitor the use of those skills. A student might even be assigned to act as an observer. Finally, we would consider how best to facilitate student reflection on the group process. The Participation Pie would work well with our graphing assignment.

In contrast, the Kagan model would have us ask, "What kind of structure fits with this content and my learning goals?" The Think-Pair-Share structure would be best if we wanted tight control of the activity whereas Team Discussion would give greater autonomy to students to organize themselves, but may not result in equal participation by all students. Numbered-Heads-Together with its strong individual accountability might be a good compromise. If this is early in the year, we would teach the purpose and procedure of the structure. Otherwise, we need only tell students that they are going to follow a Think-Pair-Share or Numbered-Heads-Together structure. Specifying the social skills and processes are very important for the Structural Approach, but they are not as explicit a part of every lesson as they are with Learning Together. However, because simultaneity and equal participation are important for the Kagans, the final answers might well be shared by group representatives writing their answers on the blackboard at the same time (Blackboard Sharing structure) or with the team representatives making a tour of other groups (Carousel Sharing structure).

The Johnsons and Kagans have also grafted additional strategies and approaches on to the core of co-operative learning. For example, both spend considerable time in their training programs on team- and class-building to create a sense of a community of learners. Both have developed teaching materials for social studies. Together, these two models give social studies teachers a rich source of practical techniques and principles to which they can refer when implementing co-operative learning.

Dick Tracy's Crime Stoppers, a.k.a. the Four Fatal Flaws

Growing up in the 1950s and 1960s, I often read the comic strip "Dick Tracy." At the end of Saturday's funny pages, there was a section called "Dick Tracy's Crime Stoppers Textbook,"

which contained hints for the amateur detective. For instance, when trying to memorize the face of a criminal to identify him later, make sure to note the size and shape of the ears and earlobes. What follows is a more serious educational version of my comic strip memories.

Paul Vermette of Niagara University probably did it best in identifying tips for stopping "crimes of co-operative learning" in his article "Four Fatal Flaws: Avoiding the Common Mistakes of Novice Users of Co-operative Learning" (1994). He considers the first fatal flaw to occur in the construction of student groups, that is, many novice users leave the choice to students with disastrous results. He argues, as I do, that teachers should build the teams.

The second fatal flaw is to launch students into a major group project before completing smaller activities to build teams and establish social skills and habits of co-operation.

The third common fatal flaw involves the issue of working in class. "To help monitor the effectiveness of co-operative learning, the teacher *needs to see it!*" writes Vermette. (The italics are his, but could have been mine.) He lists many advantages of doing co-operative work in class, for example, teachers can offer suggestions and praise to students, boost the efforts of reluctant learners or shy students, and help groups reflect on their behaviour. When teachers give students group projects to complete outside class, none of this happens. Moreover, having seen many of these group projects assigned to my daughter, I have a visceral reaction against the almost inevitable unequal participation. There is almost always someone who does not participate fully.

The fourth fatal flaw is found with group grades: "Nothing offends an industrious student more than having someone else (Paul or Paula Parasite?) do nothing and share an A!" If group grades are to be assigned, it is imperative that all students get what, and only what, they deserve.

Co-operative learning is a valuable approach to teaching and learning, worthy of attention and thoughtful implementation by secondary school teachers. Although it does demand a commitment on our part, an alignment of our values with the approach, and a willingness to address the social side of learning, there is research, practical guides, and experienced teachers, some of which are listed in the following references, to help us.

Select a lesson, preferably one you have planned. Using the example of the remake of a traditional lesson into a co-operative lesson as a guide, modify the activities and structure of the selected lesson so that it embodies Kagans' four principles of effective co-operative learning.

REFERENCES

Deutsch, M. 1949. A theory of cooperation and competition. *Human Relations* 2: 129–152.

Dewey, J. 1916. *Democracy in education.* New York: Macmillan.

Johnson, D. and R. Johnson. 1989. *Cooperation and competition: Theory and research.* Edina, MN: Interaction Book Company.

———. 1992. Approaches to implementing cooperative learning in the social studies classroom. In *Cooperative learning in the social studies classroom,* eds. R. Stahl and R. VanSickle, 45–51. Washington, DC: National Council for the Social Studies.

Johnson, D., R. Johnson, and E. Holubec. 1998. *Cooperation in the classroom,* 7th ed. Edina, MN: Interaction Book Company.

Kagan, S. 2001. Kagan structures and learning together—what is the difference? *KaganOnLine Magazine.* Available online at http://www.KaganOnline.com/KaganClub/index.html.

Kohn, A. 1992. *No contest: The case against competition.* Boston: Houghton Mifflin.

Morton, T. 1996. *Cooperative learning and social studies: Towards excellence and equity.* San Juan Capistrano, CA: Kagan.

Myers, J. 1991. Cooperative learning in history and social sciences: An idea whose time has come. *Canadian Social Studies* 26 (2): 60–64.

———. 2003a. Assessing citizenship and character using co-operative learning. *Orbit* 33 (2): 47–9.

———. 2003b. Co-operative learning: Steps toward an anti-racist education. *Orbit* 33 (3): 29–32.

Sapon-Shevin, M. and N. Schniedewind. 1992. If cooperative learning's the answer, what are the questions? *Journal of Education* 174 (2): 11–37.

Sarason, S. 1995. Some reactions to what we have learned. *Phi Delta Kappan* 7 (1): 84.

Slavin, R.E. 1989. *Cooperative learning: Theory, research, and practice.* Englewood Cliffs, NJ: Prentice Hall.

Stone, J.R. 2005. *The Routledge dictionary of Latin quotations.* New York: Routledge.

Vermette, Paul. 1994. Four fatal flaws: avoiding the common mistakes of novice users of cooperative learning. *The High School Journal,* February/March: 255–260.

ADDITIONAL RESOURCES

Bellanca, J. and R. Fogarty. 2001. *Blueprints for achievement in the cooperative classroom,* 3rd ed. Thousand Oaks, CA: Sage.

Bower, B. and J. Lobdell. 2003. *Social studies alive! Engaging diverse learners in the elementary classroom.* Palo Alto, CA: Teachers' Curriculum Institute.

Coelho, E. 1994. *Learning together in the multicultural classroom.* Markham, ON: Pippin.

DeBolt, V. 1998. *Write! Social studies.* San Juan Capistrano, CA: Kagan Publishing.

Johnson, D. and R. Johnson. 1992. *Creative controversy.* Edina, MN: Interaction Book Company.

Johnson, D., R. Johnson, J. Bartlett, and L. Johnson. 1988. *Our cooperative classroom.* Edina, MN: Interaction Book Company.

Kagan, S., L. Kagan, and M. Kagan. 2000. *Reaching the social studies standards through cooperative learning* (video and teachers' guide). San Juan Capistrano, CA: Kagan Publishing.

Stahl, R., ed. 1994. *Cooperative learning in social studies: A handbook for teachers.* Reading, MA: Addison-Wesley.

Vermette, P.J. 1998. *Making cooperative learning work: Student teams in K–12 classrooms.* Upper Saddle River, NJ: Merrill.

GROUPS

BC Cooperative Learning Association is the professional specialist association of the BC Teachers' Federation. See http://bccla.weebly.com/.

Cooperative Learning Center at the University of Minnesota. See http://www.co-operation.org.

International Association for the Study of Cooperation in Education is a group of teachers and researchers from around the world who produce a magazine called *Co-operative Learning.* See http://www.iasce.net.

Kagan Publishing and Professional Development. See http://www.KaganOnline.com.

PART 3 Implementation

Instructional Planning

Learning Resources

Student Assessment

23

Course, Unit, and Lesson Planning for Secondary Teachers

Roland Case

In this chapter I offer a framework that tracks teacher planning in social studies, history, or geography from the most abstract and general aims for an entire course to the most specific decisions about which method and resource to employ in a particular lesson. The framework consists of four levels:

- the vision for the year
- a course plan
- unit plans
- individual lesson plans

Before examining each level in detail, I offer four overall principles to guide your deliberations. I introduce these principles by drawing parallels between successful planning and the practices of experienced hikers on a long-distance wilderness trek. The image of a journey through boundless, often unfamiliar territory is a particularly apt metaphor for the challenges of course, unit, and lesson planning.

Guiding Principles of Planning

There are many insights about effective planning to draw from this analogy with trekking though wilderness terrain. These insights can be consolidated into four general principles of planning: be purposeful, build thoughtfully, draw widely and wisely, and plan loosely.

PLANNING AS TREKKING

Those with orienteering experience will know that hikers must be clear about where they are starting from and where they want to get to ultimately. Otherwise they are likely to lose their bearings in what may well be dense and confusing terrain. Without a clear sense of direction, even if they do not become completely lost, hikers may waste considerable time and energy and may fail to reach their intended destination. Although the ultimate destination may not be in view until near the end of their trip, which may be many days or weeks in length, hikers will always know the general direction to head towards in order to reach their long-term objective. Typically, they plot their route in outline form. They anticipate that their plans will change, but they recognize the value of having a clear plan, even if it is provisional. To keep themselves on track, hikers identify prominent features or landmarks within intermediate reach that will keep them working towards their final destination. These landmarks may be off in the distance, several or even many kilometres ahead, but they nevertheless serve as a beacon—as the clear visible focus of their travel. If a landmark is vaguely defined, for example, if they select a feature as vast and undefined as a mountain range or an ocean, it will not keep them on a consistent path. From time to time, especially if conditions change or the going becomes very rough,

hikers may reconsider whether or not heading towards the designated beacon is the best course to follow. Of course, the bulk of hikers' time is spent attending to their most immediate objectives—getting up the ravine, finding a suitable place to stop, checking their resources, making sure morale among the hikers is positive, and so on. They look for easy routes or pre-established paths that can expedite their travel, and they take detours if a route seems easier or if there is a site that offers an enticing diversion. They supplement the supplies they carry with resources found on the way, and they improvise should the need arise.

Although much of the trip consists of these moment-to-moment choices about which way to turn or where to step next, there is no point in staying on a path or turning towards a hill if it does not lead in the desired direction. Consequently hikers continually double-check—often in an intuitive or reflexive manner—that the specific choices they make are aligned with the more distant beacon they have set. Accordingly, they will follow a pre-established path only so long as it leads in the desired direction, and they may rejoin the path sometime later if it turns back towards their destination. Consistently, the direction hikers take is informed by the beacon they have set because, if clearly and properly determined, heading for it means they are on the track towards their ultimate destination.

BE PURPOSEFUL

The principle that planning should be purposeful is perhaps the most significant recommendation I offer. It emphasizes the need to decide where we want to take our students and to use that destination to orient everything we do. Without a clear and conscious direction, our teaching is aimless—likely amounting to little more than a string of activities leading nowhere in particular and serving no important purposes. Just as with trekkers, so too as teachers we need to set and be guided by long-, intermediate-, and immediate-term destinations:

- Our ultimate destinations are our rationale—our ideals or ultimate vision—for society and for our students.
- Our intermediate destinations are our goals for an individual unit and course.
- Our immediate destinations are our objectives for specific lessons.

The principle of being purposeful does not presuppose a "teacher-driven" approach to planning and teaching. The need to have a clear purpose is compatible with extensive student involvement in setting destinations by consensus or, to the extent feasible, in encouraging individuals to strike out in different directions. Given students' different preferences and abilities it often makes sense, even for those heading towards the same general ultimate destination, for individuals to pursue common goals by following different paths.

Effective implementation of purposeful planning implies four conditions:

- **Clear, focussed destinations.** Both in the long- and short-term, we should know what we hope to achieve with our students. Vaguely understood goals and objectives do not provide the sense of purpose that effective teaching requires.
- **Manageable destinations.** We should not expect to do it all and if we try to do too much—for an entire course or for an individual lesson—we may end up doing a superficial job that makes no lasting difference.
- **Justifiable destinations.** We cannot simply decide to pursue our own preferred direction without seriously considering students' best interests, parents' rights, and other curricular and professional responsibilities.
- **Aligned destinations.** Our long- and short-term destinations must be in alignment, so that we are continually working towards our ultimate destination. This requires that:
  - our rationale inform our goals;
  - our goals orient our objectives; and
  - our objectives determine our day-to-day decisions about teaching methods, resources, and assessment.

BUILD THOUGHTFULLY

The principle of building thoughtfully emphasizes the importance of anticipating the intermediate steps to be taken and developing the resources and tools needed to achieve our ultimate educational goals. The expression by the Chinese philosopher Lao-tzu that a journey of a thousand miles starts with a single step is especially relevant. It is not enough that we have a grand plan; we must also attend to how we will get there. Just as the trekker must decide what equipment is needed to cross a river or what supplies to sustain the team, as teachers we must also consider what our students will need to reach the desired goals and what we must do to support this growth.

Effective implementation of the principle of building thoughtfully includes at least three considerations:

- **Nurture an environment conducive to learning.** We must work to develop the type of classroom and school environment that supports the desired learning. If we want to develop student autonomy, we must nurture it by establishing a climate that encourages students to take risks and to make up their own minds. The mere planning of thoughtful lessons will not lead very far if the conditions in the classroom undermine these efforts. For example, inviting students to debate a very controversial issue before classroom trust and civility have been adequately established may lead to bitter and counter-productive results.
- **Provide meaningful contexts for learning.** A concern expressed by many teachers is that students do not perceive social studies or history to be relevant. We can help students better appreciate social studies by carefully planning activities that are motivating, and by framing our units and lessons in contexts that will resonate with students.
- **Teach the prerequisites.** Just as it is unfair to expect someone to construct an elaborate house without having the basic tools to do the job, so is it unfair to expect significant educational achievement without providing students with the intellectual tools they need for success. We must think through what students require for success at each step—for example, what knowledge, abilities, and attitudes are needed for students to become good researchers. Then we must plan how to assist students in acquiring each of these prerequisites.

DRAW WIDELY AND WISELY

The principle of drawing widely and wisely from many sources draws attention to the value of an eclectic approach to planning for content, teaching methods, and learning resources. Preoccupation with a narrow theme and over-reliance on a single method, such as lectures, or on a single resource, such as a textbook, are analogous to staying on pre-established paths long after they cease to lead in the direction that we want to head towards. We must draw imaginatively from varied sources in our quest for better ways to help our students get where we want them to go.

Effective implementation of the principle of drawing widely and wisely involves the following considerations:

- **Integrate the content of different disciplines and subjects.** We should help students make meaningful links among the disciplines within social studies, draw insights from other subjects, and connect what they study in school with their own experiences and concerns.
- **Use diverse learning resources.** We should plan to make effective use of diverse resources from computers to cartoons, from textbooks to picture books, and from feature films to guest speakers.
- **Use varied teaching methods.** We should plan for a rich array of activities from teacher-directed to student-directed, from written work to small-group conversation, and from seat-work to fieldwork.

PLAN LOOSELY

The principle of planning loosely arises because there is no guaranteed path for all students for all times. Planning is too messy and uncertain an affair to be reduced to a fixed plan. Not only will one path not work for all students, but conditions change, our students change, and we change. We should be prepared to reformulate our plans to accommodate these eventualities and the countless unanticipated turns that arise halfway though the year or in the middle of a lesson. However, this lack of predictability does not imply that planning is fanciful or useless. Planning is a deeply practical matter. The point of planning is to identify what is most worthwhile to teach and then to design a course, a unit, or a lesson that increases the likelihood that our teaching will be successful.

Effective implementation of the principle of planning loosely involves the following considerations:

- **Expect diversity.** Always expect and, to the extent possible, accommodate diversity in student interests and abilities.
- **Allow for student choice.** Entrench opportunities for student choice and self-direction as a feature of our teaching.
- **Stay flexible.** As teachers, we will be more effective if we remain open to change. Instead of viewing a lesson or unit plan as the fixed menu for the day or the month, we should look upon planning as the ongoing vehicle for

scrutinizing where we are going with our teaching and deciding what is a good way to get there.

I believe these four principles should permeate all of our planning, from decisions about the ultimate goals to our most immediate objectives. To assist in planning that embodies these principles, I offer a four-level framework:

- the vision for the year;
- a course plan;
- unit plans; and
- individual lesson plans.

These levels are akin to progressive snapshots of the earth beginning with the broadest global view and zeroing in on a particular site. Each provides increasing detail of a progressively smaller area of instruction. I begin by describing the most general level and proceed to the most specific level. Despite sequencing my discussion of the model in this order, planning should not necessarily proceed in a "general to specific" manner. Those who like to begin with the concrete will find it more productive to start with particular lessons and resources, and work from there to the more general vision. Regardless of where we start, all of us will likely move back and forth between levels as our ideas become clearer and more specific. Thus the four levels imply no particular planning sequence; but regardless of how we proceed, by the end of our planning deliberations, the issues raised at each level of the model should have been thought through in a coherent way.

Realistically, a fully completed set of plans as outlined in this framework would involve years of thinking about and trying out ideas. Nevertheless, all of us, and especially new teachers, can benefit from a deeper understanding of the considerations involved in the kind of comprehensive planning suggested by this framework. In this respect the framework is an ultimate destination. It is an invitation to strive for an ideal—even if never fully reached; only by attempting it will we come closer to where we want to be.

Creating a Vision for the Year

The most general level of planning involves creating a vision for the entire year. In effect, it involves asking ourselves the following question: "In a hundred words or less, what am I really attempting to achieve in my course this year?" The point of planning at this level is to give focus and direction to a course. Figure 23.1 illustrates a form that might be used to articulate the most general level of planning. A vision for the year may consist of three main components:

FIGURE 23.1 VISION FOR THE YEAR

Theme for the year			Grade
Rationale			
PRIORITY GOALS			**Classroom climate**
Content knowledge	Personal and social values		
Thinking	Individual and collective action		
Information gathering and communication	Other		

- **Rationale.** Our rationale should be a clear and defensible account of our educational ideals—the underlying reasons or ultimate purposes for our efforts as educators.
- **Priority goals.** Our priority goals are the handful of educational goals that will be the major focus of attention for the year. These goals represent our priorities for the year—mindful that we cannot do everything well. If our goals are met, we will have gone some way towards moving students closer to the ideals set out in our rationale.
- **Classroom climate.** The classroom climate refers to the defining qualities and procedures of the learning environment within which we hope to promote the priority goals and, ultimately, our rationale.

FORMULATING A RATIONALE

Educational rationales are descriptions of the ideal individual or society we hope to promote through education. An earlier chapter in this collection, "Four Defining Purposes of Citizenship Education," identified four broad categories of rationales for social studies, positioned along two continua:

Social acceptance/social change spectrum
- **Social initiation.** Transmitting the understandings, abilities, and values that students will require if they are to fit into and be contributing members of society.
- **Social reform.** Promoting the understandings, abilities, and values necessary to critique and improve society.

Student-centred/subject-centred spectrum
- **Personal development.** Fostering the personal talents and character of each student so that they develop fully as individuals and as social beings.
- **Intellectual development.** Developing understanding of and appreciation for the bodies of knowledge and forms of inquiry represented in the social science disciplines.

These rationales, in effect, are ways of categorizing the types of ideals that are typically offered for social studies. In the sample vision for the year, Figure 23.2, you will find elements from each of these four categories.

In thinking about our own rationale, we should be guided by two considerations: Am I clear about the ideals I am striving for? Are these justifiable ideals?

CLARITY OF FOCUS

Many of the ideals found in rationales for social studies—such as personal autonomy, historical or geographical thinking, productive citizen, or tolerant society—are potentially vague. Unless we are clear in our own minds what we mean by notions such as these, they will not serve as useful guides to our planning. Does a tolerant society mean that we will begrudgingly accept differences? And what sort of differences will we tolerate? Religious views? Alternative lifestyles? Political and economic ideologies? Perhaps we want to focus largely on racial, ethnic, and cultural differences. We may also want to pursue a more embracing vision, not merely putting up with differences but actually welcoming and accepting people because of the cultural contributions that they bring to mainstream society. These are different

FIGURE 23.2   SAMPLE VISION FOR THE YEAR

Theme for the year Canada before and after Confederation		Grade middle school

Rationale
My ideal citizen:

- is able to cope with a complex, uncertain world
- is willing and trained to think things through rigorously
- is knowledgeable about a wide range of issues
- is committed and willing to work to make the world better for all
- is emotionally mature and socially adept

PRIORITY GOALS		Classroom climate
Content knowledge - understands the complexities of and interrelationships among many of the historical and contemporary problems in Canada - has knowledge of both the ennobling and the regrettable events in Canada's past	**Personal and social values** - has empathy and respect for others - is committed to social justice - is respectful of different viewpoints - has tolerance for ambiguity - is independent-minded	- respectful, safe environment - challenge students in non-threatening ways - emphasis on self-directed learning —independent projects, peer and self-assessment - abundant opportunities for student choice - students expected to form personal opinions and support with reasons
Thinking - can competently analyze controversial issues - sees issues from varying perspectives - possesses the tools of a good critical thinker	**Individual and collective action** - is able and willing to work co-operatively with others, even in difficult situations - can plan thoughtfully to solve demanding problems	
Information gathering and communicating - can plan and conduct independent research - can effectively use media and other local sources of information	**Other**	

emphases, and clarity about the particulars of our rationale are useful when planning.

JUSTIFIED IDEALS

In deciding whether or not our rationale is justifiable we should be guided by the following considerations:

- the broad needs of our students;
- the broad needs of the local community;
- the broad needs of society generally;
- our own values as educators.

The value of a clear, justifiable rationale is that it helps us to recognize and keep to what really matters. I remember teaching an especially troubled group of grade 6-7 students. Whenever I got bogged down in the minutiae of the curric-

ulum or was frustrated by the day's events, I would remind myself of why I was there. Long before I knew to call it my "rationale," I knew that my reason for persisting was to help these students learn to take personal responsibility for their lives. I had seen too many of their peers fall by the wayside, driven by a lack of trust of others and a lack of respect for themselves, into a world of glue sniffing and other forms of self-destructive escapism. I hoped I could teach them about literature and science along the way, but not if pursuing these goals interrupted my more pressing mission of helping them take control of their lives. My justification for this "personal development" rationale was obvious. When I thought about what these students most needed in their lives and what their parents most hoped for them, of paramount importance were notions such as functional literacy, personal responsibility, and self-respect.

ESTABLISHING PRIORITY GOALS

The priority goals identify our key educational emphases for the year. If we could make a real difference in several areas, what would we hope to achieve over the year? With the students described above, my priorities included teaching them to read at a level required to understand the newspaper, to commit themselves to a task and complete it, to treat each other with respect, and to develop pride in themselves.

In deciding what to emphasize in a given year, it is useful to consider how our rationale could be advanced through the general goals for social studies. Throughout this book, the following have been identified as representative of the range of goals social studies typically seeks to promote:

- **content knowledge:** the breadth and depth of factual and conceptual knowledge students should possess about their world;
- **thinking:** the ability and inclination to assess what to believe and how to act competently;
- **information gathering and communicating:** the ability to identify information needs, extract information from varied sources, and represent this information in appropriate forms;
- **personal and social values:** the desired values that individuals are to hold about themselves and towards others; and
- **individual and collective action:** the ability to analyze problems in students' lives and in society, plan appropriate courses of action individually and in collaboration with others, put into action their plans, and evaluate the efficacy of their efforts.

We need not be bound by these categories of goals, and may prefer to use the terminology provided in the provincial curriculum or some other document. If teaching an integrated course, we would include goals not exclusively from social studies but from other subjects as well. The important consideration is not the terminology, but to identify a manageable number of priority goals that will form our emphasis for the year. We will, of course, pursue many other goals; these merely represent the handful of goals that we have set as the most productive and pressing avenues to promote our ideals. Often our rationale overlaps with our priority goals because some of the ideals in our rationale are aims that are directly promoted in social studies. Typically, however, ideals are broader aspirations, and we will emphasize only some aspect of these. For example, a "social reform" rationale might include the ideals of promoting a world without poverty, hunger, and war. In a given year, we might emphasize only a few goals that promote these ideals, for example, teaching students to treat one another respectfully and to use peer-mediation and other nonviolent forms of interpersonal conflict resolution.

The criteria for justifying a rationale are relevant to justifying our priority goals, although the focus in justifying priority goals is more on examining how our subject and we, as teachers of social studies, history or geography, can best further ideals embedded in our rationale. In deciding upon this we should consider the following factors:

- the needs and expressed wishes of our students;
- the expectations embedded in the provincial curriculum;
- the nature of our subject and the range of purposes that it is expected to serve;
- the expressed wishes of parents and the local community;
- the needs of society generally; and
- our own priorities and strengths as educators.

SHAPING THE CLASSROOM CLIMATE

Although classroom climate has not traditionally been seen as part of the defining vision of a course, it is becoming increasingly obvious that this factor plays a significant role in supporting or impeding the achievement of our goals. Many of us will have been frustrated by our inability to get students, say, to think critically about issues or to take responsibility for their learning because the prevailing mood in the class undermined our efforts. The point of including classroom climate is to identify the basic principles that ought to guide the conduct of our class if we are serious about our rationale. For example, in the sample vision for the year, one of the elements of the rationale is to promote students' willingness and ability to think things through with rigour. Students are likely to take the risks involved in thinking for themselves only if the classroom is a safe and respectful place, and only if the inevitable "challenging" required to help students probe their thinking more deeply is done in a non-threatening manner. These features must, therefore, be important operating principles for the classroom. Identifying operating principles requires thinking through the sorts of routines and norms that must be part of the daily business of our classrooms if we are to have any likelihood of advancing our rationale. See chapter 8, "Supporting a Community of Critical Thinkers," for more about nurturing classroom climate.

Developing a Course Plan

Although the vision for the year is our ultimate destination and should always be in the back of our minds, like trekkers, we will not have that vision constantly in our sights. Our conscious focus will likely be more immediate: deciding what we would have to teach in September, or in November, in order to get where we want to be in June. The purpose of the second level of the planning model—the course plan—is to set out the general sequence and structure of the pursuit of our goals by plotting the more specific objectives or outcomes that will be promoted in each unit. Just as a long trip may be broken into phases, so too the journey through the curriculum is typically divided up into units of study—usually between three and five units over the course of a year. Figure 23.3 contains a structure that might be used to lay out a course plan. The tasks in developing a course plan include:

- deciding on an appropriate focus for each unit;
- identifying specific objectives for all unit goals; and
- sequencing objectives across units.

DECIDING ON A FOCUS FOR THE UNIT

Typically, planning a course begins by identifying the unit topics or unifying ideas for each phase of the course. The topic provides the context or vehicle for promoting the goals and specific objectives that will eventually be set for each unit. Selecting a topic is a common beginning step in deciding on an appropriate focus for a unit. Surprisingly, however, identifying a topic need not determine in any definitive way what will be taught in a unit. For example, a unit on the topic "ancient Egypt" might focus on any number of studies, for instance:

- the environment's significant role in shaping human activity (for example, impact of the Nile);
- the thinking behind religious and cultural practices of other groups that may at first glance seem foreign to us (for example, studying the rationale for embalming, beliefs about reincarnation);
- the wondrous mathematical and engineering accomplishments of this civilization (for example, building of pyramids);

FIGURE 23.3   COURSE PLAN

UNIT DESCRIPTION	UNIT OBJECTIVES				
	Content knowledge	Thinking	Information gathering and communicating	Personal and social values	Individual and collective action
Unit 1 Synopsis Main goals					
Unit 2 Synopsis Main goals					
Unit 3 Synopsis Main goals					
Unit 4 Synopsis Main goals					
Unit 5 Synopsis Main goals					

- the work of archaeologists in adding to our knowledge of ancient Egypt (for example, carry out a simulated dig, read about famous discoveries).

These underlying ideas within the topic are often framed as generalizations that we want students to come to understand. Various educators have stressed the power of unpacking the underlying idea through "essential" questions (Erickson 2007, Wiggins and McTighe 2005) that guide students in "uncovering" the curriculum. The examples in Table 23.4 illustrate how underlying ideas, curricular outcomes, and guiding questions help to create a focus around which learning activities can be developed.

In an important respect, a unit topic (for example, progress, revolutions, our natural resources) is the shell within which the contents of a unit will develop. Although the most common type of topic is what is typically referred to as a theme, there are other types of unifying or central ideas of a unit. The highlighted text identifies six types of unit organizers, each of which could be unpacked into more specific essential or guiding questions.

The choice of the type of topic influences the shape or direction of a unit. For example, a unit organized around the theme of explorer Simon Fraser provides a different orientation than a project-based unit on researching, writing, and mounting a play about Simon Fraser's travels or an issue-based unit on deciding whether Simon Fraser was a hero or a rogue. Although there will be overlap in what is learned from these three units, there will likely be important differences in the outcomes. Accordingly, we should select unit topics that will best advance the goals we want to foster in each unit.

An important step in getting clear about a unit is to decide upon three or four goals that will be the main emphasis of the unit (other goals will be promoted but not stressed in the way the main goals will be) and, using these goals as a guide, to think through how the topic might best be handled. (As a theme or an issue? And what theme or issue in particular?) The partial course plan in Figure 23.5 contains a synopsis, the main goals, and the objectives for the first unit in a year-long study of nineteenth-century Canada. The main focusses of this unit are to help students learn to work effectively together in groups, to teach them about conducting independent research, and to develop a broad understanding of key events leading up to Confederation. The unit organizer—a project to create a giant timeline of events during this period—was chosen because it is a good vehicle to serve these three goals.

IDENTIFYING SPECIFIC OBJECTIVES

As we think about our unit topic and main goals, we will inevitably begin to identify specific content. At some point it becomes necessary to outline more systematically and specifically the objectives or learning outcomes for the unit. At this stage we are not concerned about teaching methods— what we will have students do during the unit—but rather on what we hope students will learn. (Research suggests that many teachers prefer to begin with the activities then decide what the objectives might be. This simply means that once deciding on a unit focus some teachers may want to jump to the next, more specific level and think about the activities that students will be involved in before identifying the specific objectives that the unit will address.)

The key challenge in identifying the specific objectives is to unpack what is involved in promoting the goals we have set for the year, and especially the main goals that we have identified for the unit. Objectives are simply more specific elements of a goal; objectives often take a lesson or two to cover, whereas goals typically refer to general aims that may take an entire unit or longer to achieve. In developing the sample unit plan, we would want to think through what is involved in promoting independent library research. What are the crucial sub-skills or tools that students will need to develop this ability and which of these are best taught in this unit? Should my students learn to use basic reference aids (for example, Google search), or should I introduce them to more advanced tools for electronic research? Perhaps my students already know how to locate information sources. In that case, I might be better advised to help them improve at extracting information from these sources.

Although it is difficult to do, the best place to begin this articulation process is by developing lists of the more specific objectives that are implied by the goals for each unit—especially the main goals for the unit. Often the curriculum guide or other professional materials are helpful in providing details about the objectives for specific goals. Of course, we will not be able to do it all in any one unit; we must set priorities about the most important objectives to pursue. As a general rule, we are well advised to do a smaller number of things very well, rather than attempt to do too many things in one unit. This is why a few goals (perhaps three or four) should be designated as the main goals for the unit. If we run out of time, we will make sure that the key objectives associated with our main goals are not sacrificed.

The following factors are particularly relevant considerations when deciding the specific objectives for a unit:

- the overall rationale for the course and the main goals for the unit;
- our students' interests and prior learning;
- the requirements of the provincial curriculum;
- our own interests and competencies as teachers;

TABLE 23.1   UNPACKING THE UNDERLYING IDEA

UNIFYING IDEA/BROAD UNDERSTANDING	CURRICULAR OUTCOMES ADDRESSED	QUESTIONS TO BE EXPLORED
Creating Canada, 1850–1890 (History Grade 8, Strand A, Ontario) Not all Canadians enjoyed the same rights and privileges in the new nation. (Ontario 2013A, 146)	• Evaluate the importance of various internal and external factors that played a role in the creation of the Dominion of Canada and the expansion of its territory. • Assess the impact that differences in legal status and in the distribution of rights and privileges had on various groups and individuals in Canada between 1850 and 1890. • Analyse some of the actions taken by various groups and/or individuals in Canada between 1850 and 1890 to improve their lives. (Ontario 2013A, 148–49)	• What was the significance of the Indian Act in the expansion of Canada? • What do her [Emily Stowe's] actions tell you about limitations on women's rights in Canada during this period? What impact did these limitations have on women? • In what ways did the rights of First Nations peoples living on reserves differ from those of other Canadians? • What impact did limited citizenship rights have on status Indians? • What were some strategies immigrants developed to cope with the environment of the Canadian Prairies? (Ontario 2013A, 148–49)
1750–1919 (Social Studies Grade 9, British Columbia) Emerging ideas and ideologies profoundly influence societies and events. (British Columbia 2015)	• [Know about] the continuing effects of imperialism and colonialism on indigenous peoples in Canada and around the world. • [Know about] global demographic shifts, including patterns of migration and population growth. • [Know about] nationalism and the development of modern nation-states, including Canada. (British Columbia 2015)	• What were the motivations for imperialism and colonialism during this period? • What continuing role does imperialism and colonialism from this period play in present-day Canada and around the world? • How did the arrival of new groups of immigrants affect Canadian identity? • Is nationalism a more positive or negative force in the world? • To what extent did nationalism bring people together or drive them apart? (British Columbia 2015)
The Sustainability of Resources (Geography Grade 9 Academic, Strand C, Ontario) The way Canada's resources are used has a direct impact on the availability of resources for the future. (Ontario 2013B, 70)	• Describe strategies that industries and governments have implemented to increase the sustainability of Canada's natural resources. • Assess the impact of Canada's participation in international trade agreements and of globalization on the development and management of human and natural resources in Canada. • Analyse the influence of governments, advocacy groups, and industries on the sustainable development and use of selected Canadian resources. • Analyse the roles and responsibilities of individuals in promoting the sustainable use of resources. (Ontario 2013B, 78-79)	• How effective are the waste management practices in your community in supporting sustainability? • What, in your opinion, are the three most important criteria that a trade agreement with another country should meet in order for it to be acceptable to Canada? • How might foreign ownership of companies extracting resources within Canada affect long-term employment prospects or sustainability policies? • What impacts do different kinds of industries have on the environment, and what can they do to operate more sustainably? • How can we balance our individual needs and wants against the need for sustainable resource use? (Ontario 2013B, 78–79)

FIGURE 23.4 SAMPLE COURSE PLAN

UNIT DESCRIPTION	UNIT OBJECTIVES				
	Content knowledge	Thinking	Information gathering and communication	Personal and social values	Individual and collective action
Unit #1 Timeline: The lead-up to Confederation **Synopsis** The class is divided into five teams that are to research and prepare a giant illustrated timeline that will be posted around the entire classroom depicting the major social, political, cultural, and economic events and people in Canada from 1815 to Confederation. Each team is responsible for researching, documenting, and illustrating major landmarks and key figures for a ten-year period. Groups must decide by consensus on the basis of agreed-upon criteria the most significant events and persons of their time period. Students are expected to share their findings orally and prepare a background sheet that all students receive. The unit will conclude with a student-created exam on events and people depicted in the timeline. **Main goals** • Learn to work effectively and co-operatively in groups. • Learn to conduct independent library research. • Develop a broad overview of events leading to Confederation.	• Understands the political, economic, social, and geographical factors leading to Confederation. • Has knowledge of key events and persons in Canada from 1815 to 1867.	• Is able to assess appropriateness of information sources for a purpose. • Is able to use criteria to reach a reasoned decision.	• Uses library reference aids to locate sources (for example, bibliography, catalogue, electronic search engines). • Uses textual aids to locate information (for example, table of contents, index, glossary, keywords, headings, legend). • Summarizes ideas in his or her own words. • Uses graphics (for example, timelines, charts, graphs) to present information. • Oral and visual communication is clear and accurate.	• Takes pride in preparing quality work. • Respects opinions and is supportive of others. • Respects the rights of everyone in the group. • Engages respectfully in group discussion.	• Understands collaboration, co-operation, compromise, consensus. • Plans how to organize the group, divide up the tasks, and schedule and monitor the work plan. • Fulfills roles and responsibilities effectively and fairly.

- the resources available in the school and district; and
- the possibilities of integration with other areas of study.

SEQUENCING OBJECTIVES ACROSS UNITS

The final task in developing a one-year overview is to develop a scope and sequence of objectives from unit to unit. The scope of objectives should be comprehensive so that over the course of a year the entire set of curricular objectives are adequately addressed. The sequence should be reasonable; for example, we should not teach objectives in an early unit that presuppose mastery of outcomes that we have planned to teach later in the year. In many cases, there may be no obvious prerequisites; for example, in teaching students to interpret visual documents it may make no difference whether we start with photographs or maps. The sequence may depend entirely on the availability of resources for the unit topics we have selected. In other cases, the sequence may be crucial. For example, we should teach simple procedures for using the internet, such as finding sites where the address is provided, prior to introducing more sophisticated variants involving student-designed searches. Although there are no hard and fast rules, the following are different ways to think about the scope and sequence of objectives over the course of a year:

- proceed from simple to more difficult;
- proceed from concrete to abstract;
- proceed from general to specific;
- proceed in chronological order (especially relevant with content objectives);

TYPES OF TOPICS OR UNIT ORGANIZERS

Theme
A theme is an idea or feature that is shared by, or recurs in, a number of separate elements. The connection among elements in the unit is that they are in some way associated with a common theme. Some types of themes are:

- **Places.** For example, Egypt, the Arctic, deserts, the moon.
- **Events.** For example, building the pyramids, making the atomic bomb.
- **Eras.** For example, the Depression, pre-Copernican Europe.
- **Concepts.** For example, harmony, time, creativity.
- **Generalizations.** For example, man is a social animal, history repeats itself.
- **Phenomena.** For example, biological change, war, globalization.
- **Entities.** For example, cities, atoms, multinational companies.

Narrative
A narrative (Kieran Egan calls it a storyform) is a series of episodes that uses a familiar structure for building upon and connecting elements in a unit. The elements are united in that each must fit the story being told. Some sample narratives are:

- developing story of a country, province, or city
- tale of a people, family, or person
- evolutionary steps in a discovery or invention
- account of a quest or adventure

Issue
An issue identifies a specific question whose answer is a value judgment about what ought to be the case. The elements are united in that each is necessary to competently address the issue. Entire units might focus on issues such as:

- Should students have a right to select their textbook?
- Are large cities better than smaller cities?
- Should further technological innovation be encouraged?

- Which innovation arising from ancient Greece has had the most significant influence on our lives?

Inquiry
An inquiry identifies a specific question whose answer is a description of how things actually were, are, or are likely to become. The elements are united in that each is necessary to competently undertake the inquiry. Entire units might focus on inquiries such as:

- What motivated/drove famous people to greatness?
- How does the natural environment deal with its "waste"?
- What will my life be like thirty years from now?
- Are we actually better in Canada now compared to sixty-five years ago?

Problem
A problem identifies a specific question whose answer is a course of action. The elements are united in that each is necessary to competently solve the problem. Instead of merely talking about what should or might occur, entire units could lead students to act on problems such as:

- Can we reduce the amount of paper wasted in school?
- How can our school be made more personal/safe?
- What can we do to protect our parks and wildlife?
- What can we do to improve working conditions in developing countries?

Project
A project involves creation of a "product" of some kind. The elements are united in that each is necessary to competently complete the project. Entire units might focus on producing objects or events such as:

- models or replicas
- a play or performance
- a diorama or mural
- a written or audiovisual piece

- process in reverse chronological order from present working back;
- proceed from near to far; and
- proceed from far to near.

Outlining Unit Plans

A more specific level of planning occurs when we take each of the units described in the course plan and begin to develop their details. As illustrated in Figure 23.6, unit plans typically consist of summary notes outlining the objectives, the proposed methods or activities, the anticipated resources that will be needed, and the suggested assessment strategy for each

lesson. A unit might contain anywhere from ten to twenty lessons. The following sequence is one way to proceed when developing a unit plan.

- Brainstorm possible teaching strategies and resources that would promote the identified goals and objectives. Supplement your own ideas by looking for teaching resources in a local school library, in a teacher's resource centre, or data bases of print and digital resources. Talk to others who have taught this topic and may be in a position to suggest ideas or resources. Assemble as many ideas and resources as you can find.
- Identify an introductory activity or activities. We all know that first impressions are important. This same principle applies to the way new units of study are introduced. The introductory lesson(s) to a unit can serve several important purposes:
  - Arouse student interest in the topic and provoke student questions.
  - Provide students with background information and set the context for what is to follow.
  - Provide the teacher with diagnostic information about the extent of students' present knowledge about the topic and attitudes towards it, as well as related skill levels.

FIGURE 23.5   UNIT PLAN

Unit topic		Grade	Unit #
Unit goals	1. 2. 3. 4.		

LESSON TITLE	SPECIFIC OBJECTIVES	METHODS/ ACTIVITIES	RESOURCES	ASSESSMENT STRATEGIES AND CRITERIA

- Help the teacher and students formulate a plan of action for studying the topic of the unit; the highlighted text, "Ways to Introduce a Unit," offers various suggestions for beginning new units of instruction in an engaging and effective manner.
- Identify a culminating activity or activities that summarize or draw attention to the main goals and provide an occasion to demonstrate and celebrate students' learning. Often the culminating activity may refer back to the introduction or be previewed at the outset of the unit so that the unit is "framed" in a coherent manner.
- Begin to flesh out the rest of the unit plan by indicating the specific lessons and order in which the unit will unfold. Specify objectives for each lesson. Check to see that all relevant objectives listed on the course plan for that unit are addressed. From the list generated above, select the teaching strategies, student activities, and learning resources that will best serve the objective(s)

WAYS TO INTRODUCE A UNIT

- **Video.** Viewing a YouTube video or short documentary is motivating and provides students with information on which to build. Students may not attain a strong grasp of its contents on the first viewing. It can be viewed again later in the unit. When choosing videos to introduce a unit, the priority should be to stimulate interest rather than to provide a great deal of information immediately.
- **Brainstorming.** Brainstorming is a useful way to ascertain the depth of students' knowledge about a topic before beginning instruction and to help them organize the information they already have into a framework. The teacher's role is to record all responses without criticism, help students expand on others' ideas, and set a time limit and stick to it. Following the brainstorming sessions the teacher helps students sort the ideas into categories using approaches such as webbing or data retrieval charts. Retain the final organization so that students can examine it at the end of the unit to see how much they have learned.
- **Discrepant Event.** A discrepant event identifies unusual aspects of a situation in order to provoke student thought. For example, tell students that as the people in a sleepy town of five hundred inhabitants left church one Sunday, they heard much shouting and general hilarity issuing from the direction of the harbour. As they raced down for a look, they saw a steamship containing four hundred men entering their harbour. Many of the men wore bright red shirts and carried backpacks with supplies. Some had picks and shovels. Ask students why they think these men descended on this town. After students have advanced a number of possible explanations, tell them that the sleepy town was called Fort Victoria and it was the future capital of the province of British Columbia. The men who arrived on the ship had just come from San Francisco because they had heard that gold had been found on the Fraser River. They intended to purchase supplies in Fort Victoria and then continue on to seek their fortunes. The first step towards British Columbia becoming a colony and then a province was because of the influx of new people due to the gold rush.

  Here is another example. Tell students that a civilization began on the banks of a river that flooded regularly. A desert surrounded the civilization, which made the climate dry and hot. Ask them for their predictions as to the likelihood of this civilization surviving and ask for their guesses as to what civilization this might have been. If students are not able to guess correctly, tell them that the civilization was that of ancient Egypt and that it flourished on the banks of the Nile River in Africa for thousands of years. Ask students to hypothesize why the civilization of ancient Egypt established itself in this particular location. They can then begin data-gathering activities to verify or refute their hypotheses.
- **Displays.** A teacher-created display can arouse interest and provide initial information about a topic. The display should be set up a week or more prior to beginning the unit so that students will have plenty of time to browse among the items in the display and to talk about them informally with other class members. Alternatively, students can create their own displays by bringing pertinent items, newspaper articles, and magazine illustrations to school, or the teacher and students can contribute jointly to the display.
- **Field Experience.** A field experience is often considered to be most effective at the end of a unit because students have a greater understanding to bring to it at that point. However, such an experience can also be useful at the beginning of a unit because of its value in piquing interest and in the information it can provide, which can serve as a springboard to the acquisition of further information.
- **Guest Speaker.** Invite a guest who has special knowledge about the unit to speak to the students. The students' parents may be willing to speak about their occupations, countries of origin, or other areas of expertise. A way of finding out whether there are parents willing to make themselves available for this purpose is to send a questionnaire home at the beginning of the school year. Other sources of speakers include retired people's organizations, consulates, government departments and agencies, and public relations departments of large companies.
- **Music.** Play a tape that is representative of the time, place, or topic. For instance, if studying a particular country, music commonly enjoyed by people there could be played. The "Huron Carol" by Jean de Brébeuf might be used to introduce the study of Aboriginal peoples in New France

continued on next page

and "The Wreck of the Edmund Fitzgerald" by Gordon Lightfoot could be used in connection with Canada's transportation links.

- **Mystery Box.** Show students a box containing several objects related to the unit. Let each student handle the box. Have students use a "twenty questions" approach to ascertaining which objects you have selected to include in the box; that is, they will be limited to twenty questions, and therefore must begin with very general questions in order to eliminate as many possibilities as they can as quickly as possible. Record the guesses on the blackboard. When twenty questions have been asked, open the box and explain each object.

- **Simulation.** A simulation can provide an extremely motivating introduction to a unit. Examples are beginning a unit on the growth of industrialization by having students simulate an assembly line or a unit on local government with a simulation in which they become members of a city council making a decision related to commercial versus recreational uses of land. Follow up with a discussion in which the simulation experience is related to understandings that will arise from the unit.

- **Story.** Stories can engage student interest in a unit of study and bring unit understandings to life. For example, read a Greek myth to begin a unit on ancient Greece, or an excerpt from *Roughing it in the Bush* by Catherine Parr Trail to introduce early life in Upper Canada.

for each lesson. Also, specify the assessment techniques (for example, a one-page report, an oral presentation, a poster) that will reveal how well students have met the objectives for that lesson. It is also very useful to specify what qualities will be looked for when assessing students' work—in other words, indicate the criteria that will be used to assess students' work (for example, the report is well organized, shows evidence of empathy for the people described, is historically accurate).

- Finally, review the draft unit plan with another person to ensure the following:
  - *Adequate emphasis on each goal.* Verify that the activities and objectives described in the unit plan match the main goals identified in the course plan. Has the unit shifted in a direction that does not do justice to the proposed emphasis? If so, either bring the unit back into line so that it promotes the main goals adequately, or change the proposed focus for the unit.
  - *Appropriate sequence.* Check to see that the lessons are ordered in such a way that the prerequisite objectives are taught in a reasonable sequence and that the unit builds towards a culminating activity, with a sense of completion for students.
  - *Reasonable flow.* Look to see if the transitions are connected or disjointed between lessons and over the whole unit. Although every lesson will not follow directly from the prior one nor lead smoothly to the next, the greater the flow of lessons, the less likely that students will be confused by the progress of the unit.
  - *Rich variety.* Review the proposed activities, resources, and assessment strategies to ascertain whether they contain sufficient variety and range. Without realizing it, the unit may rely excessively on one or two activities (for example, answering questions from a textbook) or assessment strategy (for example, journal reflections).

A sample of a partial unit plan is found in Figure 23.7.

Creating Lesson Plans

The most specific level of planning occurs at the individual lesson level. This is where we think through in considerable detail exactly what, when, and how things will be done for each lesson. The more experienced we become, the less detailed our lesson plans need to be. Although lesson planning may take different forms, I recommend dividing the planning of a lesson into the seven tasks described below and outlined in Figure 23.7.

- **Formulate lesson objectives.** Objectives specify the outcomes we hope to produce (that is, what we expect students to learn from the activities that we plan for them). These objectives will already be identified if a unit plan has been developed. Although there is no hard and fast rule, it may be unwise to have more than three objectives for any given lesson, especially if they are not closely connected to one another. Generally speaking, promoting one or two outcomes well is preferred over doing many things superficially. It is important not to confuse objectives with methods: an objective specifies the hoped-for outcome of having students complete the learning activity. Statements of method would include statements such as "Students will debate an issue" and "Students will experience what it is like to be discriminated against." A statement of the objectives is generated by asking what the students will learn by engaging in the debate (for example, learn to express their ideas clearly or to develop persuasive arguments to support their position) or what they will learn by experiencing discrimination (for example, acquire greater sensitivity to the feelings of others).

- **Introduce the lesson.** The introduction should provide an engaging and illuminating launch into the lesson.

FIGURE 23.6   SAMPLE UNIT PLAN

Unit Topic: Historic injustice in Canada[1]		Grade: 10	Unit # 3
Unit Goals	1. Understand the events, causes, and implications of the World War I internment operations and of other legally sanctioned historical injustices in Canada that have occurred over the past one hundred years. 2. Develop the ability to think historically by making	judgments about historical significance, causation, perspective-taking, and ethical considerations. 3. Appreciate the importance of educating people about past injustices.	

LESSON TITLE	SPECIFIC OBJECTIVES	METHODS/ACTIVITIES	RESOURCES	ASSESSMENT STRATEGIES AND CRITERIA
Should this event be in the curriculum?	• learn to assess the significance of various historical events • learn about the historical significance of internment operations during World War I and II	• Students identify significant events in their own lives. • Students rate the level of significance of various events, ranging from globally significant to insignificant. • Students view a video and read accounts of internments in Canada during World War I and II, and consider why the latter is typically included in the curriculum and the former is rarely profiled. • Students decide on the extent to which the topic of World War I internment should be included in the curriculum.	**Activity sheet** • chart to compare events • rating sheet for historical significance **Briefing sheets** • internment operations in Canada during World War I and II **Video** • Historical significance	Assess students' ability to: • rate the historical significance of various events • support their ratings with accurate, relevant, and comprehensive evidence
Why did it happen?	• learn to recognize when a factor is an underlying or immediate cause • learn about the causes leading to Canada's internment operations during World War I	• Introduce the concept of causation by identifying various factors that may have contributed to a fictional car accident. • Students distinguish between underlying and immediate causes. • Students examine various primary and secondary sources to gather information about the contributing role of various factors to World War I internment. • Students identify the many underlying and immediate causal factors before determining the three most important contributing factors to the event.	**Source documents** • various historical documents on the motivations behind the internment **Activity sheets** • chart to sort immediate and underlying causes • graphic organizer to represent various causal factors	Assess students' ability to: • identify possible contributing factors to various events, and distinguish intermediate and underlying causes • support their conclusions about each cause's importance to an event with accurate, relevant, and substantial evidence

continued on next page

FIGURE 23.6   SAMPLE UNIT PLAN (CONT.)

LESSON TITLE	SPECIFIC OBJECTIVES	METHODS/ACTIVITIES	RESOURCES	ASSESSMENT STRATEGIES AND CRITERIA
What were the internment camps like?	• learn to distinguish presentist from historically sensitive accounts • learn about the hardship and suffering internees endured during World War I while in the camps	• Introduce historical perspective-taking by comparing presentist and historically sensitive accounts of an event. • Introduce three strategies for adopting a historical perspective. • Students analyze primary and secondary sources to learn about life in the camp. • Students record relevant details from the sources, draw possible conclusions, and summarize what they have learned about internee experiences. • Students write a letter from the point of view of a teenager at the time explaining the internment experience.	**Source documents** • various historical documents and photographs of daily life in the camps **Activity sheets** • chart to record details and anticipate historical perspective **Video** • Historical perspective	Assess students' ability to: • hypothesize about the experience and meaning of events in light of the prevailing conditions and mindset at the time • offer a detailed, realistic, and believable account of life in the internment camps

How adequately has the government responded to various injustices?	• learn about the adequacy of official government responses to several legally sanctioned injustices in Canada
	
	• learn to draw thoughtful ethical judgments about complex historical issues
		• Students explore a fictional scenario where a student is falsely accused of a criminal act to learn about criteria for judging the adequacy of a response to a legally sanctioned but unjust act.
		
		• Students examine official government responses to one of four historical injustices in Canada (internment of Japanese Canadians in World War II, residential schools for Canada's indigenous peoples, head tax on Chinese immigrants, refusal to allow disembarkation of *Komogata Maru* passengers).
		
		• Students compare the arguments for and against the adequacy of the official response to their assigned incident, share findings with the rest of the class, and rank order the four responses in terms of their adequacy.
		
		• Students rate the government's response to World War I internment, and communicate their conclusions and recommendations in a letter to a government official.
			Activity sheets
			• rating scale to judge official responses
			• chart to compare official responses
			
			Briefing sheets
			• historical details on the event, aftermath, and government response to five historic injustices:
			  • Chinese head tax
			  • *Komagata Maru*
			  • World War I internment
			  • residential schools
			  • World War II internment
				Assess students' ability to:
				
				• offer plausible and well-supported critiques of government responses to various historic injustices
				
				• support their conclusions and recommendations with accurate, relevant, and comprehensive evidence
				
				continued on next page

FIGURE 23.6 SAMPLE UNIT PLAN (CONT.)

LESSON TITLE	SPECIFIC OBJECTIVES	METHODS/ACTIVITIES	RESOURCES	ASSESSMENT STRATEGIES AND CRITERIA
What should we all know now?	• learn about the most memorable features associated with internment during World War I • appreciate the importance of remembering key aspects of injustices and of honouring those who have suffered past injustices in order to reduce the occurrence of similar injustices	• Review the key details of the event. • Introduce four aspects about a historical incident: what went on (key events), why it happened (causes), what happened as a result (consequences), and what we might learn from the event (lessons learned). • Students apply these questions to a video of an interview about the internment operations prior to compiling what they have learned about one of the four aspects of the event. • Groups representing each of the aspects share their findings with each other and then with the entire class. • Students decide upon ten key ideas that all Canadians should remember.	**Activity sheet** • chart to assemble and rate potential features **Video** • Internee descendants	Assess students' ability to: • identify relevant and important features of the internment • explain the importance of knowing and remembering the key features they have identified

Its purpose is to create a "mindset" that will motivate students and focus their attention in ways that will increase the likelihood of their benefitting from the lesson. Suggestions for creating a mindset include:

- Establish a connection with a previous lesson.
- Explain the purpose and value of what is to be learned.
- Provide an overview of what will take place.
- Invite students to share what they know about the topic for the day's lesson.
- Involve students in an enjoyable activity or pose a question or dilemma that will arouse curiosity and set a context for what students are about to learn.

- **Develop and sequence the body of the lesson.** The body of the lesson refers to the teacher instructions and student activities that will occur during the lesson. Suggestions for planning the body of the lesson include:
  - Break down the component parts of each objective into teachable elements and think of how each can be taught.
  - Vary the types of activities so there is a change of pace.
  - Think about dividing the tasks/sessions into tightly orchestrated segments (between ten and twenty minutes' duration) to reduce the likelihood of students tiring of activities that go on for a long time.

- Although this sequence is not always appropriate, as a rough rule it is useful to think of six stages in the body of a lesson:
  - *Instructional input:* students are given new information or are introduced to a new notion (by the teacher or students, through reading or viewing).
  - *Modelling:* a demonstration (by the teacher or by the students) of what is to be done with this new knowledge.
  - *Trial run:* on their own or in small groups, students try one or two examples (or the first steps) to see if they have grasped the task.
  - *Group feedback:* issues and difficulties encountered during the trial run are discussed as a class.
  - *Application of knowledge:* students proceed with the main assignment for the lesson.
  - *Coaching:* as students work on their assignment, the teacher or students (in pairs or in cooperative groups) provide individual advice as problems and questions arise.

FIGURE 23.7 SAMPLE LESSON PLAN

Lesson title	Simon Fraser: Hero or Rogue?
Objectives	By the end of this lesson, students will: • understand the concepts of "directly observed fact" and "inference" and be able to identify inferences drawn by an author; • understand that different inferences may be drawn from the same event (and the most defensible inference is the one that is most plausible given the facts); • be able to generate and defend an interpretation of a historical event; and • know about Simon Fraser's experiences with the First Nations people.
Introduction	Mention to students that Simon Fraser was a famous Canadian explorer—among other forms of recognition, a major river and a university have been named after him. Suggest that there is some reason to suspect that history has been too kind to Simon Fraser—that possibly he really doesn't deserve his fame. The point of the lesson will be to find out exactly what sort of person he was. Before doing that, students must learn how to interpret facts.
Body of lesson	1. **Teaching about inferences** (that is, the difference between directly observable/audible fact and an inference). With little or no prior explanation perform the following gestures and ask students to explain what you are doing: • Point your finger at a student and motion for him or her to come. • Put your finger to your mouth to indicate silence. • Pretend to be thinking. After students have answered, suggest that they have interpreted or drawn an inference from what you were doing. Ask them to tell you exactly what they saw you doing. Use a chart such as the following to record student answers. <table><tr><th>DIRECTLY OBSERVABLE FACTS</th><th>INFERENCES</th></tr><tr><td>Directing index finger at student and curling it inward.</td><td>Teacher wants student to come to her.</td></tr><tr><td>Putting index finger to your lip.</td><td>Teacher is trying to quiet class.</td></tr><tr><td>Looking upward pensively and saying "Well, I wonder…"</td><td>Teacher is thinking about something.</td></tr></table> 2. **Reinforcing understanding.** Ask the class to come up with a definition of: (a) a directly observable (or audible) fact, and (b) an inference. Ask students for examples of a directly observable fact and possible inferences to be drawn. Provide several examples and discuss the inferences implied in the statements (include some that are contentious inferences). 3. **Modelling the assignment.** Direct students' attention to the first paragraph of the reading for this lesson, "The Descent of the Fraser River." Invite students to identify either directly observed facts or inferences in this paragraph. Ask students to speculate about other inferences that might be drawn from these events. For example, it is stated that "The route was so rough that a pair of moccasins was worn to shreds in one day of portaging." The wearing out of a pair of moccasins in one day is the directly observable fact. The author's inference seems to be that Fraser and his men were determined, persevering, and willing to endure great sacrifice. 4. **Application of learning.** Direct students' attention to the Student Instructions sheet (for younger students, present them orally) and the Data Recording Chart. Explain the tasks (which may be done individually or in small groups). Ask one-half of the class to focus on Simon Fraser and the other half of the class to focus on the First Nations people. Confirm that students understand what is expected before setting them to work.

Body of lesson (Cont.)	5. **Sharing of insights.** After students have had sufficient time to complete the assignment, invite them to share their findings. Begin by asking about the more interesting facts and inferences that students encountered in the text. Then ask individuals to share their assessments of the character of Simon Fraser and the First Nations people they encountered. Encourage debate and ask students to defend and qualify their answers on the basis of consistency with the evidence found in the text. Be careful to note that all First Nations people may not have the same character—some may be friendlier than others, and so on. 6. **Application of knowledge.** Based on their own deliberations and on the class discussion, ask students to list five or six words or phrases that they believe describe Simon Fraser's character fairly and five or six words or phrases describing the First Nations character(s). Students must support their character descriptions by referring to their interpretations of the events. Remind students that events may have several plausible interpretations, and their task is to decide which is the most defensible interpretation. For older students, expect them to defend their interpretations of specific events in light of other evidence in the text.
Closure	• Discuss how differences of opinion about what sort of person Simon Fraser was could be resolved by finding out more about Simon Fraser from other sources (for example, Simon Fraser's diary; the diaries of some of his companions; what is known about Simon Fraser from his friends, employers, and competitors). • What do these differing stories tell us about the study of the past? Consider the following question: What is the true nature of history: fact or inference? In your own words, explain what the question is asking and support your position by referring to examples drawn from the report about Simon Fraser's trip and an account of the trip from a First Nations perspective.

Assessment	• Evaluate each student's character profile in light of the following criteria: adequacy of support for overall conclusion, sensitivity to alternative inferences, ability to support particular inferences in light of other textual evidence.
	
	• Present students with the drawing of Simon Fraser and his crew. Pose the following questions:
	  ◆ Which one of the men in the drawing is Simon Fraser? Explain the reasons for your choice.
	  ◆ What impressions does this drawing suggest about these explorers and about the region that they are travelling through?
	  ◆ Draw your own picture of Simon Fraser and his men as seen from a First Nations perspective. On the back of your picture explain the key differences in perspective on the explorers and the region between your picture and the drawing provided.
	
	• Use these criteria to assess students' picture study:
	  ◆ Correctly identify the middle person (in the front canoe) and suggest that clothing, physical appearance, and lack of a paddle are key reasons why this person stands out from the rest.
	  ◆ The number of plausible inferences that the students suggest (for example, the region is dangerous, uncivilized, and largely uninhabited, and the explorers are daring, afraid, and determined).
	  ◆ Assess students' pictures (and explanations) in terms of the number and plausibility of inferences drawn as seen from the First Nations perspective. An additional criterion might be imaginativeness of inferences drawn.

Extension	• Ask students to write a two-page detailed account of Simon Fraser's trip from the perspective of one of the First Nations people that Simon Fraser would likely have encountered. Their account should be consistent with the directly observable facts in the attached historical report. (It is expected that they will draw different inferences from these facts.) Criteria for assessment: the major criteria are the plausibility of inferences drawn and sensitivity to alternative inferences when facts are seen from different perspectives. Other criteria might include accuracy of chronological sequence, imaginativeness of inferences drawn, and completeness of account of all the major events. • Discuss factors that affect the credibility of reports, such as: Were the witnesses physically present? Do they have an obvious self-interest? Are they trustworthy sources? Why might Simon Fraser's diary not be completely credible? Why might he be motivated to distort the truth, consciously or unconsciously? Perhaps you could introduce the concepts of primary and secondary sources.

continued on next page

STUDENT INSTRUCTIONS

SIMON FRASER: HERO OR ROGUE?

Simon Fraser is a famous Canadian explorer—among other forms of recognition, a major river and a university have been named after him. Has history been too kind to Simon Fraser? Does he really deserve this fame? What sort of person was he? What sort of people were the First Nations people that Simon Fraser encountered on his travels? Read the attached historical report, "The Descent of the Fraser River," and complete the following task(s).

Step 1

Circle all the statements in the attached report that provide any obvious insights about the character (personality traits, and personal strengths and weaknesses) of Simon Fraser and/or the First Nations people he encountered.

Step 2

Use the data recording chart to summarize what the report tells us about Simon Fraser and the First Nations people. The entries in the left-hand column should be descriptions of what occurred, the entries in the middle and right-hand column are character traits that the author and you attribute to the character of the person(s). In many cases, the author does not present directly observed facts, but simply provides his inferences. In these situations, indicate what you imagine are the facts that would have been observed. Examples have been provided on the data recording chart.

1) Simon Fraser's character: In the left-hand column, list any directly observable facts about the events and actions involving Simon Fraser. For each directly observable fact, indicate in the middle column what the author infers from the facts about his character, and in the right-hand column indicate what you infer from these facts about his character.

2) Characteristics of First Nations people: In the left-hand column, list any directly observable facts about the events and actions involving First Nations people. For each directly observable fact, indicate in the middle column what the author infers from the facts about their character, and in the right-hand column indicate what you infer from these facts about their character traits.

Step 3

1) List approximately five words or phrases that portray your assessment of Simon Fraser's character. Be prepared to defend your assessment.

2) List approximately five words or phrases that portray your assessment of First Nations people's character. Be prepared to defend your assessment.

DATA RECORDING CHART

SIMON FRASER'S CHARACTERISTICS		
Directly observable facts	Author's inferences	Your inferences
Example: The places where they had to carry their canoes were so rough that a pair of moccasins was worn out in one day.	Simon Fraser is a very determined individual—nothing will stop him.	Fraser may be determined, but perhaps he just doesn't know how to walk in this kind of countryside.
FIRST NATIONS CHARACTERISTICS		
Directly observable facts	Author's inferences	Your inferences
Example: The First Nations people said the river could not be canoed and Fraser believed them.	The First Nations people were truthful.	Perhaps the First Nations people were trying to scare Fraser.

READING[2]

On May 28, 1808, Simon Fraser led twenty-three men on an expedition to find a route from the interior of British Columbia to the Pacific Ocean along the river that Fraser imagined to be the Columbia River. Day after day they encountered obstacles as they paddled down the river. The river was a continual series of rapids and the carrying places were extremely dangerous or very long. The places where they had to carry their canoes to get around the rapids were so rough that a pair of moccasins was worn to shreds in one day. Fraser decided the First Nations people he had met were correct in saying that the river was not passable for canoes. So Fraser and his men set out on foot, carrying packs weighing eighty pounds each. In his diary, Fraser wrote that they experienced "a good deal of fatigue and disagreeable walking" but he and his men continued on their journey.

Soon they met First Nations people who told them ten more days would bring them to the sea. One villager said that he had been to the sea and had seen "great canoes" and white men. When Fraser and his party proceeded, many of the locals walked with them. Two days later, at a large village near present-day Lillooet, First Nations people told them that the river was navigable from their village to the sea, whereupon Fraser bargained for two canoes. At another village (now Lytton), the people were so friendly that Fraser was called upon to shake hands with twelve hundred of them. In return, he and his men were well fed and were able to get two wooden canoes.

Despite what the First Nations people had said about the river being navigable, the explorers soon found their way blocked by numerous rapids. Two canoes were lost. More canoes were obtained from the Native people. During this time, the explorers toiled over the roughest country they had ever seen:

> We had to pass over huge rocks assisted by the Indians.... As for the road by land, we could scarcely make our way with even only our guns. I have been for a long period among the Rocky Mountains, but have never seen anything like this country. It is so wild that I cannot find words to describe our situation at times. We had to pass where no human being should venture; yet in those places there is a regular footpath impressed, or rather indented upon the very rocks by frequent travelling. Besides this, steps which are formed like a ladder ... furnish a safe and convenient passage to the Natives; but we, who had not the advantage of their education and experience, were often in imminent danger when obliged to follow their example. [extract from Fraser's journal]

At Spuzzum, Fraser was much impressed by a number of totem poles, each fifteen feet high and "carved in a curious but rude manner, yet pretty well proportioned." Friendly First Nations living in large frame houses presented them with

Illustration by Charles W. Jefferys.

roast salmon. Near where the town of Hope now stands, they were entertained at a large village where there was a huge community house built of cedar planks. The First Nations people warned that the Natives of the coast were "wicked" and would attack them, but Fraser would not alter his plan. When these First Nations people refused to lend him a canoe, Fraser took one by force. For a short while canoes from the village followed them, their occupants waving weapons and shouting war songs, but Fraser and his men ignored them. Soon after, another group came at them "howling like wolves" and swinging war clubs, but they did not attack Fraser's group. Fraser ordered his men to paddle farther along to a second village, but the behaviour of the First Nations people forced them to turn back. On July 2, near what is now New Westminster, Fraser decided to return up the river in order to secure provisions before attempting to resume his descent to the ocean. This was the farthest point reached by the explorers. Fraser's reception by First Nations people on his return up the river was far from friendly—one group seized a canoe and began to pillage the baggage. Fraser forced a canoe from them and left a blanket in return. For several days hostile First Nations people followed them. They finally reached friendly villages and were guided over rough bridges and swaying ladders by Natives who "went up and down these wild places with the same agility as sailors do on board a ship."

Fraser finally arrived back at Fort George on August 6. Although Fraser had not accomplished his purpose of exploring the Columbia River, he really was the discoverer of the river that bears his name. Because of his voyage the confusion between the Fraser River and Columbia River was cleared up.

- **Prepare resources.** Resources refer to the instructional materials, activity sheets, readings, and questions that will be used to support the lesson.
- **Draw closure.** Closure refers to the proposed means for debriefing the students and helping them consolidate what they have learned. Closure often involves the following tasks:
  - Students summarize what they have learned.
  - Students apply learning to a new situation.
  - The teacher synthesizes key ideas and draws connections.
- **Assess student learning.** Assessment tells us how well the objective(s) have been met. Students should be provided, prior to completing an assignment, with a clear indication of the assessment, including:
  - the criteria that will be used as the basis for assessment of student learning; and
  - the standards or levels of performance for each criteria (that is, what does "very good" on the assignment look like, and how does it differ from "good"?).
- **Extend or follow up on the lesson.** The extension part of a lesson is a way to provide for those students who invariably finish early. Unless we plan educationally enriching activities for this eventuality, some students will often waste considerable class time. Extension activities are useful when the proposed lesson goes more quickly than anticipated. Extension is also useful to encourage students who may want to pursue ideas raised by the lesson further.

The sample lesson plan in Figure 23.8 illustrates many of the suggestions just described. The focus of the lesson is the concept of inference—that is, interpreting or drawing conclusions from accepted facts. In this lesson, students consider whether or not Simon Fraser is a bona fide hero by reading a historical account of his explorations and dealings with the First Nations people he encountered.

Closing Remarks

As suggested by the analogy offered at the outset of this chapter, the challenges to thoughtful planning are a lot like trying to negotiate a wilderness. Just as it is easy to lose one's way in the forest, so too is it easy to become disoriented when planning for instruction at any level. We are especially likely

Select two of three outcomes from the social studies, history or geography curriculum and develop a detailed lesson plan using the template outlined in this chapter or another of your choosing. Take care to ensure that the lesson teaches and assesses the identified learning outcomes.

to stumble if we fail to articulate or lose sight of our important educational destinations. The danger, if you will pardon the forced metaphor, is that we may lose sight of the forest through the trees. The immense volume of choices about what and how to do it, and our desire to do it all, may result in plans that are scattered and rather superficial. Setting a modest number of challenging goals and doing them well may be the best course to follow.

Having just emphasized the importance of a strong guiding direction to one's teaching, let me also caution that we should not feel bound to follow a preordained set of steps and activities when circumstances change. We need to monitor student reactions as we go, changing plans in midstream when appropriate. In addition, as we learn more about teaching, we should revisit our plans from year to year.

ACKNOWLEDGMENTS

Thanks to Mary Abbott for developing the examples found in "Unpacking the Underlying Idea."

Thanks to Penney Clark for the list found in "Ways of Introducing a Unit."

NOTE

1. The sample unit plan, "Historic injustice in Canada," outlined in Figure 23.6 is based on a publication entitled *Recognizing an historical injustice: Canada's first national internment operations, 1914-1920* (Bahl and Case 2015). The entire 146-page resource is available for free download at http://tc2.ca/pv.php.
2. This is a shortened version of "The descent of the Fraser River" by Malcolm G. Parks in *Discoverers and Explorers in Canada—1763–1911* (Portfolio II #4), illustrated by Charles W. Jefferys and published by Imperial Oil Ltd. Used with permission.

REFERENCES

Bahl, A. and R. Case, eds. 2015. *Recognizing an historical injustice: Canada's first national internment operations, 1914–1920.* Vancouver: The Critical Thinking Consortium and Canadian First World War Internment Recognition Fund. Available online at http://tc2.ca/pv.php.

British Columbia Ministry of Education. 2015. *Building student success: BC's new curriculum—Social studies 1–9.* Victoria, BC: Author. Available online at https://curriculum.gov.bc.ca/curriculum/social-studies/9.

Erickson, L. H. 2007. *Concept-based curriculum and instruction for the thinking classroom.* Thousand Oaks, CA: Corwin Press.

Ontario. 2013A. *The Ontario curriculum—Social studies grades 1–6 History and geography grades 7 and 8 (revised).* Toronto: ServiceOntario. Available online at www.ontario.ca/edu.

Ontario. 2013B. *The Ontario curriculum—Grades 9 and 10—Canada and world studies (revised).* Toronto: ServiceOntario. Available online at www.ontario.ca/edu.

Wiggins, G. and J. McTighe. 2005. *Understanding by design.* Second edition. Alexandria, VA: Association of Supervision and Curriculum Development.

24 Engaging Students in Learning History

John Fielding

It is easier to comment on how not to teach history, than it is to explain how to teach it successfully. I have only to recall the countless negative reactions I heard throughout my career from adults when I informed them that I was a history teacher. Some of their responses included: "Oh! That was my worst subject." "I hated history." "History was boring." "Names and dates, that's all it was, and I can't remember any of them!" Their responses to my question, "Why didn't you like history?" made reference to a typical list of complaints: memory work, recall, lists of names and dates, not relevant, uninteresting, the teacher talked all the time, and we didn't do anything.

I believe we can learn how to teach history effectively by considering the positive memories that people who enjoyed the subject have about history in school. Typically, positive responses come from people who had teachers who took them to historic sites, involved them in recreating history through drama, told great stories, and encouraged provocative discussions. In short, history learning was, to use the word these people often used, engaging.

What I have also learned by talking with people who enjoyed history in school is that they have continued to study and learn history throughout their lives. In most cases they continue their study not through formal academic study, but by reading history for pleasure, researching their family's history or genealogy, collecting stamps or antiques, telling stories of the past, or travelling to museums and historic sites. Their lives are richer and more interesting as a result of their enjoyment of history. The challenge for history teachers is to stimulate students' curiosity, interest, and engagement similarly.

Speaking personally, I trace the reason I studied history in university and eventually became a history teacher back to my grade 4 teacher. She was an austere woman who would slap any unsuspecting child with a ruler simply for looking sideways. But one day she did an unusual thing. She told us to get out of our seats and go to the huge windows at the side of the classroom. There we were instructed to observe the river outside. The school sat on a hill overlooking the Grand River, which flowed through the little town of Paris, Ontario. She said, "Try to imagine Father Marquette and his partner in exploration, Louis Joliet, in their birchbark canoes paddling down our river through the forested wilderness past our school. Of course, our school would not have been here!"

After a few minutes of scene-setting—dreamy gazing for some, but intense imaging for me—we were whisked back to our desks. Here the rest of the story with dates and details continued, but from that moment on I was fascinated with these explorers. I had imagined that I actually saw them. History came alive for me that day. Years later, in grade 12 and grade 13, when trying to decide what to do with my life, I couldn't get that moment with history out of my head. I now realize that my experience in that class was momentous because my teacher had engaged my historical imagination. She did this in various ways. She made history "active" because she got us to move out of our desks. She used historical facts to "create a story" of Marquette and Joliet's travel and explorations. And she made it "immediate and relevant" by encouraging us to look at locations and events in our own community.

Our first priority in teaching history is to develop strategies that arouse and engage our students' historical imaginations. It will not occur by lecturing students with lists of names, dates, and definitions for recall and test purposes. Certainly students need to learn historical facts, including names and dates, but students are more likely to understand and remember them if they are engaged by the study of history. The ineffectiveness of the traditional textbook and lecture methods were documented in a famous memory study conducted by Danielle Lapp of Stanford University. Her research concluded that we remember only 10 per cent of what we read, 20 per cent of what we hear, 30 per cent of what we see, 50 per cent of what we see and hear, and 90 per cent of what we do and say. The challenge then is to make the study of history something that students can see, do, and talk about.

Traditional Strategies for Increasing Student Interest

Like most history teachers, I have searched for years to find ways to interest my students and to make history fun. I tried many strategies before I understood the difference between lessons that are just interesting and those that are engaging and effective. Students may enjoy some activities, but they may not learn much of real substance from them. The following activities are examples of interesting but not necessarily effective strategies.

CROSSWORD PUZZLES, WORD SEARCHES, AND FILL-IN-THE-BLANKS

These activities can keep students busy and, for some students, may reinforce dates or vocabulary. However, students don't learn about historical context, and the activities don't invite imaginative re-creation of an era or event, and don't involve any of the skills of a historian. In fact, I wonder if they do much at all for learning history.

TRIVIA GAMES

With the popularity of various forms of trivia games and the annual Dominion Institute survey report about how little Canadians know about their history, there has been a push to teach young people more historical facts. History-related trivia games can be used for review or to conclude a lesson. However, for many students trivia games simply reveal how poor they are at memory work. Even those who remember the details may have little real understanding of their historical significance or context.

Traditional Engaging and Potentially Effective Strategies

There is a second category of activity that does have wonderful potential to interest students and to help them develop skills, including critical thinking and decision making. However, these activities are often deficient in another respect: they fail to engage students' historical imagination. The following activities can make history come alive for students, but typically they fall far short of this potential.

FILMS, VIDEOS, OR DVDS

Films, videos, and DVDs are more popular with students than word games. These resources can help students visualize an era or an event. However, too often students passively watch presentations without analyzing what is presented, why it is presented, and how it is being presented. While these presentations may stimulate students' interest, unless students raise questions about the experience we have to wonder what students are actually learning and if this is really an effective way of coming to understand history.

FIELD TRIPS

How can anyone be critical of a field trip? Students enjoy field trips because they include a change of scenery, involve free time, and introduce interesting places to see. Without ruining all the fun involved in a site visit (because we know our task is partly to interest students in studying history), we need to engage students in learning about the place they are visiting. We need to challenge students to think about what they are experiencing, why a site is important, and what we can learn from it. Pre- and post-field trip research and activities can make the difference between a merely entertaining outing and a significant history-learning experience.

DEBATES

Debates are a favourite activity for some teachers who like controversy and competition. The danger with debates is that students are often more interested in winning their argument than thoroughly examining an issue. I have steered clear of the "either/or" mentality encouraged by debates since I learned about Edward DeBono's PMI approach—P stands for plus or positive, M for minus or negative, and I for interesting or I wonder if. Using a PMI strategy, students would gather in groups to brainstorm an issue and then record the plus, minus, and interesting ideas. The PMI approach can lead to great discussions and thoughtful reflection.

Another alternative to the debate is the "U-shape" forum. To facilitate discussion, classes may be configured in a "U-shape." Students with polar views (either strongly agreeing or strongly disagreeing with the proposition) seat themselves at either tip of the "U"; students with mixed opinions sit at appropriate spots along the rounded part. At varying stages in the discussion, students are encouraged to move along the spectrum as their intellectual positions on the issue change. In this way, less dogmatic attitudes are encouraged. The implicit messages of the traditional debate (fixed opinions with the objective of winning the argument) are supplanted by varying messages in the "U-shaped" discussion (provisionally held positions as one tries to figure out the most defensible personal stance from a continuum of options).

POSTERS

It has become increasingly popular to ask students to create posters, especially posters encouraging immigration to Canada at the beginning of the twentieth century or recruiting soldiers for World War I. Students who like to draw or paint enjoy making posters in history class, but too often this involves little or no research. Creating posters turns into a copying exercise, and involves no critical thinking about the use of propaganda and why certain images appealed to people at that time in history. Without these latter dimensions, creating posters may have limited value in a history class.

There are always exceptions, and one approach to posters that I recently encountered involves critical examination of an issue combined with an imaginative activity. It is called "Moving to New France" (Sandwell, Misfeldt, and Case 2002, 75). In this two-part critical thinking activity, students explore the "push/pull" and "retain/repulse" factors connected with immigrating to New France in the seventeenth century. In the first task, students examine and prioritize reasons for staying and leaving a community. Students then read about four fictional persons who contemplate immigrating to New France and assess the factors affecting each person's decision to immigrate. They then determine whether their assigned French citizen would stay at home or immigrate to the New World. In the second critical thinking task, students learn to recognize a poster's implicit message, target audience, and persuasive techniques by analyzing several Canadian immigration posters. They then create a poster encouraging or discouraging immigration to New France using appropriate techniques and appealing to the interests and fears of the target audience. In the final step, students analyze each other's posters.

MIND MAPS

The sounds of moaning can be painful when we ask students to write an essay or a report. For many students, extended written work is their worst nightmare. Yet when showing a video in class or assigning material for students to read we want to see what they have understood from the activity. In place of extensive writing tasks, I have found mind map assignments to be more satisfying and effective for many students. A mind map is a visual representation of students' thoughts and thought processes. It can show how they connect ideas and reveal their understanding of cause and effect relationships. Instead of asking students to share a report by reading it to the class, I have noticed that it is more effective to ask students to explain what they have learned by referring to a mind map that they can display for the class.

TIMELINES

I used to dread starting a new topic such as the French Revolution or World War II. I wondered how students would understand what happened without having some knowledge of the sequence of events. I certainly didn't want to lecture them for forty minutes. Instead of simply giving students a timeline of key events to introduce a topic, I started asking them to evaluate the significance of these events according to a set of criteria established by the class. For example, how many people were affected by the event? Did it cause subsequent changes? Did it cost lives or save lives? Was the impact of the event short- or long-term? In order to answer these questions, students had to read and do some independent research. I assigned this as a group activity so students could divide up the research, pool their knowledge, and discuss why they assigned the rankings they did. Students made a bar graph ranking each event's significance on a scale from zero to ten. Finally, students presented their findings using their graphs. The presentations led to many a lively discussion, for the students' interpretations of events were never the same.

Less Traditional Engaging, Imaginative, and Effective Strategies

In my opinion, the most important element of an effective strategy is its ability to activate students' historical imagination. It should involve students in using and talking about their learning. Some strategies that are not merely interesting but actively engage students in an effective and creative manner include role-playing, creating tableaux, stepping into history, and writing postcards and obituaries. One word of caution, however; there are no guarantees that these activities will work for everyone. Many elements must be in place for successful results. Good research habits are needed to avoid blatantly inaccurate, false history. And students need to know that inviting different interpretations is not permission to make errors in historical fact or to impose present-day thinking and values on the past.

ROLE PLAYS

I made sure my students participated in at least one role play or tableau exercise each semester. Why? Because year after year, for more than twenty years, when I asked my students to rate their favourite lesson, most said it was role-playing an event. Keep in mind that role-playing should involve historical accuracy, not remaking history.

The challenge with role-playing is that it can take longer to prepare. The good news is, once you find a good ready-made role-playing activity, you can use it for many years. There are many suitable role plays on the internet or you can create your own exercise. You can, with a little reflection, update it every year and it will just get better every time you use it.

Role-playing puts students into decision-making situations when they are asked to re-enact events such as famous meetings (for example, the Quebec City Conference of 1865) or encounters between historic individuals (for example, an immigration simulation in the *We Are Canadians* learning package (CRB Heritage Foundation 1995) provides the resources to support elementary students in playing the parts of immigrants and immigration officials during four different time periods of the twentieth century). Role-playing helps students learn not only about the event, rules, dates, and people, it makes the event come alive. In the case of the Quebec City Conference, students learn to negotiate, compromise, and even make good impressions. While re-enacting immigration scenarios, students learn about the process and may come to feel the emotions accompanying historical debates about immigrants, immigration, and immigration restrictions.

The following list outlines various strengths of role-playing as a learning activity.

- It can help students recreate the dramatic quality of a situation or historical setting.
- Open-ended role-playing situations provide students with an opportunity to analyze a problem or controversial situation.
- It provides an opportunity for students to develop a social conscience by putting them in the shoes of another person.
- It can help students learn to view issues from the perspective of other people.

- It can sensitize students to the idea that maintaining a win-lose posture in which "I am right and they are wrong" often serves to perpetuate a problem.
- Role-playing often leads students to decision-making activities. Decision making in itself can be motivating. It empowers students: they feel they have some control over their learning when they are encouraged to make decisions.
- It allows students to combine the cognitive and the affective domains of learning. Students are encouraged to feel as well as think.

Some cautions to address when using a role-play activity are listed below.

- It is very difficult to understand how people thought in the past. Too often, we impose our thinking on the past and do not dig deep enough to begin to enter the minds of our ancestors. Students need help in building a historical setting or context for their role play.
- The real complexities and subtleties of a situation may be overlooked or simplified to an unacceptable level. Some groups may be presented in a stereotypical way (for example, women, visible minorities, people in certain jobs, and religious groups).
- People's feelings, opinions, and attitudes might not be portrayed accurately. Try as we might, we can never really feel the pain, anxiety, fear, or even the joy of the original experience. We must encourage students to thoroughly and critically research the time period they are about to dramatize.

TABLEAUX

A tableau is a striking scene or picture created by organizing students in a staged pose, often in costume. A series of tableaux can be used effectively to recreate an event, especially when a narrator describes the various scenes and the progression of events. Tableau is a variation of role-playing and can be less intimidating because, while everybody can participate, not everyone needs to speak. I have used the following guidelines to recreate events in a tableau.

- Divide the class into teams of four to six students. Each team should do the research to create their series of tableaux.
- Include three to five tableaux or frozen snapshots in a series, each representing a dramatic moment.
- Explain to the students that everyone should be in the picture and visible from the same camera angle. Students should avoid clumping together to give the picture depth.

- Each person needs to decide on an interesting pose. Some exaggeration may be required in order to convey a point. Every feature is important, for example, wide-open eyes, reaching hands, or a tilted head.
- Costumes and props can be difficult to find, but you may be able to find one prop for each student. Props can add to the scene and also help shy students who need something as a distraction.
- When the picture freezes, the narrator steps out of the tableau and describes the scene and its significance with a prepared statement. The narration should be concise and dramatic, and include no more than two or three sentences. In order to get more students involved, encourage the group to have a different narrator for each scene. Perhaps the key person in each tableau could be the narrator.
- During the rehearsal, the actors should take turns stepping out of the tableau to take on the role of director. They should look for variation in the tableau scenes, visual impact, timing, and clarity for the narrators. If a digital camera is available, pictures can be taken so that the group can see themselves to analyze and assess their visual impact.
- Remind the students that in a tableau, each actor is aware of not only his or her role but also of the relationship to each other.

The crucial aspect of this activity is the debriefing. At the end of the activity, invite students to discuss the following questions:

- What was portrayed?
- Why was it important?
- Was it a plausible recreation of the event?
- What aspects do we need to learn more about?
- Are there other interpretations of what happened?
- What have we learned from this activity?

STEPPING INTO HISTORY

Role-playing and tableau can be combined into an activity called "Stepping into History." This is a concept I developed after participating in a History Alive! workshop presented by Bert Bower from the California Teachers' Institute. This activity involves students in role-playing people in a painting or photograph. Some of my favourite photographs for this strategy are famous ones, such as "The Last Spike"[1] or "Fathers of Confederation at the Charlottetown Conference." The idea is to assign roles based on the people in the picture. Students research their characters, and then they create a conversation about the issue that is the subject or reason for the picture.

For example, in the two photographs I mentioned, the issues are obviously the building of the transcontinental railway and Confederation. This activity is excellent for stirring up the students' historical imaginations and encourages them to research, discuss, and identify people and places in history. It can also, with thoughtful help from the teacher, involve critical thinking. By asking penetrating questions, we can encourage students to recreate a realistic historical context. Otherwise, students are likely to impose the present on the past. There are opportunities for some imaginative dialogue but avoid inauthentic dialogue—that is neither good history nor good history teaching.

POSTCARDS FROM THE PAST

Creating postcards from the past is an interesting alternative to essay- and report-writing. When studying a time period or an event, whether it is the Loyalists, Confederation, or settling the West, ask students to create postcards from the perspective of individuals living in that time period. The postcard should be historically accurate—we may have to suspend some historical accuracy for the Loyalists since they were far too busy and disoriented to be writing postcards even if they had had them back in the 1780s. The postcards are to be written in the first person and should have proper postcard format, including a representative picture on the front.

This is a more useful activity than simply writing a letter or drawing a picture. It involves student research, which often does not occur if you ask them simply to draw a picture or create a poster. The purpose of the research is to ensure accurate information and realistic portrayals of the character's opinions about the matters of the day. The 5W questions (what, where, who, when, and why) can provide a template for developing the postcard narrative.

I developed "Postcards from the Past" with the help of colleagues for the Historica Fair program. For more information about this lesson, including an assessment rubric and template, consult the Historica website (www.histori.ca). The Loyalists unit developed for the Library and Archives of Canada has an excellent Postcards from the Past activity (www .archives.ca). This activity satisfies all my criteria for an effective lesson: it invites imagination, requires research, and appeals to different learning styles.

HERITAGE OR HISTORY MINUTES

History minutes is a strategy that developed out of the popular television advertisements called "Heritage Minutes." These were produced originally by the CRB Foundation Heritage Project and more recently by Historica. In preparation for their own history minute, help students choose and research a person, event, or even a popular product of the time. Divide the class into small production teams and ask them to write a storyboard for their history minute. You may want to show an actual Heritage Minute and critically analyze it as a model. Information about the actual Heritage Minutes and about this type of lesson is easily found on the Historica website. It is not necessary that students actually produce a video, although students usually want to and it teaches them other skills in a real, worthwhile way.

OBITUARY OR EULOGY

I have lots of friends who read the obituaries every day—of course, I am older than elementary students, and so are my friends. An obituary can offer a wonderful summary and interpretation of a person's life. There are excellent models in most newspapers, especially the "Lives Lived" column in *The Globe and Mail*. I like the idea of finding primary documents about famous people such as Winston Churchill, Sir John A. Macdonald, or Billy Bishop and asking students to write an obituary based on them rather than on secondary sources that have already done most of the work. Of course, this suggestion will depend on the students' age and ability level. Even writing an obituary or eulogy from secondary sources requires research, creativity, storytelling ability, and writing skills. Encourage students to present their eulogy orally.

Conclusion

My purpose in writing this chapter has been to try to encourage teachers to see the value—even the necessity—of engaging students in the study of history. I have tried to explain how this is not the same as making history fun or amusing. Rather, it involves trying to excite students' curiosity about the past. They want to be challenged, but not overwhelmed. They want to be able to think, talk, and do history. They need to be given opportunities to make decisions, walk in other people's shoes for a while, and, most of all, to be engaged imaginatively.

NOTE

1. A complete, ready-to-use "Stepping into History" lesson with the "Last Spike" photograph is available on the Historica website at http://www.histori.ca/prodev/lp.do?id=10086.

REFERENCES

CRB Heritage Foundation. 1995. *We are Canadians* (Kit #10: Changing Patterns). Toronto: Prentice Hall.

de Bono, E. 2000. *Edward de Bono's CoRT Thinking Lessons.* Oxford: Cavendish Information Products.

Sandwell, R., C. Misfeldt, and R. Case, eds. 2002. *Early contact and settlement in New France.* Richmond, BC: The Critical Thinking Consortium.

Select one of the kinds of activities discussed in this chapter and develop a lesson plan on some past event included in the curriculum. For young children this may be an important family or community incident. Focus on trying to draw students into the time period and to engage their imagination.

25 Sample Secondary Lesson
The Impact of Contact on First Nations

Serina Young

This chapter provides a detailed lesson plan that illustrates how students can use maps to make inferences about and report on the significance of the changes First Nations people experienced as a result of contact with Europeans. More specifically, students are asked to assume the role of a member of the Nlaka'pamux people living on the Thompson River in 1878 and draw a map representing the important changes in culture and world view that might plausibly have occurred in the seventy years since the Nlaka'pamux had had contact with Europeans.

This lesson uses a reconstruction of an early nineteenth-century map attributed to the Nlaka'pamux people (also referred to as the Thompson Indians) to explore the changes that occurred in their world view between 1808—the time of first European contact—and 1878, when Commissioner Sproat arrived in the area. Students begin by drawing their own freehand map of the world and discussing the world views implied in these maps. They then examine the Nlaka'pamux map and other information sources as the basis for drawing inferences about the Nlaka'pamux world view prior to contact with Europeans. Next, students read about dramatic changes that occurred in the succeeding seventy years. Students are asked to redraw the Nlaka'pamux map and explain in light of traditional beliefs, subsequent events, and human nature why the Nlaka'pamux world view might plausibly have changed by 1878 in the ways that the students' maps indicate.

In the course of working through this task, students learn about the dramatic impact on First Nations culture and world view that Europeans had. In addition, students learn that maps are valuable sources of information, not solely about the areas depicted but also about the values and beliefs of the maps' creators.

Student success in thinking critically depends on their possession of the relevant intellectual resources or tools needed for the task.[1] Below are the key tools that students are taught in this lesson:

Background knowledge
- knowledge of the Nlaka'pamux way of life and the changes that occurred between 1808 and 1878

Criteria for judgment
- criteria for visual representation of cultural change (for example, clearly indicates changes, reveals importance aspects of the cultural transformation, plausible given the evidence)

Critical thinking vocabulary
- world view
- inference

Thinking strategies
- data chart

Habits of mind
- historical perspective-taking
- geographic perspective-taking

Session One

DRAW FREE-HAND MAPS

Begin by asking students to take five minutes or less to draw freehand a map of the world. Explain that these maps will simply be used for discussion purposes. Encourage students to include as much detail as they can.

COMPARE STUDENTS' MAPS

Invite students to post their maps on the walls (allowing those who do not wish to exhibit their maps to refrain from doing so). In a gallery walk, ask students to examine each other's maps looking for similarities and differences. In particular, direct students to look for the following features:
- Which continent is in the centre of the map?
- Which countries have the greatest detail?

- Which countries have the least detail?
- What specific features seem exaggerated or under-represented?

INTERPRET MAP FEATURES

Invite students in small groups to identify the common and unique features among the maps and to speculate on the reasons why these features are included on the maps. (Why, for example, would many maps show North America in the centre of the page? Why might some other maps show Southeast Asia or Europe at the centre?) As a class, debrief each group's observations. During the course of the discussion, draw out the ideas summarized in the following account of maps as windows onto personal and cultural beliefs and values:

Maps as personal and cultural windows

A map is a way of understanding the environment and of making sense of it. It reveals people's perceptions of their world—a mirror of their culture—as it represents their view of reality. In maps, points of view are represented visually. Inevitably, certain places will be indicated and others excluded (for example, large cities are often shown on maps, but small towns may not be; some maps show roads, others show rivers, some show both). Why are certain places or physical features judged important? Why is one feature shown and not another? Maps also reflect perceptions of how things are arranged in spatial relationship with one another. They com-

municate where one place is viewed in relation to another. Because maps reveal these cultural and personal perspectives, they can serve as windows to other world views.

DRAW CONCLUSIONS ABOUT WORLD VIEW

Pose this question to your class: Using your maps, what can you infer about our perception of the world? Create an overhead transparency of "Maps as Mirrors of World View" (Blackline Master 25.1) and record student answers as suggested in the example provided.

Session Two

INTRODUCE THE STUDY OF THE NLAKA'PAMUX

Explain that students will learn about the Nlaka'pamux, a First Nations people from south-central British Columbia who speak a common language and live in communities along the Fraser and Thompson rivers. Display an overhead transparency of "Map of the Thompson and Fraser Rivers" (Blackline Master 25.2). Ask students to speculate on the point of view of the creator of this map, noting the emphasis on riverways and historic communities.

BLACKLINE MASTER 25.1   MAPS AS MIRRORS OF WORLD VIEW

FEATURE ON THE MAP	IMPLIED VIEW OF THE WORLD
Canada is in the centre of the map	the person's "universe" revolves around Canada

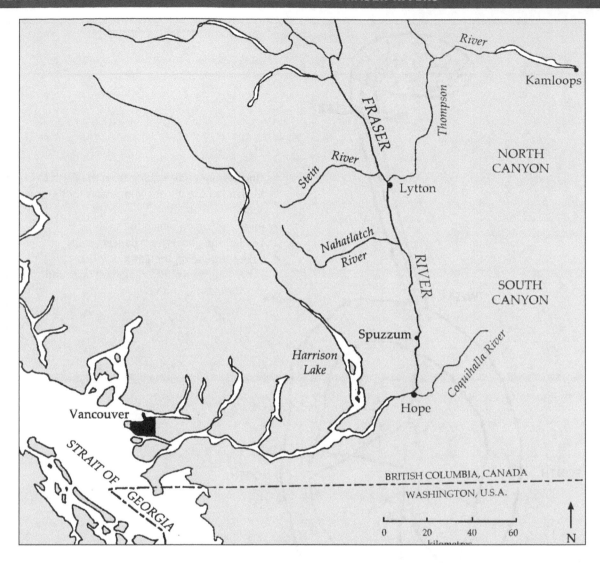

INTERPRET THE FIRST NATIONS MAP

Distribute the "Reconstructed Nlaka'pamux Map" (Blackline Master 25.3). Explain that this map is based on a map believed to have been created by a member of the Nlaka'pamux Nation around the time of initial contact with Europeans in 1808. Review the features of the map and invite students to examine the map for insights on the world view of the creators of the map, as they did with their own freehand maps. Encourage students to apply the lessons learned from their own freehand maps (for example, that a vaguely outlined South America might suggest that mapmakers had limited exposure to or attached limited significance to that continent) to this First Nation.

Distribute the briefing sheet "Nlaka'pamux Way of Life in 1808" (Blackline Master 25.4). In small groups, invite students to use the map and the background information to draw inferences about the Nlaka'pamux and how they viewed the world. Encourage students to try to imagine the perspective of Nlaka'pamux people living in that time and place. Distribute copies of "Maps as Mirrors of World View" (Blackline Master 25.1) for use in recording each group's findings.

SHARE STUDENTS' FINDINGS

After students have had sufficient time to consider the material and to record their inferences about the Nlaka'pamux world view implied by the map, invite them to share their findings with the class. Record comments on the board. Some of the ideas may refer to the centrality of water (rivers), intimate relationship with nature, the spirit world as a part of their reality, and separation from any "outside" world.

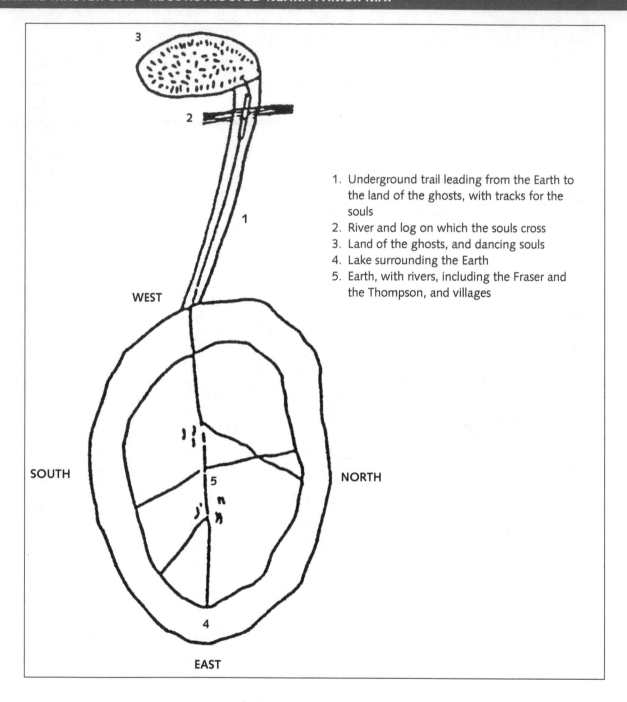

1. Underground trail leading from the Earth to the land of the ghosts, with tracks for the souls
2. River and log on which the souls cross
3. Land of the ghosts, and dancing souls
4. Lake surrounding the Earth
5. Earth, with rivers, including the Fraser and the Thompson, and villages

When the Nlaka'pamux, also known as the Thompson Indians, met Simon Fraser in 1808, they were not afraid, nor were they hostile. Their oral stories recall conducting Fraser's canoes ashore with ceremony to exchange goods and smoke. The Spence's Bridge chief ran so as not to miss the occasion and delivered a great speech to all those who had gathered.

During the summer season, the Nlaka'pamux males spent most of their time hunting, snaring, and trapping. The Nlaka'pamux ate the meat of various animals, but deer and salmon were the principal sources of food. Five varieties of salmon were abundant in the Fraser River and were dried for trading in "sticks" of one hundred fish each. Each village had its usual hunting-grounds. Women from any village could join in the picking of berries as long as it was done in the proper season. Sometimes as many as a thousand women, representing all the divisions of the Nlaka'pamux, gathered to dig roots.

There was brisk trade between the bands and also with other First Nations who inhabited the interior plateau. Two salmon sticks were traded for one tanned bison skin. One canoe might be traded for a large water-tight cedar-root basket. The Nlaka'pamux sometimes raided other groups, and they also fought among themselves. What started out as trivial quarrels sometimes ended up in bloodshed and hostilities that lingered for twenty years or more.

In the winter, the Nlaka'pamux moved into pit houses, dug a metre or more into the ground. These houses were usually round in shape and covered over by logs, sod, and earth. This was the time for social festivals to demonstrate good will and generosity. Typically this involved a host family providing food for a visiting relative. Storytelling was developed to such an art that sophisticated sign language for moments such as "bear

running," "quick," and "sudden appearance" were essential to enhance the drama. Winter was also the time when the elders would teach the young the evils of stealing and lying.

The Nlaka'pamux believed that each person has a guardian spirit acquired at a puberty ceremony. This spirit might be a natural phenomenon such as water, a heavenly phenomenon such as the Milky Way, an animal (of which the most powerful are the wolf and the grizzly bear), or everyday objects such as a root digger tool. Every year during winter ceremonials, individuals would renew their relationships with their guardian spirits.

When the body died, it was thought that the soul went on a journey down the trail to the country of souls, which is underneath and towards the sunset. The soul has a shadow—a ghost—that might remain for years among the living, trying to make the surviving family sick so they would join the soul as company.

Everything has a soul—trees, fire, herbs, and animals. Certain animals have other worlds of their own with hidden entrances. It was thought that animals entered the human world just to benefit people. If they were wrongly used, they returned to their own world. This explained why some animals sometimes became scarce. When an animal was killed, other animals did not like to see any of it wasted.

Only the shaman has the power to communicate between this world of the living and that of the souls. When a person suspected that their soul had been taken, they would seek out the shaman within two days so the shaman could overtake the soul by looking for tracks on the trail. If it was not the time for death, the shaman might carry the soul back to the individual's body in his hands.

Session Three

EXAMINE CHANGES IN WAY OF LIFE

Explain that students will now consider how the traditional Nlaka'pamux way of life was disrupted with the advent of Europeans. Distribute "Living Conditions of the Nlaka'pamux by 1878" (Blackline Master 25.5). After students have read this sheet, arrange for them in their groups to discuss the following questions:

- How might the Nlaka'pamux have felt about the changes that had occurred in their lives?
- How might these experiences have affected their beliefs and outlook on the world?

PRESENT THE CRITICAL CHALLENGE

Assign students to individually complete the following task for homework:

> Imagine that you are a member of the Nlaka'pamux people living on the Thompson River in 1878. Draw a map representing the changes in culture and world view that might plausibly have occurred in the seventy years since contact with Europeans and write an explanation of your choices.

EXPLAIN THE TASK

Ask students to imagine a minimum of five changes reflecting important features of the Nlaka'pamux world view that had occurred by 1878. Direct students to use "Accounting for the Changes" (Blackline Master 25.6) to record the following

In 1878, Gilbert Malcolm Sproat, who was the Indian Reserve Commissioner (a representative of the federal and provincial governments), arrived at Spuzzum, British Columbia with the intention of adjusting the reserves that the government had allocated to the Nlaka'pamux. They were happy that he had come because they wanted him to address an important concern: settlers had acquired land they hoped to get. As Father Grandidier wrote in the *Victoria Standard* on August 28, 1874:

> The whites came, took land, fenced it in, and little by little hemmed the Indians in their small reservations.... Many of these reservations have been surveyed without their consent, and sometimes without having received any notice of it, so they could not expose their needs and their wishes. Their reserves have been repeatedly cut off smaller for the benefit of the whites.... The natives have protested.... They have complained bitterly of that treatment, but they have not obtained any redress.

At Spuzzum, where Commissioner Sproat began his land survey, he found himself standing at the site of a tragic disaster. In one village north of Lytton, he recorded a population of 107 where Simon Fraser had earlier reported there were 400. There were decreased populations in other villages as well. In the spring of 1862, the Nlaka'pamux had been struck with smallpox. Their traditional healers were helpless in preventing the high death rates among children and elders. The deaths of elders resulted in the loss of many skillful leaders, craftspersons, and people who were most knowledgeable about religious traditions.

In 1878, Commissioner Sproat found that the majority of the population was still Nlaka'pamux; however, there were many newcomers. Most of these were single Chinese men who had come for the gold rush about twenty years earlier, and the rest were whites. A number of Native women had married these immigrants.

As Commissioner Sproat studied the issue of Native reserves, he found that the best land had already been granted to white people. He was critical of the government's land policy; nevertheless, since he felt obligated to uphold the law, he was limited in what he could do. He believed Native people and whites were equally subject to the laws of a white government.

As their lives became increasingly regulated, the Nlaka'pamux had many questions for Commissioner Sproat. Could they hunt on certain lands? Were the canneries at the mouth of the river going to take all the salmon? If they worked hard, could they reacquire their traditional land? Could they hire a teacher for their children? These were desperate cries in the face of changing, unknown circumstances.

---

information to accompany the redrawn map they completed for homework:

- In the left-hand column, identify the changes they have made to the Nlaka'pamux map of the world.
- In the middle column, indicate the implied changes in world view these represent.
- In the right-hand column, explain why each change in world view is plausible, given the information we have about the Nlaka'pamux.

DISCUSS THE CRITERIA TO CONSIDER

Emphasize that the imagined changes in Nlaka'pamux world view must be clearly identified, reflect important (not trivial) changes, and be plausible, given the available evidence. Briefly discuss with the class the factors that affect plausibility, including the following:

- **consistent with cultural beliefs of the Nlaka'pamux**—changes must grow out of or be derived from this group's traditional beliefs;
- **grounded in actual events**—changes must have some root in the events that actually happened;

- **realistic, given human nature**—changes must be consistent with what people are likely to do in such situations.

Session Four

DISCUSS RESULTS IN GROUPS

Divide students into small groups to share their maps and the implied changes in world view and cultures. Ask each group to identify the changes that are generally recognized by the group members and to rank these in order of their significance for the Nlaka'pamux people. Invite each group to list those changes that are disputed by group members.

SHARE RESULTS AS A CLASS

Arrange for each group to record its rank-ordered list of important changes and its list of disputed changes on the board. Look for patterns across the lists, and encourage students to discuss the evidence for and against their conclusions.

CHANGE IN MAP	IMPLIED CHANGE IN WORLD VIEW	EXPLANATION FOR CHANGED WORLD VIEW

Evaluation

Use the rubric "Assessing Students' Redrawn Maps" (Blackline Master 25.7) to evaluate students' maps and supporting explanations using the following criteria:

- clarity of the features in illustrating the imagined changes in world view;

- the degree to which the implied changes reveal key, as opposed to trivial, aspects of the Nlaka'pamux world view;
- the adequacy of the explanations in establishing the plausibility of the imagined changes in world view.

If it is to be used, distribute a copy to students before they begin the assignment. If so desired, this rubric can be used in student peer and self-assessment of this assignment.

	OUTSTANDING	VERY GOOD	COMPETENT	UNDERDEVELOPED
Clarity of identified features	At least five features noted by the student illustrate very clearly the implied changes in world view.	Four features noted by the student illustrate clearly the implied changes in world view.	Two or three features noted by the student illustrate somewhat clearly the implied changes in world view.	None of the features noted by the student clearly indicate the implied changes in world view.
Important changes in world view	Overall, the implied changes reveal the important aspects of the group's world view.	The implied changes reveal some important aspects but other key aspects of the group's world view are missing or incorrectly identified.	Only a few of the implied changes reveal important aspects of the group's world view.	None of the implied changes correctly indicate important aspects of the group's world view.
Explanation of changes	In every case, the explanation offers highly credible, clear reasons why the imagined change is plausible.	The explanations are generally credible and clearly explain why the imagined changes are plausible.	Some of the explanations offer credible and clear reasons why the imagined changes are plausible.	None of the explanations offer credible and clear reasons why the imagined change is plausible.

> Thinking of the intended student audience and the curriculum, critique this lesson. Be sure to identify its positive traits and its shortcomings. Discuss what you could do to improve, adapt, or extend this lesson.

Extension

EXAMINE OTHER EVIDENCE OF EUROPEAN IMPACT

Encourage students to use the internet to locate additional evidence of the effects of European contact on the Nlaka'pamux. See, for example, James Alexander Teit's collection of photographs on the Canadian Museum of Civilization's Gateway to Aboriginal Heritage website at www.civilization.ca/tresors/ethno/etf0200e.html.

EXAMINE OTHER HISTORICAL MAPS

Invite students to analyze other published historical and contemporary maps to see what can be inferred about the attitudes and outlook of the creators of these maps.

STUDY FREEHAND MAPS FROM OTHER STUDENTS

Analyze student-drawn freehand maps of Canada or of the world obtained through an exchange with students from other provinces (or countries) to determine potential differences in world views as a result of geographic location.

NOTE

1. Chapter 7 in this volume, "Teaching the Tools to Think Critically," explains each of these tools.
2. This blackline master is based on information found in Teit (1975) and Wickwire (1994).

REFERENCES

Teit, J. 1975. The Thompson Indians of British Columbia. In *The Jesup North Pacific expedition: Memoir of the American Museum of Natural History*, Vol. 1, 337–366. New York: AMS Press, first printed 1900.

Wickwire, W. 1994. To see ourselves as the other's other: Nlaka'pamux contact narratives. *Canadian Historical Review* 75 (1): 1–20.

26 Bringing the Outside In
Using Community Resources in Secondary Social Studies

Penney Clark

Garnet McDiarmid (1970) tells the story of a teacher who wrote that he did not have science in his school because the school had neither textbooks nor laboratory equipment. McDiarmid points out that the school was located in an area of uranium mines, moraines and other post-glacial deposits, running water, ponds, and abundant flora and fauna—all of which could have been exploited as fascinating sources for scientific investigation.

A similar point might be made about the availability of outside resources for social studies. Every school has many historic and geographically interesting sites to explore nearby or farther afield. Every teacher has access to local people who are willing to be interviewed or come to school to share their expertise. Many organizations will send print and video materials free-of-charge. Students in urban areas can step outside their school to investigate traffic patterns, community development, museums, and recreational facilities. Students in rural areas can visit metropolitan areas, regional industries, local historic sites, and countless other places in the surrounding area. Unfortunately, many of us overlook the educational potential of what is outside our classroom walls.

Learning to make effective educational use of the community requires that these encounters become more than "isolated experiences," unrelated to curriculum learning outcomes. As one writer warns, field trips may involve little more than "wandering in a long line (rather like a snake that has just shed its skin and is doubtful about its boundaries) through museum corridors with half-minute halts to gape at an exhibit or collect stragglers" (quoted in Oliver 1970, 22). The lost educational potential of field experiences is reflected in an episode of the television show *The Wonder Years* in which the junior high school protagonist Kevin Arnold and his classmates visit a museum. In the episode, teacher and students have very different agendas. The teacher, of course, views the trip as an opportunity to expose students to the richness of the past. For Kevin and his friends, the exhibits become a mere backdrop to more important personal concerns—who likes whom, who is going to which party on the weekend, and so on.[1]

If students lack clear curricular purposes and educational context in which to place it, embarking on a community experience can become a mere diversion from classroom routine—a welcome relief perhaps, but ultimately not an experience that furthers the goals of social studies. In this chapter, I explore the value of and strategies for effectively bringing the outside into the curriculum in the context of three types of community resources: field experiences, local experts, and materials developed by non-educational agencies.

Field Experiences

Field experiences, with the direct involvement that they entail, can foster rich understandings and promote empathy in ways that textbook study and other instructional strategies cannot. This potential is illustrated in a grade 8 student's account of his field experience in Vancouver's notorious Downtown Eastside.

> We walked outside Victory House, which is a hotel for poor people. There we met a woman called Rosie. She was 78 and wearing lots of jewelry and makeup, even though it was in the wrong place on her face. Pastor Brian said lots of artists had painted her. She definitely stood out. She seemed wired at first but turned out to be very nice. She was carrying lots of bags and today was welfare day but she hadn't picked up her cheque yet. We all went for coffee and she asked Pastor Brian to buy her a pack of smokes. There was a drug deal going on at the back of the restaurant and that felt really strange. It all felt like such a different world.

He concluded: "I felt so much that I can hardly begin to describe exactly everything I felt. I felt that if every kid could have this kind of experience the school system would be a lot better" (Corcoran and Thompson 1999, 5).

These students' attitudes towards poverty, homelessness, and mental illness were all profoundly affected by this field experience, which was part of a unit on the social problem of homelessness in Canada at a school in a wealthy Vancouver suburb. The students developed a level of empathy and understanding that would have been difficult to attain if their research had been limited to newspaper articles on the topic.

A similar power is reflected in the reminiscences reported in the highlighted text, "Mr. Hou's Harrison Hike," by David Mushens (an educational administrator in Burnaby) who took part in a seven-day historic hike, the purpose of which was to deepen students' historical understandings related to the Cariboo gold rush.

As these examples suggest, properly conceived, a field trip can become much more than a pleasant break from daily routines. It can provide information and direct experiences that enrich a wide range of social studies topics, such as:

- natural and built landscapes
- geological formations
- resource management
- tectonic and gradation processes
- historical eras
- cultural makeup of a community
- local government
- transportation networks
- industry and commerce
- architecture
- zoning
- recreation

Field experiences at art galleries and museums can enhance wide-ranging topics such as ancient civilizations or pioneer times. Field experiences, particularly those involving overnight stays, are ideal for outdoor studies and environmental investigations.

Field experiences must be carefully planned. Activities that take place prior to and following the field experience may be of equal importance to those activities that take place during it. Prior activities set the context for the experience and help students participate with inquiring attitudes. Follow-up activities allow students to clarify impressions, share ideas, and apply what they have learned. The highlighted text, "Field Trip Checklist," contains a list of logistical and educational factors to consider when organizing a field trip. I will elaborate on three sets of considerations:

- choosing a field experience;
- deciding on a site;
- developing preparatory, on-site, and follow-up activities.

CHOOSING TO GO ON A FIELD TRIP

Two factors should govern the decision to include a field experience in a social studies program: feasibility and educational efficacy. Feasibility refers to the reasonableness of undertaking the proposed activity given the typical constraints—transportation logistics, insufficient adult supervisors, expensive admission fees, safety considerations, and parental resistance due to lack of understanding of the connection between the experience and curriculum objectives. Many of these difficulties can be overcome with careful planning.

A second consideration is educational efficacy—whether the benefits outweigh the risks and drawbacks. Will the gain in learning justify the valuable class time and effort involved? Could the same learning outcomes be attained as richly and efficiently by staying in the classroom? A field experience

MR. HOU'S HARRISON HIKE

For more than twenty years, Charles Hou has led hundreds of students along the original Harrison-Lillooet Gold Rush trail. I was fortunate to be one of them. In tenth grade, at the ripe old age of sixteen, I and some sixty or so of my schoolmates began our seven-day journey with a two-and-a-half hour "cruise" up Harrison Lake on a creaky, aluminum logging boat. After vibrating, roaring, and huddling against the cold, we stepped off the dock and into the past at what is left of the town of Douglas, the original planned capital of BC.

The Harrison Hike brought Mr. Hou's students to history, helping young historians relive the adventures of prospectors bent on striking a claim in BC's gold-rich territory. The trip meant so much to me I went seven more times! During my college and university years, I continued to trek the trail with "Charlie," each year watching a fresh group of students, many of them never having camped a day in their lives, awestruck by the majesty of the forest, the power of the mighty Lillooet, and the wonder of packing the same road prospectors trekked along so many years before them.

No two trips were the same. Each brought some different aspect of history roaring into the present: gold panning, clearing trail, meeting First Nations chiefs, building a sweat lodge, singing gold-rush folk songs. And every year traditions continued, like climbing Colonel Richard Moody's lookout, braving cold Whiskey Lake, and, of course, cooking the famous buried beans.

Former Harrison hikers still approach me to reminisce about this most memorable experience of their education and even look forward to sending their own kids on what they will always call "Mr. Hou's Harrison Hike."

should be chosen only if important benefits are realized that could not be achieved in the classroom. Clear communication is helpful in assuring parents, students, and school (and school board) administration that a field experience is the best way to meet specific curriculum goals.

CHOOSING THE SITE

The key criterion in choosing a field-trip site is that it advances curricular objectives by extending and enriching areas of investigation that are being (or will be) pursued in the classroom. Field experiences should be seen as one more data source to be accessed in a unit, albeit a more intriguing one.

We need not limit our choices of field site to destination settings such as museums, local historical sites, or other typical attractions. A field experience might be as simple as a walk through the neighbourhood to record the range of home types, or a trip to the shopping mall to observe product marketing, if these will help attain curriculum objectives.

In considering alternatives, a site should not be rejected out-of-hand merely because most students may have been there before. Retired teacher Bill Willson commented that he was always amazed at how many of the students in his senior geography classes had never walked Vancouver's Stanley Park seawall. We cannot assume that all students will have had these seemingly common experiences. As well, a family excursion can and should be quite a different experience than a structured field trip. During a field experience, students observe with particular purposes in mind, which guide their information gathering. Also, field trips offer opportunities for in-depth activities. In this case, students examined the twenty-metre cliff that forms Prospect Point as visible evidence of the area's fiery creation. This columnar blocking of andesite in its dyke of cooled magma is just one of the many things at this common Vancouver site that can bring to life the vocabulary, concepts, and pictures from students' geography lessons.

Table 26.1, "Range of Field Sites," outlines various possibilities available in many communities, and suggests ques-

FIELD TRIP CHECKLIST

Early preparation
☐ Review school and district policies regarding field trips.
☐ Obtain information about the field trip, including talking to other teachers who have organized similar outings.
☐ Clarify educational objectives. Make them as concrete as possible.
☐ Obtain permissions from principal and on-site authorities.
☐ Book trip and arrange transportation.
☐ Make students aware of objectives and solicit student input.
☐ Visit site. Could take along a student committee.
☐ Arrange for helpers.
☐ Inform parents of the purpose of the trip, departure and arrival times, eating arrangements, costs, supervision arrangements, and any special clothing or equipment requirements.
☐ Obtain permission from parents or guardians.

Just prior to trip
☐ Provide checklist for students:
  ◆ money
  ◆ equipment
  ◆ clothing
  ◆ food
☐ Collect money, if required.
☐ Prepare students logistically:
  ◆ discuss safety issues
  ◆ could role-play expected behaviour
  ◆ review rules of conduct
  ◆ establish work groups and buddy system

☐ Brief adult helpers:
  ◆ discuss purposes of trip
  ◆ discuss duties
  ◆ discuss safety issues
☐ Prepare students educationally:
  ◆ review objectives
  ◆ share students' prior knowledge about the place
  ◆ assign individual and group tasks

On the trip
☐ Use the travel time to the site as part of the experience (for example, have students take note of types of buildings, industries, and transportation observed en route).
☐ Once on site, point out boundaries and key spots (for example, washrooms, meeting area, lost and found space).
☐ Elicit student questions and discussion.
☐ Remind students about gathering and recording data:
  ◆ go over charts to be filled in or questions to be answered
  ◆ assign one or more students to take photographs as a record of the trip
  ◆ create field sketches
  ◆ interview people on-site
☐ Plan for return trip (for example, take a different route back to the school to capitalize on the commuting and what can be observed while travelling).

Follow-up
☐ Organize, synthesize, and present collected data.
☐ Formally thank hosts and helpers.
☐ Evaluate trip.

TABLE 26.1   RANGE OF FIELD SITES

FIELD SITES	FOCUS QUESTIONS OR TASKS
School • physical layout • roles of various staff members	• What types of rooms are in our school (for example, classrooms, offices, gym)? How is each one used? • What types of occupations are there in our school? What tasks do people do? How are these tasks important? • How could the physical layout be altered to better meet the needs of the people who use the school?
Local neighbourhood • modes of transportation • safety measures (for example, crosswalks, sidewalks, signs, fire hydrants)	• How do people get to work and to school? What do people in the neighbourhood think of the transportation services? How could they be improved to better meet people's needs? • What safety features are in our neighbourhood? What is the function of each? Are other safety features needed? How could we go about getting them?
Public services • fire station • police station • public library • public health unit	• What places in our community provide services? Which services does the government provide? Which services are special to our community and which are provided in most communities? • Are other services needed in our community? How could we go about getting them?
Retail businesses • grocery store • bakery • shopping mall	• Which places sell goods? Are there enough goods and services available in our community? Do all communities need goods and services from other communities?
Manufacturing or commercial sites • assembly line • newspaper plant • warehouse • advertising agency	• What is the product(s) here? Where does the facility fit in terms of the product's production, distribution, marketing, or sale? What happens at this site? What happened to the product before it arrived at this site? What happens next? • Is it safe working here? Why or why not?
Community celebrations • multicultural festivals • Remembrance Day ceremonies • heritage days	• What things do people in our community choose to celebrate? • What is the history of this event? • Why are these celebrations important to people in this community?
Historical sites • restored homes, forts, and villages • graveyards and monuments • museums (local and provincial)	• What can we learn about the past at this site? Is it important to maintain sites like this one? Why or why not? • What might life have been like when people lived and worked here?
Resource development sites • mines • lumber mills • farms • refineries	• What resource is being developed? Give a step-by-step description of the process used to develop this resource. • What are the environmental effects of development of this resource? What environmental protection measures are used here? Are these measures sufficient? • Where does the product(s) go? How are transportation systems used to transport the product from this site?

TABLE 26.1   RANGE OF FIELD SITES (CONT.)

FIELD SITES	FOCUS QUESTIONS OR TASKS
Environmental preservation sites • fish hatchery • water-treatment plant • landfill facility	• What happens at this facility? • How does it contribute to environmental preservation? • Does this site create any pollution?
Government operations • all-candidates meeting • provincial legislature in session • city council in session • ratepayer meeting on a local issue • mock trial in a courtroom	• All-candidates meeting: Choose two election issues. What is each candidate's stance on these issues? Which issues seem to be of most concern to the audience? Who are the strongest candidates? Why? • Simulated city council meeting: What strategies did you use to try to win others over to your point of view? How successful were you? Did you change your position in any way based on what others said? • Actual city council meeting: Describe the decision-making process used by the city council. Were points in favour of each argument taken into consideration? Did some opinions seem to carry more weight than others? What recommendations would you offer to city councils about the process of making decisions?
Transportation and communication venues • railway station • bus depot • port facilities • television station • post office • airport	• How are things organized so that employees work together to keep things running smoothly? Draw a flow chart. • Describe what it would be like to work at a job at one of these sites. • What are some examples of the technology used at this facility?

tions or tasks to focus these experiences. There has been no attempt to assign sites according to grade level. Many sites visited in the primary years for one purpose may well be re-visited in later grades for other purposes.

PREPARATORY ACTIVITIES WITH STUDENTS

Prior activities set the context for the experience, and help students participate with an inquiring attitude. First and foremost, students need to be aware of field-trip objectives. For instance, the reason for a trip to a local court house might be to discover the legal services offered to community groups (and how these services are delivered). A second objective might be to explore how these services or their delivery might better meet people's needs. Such a trip could be part of a larger unit on civil society. Do not assume that students will automatically make the connections between their experiences on the trip and other learning activities. The objectives to be addressed should be discussed explicitly.

Provide students with site-related pamphlets, posters, websites, kits of sample items, or video programs that preview the field experience. Students can use these materials to generate questions to guide their observations at the site. The

teacher can also give key questions to the students.

Prior to the trip, a permission form providing basic facts about the trip, such as the one shown in Figure 26.1, should be sent home. There is nothing more frustrating than planning a field trip only to discover that after all the work is done not every student can come on the trip. Secondary school field trips can be logistical nightmares because each student in your class may have a different timetable involving a variety of subjects and subject teachers. Legitimate concerns or conflicts with other subject teachers may mean individual students have to remain behind so that they do not miss specific skills, classes, or scheduled examinations.

Planning well in advance of the field trip in consultation with colleagues may help avoid the disappointments and conflicts that you and individual students may be subjected to because of scheduled exams, poor marks, or other problems.

Even better, working with administration to schedule field trips can reduce subject conflicts to a minimum. For example, scheduling double periods into afternoon classes at least once a week can alleviate the problem of having to negotiate around times scheduled for other subjects. This gives the subject teacher the opportunity to pull their students out of the school for an extended period of time without af-

FIGURE 26.1   SAMPLE FIELD TRIP PERMISSION FORM

In conjunction with their local history study, our class will be visiting McAdam Heritage Home. Volunteers at the home will engage students in activities that people living in the home would have done in the late 1800s.

Date of trip _____

Destination _____

Duration _____

Transportation _____

Time leaving school _____   Time of return _____   Cost to student _____

Items to bring _____

Teacher's name _____   Phone _____

- -

Please return this section

I give my permission for _____ to participate in the trip to the McAdam Heritage Home on October 3, 2006.

Signature _____ (parent/guardian)

Phone number: Home _____   Work _____

Emergency contact _____

---

fecting other classes. Alternatively, create student schedules that integrate two or three classes that travel as a block to designated courses. This strategy has several advantages. First, it allows teachers to team teach and integrate subjects around common themes (Comparative Civilizations and Literature, Social Responsibility and Environmental Studies). It also allows subject teachers to team up for field trips related to common themes.

Considerable preparation is required if interviews or surveys are to be conducted at the site. The highlighted text, "Advice on Conducting Interviews and Surveys" offers suggestions for carrying out interviews and surveys.

ACTIVITIES AT THE SITE

An ideal field experience is structured and purposeful. Students observe and record their observations in an organized manner. Here are some approaches to recording information at the site:

- **Tally sheets.** Students may find tally sheets useful if they are looking for specific information that can be counted. The following example shows how students might calculate on a tally sheet how much traffic goes over the school crosswalk during a specific period of time. Students could also use a tally sheet to solicit opinions for a survey.

TRAFFIC OVER A CROSSWALK	
TIME PERIODS	**NUMBER OF PEOPLE**
8:00–8:15	///
8:15–8:30	////
8:30–8:45	
8:45–9:00	////
...	

- **Maps.** A simple street map of the community can be used to record the location of community features such as housing types (for example, apartments, single-family dwellings, duplexes).
- **Note-taking sheets.** Encourage students to record responses during the field experience on sheets with teacher- or student-made questions. The questions should direct students to the features of the site that relate to the intended understanding, especially those that students may not notice otherwise.
- **Photographs/video.** One or more students could record important aspects of the trip by means of photo-

ADVICE ON CONDUCTING INTERVIEWS AND SURVEYS

Preparation

- Decide what information is needed to meet the research objectives.
- Consider whether survey or interview is the better format to obtain the required information. Use surveys when a minimal amount of common information is needed from a fairly large number of people. An interview works best when smaller numbers are involved and the answers may be lengthy or need to be clarified.
- Research background information before the interview or survey. The more information you have, the more pertinent your questions are likely to be.
- Decide on the type of questions to ask: questions where people can indicate YES/NO or AGREE/DISAGREE, or the type where people explain their answers. Generally with interviews it is preferable to avoid questions that could be answered with a simple "yes" or "no" because these may not be particularly enlightening. Long answers on surveys involve more work from the respondents and may be more difficult to interpret and categorize.
- Generate a list of possible questions and select those questions that most clearly and directly address the desired information.
- Decide on the "sample" (the group who will answer the questions). Check with possible respondents beforehand that they are comfortable sharing information on the research topic.
- Discuss as a class the guidelines for effective interviewing.
- Provide an opportunity for students to practise interviews with peers, parents, or other familiar individuals.

Survey guidelines

- Decide whether each respondent will be asked questions or if they will fill out the form on their own. Response rates are lower when respondents fill out their own forms because some will not do so.
- Decide whether responses will be anonymous. This will depend on the type of questions and respondents' wishes.
- Provide information on the survey in an accompanying letter. The information should include why the survey is being conducted, who is conducting it, and how the person can find out the results of the survey.

Interview guidelines

- Clearly state who you are, your purpose, how the information will be used, and how long the interview is expected to take.
- Visit with the interviewee for a few minutes before and after the interview. This will help you to see the interviewee as a person and to make the interviewee feel comfortable.
- Allow the interviewee time to think about the question before responding.
- Clarify ambiguous responses. Restate the question using other words. Or say, "Is this what you meant?" and restate the intended meaning of the response.
- Ask new questions that grow out of the interviewee's comments. By sticking to the prepared questions, valuable opportunities to delve deeper and explore ideas may be missed.
- Use a tape recorder (with the interviewee's permission) or notes to record the interview. Use the interviewee's exact words in the notes. Choice of words may be an important indicator of feelings.
- Summarize the main points for the interviewee at the end of the interview. Don't offer comments that could be interpreted by the interviewee as critical of their responses.
- Thank the interviewee at the end of the interview.

Follow-up

- Send a thank-you note to all interviewees.
- Summarize impressions in writing as soon as possible after the interview. Tabulate survey results by adding up the totals of similar answers and clustering common themes contained in open-ended answers.
- Prepare an oral and/or written report of the results.
- Send a copy of the report to all those who wish to have it.

---

graphs or video. These visual records assist in making detailed observations following the trip and in preparing PowerPoint presentations, bulletin boards, class booklets, or websites.

- **Sketches.** Drawings are a useful way to record information because students can focus on particular details rather than record everything as a camera would.
- **Journals.** Students could record impressions in a journal, perhaps writing in the role of someone working at a site or living in a particular historic time.
- **Interviews.** It may be appropriate for students to con-

duct interviews at the site. A chart, such as the one in Figure 26.2, could be used by secondary students to record interview information.

Think of a particular site that would enhance the study of a topic in the social studies curriculum. Develop an activity sheet based on one of the ideas discussed above that would structure students' experiences while at this site. Focus the activity so that the field experience provides students with insights that they could not achieve from a classroom-based study.

FIGURE 26.2 STRUCTURED INTERVIEW FORM

Interviewer _____   Interviewee _____

Date _____   Place _____

1. Question	Response
2. Question	Response
3. Question	Response
4. Question	Response
Other points made during the interview:	

FOLLOW-UP ACTIVITIES

After a field experience three kinds of activities are helpful:

- Students organize and interpret the data they have gathered.
- Students share their findings with others.
- Students review and assess the experience itself, including its preparatory and follow-up activities.

In preparation for interpreting data, students should review their notes, diagrams, photographs, drawings, or other records and then select and organize this information. (The pre-visit questions or the recording charts provide an organized format for the data.) Students should then interpret and draw conclusions from the information. This might include asking questions such as the following:

- Is there a particular point of view from which this information was presented?
- Is there another side to this story?
- What conclusions can I draw from this information? Does other evidence support these conclusions?
- Was I able to answer all my questions or do I need to consult other sources?
- What other questions arise now that my original questions have been answered?

Encourage students to develop effective and interesting ways of presenting their findings. Presentation formats include individual or group bulletin board displays, models, photo albums, stories, reports, letters, poems, tape recordings, journals, articles in the school newspaper, a play to be put on for other classes, and so on. Choices are as varied as for any other kind of research. (See chapter 12, "Escaping the Typical Report Trap," in this volume for other ideas.)

Finally, it may be useful to invite students, orally or in writing, to review and assess the field experience itself. Students could address the following questions:

- What were our purposes in engaging in this community experience?
- Did we achieve our purposes? Was the trip interesting?
- Are there things we could have done differently in order to achieve our purposes?
- Was the trip the best way to obtain the needed information?
- What were some of the pleasant and unpleasant surprises we encountered? How could we reduce the possibility of encountering the unpleasant surprises in another field experience?

Local Experts

Local resource people provide students with unique learning opportunities to initiate relationships with adults they may not normally meet. Students enjoy asking their own questions, receiving first-hand responses to those questions, and drawing their own conclusions.

Alan Sears (1999) writes of his experiences in using

local experts to support a grade 11 modern history course he taught.

I had been struggling to make the turmoil of the 20th century more real for them [his students] and decided to assign students the task of interviewing someone who had been involved in an international conflict. Students were to find an individual who met one of the following criteria:

- A veteran of the armed forces who had served in the First or Second World War, in an area of conflict such as Korea, or with a Canadian peace-keeping mission. The person may have served in the Canadian armed forces or those of another country.
- A civilian who had lived in a war or occupation zone such as Holland during the Second World War, in Britain during the blitz, or in Vietnam during the more recent conflict in that country.

The purpose of the interview was to foster an intimate personal view of modern conflict. Students were to inquire into the individual's views on the causes of conflict, the morality of it, the actual events, the areas involved, the strategies and equipment used, and the effects and consequences. The interviews consisted of a minimum of 25 questions, some of which were made up in class. After the interviews were completed, the information was presented in a formal essay.

Prior to assigning the interview task, I contacted the local branch of the Royal Canadian Legion and arranged for volunteers to be interviewed in the event that some students were unable to find their own interviewees. Out of 60 students, only 14 needed this help.

The quality of the final assignments was exceptional and the range of topics covered was fascinating. I had been afraid that students would get a rather narrow view of conflict from completing their own interviews, but this problem was avoided by having students share information and insights with the rest of the class. Interviewees ranged from a woman whose war-time role in the British Home Army involved gassing rabbit warrens to prevent the pests from eating much needed produce, to a man who spent four years as a prisoner of war in Japan (221–222).

SOURCES OF EXPERTS

If given the opportunity, many people are willing to come to the classroom and share their expertise with students:

- **Parents.** It is easy to forget this rich source that is so close at hand. Every classroom will have parents who have travelled widely. Many parents may have come to Canada as immigrants. Parents will also have a variety of occupations and interests. It can be useful to send a form home at the beginning of the year outlining topics that the class will be exploring, and asking for parents who have some related expertise to share it.
- **Industry and commerce representatives.** Chambers of commerce, public relations departments of large firms, business lobby groups, owners of small businesses, and professional people such as doctors and lawyers are often prepared to come to schools or to arrange for interviews.
- **Interest and service groups.** Representatives from community organizations such as local historical societies, environmental lobby groups, veterans' organizations, and ethnic group associations are often prepared to meet with students. Museums sometimes provide resource people, as well as kits of materials for classroom use.
- **Government officials.** Politicians are often willing to visit schools to present their perspectives on pertinent issues and to answer student questions. Local law courts, police departments, embassies, and consulates are other possibilities.
- **Individuals with unique backgrounds.** Some people have unique life experiences to share. Such people might include Holocaust survivors, refugees from war-torn countries, and workers for humanitarian organizations in developing countries. The possibilities are limitless.

PREPARATION

Hosting a resource person is likely to be a profitable experience only if both students and guest are adequately prepared. In her article "Beyond Guest Speakers," Diana Hess (2004) discusses the futility of having guests who lecture the class for thirty minutes and answer a few vague or irrelevant student questions. A guest expert's visit is far more likely to be a meaningful experience if there is genuine interaction between the resource person and students. This may mean that the guest does not simply speak to the class but shares artifacts, documents, or issues for students to examine and discuss. The highlighted text, "Checklist for Guest Experts," suggests planning ideas to ensure a meaningful experience.

CHECKLIST FOR GUEST EXPERTS

Students

- ☐ Discuss the objectives of the visit with students.
- ☐ Emphasize that the guest is volunteering valuable time, and therefore students should be on their best behaviour.
- ☐ Help students formulate questions ahead of time. The questions should be in keeping with previously established objectives. They could be listed on the blackboard and then students could choose the most appropriate questions. These questions could be recorded on chart paper.
- ☐ Appoint recorders to record the guest's responses.
- ☐ Involve the class in choosing students to introduce and thank the guest.
- ☐ Allow unstructured time at the end of the session for casual interaction between students and the resource person.

Resource person

- ☐ Consider whether the guest is the best resource for students for this particular topic. Consider alternatives such as audiovisual materials, library resources, and so on.
- ☐ Consider timing. Scheduling the guest's visit for the end of a unit of study rather than at the beginning means that students will have greater background knowledge. This may make the session more rewarding for both students and guest.

- ☐ Discuss with the guest the purpose of the talk, how it fits into the theme of the unit of study, and what the individual can offer to students. Point out aspects that are of particular interest to students. Encourage the guest to do more than simply talk at students; perhaps the guest can bring in materials for the students to examine or develop a topic for students to discuss.
- ☐ Discuss the length of the session. The guest may not be used to being with students at this grade level. Alert the guest to questions that the students may ask.
- ☐ Help the guest prepare content and visuals. Point out the value of interactive learning and the use of visual aids to increase student interest.
- ☐ Determine whether the guest requires specific directions to the school or if transportation arrangements need to be made.
- ☐ Determine audiovisual equipment needs and arrange for necessary equipment to be available.
- ☐ Arrange to meet the guest in advance of the scheduled time.
- ☐ Send the guest a written note of appreciation.

FOLLOW-UP ACTIVITIES

Follow-up activities should provide students with opportunities to compare ideas provided by the expert and previously acquired information, interpret the lessons learned, draw conclusions, and develop further questions. The visit should be acknowledged with a written thank-you letter. Students might also send copies of pictures, stories, or other projects to the visitor.

We have been looking at how to bring the outside in by using our community. As members of a global community, technology offers us the ability to send our students into the world virtually to explore times and places they could never visit. We can also bring guests from around the world into our classes for virtual interviews. Like traditional field trips and interviews, the virtual ones have great potential to enhance student interest and learning in social studies. However, unless the trip or visit is meticulously planned, the virtual experience could become another Franklin expedition.

Community-Developed Materials

In addition to the community resources already discussed—field experiences and resource people—community organizations offer an amazing variety of materials for teachers and students:

- **Consulates.** A vast array of materials are available from some countries (for example, Japan, Switzerland).
- **Federal agencies.** Many national government agencies (for example, Canadian International Development Agency, Library and Archives Canada, National Film Board, Canada Revenue Agency, Citizenship and Immigration Canada) are rich sources of print, electronic, and video resources.
- **Provincial and local services.** Materials are available from fire and law-enforcement services, municipal and provincial bodies, and many local agencies. Museums often have kits of materials that schools can borrow.
- **Political parties.** The websites of major political parties contain information about the party, its organization, and its position on key issues.
- **Resource industries.** Industry associations often work with teachers to develop teaching materials (for example, provincial mining or forestry associations).
- **Environment and development organizations.** Non-governmental groups (for example, Greenpeace, Western Canada Wilderness Committee) can provide materials.

VIRTUAL FIELD TRIPS

An effective model that has been embraced by teachers worldwide is WebQuest, developed by Bernie Dodge, a professor of educational technology at San Diego State University.[2]

Elements of WebQuests

- Introductory information sets the stage and provides background data to stimulate students' curiosity.
- Task that is engaging and is the ultimate focus for the quest.
- Resources needed to complete the task. These are easily accessible, relevant, and selected by the teacher. These include the web sources for all the databases and museums required as well as the e-mail addresses of experts in the area.
- A process that is clearly established in a step-by-step manner.
- A guide on how to organize information. The guides often provide students with specific models for designing

effective graphs, tables, or puzzles that are required to complete their quests.
- An assessment that students understand before they start the quest.
- A conclusion that brings closure to the quest and reinforces what the participants have learned.

Cautions

- Allow time for planning; become familiar with the quest and the range of options offered within it.
- Ensure that the main questions students are asked to research are not simply factual questions, but require critical thinking.
- As with any other instructional design, it must be adapted to student needs, interests, and abilities.
- Allow sufficient class time to use the quest well.
- Book computer labs in advance to avoid last minute organizational glitches.

Community-developed resources may be particularly useful in providing information that presents an alternative, more current perspective than that found in textbooks. Because these materials may not have been originally intended

GOVERNMENT-RELATED RESOURCES

The Library of Parliament website has two very helpful compilations of annually updated resources and programs about parliamentary democracy and citizenship education.

- "Background Resources for Educators" lists resources produced by parliamentary groups, organized under three headings:
  - Parliament
  - Senate
  - House of Commons
    This document can be found online at www.parl.gc.ca/information/about/education/resources/index-e.htm.
- "Links to External Organizations" lists contact information and educational resources available from numerous federal and provincial departments and educational organizations organized under six headings:
  - Information about Parliament
  - Parliamentary history
  - Multimedia
  - Professional development
  - Youth programs and contests
  - Provincial and territorial assemblies
    View this document at www.parl.gc.ca/information/about/education/resources/related/index.asp?Language=E.

for use in classrooms, the information and views contained in them must be scrutinized carefully. The following questions may help teachers critically examine these materials:

- What are the aims of the organization? Are these acceptable in a public education system?
- How are these aims reflected in the materials available to teachers and students?
- Does the organization have any formal ties to education or the production of educational materials?
- How suitable are the materials for classroom use and what levels might they be appropriate for? Can they be adapted for use?
- Which curricular objectives can these materials be used to help attain?
- If the organization provides human resources for classroom or professional purposes, how can these resources be used to enhance social studies?

Conclusion

In an interview, social studies teacher Charles Hou commented:

> It just seems to me that field trips help students connect to history and make it more real. Students use all of their senses on a field trip. They don't really remember much of what they learn in school; but this is something they will remember for the rest of

their lives. Field trips are the best way of teaching. A lot of teachers get discouraged, but they are the best way of teaching (cited in Clark 2000, 4).

A rich social studies program requires access to a wide array of resources, including those in the community. Community resources offer important experiences and insights that can deepen student understanding of social studies. Careful preparation is the key to making the most of such resources. Preparation includes carefully choosing a field-trip site or resource person, making students aware of the purposes for using the resource, and helping students develop questions to guide their discovery. Most importantly, unlike the teacher described at the beginning of this chapter, let us not ignore the exciting possibilities all around us. The rewards are immense.

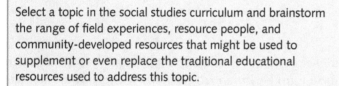

Select a topic in the social studies curriculum and brainstorm the range of field experiences, resource people, and community-developed resources that might be used to supplement or even replace the traditional educational resources used to address this topic.

NOTES

1. I would like to thank Marjorie Redbourn, a student in a Simon Fraser University social studies methods class, for reminding me of this episode of *The Wonder Years* and its applicability to field experiences.
2. Thanks to Bill Willson, who is a retired social studies teacher and sessional instructor at the University of British Columbia for his ideas regarding WebQuests.

REFERENCES

BC students team up to build school in Kenyan village. 1999. *BC Education News*, April: 5.

Clark, P. 2000. Making social studies real. *Canadian Social Studies* 34 (2): 4.

Corcoran, L. and T. Thompson. 1999. City reflections. *The Newsletter of Rockridge School*, May: 2–5.

Hess, D. 2004. Beyond guest speakers. *Social Education* 68 (5): 347–348.

McDiarmid, G.L. 1970. The value of on-site learning. *Orbit* 1 (3): 4–7.

Oliver, H. 1970. Philadelphia's parkway program. *Orbit* 1 (3): 22–23.

Sears, A. 1999. Using interviews in social studies. In *The Canadian anthology of social studies,* eds. R. Case and P. Clark, 221–225. Vancouver: Pacific Educational Press.

27 Using Primary Documents in Social Studies and History

Ruth W. Sandwell

Teachers are increasingly urged to include primary documents—records or evidence of the past created in the past—in their teaching of history and social studies. Primary documents have clear advantages over textbook accounts. Historical documents such as diaries, photographs, letters, and even house-by-house census manuscripts provide personal points of entry into history. They can offer eye-opening perspectives for students who believe that history is impersonal and therefore irrelevant to their lives. Criminal trials, inquests, and newspapers offer a sense of immediacy about the past, providing students with a window on history that is more urgent and interesting than textbook histories. However, the usefulness of primary documents is not limited to their ability to entertain students. Initially engaged by the immediacy or personal nature of primary documents, many teachers use primary sources as a "hook" to draw students into historical thinking. In the process of thinking critically about these documents, students develop a deeper understanding of the content—the larger events, themes, and issues of history—in meaningful ways that are likely to be remembered beyond the final exam. Students who learn to use primary documents effectively learn how to "do" history like historians, interpreting evidence to piece together a narrative of historical explanation and to make richer sense of the everyday world around them.

Despite these advantages, their potential is not always realized for at least three reasons:

- difficulties in finding useful documents,
- challenges in using documents to advance an already crowded curriculum,
- uncertainty about how to teach students to analyze them critically.

I address each of these challenges, providing suggestions for finding and using primary documents effectively. I conclude by arguing that use of primary documents is not only possible for busy teachers who need to meet specific curriculum requirements, but also central to the very reasons for teaching history.

The "What" and "Where" of Primary Documents

Teachers are often uncertain about what constitutes a primary source, what kinds of information primary documents contain, or where to find historical documents appropriate for classroom use. This section defines primary documents and explores the particular benefits that primary documents can offer to teachers of social studies and history. I provide examples of how historians use historical documents, and where they might be found.

DEFINING PRIMARY DOCUMENTS

Primary documents are those records created in the past, at or close to the time under study, that have survived into the present. Historians have traditionally used a wide variety of written records, from personal diaries created by a child to statistical records kept by government departments, as the foundation for their historical investigations. More recently, historians have been drawing on non-document records, including photographs, moving pictures, the spoken word, and even architectural plans or botanical (plant) inventories to find clues about how people lived in the past. All of these primary documents are, in an important sense, the "raw materials" that historians work with as they attempt to figure out what happened in the past, and what it means to us in the present.

Ultimately, primary documents are our sole sources of

evidence about the past. But what they reveal depends on the questions that historians ask. For example, statistics about factory wages in Canada in 1914 might be used by a historian to prove any number of conclusions, including the following:

- women were paid less than men,
- the economy in Canada was in a slump in that year,
- Montreal was the leading manufacturing centre in Canada in the pre-war years,
- the Canadian government was more interested in factory work (since it collected these kinds of statistics) than it was in child-raising practices (about which few statistics were collected).

As the historian E.H. Carr explains in his famous book, *What is History?*:

> The facts are really not at all like fish on the fishmonger's slab. They are like fish swimming about in a vast and sometimes inaccessible ocean, and what the historian catches will depend, partly on chance, but mainly on what part of the ocean he chooses to fish in and what tackle he chooses to use—these two facts being, of course, determined by what kind of fish he wants to catch. By and large, the historian will get the kinds of facts he wants (1961, 23).

The uses to which primary sources can be put, in other words, have as much to do with the questions asked by the historian using them as they do with the "facts" they contain.

IDENTIFYING PRIMARY DOCUMENTS

There are literally millions of potentially usable primary documents. Fortunately, school boards, ministries of education, and other educational organizations have compiled collections and lists of primary documents. It is well worth the time to examine these sources. Many of these guides to primary sources are available online.

In Table 27.1 are listed examples of primary documents routinely used by historians, with a brief description of what they contain, and suggestions about where you might find them.

TABLE 27.1 COMMON DOCUMENTS AND WHERE TO FIND THEM		
KIND OF RECORD	**DESCRIPTION**	**WHERE TO FIND THEM**
Family records	Personal letters, diaries, family photographs, newspaper cuttings, inventories of possessions, clothing.	Attics, basements, shoe boxes, archives, museums, historical societies.
Census records	A wide variety of information about individuals and families, household by household, before 1901 across Canada, including age, marital status, place of birth, ethnicity, date of immigration to Canada, income, and employment. The aggregate data (the "counting up" of the information in the household census material) is available for all censuses.	The government of Canada protects individual information on the Census of Canada for 94 years and makes it available to the public in archives and online after that time period. Aggregate (non-individual) data is available as soon it is generated by Stats Canada, which has also compiled historical statistics for public and educational use on their website at http://www.statcan.ca/english/freepub/11-516-XIE/sectiona/toc.htm.
Wills and probate files	Provincial governments across Canada obtained and preserved in their archives copies of all wills that were legally registered. They contain information about the individual, as well as family and community relations, and property. Probate files, created when a will is put into effect, provide detailed information about the deceased person's financial status, including lists of possessions.	Provincial and local archives.
Cemetery records	Cemetery headstones often contain a wealth of information about individuals and the families and communities in which they lived.	Local historical societies are good places to find listings or "rubbings" of cemetery stones. Many offer cemetery tours.

TABLE 27.1   COMMON DOCUMENTS AND WHERE TO FIND THEM (CONT.)

KIND OF RECORD	DESCRIPTION	WHERE TO FIND THEM
Birth and death records	The federal and provincial governments have been keeping track of vital statistics (records of births and deaths) and publishing these statistics in annual reports in the Vital Statistics portions of the Sessional Papers for over 140 years. These records provide information about individual family members, but also provide a lot of statistical information that helps us understand how people lived and how and why they died.	National registers are now available for much of Canada online from some provincial archives and the National Archives of Canada (www.archives.ca); for earlier time periods, and particularly in Quebec, parish records of births, marriages, and deaths can be found in churches, local historical societies, or church archives.
Old maps	Useful for understanding how a place and the people in it have changed, and what remains the same.	Local, provincial, and national archives; local historical societies; museums; a variety of online sources.
Photographs and moving images	Rich source of information about and impressions of people, places, and events.	Personal papers; local, provincial, and national archives.
Household artifacts	Items in use in everyday life in the past can provide real insights into how people lived before electricity or indoor plumbing.	Flea markets, second-hand stores, church bazaars, basements, museums, local historical societies.
Newspapers	Historic newspapers provide an up-close view of particular events as seen at the time. Each edition also provides a snapshot of news, local events, advertising, and letters to the editor that can provide great insight into local as well as national and international views.	Newspapers are available on microfilm and online through most municipal and university libraries. Indexed newspapers are the easiest to use, because you can search by topic through time. Ask the librarian or archivist for an index list.
Court records	Criminal trials, inquests, depositions, and civil cases provide an excellent view of conflicts in society, and what people thought of them.	Provincial or national archives.
Historical textbooks	A number of university libraries across the country have collections of textbooks used in elementary and secondary schools in the nineteenth and twentieth centuries.	University libraries, school archives, local museums and archives.
Military records	There are a wide variety of records pertaining to the military and war generally. They can include enlistment and war pension information.	Department of National Defense, national archives.
Business and industry records	Business records can provide detailed information about the kinds of industry in Canada, as well as information about work and employment conditions experienced by people in the past. Many Canadian towns are or have been single resource communities, and company records may provide detailed information about the wider community, its problems, and its successes.	Records of local and national businesses may have been deposited in local, provincial, or national archives. Occasionally, businesses themselves create and maintain their own archives that are open to the public (such as Rogers Sugar in Vancouver).
Local government records	These records are generally the official records created in the running of a municipal or local government. They can reveal a wealth of information about a community, from police records to agricultural fairs to protests against commercial development to welfare rolls.	Municipal or local archives.

LOCATING PRIMARY DOCUMENTS ONLINE

The internet is largely responsible for the recent burst of interest in primary documents in teaching. Before documents were available online, researchers had to visit archives in person, and hunt through multiple card catalogues. Prior to large scale computerization of primary documents, educational publishers assembled small selections of primary documents useful in teaching, the most famous being the "Jackdaws" series. Jackdaws provided file folders with reproductions of a variety of primary sources—letters, photographs, government reports—about a particular issue or event, and students were guided through their interpretation with supporting materials. Finding primary documents has become much easier now that many archival documents are available—and fully indexed—online. At the end of this chapter is an extensive list of searchable databases of primary documents useful in secondary school teaching in Canada, and many provide grade-appropriate online support materials.[1]

> Identify a topic in the curriculum dealing with a historical event or person. Think of three kinds of primary document that you might use as an entry point to raise important themes connected with the historical topic you have identified. List several questions to ask students to guide them in thinking about the bigger issues raised by each kind of document.

The "How" and "When" of Primary Documents

Before discussing how and when primary documents might be most effectively used in the classroom, a more general point needs to be emphasized. Primary sources are the *only* authentic connections between the past and the present. Without evidence available in the present that is "left over" from the past, we have no sure way of knowing "what happened" or what it meant. Professional historians may have greater skill at finding and interpreting evidence from the past than other people, and they certainly have a greater knowledge of how other historians have used the available evidence, but, in the end, all historians "do" is to interpret evidence from the past available through primary documents, usually in the context of what other historians have written. While history is generally defined as "the story of the past" or "what really happened"—as a finished product, as a fixed body of knowledge—the study of primary documents introduces students to the idea that history is not simply "what happened." Instead, they learn

that history is *an active process of developing knowledge, an act of interpretation.* As one of my student teachers put it, using primary documents in the history and social studies classroom teaches students that history is a verb, not a noun.

INTRODUCING THE IDEA OF PRIMARY DOCUMENTS

Students need time and practice to get used to the idea that history is a contextualized dialogue about evidence (usually written documents) from the past, and that students can participate in that dialogue, if only as beginners, by finding and analyzing primary documents. Students need to learn, in other words, how to engage critically with the evidence contained in primary documents, and to recognize that this activity is "doing" history. The following activities illustrate some of the ways to introduce students to the role of primary documents in the construction of history:

- ask students to keep a record of the documents they create in a given week, of the "traces" that they are leaving behind for future historians to find (phone message, e-mail, homework);
- arrange for students to create a journal, diary, or short essay that they might leave for historians of the future;
- get students to create a "time capsule" that best represents their lives, the lives of their family, or their school;
- invite students to write a history of their lives or of their family based only on the documentary evidence available in their home.

The highlighted text, "Seeing Myself in the Future's Past," describes in detail an activity to introduce students to the idea that primary documents are the "raw materials" or the building blocks on which they can base their interpretations of the past.

SUGGESTIONS FOR EMBEDDING PRIMARY DOCUMENTS

Of all the reasons given for not using primary documents in the classroom, concerns about curriculum coverage are the most frequently heard. Many teachers feel that primary document analysis is simply too time-consuming within an already overcrowded curriculum. It can seem impossible to take the time necessary to examine a primary document about a particular issue or event when there is so much other information to cover. Moreover, many teachers may be uncertain how to use primary sources to their full advantage, as ways of teaching content knowledge, research skills, and critical thinking.

Although most teachers feel constrained by curriculum

SEEING MYSELF IN THE FUTURE'S PAST

Introduce the following scenario to students:
A historian of the twenty-third century, feeling that teenagers have been misunderstood through time, wants to write a history of teenagers. The historian wants to know about all aspects of teenage life, from work, family life, and formal education to leisure activities, social life, and personal issues of concern to the twenty-first century teenager. Explain that while historians read a lot of things written by other historians, the books and articles they write are based on their own research into evidence created in the past—called primary documents—that have been preserved into the present. Students are to suggest answers to the following question:

> What records will the students in the class have left behind that this historian might use to understand teenage life? What records about their life will have been created and might be preserved for that historian to find?

Record their responses on the board, encouraging students, if needed, with the following suggestions. Issues to raise about the creation or preservation of each source are in parentheses.

- diaries and journals (Who will keep them? Will they make it into a public archives, as hundreds of thousands have in the past?)
- e-mails (Will they be preserved? Will they be machine-readable in the future?)
- credit card bills (Where will they be stored? Will historians have access to them?)
- home movies (Will the technology still exist to view them?)
- photographs (Who will preserve them? Will they be in public archives?)

- school records stored by the school and then by the provincial archives, as required by law (Who will have access to them in the future? If they are kept by individuals, who will preserve them and who will have access to them?)
- school work (How will this be preserved?)
- clothing (How will someone in the future understand what the clothing "means"?)
- music (How will someone in the future understand what the music means? Will the technology exist to listen to it?)
- court records—juvenile court records may become part of the public domain after 100 years
- census records—every Canadian will appear on the census if they are in Canada in a census year, even though their individual information will not be available to historians for 96 years
- birth, marriage, and death records (What might these tell someone in the future about teenage life—AIDS statistics, car accidents, teenage pregnancy?).

In pairs, ask students to rank the three sources from the list that will be most useful to the historian wanting to learn about teenagers in the early twenty-first century. Explain how to complete the chart below using one source (e-mails, Visa bills, photographs) as an example.

After completing the chart, arrange for each group to present its best sources to the class. Discuss the limits and potential misrepresentations that arise when historians draw conclusions from the available sources that may be partial and incomplete. As an extension, invite students to identify the very worst source for representing their lives, and to write a one-page history based on that source. Debrief how this would misrepresent their lives.

SOURCE	WHAT WILL THE HISTORIAN LEARN ABOUT ME?	WHAT INFERENCES ABOUT TEENAGE LIFE MIGHT THE HISTORIAN DRAW FROM THIS EVIDENCE?
Best source:		
Second best:		
Third best:		

requirements, Canadian history and social studies teachers have considerably more freedom in their selection of materials within the curriculum than do most other teachers. Teachers are more likely to find the time and enhance their coverage of the curriculum if they attend to four principles when embedding primary documents in their teaching.

ILLUSTRATE MORE THAN ONE CURRICULAR THEME, ISSUE, OR EVENT

Primary documents must be explicitly connected to the broad themes in the curriculum. When choosing a primary document, teachers should ask themselves (and their students) what "big idea" the source represents. In fact, the most effective primary sources will address multiple objectives within the curriculum. For example, an examination of World War I posters might allow students to explore various themes from Canadian history and identity from nationalism to women's participation in society to conscription to regionalism. Finding primary documents that illuminate several issues or events helps to allay fears that document analysis takes up too much time because it is covering too little subject matter. The strategy in Figure 27.1 is useful in helping students draw insights from primary documents about an individual's

| FIGURE 27.1   IDENTIFYING PERSPECTIVES |

Provide two supporting reasons from the historical documents for each rating.

LOYALTY TO CANADA					
	5	4	3	2	1
	strongly unpatriotic				*strongly patriotic*
Clues from the document			**Possible conclusions**		
•			•		
•			•		
Questions					

VIEWS ON IMMIGRATION					
	5	4	3	2	1
	very welcoming				*highly restrictive*
Clues from the document			**Possible conclusions**		
•			•		
•			•		
Questions					

ECONOMIC VALUES					
	5	4	3	2	1
	strongly socialist				*strongly capitalist*
Clues from the document			**Possible conclusions**		
•			•		
•			•		
Questions					

or groups' perspectives on a range of topics. Students are expected to look for clues in a primary document that suggest how a particular individual or group might have felt about the identified issues.

USE PRIMARY DOCUMENTS TO ADD VALUE TO EXISTING RESOURCES

Primary documents work best when they add value to existing resources in at least two ways:

- **enhance content knowledge:** add value to the textbook and other resources by exemplifying, extending, or even contradicting key facts in the textbook.
- **engage students:** draw students into a topic by presenting an immediate and often vivid and dramatic perspective on a topic.

A letter describing life in the trenches at Passchendaele can reinforce "facts" about World War I, and a testimonial about child labour in a nineteenth-century factory will help

PERSONALIZING THE PAST

Typical textbook account of Jewish immigrants (1930–1948)

During the 1930s, "isolationism"—the desire by many Canadians not to get involved in European conflicts—became very strong. The economic collapse, or Great Depression, that occurred in this decade resulted in the Canadian government taking measures to prevent immigration into Canada. Many Jews who wanted to escape persecution in Nazi Germany were refused entry into Canada during this time. In one instance, 907 Jewish refugees aboard the *S.S. St. Louis* were refused entry into Canada. The ship was forced to return to Nazi Europe. Between 1933 and 1945 Canada admitted only 5,000–8,000 refugees, the worst record of any large non-European country (Misfeldt and Case 2002, 74).

Excerpt from an interview with Mariette Rozen, a Jewish war orphan who arrived in Canada in 1947 (reported in Miller 1997).

Arrival in Canada
I arrived in Canada on December 2, 1947. I was twelve years old but with the mind of an old person. I wore a name tag, pinned to my coat with a safety pin. We went into a building with bars on the window. It looked like a prison to me and I worried that I had done something wrong. We had been told that Canada was a free country and that we would be welcome, but when we arrived, we were guarded like we were in a prison camp.

   What they put us through when we arrived in Halifax was terrible. The customs officers took everything we had, and we were too afraid to mention this to anyone. I still had a little diamond ring that my sister Sara had given me, and I tried to hide it. Throughout the entire war I had saved the ring. They removed the diamond, took my money and loose coins. I think the custom officers took advantage of us but we didn't want to make trouble so none of us ever reported those things. Finally, after they examined us, we were put on a train across Canada. On January 3, 1948 we arrived at the train station at the foot of Granville Street in downtown Vancouver.

Becoming Canadian
I had no expectations about what Canada would be like, none.

Mariette Rozen

For a long time afterwards, I wanted to hide who I was and where I had come from. I didn't want to associate with other survivors, because I did not want to be identified as a survivor. My siblings and I were like strangers. Because we had been separated throughout the war, we were not bonded like most families. We loved each other but we seemed to have nothing in common. That's what the war did to us. To this day, I have trouble trusting people.

   We were all worried about who we were going to live with in Canada. When we arrived in Vancouver I was separated from my sister and brothers. We all went to live in different homes. I went to live with my foster parents, Joe and Minnie Satanov, who were childless. When Mr. Satanov came to the train station and saw me, he said, "I want that little girl." The social worker Jean Rose, took me to their great big house. Mrs. Satanov was in the kitchen ironing and didn't even look my way when I arrived. I knew right then that she didn't want me but I had no choice and I was too tired. They took me to my room and Jean Rose said good-bye. I asked for Esther's, Jacques' and Henri's phone number and I called them right away and told them to come and get me.

students remember key issues about employers and employees, long after the textbook section on war or industrialization has been forgotten. So too, primary documents can engage students in issues as arcane and seemingly remote as Canadian confederation debates and the conscription crisis by expressing a sense of urgency or representing the issues in very personal ways.

The use of primary documents to enrich information found in textbooks and to provide a gripping hook to draw students into the topic is illustrated in the highlighted text, "Personalizing the Past." It suggests supplementing a typical secondary account of Canada's response to attempts by European Jews to escape Nazi persecution with a young Jewish girl's autobiographical account of her arrival in Canada just after the war. As you read both accounts, image the deficiency in students' appreciation of the meaning of Canada's response if they had read solely the textbook account.

MAKE THE TEXT AND CONTEXT ACCESSIBLE TO STUDENTS

Historians best describe their work as being about "text" and "context." "Text" does not refer to textbooks, but to the primary documents that they use as the sources of evidence about the past. "Context" refers to the material other historians and writers have written and published on the historical topic. The challenges of historical text and context are vexing to social studies and history teachers: How can we help students learn to read the primary document for literal meaning and acquire the background knowledge about the topic they need in order to make sense of and contextualize what they are reading? The more students understand the text and historical context, the better equipped they are to benefit from use of primary documents. The activity in the highlighted text, "Pre-Reading Historical Documents," illustrates a strategy for preparing students to read a primary document by inviting them to anticipate its contents based on the clues found in a list of key vocabulary provided by the teacher. Other ideas for tools to help students interpret cartoons, photographs, maps, and other primary documents are found in the Learning Centre Toolkit available on the Library and Archives Canada website (www.collectionscanada.gc.ca/education/008-3000-e.html).

The more knowledgeable a teacher is about the subject, the easier it is to select appropriate documents and to provide the context that will help him or her use these documents to advance the curriculum. Teachers who are worried about providing adequate background context might want to purchase a university level textbook for the period covered by the course they are teaching.

PRE-READING HISTORICAL DOCUMENTS[2]

Prior to sharing a primary document for students to interpret, invite them to anticipate its contents based on key terms you have extracted from the document. Make a list of 15 to 20 words that are key to interpreting the text or will be difficult for students to understand. Explain any words from the list that are unfamiliar to students. Invite students to use the words to anticipate the contents of an as-yet-unseen document. Indicate that they are to use five questions known as R.A.F.T.S. (Role, Audience, Format, Topic, Strong Verb) to guide their investigation:

R the **role** from which the author created the document (for example, a government official, a concerned citizen, a business leader, someone with much or little power)
A the **audience** for whom the writing was intended (for example, themselves, the writer's peers, the general public, a social superior, a government official)
F the **format** in which the document was written (for example, official letter, formal essay, post card, diary)
T the **topic** about which the document is written (for example, a recent event, problems in the community, plans for the future)
S a **strong verb** that best captures the tone or overall purpose of the document (for example, plead, persuade, complain, inform).

Encourage students to answer as many as possible of the R.A.F.T.S. questions using the list of key words as clues. Invite students to summarize their preliminary conclusions about the document using the following structure:

I think _____ role _____ created
a _____ format _____ about
_____ topic _____ to
_____ strong verb _____ directed
to _____ audience _____ .

Encourage students to support their tentative conclusions with evidence and to challenge alternative interpretations presented by others in the class. Students are now ready to view the actual document and assess their conclusions about its contents.

INVITE CRITICAL THINKING, NOT JUST RECITATION OF FACTS

Unfortunately, primary historical documents are often used to emphasize only superficial and the most accessible aspects of the documents, and leave untapped the documents' deeper potential to stimulate critical thinking and historical understanding. Recent research suggests that students are most comfortable using primary documents—particularly those available on the world wide web—to simply get to the answer that they think the teacher wants as quickly as possible. When designing lessons that use primary documents, teachers can best use their potential to stimulate critical thinking by asking students questions that do not simply require them to find particular pieces of information, or come up with a single right answer. Instead, lessons should be framed that require students to think critically by offering a judgment based on criteria.

One way to promote critical thinking is to provide students with more than one primary document to analyze. This allows us to invite students to assess the relative merits of various records. For example, students might compare the representation of a single event in three different sources—a newspaper, a trial record, and a diary—and decide which account provides the clearest picture of life at the time under study. They might compare the coverage of a single event in three different newspapers. Alternatively, we might ask students to draw conclusion about an event based on several sources. As Figure 27.2 illustrates, students might be asked to analyze letters to the editor, statistical data, and Hansard records in an attempt to understand historical attempts to support bilingualism in Canada.

The "Why" of Using Primary Documents

While many teachers appreciate the interest and enthusiasm that primary documents stimulate in their students, there remains a lingering uncertainty about just what, exactly, the study of primary documents accomplishes in the history classroom. If history is a narrative about facts already

---

FIGURE 27.2   USING MULTIPLE SOURCES

In 1927, the post office issued bilingual stamps to commemorate Canada's sixtieth anniversary, and continued to do so. In 1934, R.B. Bennett created the Bank of Canada and authorized the printing of bank notes in either French or English. In 1936, Mackenzie King decided that the bank should end this practice and provide bilingual bank notes in both French and English. Based on the historical documents, argue whether or not Canada should have adopted bilingual currency in 1936.

Document #1

It is an insult to any loyal Protestant to think that every time we post a letter we have to lick a bilingual postage stamp, and every time we buy a postcard or money order, we are insulted by the French language being given equal prominence with English.... If the French get away with this it will not be long before they will give us bilingual coins and Federal bills.

Letter to the editor, The Sentinel and Orange and Protestant Advocate, *Chatham ON, March 14, 1929*

Document #2

Are official bilingualism and the equality of the races in the Constitution rights or are they myths? Are they legal and political realities or simply oratorical devices for the first day of July for naive French Canadians? If the contract of 1867 was not a fool's bargain, why does a single race reserve for itself the rights to use its own language, and nothing but its own, on one of the principal official documents which affirms at home and abroad the national character of the state.

L' Action Nationale, *Montreal, February 1933*

Document #3

Ethnic breakdown of population

Ethnic Origin	Percent
French	28%
English	26%
Scottish	13%
Irish	12%
German	5%
Scandinavian	2%
Hebrew	2%
Ukrainian	2%
Other	10%

Canadian Census, *1931*

Document #4

I have been amazed...to see this house spending a day and a half discussing what to many people in Canada is a very trivial aspect of this bill.... I cannot help feeling that if the hon. members had used as much energy and as much heat in getting money into the pockets of the people as they have in worrying about the language in which the money is printed, we would be a great deal further ahead. Being a Scotsman, I am glad to get a dollar whether it is printed in Siamese or Chinese, provided I can buy something with it.

T.C. Douglas, House of Commons Debates, *June 16, 1936*

"discovered" and interpreted by expert historians, what is the point of asking students, with their limited experience and knowledge, to examine documents from the past? Isn't the analysis of primary documents more "busy work" added to the real work of the course as a diversion or entertainment for the students (Barton 2005)?

In his well-known study, Samuel Wineburg (1991) asked students and historians to think aloud as they read historical texts, both primary and secondary. He noted that whereas historians entered into a complex dialogue with the multiple meanings of the text, students were usually able to marshal only one kind of question about what they were reading: is it true? With little familiarity with primary documents, without the appropriate background information, and without an understanding of the processes of critical inquiry, students were unable to engage in discussions of how to construct historical knowledge from the documents.

Wineburg's research helped to promote the use of primary documents in history classrooms, but recent research suggests that they are seldom used to promote critical inquiry. With proper instruction, researchers such as Keith Barton (1997), Stella Weinert (2001), and Bruce Van Sledright (2002) have demonstrated, students as young as 7 years old are able to learn and apply sophisticated understandings of historical selection and construction, learning to deal with complex narratives and conflicting evidence. However, even when students have been taught how to interpret documents critically, they are often reluctant to use these skills.

Instead, students often prefer to follow the path of least resistance in getting to the answer that they think the teacher wants. As Barton (1997) notes, "rather than evaluating information from multiple sources, students move directly to search engines to find the sites they thought would give them all the necessary information to accomplish the task." Even after intensive training sessions where students have demonstrated their skills at evaluating complex historical evidence, students are more likely to give whatever answer they think the teacher wants by guessing at an answer, justifying their answer by saying "I just kinda know."

One of the reasons for this unwillingness to think critically about history appears to be a deep attachment by many students to the belief that history is, quite simply, not about the process of interpretation, but about facts, information, and absolute knowledge. While some students demonstrate sophisticated understanding of the past as a constructed narrative, the vast majority accept the past as a given or as simply inaccessible. For these students, critical inquiry is seen as irrelevant to the study of history.

While students are capable of critical analysis, students tend to revert when approaching historical documents to one question: Is it true? (Wineburg 1991; Grant and VanSledright

2001). Since no account *could possibly* be unequivocally true, students' attempts to analyze primary documents as "the truth" or "the facts" immediately collapse. What they collapse into, most commonly, is attempts to discover the primary document's bias (Seixas 1998; Barton 1997). Bias has the advantage for students and many teachers of looking like both a foundational truth ("every point of view is biased") and a tool for critical inquiry ("by uncovering the bias, we can critically examine the truth behind the document").

Discussions of bias, though certainly valuable in some areas of historical study, when applied to the study of primary documents usually serve only to reduce students' potential for understanding history. This is because bias is used to describe the very things that need to be explained in critical historical inquiry: What are the factors that can explain why the author of the primary document represented the world the way he or she did? What were the economic forces, social influences, historical chronology, family situations, ethnic origin, or gender and age factors that made the world look the way it did for the person creating that document? Examined through the lens of "bias," the complexities of historical interpretation get reduced to simplistic and stereotyped impressions about the self-interest of the person who created the document.

Once students identify the bias of the document's creator, they believe that they have satisfied the requirements of critical analysis. Students routinely declare the document biased and conclude that it is therefore unworthy of consideration (Wineburg 1991). Discussion then moves on to another topic. When students are challenged about the usefulness of the term "bias," they typically declare, with some frustration, that it is, after all, impossible to find a single truth about what happened, and so every interpretation can only be "just his or her own opinion" (Barton 1997).

For these students, then, at an important level, historical knowledge is not so much irrelevant as impossible to obtain. Their encounters with primary documents represent a process of swinging wildly between two opposite and mutually contradictory beliefs: the complete belief in the single coherent truth tantalizingly implied by the word "bias," and a belief in the impossibility of any knowledge, underwritten by a kind of relativism (Grant and Van Sledright 2001). Historians, I would argue, spend their days contemplating how we negotiate that livable and comprehensible middle ground between complete relativism and absolute truth. How to do this defines the discipline of history.

Given the emphasis on "the facts" and history as a single truth, it is really not surprising that North American students find irrelevant and meaningless the kinds of critical inquiry so relevant to historians. Students need to experience the idea that history is an open but disciplined dialogue about evidence. They will not encounter this idea if history is presented through lectures and textbooks as a series of facts, the knowledge of which is measured by standardized tests. Sadly, most will not encounter this idea of history as a process of critical inquiry at university either, because historical knowledge, though perhaps in a more complex way, is still presented there through lectures and scholarly monographs as a series of more or less self-evident facts—a product, rather than a process, of inquiry. It is no wonder that many students see document-based inquiry as busy work added to the real course material.

The disconnect between what historians do and what history teachers teach their students highlights yet again the question: Why teach history at all? History does not just allow us to learn lessons from certain events in the past. This kind of critical inquiry is exactly the kind of complicated and compassionate process of knowledge-building that we need to have to understand our contemporary world. How do we know what accounts in the media make sense in terms of evidence and interpretation? How do we evaluate the significance of a particular event in our own lives, or in the lives of others? How do we find the language to talk about the kind of world we want for humanity? The process of historical inquiry—the dialogue among people about evidence from the past—is the best way to explore who we were and are, and how we can turn that into who we as the human race want to be (Barton and Levstick 2004).

Conclusion

If teachers believe that history is the true facts about "what really happened" organized within a clearly defined "master narrative" of national development or progress, then primary documents will indeed have only a limited appeal. Usually written by one person from one point of view, and often a clearly biased or openly contradicted one at that, primary documents do not always lend themselves to teaching the coherent narrative that passes for history in so many provincial and territorial jurisdictions. Ironically, the same documents that provide the foundation of historical research can seem irrelevant to teaching history. As students encounter primary documents, they gain an opportunity to open up to inquiry the ways that knowledge is constructed from evidence. They are learning to think like historians. The point is *not*, however, to change every student into an amateur historian but to give students the tools to think cirtically and creatively about human societies, including our own. I have suggested where to find and how to select and use primary documents that work within curricular constraints. I have discussed how teachers can use primary documents to support the coherent narrative of history presented in most Canadian history and social studies curricula. But I have also suggested how teachers can take full advantage of the fragmentation and dissonance of primary documents to teach a history that involves students in the meaningful, active, and disciplined construction of knowledge.

Assemble at least two primary documents that pertain to a historical topic in the curriculum. Design a lesson to help students use these documents to learn about a broad theme or "big idea" of the curriculum. Provide details and sample resources indicating how you will teach students to analyze the sources and interpret them in light of background information about the topic.

NOTES

1. Thanks to Marian Press in the Education Commons of the Ontario Institute for Studies in Education of the University of Toronto for her help in assembling the list of websites supporting the use of primary documents.
2. I am grateful to my colleague Garfield Gini-Newman for developing this strategy.

REFERENCES

Barton, K.C. 1997. "I just kinda know": Elementary students' ideas about historical evidence. *Theory and Research in Social Education* 25: 407–430.

———. 2005. Primary sources in history: Breaking through the myths. *Phi Delta Kappa* 86 (10): 745–753.

Barton, K. C. and L.S. Levstik. 2004. *Teaching history for the common good.* London: Lawrence Erlbaum Associates.

Carr, E.H. 1961. *What is history?* Middlesex, UK: Penguin Books.

Grant, S.G. and B. Van Sledright. 2001. *Constructing a powerful approach to teaching and learning in elementary social studies.* Boston: Houghton Mifflin.

Miller, F. 1997. *Journey to Canada: The war orphans project 1947–1949.* Vancouver: Vancouver Holocaust Education Centre. Available online at the "Open Hearts/Closed Doors: The War Orphans Project," http://www.virtualmuseum.ca/Exhibitions/orphans/english/biographies/rozen/chapter1.html.

Misfeldt, C. and R. Case, eds. 2002. *Immigration in 20th century Canada.* Vancouver: The Critical Thinking Consortium and the British Columbia Ministry of Education.

Seixas, P. 1998. Student teachers thinking historically. *Theory and Research in Social Education* 26 (3): 310–341.

Van Sledright, B.A. 2002. Fifth-graders investigating history in the classroom: Results from a researcher-practitioner design experiment. *Elementary School Journal* 103 (2): 131–160.

Weinert, S.R. 2001. Young children's historical understanding, Unpublished master's thesis. Vancouver: Centre for the Study of Curriculum and Instruction, University of British Columbia.

Wineburg, S. 1991. On the reading of historical texts: Notes on the breach between school and academy. *American Educational Research Journal* 28 (3): 495–519.

SUPPLEMENTAL READING

Lee, P. and R. Ashby. 2001. Progression in historical understanding among students ages 7–14. In *Knowing, teaching and learning history: National and international perspectives*, eds. P. Stearns, P. Seixas, and S. Wineburg, 199–222. New York: New York University Press.

Levstik, L.S. and K.C. Barton. 2001. *Doing history: Investigating with children in elementary and middle schools.* Mahwah, NJ: Erlbaum.

Milson, A.J. 2002. The internet and inquiry learning: The integration of medium and method in a sixth grade social studies classroom. *Theory and Research in Social Education* 30 (3): 330–353.

Milson, A.J. and P. Downey. 2001. WebQuest: Using internet resources for cooperative inquiry. *Social Education* 65 (3): 144–146.

Paxton, R.J. and S.S. Wineburg. 2000. Expertise and the teaching of history. In *Routledge international companion to education*, eds. B. Moon, M. Ben Peretz, and S. Brown, 855–864. London: Routledge.

Pope, D.C. 2001. *"Doing school": How we are creating a generation of stressed out, materialistic, and miseducated students.* New Haven: Yale University Press.

Sandwell, R.S. ed. 2006. *To the past: History education, public memory and citizenship education in Canada.* Toronto: University of Toronto Press.

Seixas, P. 1993. The community of inquiry as a basis for knowing and learning: The case of history. *American Educational Research Journal* 30 (2): 305–324.

———. 1996. Conceptualizing the growth of historical understanding. In *Handbook of education and human development: New models of learning, teaching, and schooling*, eds. D. Olson and N. Torrance, 765–783, Oxford: Blackwell.

Stodolsky, S.S., S. Salk, and B. Glaessner. 1991. Student views about learning math and social studies. *American Educational Research Journal* 28: 89–116.

Wertsch, J.V. 2001. Is it possible to teach beliefs, as well as knowledge about history? In *Knowing, teaching and learning history: National and international perspectives*, eds. P. Stearns, P. Seixas, and S. Wineburg, 38–50. New York: New York University Press.

Wilson, S.M. 2001. Review of history teaching. In *Handbook of research on teaching*, ed. V. Richardson, 527–565. Washington DC: American Educational Research Association.

Winebury, S. 2001. *Historical thinking and other unnatural acts: Charting the future of teaching the past.* Philadelphia: Temple University Press.

OTHER RESOURCES

GATEWAY SITES

Academic Info: Canadian History
http://www.academicinfo.net/canhist.html
Links to Canadian history websites, principally those with some full text documents.

Canadian Archival Resources on the Internet
http://www.archivescanada.ca/car/menu.html
Provides a comprehensive list of links to Canadian archives and associated resources on the internet. These include links to individual repositories, multi-repository databases, archival listservs, archival associations, educational opportunities, and other related sites.

Canadian Institute for Historic Microreproductions
http://www.canadiana.ca/en/cihm
CIHM was established in 1978 to locate early printed Canadian materials (books, annuals, and periodicals), to preserve their content on microfilm, and to make the resulting collections available to libraries and archives in Canada and abroad. A wide selection of these materials is now available, in searchable form, online.

MERLOT
http://history.merlot.org/
Links to online learning materials are collected here, along with annotations such as peer reviews and assignments.

Schoolshistory.org.uk
http://www.schoolshistory.org.uk/
Based on the history curriculum for the United Kingdom, but an incredible gateway to teacher's resources.

The History Guide: Resources for Historians
http://www.historyguide.org/resources.html
Links to a wide range of history resources.

PRIMARY DOCUMENTS ONLINE

Collections Canada (Library and Archives Canada)
http://www.collectionscanada.gc.ca
A number of online historical research tools including a searchable database of over 600,000 Canadians enlisted in the Canadian Expeditionary Force (CEF) during World War I (1914–1918) along with scanned images of 765,000 Attestation papers; the Colonial Archives database with over 35,00 images; and Western Land Grants issued in Manitoba, Saskatchewan, Alberta, and the railway belt of British Columbia, c. 1870–1930.

Digital History Archives of New Tecumseth
http://news.ourontario.ca/44743/data
Site of digitized newspaper clippings and images of the history of the town of New Tecumseth.

Documents of World War II
http://www.mtholyoke.edu/acad/intrel/ww2.htm
Transcribed documents from World War II.

Early Canadiana Online
http://eco.canadiana.ca/
A full-text online collection of more than 3,000 books and pamphlets. Includes some local histories, directories, and biographical collections. The contents of this virtual library are part of the Canadian Institute for Historical Microreproduction (CIHM) collection.

Historical Text Archive
http://historicaltextarchive.com
A gateway to historical web sites, with an emphasis on those with primary texts online.

In Search of Your Canadian Past
http://digital.library.mcgill.ca/countyatlas
The Canadian County Atlas Digital Project presents the Ontario county atlases (43 in total) online in digitized form.

Local and Alberta Histories Collection
http://www.ourfutureourpast.ca/loc_hist
Growing collection of digitized books on Alberta local history.

Making of America
http://quod.lib.umich.edu/m/moagrp
Making of America (MOA) is a digital library of primary sources in American social history from the antebellum period through reconstruction.

Salem Witchtrials: Documentary Archive
http://etext.virginia.edu/salem/witchcraft/home.html
Both scanned and transcribed primary sources for the Salem witch trials.

The Champlain Society Digital Collection
http://link.library.utoronto.ca/champlain/search.cfm?lang=eng
The collection contains thirty-three of the Champlain Society's most important volumes (approximately 16,000 printed pages) dealing with exploration and discovery over three centuries. It includes first-hand accounts of Samuel de Champlain's voyages in New France as well as the diary from Sir John Franklin's first land expedition to the Arctic, 1819–22.

The Gateway to Northwestern Ontario History
http://ourontario.ca/gateway/search.asp
Photos, books, drawings, and artifacts from libraries and museums of northwestern Ontario. This includes the full text of some books, many photos of people, and a searchable version of the Thunder Bay News Index.

HISTORY FOR THE CLASSROOM

British Library Online Gallery
http://www.bl.uk/onlinegallery/index.html
Digital collections, exhibitions, and themed tours on British history put together from the British Library's collections.

Historica
http://www.histori.ca
The website of the foundation devoted to Canadian history education. Includes the Canadian Encyclopedia Online as well as lesson plans, resources, and current articles.

Martha Ballard's Diary Online
http://dohistory.org/diary/index.html
Martha Ballard wrote in her diary nearly every day for twenty-seven years from January 1, 1785 to May 12, 1812 for a total of almost 10,000 entries. The full diary is online, along with suggested ways of using it to "do history."

Great Unsolved Mysteries in Canadian History
http://www.canadianmysteries.ca
A multiple-award winning collection of historical documents and supporting teacher materials (MysteryQuests) on twelve infamous events in Canadian history from early Viking exploration of Eastern Canada to the Klondike Gold Rush, and from the great fire of 1734 in Montreal to the death of Herbert Norman in 1957.

World War I: Trenches on the Web
http://www.worldwar1.com
A superb interactive site that shows what can be done with history on the web.

28 Training the Eye of the Beholder
Using Visual Resources with Secondary Students

Penney Clark

The statement "a picture is worth a thousand words" is a truism. Photographs, paintings, films, and other visual resources can convey immense detail at a glance—detail that would take pages of print to describe. They can depict nuances of colour, texture, and facial expression that are difficult to convey in words. They may also be artifacts that provide rich historical insights. Certain photographs are so powerful that they come to represent an era, such as the poignant image of John Kennedy, Jr. saluting his father's coffin, Pierre Elliott Trudeau pirouetting behind the queen, or the sole Chinese student in front of sixteen tanks in Tiananmen Square. Much of Canada's early history (and that of other countries, too, for that matter) was recorded for posterity by painters, before photography came into common use. For example, Paul Kane produced more than a hundred oil paintings of aboriginal people based on sketches done in his travels from the Great Lakes to Vancouver Island between 1845 and 1848. We are indebted to Frances Ann Hopkins, whose husband was the secretary to George Simpson, governor of the Hudson's Bay Company, for her detailed paintings of the voyageurs on several canoe journeys that she took with them between 1858 and 1870.

Given their importance, visual resources should be a key part of a social studies program. If students are to make effective use of visual resources, they first need to see them as an important part of the variety of information sources available to them. Yet visuals are often overlooked. For instance, pictures in textbooks are ignored while students scour the print segments for information. Students need to learn to examine pictures from a critical perspective. They are not only a rich source of information and insights, but deliberate constructions, rather than mere reflections, of reality; and as constructions, they represent their creators' purposes and perspectives. Coupled with this is the need to examine visuals actively to uncover the meanings that lie under their surface images. In order to make them yield all that they have to offer, students must spend time studying them and learn to ask compelling questions about them.

This chapter discusses the thoughtful classroom use of photographs and paintings, as well as visual resources with an audio component, such as videos, films, and CD-ROMs.

Paintings and Photographs

The most abundant and accessible visual resources are photographs and paintings. Most authorized textbooks are full of them. Other sources include:

- travel brochures
- calendars
- newspapers
- magazines
- government publications
- discarded textbooks
- store advertising displays
- CD-ROM encyclopedias
- archives and museums
- the internet
- art books
- family albums
- public relations material
- art galleries

In this section, I look at concerns about interpreting paintings and photographs at face value and offer a few strategies for "interrogating" these visual resources.

PAINTINGS

Paintings (and other art forms) can give students a powerful sense of how the world was viewed in the time and place in which they were produced. However, students need to be aware that paintings are not necessarily intended to represent events as they actually happened. For instance, a famous painting showing the death of the French commander, Marquis de Montcalm, at the Siege of Quebec shows him dying on the battlefield. In fact, he died the next morning in Quebec. An equally famous painting of the death of General Wolfe, the British commander, depicts people who weren't actually present, and some who were there are not shown.

Students should discuss why artists do not always represent events as they actually happened. One of the reasons for altering the details is to represent the artist's social and political purposes. Students can see the influence of national perspective on the depiction of events by comparing paintings by different artists on a particular incident. For example, American artist John Trumbull's painting of the death of the American commander Richard Montgomery during the 1775–76 American invasion of Quebec shows Montgomery as the centre of attention. The painting by British artist Johan Frederick Clemens shows a chaotic battle scene with many more things happening at once. It is interesting to note that neither painting is authentic in that Montgomery died on the battlefield on December 31, but his frozen body was not found until the next day.[1]

Students can use historical paintings to construct a written account of life in a particular place at a particular time in the past. For instance, Peter Rindisbacher, a Swiss settler who lived at Red River from 1821 to 1826, created numerous drawings and paintings depicting the activities of aboriginal people in the area. (*Life at Red River: 1830–1860*, a text in the Ginn "Studies in Canadian History" series, contains reproductions of several Rindisbacher paintings.) Students could examine these paintings and then write a few paragraphs describing what they see. They might also compare the information extracted from the drawings and paintings to information extracted from written sources and attempt to account for any differences.

It is important for students to be aware that paintings, like other visual sources, need to be interrogated for the messages that lie beneath the surface. In one activity, students are asked to examine the use of symbols in two early Renaissance Flemish paintings depicting weddings—Jan Van Eyck's *Giovanni Arnolfini and His Bride* and *The Peasant Wedding* by Pieter Bruegel—and then create their own artwork using symbols from this period. Students are provided with background information about the symbolism in the paintings. For instance, Van Eyck's painting uses religious symbols such

as a burning candle in the chandelier, which represents the ever-present, all-seeing Christ; the couple's shoes have been removed, which suggests that they are standing on "holy ground"; and a little dog symbolizes faithfulness. Bruegel has painted his peasant wedding scene in a solemn, respectful way that suggests that he saw peasant life as preferable to the city life of the time. Students are asked to identify the actions, gestures, and expressions of people; choice of colours and objects used as symbols in the paintings; speculate about the symbolic meaning behind each and provide a plausible explanation for each symbol. Students then create an artwork using symbols from the early Renaissance period to portray an aspect of that age. Finally, they write a commentary on the symbolism used in the work of another student (Case, Daniels, and Schwartz 1999, 49–54). Other strategies for deconstructing these messages will be presented in a later section of this chapter.

PHOTOGRAPHS

"While photographs may not lie, liars may photograph" (Lewis Hine, quoted in Everett-Green 1996, E1). Students (and many others) tend to take photographs at face value, while they are ready to accept that drawings and paintings represent the perspectives of their creators (Gabella 1994). It is difficult to repudiate the visual evidence of a photograph because it is a record of a particular moment in time. Students may not stop to consider that even photographs are not always what they seem and that the person behind the camera will likely have constructed the picture to suit particular purposes. Photographic evidence may be unreliable in four ways:

- Photographers or subjects may stage photographs in order to deliver a particular message.
- Photographs may depict an atypical situation or event that is not representative of the people or circumstances shown.
- Photographs may be deliberately altered.
- Photographs may exclude important aspects of a situation.

STAGED PHOTOGRAPHS

Photographers may arrange subjects or objects in a photo in order to deliver a particular message. For example, a famous photo by Alfred Eisenstaedt shows a sailor and a nurse kissing in the middle of a crowd on VJ Day (official end of the fighting between the Allies and Japan in World War II). The photographer had two people pose for the shot. He did not happen upon a spontaneous eruption of joy, as most people who see the photograph imagine. Such photos are clever and capture the imagination, but they are not "real," in that they would not have happened without the photographer's intervention.

Photographs can be "created" in much less dramatic ways than the VJ Day example. It was common practice for nineteenth-century photographers, intent on preserving traditional images of Native people for posterity, to stage their photographs. For instance, Edward S. Curtis, who photographed Native peoples from Alaska to the American Southwest, used wigs and costumes, as well as other props, so his subjects would appear as he imagined First Nations people to have looked before being affected by white culture.

In other cases, it is not so much that the photos have been deliberately staged, but rather that the reality they are intended to convey has been slightly altered to suit the momentous occasion of the photograph itself. For instance, the photograph below shows children dressed in ragged and dirty clothing, yet with freshly scrubbed faces. Someone has prepared the children for this photograph. Students have to be aware of such anomalies so that they do not take such photographs at face value (no pun intended). It is interesting to speculate about the photographer's motives and the effect on the audience of seeing poorly dressed children with fresh faces.

A photograph may also, in some sense, be staged by its subjects. Joy Kogawa, in *Obasan*, a novel about a Japanese family that was transported first to an internment camp and then to an Alberta beet field, says of a photograph of another Japanese family taken at the time: "'Grinning and happy' and all smiles standing around a pile of beets? That is one telling. It's not how it was" (1981, 197). This photo did not reflect the reality of the lives of the subjects of the photo. The camera can create its own reality.

Students need to learn to look beyond distortions created by photographers or subjects to examine other evidence that photographs may offer. J. Robert Davison (1981–82) describes a photograph labelled "Indians, Fraser River," taken about 1868 by photographer Frederick Dally. The photograph, which appears on the following page, shows a group of Native people "praying." However, the photographer contradicts the evidence of the photograph by writing underneath, "Indians shamming to be at prayer for the sake of photography."

GRAFLEX CAMERA PHOTOGRAPH

THE SHAME OF THE CITY—CAN WE GIVE OUR CHILDREN NO BETTER PLAYING SPACE?

"The shame of the city: Can we give our children no better playing space?"—*Winnipeg, 1912*
Library and Archives Canada (C-030947)

"Indians shamming to be at prayer for the sake of photography. Fraser River." —Frederick Daly
British Columbia Archives (E-04419)

Above the photo is written, "At the priests [sic] request all the Indians kneel down and assume an attitude of devotion. Amen." Even without the help of the caption, close examination of the photograph reveals that it is a sham:

> The two priests have set a fine, holy example, but their spiritual and physical distance from the group is palpable; they are easily picked out standing (here kneeling) apart—curiously not aloof, for in this case it is the Native group that is aloof. They have gone along with the play, but there is little conviction. Some emulate the priests, but only tentatively, as if they were unsure of what exactly constitutes an "attitude of devotion." A few others seem to have thought it barely worth the effort. They have pulled their dignity and their pride around them like their blankets, refusing the pious assault on their spirit (Davison 1981–82, 2).

Much can be ascertained from such a photograph and its captions. It can be used to demonstrate to students that critical examination of a visual resource can reveal messages that are not evident at first glance. Students could discuss why it might be in the best interests of the priests to have such a photograph taken and how it might be used. Also, it would be interesting to consider why the photographer, in writing his captions, refused to go along with the sham. Students could examine other photographs and their captions to determine how a caption can alter the message conveyed by a photograph.

UNREPRESENTATIVE IMAGES

A second way photographs lead viewers to draw unwarranted conclusions occurs when they are highly unrepresentative of the reality of the person or the situation. The famous photograph showing candidate Robert Stanfield fumbling a football kickoff during a national election campaign is an example of this. The photograph, which was widely reprinted, left the impression that Stanfield was an incompetent bungler. Other evidence does not support this impression. Students could be shown such a photograph and asked to locate additional evidence that supports or refutes the impression conveyed by the picture. They could then be asked to draw a conclusion about the person or event based on the wider array of evidence that they now have at hand. They should also consider the power of such impressions, where connections can be made that are not warranted. In this case, competence in football is not related to competence in politics or, for that matter, governing, but these connections were made.

Daniel Francis (1996) points out that early photography technology was instrumental in developing an image of nineteenth-century aboriginal people that was less than accurate. Francis says:

> A mask-like quality was particularly pronounced in early photographs, because exposure times were prolonged and subjects had to keep themselves and their expressions immobile for up to half a minute. Since photographs were often the only glimpse most non-natives got of native people, this simple technological imperative may have contributed to the stereotype of the grim, stoical, cigar-store Indian (2).

Here, the camera has created rather than captured unrepresentative images. The result is the same—a misleading impression is created.

To help students appreciate that photographs may lead viewers to draw unwarranted conclusions, students could role-play particular historical events while another student takes photographs at dramatic moments. Invite students to examine the photographs and discuss what they convey about the event and what is misleading. Students might also speculate about the conclusions historians using family photo albums as evidence might draw about contemporary family life. Using their own family albums as an example, students may conclude that a historian would judge the family to be avid travellers and partygoers, without realizing that these were the types of events that family members recorded by means of photographs. Such albums often do not record the more typical routines of a family.

ALTERED PHOTOGRAPHS

With the advent of digital technology, photographs are "as malleable as clay" (Grady 1997, A23). People can be moved from one location to another, objects can be placed in the photograph, unwanted people can be removed, and so on. However, these sorts of alterations did not suddenly appear with the advent of the computer. They have occurred since photography was invented. Stephen Jay Gould describes his unearthing of "conscious skulduggery" (1981, 171) in the work of psychologist H.H. Goddard. Goddard maintained that the "feeble-minded" could be recognized by their facial characteristics and "proved" this point by means of photographs of poor families. Seventy years after publication of the photographs, examination by experts revealed that facial features had been altered to make the people appear mentally disabled. Communist regimes have rather routinely altered historical evidence, including photographs, to suit current political thinking. For instance, in *The Book of Laughter and Forgetting*, Milan Kundera (1980) describes a scene on the balcony of a palace in Prague in 1948 where Communist leader Klement Gottwald was addressing hundreds of thousands of Czechoslovakian people. Photographs of the group on the balcony were reproduced widely in posters and textbooks. However, after Vladimir Clementis, who was on the balcony and in the photographs, was executed for treason in 1952, his image was removed from the photographs—which, once doctored, showed a bare palace wall where he had stood.

More commonly, a photograph intended for publication will be cropped before printing in order to suit layout requirements, sometimes radically altering its meaning in the process. Students can apply two L-shaped frames to photographs from magazines and newspapers in various ways in order to see for themselves how the meaning can be altered by the practice of cropping.

SELECTIVE FOCUS

Photographs can also exclude; that is, they may only represent "part" of a story. An example of this is the famous photo, which has appeared in many textbooks, of Donald Smith and other dignitaries at the Last Spike ceremony to mark the completion of the Canadian Pacific Railway at Craigellachie, British Columbia. It is important in such a case to ask who is included and who excluded. Another, less famous photo shows the labourers who had built the railway holding their own Last Spike ceremony while they waited for the train that would take them back east. A comparison of these two photographs, which appear on the next page, can be used to show that the historical record is selective. However, it is not only the first photo that excludes. Encourage students to note who is missing from the photograph of the labourers as well. Even though there was a large contingent of Chinese workers on the railway, they are not represented in the second picture. This, too, tells students something about historical perspectives. Many textbooks dwell on the activities and achievements of prominent Caucasian men, while ignoring those of working-class people, people of other races, and women.

In the highlighted text is a question sequence that could be used with the two Last Spike photographs. Similar questions aimed at helping students consider who is excluded, as well as who is included in the photos, could be posed about many historical pictures. For instance, there is a photo showing the Fathers of Confederation at the Charlottetown Conference. Since historians (Cuthbert Brandt 1992) have acknowledged that the social aspects of the Conference were key to its success, it seems fair to ask why the politicians' wives, who organized these social events, do not appear in official photographs.

STRATEGIES FOR INTERROGATING PHOTOGRAPHS AND PAINTINGS

There are many different kinds of questions that we might use with students to help them examine photographs and paintings (as well as other visual resources) critically. We might ask students to:

- attend carefully to detail;
- consider geographic data (for example, climate, landscape);
- consider historical data (for example, type of clothing, hairstyles, furniture);
- consider sociological data (for example, social class, relationships);
- consider emotional context (for example, feelings of people depicted);
- consider aesthetic qualities (for example, general appeal, use of colour, light, texture); and
- consider photographer's or artist's perspective and purpose (for example, intended audience, messages conveyed).

DECONSTRUCTING THE LAST SPIKE

Questions to ask about these pictures:
- What is happening in these two photographs?
- What features signal that an important event is occurring?
- Who is included in the first photo (for example, William Van Horne, who was in charge of the project to build the railway; Donald Smith, a financial backer; and Sir Sanford Fleming, an engineer)?
- Do you see the young boy in the first photo? Who do you think he might be? How do you think he found himself in the photo?
- Do you recognize anyone in the second photo?
- Why would there be recognizable faces in the first photo but not the second?

- Why do you think the labourers were not featured in the more famous photo?
- Why do you think the labourers chose to stage their own ceremony?
- Why do you think the first photo has been included in many Canadian history books and the second has been included in far fewer?
- Who is missing from the labourer's photo?
- Who "built" the railway?
- What does this tell us about our perspectives on history?

"Hon. Donald A. Smith driving the last spike to complete the Canadian Pacific Railway"
—*November 7, 1885, Alexander Ross, Ross, Best & Co., Winnipeg*
Alexander Ross/Library and Archives Canada (C-003693)

"Hon. Donald A. Smith driving the last spike to complete the Canadian Pacific Railway"
—*November 7, 1885, Alexander Ross, Ross, Best & Co., Winnipeg*
Library and Archives Canada (C-014115)

Questions that fit within one category may not necessarily be asked all at once. It may be helpful to follow a sequence that stems logically from students' responses. Two examples of the use of these questions to interrogate visuals are shown in the highlighted areas on the following pages. The first example uses the painting "Canoe Manned by Voyageurs Passing a Waterfall" by Frances Ann Hopkins. The second example uses the drawing "A Jesuit Preaching to the Indians" by C.W. Jeffreys to demonstrate how students can be guided through a process intended to reveal both the explicit and the implicit messages that a visual conveys (based on a lesson in Sandwell, Misfeldt and Case 1999).

The following framework (adapted from the Ontario Ministry of Education 1989, 137–138) supports students in examining the aesthetic features of photographs and paintings by focussing on techniques (for example, use of light, focus, and frame) that highlight or subdue various aspects of a picture. These questions can be used with any of the visuals discussed in this chapter.

- **Subject.** What is the photograph or painting about? Does the photographer or painter wish us to think about an object, a place, a person, an event, or an idea? Is the subject unusual or revealing? Does the subject have an impact on the viewer? Is the subject representational or universal?
- **Frame.** In what way has the subject been isolated from its surroundings? Are there particular objects that become more interesting to us as a result of the frame established by the photographer or painter? What new meaning between objects or people is created within the frame? What comparisons, contrasts, or tensions are created by the framing? What effects has the point of view had on the meaning of the subject?
- **Light.** Students should examine the use of light in terms of its quality (for example, sunlight or artificial light), quantity (for example, under- or overexposure), and angle (for example, how the subject is lit, whether a flare was used). Guide their discussion with questions such as the following: How has light been used creatively to create the overall effect? Is the subject lit from a specific angle? Do lines of light and shadow create or enhance the meaning? What reasons do you think the artist had for using light the way he or she did?
- **Focus.** How much detail is in focus in the picture? Did the artist isolate certain elements and leave the rest fuzzy? Has the artist used "sharp" or "soft" focussing to create a specific mood? Did the artist make the best choice in the details emphasized in the photographs? Is the picture too "busy" with sharply focussed details?

Select three or four pictures pertaining to a particular topic in the curriculum (for example, a specific community, historical event, or time period). Develop a lesson where you teach students to read the pictures and notice the similar and contrasting information contained in them.

Audiovisuals

Audiovisual resources—CD-ROMs, videos, films—have many positive features that make them useful in teaching social studies. Students with different learning styles may benefit from their use because they deliver information through both auditory and visual means. They provide alternative ways to gather information for less capable readers. In some cases, they can be more useful for data gathering than field trips because they focus on the most important aspects of the experience and eliminate extraneous details. They can convey a great deal of information in a relatively brief span of class time. Through such methods as animation, slow motion, time-lapse photography, and microphotography, they allow students to view scenes they would otherwise not have an opportunity to observe. Those that use motion have their own advantages. For instance, processes that can be difficult to visualize when described in print can be seen in action. Motion can also add to student interest. Finally, they can be more motivating than many other resources, because they are usually less intimidating than textbooks, as well as being colourful and appealing.

Historian Graeme Decarie has warned us to "beware of technologies standing under streetlights, calling, 'Hi, sailor'" (1988, 98). He was referring to the production and indiscriminate classroom use of poor-quality (both technically and in terms of meeting curriculum objectives) audiovisual aids of various kinds. He urged teachers to choose such resources carefully and use them selectively. With the advent of computer technology, there are many more audiovisual materials available than there were a decade ago. Therefore, it is more important than ever that they be chosen carefully and used selectively.

The type of audiovisual technology chosen will depend on its accessibility and the purpose for which it is being used. Specific audiovisual resources should be selected for classroom use based on criteria such as interest, accuracy and currency of content, conceptual level, whether content fits intended purposes, quality of photography and sound, and the way in which information is organized for presentation.

INTERROGATING A PAINTING

"Canoe Manned by Voyageurs Passing a Waterfall"—1869, Frances Ann Hopkins
Library and Archives Canada, Acc. No. 1989-401-1

Attend carefully to detail
- Describe the people you see in this painting. Note the clothing and various types of headgear.
- What are the people doing?
- What objects do you see? Describe them.

Geographic data
- What is in the foreground of the painting? The background?
- Where do you think these people are?

Historical data
- What can you learn about the voyageurs from this painting?
- What questions would you like to ask the artist about the lives of the voyageurs?

Sociological data
- Who are the woman and man in the centre of the canoe? What clues suggest this?

- Why do you think they are not paddling? Is this explanation supported by anything in the painting?

Emotional context
- How do you think the voyageurs felt about having the well-dressed man and woman in the canoe with them? How might their presence affect the behaviour of the voyageurs?
- What aspects of this painting convey a sense of tranquility?

Aesthetic qualities
- How is light used in this painting? What is the purpose of this use?
- What are some of the ways the artist has made the painting artistically pleasing?

Photographer's or artist's perspective and purpose
- Why do you think the artist chose to paint a journey by voyageurs?
- Why might the artist have chosen to convey the voyageurs amid such a tranquil scene?
- Do you think the artist has a positive feeling for voyageurs?

HELPING STUDENTS BECOME CRITICAL VIEWERS

As with other visual resources, it is important to help students see that these resources have been created by human developers with particular perspectives and for particular purposes. Like the other resources, these must be actively investigated in an effort to reveal the messages that lie underneath the sur-

face. Below are sample questions (adapted from Cates 1990) for deconstructing an audiovisual resource:

- **Dialogue.** Notice consistent use of words that have positive or negative connotations. What is the effect of using the word "cheap" instead of "inexpensive," or "conceited" in place of "high self-esteem," or "forthright" instead of "domineering"?

REDRAWING EARLY CONTACT

Visuals can have both explicit and implicit messages. Students can be helped to access the explicit messages by means of the 5W questions, a technique used by reporters:

- Who are the people in the drawing?
- What are they doing?
- Where does the drawing take place?
- When did it take place?
- Why is the action happening?

In order to help students access implicit messages, introduce the concept of point of view or perspective. Explain that the artist has drawn the picture from a particular point of view or perspective and ask the class to identify this perspective. As a clue, ask students to consider the difference between the following titles for the Jeffreys drawing:

Jeffreys' title: A Jesuit Preaching to the Indians
Alternative title: The Algonquins allow the priest to explain his religion

- Based on the title, whose position or viewpoint has the artist presented in the drawing (that is, aboriginal people, the European priest, or a balanced perspective)? Offer evidence from the drawing as to why the European perspective seems to dominate the picture.
- Another dimension or point of view is the artist's attitudes towards each of the groups in the drawing. Direct students to consider the qualities or character traits that the European priest seems to possess and compare these with those shown by the aboriginal peoples.
- Introduce the "iconic" dimension. Create a chart such as the one below and record students' interpretations and supporting evidence for each symbolic message:

SYMBOLIC MESSAGE	
Inference	Evidence
Bringing Christianity to the receptive Indians	the cross (symbolizing Christianity towers above the heads of everyone)

A Jesuit Preaching to the Indians

"A Jesuit Preaching to the Indians"—*1934, C. W. Jefferys*
Library and Archives Canada (ICON113250)

- Students could be asked to interpret the implicit message of another Jeffreys drawing, in terms of dominant focus (artist's point of view), implied European qualities (the artist's attitudes towards the aboriginal peoples), implied aboriginal qualities (the artist's attitudes towards the aboriginal peoples), and symbolic message (artist's overall theme or message).
- Students could be asked to consider how the aboriginal peoples might have viewed their early encounters with missionaries (for example, Would aboriginal people understand what the cross meant? What theories might aboriginal people have about how the missionaries came to their land?)

- **Actors.** Is there any relationship between the type of character played and the physical appearance of the actor? For instance, do homely actors play "bad guys," while attractive people play the "upstanding characters"? Are people of a particular race overrepresented among the evil characters?
- **Character development.** Are characters stereotypical (for example, are Native people presented as uniformly good or uniformly bad, or are attractive blonde women presented as unintelligent)?

- **Colour and lighting.** Is the depiction light and airy, dark and brooding, or some variation of this? Are some scenes lighter and brighter than others? What is the content of these scenes? What about the darker scenes? Are any scenes in black and white? Why do you think this is the case?
- **Music.** Can you find examples where the choice of music or its volume influences the way you view particular characters or events?
- **Camera angle and choice of shot.** Is the action ever

shown from the viewpoint of a character? If so, in what cases and for what purposes?

- **Selection and arrangement of scenes.** Does the film alternate among different viewpoints, places, or people? Are different viewpoints given equal time and emphasis?
- **Overall impression.** What is the developer of this resource attempting to convey through use of some of the devices presented here?

Use of audiovisual resources need not be limited to those developed specifically for classrooms. Popular films, for example, can be used to help students learn to analyze a medium to which they receive constant exposure in their daily lives. This is important to do for the following reasons: many people are predominantly visual learners; films present details graphically that may not necessarily be communicated through writing; their dramatic telling can amplify and illuminate themes and ideas from history; they are an important art form in their own right because of their pervasiveness in our culture; and they are a gauge of the tastes and ideologies prevalent in North American culture (Johnson and Vargus 1994).

Peter Seixas (1994) has used the 1989 Kevin Costner film *Dances with Wolves*, in conjunction with the 1956 John Ford film *The Searchers*, to determine how students' ideas about a currently popular historic film are challenged by viewing an older film with differing perspectives on Native-white interactions. Students endorsed segments in *Dances with Wolves* as "true" windows on the past because they were congruent with their own views. The moral stance of the movie, with its critical view of the US army and westward expansion and the Sioux as their victims, was in keeping with revisionist popular culture. *The Searchers,* on the other hand, with its depiction of Native people as violent and vengeful, represents an earlier view of Native-white interaction during the period of settlement of North America. The contrasting historical interpretations posed a moral dilemma for most of the students. While Seixas used the two films for research purposes, contrasting film clips can be used to develop students' sense of the problematic relationships between historical evidence and historical interpretation. The use of popular film is an engaging way to help students develop such understandings.

IDEAS FOR USING AUDIOVISUAL RESOURCES

This section discusses previewing, viewing, and follow-up activities for use with audiovisual resources. It is, generally speaking, not sufficient merely to turn on the video machine and let students sit back and watch the show. These following activities are helpful in turning what may simply be an entertaining interlude into an educational experience.

PREVIEWING ACTIVITIES

Previewing activities should arouse interest, build background knowledge, clarify purposes for viewing, and reveal what students already know about a topic. In order to arouse interest and build background knowledge, teachers might briefly describe the topics to be explored in the audiovisual resource and ask students to bring pertinent newspaper and magazine pictures and articles to class. These materials could form part of a bulletin board display that would evolve throughout the unit of study. In order to clarify purposes for viewing, students can be given key questions that identify main ideas, establish relationships among different aspects of a topic, or help students examine the material for accuracy, authenticity, or bias. These questions need not be numerous; one general question may be quite sufficient. The important point is that students have the questions prior to, rather than following, the viewing to provide a focus or purpose for their viewing. Students can be assigned different questions and therefore have different purposes. They pool their information following the viewing. A previewing activity might also consist of a discussion of students' prior knowledge of the topics dealt with in the audiovisual. They could record what they already know in a retrieval chart (such as Figure 28.1, which is intended for use with an audiovisual resource on an assigned Canadian region).

After viewing, students can refer back to their charts to add to and confirm the accuracy of the information they recorded prior to viewing.

Previewing activities signal to students that the viewing is to be an educational rather than a recreational experience. Because videotapes in particular, and also CD-ROMs, are accessible in many homes, students develop a mindset that such materials are for pleasure use only. Unless reminded by means of such previewing activities, students may not view them with the same intensity that they might read a textbook or other "serious" information source.

VIEWING ACTIVITIES

The purpose of viewing activities is to give students a focus while encountering the resource. It is preferable that students not take detailed notes during the viewing because there is a danger that the recording task will occupy their attention to such an extent that they will miss important points. Audiovisuals can be stopped frequently in order to check on student comprehension and to discuss and clarify points made. The entire audiovisual need not be viewed if only a portion is appropriate to curricular intents. If the entire audiovisual is pertinent, one viewing can be insufficient to allow students to

FIGURE 28.1   DATA KNOWLEDGE CHART

Region of Canada _____

	PRIOR KNOWLEDGE	ADDITIONAL KNOWLEDGE
Topography		
Climate		
Vegetation		
Natural resources		
Industries		
Major cities		
Transportation and communication		
Wilderness preserves		

cope well with the information. It may be best to view it in its entirety once and then show selected portions a second time, or as many times as necessary.

FOLLOW-UP ACTIVITIES

Following the viewing, students might record and then compare their responses to questions asked during the previewing phase. If there are discrepancies, pertinent sections of the audiovisual can be viewed again to determine why. If students have recorded hypotheses prior to viewing, they might confirm their accuracy. Other follow-up activities might relate the material in the audiovisual to the ongoing unit of instruction in which they are engaged. For example, students might use an audiovisual resource as one of a set of information sources to prepare for a talk or a report that they will prepare.

The example in Figure 28.2 (adapted from Clark 1991) of an approach to previewing, viewing, and follow-up activities is an adaptation of the well-known SQ3R (Survey, Question, Read, Record, Review) strategy for dealing with print material. Its purpose is to provide students with a structured

format that gives them purposes for viewing, ways to record information, and ways to summarize the information once recorded. Students can then proceed to more sophisticated strategies involving probing underneath the surface discourse for the author's purpose, and so on. They may also wish to view the resource a second time.

Conclusion

Visual resources should be a key part of a social studies program. They add interest and variety. Their use teaches students that the print medium is not the only means by which

Select a video resource that has been recommended for use in a particular grade level. Identify specific outcomes in the curriculum that might be addressed using this resource. Design an activity and student support material to achieve these outcomes using the selected resource.

FIGURE 28.2   VIEWING GUIDE

SURVEY. Listen to your teacher read you a brief summary of the video. List five topics you think will be addressed in this video.

1. _____

2. _____

3. _____

4. _____

5. _____

QUESTION. Create a question about an important aspect for each of the above topics. Write your questions on the lines below.

1. _____

2. _____

3. _____

4. _____

5. _____

VIEW AND RECORD. View the video to find the answers to your questions. Record your answers below. All of your questions may not be answered in the video. You may want to check other sources for those answers.

1. _____

2. _____

3. _____

4. _____

5. _____

REVIEW. Review your answers above. Use this information to write a summary of the video.

_____

_____

_____

_____

information is attainable. However, visual resources, like other learning resources, represent the perspectives of their creators. Visual resources are particularly seductive sources of misleading information because of the powerful effect they can have on the viewer. Therefore, students need systematic strategies for interrogating this source of information and they should view these resources with the same healthy scepticism with which we would want them to view any other resource.

NOTE

1. Trumbull's painting of the death of Montgomery can be viewed at http://en.wikipedia.org/wiki/Invasion_of_Canada_(1775); Clemens' painting can be viewed at http://explorer.monticello .org/?s1=0|s4=4_42.

REFERENCES

Case, R., L. Daniels, and P. Schwartz. 1999. *Critical challenges in social studies for junior high students.* Vancouver: The Critical Thinking Consortium.

Cates, W.M. 1990. Helping students learn to think critically: Detecting and analyzing bias in films. *Social Studies* 81: 15–18.

Clark, P. 1991. *Government in Canada: Citizenship in action.* Montreal: National Film Board of Canada.

Cuthbert Brandt, G. 1992. National unity and the politics of political history. *Journal of the Canadian Historical Association* 3: 2–11.

Davison, J.R. 1981–82. Turning a blind eye: The historian's use of photographs. *BC Studies* 52: 16–35.

Decarie, G. 1988. Audio-visual aids: Historians in Blunderland. *Canadian Social Studies* 23 (2): 95–98.

Everett-Green, R. 1996. Photography's white lies. *Globe and Mail,* November 9.

Francis, D. 1996. *Copying people, 1860–1940.* Saskatoon, SK: Fifth House.

Gabella, M.S. 1994. Beyond the looking glass: Bringing students into the conversation of historical inquiry. *Theory and Research in Social Education* 22 (3): 340–363.

Gould, S.J. 1981. *The mismeasure of man.* New York: Norton.

Grady, M. 1997. Photography as "monster." *Vancouver Sun,* May 17.

Johnson, J. and C. Vargus. 1994. The smell of celluloid in the classroom: Five great movies that teach. *Social Education* 58 (2): 109–113.

Kogawa, J. 1981. *Obasan.* Boston: David R. Godine.

Kundera, M. 1980. *The book of laughter and forgetting.* New York: Knopf.

Ontario Ministry of Education. 1989. *Media literacy resource guide.* Toronto: Queen's Printer.

Sandwell, R., C. Misfeldt, and R. Case. 2002. *Early contact and settlement in New France.* Vancouver: The Critical Thinking Consortium and British Columbia Ministry of Education.

Seixas, P. 1994. Confronting the moral frames of popular film: Young people respond to historical revisionism. *American Journal of Education* 102 (3): 261–285.

SUPPLEMENTARY READINGS

Allen, R. 1994. Posters as historical documents: A resource for the teaching of twentieth-century history. *Social Studies* 85 (2): 52–61.

Allen, R.F. and L.E.S. Molina. 1993. Snapshot geography: Using travel photographs to learn geography in upper elementary schools. *Canadian Social Studies* 27: 62–66.

Braun, J.A. and D. Corbin. 1991. Helping students use videos to make cross-cultural comparisons. *Social Studies and the Young Learner* 4 (2): 28–29.

Burke, P. 2001. *Eyewitnessing: Uses of images as historical evidence.* Ithaca, NY: Cornell University Press.

Considine, D.M. 1989. The video boom's impact on social studies: Implications, applications, and resources. *Social Studies* 80 (6): 229–234.

Downey, M.T. 1980. Pictures as teaching aids: Using the pictures in history textbooks. *Social Education* 44 (2): 92–99.

Felton, R.G. and R.F. Allen. 1990. Using visual materials as historical sources: A model for studying state and local history. *Social Studies* 81 (2): 84–87.

Hennigar-Shuh, J. 1988. Learn to look. *History and Social Science Teacher* 23 (3): 141–146.

Jackson, D. 1995. A note on photo CDs: A valuable resource for the classroom. *Canadian Social Studies* 30 (1): 28–29.

Morris, S. 1989. *A teacher's guide to using portraits.* London: English Heritage Education Service.

Nelson, M. 1997. An alternative medium of social education—The "horrors of war" picture cards. *Social Studies* 88 (3): 100–107.

Osborne, K. 1990. Using Canada's visual history in the classroom. In *Canada's visual history,* 1–19. Ottawa and Montreal: National Museum of Civilization and National Film Board of Canada.

Pazienza, J. and G. Clarke. 1997. Integrating text and image: Teaching art and history. In *Trends and issues in Canadian social studies,* eds. I. Wright and A. Sears, 275–294. Vancouver: Pacific Educational Press.

Segall, A. 1997. "De-transparent-izing" media texts in the social studies classroom: Media education as historical/social inquiry. In *Trends and issues in Canadian social studies,* eds. I. Wright and A. Sears, 328–349. Vancouver: Pacific Educational Press.

Seixas, P. 1987. Lewis Hine: From "social" to "interpretive" photographer. *American Quarterly* 39 (3): 381–409.

Sunal, C.S. and B.A. Hatcher. 1986. How to do it: Studying history through art. *Social Education* 50 (4): 1–8.

Werner, W. 2000. Reading authorship into texts. *Theory and Research in Social Education* 28 (2): 193–219.

———. 2002. Reading visual texts. *Theory and Research in Social Education* 30 (3): 401–428.

———. 2004. Towards visual literacy. In *Challenges and Prospects for Canadian Social Studies,* eds. I. Wright and A. Sears, 202–215. Vancouver: Pacific Educational Press.

OTHER RESOURCES

Internet resources

Canadian Museum of Civilization: http://www.civilization.ca

CanPix Canadian Gallery: http://northernblue.ca/canchan/canpix/gallimag.php

Library and Archives Canada: http://www.collectionscanada.gc.ca

McCord Museum "Keys to History": http://www.mccord-museum.qc.ca/en/

Royal BC Museum "Amazing Time Machine": http://royalmuseum.bc.ca/exhibits/bc-archives-time-machine/

Royal Ontario Museum: http://www.rom.on.ca

A Scattering of Seeds: http://www.whitepinepictures.com/seeds

United States Holocaust Memorial Museum: http://www.ushmm.org

WebMuseum, Paris (also known as LeWebLouvre): http://www.ibiblio.org/wm

Films using paintings

National Film Board of Canada. 1972. *Paul Kane goes west.* Montreal: Author. A source of Paul Kane paintings depicting Canada's early history.

———. 1977. *Pictures from the 1930s.* Montreal: Author. Juxtaposes paintings produced during the Depression with newsreel footage about both domestic and international events. Features female artists such as Emily Carr and Paraskeva Clark.

————. 1980. *A visit from Captain Cook.* Montreal: Author. Illustrates how European artists projected their own ethnocentric perspectives on what they observed and recorded.

CD-ROM on Canadian history

National Film Board of Canada. 1997. *Canada's visual history.* CD-ROM. Montreal: National Museum of Civilization and National Film Board of Canada. This rich source of visual information deals with Canada's social and economic history. Includes visuals from pre-European contact to the recent past. Includes articles by Canadian historians and suggestions for further reading.

Videos on Canada

National Film Board of Canada. *Postcards from Canada.* Montreal: Author. Includes stunning postcard-like images from coast to coast.

————. *Transit series.* Montreal: Author. Individual titles are:

AIR: Climate
WATER: Reserves and Networks
LAND: Territory and Resources
FIRE: Energy
LIFE: People, Fauna and Flora

These documentaries examine Canada's geography from five different themes. The cinematography is stunning.

National Film Board (NFB) resources contact:
National Film Board of Canada
P.O. Box 6100, Station Centre-Ville
Montreal, Quebec H3C 3H5
NFB website: http://www.nfb.ca/store

29

Teaching History Through Literature

Penney Clark

My most cherished memories from the years I spent teaching public school are of the times I read to my students. I could be assured for those brief moments of having everyone's rapt attention, something that occurred only rarely on other occasions, I must admit. For some students, it must have been the highlight of a school day. It allowed them to lose themselves in the moment without the anxieties attached to assessment, for I never assessed these experiences in any formal way. For other students, it was simply an opportunity to travel to a different time and place, gaining insights that their textbook and other materials could not provide.

The evocative power of stories is illustrated in the following passage about the 1917 Halifax explosion from the novel, *Irish Chain*:

> My eyes saw terrible sights: a woman hanging lifeless over a windowsill; a man crushed beneath the collapsed wall of a house; a girl leading her little brother, his face a bloody pulp; a dray horse dead under the wagon it had recently pulled. My eyes saw all this horror, but my brain did not register it as I calmly picked my way over the rubble. I did, though, have the presence of mind to pull Winnie close to me and bury her face in my coat. I couldn't be sure whether she shared my nightmare or not. She shivered uncontrollably now, her skin a pale shade of blue that worried me desperately.... Then I'd find Mam and Da so they could help Winnie (Haworth-Attard 2002, 113).

The events of the novel are described from the perspective of thirteen-year-old Rose Dunlea, a member of a large Irish family living not far from the harbour. Rose must deal with the loss of, and injuries to, beloved family members, as well as her own guilt because she thinks her prayer to God to help her avoid school has caused the explosion. This passage is in stark contrast to the following textbook account of this event:

It killed 1900 people immediately. Thousands more were blinded or injured. A gigantic wave created by the blast swept through the harbour, adding to the destruction. The death toll eventually swelled to over 2000. The exact number of deaths was never known.

The blast was one of the worst disasters in Canadian history. It was the most powerful artificial explosion the world had yet known (Francis et al. 1998, 65).

The differences in perspective are striking. The novel account is told in the first person and is steeped in emotions, both Rose's and the reader's. The reader cares about Rose and what is to become of her because there has been an opportunity to experience her as a person. The textbook account clinically sets out the facts. Like the calamities people read about in the newspaper on a daily basis, it is difficult to relate to events so far off that do not involve anyone we know.

There is no particular reason for singling out this textbook. In fact, it happens to be a very good text. The point is that textbooks, by presenting only the bare facts, do not capture the whole story. They rarely develop students' sense of what it actually felt like to be in a particular situation. The reader gets little sense of how people reacted emotionally to the circumstances being described. Nor does the reader react emotionally. It is only by telling the stories of individuals, and seeing events through their eyes, that these feelings can be conveyed in a way that creates empathy in the reader.

In summary, the prime reasons for using novels in the teaching of history are to help students personalize events, to develop historical empathy—a strong sense of what it actually might have been like to have those experiences—in a way that textbooks cannot. Children's author Heather Kirk has referred to this as the "emotional sustenance" that novels can provide (1996, 19).

This chapter focusses on historical literature about Canada intended for middle and secondary school students. I attach an extensive annotated bibliography organized chronologically by historical era that represents a wide range of reading level. It includes a few picture books, such as *A Dog Came Too* by Ainslie Manson, since their visuals can be useful in a secondary classroom. Many senior high school students read adult fiction and they should, of course, be encouraged to do so. However, I have not included adult fiction in the bibliography because the possibilities are limitless. I use the term "literature" in a broad sense, incorporating non-fiction such as biographies, as well as fiction.

What is Historical Fiction?

In an effort to identify the kind of historical fiction of interest to history teachers, I want to distinguish it from two related genres—past-time fantasies and costume novels.

HISTORICAL FICTION AND PAST-TIME FANTASIES

There is some controversy about the term "historical fiction" among people who examine and write about adolescent and young adult fiction. According to Charlotte Huck et al., historical fiction encompasses "all realistic stories that are set in the past" (2001, 464). Sheila Egoff and Judith Saltman (1990), in *The New Republic of Childhood*, endorse this definition and exclude "past-time fantasies" that involve a contemporary protagonist travelling to the past and taking part in events there. I choose to include past-time fantasies myself because not doing so would involve overlooking useful novels for the history classroom such as Karleen Bradford's *The Other Elizabeth* (1972), Janet Lunn's *Root Cellar* (1981), and Kevin Major's *Blood Red Ochre* (1989). Time travel is a literary device to allow the narrator to legitimately express contemporary views on past events without being open to accusations of anachronism.

HISTORICAL FICTION AND COSTUME NOVELS

"Historical fiction may focus on a particular time period, a historic event, or a historic social issue or phenomenon" (Courtland and Gambell 2000, 25). A distinction is often made between the historical novel, which is "wholly or partly about public events and social conditions which are the material of history" (Walsh 1972, 19), and the costume novel, which, in effect, simply chooses a place and time from the past as stage props. Children's fiction writer Paton Walsh asks, "Can we imagine the plot and characters set in any other period? If we can, then the book is not in any organic way *about* its historical period. It may be a very good book, but it is not a historical novel" (19). Kit Pearson's *Guests of War* trilogy, the story of two British children sent to Toronto

during World War II to escape the bombs falling on Britain, is an outstanding example of a historical novel because it is firmly set in its time and place. Kirk (1996) calls it,

> complex and mature in subject matter, discussing as it does the results of peaceful colonialism on the mentality of Canadians during World War II: the unquestioned loyalty to Britain, the indifference to the plight of Jewish and Dutch children, the smugness about our own safety and affluence, and the incomprehension of the emotional trauma caused by first-hand experience of war (18).

Egoff and Saltman (1990) consider the first two books of Marianne Brandis' Upper Canada trilogy, *The Tinderbox* (1982) and *The Quarter-Pie Window* (1985) as "costume novels." (The third novel, *The Sign of the Scales*, was not published until 1990). They describe these books as "not contain[ing] the slightest mention of a historical event (a war or rebellion) or a social situation (the plight of homeless boys or labour disputes). These are individual life stories that could take place today but are set in the past" (124). I have included these "costume novels" in the annotated bibliography because, although they may not mention historical events, they may still be of interest to students, help them empathize with people in the past, and provide information about details of daily living. Marianne Brandis recently described the painstaking research used to verify the historical details that she included in this trilogy. She said that "for each book I've written, I used (not necessarily read from cover to cover) several hundred books on dozens of subjects, not to mention maps and pictures and museums and actual places and occasionally interviews with experts" (Draper 2002, 89). With their teacher's help, students can turn to their textbooks and other non-fiction resources in order to locate the events of the novel within a broader historical context.

Recent Developments

Teachers of Canadian history may want to be mindful of the following recent trends when planning to use juvenile and young adult historical fiction:

- **Emphasis on historical fiction about Canada.** There has been an outpouring of Canadian fiction for youth over the past thirty years. Increasingly that fiction has been historical. In fact, some of the leading writers of adolescent fiction in Canada, such as Jean Little, Kit Pearson, Julie Lawson, and Sarah Ellis, are writing historical fiction at this time. All of these authors have written books in the recent Dear Canada series published by Scholastic.

- **A focus on the more recent past.** Most Canadian adolescent fiction concentrates on the relatively recent past, examining such events as the building of the Canadian Pacific Railway, the Cariboo gold rush in British Columbia, experiences of the British Barnardo "home" children, the Great Depression, and home front events during the two world wars.

- **Greater realism.** Geoffrey Trease (1983), in reflecting on his fifty years as an author of historical fiction for young people, commented on how very restricted such writing once was. He pointed to the absence of a number of aspects of life that now appear in novels for youth, such as liquor, parents with serious moral weaknesses, swearing, and adolescent romances.

- **Proliferation of female protagonists.** Jane Austen (1917, 1975) had a character say, "[History] tells me nothing that does not either vex or weary me.... the men all so good for nothing, and hardly any women at all" (96). For years, teachers, librarians, and parents have lamented the paucity of female protagonists in adolescent and young adult fiction. That situation has changed to the point that a majority of such fiction now features females. For example, the books in the Dear Canada series all have female protagonists.

- **Blurring of fiction and non-fiction.** Barbara Greenwood has emerged as a master of the technique of combining fiction and non-fiction. Several of her books—*Gold Rush Fever* (2001), *The Last Safe House* (1998), and *A Pioneer Story* (1994)—weave historical background information around a fictional narrative. *The Story of Canada* (1992) is another example of this approach. This wonderful book was co-written by children's fiction author Janet Lunn and historian Christopher Moore. While primarily a reference book for a juvenile audience, it also contains fictional narratives.

The Dear Canada series is written in the first person, as if the protagonist is writing in her journal. These books are, in fact, pure fiction. At the end of each book, following the fictional narrative, is historical background information, maps, photographs, and other primary source accounts. *Eleonora's Diary* (1994) is the authentic journal of a young girl, written over a thirteen-year period, and preserved by her family for 150 years. Caroline Parry provides lengthy explanations of the historical background to events described by Eleonora, a glossary of archaic terms, photographs, maps, and an ongoing discussion of how she has gone about constructing a historical record of Eleonora's life.

- **Canadian biographies for juvenile audiences.** Increasingly, Canadian biographies for young audiences are blurring the line between fiction and non-fiction. Connie Brummel Crook's three-volume biography of Nellie McClung (1994, 1998, 1999) is fictionalized. The author takes a great deal of licence with the documented material, including invented conversations, Nellie's unrecorded thoughts, and undocumented events that may or may not have occurred. Susan Merritt's popular three-volume series, *Her Story: Women from Canada's Past* (1993, 1995, 1999) fits within this genre. She includes such luminaries as Laura Secord, Pauline Johnson, and Emily Carr as well as some women who are not well known, such as former slave and early Saltspring Island settler Sylvia Estes Stark.

Select a piece of historical fiction from the bibliography at the end of this chapter that fits with a period or event covered in the curriculum. Select specific passages or chapters from the historical novel and explain how these could be used to enhance students' understanding of the content and skill outcomes in the curriculum.

Cautions

The most significant educational concerns with the use of literature to teach about history are inaccuracies and presentism.

INACCURACY

Historical inaccuracy can be a problem for the simple reason that the first purpose of authors of fiction is to entertain, not to inform. Charles Frasier, author of the adult novel *Cold Mountain*, has talked about this:

> Not long ago I met a reader who told me her husband was convinced that at some point in *Cold Mountain*, I began making things up. Her husband wondered when that was. I said I knew exactly at what point I began making things up. It was on page one. That exchange keeps coming back to me, largely because its assumptions raise any number of questions...about how historical fiction works and, indeed, what its goals as a genre should be. Where, for example, should we place the balance point between the history and the fiction? (I'm supposing, perhaps unfairly, that the husband would position it to leave a great weighty length of history and only a bare nub of fiction, just enough to keep the plot rolling along.) Might we wish to limit

historical fiction to a retelling—or repackaging—of so-called actual past events? To what extent are we writers free to introduce well-known historical figures into our work and have them carry on conversations and commit acts we cannot verify? Are we free to lash them with emotions they never actually felt?

…It worked best for me to let the fiction drive and the history ride (2001 , 312–313).

We have to recognize that, in using fiction to aid in the teaching of history, we are engaging in an activity not intended by the author. The author of a fictional work does not necessarily have a responsibility to be historically accurate, although the worth of the work is increased if she or he is. The same point can be made about historical films.

However, as Egoff and Saltman point out, while "accuracy is an asset; plausibility is essential" (1990, 104). In spite of their desire to "let the fiction drive," it is reassuring that many authors report taking great delight in amassing the historical details necessary to paint a rich and (mostly) accurate picture of the past. One of these is well known author of adolescent fiction, Jean Little:

> It is the small details that make historical fiction work, I believe. You need to know what hymns they sang, what their family traditions were, what sayings were passed down, what riddles were set, what advice was given to children, what chores they had to do, what books they read, what games they played, what gave them nightmares. Finding these bits and pieces is like going on a treasure hunt—deeply satisfying when you stumble on a tiny bit that brings your whole scene to life (1996, 96–97).

Janet McNaughton has commented on the question of accuracy she confronted when writing the novel, *To Dance at the Palais Royale* (1997), about Aggie Maxwell, a teenage girl who emigrates from Scotland to Toronto. In the end the author explained the "message" she wished to send to her young readers and her alteration of the facts to create this effect. For instance, she manipulated circumstances in order to portray interactions between the British-born protagonist, Aggie, and Rachel Mendorfsky, a Jewish woman from Russia. As McNaughton acknowledges, it is unlikely that such interactions would ever have actually taken place. She explained that "Toronto was on the verge of becoming one of the great cosmopolitan cities of all time. And in an odd way, I felt it would be untrue to the future if my view of the past portrayed Toronto as nothing but that outpost of the empire" (18). And yet Toronto in the 1920s was indeed an "outpost of Empire." McNaughton fabricated her story in order to portray the city that Toronto would become rather than the city it was during this period. It seems an odd decision. Such a decision would be unacceptable to a historian, but for a novelist, it is poetic licence. This willingness to play with the facts raises important questions for history teachers.

PRESENTISM

The term presentism refers to the placing of "present-day culturally contingent values, conventions and judgments upon the people of the past, people whose cultural frameworks were quite different" (Seixas 1993, 352). Authors often use "presentism" intentionally in an attempt to make protagonists more familiar, convincing, and realistic to their contemporary readers. In this way, the characters from different time periods become recognizable as people the reader might know in their own lives.

Some authors of juvenile fiction establish a legitimacy in viewing events from a contemporary perspective by creating lead characters who go back in time. For example, Janet Lunn used this device in *The Root Cellar* (1981) to involve a contemporary girl in the American Civil War. Similarly, Ann Walsh employs it in *Your Time, My Time* (1984) in order to allow a contemporary girl to fall in love with a boy living in the gold rush town of Barkerville in 1870. As mentioned previously, Egoff and Saltzman (1990) refer to these kinds of books as "past-time fantasies."

Janet McNaughton (1997) described how she struggled with presenting behaviour that would be considered child abuse today, but which was perfectly acceptable, and even laudable, parental behaviour in Scotland of the 1920s. In her novel, the younger children in the family are whipped by their father for stealing from the collection plate at church. McNaughton includes this punishment because it was appropriate to the period. However, she wanted her readers to realize that she did not approve of the father's action. She had the minister approve of the father's actions to indicate that they were acceptable within that historical community. In opposition, the protagonist Aggie, with whom the reader was intended to empathize, strongly disapproved of the punishment.

Choosing Literature for Teaching History

There are many specific considerations when selecting individual pieces of historical fiction to use in the history classroom. In addition, because of the significant likelihood of historical inaccuracies, teachers may want to use multiple sources—drawing on fiction and non-fiction—when using literature to teach history.

CRITERIA FOR SELECTION

It is necessary to choose carefully when selecting from the wealth of available historical literature. The criteria for these choices are not the same as those for choosing a novel in an English course. The English teacher is likely to be concerned with exposing students to high quality writing, sparking students' interest in different literary genres, teaching about literary conventions, and exposing students to the sheer joy of reading. The history teacher is primarily concerned with the historical content, although high quality writing is also important. From a historical perspective, a novelist's emphasis on setting—illuminating a particular place and historical period in the curriculum—is perhaps more important than character and plot development. If the historical background serves merely as "set decoration," then the novel, while perhaps an excellent choice for an English classroom, may not assist in the teaching of history.

The highlighted section, "Selection Criteria for Historical Fiction," describes suggested criteria for use in selecting literature for historical purposes.

USING DIFFERENT HISTORICAL SOURCES

The historical information presented in literature is "strongly colored by the author's point of view and the reader's identification with particular characters" (Levstik 1986, 16). For this reason, Linda Levstik (1990) encourages history teach-

ers when using fiction to provide several historical sources, thereby offering students opportunities to compare accounts and to consider whose perspectives are at the forefront and whose are missing. This approach is illustrated by the example found in the highlighted text, "Comparing Literature and Other Accounts," involving a comparison of five different accounts of World War I.

Ideas for Using Literature in the History Classroom

Ideally, history teachers would have access to class sets of historical literature for use with their students. Since this will not always be the case, it is useful to consider ways that teachers can use literature that do not require purchasing quantities of books. Here are a few ideas:

- Choose a novel that is already required reading for your students' English course. Find out what activities the English teacher has planned. Complement these activities with others that meet social studies objectives.
- Read an excerpt from a single copy of a novel to provoke student discussion, set a mood, or provide background information about quotidian details often not found in textbooks. These passages might focus on details of food preparation and storage, the components of typical meals, household routines, appearance of rooms, clothing, hairstyles, architecture, or forms of transportation.
- Read aloud to students for the first ten minutes of each class.

SELECTION CRITERIA FOR HISTORICAL FICTION

- **Does it tell a compelling story?**
  Will students be interested in following the story? Is the novel well written? Are the historical facts a natural part of the plot?
- **Will readers learn about the historical period?**
  Are the experiences and dilemmas of the characters rooted in the historical period? Is there some indication of the broader context in which the events of the novel take place? Is there something to be learned about the time and the place from the characters' experiences?
- **Are background details indicative of the time and place?**
  Are documented historical events presented accurately? Do characters' actions seem plausible, given the historical circumstances in which they find themselves? Is the reader provided with accurate information about such daily details as food preparation, clothing, chores, medical practices, grooming habits, childcare routines, etiquette, social

interaction, work, and recreational activities? Is language use authentic to the class and gender of the people speaking? to the time? to the place?
- **Does it complement the perspective of other resources?**
  Does it portray a perspective(s) about the event or period not found in other resources, such as the textbook? Typically, textbooks are written in the third person, "voice of authority" mode. A novel has a personalized voice. It may present events from the point of view of a child, a female, a racial minority, the working class, the elderly, or other group often not well represented in other resources.
- **Does it offer "emotional sustenance"?**
  Will readers be emotionally involved in the events of the novel? Will they feel empathy for the characters? Will they care what happens to them? If not, they might as well simply read their textbooks. Literature is supposed to provide something the textbook cannot.

COMPARING LITERATURE AND OTHER ACCOUNTS

- Divide students into five groups. Each group examines a different source:

  Group 1: Painting of a battle scene by a Canadian war artist (*Canvas of War* by D.F. Oliver and L. Brandon (2000) is a collection of such paintings).

  Group 2: Textbook excerpt.

  Group 3: Photographs (*Marching to Armageddon* by war historians Desmond Morton and J.L. Granatstein (1984) contains paintings and recruitment posters).

  Group 4: Primary source excerpts such as letters from the front, journal entries, newspaper accounts (The Memory Project Digital Archive by the Dominion Institute available at www.thememoryproject.com/digital-archive/index.cfm or *Canadians at War*, Canadiana Scrapbook series, edited by Donald Santor (1978) are good sources).

  Group 5: Literature excerpt (*Rilla of Ingleside* by L.M. Montgomery (1921) is a particularly powerful example of the hardships and heartbreak endured by people on the home front. *Brothers Far From Home* in the Dear Canada series deals with similar content for students who are a little younger.)

- Each group writes a paragraph describing what it learned about World War I from its source. Each group records its paragraph on chart paper and reads it aloud to the class.
- Students compare the accounts and discuss statements that are contradictory or inaccurate. If necessary, they consult another source to confirm or refute such concerns.
- Students individually write a comprehensive account, taking into consideration perspectives presented in all the sources.
- As a class, discuss the following questions:
  - ◆ How is each source useful in expanding our understanding of the events of World War I?
  - ◆ What are the limitations of each source?
  - ◆ What are questions that you could ask of each source and expect to find answers?
  - ◆ Which source makes you want to learn more?
  - ◆ How does using a range of resources help a historian develop a rich account of the war?

- Provide a list of books found in the library on a particular historical period or event and ask students individually to prepare a report or project on a book of their choice.
- Recommend supplementary books to interested students related to the topics in your social studies or history courses.

Although the teaching activities will likely be tailored to the particular literary selection and teaching objectives, the highlighted text, "Questions to Use With Historical Novels," suggests a range of questions that are broadly applicable across many historical novels.

QUESTIONS TO USE WITH HISTORICAL NOVELS

Sample questions that could be used with any historical novel:
- Describe the protagonist.
- What can you learn about:
  - ◆ expectations of children
  - ◆ public education
  - ◆ male and female occupational roles
  - ◆ homes
  - ◆ class structure
  - ◆ differences between urban and rural life
- Are the protagonist's actions realistic for the time and place? Support your answer.
- Are there details that are not historically accurate? Explain.
- Do you consider the novel to be plausible historically, in spite of any inaccuracies?
- How important is it that a novel be historically accurate?

Comparing two historical novels about the same period.
- Does one protagonist seem more realistic than the other in the context of the historical period in which they lived? Explain.

Possibilities for comparison: (These novels are all included in the bibliography at the end of this chapter.)
- World War I: Margaret in Barbara Haworth-Attard's *Flying Geese* with Eliza in Jean Little's *Brothers Far From Home* or Rose in Haworth-Attard's *Irish Chain;*
- "Home" children: Rosetta in Linda Holeman's *Promise Song* with Maggie in Troon Harrison's *A Bushel of Light;*
- War of 1812: Dan in Marianne Brandis' *Fire Ship* with Tom in Eric Walter's *The Bully Boys.*

Concluding Thought

In this chapter, I have suggested that historical literature can deepen and enrich a history program by allowing readers to vicariously experience events in other times and places. Through literature, middle and secondary school history students can feel the pain, the pleasure, the fear, and the affection of people of other times. There is a wealth of available literature that can be used in the teaching of history both about Canada and in relation to other historical topics. It would be a shame not to use it.

Select a piece of historical fiction from the bibliography at the end of this chapter that fits with a period or event covered in the curriculum. Offer a brief critique of the historical accuracy and sense of time and place represented in the novel. Locate several non-fiction sources that would help students see the historical anomalies found in the novel. Explain how you would use these other sources to enhance students' understanding of the limitations and strengths of the novel as a source of historical insight about the chosen period or event.

ACKNOWLEDGEMENTS

This article is adapted from Penney Clark, Literature and Canadian history: A marriage made in heaven? *Canadian Social Studies* 37 (1). Available online at www.quasar.ualberta.ca/css/Css_37_1/index37_1.htm.

REFERENCES

Austen, J. 1817; 1975. *Northanger abbey.* London: The Folio Society.

Brandis, M. 1982. *Tinderbox.* Erin, ON: Porcupine's Quill.

———. 1985. *The quarter-pie window.* Erin, ON: Porcupine's Quill.

———. 1990. *The sign of the scales.* Erin, ON: Porcupine's Quill.

———. 1992. *Fire ship.* Erin, ON: Porcupine's Quill.

Courtland, M.C. and T.J. Gambell. 2000. *Young adolescents meet literature: Intersections for learning.* Vancouver: Pacific Educational Press.

Crook, C. Brummel. 1994. *Nellie L.* Toronto: Stoddart Kids.

———. 1998. *Nellie's quest.* Toronto: Stoddart Kids.

———. 1999. *Nellie's victory.* Toronto: Stoddart Kids.

Draper, Gary. 2002. An interview with Marianne Brandis. *Canadian Children's Literature* 105–106: 82–99.

Egoff, S. and J. Saltman. 1990. Historical fiction. In *The new republic of childhood: A critical guide to Canadian children's literature in English,* 103–130. Toronto: Oxford University Press.

Francis, D., J. Hobson, G. Smith, S. Garrod, and J. Smith. 1998. *Canadian issues: A contemporary perspective.* Toronto: Oxford University Press.

Frazier, C. 2001. Some remarks on history and fiction. In *Novel history: Historians and novelists confront America's past (and each other),* ed. M.C. Carnes, 311–315. New York: Simon and Schuster.

Greenwood, B. 1994. *A pioneer story: The daily life of a Canadian family in 1840.* Toronto: Kids Can Press.

———. 1998. *The last safe house: A story of the Underground Railroad.* Toronto: Kids Can Press.

———. 2001. *Gold rush fever: A story of the Klondike, 1898.* Toronto: Kids Can Press.

Harrison, T. 2000. *A Bushel of Light.* Toronto, Stoddart Kids.

Haworth-Attard, B. 2001. *Flying geese.* Toronto: HarperCollins.

———. 2002. *Irish chain.* Toronto: HarperTrophy Canada.

Holeman, L. 1997. *Promise song.* Toronto: Tundra Books.

Huck, C.S., S.Hepler, J. Hickman, and B.Z. Kiefer. 2001. *Children's literature in the elementary school,* 7th ed. New York: McGraw-Hill.

Kirk, H. 1996. No home or native land: How Canadian history got left out of recent historical fiction for children by Canadians. *Canadian Children's Literature* 87: 8–25.

Levstik, L. 1986. The relationship between historical response and narrative in a sixth grade classroom. *Theory and Research in Social Education* 14: 1–19.

———. 1990. Research directions mediating content through literary texts. *Language Arts* 67: 848–853.

Little, J. 1996. My historical fictions. *Canadian Children's Literature* 83: 94–97.

———. 2003. *Brothers far from home.* Markham, ON: Scholastic Canada.

Lunn, J. 1981. *The root cellar.* Markham, ON: Puffin Books.

Lunn, J. and C. Moore. 1992. *The story of Canada.* Toronto, ON: Lester Publishing and Key Porter Books.

Major, K. 1989. *Blood red ochre.* New York: Dell.

McNaughton, J. 1996. *To dance at the Palais Royale.* Toronto: Stoddart Kids.

———. 1997. Interpreting the past. *Children's Book News* 20 (2): 17–18.

Merritt, S. E. 1993. *Her story: Women from Canada's past.* St. Catherine's, ON: Vanwell.

———. 1995. *Her story II: Women from Canada's past.* St. Catherine's, ON: Vanwell.

———. 1999. *Her story III: Women from Canada's past.* St. Catherine's, ON: Vanwell.

Montgomery, L.M. 1921. *Rilla of Ingleside.* New York: Frederick A. Stokes.

Morton, D. and J.L. Granatstein. 1989. *Marching to Armageddon: Canadians and the great war, 1914–1919.* Toronto: Lester and Orpen Dennys.

Oliver, D.F. and L. Brandon. 2000. *Canvas of war: Painting the Canadian experience, 1914–1945.* Vancouver: Douglas and McIntyre.

Parry, C. 1994. *Eleanora's diary: The journals of a Canadian pioneer girl.* Richmond, Hill, ON: Scholastic Canada.

Santor, D. 1978. *Canadians at war: 1914–1918.* Canadiana Scrapbook series. Scarborough, ON: Prentice Hall.

Seixas, P. 1993. Popular film and young people's understanding of the history of Native American-white relations. *The History Teacher* 26 (3): 351-370.

Trease, G. 1983. Fifty years on: A writer looks back. *Children's Literature in Education* 14: 149–159.

Walsh, A. 1984. *Your time, my time*. Victoria, BC: Beach Holme Publishers.

Walsh, J.P. 1972. History is fiction. *The Horn Book Magazine* 48 (1): 17–23.

Walters, E. 2000. *The bully boys*. Toronto: Viking.

SOURCES OF IDEAS FOR HISTORICAL LITERATURE

Canadian Book Review Annual
http://cbraonline.com/home/

CLWG: Children's Literature Web Guide
http://www.acs.ucalgary.ca/~dkbrown/index.html

CM: Canadian Materials
http://www.umanitoba.ca/cm/index.html

Library and Archives Canada: Read Up On It!
http://www.collectionscanada.gc.ca/read-up-on-it/index-e.html

Saskatoon Public Library: How Novel! Canadian Young Adult Literature
http://spldatabase.saskatoonlibrary.ca/internet/HowNovelQuery.htm

CANADA HISTORICAL FICTION AND BIOGRAPHY

VIKING EXPLORATION

Henighan, Tom. 2001. *Viking quest.*
Describes the experiences of fifteen-year-old Rigg, son of Leif Eriksson, in an early eleventh-century settlement in Vinland.

NEW FRANCE

Martel, Suzanne. 1992. *The king's daughter.*
Describes life in New France from the point of view of a recently arrived *fille du roi*.

Trottier, Maxine. 2003. *Alone in an untamed land: The* filles du roi *diary of Hélène St. Onge* (Dear Canada series).
Describes life in New France from the point of view of a recently arrived *fille du roi*.

FUR TRADE

Manson, Ainslie. 1992. *A dog came too.*
This beautiful picture book depicts the 1793 journey of Alexander Mackenzie and his men overland to the Pacific Ocean. The focus is on a faithful dog who did actually make the journey.

Thomas, Audrey. 2001. *Isobel Gunn.*
This fictional account is based on the true story of a woman who came to Canada disguised as a man, and who worked as a fur trader until giving birth to a child.

Thompson, Margaret. 2000. *Eyewitness.*
Six-year-old Peter lives in Fort St. James, New Caledonia, in the 1820s. He meets the future governor of Vancouver Island and New Caledonia, James Douglas, Hudson Bay Company Governor Sir George Simpson, chief trader James McDougall, and Carrier Chief Kwah.

EXPULSION OF THE ACADIANS

Downie, Mary Alice. 1980. *Proper Acadian.*
A boy chooses between deportation and family ties.

BATTLE OF PLAINS OF ABRAHAM

Henty, G.A. 1896, 2001. *With Wolfe in Canada—Or the winning of a continent.*
This reprinted book tells an imperialistic tale of a heroic British lad at the Battle of the Plains of Abraham.

LOYALISTS

Bradford, Karleen. 2002. *With nothing but our courage: The Loyalist diary of Mary MacDonald* (Dear Canada series).
Describes the fictional experiences of a family of Loyalists who settle in the colony of Quebec. The diary is accompanied by historical notes and photographs.

Crook, Connie Brummel. 1991. *Flight.*
John W. Meyers (the founder of Belleville, Ontario, and an ancestor of the author) and his family flee the American Revolution.

Crook, Connie Brummel. 1995. *Meyers' creek.*
Tells the fictionalized experiences of John W. Meyers and his family as they build a new life in the colony of Quebec. A sequel to *Flight*.

Crook, Connie Brummel. 2001. *The hungry year.*
Twelve-year-old Kate cares for her two younger brothers in a wilderness cabin during the harsh winter of 1787.

Downie, Mary Alice and John Downie. 1971. *Honor bound.*
Loyalist family leaves the United States after the American Revolution and settles in Quebec.

Lunn, Janet. 1997. *The hollow tree.*
Phoebe Olcott makes a dangerous journey to deliver a message carried by her cousin, Gideon, who has been hanged as a British spy during the American Revolution. She marries and settles on an island in Lake Ontario.

WAR OF 1812

Bradford, Karleen. 1982. *The other Elizabeth.*
Elizabeth travels back in time to 1813 and saves the life of one of her ancestors.

Brandis, Marianne. 1992. *Fire ship.*
Describes the 1813 devastation of York by the Americans, from the point of view of Dan, a boy who has recently emigrated from the United States.

Crook, Connie Brummel. 1994. *Laura's choice.*
Tells the story of Laura Secord and the War of 1812.

Ibbitson, John. 1991. *1812.*
An orphaned boy loses his farm and fights with General Brock.

Pearson, Kit. 2002. *Whispers of war: The 1812 diary of Susanna Merritt* (Dear Canada series).
Describes the fictional experiences of Susanna and her family, who are living on the Niagara peninsula. The diary is accompanied by historical notes and photographs.

Sass, Gregory. 1985. *Redcoat.*
A working-class boy joins the British army and travels to Upper Canada to serve under General Brock. Egoff and Saltman call this "the harshest book in Canadian children's fiction" (1990, 118).

Walters, Eric. 2000. *The bully boys.*
Describes the adventures of fourteen-year-old Tom Roberts with the British lieutenant James Fitzgibbon and his Bully Boys. Lighthearted, humorous account.

IMMIGRATION TO UPPER AND LOWER CANADA

Bilson, Geoffrey. 1982. *Death over Montreal.*
Jamie Douglas travels from Scotland, only to arrive in Montreal during a cholera epidemic. He helps a naturalistic healer with his work.

Lunn, Janet. 1986. *Shadow in Hawthorn Bay.*
Mary Urquhart follows her cousin Duncan from the Highlands of Scotland to the wilderness of Upper Canada.

Parry, Caroline. 1994. *Eleanora's diary: The journals of a Canadian pioneer girl.*
The author takes an actual diary recounting the experiences of a British immigrant family in Simcoe County, Ontario, and adds historical details, maps, photographs, drawings, and explanations.

UPPER CANADA/CANADA WEST (1800–1860s)

Brandis, Marianne. 1996. *Rebellion: A novel of Upper Canada.*
Describes the 1837 Rebellion from the perspectives of three teenagers.

Brandis, Marianne. Trilogy: *The tinderbox* (1982); *The quarter-pie window* (1985); *The sign of the scales* (1990).
Describes rural Upper Canada and the new town of York during the 1830s.

German, Tony. 1982. *Tom Penny and the grand canal.*
Describes the adventures of sixteen-year-old Tom Penny during the "canal fever" period of the 1830s

Greenwood, Barbara. 1994. *A pioneer story.*
Provides details of life on a backwoods farm in 1840.

Greenwood, Barbara. 1984. *A question of loyalty.*
A family who supports the government protects a young rebel in the aftermath of the 1837 Rebellion.

Greenwood, Barbara. 1990. *Spy in the shadows.*
Describes the Fenian raids across the Niagara River in 1866.

Lunn, Janet. 1981. *The root cellar.*
Rose is transported to Upper Canada and the American Civil War.

RED RIVER SETTLEMENT

Matas, Carol. 2002. *Footsteps in the snow: The Red River diary of Isobel Scott* (Dear Canada series).
Describes the fictional experiences of Isobel and her family, who travel from Scotland to settle in Rupert's Land. Diary is accompanied by historical notes and photographs.

CHILD LABOUR

Freeman, Bill. 1975. *Shantymen of Cache Lake.*
Meg and John find work in the same Ottawa Valley lumber camp where their father died. They carry on his work of starting a union. This book provides many technical details about logging in the mid-nineteenth century.

Freeman, Bill. 1976. *The last voyage of the Scotian.*
Meg and John are crew members on a windjammer that travels from Quebec to Jamaica with a load of squared timber, then on to Liverpool with a cargo of sugar cane, and, finally, back to Halifax with a load of immigrants. Sequel to *Shantymen of Cache Lake.*

Freeman, Bill. 1983. *Trouble at Lachine mill.*
Child labour replaces striking workers in a Montreal shirt factory in the 1870s. Historical photographs.

Gaetz, Dayle Campbell. 1998. *Living freight.*
An orphaned girl leaves a sixty-hour work week in an English mill to move to colony of British Columbia, where she works for the family of James Douglas.

UNDERGROUND RAILROAD

Greenwood, Barbara. 1998. *The last safe house: A story of the Underground Railroad.*
Eleven-year-old Eliza travels from a southern plantation to St. Catharines, Canada West. This book is a combination of fiction and historical information.

Smucker, Barbara. 1978. *Underground to Canada.*
Julilly, a slave, escapes to Canada via the Underground Railroad.

ARCTIC EXPLORATION

Godfrey, Martyn. 1988. *Mystery in the frozen lands.*
Depicts life of nineteenth-century explorers through an expedition searching for John Franklin.

CARIBOO GOLD RUSH

Duncan, Sandy Francis. 1997, rev. ed. *Cariboo runaway.*
Two children set out on a dangerous journey, travelling from Victoria to Barkerville in search of their missing father, who is a prospector.

Walsh, Ann. 1984. *Your time, my time.*
Fifteen-year-old Margaret Elizabeth Connell is transported back in time to the Barkerville of 1870. She meets Judge Matthew Baillie Begbie, falls in love with a boy of the time, and deals with death.

Walsh, Ann. 1988. *Moses, me and murder.*
Twelve-year-old Ted MacIntosh and his friend Moses work to solve a murder in Barkervillle at the height of the gold rush.

Walsh, Ann. 1998. *The doctor's apprentice.*
Fourteen-year-old Ted MacIntosh is an apprentice to a doctor in Barkerville at the height of the gold rush and during the fire of 1868. Sequel to *Moses, me and murder.*

BUILDING THE CANADIAN PACIFIC RAILWAY

Bright, Elizabeth. 2001. *Lambs of Hell's Gate.*
Mui travels from China and then up the Fraser Canyon in search of her brother.

Lawson, Julie. 2002. *A ribbon of shining steel: The railway diary of Kate Cameron* (Dear Canada series).
Describes the fictional experiences of twelve-year-old Kate as she observes the building of the Canadian Pacific Railway (CPR) through the Fraser Canyon. The diary is accompanied by historical notes and photographs.

RIEL RESISTANCES
1869 AND 1885

Truss, Jan. 1977. *A very small rebellion.*
The story is accompanied by background information on both resistances.

1885

Boyle, B.J. 2000. *Battle cry at Batoche.*
The events of the 1885 Riel Resistance are viewed through the eyes of fifteen-year-old twins, whose uncle is a Hudson's Bay Company employee, and a Cree boy, who are befriended by Gabriel and Madeleine Dumont.

Richards, David. 1993. *Soldier boys.*
Describes the experiences of a bugle boy with the Winnipeg Rifles and a Métis boy who meet at the battle of Fish Creek.

Scanlan, W.J. 1989. *Rebellion.*
Fifteen-year-old Jack is captured by the Métis after the Battle of Duck Lake during the 1885 Resistance.

"HOME" CHILDREN (1860s–1930s)

Harrison, Troon. 2000. *A bushel of light.*
Fourteen-year-old Maggie, an orphan sent to Canada by the Barnardo Society, is trapped in an unhappy situation on an Ontario farm. She is torn between running away to find her twin sister and feelings of responsibility towards neglected four-year-old Lizzy.

Holeman, Linda. 1997. *Promise song.*
Two orphans, fourteen-year-old Rosetta and her younger sister Flora, travel from England to Canada. Upon arrival, the sisters are separated, but manage to be reunited after many tribulations.

Little, Jean. 2001. *Orphan at my door: The home child diary of Victoria Cope* (Dear Canada series).
Describes the fictional experiences of two home children in Guelph, Ontario. The diary is accompanied by historical notes and photographs.

KLONDIKE GOLD RUSH

Greenwood, Barbara. 2001. *Gold rush fever: A story of the Klondike, 1898.*
Thirteen-year-old Tim and his older brother make the hazardous journey from Seattle to the Yukon and spend a year in the gold fields. This book is a combination of fiction and historical information.

Hughes, Monica. 1974. *Gold fever trail.*
Two children travel from Victoria to the Klondike to find their father.

Service, Robert W. 1986. *The cremation of Sam McGee.*
Service's famous poem is illustrated by Ted Harrison's paintings.

TURN OF THE CENTURY

Barkhouse, Joyce. 1990. *Pit pony.*
Gives a portrayal of life in a company mining town in Cape Breton.

Hutchins, Hazel. 1994. *Within a painted past.*
Alison travels through time to nineteenth-century Banff and the Alberta foothills area.

McGugan, Jim. 1994. *Josepha: A prairie boy's story.*
A fourteen-year-old immigrant boy on the Prairies must attend school with younger children because he cannot speak English.

Montgomery, L.M. 1908. *Anne of Green Gables.*
This internationally acclaimed book depicts social mores and daily life in rural Prince Edward Island in the latter half of the nineteenth century.

Tanaka, Shelley. 1996. *On board the Titanic.*
Tells the fictionalized story of two of the *Titanic's* survivors. Lots of factual detail and explanations provided, as well as many photographs and original illustrations.

Wilson, Eric. 1997. *Trapped in ice.*
This novel is based on accounts of the ill-fated Canadian Arctic expedition of 1913.

CANADA AND WORLD WAR I

Granfield, Linda. 1995. *In Flanders Fields: The story of the poem by John McCrae.*
Each line of the poem is accompanied by a vivid full-page illustration. Includes a biography of McCrae and a description of the writing and legacy of the poem.

Haworth-Attard, Barbara. 2002. *Irish chain.*
Rose and her family experience the devastating effects of the Halifax explosion.

Haworth-Attard, Barbara. 2001. *Flying geese.*
Twelve-year old Margaret and her family leave their farm in Saskatchewan to live in London, Ontario, where they deal with poverty and the anxiety of having a son and brother overseas. The theme of quilting as a means of expression for women weaves through this book.

Little, Jean. 2003. *Brothers far from home: The World War I diary of Eliza Bates* (Dear Canada series).
Eliza and her family live in Uxbridge, Ontario. Her two brothers and their friend are overseas.

Little, Jean. 2007. *If I die before I wake: The flu epidemic diary of Fiona Macgregor* (Dear Canada series).
Describes the horrors of the global flu epidemic that erupted at the end of World War I.

Major, Kevin. 1995. *No man's land.*
Describes the men of the Newfoundland Regiment at the Battle of the Somme in 1916.

Montgomery, L.M. 1920. *Rilla of Ingleside.*
This poignant story describes the anguish of life on the home front in rural Prince Edward Island. Rilla is Anne Shirley's (of *Anne of Green Gables*) youngest daughter.

Whitaker, Muriel, ed. 2001. *Great Canadian war stories.*
As Whitaker puts it, "These are stories of individuals, generally taking the form of fiction based on personal experience." Adult book.

WINNIPEG GENERAL STRIKE

Bilson, Geoffrey and Ron Berg. 1981. *Goodbye Sarah.*
Mary Jarrett's father is an organizer of the General Strike. The family endures financial hardship and Mary's relationship with her best friend is destroyed as a result of tensions related to the strike.

1920s

Doyle, Brian. 2001. *Mary Ann Alice.*
Describes loss of farmland on Gatineau River due to damming for hydroelectric power.

Ellis, Sarah. 2001. *A prairie as wide as the sea: The immigrant diary of Ivy Weatherall* (Dear Canada series).
Describes the fictional experiences of a British family who emigrate to Saskatchewan and their initial experiences there. The diary is accompanied by historical notes and photographs.

Hunter, Bernice Thurman. 1995. *Amy's promise.*
Describes family interactions in Toronto.

McNaughton, Janet. 1996. *To dance at the Palais Royale.*
Aggie, a seventeen-year-old Scottish girl, travels to Toronto to work as a domestic servant. The novel explores poverty, class interaction, and ethnicity.

Smucker, Barbara. 1980. *Days of terror.*
Describes the persecution of Russian Mennonites and their emigration to Canada.

GREAT DEPRESSION PERIOD

Hunter, Bernice Thurman. Trilogy: *That scatterbrain Booky* (1981); *With love from Booky* (1983); *As ever, Booky* (1985).
Booky and her loving family cope with unemployment and poverty in Toronto.

Kurelek, William. *A prairie boy's summer* (1975); *A prairie boy's winter* (1973).
Kurelek's paintings depict rural life on the Prairies.

Mitchell, W.O. 1947. *Who has seen the wind?*
Canadian classic depicts life on the Prairies during the Depression. Adult book.

Morck, Irene. 1999. *Five pennies: A prairie boy's story.*
Morck gives a loving portrayal of her father's life as a member of a large family living on farms in Saskatchewan and Alberta from 1916–1939.

Nodelman, Perry. 2007. *Not a nickel to spare: The Great Depression diary of Sally Cohen* (Dear Canada series).
Sally faces anti-Semitism in Toronto during the Great Depression.

Slade, Arthur. 2001. *Dust.*
Fantasy novel takes place in rural Saskatchewan where children are being kidnapped.

Taylor, Cora. 1994. *Summer of the mad monk.*
Twelve-year-old Pip and his family cope with the difficulties of living in the Dust Bowl of rural Alberta. Pip suspects an immigrant blacksmith is Rasputin, the infamous figure from the Russian Revolution.

CHINESE IMMIGRANT EXPERIENCES

Chan, Gillian. 1994. *Golden girl and other stories.*
Five stories explore intergenerational conflict and teenage bullying in the small Ontario town of Elmwood.

Chan, Gillian. 2003. *An ocean apart: The gold mountain diary of Chin Mei-ling* (Dear Canada series).
Chin Mei-ling and her father live in Vancouver's Chinatown. They are saving in order to bring Chin Mei-ling's mother and younger brother from China.

Chong, Denise. 1995. *The concubine's children.*
This biographical account describes the author's mother's and grandparents' experiences in Vancouver and Nanaimo Chinatowns. Adult book.

Choy, Wayson. 1995. *The jade peony.*
Set in Vancouver's Chinatown in the late 1930s and 1940s, this novel describes the mingling of new immigrants with people who have lived there for many years. Adult book

Lawson, Julie. 1993. *White jade tiger.*
Jasmine travels through time to Victoria's Chinatown in the 1880s.

Yee, Paul. 1986. *The curses of third uncle.*
Lilian Ho, who is living in Vancouver's Chinatown in 1909, is learning New World ideas about possibilities for females. The novel is set against a backdrop of a struggle to overthrow the Chinese emperor.

Yee, Paul. 1989. *Tales from gold mountain: Stories of the Chinese in the New World.*
These eight stories represent the nineteenth-century Chinese experience in Canada.

Yee, Paul. 1994. *Breakaway*.
Describes financial hardship and racial intolerance from the point of view of Kwok-Ken Wong, an eighteen-year-old Chinese soccer player living on a mudflat farm by the Fraser River during the Great Depression.

Yee, Paul. 1996. *Ghost train*.
Haunting picture book depicts the sacrifices made by Chinese immigrants involved in the building of the Canadian Pacific Railway. Powerful illustrations by Harvey Chan.

CANADA AND WORLD WAR II

McNaughton, Janet. 1994. *Catch me once, catch me twice*.
Describes home front in St. John's, Newfoundland, 1942; family relationships, friendships, class issues, and anguish about a father who is missing in action overseas.

Little, Jean. 1977. *Listen for the singing*.
A German-Canadian family living in Toronto is affected by anti-German sentiment.

Whitaker, Muriel, ed. 2001. *Great Canadian war stories*.
As Whitaker puts it, "These are stories of individuals, generally taking the form of fiction based on personal experience." Adult book.

JAPANESE INTERNMENT

Garrigue, Sheila. 1985. *The eternal spring of Mr. Ito*.
Explores the effects of the attack on Pearl Harbor on the relationship between a British war evacuee living in Vancouver and a Japanese Canadian gardener.

Kawaga. Joy. 1986. *Naomi's road*.
A family is moved from Vancouver to an internment camp near Slocan, BC. Based on the adult novel, *Obasan*, by the same author.

Takashima, Shizuye. 1976. *A child in prison camp*.
Describes experiences of a Japanese Canadian family living in a Canadian internment camp.

Trottier, Maxine. 1999. *Flags*.
After the neighbour of a young girl goes to an internment camp, she vows to remember his legacy.

Walters, Eric. 2000. *Caged eagles*.
Japanese Canadian family from a fishing village on the northwest coast of British Columbia is sent to an internment centre in Vancouver and then to a sugar beet farm in Alberta.

BRITISH CHILDREN IN CANADA

Bilson, Geoffrey. 1984. *Hockey bat Harris*.
David Harris is evacuated from Britain in order to live with a family in Saskatoon. There are tensions because he is worried about his mother in England and his father on active duty in Egypt.

Pearson, Kit. Guests of War series: *The sky is falling* (1989); *Looking at the moon* (1991); *The lights go on again* (1993).
Norah and Gavin are evacuated to Toronto, where they live with a wealthy matron and her adult daughter. There, they confront adolescence, unfamiliar cultural mores, and people who cannot understand the emotional pain of those who have had firsthand experience of war.

POST-WORLD WAR II

Boraks-Nemetz, Lillian. 1994. *The old brown suitcase: A teenager's story of war and peace*.
A Jewish girl adjusts to life in Canada, while dealing with memories and emotions related to her war experiences in Europe.

Carrier, Roch. 1979. *The hockey sweater*.
This classic tale of Canada's two solitudes is told from the point of view of a boy living in rural Quebec.

Doyle, Brian. 1984. *Angel square*.
Explores racial tensions in Ottawa.

Hewitt, Marsha and Claire Mackay. 1981. *One proud summer*.
The one hundred-day millworkers' strike in Valleyfield, Quebec, in 1946 is described from the perspective of thirteen-year-old Lucie.

Ibbitson, John. 1993. *The night Hazel came to town*.
Describes the experiences of a copy boy working for the *Toronto Telegram* during the Cold War period of the 1950s.

Pearson, Kit. 1987. *A handful of time*.
A twelve-year-old girl travels back to the 1950s, to one of her mother's childhood summers at the lake.

Razzell, Mary. 1994. *White wave*.
Set in British Columbia, this novel traces a girl's journey towards self-discovery, part of which involves coming to know her father, who returns from service in the navy.

Sheppard, Mary C. 2001. *Seven for a secret*.
Three fifteen-year-old girls in a fictional coastal village in Newfoundland in the early 1960s cope with impending adulthood and secrets from the past.

ABORIGINAL PERSPECTIVES

Clark, Joan. 1995. *The dream carvers*.
A Greenland Viking in Newfoundland is captured by a Native clan.

Harris, Christie. 1966, 1992. *Raven's cry*.
Illustrated by Bill Reid, this book explores the impact of European culture on the Haida.

Hudson, Jan. 1984. *Sweetgrass*.
Sweetgrass, a fifteen-year-old Blackfoot, breaks a tribal taboo to save her family from starvation and smallpox.

Major, Kevin. 1984. *Blood red ochre*.
The story of a contemporary girl and boy living in Newfoundland is mingled with the story of Dauoodaset, one of the last of the Beothuk.

Maracle, Lee. 1993. *Ravensong: A novel*.
Seventeen-year-old Stacey lives in a Native village, but attends school in a nearby town. It is the early 1950s and she is struggling to learn how to balance the values of the two cultures.

Olsen, Sylvia with Rita Morris and Ann Sam. 2001. *No time to say good-bye: Children's stories of Kuper Island residential school.*
This fictional account describes the experiences of five Tsartlip First Nations children at a residential school.

Sterling, Shirley. 1992. *My name is Seepeetza.*
This is a fictional account of one girl in an aboriginal residential school.

Taylor, Cora. 2002. *Buffalo hunt* (Our Canadian Girl series).
Angélique, a Métis girl living near Batoche in 1865, experiences a buffalo hunt.

STORY COLLECTIONS

Barkhouse, Joyce. 1992. *Yesterday's children.*
Twelve stories set in Atlantic Canada in different time periods.

Harrison, Dick, ed. 1996. *Best Mounted Police stories.*
Reprinted stories organized into four sections: The Trek West and the Early Days, The North-West Rebellion and After, the Gold Rush and the North, the Twentieth Century. Adult book.

Hehner, Barbara. 1999. *The spirit of Canada.*
Includes legends, stories, poetry, and songs written by Canadian authors. Includes 150 illustrations by 15 Canadian children's artists.

Pearson, Kit, ed. 1998. *This land: A cross-country anthology of Canadian fiction for young readers.*
Pearson has selected twenty-two, mostly historical, pieces that are representative of the best of Canadian fiction for adolescents.

Walsh, Ann, ed. 2001. *Beginnings: Stories of Canada's past.*
Fourteen stories describe historical "firsts," including a first meeting between First Nations and Europeans, the first *filles du roi* in New France, and a young woman's first opportunity to vote.

BIOGRAPHIES

Braid, Kate. 2001. *Emily Carr: Rebel artist.*
Detailed biography accompanied by a timeline of major events in Carr's life and black-and-white photographs.
Other books in this series include:
    Bowen, Lynne. 1999. *Robert Dunsmuir: Laird of the mines.*
    Chalmers, William. 2000. *George Mercer Dawson: Geologist, scientist, explorer.*

Keller, Betty. 1999. *Pauline Johnson: First aboriginal voice of Canada.*
Margoshes, Dave. 1999. *Tommy Douglas: Building the new society.*
Wilson, John. 1999. *Norman Bethune: A life of passionate conviction.*
Wyatt, Rachel. 1999. *Agnes Macphail: Champion of the underdog.*

Crook, Connie Brummel. Trilogy.
A fictionalized biography of Nellie McClung.
Nellie L. (1994). Childhood, ages 10 to 17.
Nellie's quest. (1998). Schoolteacher.
Nellie's victory. (1999). Marriage, family life, and political activism until 1914.

Hancock, Lynn. 1996. *Nellie McClung: No small legacy.*
Adult level biography. Includes two of McClung's short stories.

MacLeod, Elizabeth. 1999. *Alexander Graham Bell: An inventive life.*
Uses a visual approach. Surrounding the text on each two-page spread are photographs, newspaper excerpts, editorial notes, as well as a cartoon of Bell with a word bubble in which he makes a comment on the information provided.

Martin, Carol. 1996. *Martha Black: Gold rush pioneer.*
Entertaining biography, accompanied by photographs.

Merritt, Susan E.
Her story: Women from Canada's past. Vol. I (1993).
Her story: Women from Canada's past. Vol. II (1995).
Her story: Women from Canada's past. Vol. III (1999).
Sixteen biographies in the first two books and fourteen in the third, deal with women from different walks of life and different time periods. Black-and-white photographs and paintings depict the people and the times.

NON-FICTION (REFERENCE)

Lunn, Janet and Christopher Moore. 1992. *The story of Canada.*
Written by a children's author and a historian, this beautifully illustrated history deals with the Ice Age to 1992. Listed in *Great Canadian books of the century* (Vancouver Public Library).

30

Images of the Past
Using Film to Teach History

Stuart Poyntz

Introduction

Most of us spend more time learning about the past through film and television than through any other media. Should this surprise us? Not really. The study of history, like so much of our lives, has been dramatically remade by the expansion of visual media. In fact, movies and television have never been more powerful and popular as a way of encountering the past. Evidence of this trend is found in the increase in history documentaries on television, the development of the History Channel, the production of major historical mini-series,[1] the rebirth of the Hollywood historical drama,[2] not to mention an array of World War II epics,[3] a series of historical literary adaptations,[4] and any number of other critically acclaimed productions.[5]

Some find these developments troubling, especially in relation to teaching history in the classroom. A common criticism is that films contain "poor information load" (Jarvie, quoted in Rosenstone 1995, 26) because they provide partial or distorted accounts of the story of the past, and moreover, they fail to engage in exactly the sorts of debates historians have about what constitutes history. Movies do not typically defend, footnote, or problematize their interpretations of the past, and because of this, some argue they distract from rather than aid us in understanding history.

For educators, there is at least some truth to these concerns, if only because many Hollywood movies are so clearly made as marketing exercises rather than as credible historical accounts. Michael Bay's forgettable *Pearl Harbor* (2001) comes to mind here, as does Roland Emmerich's *The Patriot* (2000). In both movies, the past is just a resource far enough removed from our lives that it can be reshaped to fit any marketing spin a producer would like to put on it. How else is one to explain that in *Pearl Harbor* the ending of the film is changed depending on the intended national market (Japan or America). Similarly, in *The Patriot*, why else is history whitewashed to exclude difficult truths about America's history of slavery?

However, educators know how enticing, effective, and useful movies can be, especially for teenagers who may feel that the past is a distant and unknowable place. Historical films are recognized for their value in generating student interest in a specific period or event from the past. Despite their flaws, they can also be used to contribute in more substantive ways. The highlighted section, "Opportunities to use Historical Films," suggests several entry points for using historical movies to expand and deepen students' understanding of the past.

Perhaps the real question is not whether or not to show movies in the classroom, but how to use movies to help students understand history. In what follows, I look at this question in two parts. I begin by looking at how mainstream Hollywood approaches the past. I discuss the primary codes or cinematic conventions—the "language" that popular movies use in creating historical representations—and how these shape our experience of history on-screen. Students must learn the importance of recognizing and reading these codes. Secondly, I assess how Hollywood representations contribute to historical understandings and misunderstandings. I explore the ways that movies represent the past well and their pitfalls. Throughout these two discussions, I refer to various popular and critically acclaimed movies and I suggest activities to engage students critically with movies in the classroom.

Representation and Cinematic Codes

Peter Seixas suggests that teenagers tend to view "popular historical film as if it were a window on the past" (1996, 770). He identifies six aspects of movies that influence this perception:

- movies conform to students' understanding of human nature;
- historical characters in film are depicted in very familiar ways;

OPPORTUNITIES TO USE HISTORICAL FILMS

- **Introduce a topic.** Movies are helpful for introducing a unit, especially as a means of drawing students' attention to the central themes and issues you want to explore in future classes.
- **Create a controversy.** Movies can be used to raise or even crystallize controversies or debates at the conclusion of a unit. In this way, they can be helpful to set up a debate about issues students will need to explore further in a final project.
- **Use as information source.** Movies can provide students with a great deal of information about the past. For instance, Oliver Stone's *JFK* (1991) provides in depth treatment of key issues in the assassination of Kennedy.
- **Highlight the meaning of an event.** The opening 15–20 minutes of a movie are often useful sources of iconic images that highlight the film director's interpretation of major historical themes or the significance of key historical events. Use short clips from the opening of the film to draw students' attention to one or more key images that define the filmmaker's understanding of the past.
- **Highlight specific events.** At their best, movies can show us a representation of what a historical era was like. Use short clips from a movie to provide students with constructions of key places or dramatic events from the past, especially as a way to introduce this time and place.
- **Create a sense of the times.** Film music on its own can be very effective at constructing the mood or sensibility of a specific period—for instance, the jazz era as depicted in Francis Ford Coppola's *The Cotton Club* (1984). Use a short clip that includes music to capture the atmosphere and feel of a historical period.

- cinematic and school accounts of the past are very similar;
- recent film releases are seen to reflect up-to-date knowledge of the past;
- the technical sophistication of films produces a sense of verisimilitude;
- the emotional impact of movies creates a sense of proximity between the past and the student's present.

The sway that popular films have over students is a major obstacle to using movies in the classroom—as much as movies can make students believe accounts of the past, they can also deceive students about the past. If students are to resist the distorting allure of film, they must understand five dominant codes or conventions that directors and screenwriters employ in histories on film:

- cinematic realism
- linear plot structure
- the heroic perspective
- visual and audio techniques
- use of detail.

CINEMATIC REALISM

The most general code in Hollywood cinema is the desire to produce "cinematic realism"—the sense that what we see on screen *is* as it was. Realism of this sort is produced through seamless continuity editing and emotionally direct sound tracks that leave us feeling as though everything on screen is as it should be. We're not watching a metaphor or a symbol of the past; rather, we are watching *the* past. Of course, many of us know movies are manipulated, and yet, like written history, when movies work, we tend to forget that the whole enterprise is constructed. We experience verisimilitude, a feeling of sameness between two realms of experience—the one on screen and the one we imagine to be a real past. Hollywood realism is just the way mainstream filmmakers make the past seem familiar. And when movies accomplish this feat, audiences find it very difficult to distinguish representations that help our historical understanding from those that hinder it.

The remaining four codes of representation that I discuss are actually techniques that filmmakers employ to generate a cinematically realistic style.

LINEAR PLOT STRUCTURE

A very common code used to build credibility is the linear plot structure that shapes most mainstream movies. Through this structure, movies tell history as stories with a beginning, a middle, and an end. They also include "a moral message and (usually) a feeling of uplift" (Rosenstone 1995, 55). The stories generally imply that humanity is making progress and that things are getting better. A few history movies run counter to this tradition, including Oliver Stone's *JFK* (1991), which suggests that American democracy is under threat from forces inside the U.S. government. Even in *JFK*, we are reassured when New Orleans attorney Jim Garrison (played by Kevin Costner) tells us how corrupt the government is because it signals "that the problems of the security state will be exposed" (Rosenstone 1995, 56).

History movies, like most other mainstream historical accounts, are organized around a specific period, personality, or set of events, and these events and persons are explained in a manner that is self-contained, largely unambiguous, and has closure. Rarely does Hollywood give us ambiguous endings, alternative possibilities, information, and details not fully exhausted by the plot, or uncertainties in our understanding of major events. Even in a very good movie like Daniel Vigne's *The Return of Martin Guerre* (1982),[6] which included historian Natalie Zemon Davis as an advisor, the story offers such "powerful simplicity" that Davis had cause to ask: "Where was there room in this beautiful and compelling…recreation of a [sixteenth-century French] village for the uncertainties, the 'perhaps,' the 'mayhavebeens' to which the historian has recourse when the evidence is inadequate or perplexing" (Davis, quoted in Rosenstone 1995, 58). There is little room for such ambiguity since this and other popular movies avoid uncertainty by offering us false clarity about the past.

THE HEROIC PERSPECTIVE

Another cinematic code refers to the way perspective is generated in history movies. Individual heroes or heroines are typically the key figures in a film because they are our emotional entry points into the past. Such figures may be famous (T.E. Lawrence in David Lean's 1962 epic, *Lawrence of Arabia*) or little known (Oskar Schindler in *Schindler's List* (1993)), but they are at the centre of the story, anchoring our relationship to the past. Large movements of people or other social forces are rarely important in Hollywood. Instead, mainstream movies tend to reduce those "difficult and insoluble social problems" that often drive history to the personal transformation of the main protagonists (Rosenstone 1995, 57).

Benardo Bertolucci's *The Last Emperor* (1987) offers a stunning and remarkable example of this tendency. Bertolucci's film tells the story of Pu Yi, the last man to occupy the Dragon Throne in China. After ascending the throne at the age of three in 1908, Pu Yi was forced to abdicate at the age of seven as China began its twentieth-century march from feudalism to war to revolution and, eventually, a state of relative stability. Throughout these massive historical transitions, the happiness of a single man is used to stand in for the fate of the Chinese people. Of course, Pu Yi's life was unique and highly unusual, and the film is equally magnificent. It was shot on location in the Forbidden City (with its 9,999 rooms) and is filled with authentic costumes and thousands of extras. But this story becomes a lens through which the historical tremors that shaped the most populous nation on earth is understood. In this sense, *The Last Emperor* is a strange mix of historical detail and myopic il-

lusion, a film of great beauty and a peculiarly narrow view of history.

VISUAL AND AUDIO TECHNIQUES

Specific technical elements are another device used to draw audiences emotionally and intellectually into a movie. Mainstream cinema uses "the special capabilities of the medium—the close-up of the human face, the quick juxtaposition of disparate images, the power of music and sound effect—to heighten and intensify" audience responses to stories (Rosenstone 1995, 59).[7] Understanding the purposes to which these visual and audio tools are used helps us see how they influence our perceptions of the past. For example, the meaning of shots in films is importantly determined by the positioning of the human form in the frame as suggested by these common camera angles:

- **long shots and full shots** show characters at a distance and are chosen to highlight the environment or setting in which a story takes place;
- **medium shots** show characters from about mid-thigh up and might be called "relationship" images, in that they are used to show the dynamics of character development;
- **close-ups** are generally emotion shots and are meant to create a sense of intimacy or suspense;
- **extreme close-ups** are typically used for symbolic purposes to highlight central metaphors.

While camera angles set the dynamics of power on screen, a film's moral dilemmas are typically indicated through lighting. Low-key lighting (the use of shadows and directed pools of light to create atmosphere) suggests mystery or uncertainty; high contrast lighting (harsh lines of light combined with dramatic streaks of blackness) tends to suggest anxiety or confusion. This style is also used to suggest corruption and threats to a movie's main characters.

Typically, movie's emotional tones are framed through the audio environment. The soundtrack is most obviously used in this way. Sound effects add mood or atmosphere and when used well (as, for instance, in Gilles MacKinnon's 1997 World War I film, *Regeneration*) they highlight a character's "internal voice." In one scene in *Regeneration*, for instance, Billy Prior, a working-class officer, is hypnotized so he can recollect the battlefield experience that left him unable to remember the recent past. As the scene unfolds, Prior returns to the trenches and his horrifying experience is made real through startling sound effects. We hear the expected sounds of battle, including explosions and the sounds of men screaming, but at key moments the sound track eliminates all these noises. In their absence, we hear a low, grating hum along with the sounds of boots sloshing through the muck. The battle rages on around Prior but the sound effects create the feeling that we have entered the mind of a man psychologically falling apart.

USE OF DETAIL

Filmmakers use historical practices (customs, mannerisms, language patterns, accents) and artifacts (clothes, weapons, utensils, lighting fixtures) to create the right "look" for the past. The selection of these historical details highlight three ways in which filmmakers' representations shape our understanding of the past:

- They influence which parts of the historical record are retained in popular culture and which are not by including or excluding certain details and artifacts.
- They decide on the experience of historical proximity audiences will feel by choosing how they will include and use details from the past.
- They influence the accuracy of popular impressions of a historical event portrayed in a movie depending on their level of fidelity to or disregard for the historical record.

Not surprisingly, mainstream movies often exaggerate or downplay events from the past in order to simplify the moral dimensions of the story or to contain anachronisms that will appeal to movie goers. In effect, Hollywood encourages audiences to believe we are *in* history (because the visible objects and practices seem right) when in fact history is as always a text that has been manufactured for us.

Select a film related to a historical person or event you have studied or read about. Using the five cinematic codes introduced in this chapter, identify how each code is used in the film to influence the message about the past. Prepare a brief report assessing the strengths and weaknesses of the film as a historical account.

Film and Historical Understanding

Having identified the range of codes and the work they do in constructing a sense of historical realism, I now consider their impact on students' historical understanding. Peter Seixas suggests that the real task of historical understanding is to organize "our collective experiences of the past—the traces and presentations of the past that we encounter in the present—in such a way that they provide a meaningful context for our present experience" (1996, 767). We encounter the past con-

stantly in our lives, through movies, news reports, museums, textbooks, still images, family and community, and any number of other artifacts, anecdotes, and documents. To develop historical understanding requires assessing how these traces and accounts fit into the stories we take to be meaningful in our lives. As was explored in greater detail in chapter 9, "Portals to Understanding," Seixas delineates six concepts central to historical understanding:

- historical significance;
- evidence and interpretation;
- continuity and change;
- cause and consequences;
- historical perspective taking;
- moral judgment.

I want to use these concepts to highlight how media representations influence students' sense of the past.

HISTORICAL SIGNIFICANCE

To say historical events have significance is to say they add something important to the way we imagine our present lives. The past becomes significant when we negotiate "connections between historical events and issues of concern in our time" (Seixas 1996, 769). "What makes any particular event significant," Seixas continues, "is the richness and complexity of its connections to other events and processes, and ultimately to ourselves" (768). The value of learning about the history of, for instance, Louis Hippolyte LaFontaine and Robert Baldwin is not simply to get the facts straight about life in nineteenth-century Canada, but also to assess how their great compromise established a framework for democratic government and respect for minorities that remains crucial to the country today.

In relation to film, this consideration is important because movies are very effective at recasting our perceptions of what historical facts and events are significant and what are not. For instance, filmmakers reconstruct the importance of historical events by using music or sound effects in such a way that may be exciting or dramatic, but may not have anything to do with the significance of that event in history. Similarly, filmmakers influence audiences' sense of importance by including or excluding certain details from the historical record. An interesting example of this is Martin Scorsese's epic of nineteenth-century violence, *Gangs of New York* (2002). *Gangs* begins in 1846 and largely tells a tale of violence, turf wars, and brutal anti-immigrant politics in the Five Points area of New York City. While filled with remarkable historical details, what stands out most for critic Robert Snyder is a very significant absence. In Scorsese's telling, the history of New York's most famous nineteenth-century slum turns into a story about people who "spend their days fighting in the streets and their nights fornicating on the docks. But the film ignores what most New Yorkers did back then with their days and nights: work" (Snyder 2003). Mid-nineteenth- and early twentieth-century New York is also famous for the "struggles of... workers for shorter hours, better pay and safer working conditions" (Snyder 2003). Gang violence happened, but it was a small part of the cast of daily life. Consequently, Scorsese's film leads audiences to forget New York City's great legacies to the world, including but not limited to the opportunities the city has long provided for working people to create better lives for themselves and their families. By modifying the historical record to exaggerate specific elements, this movie distorts the significance we assign to past events.

EVIDENCE AND INTERPRETATION

A second key concept refers to the role of evidence and interpretation in historical understanding. When we talk about historical evidence, we are asking how we assess and interpret the traces and accounts we find of the past. On what grounds should these be accepted and with what reservations? These questions have specific relevance to the use of film in history teaching because movies do not just render aspects of the past significant, they also shape what we believe *is* history.

Filmmakers influence a film's perceived credibility largely through the use of historical details in the setting, costumes, and music. Daniel Vigne's *The Return of Martin Guerre* (1982) is a useful example. The film is memorable in the way it appears soaked in the details of mid-sixteenth century French life. From its painterly images of smoke emanating from buildings at just the right time of year, to details about farm life and the motivations that underlie the actions of Martin Guerre's wife, Bertrande de Rols, the film is like a window into a medieval French world. As one writer noted: "anyone other than an expert ... is confronted with a ... story that is unproblematic and uncontested in its view of what happened and why" (Rosenstone 1995, 58). Of course, there are inaccuracies in the movie but the point is that its attention to detail exemplifies how movies fortify a credible vision of the past.[8]

Other film codes relevant to questions of evidence include filmmakers' modifications of the historical record to serve cinematic purposes. The furor following the release of *The Patriot* is illustrative. The filmmakers offer up such sentimental and confused images of African Americans that director Spike Lee suggested the film "dodged around, skirted about or completely ignored slavery." Mel Gibson's character, Benjamin Martin, is based on a historical figure named Francis Marion. In the movie, Martin does not own slaves and is a pacifist who attempts to stay out of the war. However, according to the historical record, Francis Marion was a racist who owned slaves and was known to abuse them. Conveniently, the filmmakers eliminated these facts from the story.

More generally, the ability of filmmakers to use sympathetic or unsympathetic characters to encourage viewers to believe the historical account offered on screen is an important use and misuse of evidence. So, too, is the way filmmakers use visual techniques such as extreme close-ups to corroborate or refute claims made in the story. By using techniques like close-ups or emotion-inducing juxtapositions of important images, filmmakers revise or reinterpret evidence from the past.

Figure 30.1 suggests several activities to help students appreciate the ways in historical films manipulate historical evidence and interpretation.

CONTINUITY AND CHANGE

Continuity and change are yet another set of concepts relevant to the development of historical understanding. These pairs of concepts draw attention to the many features that are relatively constant and to the continuous changes over specific periods.

Questions of continuity and change are especially relevant to film representations because filmmakers have a remarkable ability to influence viewers' perceptions of the similarities and differences between historical and contemporary times. The most common tendency in film, rooted in the frequency of anachronisms, is to exaggerate the extent to which things are the same now as they were in times past. To extend our earlier discussion of *Gangs of New York*, by casting mid-nineteenth century life as a cauldron of brutality and revenge, Scorsese overplays a linkage between historic violence in American cities and the violence associated with inner city American life today. By doing this, the film suggests a kind of continuity that serves to naturalize violence as a way of life. It has always been there, the film seems to imply, and perhaps that is why things are as they are now.

CAUSE AND CONSEQUENCE

Historical causation and consequences are other key aspects of our understanding of history. Questions of power are at the heart of these issues and, over the past thirty years, discussions about who made decisions in history and why have focussed on how we envisage previously marginalized actors on the historical stage. Here investigations examine the ways in which historical agency is developed and exercised by

FIGURE 30.1 ACTIVITIES INVOLVING EVIDENCE AND INTERPRETATION

Assess Omissions and Inaccuracies

Invite students to identify inaccuracies in a movie and to assess the significance of those inaccuracies or omissions. Working in small groups, ask students to use the world wide web to research a history film you have seen recently in class. One website to look at is the Internet Movie Database at www .imdb.com. On this site, you will find a button for "goofs," which details errors made in the film. In addition, encourage students to search under the film title for other websites describing history errors in the movie. Ask students to locate at least three major inaccuracies and a chart such as the one illustrated below to document the flaws and their impact on how we think about the past.

Evidence in Film

In response to the way filmmakers ignore or reshape historical evidence, Natalie Zemon Davis (2000) has suggested that filmmakers make their movies more historically interesting and faithful by committing to the following principles:

- Be willing "to tell audiences … what they have done to shape a story" (131). For instance, filmmakers could place a legend alongside the final credits where they indicate how they have altered names, people, and events from the actual story.
- Include references to key primary documents in the stories rather than legends in order to give viewers an idea of where the story comes from and where the historical record can be found.
- Experiment with multiple character perspectives so that audiences do not rely too strongly on one character as their guide to history.

In small groups, ask students to apply one of Davis' ideas to a film seen recently in class. Working with either a specific scene or the entire film, invite students to show how Davis' ideas could be applied (explaining, for instance, how the introduction of multiple character perspectives would help audiences see that history is different depending on who is doing the telling).

Rework a Historical Scene

Working in small groups, invite students to select a scene or series of scenes (up to three) from a history film screened in whole or in part in class. The chosen scenes should focus on significant historical elements that the filmmakers have clearly invented. Encourage students to conduct web-based research about the making of the movie to ascertain inaccuracies in the movie. As mentioned above, the Internet Movie Database (www.imdb.com) is good website to begin this research. Once their research is complete, ask students to rewrite the scenes so that the film is, as much as possible, historically accurate. Direct students to produce a script that includes characters, settings, specific costumes, and other elements that make the scene both historically credible and consistent with the rest of the film. Remind students that filmmakers are entitled to some artistic licence, so it is not necessary that the rewritten scenes be held hostage to the precise details of the historical record, but they should honour the larger truths of history.

ALLEGED INACCURACIES/ OMISSIONS	THE FACTS ACCORDING TO THE HISTORICAL RECORD	THE IMPACT ON HOW WE THINK ABOUT THE PAST

relatively powerless groups, including, women, peoples of colour, First Nations, and the working class. But these concerns for what Seixas has called, "a democratic sense of historical causation" are also very important in regards to young people because so often historical change is taught in schools as the domain of elites rather than as a possibility for various social groups and organizations (Seixas 1996, 777).

Movies are significant in this regard. This influence is exercised most commonly by focussing on the role of individuals in history as opposed to the collective work of many. Because most films unfold though a particular character's eyes—for instance, Mel Gibson as William Wallace in *Braveheart* (1995)—the effect is to systematically accentuate the achievements of individuals.

An interesting counter-example is John Sayles' *Matewan* (1987), a remarkable film about a West Virginia coal-mining town and the people who fought to protect workers and the community in the 1920s. Set around the so-called Matewan Massacre, Sayles' movie tells the story of a union (the United Mine Workers) that must overcome its white members' racism (against black and Italian immigrant workers) in order to ensure a short-lived victory over the brutal tactics of the Stone Mountain Company. Based on a famous battle that took place in the midst of Virginia coal-mining country, *Matewan* foregrounds the union organizer Joe Kenehan as the story's tragic hero, yet it is the people of the community and the union members who overcome a self-defeating bigotry to challenge the company's union-busting cruelty that are the agents of change in the film. In this sense, *Matewan* stands in contrast to so many Hollywood movies that offer individuals as the agents of social change and fail to recognize how a people acting collectively can alter the course of history.[9]

HISTORICAL PERSPECTIVE TAKING

Another aspect of historical understanding has to do with the way we encounter people, societies, and periods from the past that are necessarily different from our own time. Part of understanding our own continuity with and difference from the past arises from unearthing the motivations of those whose lives we are removed from. But the catch here is that it is no help to understand the lives of others only through our own values; the real work of historical understanding comes about by clarifying the terms others used to justify their actions and assessing these in relation to our own values. Seixas suggests that we must be open to the "possibility that [historical] actors differ from us in ways so profound that we perpetually risk misunderstanding them" (1996, 776).

Steven Spielberg's *Amistad* (1997) offers an interesting example of filmmakers' attempts to avoid having modern audiences identify with and understand historical positions. The film tells the story of African slaves fighting for their lives and freedom in 1830s and 1840s America. Former US President John Quincy Adams is shown making an appeal before the Supreme Court based on his regard for the character Cinqué and other Africans who are trying to free themselves. As one writer commented, Spielberg's Adams speaks in a manner that is "sentimental and romantic," and far different than what Adams actually said during his real address to the court in February and March of 1841.[10] As we hear him on screen, Adams sounds like the kind of US president one would want to see in office today. He embodies a contemporary liberalism and respect for universal human rights, yet Adams' actual words reflected the sentiments of a former US President living out the last decades of slavery. While we might wish that Adams' view of Cinqué and the other Africans were closer to our own, this was not the case. By falsifying the historical record, the filmmakers are disrespectful of their audiences, who, it is implied, cannot conceive of how our understanding of freedom has changed in the past 160 years.

The problem of presuming that modern audiences cannot appreciate the realities of previous times and people has been raised most forcefully in regards to the Holocaust, an event often discussed in high school classrooms in conjunction with screenings of Steven Spielberg's *Schindler's List* (1993) or, more recently, Roman Polanski's *The Pianist* (2002). The Holocaust has been called a "limit event" for human understanding: it is so grotesque and violent in its intentions—to annihilate *a people*—and its effects—the death of six million Jews—that it "ruptures and is ultimately outside of" the continuum we call history (Hansen 1997, 84). It is different in a way that is impossible to imagine from our contemporary standpoint. In the words of director Claude Lanzmann, "The Holocaust is above all unique in that it erects a ring of fire around itself, a borderline that cannot be crossed because there is a certain ultimate degree of horror that cannot be transmitted. To claim it is possible to do so is to be guilty of the most serious transgression" (1994, 14). Lanzmann's position forces us to ask whether one of the great strengths of fictional cinema, its ability to make us feel intimate with history, should be avoided altogether in the case of the Holocaust. By making us feel as if we can understand an event of such horrifying magnitude, Hollywood movies misunderstand the awful distinctiveness of this history.[11]

In contrast, others suggest that while it is necessary to understand the distinctiveness of the Holocaust and other violent events in twentieth-century history, if we do not use all our resources, including film, to build empathy with and understanding of the past, we risk abandoning our connections to history altogether (Elsaesser 1996). Even if Hollywood fiction films such as *Schindler's List* have their problems,[12] they are a potentially useful resource provided we understand their difference from the past.

Figure 30.2 describes two activities to develop students' ability to get inside the perspective of a historical figure and to identify the historical perspectives presented in film.

MORAL JUDGMENT

A final concept related to historical understanding concerns the moral judgments we make about past actions and events. Often we are not conscious of making these judgments because they are made for us. For example, school textbooks have typically offered up "an underlying message [about] the growth of democracy, knowledge and enlightenment

---

FIGURE 30.2 ACTIVITIES INVOLVING HISTORICAL PERSPECTIVE-TAKING

Conduct a Historical Interview

Working in small groups, invite students to select a historical figure who interests them or who has been the focus of classroom discussion. Ask students to research and write the script for an imaginary five-minute television interview with their historical figure. A five-minute interview is approximately five pages of text. Suggest to students that they frame the interview around a controversy or conflict associated with their chosen subject. The purpose of the interview is to invite students to confront their subject with questions that students want to ask in order to learn more about the person and the period. To make the interview as believable as possible, ask students to write the responses for their subject with reference to what we know about the prevailing beliefs and values of the time. Discourage students from simply making up answers for their subject. Instead, ask students to construct plausible responses based on what is known about the individual and the historical context in which the person lived.

Identify Iconic Images

Directors often turn to iconic images to suggest a larger, symbolic meaning in the story. Iconic or dramatically significant images are useful in this way because they are efficient—the images stand as metaphors that represent ideas in one shot—and, more importantly, as a medium, movies

work best when they *show* ideas rather than *tell* us about history. For instance, in *Dances with Wolves* (Kevin Costner, 1990), Kevin Costner plays John Dunbar, a soldier who is sent to the frontier to make contact with Native peoples. In the film, Dunbar is a Christ-like figure who comes to understand the noble dignity of the Lakota people. To make this point clearly, during the film's opening sequences, Costner is shown riding a horse with arms stretched wide in the image of Christ on the cross. This shot takes place in the midst of a pitched battle between armies from the North and the South and serves to define John Dunbar as a special kind of figure. In a very different film, director Ridley Scott uses an extreme close-up on an eyeball in the opening of *Blade Runner* (1982) to alert audiences to the fact that the movie is about our belief in the eye as the window into the human soul. The film's story will ultimately challenge this belief and Scott makes us aware of this from the outset.

Ask students to look for one or more images from a film screened recently in class that provides an iconic message about some historical event or person. Using the chart below, direct students to describe the iconic image in detail. Then they are to identify the message conveyed by the image. Finally, ask students to offer an opinion about why they think the filmmakers chose this image in light of the account presented in the movie.

ICONIC IMAGE	THE MESSAGE THAT THE IMAGE IS INTENDED TO SUGGEST IN RELATION TO THE STORY	WHY THE IMAGE FITS THE HISTORICAL ACCOUNT OFFERED IN THE FILM

through time" (Seixas 1996, 773). Here, notions of progress and decline, while implicit to the texts, are often left unacknowledged. More recently, as questions of narrative and the structure of how history is conveyed to audiences has become of greater concern in the discipline of history, this tendency has waned. In its place are more complex readings of both the advance and decline of cherished values and experiences.

In regard to media, a number of film codes significantly influence young people's moral assessments of the past. The most crucial way in which this takes place has to do with Hollywood's tendency to impose a positive resolution on the dilemmas and contradictions of history. As noted earlier, mainstream movies' tendency towards closure leaves few questions unanswered. Hollywood's bias towards the happy ending suggests that things are getting better. An interesting example of this tendency in a recent Canadian television event is the epic CBC series, *Canada: A People's History* (2000–2001). It is perhaps the greatest and most successful production of a national history in this country. However, Lyle Dick also points out that the series is plotted "as the inexorable progress, through many challenges, of the Canadian people from different origins to their collective realization" in our current nation (2003, 6). The problem, however, is that by the end of the series a number of conflicts and unresolved tensions go untreated. For instance, "the status or rights of First Peoples, racial minorities, women, … lesbian and gay people, the homeless, the unemployed, and others" are given short shrift so that the larger tale of progress towards unity can be upheld. In this way, *Canada: A People's History* could be accused of modifying the historical record to exaggerate the positive assessment of our nation's past, as opposed to laying bare the conflicts and struggles that still remain part of our present.

Movies also have an impact on the way audiences come to judge an event through the inclusion or exclusion of certain details that construct a positive or negative light. As well, viewing historical events through a sympathetic character's eyes will likely colour our judgments of an event. In addition, filmmakers use audio and visual techniques such as music and extreme close-ups to communicate and shape a desired moral judgment.

Figure 30.3 describes two activities to help students appreciate how films influence the moral judgments that audiences are likely to make about historical people and events.

Public Performance Rights

As many educators will know, by law, to show films in the classroom requires that the school or school district purchase a public performance licence. Such licences are required for the screening of any copyright-protected film outside of one's home. This applies to pre-recorded home VHS/DVD movies that have been purchased or rented from any retail or rental stores or to movies your school may own as resources. Besides the National Film Board (www.nfb.ca), two companies in Canada provide public presentation licences for the vast majority of movies teachers will want to use in their classrooms—Audio Ciné Films (www.acf-film.com) and Criterion Pictures (www.criterionpic.com). Increasingly, schools and school districts are purchasing annual public performance licences to give their teachers full access to the catalogue of movies available through these organizations. Speak with your library resource teacher or the learning resource contact at your school district to find out if your school has such a licence and what films this licence covers.

Unfortunately, public performance licenses are not inexpensive. Fees depend on whether a licence has been purchased on a school or district-wide basis (the latter tends to reduce the cost per film screening substantially), or whether a licence is needed for each film screening (which tends to raise the costs to approximately $100.00 or more per film).

Conclusion

In an age when we encounter more and more historical images throughout our lives, it is difficult to distinguish between these images in order to know how to assess their importance and credibility. This is not only true for the layperson, it is also increasingly the case for historians who use cinema as an introduction to fields outside of their own areas of specialization. But if historians are doing this, we should neither be surprised nor unnecessarily concerned that the rest of us are learning about the past through screen drafts of history.

FIGURE 30.3   ACTIVITIES INVOLVING MORAL JUDGMENTS

Historical Progress

Use the following activity sheet when screening a history film in class to help students assess the film's overall positive message. Invite students to defend their answers in the bottom section by identifying specific events and scenes that crucially support the film's message of moral progress.

The film's overall moral judgment about the key event or person:	

Identify specific events or scenes in the film that reinforce the overall moral judgment	
SCENES OR EVENTS IN THE FILM	**HOW THEY SUPPORT THE MORAL JUDGMENT**
1.	
2.	
3.	
4.	
5.	

Rewrite the "Hollywood Ending"

Many mainstream movies and television series alter the historical record in order to reinforce a positive or up-lifting ending. Using a film screened in class, ask students to rewrite the end of the movie with a different moral conclusion. For example, if the film ends with an uplifting assessment and vindication, rewrite the final sequences into a less flattering or at least a more ambiguous moral resolution. Direct students to ensure that the revised ending is consistent with the historical record and fits with the rest of the film.

Select a film related to a historical person or event in the curriculum. Use the six concepts of historical understanding discussed in this chapter as lenses to help you identify how the film both contributes to and undermines historical understanding. For example, does the film exaggerate the significance of particular events or offer an excessively flattering assessment of a character? Prepare a brief report cataloguing the strengths and weaknesses of the film in enhancing students' historical understanding.

Rather, what is needed are the critical visual literacy tools to engage with these representations critically so that we and our students can make judgments about what stories to trust and what images need to be discarded into the dustbin of history.

NOTES

1. Recent examples in Canada include Starowicz's *Canada: A People's History* (2000–2001) and Dando's *The Canadian Experience* (2003–2005), in the US, Ken Burns' series on *The Civil War* (1990), *Baseball* (1994), and *Jazz* (2001) have been especially popular.

2. See, for instance, Steven Spielberg's *Amistad* (1997), Shekhar Kapur's *Elizabeth* (1998), Luc Besson's *Messenger: The Story of Joan of Arc* (1999), Roland Emmerich's *The Patriot* (2000), Philip

Kaufman's *Quills* (2000), Martin Scorsese's *Gangs of New York* (2002), and Peter Weir's *Master and Commander: The Far Side of the World* (2003).

3. Two of the most important examples include Steven Spielberg's *Saving Private Ryan* (1998) and Terrence Malick's *The Thin Red Line* (1998).

4. For instance, Patricia Rozema's *Mansfield Park* (1999), Alan Parker's *Angela's Ashes* (1999), and Robert Altman's *Gosford Park* (2001).

5. This list includes Atom Egoyan's *Ararat* (2002), Alexandr Sokurov's *Russian Ark* (2002), André Heller and Othmar Schmiderer's *Blind Spot: Hitler's Secretary* (2002), Eugene Jarecki's *The Trials of Henry Kissinger* (2002), and Errol Morris' *Fog of War* (2003).

6. Set in rural France in 1542 and based on a French legend, *The Return of Martin Guerre* tells the story of a young man who disappears suddenly from his wife and community. He returns years later a changed man. His wife accepts him wholeheartedly, but there are nagging doubts about his true identity. Not least because he is so much a better man than the one who left. Eventually, Guerre's in-laws challenge his claims, which forces the local magistrate to rule on his identity.

7. Giannetti and Leach (1998) offer an interesting overview of the use of these techniques in mainstream cinema. See Poyntz (2001; 2001a) for classroom activities suitable for secondary school students related to these techniques.

8. For an interesting discussion of these, see Natalie Zemon Davis' (1983) book *The Return of Martin Guerre*.

9. The British director Ken Loach has also made a number of pictures on the role of collectivities in changing history, including *Land and Freedom* (1995) and *Bread and Roses* (2000).

10. For the record, in Adams' speech to the US Supreme Court, "he genuinely applauded the actions of Cinqué and his fellows to free themselves, but in comparing their heroism with the 'Lilliputian trickery' of the American rulers of a great Christian nation, he said: 'Contrast it [the Lilliputian trickery of the US secretary of state] with that act of self emancipation by which the savage, heathen barbarians Cinqué and Grabeau liberated themselves and their fellow suffering countrymen from Spanish slave traders…Cinqué and Grabeau are uncouth and barbarous names. Call them Harmodius and Aristogiton'" (quoted in Davis 2000, 128).

11. Claude Lanzmann is the most important proponent of this argument in the film world. His film *Shoah* (1985) is a remarkable and deeply affecting documentary that refuses to show historic images of Holocaust victims. See Bartov's (1997) review of Lanzmann's stance on representation of the Holocaust and the relationship of *Schindler's List* to this position.

12. Criticisms of *Schindler's List* include the fact that it focusses on who was saved rather than all those who died; it relies on style, effects, and glamour (including a star-studded cast) to generate excitement and market appeal; and it tells the story of its Jewish characters through "the perspective of the perpetrators, the German Gentile Nazi (Oskar Schindler) turned resister" (Hansen 1997, 82–83).

REFERENCES

Altman, R., dir. 2001. *Gosford Park*. USA Films.

Bartov, O. 1997. Spielberg's Oskar: Hollywood tries evil. In *Spielberg's Holocaust: Critical perspectives on* Schindler's List, ed. Y. Loshitzky, 41–76. Bloomington, IN: Indiana University Press.

Bay, M., dir. 2001. *Pearl Harbor*. Touchstone Pictures.

Bertolucci, B., dir. 1987. *The Last Emperor*. Yanco Films Limited.

Besson, L., dir. 1999. *Messenger: The Story of Joan of Arc*. Gaumont.

Burns, K., dir. 1900. *The Civil War*. American Documentaries Inc.

Burns, K., dir. 1994. *Baseball*. Florentine Films.

Burns, K., dir. 2001. *Jazz*. British Broadcasting Corporation (BBC).

Coppola, F., dir. 1984. *The Cotton Club*. Zoetrope Studios.

Costner, K., dir. 1990. *Dances with Wolves*. Tig Productions.

Dando, S., dir. 2003–2005. *The Canadian Experience*. Canadian Broadcasting Corporation (CBC).

Davis, N.Z. 1983. *The Return of Martin Guerre*. Cambridge, MA: Harvard University Press.

———. 2000. *Slaves on screen: Film and historical vision*. Cambridge, MA: Harvard University Press.

Dick, L. 2003. National history, epic form, and television: Two examples from Canada and the United States. Conference paper presented at the University of New Brunswick, October.

Egoyan, A., dir. 2002. *Ararat*. ARD Sélection.

Elsaesser, T. 1996. Subject positions, speaking positions: From *Holocaust, Our Hitler*, and *Heimat* to *Shoah* and *Schindler's List*. In *The persistence of history: Cinema, television, and the modern event*. ed. V. Sobchack, 145–183. New York: Routledge.

Emmerich, R., dir. 2000. *The Patriot*. Columbia Pictures Corporation.

Gibson, M., dir. 1995. *Braveheart*. Icon Productions.

Giannetti, L. and J. Leach. 1998. *Understanding movies: Canadian edition*. Scarborough, ON: Prentice Hall Allyn and Bacon Canada.

Hansen, M.B. 1997. *Schindler's List* is not *Shoah*: Second commandment, popular modernism, and public memory. In *Spielberg's Holocaust: Critical perspectives on* Schindler's List, ed. Y. Loshitzky, 77–103. Bloomington: Indiana University Press.

Heller, A. and O. Schmiderer, dirs. 2002. *Blind Spot: Hitler's Secretary*. Dor Film Produktionsgesellschaft.

Jarecki, E., dir. 2002. *The Trials of Henry Kissinger*. British Broadcasting Corporation (BBC).

Kapur, S., dir. 1998. *Elizabeth*. Polygram Filmed Entertainment.

Kaufman, P., dir. 2000. *Quills*. Fox Searchlight Pictures.

Lanzmann, C., dir. 1985. *Shoah*. Historia.

Lanzmann, C. 1994. Why Spielberg has distorted the truth. Originally published in *Le monde*. Reprinted in *The Guardian Weekly*, April 3.

Lean, D., dir. 1962. *Lawrence of Arabia*. Horizon Pictures (II).

Loach, K., dir. 1995. *Land and Freedom*. BIM.

Loach, K., dir. 2000. *Bread and Roses*. Parallax Pictures.

MacKinnon, G., dir. 1997. *Regeneration*. British Broadcasting Corporation (BBC).

Malick, T., dir. 1998. *The Thin Red Line*. Fox 2000 Pictures.

Morris, E., dir. 2003. *Fog of War*. Sony Pictures Classics.

Parker, A., dir. 1999. *Angela's Ashes*. David Brown Productions.

Polanski, P., dir. 2002. *The Pianist*. R.P. Productions.

Poyntz, S. 2001. *Visual storytelling and the grammar of filmmaking, part 1*. History of Film Study Guide Series, 02. Vancouver: Pacific Cinémathèque.

———. 2001a. *Visual storytelling and the grammar of filmmaking, part 2*. History of Film Study Guide Series, 03. Vancouver: Pacific Cinémathèque.

Rosenstone, R.A. 1995. *Visions of the past: The challenge of film to our idea of history*. Cambridge, MA: Harvard University Press.

Rozema, P., dir. 1999. *Mansfield Park*. Arts Council of England.

Sayles, J., dir. 1987. *Matewan*. Cinecom Entertainment.

Scott, R., dir. 1982. *Blade Runner*. Blade Runner Partnership.

Scorsese, M., dir. 2002. *Gangs of New York*. Miramax Pictures.

Seixas, P. 1996. Conceptualizing the growth of historical understanding. In *Handbook of education and human development: New models of learning, teaching, and schooling*, eds. D. Olson and N. Torrance, 765–783. Oxford: Blackwell.

Snyder, R. 2003. "Gangs of New York" gets New York City wrong. *Open democracy*. Available online at http://www.opendemocracy.net/arts-Film/article_890.jsp.

Sokurov, A., dir. 2002. *Russian Ark*. The State Hermitage Museum.

Spielberg, S., dir. 1993. *Schindler's List*. Universal Pictures.

Spielberg, S., dir. 1997. *Amistad*. Dreamworks SKG.

Spielberg, S., dir. 1998. *Saving Private Ryan*. Amblin Entertainment.

Starowicz, M., dir. 2000-2001. *Canada: A People's History*. Canadian Broadcasting Corporation (CBC).

Stone, O., dir. 1991. *JFK*. Warner Bros. Pictures.

Vigne, D., dir. 1982. *The Return of Martin Guerre*. Dussalt.

Weir, P., dir. 2003. *Master and Commander: The Far Side of the World*. Twentieth Century Fox Film Corporation.

FILM RESOURCES ON THE WORLD WIDE WEB

Media Awareness Network
http://www.media-awareness.ca

Internet Movie Database
http://www.imdb.com

National Film Board of Canada
http://www.nfb.ca

31 Resource-based Learning in Geography

Andrew Griffin, Wayne Andrew, and Kendall Taylor

Introduction

The discipline of geography is the study of people, places, and environments through spatial and ecological perspectives. A rich variety of resources are available to help students encounter, understand, and respond to their world. However, in many classrooms this potential is unrealized for three reasons:

- **Heavy reliance on facts.** The geography component in a social studies course is often preoccupied with teaching superficial facts about places rather than developing understanding of relationships. This has been referred to as a "capes and bays" approach in which students memorize places that can easily be looked up in a gazetteer. Teaching "facts" for their own sake can be especially problematic in geography because there are reams of statistics, information, and other details to learn.
- **Overuse of the textbook.** Textbook readings and exercise rather than critical thinking and hands-on tasks dominate much instruction in geography. Geographical information is available in many forms and from many sources. Clearly, textbooks can be useful for acquiring background information. However, excessive reliance on them as a substitute for teaching is unlikely to excite students about geography. Most students hate hearing the instruction "Open your books to page 103 and answer questions 1–15."
- **Simplistic use of maps.** Nothing turns students off learning geography more rapidly than seemingly useless, and often trivial, "skill and drill" activities. Perhaps the most common of these is the teaching of so-called map skills that so often characterizes the initial weeks of many secondary school social studies programs. Some students complain that they are put through this ordeal virtually every year of their secondary schooling, and see it as little more than a "colouring-book" exercise, one that rewards neatness rather than cartographic understanding. Maps can provide opportunities to engage students in geographical thinking, if used in purposeful ways.

In this chapter, we offer ideas to overcome these deficiencies and unleash the power of geography by encouraging more effective use of a broader range of educational resources. We believe a richer, resource-based approach to geography teaching can be fostered in three ways:

- build on experiential learning;
- use multiple learning resources, including electronic technologies;
- draw upon cross-curricular links.

Build on Experiential Learning

Experiential learning identifies the use of "real life" situations and "hands-on" experiences—whether in the field or in a laboratory—to make learning more relevant and engaging for students. It is "experiential" because students directly encounter the material being studied. Some consider experiential learning to be the opposite of cognitive learning, where students merely engage the object of study in the abstract or through print and images. The study of geography allows for implementation of both approaches. Some geographical concepts are better learned in a theoretical way (cognitively), whereas many others are better learned experientially. Computers, for example, allow a wide variety of theoretical modelling to take place in the areas of weather or climate prediction. On the other hand, constructing the classic erupting volcano project provides an example of concrete or hands-on learning. Of course, the experience would be even more powerful if they witnessed an actual eruption.

Making a distinction between experiential and cognitive learning is potentially misleading because students must have information before they take part in real-life scenarios. There is little value in having students wander through a field study without the concepts and information they need in order to make sense of what they are experiencing. In creating authentic learning experiences, we must remember the importance of background knowledge.

There are countless opportunities in geography to engage students in experiential learning by accessing resources in the local community. Many of these opportunities are described in chapter 26, "Bringing the Outside In." We want to add to these ideas by encouraging the use of field studies and by suggesting how mapping and other forms of graphic representation can enhance the value of these experiences.

Field studies in geography are the original form of experiential learning. Students learn from real-life experiences. Fieldwork does not require going to exotic places. The schoolyard itself provides opportunities for many activities: information about plant and animal patterns, erosion, weather, and human interactions can all be gathered around the schoolyard. The neighbourhood is a valuable place for land use studies, examinations of traffic flow, and many more activities.

THE ROLE OF MAPS

Maps are the most important tool in geography. Geographical understanding comes from observing the world, finding patterns and networks of relationships, then mapping this knowledge. Students find the products of others' geographical investigations, presented as lists of phenomena, features, or symbols to be learned through skill and drill techniques to be meaningless rituals at best. Doing geography, exploring and mapping the world in a way that is significant and meaningful to students, holds the promise of greater engagement and more positive attitudes towards the subject.

Maps are the representation of geographical knowledge. They show the distribution of human and natural features on the earth's surface, surveyed and arranged in graphic form for some purpose, be it navigation, land-use planning, military strategy, or finding a tourist attraction. Maps are spatial narratives written in cartographic symbols that tell a story. Students who are encouraged to create their own maps, to tell their own stories as visual representations of their geographical understandings, may find the process both more stimulating and more meaningful than getting marks for colouring inside the lines.

Student can record local area observations in a variety of ways. They can record information as field notes, draw sketch maps of phenomena observed, or take photographs. Returning to the classroom with these data, students can then make a variety of maps, graphs, diagrams, or flow charts. Working individually or in groups they can map human and physical features, economic activities, traffic flows, land use, and other spatially distributed phenomena. It is useful to get them to make as many different maps or representations as possible of the same area in order to recognize the multiplicity of geographical narratives represented in a single landscape.

The supermarket is a good place to map complexity and global interdependence. Arrange for students to conduct a scavenger hunt in which teams win prizes for identifying the largest number of countries providing the products on the store shelves or for finding the greatest number of products from different continents. Students map the story of various foods from the primary producers in the country of origin to the various processing and distribution stages through which it flows en route to the local supermarket. Such geographical narratives can be developed for a wide range of phenomena, such as plotting the global diffusion of soccer, fashion, or trends. Inviting students to explore the geography of HIV/AIDS, SARS, or other diseases is a powerful vehicle for demonstrating the complexity of global interconnectedness in an era of individual mobility, rapid transportation, and personal freedoms.

This is not the place to explore all the different kinds and uses of maps, but we want to discuss two kinds of maps that offer useful lead-ins to geographical field work: mental maps and green maps.

MENTAL OR COGNITIVE MAPPING

A person's perception of the world is known as a mental map, also called a cognitive map. A mental map is an individual's own internal map of their known world. Mental maps are drawn from memory by recording key features as accurately as possible. They help make students aware of their spatial knowledge and perceptions of environments at different scales. Since mapping and spatial patterns are fundamental building blocks for geography, it is useful to encourage students to work from mental maps. They provide a good introduction to many geographical themes.

An interesting activity is to ask students to draw mental maps of particular places or activities. These drawings may illustrate various spatial dynamics such as:

- "action spaces" over a week (the spaces where an individual undertakes specific activities over a certain period of time, for example, visiting friends, shopping, or various forms of recreation);
- connections to the community (where they shop or eat);
- connections to various regions of the world (for example, family migrations, cultural and linguistic ties);
- the physical features of the local landscape;
- the route to school, the playing fields, or the cinemas.

Arrange for students to share their completed maps with other students and discuss the patterns on their maps. Moving on from mental maps to "scales" on maps, using maps as tools, reading maps for information, and investigating other map attributes follow from this step.

GREEN MAPS

Green maps focus on environmental features. They invite students to reflect on the relationship between people and the natural environment. The following categories of features are typically found on green maps:

- gardens, parks, naturally beautiful places, wildlife habitats, zoos;
- eco-businesses, farmers' markets, environmentally sound architecture, energy-saving features;
- places that are pedestrian-friendly, bike lanes, diamond lanes, bike paths, public transit routes;
- ecotourism destinations, history and culture destinations;
- renewable power plants (hydro), water plants, sewage treatment plants, waste disposal locations, recycling locations;
- geologic, water, and any other natural features.

An international organization found at www.greenmap .org provides students with opportunities to compare their maps with other green maps from students around the world.

Student instructions for creating a green map of their lo-cal neighbourhood or region are found in Figure 31.1. This activity is intended to help students realize that maps are subjective records that capture particular interests and are directed at particular audiences.

OTHER FORMS OF GEOGRAPHICAL REPRESENTATION

Clearly, maps are the preeminent tool in building geographical understanding. However, geography lends itself to the use of a wide variety of graphic organizers. These help students gather, arrange, and evaluate information from field studies and other sources. The data chart in Figure 31.2 is but one example of the use of graphic organizers to structure the collection of field data. Table 31.1 contains ten additional types. There are many more.

Select two or three people—preferably with different backgrounds and experiences—to draw mind maps of a similar area, perhaps the local community, Canada, or the world. Compare the maps to identify what you can learn about the individuals and their views of the profiled region. Write a brief analysis of how personal backgrounds and experiences shape the sense these individuals make of the world.

FIGURE 31.1   GREEN MAP OF LOCAL BIOREGION

Task
Create a green map of your local neighbourhood or region.

Objectives
To record:
- the key natural and human characteristics of your local region;
- the significant ways that people contribute to the local natural environment;
- how to organize the information placed on the map.

Preparation
- Choose an area to explore.
- Choose a target audience. Who will be the user of your map (neighbours, city residents, tourists, students, government planners, businesses)?
- Select a base map for the area (your teacher can provide this). Obtain two copies of this base map: one for use as a rough copy for surveying the site and recording field notes, and the second to create your final copy.
- Review the Green Map System Icons on the website

(www.greenmap.org/greenhouse/about/iconintro) before undertaking your field observations.

Field survey
Use the "survey organizer" shown on the next page to gather information. Complete this chart and note the locations. You will be plotting these locations on the surveying map. Name these sites. You are to map major roads, pathways, waterways, and human and natural features that you identify and label "green" features.

Final product
- Use the rough map and your chart to assemble the information on a blank piece of paper.
- Make the Green Map System Icons you need.
- Trace the major features of your survey area: major roads, pathways, waterways, and human and natural features.
- Place the Green Map System Icons in the correct locations on your map.
- Create a legend of the icons used.
- Provide a title that summarizes the message of your map.

FIGURE 31.1   GREEN MAP OF LOCAL BIOREGION (CONT.)

GREEN MAP SURVEY ORGANIZER			
Title:			
Target audience:			
Category	**Names of sites**	**Location notes**	**Why are these sites "green"?**
gardens, parks, naturally beautiful places, lookouts, wildlife habitats, zoos			
ecobusinesses, farmers' markets, environmentally sound architecture, energy saving features			
ecotourism destinations, history and culture destinations			
renewable power plants (hydro), water plants, sewage treatment plants, waste disposal or recycling locations			
geologic, water, and any other natural features			

TABLE 31.1 TYPES AND USES OF GRAPHIC ORGANIZERS

GRAPHIC ORGANIZER	GEOGRAPHIC USE
Venn diagram	comparing similarities and differences
Evidence-conclusion chart	recording data and offering conclusions
Web chart	developing ideas and showing their relationships
Comparison chart	compare and contrast data
Donut chart	identifying parts to a central theme
Fishbone chart	organizing information on several parts of a topic
Flow chart	charting movement of goods, people, or ideas
Know/wonder/learn chart	research method to identify unknowns
Line graph	sequencing events over time
Bar graph	comparing data across categories

Use Multiple Learning Resources

Using many different resources is key to active learning in geography. The use of multiple resources does not mean simply using different resources from one activity to the other, but also using diverse resources within the same activity. We have just discussed the use of field studies in various local settings as one of the richest sources of geographical information. Table 31.2 lists a sampling of the sources for geography-related print and electronic resources beyond the textbook.

The physical regions of Canada or comparisons of regions around the world are common topics in the curriculum. Table 31.3 describes how various aspects of each region could be examined using different kinds of learning resources.

It will not be enough to engage students simply by increasing the number of different resources they consult. Although this may be of some benefit, it is as important that we invite students to think through or use the information

TABLE 31.2 PRINT AND ELECTRONIC RESOURCES	
POTENTIAL SOURCES	**EXAMPLES OF RESOURCES**
Curriculum resource documents	provincial/territorial ministry directives and requirements, often with support materials or exemplars
Atlases—paper	map reference books such as: • *Canadian Oxford School Atlas* • *Pearson School Atlas* • *Nystrom Atlas of Canada* • *Nystrom Atlas of World History*
Atlases—electronic	• Atlas of Canada: www.atlas.gc.ca • The Canadian Atlas Online: www.canadiangeographic.ca/atlas
Globes and wall maps	PMR Learning Materials Cramm Publications Nystrom
Simulations	SimCity: http://simcitysocieties.ea.com/about.php
Professional organizations	Ontario Association for Geographic and Environmental education (OAGEE): www.oagee.org Canadian Council for Geographic Education (CCGE): www.ccge/org
Professional magazines	monograph teaching issues and materials written by teachers for teachers: www.oagee.org
Geographic magazines	Canadian Geographic: www.cangeo.ca National Geographic: www.nationalgeographic.com
Newspapers	local newspapers national newspapers
Library or resource centre	school resource centres community libraries college/university libraries
Videotapes, CD-ROMs, DVDs	many organizations put materials into electronic format (for example, OAGEE Geokit Canada)
Government of Canada websites	Statistics Canada: www.statcan.ca Atlas of Canada: www.atlas.gc.ca Environment Canada's Greenlane: www.ec.gc.ca/default.asp?lang=En&n=FD9B0E51-1 Environment Canada's Weather Office: www.weatheroffice.gc.ca/canada_e.html
Provincial/territorial government websites	each level of government operates a main website and many departmental links that are useful to geographers (for example, Prince Edward Island—www.gov.pei.ca)

TABLE 31.3 DIFFERENT WAYS OF STUDYING REGIONS

ACTIVITY	RESOURCE SOURCE
Sketch mapping. Students sketch major resource locations in each region.	print or online atlases
Diagramming. Students draw diagrams of various industrial methods.	yearbooks and industry documents
Graphing. Students create graphs (circle, bar, or line) to illustrate population patterns.	immigration statistics from Statistics Canada's Canada Yearbook and world almanacs
Thematic mapping. Students use flow arrows to show transportation patterns.	tables of transportation operations in each region
Photographs. Students compare the physical features of each region by studying photographs.	photographs found in textbooks, calendars, or coffee table books
Climate graphs. Students make climate graphs for selected locations and explain the climate's impact on environmental concerns.	monthly climate statistics on precipitation and temperature for selected communities from the Environment Canada weather office

they acquire. This point has been made in many of the chapters in this volume, notably chapter 4, "Beyond Inert Facts." The activity described in Figure 31.2 illustrates a meaningful challenge to help students think about the significance of the physical and human features of diverse locations as they collect information from a variety of resources.

The most exciting recent developments in learning resources for geography are grounded in electronic technologies. These include a wide range of geographical or geospatial information systems (GIS). In Canada, GIS is better known as Geomatics. These systems are used to capture, store, manage, and present spatial (or geo-referenced) data about the earth. GIS allow teachers and students to create and analyze many kinds of maps of the local area, be it the schoolyard, neighbourhood, or city on any number of themes from bike paths to crime scenes. Many school authorities have purchased district GIS software licenses for products like the ESRI GIS School Program.

Simulation games such as "SimCity" (simcitysocieties .ea.com/about.php) are potentially powerful electronic resources that can engage students in learning about geography as they adopt roles, make decisions, and face the consequences of their choices. Online maps and photographs and electronic sources of statistical information are available from many agencies, including those mentioned earlier. For more ideas on computer-based resources in geography, see chapter 14, "Integrating Computer Technologies in Secondary Social Studies."

A very successful GIS project, described in the highlighted text, "Sample GIS Activity," illustrates how data about the local community drawn from a variety of electronic sources and analyzed using diverse computer-based tools, can help students learn about the relevance of geography and develop sophisticated conceptual understanding and skill mastery. In this project, students plotted crime areas where robberies occurred in their home city of Peterborough, Ontario. The patterns provided a model for predicting where future crimes might be committed. They presented their conclusions to local community policing authorities who visited the school and discussed the importance of these projects in helping to solve crimes.

FIGURE 31.2 WHERE WILL I LIVE?

Making decisions is hard sometimes. One of the most important decisions you may make in your life is where to choose to live. This decision-making activity will help you to explore Canadian culture and landscapes and to understand regional differences in deciding, "Where is the best place for me to live?" Your task is to identify criteria for determining the best place for you to live in Canada, select five possible locations, gather information from your textbook, atlas, websites, and other supplied resources, and evaluate these options in light of your identified criteria identified. Use the Rating Locations chart to help you compare the relative merits of each option.

continued on next page

FIGURE 31.2   WHERE WILL I LIVE? (CONT.)

Step 1

Identify criteria for an optimal location:

* Make a heading list of the ten most important factors influencing a person's decision to live in one place rather than another. Examples include weather and climate, landscapes, types of industry and job opportunities, culture, recreational opportunities, and degree of urbanization. Beside each heading, state what you think would make that factor ideal and what would be less than desirable. For example, for weather and climate you might specify "mild climate with short winters and warm but not hot summers."
* Re-read your list and select the five most important criteria.

Step 2

* Select five geographically separated places you might consider living in Canada.
* Select locations based on their differences.

Step 3

* Weight the factors on a scale of 1 to 5 with 5 being the most important criteria relative to the others and 1 being the least important. Two or three factors may have the same weighting but not all five.
* Record the reasons for your assigned weighting of each factor.

Step 4

* Research each of the five locations. Use the available resources to help to judge how well each location meets the five criteria. For example, you may find information at the Environment Canada weather website to judge whether or not the climate consists of "short winters and warm but not hot summers."

Step 5

* Based on your research, rate the locations based on how well they satisfy each of the criteria. The location that rates the highest on a specific criterion gets a 5; the lowest rated gets a 1.

Step 6

* Multiply the rating for each criterion by the assigned weighting for that criterion. This process will magnify the effect of each criterion on your overall decision. Write the multiplied number in the score box.

Step 7

* Total the weighted scores for each location. Compare the five locations. The ones with the highest weighted scores are the best given the criteria you are using.

Step 8

* Select one location and, based on your identified criteria, evaluate whether or not this is a place where you might actually choose to live.
* What are the strengths and drawbacks of a decision-making process such as this one?

RATING LOCATIONS					
LOCATION	**CRITERIA**				
	Rating: Weighting: Score:	Rating: Weighting: Score:	Rating: Weighting: Score:	Rating: Weighting: Score:	Rating: Weighting: Score:
	Rating: Weighting: Score:	Rating: Weighting: Score:	Rating: Weighting: Score:	Rating: Weighting: Score:	Rating: Weighting: Score:
	Rating: Weighting: Score:	Rating: Weighting: Score:	Rating: Weighting: Score:	Rating: Weighting: Score:	Rating: Weighting: Score:
	Rating: Weighting: Score:	Rating: Weighting: Score:	Rating: Weighting: Score:	Rating: Weighting: Score:	Rating: Weighting: Score:
	Rating: Weighting: Score:	Rating: Weighting: Score:	Rating: Weighting: Score:	Rating: Weighting: Score:	Rating: Weighting: Score:
Total points					

SAMPLE GIS ACTIVITY: ANALYSIS OF BREAK-AND-ENTER INCIDENTS

This extended activity is one of a set of GIS analysis projects created at Thomas A. Stewart Secondary School in Peterborough. It describes how to simulate the practice of geographic profiling to narrow down where suspects might live.

Introduction

Students enjoy studying their own communities and tackling real issues. The activities described below use local area data sets from ESRI Canada and DMTI Spatial (www. esricanada.com/english/3717.asp) along with data from the Peterborough and Lakefield Community Police Service (www. peterboroughpolice.com) to display and analyze the patterns of break-and-enter incidents for the City of Peterborough for a few months in the year 2000.

ArcView GIS and the Spatial Analyst and Network Analyst extensions are used to conduct the study. A GIS such as IDRISI would be an inexpensive substitute (www.clarklabs.org). Caution students about generalizing from these data, given the small sample size.

Many skills are used in this analysis. Students should have considerable experience with ArcView GIS before attempting the project.

Expectations

The following expectations from the Geomatics: Geotechnologies in Action course in the Canadian and World Studies curriculum for Ontario are addressed by this project:

* Describe the extension of geomatics applications into non-traditional domains (for example, criminology, marketing, medicine).
* Identify sources of data, maps, images, and other geographic products (for example, government, private companies, the internet).
* Identify the areal units by which data are commonly aggregated (for example, enumeration areas, census tracts, school districts).
* Describe the structure of a database and explain basic database functions, including querying.
* Explain key analytical operations in GIS (for example, reclassification, overlaying, buffering).
* Use GIS software appropriately to perform analytical operations (for example, overlay analysis, route determination, database querying, simple image analysis).

Create the database

The first step is to create or import a database file for the break-and-enter incidents. The local police department may be willing to provide the data. Alternatively, collect crime statistics from the local newspaper. Creating the database from scratch is time-consuming. The table may be created from within your GIS or in spreadsheet or database software that can save files in the necessary format (for ArcView GIS, the preferred format is dbase).

Geocode the break-and-enter incidents

Once the data has been entered, it needs to be geo-coded so that students can display it on the map. The table of break-and-enter incidents contains addresses and these will be matched to the names in the existing street network. A layer of points is then displayed on the map. Image 1 shows the distribution in Peterborough, Ontario. Students should examine and describe the pattern carefully.

IMAGE 1

Determine the density of incidents

The Spatial Analyst Extension allows ArcView GIS to perform raster analysis and answer the question, "Where is the density of break-and-enters the greatest in Peterborough?" From the *Analysis* menu, *Calculate Density* produces a surface similar to that shown in Image 2. The concentration of criminal activity can be readily seen and again the pattern can be described.

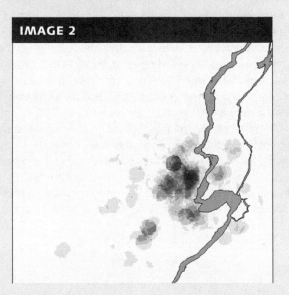

IMAGE 2

continued on next page

Display break-and-enter incidents by enumeration area

Enumeration areas are Statistics Canada's smallest spatial unit and the boundaries are included in the local area data set. You can examine break-and-enter incidents by enumeration area by performing something called a spatial join. This join takes the enumeration areas' identification numbers and assigns them to the break-and-enter incidents. The GIS can then be used to summarize the number of times a break-and-enter incident has occurred within each area and display the tally as a graduated colour map (see Image 3). The local area data set comes with a variety of information (for example, income, unemployment, age distribution) that students could use to begin to explain the break-and-enter distribution.

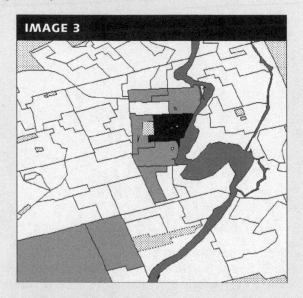

IMAGE 3

Simulate geographic profiling

The next analysis is a very simplistic attempt to show the process of geographic profiling as introduced by Kim Rossomo when he was with the Vancouver City Police Department. His work was highlighted in *Canadian Geographic* (1996) and he has written a book entitled *Geographic Profiling* (2000). Geographic profiling is an investigative methodology that uses the locations of a connected series of crimes to determine the most probable area of offender residence. It is generally applied in cases of serial murder, rape, arson, and robbery, though it can be used in single crimes (auto theft, burglary, bombing) that involve multiple scenes or other significant geographic characteristics. Environmental Criminology Research Inc. (ERCI) makes the software used in this type of analysis (www.geographicprofiling.com/index.html).

In this simplified student activity, seven fictitious suspects' residences were introduced along with a series of 17 crime scenes. Students assessed which suspect was most likely to have committed the crimes in a particular area of the city by buffering the crime scenes. The suspect was assumed to avoid his/her immediate neighbourhood, but was unwilling to travel too far to commit the crimes. Image 4 shows the buffer zones and the most likely suspects' residences.

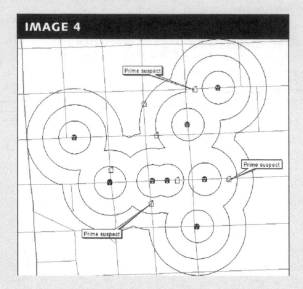

IMAGE 4

Query the database

Show students the database functions of the GIS, by posing a series of questions about the data. The questions depend on the attributes of the database you have created. In ArcView GIS, answers are found by using the Query Builder. Sample questions include:

- How many of the break-and-enter incidents were unsolved?
- How many were by forced entry?
- How many break-and-enter incidents occurred during the early afternoon?
- In how many cases was the value of goods stolen over $500?
- How many times were schools the target?

Plan a fast response route

Finally, ask students to use the Network Analyst Extension to plan the fastest response route from the police station to a crime scene. The route chosen should consider distance, and other factors such as location of stop lights, one-way streets, and road repairs.

As shown in Image 5, the required layers include a street network and two stops, the crime scene and the police station.

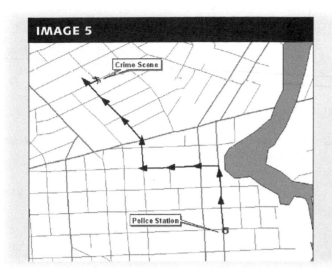

IMAGE 5

Conclusions

Students enjoyed working with local data. Using GIS to investigate local crime records helps students develop expertise with the software and spurs them to do a lot of thinking.

DRAW UPON CROSS-CURRICULAR LINKS

"Cross-curricular ventilation" is a term we coined to refer to occasions for interdisciplinary connections. There are many links between geography and other subjects, and to the unique resources found in these areas. Table 31.4 lists a sampling of the opportunities found in various subjects to reinforce and extend geographical concepts using varied learning resources.

TABLE 31.4 CROSS-CURRICULAR LINKS TO GEOGRAPHY

SUBJECT	EXAMPLES OF USES	LINKS TO GEOGRAPHIC TOPICS
English	descriptive novels or passages from them journals and diary-writing letters to editors	travel and tourism world issues
Chemistry	composition of mineral resources patterns of pollutants	environmental economics
Physics	gravity and its impact on tides and lunar cycles, radiation impact on earth	physical geography earth sciences
Geology	rock formations and patterns	physical geography earth sciences
Biology	ecological studies, such as Canadian eco-zones	environmental eco-zones
Mathematics	mean, median, average, standard deviation, and other statistical uses	GIS
Family studies	food preparation and distribution around the world	world issues
Health and physical education	medical issues and patterns sports patterns Olympics	Canada world geography
Music	Stompin' Tom Connor's Canada songs impart a sense of place world issues captured in song and verse	Canada world issues
Art	landscapes cityscapes cartography	projects and presentations for any topic

Not only do these cross-curricular links help to reinforce key geographical concepts and skills, they expand students' appreciation of the role and uses of geography and of the range of sources of geographical information.

Conclusion

The power of geography lies in its ability to bridge the gap between the earth and the classroom, the world and your students, and the gap between theory and practice. The problems mentioned at the outset of this chapter are faced daily by classroom teachers and their students. The suggestions for experiential and resource-based activities are evidence of the potential to offer interesting and challenging lessons that will help students understand and appreciate their "place" and those of others in the world.

ACKNOWLEDGMENT

We are grateful to Stan Garrod for his thoughtful ideas on the use of maps to tell the story of a place or phenomenon.

REFERENCES

Grescoe, T. 1996. Murder he mapped. *Canadian Geographic* 116 (5), September/October: 48–52.

Rossomo, D.K. 2000. *Geographic profiling.* New York: CRC Press.

32 Four Principles of Authentic Assessment

Roland Case

There is a common saying in educational circles: "What is counted counts." This expression implies that the truly important learning objectives are those we assess. Student sensitivity to this maxim is implied by their common refrains: "Is this on the test?" and "Will it be for marks?" Consequently, if we value critical thinking or the ability to apply knowledge in new contexts, then we should be concerned that our assessment practices reflect these goals. Unfortunately, most assignments and tests emphasize recall of information. The effect of this is to signal to students that what really matters is remembering facts.

This shortcoming will not be redressed simply by devoting more attention to assessing other goals. Ironically, many ways in which thinking abilities are currently assessed are self-defeating. The "timed" nature of tests and the "once-over and one-time nature" of many assignments do not invite thoughtful student reflection. Advocates of "higher" standards typically call for raised expectations of student performance and for expanded testing. It is not obvious that these steps enhance student learning. High-achieving students who are motivated by grades may already be trying their best, and may be distracted from genuine learning by heightened fears of not doing well on the test. Lesser-motivated students may be doubly discouraged by raising the "educational bar" even farther out of their reach and by constantly reminding them of their inferior performance (Assessment Reform Group 2002, 4). In addition, many important educational goals—such as student responsibility, real-life problem solving, reflection, and empathy—are rarely measured. In the rush to "teach to the test," less time may be devoted to these goals. Numerous research studies suggest that many of our system-wide and classroom-based assessment practices inhibit genuine learning.

Overcoming what many regard as the negative effects of common assessment practices is the driving motive for what is referred to as "authentic assessment." The term "authentic" refers to measuring the real, actual, or genuine thing as opposed to measuring a poor substitute. The aim is to supplement traditional assessment practices with "alternative" approaches that offer more meaningful and productive ways of assessing students (Gronlund and Cameron 2004, 10). Although writers describe authentic assessment in varying ways, three interrelated purposes underlie this movement:

- **Greater "authenticity."** Advocates of assessment reform seek a closer fit between the attributes and abilities actually measured by an assessment device and the educational goals that we most value. Too often we assess what is easiest to measure (for example, whether or not students can remember information) and neglect what is more difficult to assess yet nonetheless important (for example, students' ability to think critically and to use their knowledge to solve realistic problems).
- **Supporting learning.** Advocates of assessment reform are committed to using evaluation to help students learn. Often assessment interrupts or discourages learning. We can enhance learning by making assessment tasks more meaningful, by demystifying the process, and by involving students in assessing their efforts and those of fellow students.
- **Fairness to all students.** Advocates of alternative assessment are concerned that some students are penalized by current assessment practices, not because these students know less, but because of the methods and the conditions under which assessment occurs. For example, some students struggle to communicate what they know under the pressure of a single, timed written examination.

In this chapter, I explore four principles for guiding our assessment practices in more authentic ways:

- Focus assessment on what really matters;
- Ensure that assessments are valid indications of student competence;
- Use assessment to support student learning; and
- Develop assessment practices that use the teacher's time efficiently.

In the two follow-up chapters, I discuss ways of nurturing student ownership of assessment and suggest how to develop and use assessment strategies to further these principles. Before proceeding with these principles, I invite you to assess an assessment device that I used in my own teaching.

Assessing my Assessment

Years ago, after graduating with my teaching certificate, I proudly developed a marking sheet for a research project my students had just completed. Towards the end of a unit on India, I asked students to select an aspect of India (for example, climate, religion, geography, customs) they wished to pursue through independent research. I instructed them to consult several library resources on the basis of which they were to prepare a written report. The report was to include several visuals (for example, charts, graphs, maps) and, unlike previous efforts, these visuals were to clearly connect to ideas in the text. To discourage mere copying of reports from published sources, students were to submit research notes with their final report. When the project was completed, I evaluated and returned their work with a Research Report Assessment sheet (Figure 32.1) attached to the front of each assignment.

Make a written list of the strengths and weaknesses of my marking sheet. Imagine that I am a student teacher and you are supervising my teaching practicum. Decide the grade you would assign to my assessment practices based on the following scale:

outstanding	A+/A
very good	A-/B+
good	B/B-
satisfactory	C+/C
poor	C-/D
very poor	F

Since developing this assessment device I have asked several hundred pre-service and practising teachers to assess my early effort at assessment. The grades assigned to my marking sheet have ranged the entire spectrum from "outstanding" to "very poor" with the vast majority (approximately 90 per cent of responses) dividing fairly evenly between "good," "satisfactory," and "poor." This variance is cause for some concern. As professionals, how can we have confidence in our assessment practices if there is such latitude in our conclusions about the quality of my marking scheme? This lack of agreement is especially disturbing since our assessments have poten-

FIGURE 32.1 RESEARCH REPORT ASSESSMENT

1. Bibliography (1 mark for each book)   /4

2. Notes
      very good (3)
      good (2)
      satisfactory (1)
      poor (0)   /3

3. Charts, maps, drawings, etc.
                    #1   #2   #3
      a) neat:
      b) accurate:
      c) relevant: /9

4. Text
      a) neatness: /2
      b) spelling, grammar, punctuation:
         (1/2 mark off per error)   /5
      c) coverage of major points:
         all (5)
         almost all (4)
         most (3)
         some (2)
         few (1)   /5
      d) well written:
         good (2)
         satisfactory (1)
         poor (0)   /2
                                 /14

5. Comments:

TOTAL   /30

tially profound effects on our students. For example, if I was a secondary student and if this assessment was typical of my evaluations, it would have the following consequences:

- "Outstanding" would qualify me for university scholarships.
- "Very good" would enable me to attend the university of my choice, but not on scholarship.
- "Good" would allow me to get into a university, but perhaps not my first choice.
- "Satisfactory" would mean I would be lucky to get into a community college.
- "Poor" would prevent me from directly continuing post-secondary studies.
- "Very poor" would require that I repeat the grade.

Although I do not wish to infer too much from my informal survey, it suggests considerable inconsistency in our understanding of what counts as good assessment. As indicated earlier, I believe there are four principles, which if better understood and implemented, would improve this predicament. My present purpose is to explain the implications and importance of the four principles. Although there are other principles and other ways of expressing the ones I suggest, the four principles offer a reasonably comprehensive set of considerations for improving our assessment practices.

At the close of the chapter, I will ask you to revisit your initial assessment of my assessment in light of what I hope will be a clearer, more thorough grasp of these key principles. Just as we should use criteria to assess our students' work, so too should we use the principles of authentic assessment as the basis for judging our assessments. The implicit message in my chapter is that we should neither be satisfied with, nor confident in, our assessments of students' work until we have seriously scrutinized our own assessment practices. Let us now look in turn at the four principles that I recommend as a basis for this assessment.

Focus on What Really Matters

The most significant question to ask ourselves when judging our assessment practices is whether or not we are assessing what really matters. Are the criteria we are using—consciously or not—to judge students' work reflective of the most important educational objectives? As suggested above, what teachers assess has important implications for what students consider important and ultimately what they learn. Do our assessment practices do justice to the breadth and complexity of the goals of social studies? Assessments that are skewed towards a limited range of desired outcomes, for example, outcomes related exclusively to factual knowledge, fail to assess and possibly inadvertently discourage student growth along other desired dimensions. This concern is at the root of much of the criticism of standardized testing. Many standardized tests used to evaluate students, teachers, and schools focus on those curriculum outcomes that are easily measured by machine-scoreable questions. This leaves a considerable gap between the outcomes that schools are expected to promote and the outcomes used to measure school performance. In a study from the University of Wisconsin, the overlap between the curriculum and the test for one subject was just 5 per cent (cited in Simmons 2004, 37). The author suggests that the effect is to undervalue some of the most important life skills such as critical thinking and problem solving.

The most shocking realization when I first had occasion to look back at my marking sheet was the imbalance in my assessment. One-third of the total mark for the project (10 marks out of 30) dealt with mechanics (that is, neatness, spelling, and punctuation). Although these are appropriate criteria to use, it now strikes me as mistaken that I would weigh these twice as much as I did the content of the report (the extent to which the report addressed the main ideas accounted for only 5 out of 30 marks). Notice the consequences of this kind of weighting: students who knew a lot about their topic, but who did not write in standard English, might fail the assignment. On the positive side, the fact that I placed some value on information gathering (the use of multiple references and on the taking of competent notes) and on content knowledge (that is, the need for students to cover the main points of the topic) showed some sensitivity to the importance of these goals. Regrettably I did not appear to attach any special importance to the students' ability to think about the material they were researching.

Over the course of a unit or term (not necessarily on any given assignment), we should assess for all relevant goals, and the emphasis assigned these goals should reflect their relative importance. Completing what is called a "table of specifications" is one strategy for checking that each goal is weighted appropriately in one's overall assessment plan. At the end of a reporting period, list all the graded assignments and tests. Record in a table similar to Table 32.1 the amount of marks devoted to each goal. In Table 32.1, the five main goals are indicated in the left-hand column, and the different assessment strategies appear across the top of the chart. The column on the far right reports the percentage of marks assigned to each goal: for example, understanding of key concepts is worth 40 per cent of the total marks (160/400). Be prepared for a surprise when you discover the importance you actually attached to the various goals. The actual weighting of marks should be matched against the importance these goals deserve according to the curriculum and your own professional sense of what really matters, given the students you teach. Although not always possible, setting up a table of specifications beforehand, or partway through a term, allows you to make adjustments for any imbalances in the weighting of certain goals.

Provide Valid Indications

A second consideration in authentic assessment is validity. Although validity has a long history as a complex technical term, in the context of authentic assessment it can be defined as a close fit between the kinds of attributes actually measured by an assessment device and the intended educational goals. In simplest terms, an assessment strategy is valid if it actually assesses the outcomes it claims to assess.

My intention with the marking sheet on the research project was to assess students' ability to identify and use

TABLE 32.1 SPECIFICATION OF GOALS ASSESSED

UNIT GOALS	ASSESSMENT STRATEGIES						
	Quizzes	Activity sheets	Group project	In-class observation	Research report	TOTAL MARKS	% OF TOTAL MARK
Critical thinking about issues	15	–	–	20	25	60	15
Information gathering	15	–	20	–	25	60	15
Recall of factual information	50	30	–	–	–	80	20
Understanding of key concepts	20	20	70	–	50	160	40
Co-operation with others	–	–	30	10	–	40	10
TOTAL	100	50	120	30	100	400	100

multiple sources of information. I now doubt that assigning a mark for each reference in the bibliography measures this ability. Students could score very well on this part of the assignment even if they did not actually use more than one of the books listed in their bibliography. For that matter, I could not be sure that students knew how to find books on their topic—perhaps someone had obtained the books for them. My reliance on the number of references in the bibliography was not a valid indicator of students' research abilities. If I wanted to assess the students' ability to locate and find appropriate sources, I should have created a task in the library where students would be expected to retrieve and assess relevant sources. I could have measured their ability to make use of multiple sources by assigning marks to students who cited several sources of relevant information in their final report. The outcome measured in the "coverage of the main points" section of my marking scheme is equally problematic. Students may have written on all the main points without really understanding what they had put down. If I was serious about finding out if they had gained any understanding of the topic, I would have been better advised to ask students to tell me orally in their own words what they had found out.

The importance of validity was first brought home to me when I was preparing my grade 6 students for a day-long field trip. Several weeks before beginning to plan for a picnic lunch on our field trip, we practised answering word problems like the following:

> If there are thirty students in the class and students want on average two sandwiches each, how many slices of bread will be required? How many loaves of bread will we need if there are twenty slices of bread in each loaf? What will be the total cost if bread sells for $1.25 per loaf? How much must each student contribute to cover the cost of the bread?

Despite their ability to successfully solve these kinds of word problems (as determined by a quiz), my students were incapable of determining how much money each would have to bring for lunch on our field trip. They made no connection between the arithmetic we had been doing and the challenge before them. Even after the connection was explained, they were unable to solve the problem. In the word problems I had provided, all of the mathematical "ingredients" had been supplied to them. Not only did they not know the answers to the real-life questions (that is, the number of sandwiches we would want, the number of slices in a loaf, and the actual cost of bread), beyond getting an adult to tell them, they had no idea how they could come up with the answers. This is one of the dangers when assessment is based largely on isolated assignments and quizzes.

Although I had taught my students to solve word problems on costing lunches, I had not taught them how to cost the lunch. As Grant Wiggins suggests, "school tests make the complex simple by dividing it into isolated and simplistic chores—as if the students need not practise the true test of performance, the test of putting all elements together" (1989, 706). My students' mastery of all the requisite competencies involved in this task and their ability to integrate them successfully were tested only when they were charged with planning the actual lunch. Significantly, I would never have realized the gaps in their abilities, and subsequently addressed them, unless I had assigned this "real-life" assessment task. If we do not assess beyond isolated competencies in artificial situations, we are unlikely to know whether students are able to use their knowledge in significant ways.

Another factor affecting validity is the conditions under which the assessment occurs. The use of "surprise" tests and a failure to make clear to students the basis upon which they will be judged may impair students' abilities to show what they actually know. Instead, students may be rewarded for anticipating what the teacher wants. As well, traditional timed tests reward students who perform well in on-the-spot situations and may discriminate against students who are equally knowledgeable but are unable to perform under contrived conditions. A very common concern for validity, especially acute with students whose first language is not English, is that students' answers may be a function of their written fluency and not their understanding of the content. Although this obstacle cannot be completely overcome, there may be ways to mitigate its effects:

- Assignments and questions should be explained orally to students, and perhaps have someone translate the instructions and make frequent use of visual aids and other low vocabulary prompts.
- Whenever feasible, allow students to represent their answers in graphic form, orally, in written point form, or perhaps even in their native tongue.
- Whenever appropriate, offer alternative assignments, reduced expectations, or additional assistance to offset any language impediment.

Besides being careful when developing measures to devise questions or tasks that capture what we intended, validity may also be enhanced by using several devices of different sorts to gather information about student achievement. The point of considering a variety of approaches is to increase the likelihood of finding a valid way to assess the desired outcomes. If, for example, the ability to solve real-life problems is an important goal then, at some point, we should assess the students' ability to act on a real problem and not be satisfied by asking students to list the factors they would consider in a hypothetical context. An observation checklist or rating scale may be particularly effective in assessing student performance in group projects and class presentations. Having students keep a journal while participating in a project or a simulation activity may provide rich information about student attitudes towards themselves and others. For example, while preparing for a class discussion or debate, students might comment on their reflections about expressing and defending their positions, or about working with others.

Use Assessment to Support Learning

Advocates of assessment reform are emphatic about using assessment to enhance learning. The enhanced emphasis on using assessment to support learning is reflected in the distinction between the traditional phrase "assessment of learning" and the more recently introduced notion of "assessment

for learning" (Assessment Reform Group 1999, 2). In their review of numerous studies, this group concludes that students would be better motivated and learn more if assessment practices focussed more on supporting learning than on measuring learning (Assessment Reform Group 2002, 10). More recently, educators are talking about assessment as learning to heighten awareness of the potential to use assessment tasks as opportunities for learning, not simply to provide formative feedback (British Columbia Ministry of Education 2005, 23–24). Self-assessment is an example of an assessment task that is also a learning task as students examine their own work and think through its strengths and shortcomings.

Greater validity of assessment measures is in itself an attempt to use assessment to support learning. As suggested by the example about planning for the field trip lunch, if an assessment does not capture what it is we really value, then we are less likely to know when we have succeeded (or have failed to succeed) in reaching our objective. Only after the real-life task did I realize that my students could not calculate the cost of our lunch. Assessment practices can support learning in at least four other important ways:

- clearly communicate expectations;
- involve students in the assessment process;
- provide helpful feedback on learning; and
- provide opportunities and incentives for students to improve.

COMMUNICATE EXPECTATIONS

If students know clearly what is expected of them they are more likely to succeed at the task. One of the most obvious ways in which I could have used my assessment practices to support learning was by presenting students with the marking sheet before they embarked on the research assignment. As it was, they saw the criteria only after they had completed their report. If my measure had had validity and had focussed on the important goals, I would have been signalling to students what was important and what they were required to do to demonstrate their learning. But because of its flaws, had I distributed my original marking sheet beforehand, unwittingly I would have been encouraging students to attend to the technical dimensions more than the content. The fact that I instructed students to select graphs, charts, and maps that related to their text and that I assessed for this, encouraged students to attend to this feature in their reports.

Students may be even clearer about expectations if they are informed specifically about the "criteria" upon which they will be marked and the importance of those criteria (that is, the number of marks assigned to each criterion) and the "standards" for achievement of these criteria. Because the concepts of criteria and standards are often used interchangeably, let me explain the distinction drawn between these two terms.

Criteria are the features or attributes that provide the grounds for judging quality. Sample criteria include:

- historical accuracy
- originality of ideas
- use of several sources
- clarity of presentation
- depth of answer
- active participation in project
- openness to new ideas
- flow/structure of the paper
- neatness
- spelling accuracy

Standards are the benchmarks, performance levels, or degrees of achievement of a given criterion (that is, "high" and "low" standards). Standards can be binary (for example, correct/incorrect, pass/fail, satisfactory/unsatisfactory) or have multiple levels (for example, A$^+$ to F, outstanding to very weak, well above expectations to not yet meeting expectations). Sample standards for three criteria are listed in Table 32.2.

My grade 6 students might have been better able to succeed had I clearly indicated all the criteria and standards for assessment. When assessing their notes I merely indicated whether they were "very good," "good," and so on, without indicating the basis for this assessment. What criteria was I using? Was it the neatness of the notes? Conciseness? Amount of notes? Or, perhaps all of these? Furthermore, even if students knew the criteria, they may still not know what distinguished a "good" from a "satisfactory" standard of note-taking. And yet, if I wanted them to improve, this is precisely the understanding they require. I did a slightly better job of communicating the criteria and standards for the "main points": my criterion was the amount of coverage and my standards were distinguished by the number of main points covered (for example, all, most, a few). Besides supporting learning, another powerful reason for clearly articulating standards is that it reduces inconsistency and arbitrariness in assessments. I now wonder when I look at the standards I offered for "coverage of main points" if there is any real difference between "almost all" and "most" points and between "some" and a "few" points. If there is no clear distinction between these performance levels, how can I have reliably distinguished among them?

In the spirit of living the principles I preach, I offer in Figure 32.2 detailed descriptions of performance levels or standards for each of the four principles that I offer as the criteria for judging authentic assessments. After you have finished reading about all four of these principles, and have a clear understanding of what each involves, I will ask you to use this assessment rubric to reassess your original judgment of my marking sheet. For the time being, I offer this as an example of a way in which we can support learning by clearly articulating the standards for our assessment criteria. Read

TABLE 32.2	SAMPLE STANDARDS	
CRITERION	STANDARDS	DESCRIPTIONS OF PERFORMANCE LEVELS
Historical accuracy	excellent	no factual inaccuracies
	good	at most, a few minor factual inaccuracies that do not affect the conclusion
	satisfactory	one major inaccuracy and several minor factual inaccuracies
	unsatisfactory	several or more major factual inaccuracies that completely undermine the conclusion
Depth of answer	in-depth	all main topics are analyzed in a probing and careful manner
	modest depth	although there is evidence of careful analysis, some aspects are not addressed in much depth
	superficial	for the most part, topics are not addressed superficially
Spelling accuracy	excellent	zero errors
	very good	at most 2 errors
	good	between 3 and 5 errors
	satisfactory	between 6 and 9 errors
	poor	10 or more errors

my descriptions of each standard and decide if you would recognize what each involves.

INVOLVE STUDENTS IN ASSESSMENT

Involving students directly in the assessment process is another way to support learning. The next chapter in this collection, "Building Student Ownership of Assessment," has more to say on each of the following areas for student involvement:

- **Setting criteria and standards.** Joint teacher and student negotiation of the criteria upon which students are to be judged increases student understanding of what is expected and ultimately of their performance in light of these expectations. Students can also be involved in deciding upon standards—by articulating what might be required in order for the work to be regarded as excellent, good, and so on.
- **Creating assessment tasks.** Another way to involve students is by inviting them to assist in developing the tasks upon which they will be assessed.
- **Self- and peer assessment.** Involving students in self- and peer assessment can greatly enhance their learning. The very exercise of assessing their peers on the specific criteria related to the lesson would likely reinforce the students' own understandings of what is expected of them. Furthermore, involving students in assessment encourages students to take greater ownership of their learning. An important dimension of self-assessment is communicating the results to others—either to the teacher, their peers, or parents.

PROVIDE FEEDBACK ON LEARNING

We can enhance learning by helping students see how they might improve. Providing students with useful feedback must go beyond assigning a mark or offering a brief summative comment. For example, in my marking scheme, I provided students, albeit after the fact, with a detailed breakdown of how well they did on each aspect, with a place for general comments. This helped them understand what they did well and where more attention was needed.

Although some students may be concerned exclusively with their mark on an assignment, Paul Black and Dylan Wiliam (1998) have found that this leads to no improvement in student achievement—marks are entirely about assessment of learning, not assessment for learning. In fact, they conclude that grading and other forms of comparative feedback actually get in the way of learning and are especially demotivating for less accomplished students. Because of the negative effects of repeated failure, some educators recommend providing scores only at the end of the grading period when it is necessary to prepare an evaluation report. According to the Assessment Reform Group (2002, 10), ideally teachers should assign marks only if students have a good chance of succeeding. In the interim, students should be provided with abundant feedback and encouragement.

If we want students to improve, our feedback must clearly communicate what has been successfully done, where improvement is needed, and how to do this. A carefully prepared rubric can go a long way in providing this feedback, both in terms of indicating how students have done and what might be done to improve their performance. In my own experience, students benefit most from the use of rubrics when marks are not indicated. The lack of a summative judgment requires them to read the descriptors more carefully and encourages them to believe that it is not too late to improve. Other methods of providing effective feedback include:

- very specific written teacher comments;
- teacher conferences;
- comments by fellow students explaining areas for improvement;
- large and small group discussion of answers; and
- exemplars—samples of high-quality performance—of student work, so long as improvement requires more than simply copying the ideas in the exemplar.

PROVIDE OPPORTUNITIES AND INCENTIVES TO IMPROVE

Where feasible, use assessment to encourage students to learn on their own and to revise and rethink their work. Possible strategies include establishing a habit of assessing key objectives in subsequent units, and making it clear to students that certain abilities will be assessed routinely. Some students may be motivated by supplemental tests or makeup assignments for those who make some effort to improve their understanding. One of my most counter-productive assessment habits as a public school teacher was my penchant for "one-shot" efforts. Rarely did I ask students to seriously revise their work—if work was revisited it was only to tidy up typos or add a missing sentence or two. Now, in my university teaching, I no longer have one-time assignments. In my graduate class, for example, instead of writing three different papers, my students write the same paper three times. The first and second drafts are distributed to everyone in the class for critique. In the first draft, students show largely what they could do before the course. The significant improvement—the deeper, more insightful learning—occurs with the two subsequent revisions where students work through the ideas raised by their colleagues and by me.

FIGURE 32.2 ASSESSING THE ASSESSMENT

	HIGHLY EVIDENT	MOSTLY EVIDENT	PARTIALLY EVIDENT	COMPLETELY ABSENT
Focusses on the important goals	6	4	2	0
	The weighting of marks closely matches the important objectives of the assignment.	The weighting of marks generally matches with the important objectives of the assignment.	The weighting of marks is out of balance with important objectives of the assignment.	The weighting of marks misses or seriously under-represents all the important objectives of the assignment.
Provides valid indications of student ability	6	4	2	0
	The assignment and the marking scheme directly measure student ability on all intended outcomes.	The assignment and the marking scheme measure in a fairly direct way student ability on important intended outcomes.	The assignment and the marking scheme are unlikely to measure student ability on some of the key intended outcomes.	The assignment and the marking scheme measure student ability in a superficial, contrived, or distorted manner.
Supports student learning	6	4	2	0
	The device very clearly identifies the criteria and standards and provides very helpful feedback for improvement. Has significant potential to reinforce and encourage important student learning.	The device is generally clear about the criteria and standards and provides some helpful feedback for improvement. Has some potential to reinforce and encourage student learning in some major areas.	The device contains significant gaps or ambiguities in communicating the criteria and standards and offers little helpful feedback for improvement. Key aspects of the assessment fail to reinforce and encourage student learning.	The device is very vague or confused about the criteria and standards, and offers no helpful feedback for improvement. Offers nothing to support, and may discourage, significant learning.
Uses teacher time efficiently	3	2	1	0
	The assessment and feedback method very efficiently uses teacher time in providing significant information to students.	The assessment and feedback method is somewhat efficient in its demands on teacher time relative to the rewards.	The assessment and feedback method is somewhat inefficient in its demands on teacher time.	The assessment and feedback method requires very extensive teacher time relative to what it communicates.

Outstanding (A+/A): 19–21
Very Good (A–/B+): 16–18
Good (B/B–): 12–15
Satisfactory (C+/C): 9–11
Poor (C–/D): 5–8

Total: /21

Grade:

Before inviting students to undertake serious revision, we should ensure that they have meaningful input as to how they did initially and what they might do to improve. Since elementary and secondary students may be less motivated to engage in subsequent revisions than are students in graduate school, we must encourage them in this regard:

- Ask students to redo only a part of the original assignment (for example, the two worst [or preferred] answers, or the opening and closing paragraphs of an essay).
- Create additional incentives for revising a draft (for example, revised assignments might be exhibited in a fair, submitted to the newspaper, published in a book, or otherwise shared with adults or other students).
- Comment on but do not mark the initial mandatory draft. Establish that only the revised draft "counts" for marks.
- Ask students weeks or months later to revisit an earlier work to see how much they have progressed in the intervening time.

When encouraging students to learn from feedback, it is not simply a matter of them redoing completed assignments, but also formulating plans to use the lessons learned to improve upcoming projects. For example, we might ask students to identify a learning goal, anticipate an obstacle they might face, and suggest how they might overcome it.

Using Teachers' Time Efficiently

The final, perhaps one might say the bottom-line, criterion of good assessment is efficient use of teacher time. Although efficiency has no direct relationship to authentic assessment, the incredible press on teachers' time means that changes, however desirable, are unlikely to occur if they are more time-consuming. Generally speaking, marking sheets, including the one I developed for the independent research project, are efficient assessment tools. Once familiar with the layout it is easy to complete the sheet quickly because it keeps the assessor focussed and saves having to repeatedly write out the same comments. Rubrics are great savers of marking time, but they require considerable up-front development time. For this reason, I am inclined to develop rubrics for major projects during the year—starting with the one that causes the biggest marking headache—and when I want students to undertake peer or self-assessment.

Clearly articulated criteria and standards, communicated beforehand, increase the likelihood of students providing what the teacher is looking for, and help focus the teacher's attention when marking assignments. Clear expectations reduce the likelihood of protracted discussions with students who complain that they did not know what was required of them.

Student peer and self-assessment can save teacher time provided students are adequately trained in the practice. It saves time because it means that students are giving each other feedback that otherwise the teacher would have to give. Developing students' abilities to assess their own work and their peers' work may be one of the more efficient "learning" strategies. In my university teaching, I marvel at how much graduate students learn about (and improve upon) their own writing from frequent opportunities to critique the work of fellow students. They are better able to appraise their own writing after noting the similar strengths and weaknesses in others' writing and they benefit considerably from other students' critiques of their own work. But perhaps the biggest efficiency arising from self-assessment comes from a shift in the perceived ownership of learning. When students truly realize that they, and not the teacher, have primary responsibility for the grade they receive, the relationship between student and teacher changes. There is less need for the teacher to chase after the students and drum the information into them. Students acquire more independence, self-reliance, and commitment—and, and as a result, more is learned.

A Final Reflection

Return to your initial assessment of my marking sheet. While reviewing any notes you took, consider the merits and oversights in your earlier thoughts about my device. Use the assessment rubric presented earlier to reassess my marking sheet. What grade do you now think that it is worth? Even if your assessment is largely unchanged, do you now have greater confidence in the grade you assigned? Is it a fairer, more valid assessment? Are you clearer about how you might help me improve my assessment practices? I hope the answer is yes to all these questions, and to one further question: Do you have a better understanding of principles to follow in making your assessment practices more authentic?

ACKNOWLEDGMENT

I am grateful to Rosemary Evans of Branksome Hall School for her helpful suggestions when revising this chapter.

Select an assessment device (for example, a quiz, end-of-unit project, an observation checklist) that you have developed or that is included in a teaching resource. Use the rubric "Assessing the Assessment" to evaluate this device. Based on what you have learned about the four principles discussed in this chapter, suggest ways to make the device more authentic.

REFERENCES

Assessment Reform Group. 1999. *Assessment for learning: Beyond the black box.* Cambridge, UK: University of Cambridge. Available at http://arg.educ.cam.ac.uk/publications.html.

———. 2002. *Testing, motivation and learning.* Cambridge, UK: University of Cambridge. Available at http://arg.educ.cam.ac.uk/publications.html.

Black, P. and D. William. 1998. Inside the Black Box: Raising Standards Through Classroom Assessment. *Phi Delta Kappan* 80 (2): 139 –148. Available at http://www.pdkintl.org/kappan/kbla9810.htm.

British Columbia Ministry of Education. 2005. *Social Studies 10: Integrated Resource Package 2005* (Response Draft). Victoria, BC: Author.

Gronlund, N.E. and I.J. Cameron. 2004. *Assessment of student achievement* (Canadian edition). Toronto: Pearson Education Canada.

Simmons, N.E. 2004. (De)grading the standardized test. *Education Canada* 44 (3): 37–39.

Wiggins, G. 1989. A true test: Toward more authentic and equitable assessment. *Phi Delta Kappan* 70: 703–713.

33 Building Student Ownership of Assessment

Roland Case

Years ago, I read an article entitled "So, What Did I Get on my Muffin?" The author, a home economics teacher, suggested that this was a common student response to returned assignments (Emblem 1994). The upsetting element of this comment is the student's apparent lack of recognition that marks are earned. Rather it seems the student views teachers as random dispensers of marks. Consequently, assessment is like gift-giving at holiday time. Students present the teacher with a product and hope the teacher reciprocates by "giving" them good marks. If students are lucky and the teacher is in a favourable mood, they get a good mark; if the teacher doesn't like how students chose to do the assignment, they get a lousy grade.

Since reading this article, whenever my university students' comments revealed an absence of personal responsibility for the mark I had awarded them, I would think to myself, "Oh, you don't like what I gave you for your muffin." Naturally, I was disappointed by these incidents because they signalled my failure to promote student ownership for learning. I began to explore ways of communicating the evaluation criteria (criteria are the qualities we look for in student assignments) and eventually by making more transparent the standards for evaluation (standards specify the extent to which the criteria are met). These were improvements, but I continued to own all the assessment cards—I was simply being more explicit in communicating to students what the rules were. Gradually I learned to share responsibility for assessment with my students by negotiating the criteria, jointly articulating the standards, and eventually involving students in peer and self-evaluation.

After several years of trial and error, I recall a student commenting that in previous university courses he would regularly ask what he had to do to get an "A." If he thought the instructor's requirements were too onerous, he would ask what was needed for a "B." In these classes, the standards were external to the student. Fortunately, the student felt differently about my course. Because he had participated in setting the criteria and standards, he didn't feel that they were simply my priorities, and he didn't have to worry or guess what mark I would give him because the assessment rubrics were there for him to apply. He saw my job as corroborating his assessments; I was no longer the dispenser of marks. At the end of the course, he remarked that for the first time in his university career he hadn't done the bare minimum to get an acceptable grade. Instead, he wanted to do his best—the marks weren't a factor, because he knew they would come. He knew what his "muffin" was worth because he had contributed to setting the rules for evaluating his achievement.

In this chapter, I discuss the challenges to and strategies for building student ownership of assessment. In particular, I explore four areas:

- creating meaningful assessment tasks;
- setting criteria;
- establishing standards; and
- supporting peer and self-assessment.

Creating Meaningful Tasks

I want to start by making a somewhat obvious point about the relationship between assessment and learning activities. We will be hard pressed to build student ownership in assessment if students are turned off by the tasks and assignments that are being assessed. Students are less likely to take ownership for how well they do if they don't care about the work they are doing. We would be well advised to keep three principles in mind when thinking of assessment tasks:

- **Less is more.** Students are more likely to be drawn into their work if they have more time to do it and if there is less of it—both in terms of the size of the individual tasks and the frequency of assignments. For example, instead of posing a dozen test questions, reduce the number by half and encourage students to do a more thorough job of the questions that are asked. We might learn as much about students' knowledge of a topic by asking them to provide a detailed labelled diagram than we can by requiring an extended written explanation. Rather than grading homework assignments every week or research projects every second month, reduce their frequency and devote more time to helping students learn to better complete these tasks.

- **Students can contribute.** Another way of increasing the likelihood of students buying into an assessment task is to involve them in creating the task.
  - Ask students to draft examination questions and sample answers that are actually used as the basis of an end-of-unit test.
  - Provide students with a list of specific outcomes you wish to assess and invite them to propose projects or activities that are feasible to accomplish and would enable students to demonstrate their understanding of the intended outcomes.
  - Invite students to develop "source materials" for use in an assessment. For example, students might prepare accounts of various events containing four or five deliberately placed errors that other students would be expected to detect, or students might construct profiles of mystery famous people or historical events that other students would identify based upon the clues provided.
- **Assessments don't have to be boring.** We can go a long way towards increasing student "buy-in" by making our assessment tasks more interesting and relevant. Here are a few examples.
  - Game-show-type contests can be use to replace multiple-choice written quizzes.
  - Instead of a research essay on immigration, students might draft and send a formal brief to the minister responsible for immigration, or prepare and present an application for permanent residency in Canada to a mock immigration tribunal.
  - A biography of a famous person can be made more interesting by converting it into a request for a candid letter of reference or for responses to a census or attitude questionnaire completed from that person's point of view.

The opportunities to develop engaging assessments are limited only by our imagination.

Setting Criteria

Inevitably, when we assess something we rely on criteria. For example, if I announce that a particular movie is wonderful, I will have reasons for this assessment such as it had an excit-ing plot, breathtaking cinematography, and engaging actors. These reasons reveal the implicit criteria forming the basis for my assessment of the movie. Unless we are explicit about our criteria, our assessments may be misleading since different people may employ different criteria. For example, someone else might judge the movie unfavourably because of the trivial message, implausibility, and lack of originality. Neither of us will be able to reconcile our assessments until we recognize the different criteria we used. This problem is even more acute if our assessments are based on narrow or inappropriate considerations. The problems of differing and, in some cases, dubious criteria may explain why some students have such vague ideas about what their work is worth.

Thus, the first challenge in building student ownership is to ensure that our assessments are based on a *relevant, representative,* and *manageable* set of criteria that are *clear* to students. These four considerations are, in effect, the criteria for identifying and justifying assessment criteria. Understanding these criteria for good assessment will help to ensure that the criteria we set on our own or in consultation with students are sound. Certainly, if we want students to set their own assessment criteria, we will want them to recognize when these four considerations are present.

RELEVANT CRITERIA

How do I know whether the criteria I select (or those that students generate) are good criteria for assessment? This is essentially a question about the relevance of the criteria, and relevance depends largely on the purpose of the assignment. For the most part, the objectives or curriculum outcomes for the activity should direct what we look for when assessing students' work. In social studies, it would not be relevant to evaluate a report or other piece of extended writing largely on the basis of grammar and punctuation. An emphasis on this set of assessment criteria is more appropriate in language arts or English composition because one of the main goals of these subjects, unlike in social studies, is mastery of the technical aspects of written expression. Rather, a piece of extended writing in social studies should focus (for the most part) on criteria such as clarity of communication, ability to use information to support a position, accuracy of information, and depth of analysis. These are the kinds of outcomes that social studies seeks to promote. On any individual assignment, the criteria should relate to the particular objectives for that assignment, which in turn should be connected to the more general goals or intended outcomes of social studies. Two strategies to help identify relevant criteria are as follows:

- **Consider the purpose.** One way to determine the relevance of a criterion is to consider the curricular intent or purpose of the learning activity. For example, two common purposes for writing a paragraph are to communicate ideas and to persuade people to accept a position. Any criteria that affect these purposes will be potentially relevant considerations (for example, clarity of expression, use of examples, organization of ideas, number and quality of arguments, amount and quality of supporting evidence). Conversely, it would be largely irrelevant whether the paragraph was written in the first or third person, unless the purpose of the paragraph was to make the reader feel as though the writer actually experienced the event being described.

- **Think of specific sample responses.** Thinking of very good and very poor sample answers is also effective in identifying criteria. For example, share with students a poorly written paragraph and an especially well-written paragraph. Ask them to identify what makes the outstanding paragraph so good and the inferior one so poor.

Interestingly, the poor examples are often more useful in identifying criteria. In Figure 33.1 students consider three sets of notes summarizing a short passage about the Inuit's use of the seal and the caribou. By considering the strengths and weaknesses of each set of notes, students learn to identify the relevant criteria for good notes.

REPRESENTATIVE CRITERIA

Assessment criteria should include a representative range of the important considerations. For example, when deciding on the merits of a proposed solution to a social problem, it would not be sufficient to consider only whether the solution was likely to be effective in addressing the problem. Other important considerations include fairness to all sides and feasibility. Articulating a representative range of criteria helps students recognize the full set of requirements for a particular

---

FIGURE 33.1   SAMPLE NOTES

Below is a short passage on the Inuit's use of the seal and the caribou and three sets of notes summarizing this text. Identify the strengths and weaknesses of each set of notes.

RESEARCH TOPIC: Inuit use of seal and caribou

TEXT: In the fall, the Inuit hunt caribou with bows and arrows. The caribou have spent the summer grazing and are now fat. As well, their coats are getting thicker to protect them during the long winter. Caribou are also hunted in the late spring as they migrate north for the summer. The caribou are very important to the Inuit. The Inuit kill many caribou because much food and many skins are needed.

SAMPLE NOTES

#1	#2	#3
• bows and arrows • fall • coats • migrate north • important • kill • hides	• kill caribou in fall when they are fat • thick coats • also hunt in late spring • important for food and hides • many caribou needed	• Inuit hunt caribou with bows and arrows in fall • caribou have spent summer grazing • now they are fat • their coats are getting thicker • thick coats protect them during the long winter • Inuit also hunt caribou in late spring when caribou migrate north for summer • caribou very important to the Inuit • they kill many because much food and many skins are needed
Strengths:	Strengths:	Strengths:
Weaknesses:	Weaknesses:	Weaknesses:

curriculum expectation. Table 33.1 gives some of the relevant criteria that may be applied to a sampling of social studies assignments.

MANAGEABLE NUMBER OF CRITERIA

Another factor to consider is the number of criteria for any given assignment. Obviously, younger students will be able to deal with fewer criteria than older students. Very young students may be able to handle only one or two criteria. Even with older students, it may be overwhelming to introduce many criteria at any one time. Although no one assignment need address the full range of criteria for a particular curriculum outcome, the broader range of relevant criteria can be assessed over the unit or term. One way to avoid overburdening students with too many criteria is to frame them in broader, more general terms that subsume several specific criteria. For example, "effective presentation manner" may be used in lieu of specifying several more detailed criteria, such as clarity and audibility of voice, posture, and eye contact. However, if the presentation is a major part of the assignment, then it may be unwise to lump these more specific criteria under the broader heading.

CLEAR TO STUDENTS

A final consideration is the need for clearly articulated criteria. Obviously, students will better understand both what is wanted of them and how well they have succeeded in completing their assignment if the basis for assessment is clearly specified. One of the most confusing tendencies is to identify criteria in vague terms such as "active listener" or "creative." Students must understand more precisely what we mean by them in order for criterion-based assessment to be effective. We are better off substituting more specific terms for ambiguous concepts such as "creativity" (for example, offers ideas not mentioned in class or that is not a very obvious possibility) and "active listening" (for example, attends carefully to what others say, refers to other students' ideas during discussions).

Assessment criteria can be articulated in two ways—in *descriptive* or *qualitative* terms. The type of terms used to specify criteria has implications for the quality of direction we provide students:

- **Descriptive criteria** specify the desired features entirely in directly observable or immediately identifiable terms that describe what is required. For example, descriptive criteria for assessing a paragraph may include:
  - Opens with a statement of position.
  - The body must contain three reasons for the position.
  - Closes with a summary statement.
- **Qualitative criteria** specify the desired features in evaluative terms—in terms of attributes or qualities that characterize the effectiveness of each constituent part. For example, qualitative criteria for assessing a paragraph may include:
  - Opens with a *clear* and *accurate* statement of position.
  - The body of the paragraph contains *plausible* and *relevant* reasons for the position.
  - Closes with a *concise* and *powerful* summary statement.

Articulating criteria in descriptive terms has the ad-

TABLE 33.1 SAMPLE CRITERIA FOR ASSESSING SAMPLE ACTIVITIES	
Justification for a conclusion	• Is the information factually accurate?
	• Does the answer reveal depth of understanding?
	• Are the reasons supported with evidence?
Oral presentation	• Is the presentation thoughtfully structured?
	• Is it presented in a clear manner?
	• Does the presentation engage the audience?
Plan to solve a problem	• Is the solution doable?
	• Is it fair to all parties?
	• Will the solution solve the problem?
	• Is the solution safe to implement?
Co-operative group work	• Did students apply themselves to the task?
	• Were students willing to take turns?
	• Did students show sensitivity to the feelings of others?

vantage of being easier for students and teachers to recognize—for example, we simply look for the required number of sentences and reasons, and check that the closing sentence offers a summary. With younger students and generally in the early stages of students' work on a topic, it *may* be appropriate to specify criteria largely in descriptive terms—simply expecting students to come up with three reasons (for that matter, even one reason) for their position. The use of descriptive criteria makes most sense if our sole concern is that students understand the concept (for example, that they know what a reason or a topic sentence is).

The disadvantage of descriptive criteria is that they may not allow us to distinguish when the desired feature has been competently completed. For example, the three "reasons" provided may be largely irrelevant to the position taken, or the opening sentence may be confusing. With descriptive criteria, students may simply include the identified component without any attention to its quality. For this reason, we may be better advised to assess knowledge of concepts such as reason or topic sentence prior to asking students to use them in a paragraph. We might do this by asking students to provide a definition, recognize examples and non-examples, and offer a sample of each. Once students show their understanding, we will want to teach them what is required for effective application of these concepts. After all, it is not just any three reasons that we seek, but three "plausible" and "relevant" reasons.

Qualitative criteria identify those qualities that indicate effective application of the concept. In applying qualitative criteria we must judge the extent to which the requirements have been met (for example, how "clear" is the synthesis or how "plausible" are the reasons). Of course, we will need to help students recognize what is involved in satisfying these qualitative requirements.

There are various ways to foster students' understanding of assessment criteria.

- Provide students with clear indicators of what may be involved in satisfying the criterion: "I know I am being *friendly* when I …
    - compliment others on their work,
    - offer to help others before they ask me to,
    - use friendly words and smile, and
    - am willing to share my supplies and my ideas."
- Ask students to provide concrete indicators of each criterion: What does it look like? Sound like? Feel like? As suggested in the highlighted text, "Generating Criteria," students can be aided in making the transition from descriptive to qualitative criteria by adding an additional question: "What are the underlying qualities that make these actions and words effective?"
- Invite students to restate in their own words the criteria for an assignment.

- Provide student samples that meet and do not meet the assigned criteria and ask them to compare these samples (for example, Which of the three examples of notes on Inuit use of seal and caribou meet the criteria for clear, comprehensive, and concise note-taking?).

DECIDING UPON CRITERIA

Before leaving the discussion of criteria, it is worth considering the question: "Who should set the criteria?" As is the case with virtually all educational decisions, the answer depends on the circumstances. While, generally speaking, it may be desirable to involve students in establishing assessment criteria, there are times when this is not feasible or worth the effort required. For example, if students lack knowledge of the topic, they may be able to offer little to the discussion about criteria. In these situations, students would need to learn more about the topic before discussing criteria. For major assignments or assignments in which student ownership is especially important, it may be worthwhile to devote the time needed to jointly set criteria; on other occasions, it may be sufficient simply to invite students to comment on or suggest additions to the criteria you propose. In most occasions, the class as a whole should be able to agree on the criteria; however, it may sometimes be useful to allow individual students to add unique criteria of their own. Sharing samples of exemplary and non-exemplary performance, as was suggested with the three versions of notes described earlier, provides a valuable focus for class discussions of criteria.

> Imagine you have just asked students to create an information drawing or poster about a particular community or country. Identify, in terms that would be clear to students, three or four relevant and representative criteria drawn from the curriculum outcomes for a particular grade. Explain how you would ensure that all students understood the learning objectives for this task.

Establishing Standards

Identifying assessment criteria is only the first step in building student ownership of assessment; we must then decide what counts as meeting these objectives. As suggested earlier, this is a matter of articulating the levels of achievement or standards for each criterion. The task of specifying standards is a matter of deciding the degree to which each criterion has been met

GENERATING CRITERIA[1]

As a first step in generating criteria, ask students to brainstorm what success on a task looks and sounds like. The focus in the following example is harmonious group work. In two columns as indicated below, record student suggestions about what harmonious groups look and sound like (typically these will be identified in terms of descriptive criteria). Ask students to look for the qualities underlying or implicit in these sights and sounds—these are likely to be qualitative criteria. For example, students nodding at each other or saying, "that's a good idea" are examples of supportive behaviour. After identifying the underlying qualities for all the suggested actions and words, ask students to review their list of criteria:

- Are all the suggestions relevant? (For example, it might have been suggested that the "look" of a harmonious group requires that everyone be sitting down.)
- Is the list representative of the important features of a harmonious group?
- Should some criteria be eliminated or combined to make the list a more manageable number?
- Is each criterion clearly stated (that is, does everyone know what each means)?

HARMONIOUS GROUP WORK	
Looks like	**Sounds like**
students smile at each other students look at each other students nod to each other	"What do you think about this?" "That's an interesting idea." "Are you okay?"
Underlying qualities	
are supportive/encouraging of each other are interested in the ideas of others are sensitive to each other's feelings	

(for example, What would a "clear" position statement look like? How would this differ from a "very clear" position statement?). Articulating standards is important for three reasons:

- **Supports student learning.** There is immense educational value in helping students recognize when their work meets or fails to meet certain standards. Students may know that their report will be assessed on criteria, such as clarity and organization, but it is another matter for them to appreciate what a very clear or moderately well-organized paragraph looks like. Standards communicate to students what is required to succeed (partially or completely) in meeting these criteria. Instead of learning simply that they did well, articulating standards helps students learn what "doing well" means, and what doing even better would require.
- **Facilitates fair grading.** Articulating standards is necessary if we are to translate performance on an assignment into a grade or other summative judgment. What does "at grade level" look like and how does this differ from "above" or "below" grade level? How good is 30 out of 35? Is it "outstanding," warranting an A or an A+? Or is it "very good," warranting a B or B+? Perhaps it warrants some other grade? Teachers and students should share

a common understanding of the basis for these performance levels, which means we need to be clear about the standards we are using. This is especially true when students take part in peer and self-assessment. When a single teacher assesses a class set of assignments, there is some expectation that a common set of standards will have been applied even if the standards were not explicitly articulated. Consistent standards are unlikely when thirty different students are assessing themselves and others.

- **Builds student ownership.** Making the bases for our assessments more explicit assists in changing students' mindsets from one of "What grade did you *give* me?" to one of "Where along this scale does my work fall?" If the standards are well articulated and students are trained in making careful, fair-minded assessments of their work and that of their peers, the teacher's role in assessment becomes less prominent, relegated increasingly to checking the soundness of students' assessments.

JUSTIFYING STANDARDS

Although judgment is inevitable in justifying standards, the decision should not be arbitrary. Standards, whether in the form of letter grades or in evaluative terms such as "excellent" and "poor," can be justified on either norm-referenced or criterion-referenced bases.

- **Norm-referenced standards** are determined by how well a particular product or performance matches the work of a normal or typical population (for example, Is this a "typical" performance for a grade 6 student? Would only about thirty per cent of the class meet this level? Would this be within the top ten per cent of the province?). Norm-referenced judgments are based on the extent of students achieving a given level. For example, some universities insist that not more than twenty per cent of students in a given class receive an "A." Notice that with norm-referenced standards, it is theoretically impossible for all students to get a top score—students are rated relative to how well other students perform. To this extent, norm-referenced standards may discourage co-operation among students, because as students do better, the standard becomes higher for everyone.
- **Criterion-referenced standards** are determined by benchmarks that are not directly dependent on how well others in the population perform, but on an external reference (for example, what is needed in order to read the newspaper, be understood by an intelligent reader, successfully meet an agreed-on goal). Criterion-referenced judgments are based on expectations that are not dependent on what the average student is likely to achieve, but on an independent level of expectation. With criterion-referenced standards, it is theoretically possible for everyone to achieve a high rating.

Neither norm-referenced nor criterion-referenced standards should be arbitrary—there should be a reasonable basis for setting each level. Criterion-referenced standards may be justified in terms of what would likely be required in order to be employable, or to read and understand the newspaper, or complete a task (for example, by grade 3, students should be able to write a clear, four-sentence paragraph; after completing the unit, students should have mastered 80 per cent or more of the content on this exam; by the end of elementary school, students should be able to draw warranted inferences from newspaper articles). Norm-referenced standards may be justified in terms of the places available in the next educational level or a "normal" distribution of the population (for example, the bell curve—the top 10 per cent get "excellent," the next 20 per cent get "good," and so on)—or a comparison with what "average" students have done in previous years.

Pre-established standards in certain areas are available from provincial ministries of education. For example, Table 33.2, developed by the British Columbia Ministry of Education (2001, 19, 61, 139), summarizes performance standards for three aspects of social responsibility at various grade ranges.

When setting standards for our own assignments, we should be sensitive to both norm- and criterion-referenced considerations. There is little merit in adopting a criterion-based standard that either no student could meet because it is too demanding or would challenge no one because it is too easy. In other words, we should temper this standard with norm-referenced expectations. Conversely, it seems counter-productive to decide beforehand on norm-referenced grounds that on a given assignment only the top five students will be allowed to do "very well" and at least five students must do "poorly." Rather, we should rely on published guidelines, past experience, and our own professional intuitions about what are fair and educationally realistic expectations. In justifying the standards articulated in the "thoughtful report" example appearing below, I tempered my impression of a truly masterful essay to accommodate the reasonably expected abilities of secondary students—I should not require them to operate at a level expected of graduate students. Just as with the setting of criteria, it would be appropriate to ask students to comment on the reasonableness of the proposed expectations. Or perhaps in some circumstances, we can help students set the standards for "good" and "very good" performances on an assignment.

COMMUNICATING STANDARDS

Assessment standards that are identified simply by a set of labels (for example, excellent, good, satisfactory, poor) offer little help to students. These labels identify the levels but don't explain or articulate what is required for each. The most common way of articulating standards is through an assessment rubric, which is a scale describing the criteria and standards for an assignment or test. Two types of scales are used in rubrics:

- **Holistic scales** cluster criteria so that the description of standards for all criteria are aggregated—one would make a single overall judgment about an assignment taking into consideration all the criteria. The rubric in Figure 33.2 offers a holistic scale for judging which one of five descriptions best characterizes the overall thoughtfulness of a report on a social issue.
- **Analytic scales** specify the standards for criteria separately, and one would make judgments for each criterion used to assess an assignment. The rubric in Figure 33.3, "Self-assessment of Role Play," discussed later in this chapter, is an analytic scale used to self-assess students' performance in a decision-making simulation on four criteria—acting in role, contributing ideas, supporting others, and seeking a "win-win" solution.

TABLE 33.2   SAMPLING OF STANDARDS FOR SOCIAL RESPONSIBILITY

ASPECT	EXCEEDS EXPECTATIONS	FULLY MEETS EXPECTATIONS	MEETS EXPECTATIONS (MINIMUM LEVEL)	NOT YET WITHIN EXPECTATIONS
Contributing to the classroom and school community (kindergarten–grade 3 expectations)	• welcoming, friendly, kind, and helpful • participates in and contributes to classroom and group activities; often takes on extra responsibilities	• usually welcoming, friendly, kind, and helpful • participates in and contributes to classroom and group activities	• usually friendly and, if asked, will help or include others • may need prompting to participate in and contribute to classroom and group activities	• often unfriendly or disrespectful of others • generally reluctant to participate in and contribute to classroom and group activities
Solving problems in peaceful ways (grade 4–5 expectations)	• considers others' views, and uses some effective strategies for resolving conflicts; takes responsibility and shows good judgment about when to get adult help • can explain an increasing variety of problems or issues and generate and evaluate strategies	• tries to manage anger, listen to others, and apply logical reasons to resolve conflicts; usually knows when to get adult help • can explain simple problems or issues and generate and select simple, logical strategies	• tries to state feelings and manage anger; often needs support to resolve conflicts, frequently overestimating or underestimating the need for adult help • can identify simple problems or issues and generate some strategies; tends to rely on the same strategies for all problems	• does not take responsibility or listen to another's views in a conflict situation; tends to blame and put down others • has difficulty stating problems or issues, and may be unable to suggest or choose appropriate strategies
Valuing diversity and defending human rights (grade 8–10 expectations)	• respectful and ethical; speaks out and takes action to support diversity and defend human rights, even when that may not be a popular stance	• respectful and fair; increasingly willing to speak up or take action to support diversity and defend human rights	• usually supports those who speak up or take action to support diversity and defend human rights	• sometimes disrespectful; may stereotype or avoid those perceived as different in some way

An advantage of holistic scales is that we need make one judgment only. This often reduces the time required to assess student work. The disadvantage of holistic scales is that students may overlook particular criteria embedded in the global descriptors. On the other hand, analytic scales focus students' attention on each aspect of an assignment. When self-assessing, it may be easier to begin with analytic scales so students can attend to one criterion at a time. Having said this, the difference between analytic and holistic scales may be a matter of degree: specific criteria can always be clustered into more general categories, thereby modifying an analytic scale so that it more closely resembles a holistic scale. The social responsibility rubric shown earlier is a modified analytic scale. The ministry has grouped several criteria within each of the three general categories of contributing to community, solving problems, and defending human rights.

Another variable in assessment rubrics is the level of detail in the descriptions of performance levels—rubrics can be fully articulated or skeletal in their detail (Mertler 2001):

• **Fully articulated rubrics.** The most elaborate rubrics richly describe each level of performance. These "fully articulated" rubrics are difficult to develop, requiring numerous revisions before balanced and precise descriptions are produced. Unless the descriptions of standards are clear and mutually exclusive (i.e., no overlap between descriptors), the rubric is unreliable. Fully articulated rubrics may be worth the effort, especially for major

FIGURE 33.2 HOLISTIC RUBRIC: THOUGHTFUL REPORT

SCORE	DESCRIPTION OF REPORT
4	**Accomplished and very thoughtful.** The report clearly identifies all the main ideas of the issue. The discussion explains the important points carefully and with lots of detail. Personal opinions are well explained and supported with convincing examples and believable reasons.
3	**Competent and thoughtful.** The report is generally clear about the main ideas of the issue. The discussion explains most of the important matters in a careful manner. Personal observations are generally supported with relevant examples and believable reasons.
2	**Some thoughtfulness, but flawed.** The report identifies some of main ideas of the issue, but misses other important ones. The discussion explains some important points, but often states the obvious or overlooks basic points. Personal opinions are supported with a few reasons and examples that are not always convincing.
1	**Little or no thoughtfulness.** The report does not clearly identify any of the main ideas of the issue. The discussion does very little to explain the important points. Personal opinions are not supported with relevant examples and believable reasons.
0	**Not done.** No report submitted.

projects involving student self- and peer assessment. The elaborate descriptions provide considerable guidance, clarity, and consistency, which are especially important when students adopt an assessor's role. However, because they are difficult to produce, it may be wise to use fully articulated rubrics with major projects where the time required to develop the rubric will pay off in terms of enhanced student achievement.

- **Skeletal rubrics.** On a more regular basis it may be advisable to use less elaborate rubrics in which the descriptions for each level are not articulated in detail. In most of these cases, standards can be delineated using a single word or phrase describing various levels of performance—"always," "often," "occasionally," and "rarely."

See the rubric in Figure 33.3 for students to use in self-assessing their efforts during a role play of a simulated town hall meeting. Where possible, use words that clearly communicate the basis for distinguishing between each level (for example, quantity of correct answers, degree of clarity, extent to which criterion is present) rather than words such as "excellent" or "poor," which are vague evaluative terms and, therefore, less specific about the differences between levels.

Recently, educators have expressed concerns about the misuse and negative implications of rubrics. For example, Alfie Kohn reports a teacher's observation that her students appear "unable to function unless every required item is

GUIDELINES FOR DEVELOPING FULLY ARTICULATED RUBRICS

- **Generating criteria.** Brainstorm criteria for assessing the assignment for which the rubric is being developed.
- **Prioritizing criteria.** Select the most important and relevant criteria, justified in light of curriculum expectations and your purpose for the assignment.
- **Consolidating criteria.** Cluster criteria around common themes. Consider rephrasing some criteria more generally to reduce the number of specific criteria. Make a provisional selection of a manageable number of criteria, organized into categories (for example, presentation,

content, research). Be especially careful about vague terms such as "creativity" and "critical thinking." Where possible, use precise criteria (for example, goes beyond the obvious, questions the accuracy of the author's claims, offers evidence to support position).

- **Setting levels.** Decide on the number of performance levels or standards to specify—rubrics commonly articulate between three and five levels. With younger students, three levels may be most appropriate. More than five levels may

continued on next page

be too difficult to distinguish for any students. Besides, it is always possible to assign a mark midway between two levels.

- **Selecting the variables to distinguish performance levels.** Each level of performance can be distinguished in two ways:
  - alter the extent and degree to which the criterion has been met. For example, performance levels for "clear explanations" may range from "*every important* idea has been *clearly* explained" through "the *most important* ideas are *generally clearly* explained" to "*no clear* explanations are provided."
  - add an additional condition at certain levels of performance. For example, the highest performance level for "clear explanations" may be distinguished by inclusion of an additional expectation ("every main idea has been clearly explained in the students' own words") that is not present in the other descriptors ("the main ideas are generally clearly explained" or "no clear explanations are provided").

Many rubrics are flawed in their use of variables to distinguish performance levels in two ways:

  - use of quantitative variables to distinguish entirely descriptive criteria. For example, performance levels for "provides reasons" may range from "provides *three or more* reasons" through "provides *two* reasons" to "*no* reasons provided." The problem rests with reliance on purely descriptive features. Is a student who provides three reasons that are irrelevant and unsound actually performing at a higher level than a student who provides only one irrelevant, unsound reason?
  - use of inconsistent variables across performance levels. For example, it would be inappropriate to distinguish levels for "provides reasons" with descriptors that range from "provides several *plausible* reasons" through "provides a few *clear and relevant* reasons" to "reasons are *not supported with any examples*"). The problem arises because different *kinds* of variables (plausible, clear, relevant, supported with examples) are used at each level. Performance levels should be distinguished by varying the degree of achievement for common variables.

- **Draft polar descriptors.** Begin by describing the standards at the very top and the very bottom of the scale: What would the best performance look like? What would the worst level of performance look like? Decide whether the performance is better articulated in a single description (making it a holistic scale) or whether, for ease of preparation and clarity to students, discrete descriptions are more useful (making it an analytic scale). Because it is better to start with the best that students can achieve rather than the worst, many assessment experts recommend describing the highest performance level on the left-hand side of a rubric and the lowest level on the right-hand.

- **Draft intermediate descriptors.** The most difficult task in creating a rubric is describing the in-between standards. It may be helpful to look at existing rubrics for ideas on the kinds of words to use in distinguishing different gradations of performance. An advantage of using an odd number of performance levels (three or five levels) is that the intermediate levels can be distinguished by splitting the difference between the poles. For example, on a five-point scale, the third level would be exactly midway between the descriptions of a "one" and a "five," and the second level would then be midway between the descriptions of a "one" and a "three." With an even number of levels, it is necessary to divide the distance between the poles into equal intervals. For example, on a four-point scale, the second level is one-third of the distance between the descriptions of a "one" and a "four," and the third level is two-thirds the distance between a "one" and a "four."

- **Refine draft.** After developing an initial version of the rubric, check that the descriptors distinguish variables in mutually exclusive and precise terms, and that the intervals between the levels are "approximately equivalent" (i.e., the amount of improvement between any two levels should be roughly the same). This step is the most demanding and frustrating since it is difficult finding precise words to distinguish each performance level for each criterion. Very subtle changes in wording may make all the difference between a reliable rubric and one that provides little guidance. Be especially careful about the use of vague terms such as "good" or "successful," since the very point of articulating standards is to operationalize for students what these kinds of terms look like.

- **Finalize the performance levels.** Assign labels to each level and decide, in light of the relative importance of the criteria, the weight to be attached to each criterion. If appropriate, decide on the grade to be awarded for each range of marks by asking the following sorts of questions: "If a student received 15 out of 20 marks on this assignment, what grade does this mark deserve?" "What about a 10 out of 20?" Translating a mark to a grade requires deciding whether to use criterion- or norm-referenced standards. Will it be based on what percentage of the class will be allowed to receive an A, B, C, and so on (hence norm-referenced), or is there an independent benchmark to which we can refer (hence criterion-referenced), or should it involve a balancing of both considerations?

- **Pilot the rubric.** Before using a rubric in an actual assessment situation, score a sample of assignments to uncover any unanticipated problems or flaws. If this is not feasible, ask for critical feedback from someone who has not participated in developing the rubric (for example, Based on these descriptions, would you know what a "good" or "fair" assessment requires? Does the weighting of marks seem reasonable? Are the levels clearly distinguished?)

spelled out for them in a grid and assigned a point value" (2006, 13). Rather than building ownership in learning, for some students rubrics have accentuated their focus on doing things simply for the marks. These problems can be lessened by ensuring that assessment criteria reflect important curriculum outcomes and by articulating assessment standards in qualitative terms that reflect the intent of the assignment.

In addition to providing or involving students in developing rubrics, we can help students understand assessment standards in several ways:

- Provide actual samples of previous students' work at each performance level.
- Provide a set of standards and ask students to assess their own work and identify what would be required to bring it up to the next level.
- Ask students to prepare a sample answer to match each performance level on the scale. For example, students might write a "weak," "good," and "excellent" answer to a question.

Supporting Peer and Self-Assessment

It is essential when building ownership for learning that we involve students in assessing their own work and that of their peers. This can be as simple as inviting students to informally review an assignment in light of several identified criteria or as formal as assigning a mark based on an assessment rubric.

The highlighted text, "Introducing Peer Critique," contains detailed suggestions for grooming students as self- and peer assessors. Below are a few general guidelines to consider:

- Begin by critiquing the work of those not in the class. Before asking students to put their work on the line, invite the class to critique something you have produced (for example, an essay you wrote as a student, a mock presentation you make). When it is time for peer critique, start with group assignments so the responsibility is shared among several students. Ensure that the early instances of critique are low-risk, relatively easy to perform, and have an obvious benefit (for example, bonus marks).

FIGURE 33.3 SELF-ASSESSMENT OF ROLE PLAY

During the meetings I acted in role ... ☐ almost never ☐ about half the time ☐ all of the time	Evidence to support my evaluation:
During the meetings I contributed my ideas ... ☐ almost never ☐ a few times ☐ whenever appropriate	Evidence to support my evaluation:
During the meetings I supported other people's ideas ... ☐ almost never ☐ a few times ☐ whenever appropriate	Evidence to support my evaluation:
During the meetings I worked to find a "win-win" solution ... ☐ not at all ☐ made an effort ☐ worked very hard	Evidence to support my evaluation:
I made my greatest contribution during the meetings when I ...	

- Emphasize peer and self-assessment as critique—seeing the positives, not just the negatives. In the early days of peer critique, do not allow negative comments—only allow positive remarks. A good indication of when to allow comments about concerns/weaknesses is when students start asking each other for what is "wrong" with their work.
- Establish and model a few simple guidelines for giving peer critique: perhaps students should (1) start with two (or more) positive comments before offering a (single) concern, and (2) phrase negative comments in the form of a query (for example, I'm not sure I understand why you did it this way. Could you help me see what you had in mind?).
- Make sure students understand the criteria and standards they are to use in assessing their work and the work of others. Because of the inconsistent standards that dif-ferent students will apply, it may be best to limit peer or self-assessment to informal critique unless there is a rubric for students to use.
- Until students demonstrate the ability and commitment to assess conscientiously and fairly, it is ill-advised to use their assessments for awarding marks. Because teachers have the ethical and legal responsibility for assigning grades, reserve the right to veto any student-assigned mark that is clearly unwarranted.
- Provide feedback to students about the quality of their assessment judgments. In order to signal to students that peer and self-assessment are important, you may want to assess their assessments. The rubric in Figure 33.4 might be used to assess students' self-evaluation of the role play illustrated earlier.

INTRODUCING PEER CRITIQUE

When introducing students to peer critique, it is advisable to model the procedure initially in a whole class setting, with an assignment volunteered by a student(s) willing to undergo public scrutiny (alternatively, use a former student's assignment). Afterwards, students can repeat the process with their own assignments in small groups.

Review the criteria

Begin by reviewing two sets of criteria with students—the criteria related to the assignment being critiqued and the criteria for peer critique.

- *Criteria for judging the assignment.* Review with students, perhaps with an overhead transparency or a checklist distributed to each student, a handful of criteria that students are to consider when commenting on the selected assignment. Limit the number of criteria to four or five, especially if students are new to the enterprise. You might also ask students to look for specific strategies that contributed or did not contribute to achievement of the criteria (strategies for achieving clarity include using specific examples, supplementing oral comments with visual aids, limiting the number of points made).
- *Criteria for peer critiques.* Explain to students that just as there are criteria for judging the merits of an assignment, so too there are criteria for successful critiques. Explain the following criteria:
  - *respectful*: comments should not be mean-spirited, insulting, or condescending (stress the importance of this criterion)
  - *relevant*: comments—whether positive or negative—should not be trivial or off-topic but connected to the criteria for a successful assignment
  - *specific*: comments should identify particular aspects rather than very vague remarks (using an example, illustrate the value of specific compared to vague comments)
  - *constructive*: draw attention to the fact that the primary purpose of critique is to improve performance—not to belittle or to criticize; therefore advice on how to improve is preferable to comments that merely note areas of strength and weakness

Examine the assignment

While examining the assignment to be critiqued, invite students to make written notes in light of the criteria discussed. It may be sufficient for students to record comments in two columns—"Positive Features" and "Areas for Improvement." A more sophisticated approach is to subdivide the columns into rows, one for each criteria that students are to consider. Students would then explicitly look for "positive features" and "areas for improvement" for each criteria. In the following chart, students would indicate the criteria they are considering for both strengths and "Areas to think about."

Set the terms of the critique

Once the assignment has been reviewed, structure the sharing of the critique in the following manner:
- *Lead with the positives.* I firmly believe that critiques should always begin with "unqualified" comments on

the "strengths" of the assignment. This reduces the considerable anxiety that all of us feel when we subject our work to scrutiny. Even when reminded about starting with the positives, students have a tendency to slip into qualified (partly negative) comments. Politely interrupt whenever apparently positive comments begin to take on an implied criticism. As well, students will often have difficulty coming up with positive comments—not because they are not there in the assignment but because we are prone to notice what is wrong. Beforehand, prepare a list of positive comments to infuse into the discussion in the event that student-generated comments are not forthcoming. Remind students that the point is not to show off or to make others feel inadequate, but to help fellow students produce the best possible product.

- *Suggest areas for improvement.* Only after abundant expression of the strengths should concerns or areas of improvement be expressed. Encourage students to provide specific suggestions about how the assignment might be improved.

Coach the recipient of the critique

Just prior to the critique, encourage the student (or group of students) receiving the critique to assume an active listening role—limiting comments to asking for clarification or elaboration, checking for understanding and whether or not ideas offered by individual commentators are shared by others in the class. Encourage recipients not to be defensive, and not to feel that they should defend what they have done. Their role is to hear what others have to say, and after the critique is over, to decide for themselves which, if any, of the comments are worth acting upon. Praise students for agreeing to subject their work to public scrutiny.

Debrief the critique

Close the activity by asking for student observations, beginning with the recipient(s) of the critique. The teacher's role throughout should be to acknowledge how difficult peer critique can be, especially for recipients, but to stress that the experience can be very fruitful when the criteria of peer critique are well met. Encourage students to integrate the comments from the critique of their assignment into their final draft.

STRENGTHS

CRITERIA	NOTES

AREAS TO THINK ABOUT

CRITERIA	NOTES

FIGURE 33.4 ASSESSING STUDENTS' SELF-ASSESSMENT OF THEIR ROLE PLAY PERFORMANCE

	WELL DEVELOPED	COMPETENT	UNDERDEVELOPED
Justification for self-assessments	Offers clear and specific evidence to support each self-assessment and the evidence is highly consistent with the assigned rating.	Offers some evidence to support each self-assessment and the evidence is generally consistent with the assigned rating.	Offers no evidence to support any of the self-assessments or the evidence is clearly inconsistent with the assigned rating.
Reasonableness of personal ratings	Every one of the ratings seems completely deserved given the student's performance in the role play.	The ratings seem generally deserved given the student's performance in the role play.	The ratings seem completely undeserved given the student's performance in the role play.

Conclusion

There are, of course, many other factors to consider and issues to explore in learning to build student ownership of assessment. As well, there are many practical hurdles to overcome as we unpack the "black box" of assessment for our students. My own experiences have convinced me of the importance, for educational and ethical reasons, of ensuring that students clearly understand and have some ownership of assessment of their work. In fact, class discussions about previously vague criteria and unarticulated standards have led to fruitful examination by me and my students about what it is that students need to learn. Being clear and committed to the criteria and standards for assessment can only lead to improved teaching and learning.

ACKNOWLEDGMENT

I am grateful to Robert Hogg of the Alberta Assessment Consortium and Rosemary Evans of Branksome Hall School for their helpful suggestions in preparing this chapter.

NOTE

1. This example was suggested by Tom Morton, a secondary school teacher in Vancouver.

REFERENCES

British Columbia Ministry of Education. 2001. *BC performance standards: Social responsibility—A framework*. Victoria, BC: Ministry of Education, Student Assessment and Program Evaluation Branch, Province of British Columbia. Available at http://www.bced.gov.bc.ca/perf_stands/social_resp.htm.

Emblem, S. 1994. So, what did I get on my muffin? *SnapShots* 4 (2): 4–5.

Kohn, A. 2006. The trouble with rubrics. *English Journal* 95 (4): 12–15. Available at http://alfiekohn.org/teaching/rubrics/htm.

Mertler, C. 2001. Designing scoring rubrics for your classroom. *Practical Assessment, Research and Evaluation* 7 (25). Available at http://pareonline.net/getvn.asp?v=7&n=25

Nicol, J. and R. Case, eds. 2003. *The resourcefulness of the Inuit*. Richmond, BC: The Critical Thinking Consortium.

Northey, D., J. Nicol, and R. Case, eds. 2003. *Brazilian rainforest*. Richmond, BC: The Critical Thinking Consortium.

34 Assessment Strategies for Secondary Classrooms

Roland Case and Stefan Stipp

In this chapter we explore six common strategies for student assessment:

- regular written assignments;
- quizzes and tests;
- in-class observations;
- essays and research reports;
- projects or culminating tasks; and
- portfolios.

The principles to guide teachers in their assessment practices were discussed in chapter 32, "Four Principles of Authentic Assessment":

- Focus assessment on *what really matters*.
- Assessments must provide *valid indications* of student competence.
- Use assessment to *encourage student learning*.
- Assessment practices must *use teachers' time efficiently*.

The first two of these principles focus on developing assessment strategies that are valid measures of the important goals we have set for our teaching. Distinguishing between an assessment *target* and an assessment *strategy* helps to explain the nature of this requirement. An assessment target is the learning outcome we hope to assess (for example, understand key concepts, ability to think critically, ability to read maps). The assessment strategy is the means by which we will find out how well students have met the target. For example, we might assess students' ability to read a map using any number of strategies including in-class assignments, map-related questions on a quiz, in-class observations of group work, or a culminating project involving map reading. There is no single best assessment method. Each strategy has its merits and shortcomings depending on the target and context of the assessment. The ultimate decision about which strategy (or strategies) to use for a particular assessment target depends on the validity of the measures, how best to support student learning, and the most efficient use of teacher time.

Before looking at how to select and develop assessment strategies consistent with these principles, we begin by considering the advantages and disadvantages of six common strategies, and what can be done to maximize their effectiveness. In Table 34.1 is a thumbnail sketch comparing the main kinds of assessment strategies used in secondary grades. As we will see, these strategies overlap in many respects, but it is useful to distinguish them for discussion purposes.

Regular Written Assignments

The most frequent sources of evidence of student achievement are the activity sheets and written tasks completed by students as they learn each day. In some respects, these are ideal assessment opportunities—they are frequent, provide tangible evidence of learning, and are a seamless part of instruction. Despite these advantages, there are concerns associated with the use of written assignments. The most obvious issue is the impediment presented by second-language learners and others who struggle to write. Another concern is the implications of regularly attaching marks to written assignments for students who need more time to learn.

FRAMING ASSIGNMENTS FOR WEAK WRITERS

Written assignments can be framed for use with poor writers. One approach is to arrange for other students to record non-writers' answers. Another approach is to allow students to communicate their answers orally or in point form. As suggested by the example in Figure 34.1, students can communicate their understanding of the concept of globalization

TABLE 34.1   STRENGTHS AND SHORTCOMINGS OF COMMON ASSESSMENT STRATEGIES

	STRENGTHS	SHORTCOMINGS
Regular written assignments	• allow for ongoing feedback • involve no extra work to prepare since they are part of the instructional plan • can provide for in-depth work	• present difficulties for students who have difficulty writing or who are unable to write • may not build from one assignment to the next • penalizes students who need practice time before they are ready to be assessed • may involve considerable marking on an ongoing basis
Quizzes and tests	• may be quick to mark, especially if they involve multiple-choice questions • provide a summary snapshot of student learning • can assess for a breadth of information	• may focus largely on recall of factual information • often don't address a broad spectrum of curriculum outcomes • may cause stress for some students • tend to focus on short-term learning
In-class observation	• may reveal insights that would not otherwise be identified by other types of assessment • can assess abilities that are difficult to capture on paper • allow for immediate feedback • require no after-school marking	• hard to manage, given the real-time demands of teaching a class • difficult to observe every student equally • one-time efforts may not present a true picture of students' abilities
Essays and research reports	• allow for ongoing feedback • can provide for in-depth study of a topic	• may involve a lot of student homework • are typically time-consuming for teachers to mark
Projects and culminating tasks	• can be more fun, engaging, and worthwhile than other assessment tasks • can draw together learning over a unit • can assess for breadth of knowledge and abilities • often further students' learning while they complete the task	• may require considerable in-class and out-of-class time relative to the educational benefits • students can become bored if tasks drag on or are seen as "make work" • may be difficult to use common criteria when assessing different student projects
Portfolios	• build student ownership in learning and assessment • are effective at tracking growth over time • encourage student goal-setting and self-monitoring • deepen students' understanding of core content and help them see the "big picture" • can be used to assess a wide range of abilities • create opportunities for informed communication among students, parents, and teachers	• can become the mere accumulation of "stuff" • may require a lot of time to review and evaluate • must be implemented carefully so that they don't become overwhelming or a make-work project

FIGURE 34.1   RECOGNIZING LEVELS OF GLOBALIZATION

Border crime

A person sneaks across the border from Canada into the United States, commits a crime, and returns without ever being caught.

Migrant crime

A person who moved to the community twenty years ago from another part of Canada robs a local grocery store.

Armed robbery

A person robs the local grocery store using a gun that was purchased legally in Canada, but originally manufactured in the United States.

Prosecution

A person commits a crime in another country, returns home to Canada, and is arrested under an international agreement authorizing home countries to prosecute certain crimes domestically to avoid the problems of trying to bring the person to justice in the foreign country.

Criminal court

An international criminal court is authorized to bring persons to trial for war crimes committed in any country that has signed the treaty to establish the court. Some of the world's major powers don't sign the treaty.

Task force

Several countries assemble for a conference to co-ordinate a task force to address the problem of trafficking in illegal drugs between their countries.

---

by placing cards along a continuum. In this case, the teacher would read each scenario and students would arrange the cards along a continuum ranging from "entirely domestic to "thoroughly globalized."

MARKING REGULAR ASSIGNMENTS

There is little disagreement about the value of providing quality feedback (whether from the teacher or from fellow students) on virtually every assignment students complete. It is another matter whether each of these assignments should be graded for reporting purposes. For years it was commonly recommended that teachers assess students on a large number of assignments to ensure that students would not be penalized significantly for an occasional poor performance. This practice has begun to be questioned because of the unfairness of assessing students before they have had ample opportunity to learn what is expected of them. More recent thinking recommends that only students' best work be assessed. Since the primary purpose of classroom assignments is to help students learn, holding students accountable for their performance while they are still learning is considered unfair. This is analogous to a theatre critic reviewing a play midway into the rehearsal period. No doubt some of the actors will have their roles in good shape but many others, including those who may deliver the finest performances on opening night, may still be exploring their character. A parallel concern arises over the penalizing effect on students who end up mastering the material but do not do so as quickly as other students. Imagine a situation where three assignments are focussed on

the same outcome (for example, understanding how to read maps). Suppose the following results are recorded for two students over the course of a unit:

	Assignment #1	Assignment #2	Assignment #3	Average mark	Best result
Mindy	8	8	8	8 or B+	8 or B+
Chan	4	6	10	6.7 or B-	10 or A

When reporting on student achievement, it would be misleading and unfair to assign Mindy a "B+" and Chan a "B-" since it could be argued that Chan's understanding of the curricular outcome is superior to Mindy's understanding. The averaging of marks on a particular outcome can have a discouraging effect, since students who struggle to learn a topic will realize that even if they do very well on the final opportunity, their mark will be averaged down because of earlier poor performances. The problems with not allowing opportunities for students to learn without penalty are the reasons behind a popular adage that suggests "assess often and mark rarely."

Ensuring that we assign marks to students' *best* efforts does not necessarily mean that only the *final* effort should be graded. On any given day, students may do poorly for reasons unrelated to their knowledge of the topic. It would be unfair to penalize students who did well all term simply because they were distracted when the final assignment was completed. Another concern in relying exclusively on a final assignment is that the assignments over a term may not assess identical outcomes. If the three assignments in the above example did not assess the same topic, then the last assignment should not be the sole basis on the mark for the unit. The solution is to provide opportunities to learn without being graded and to grade students only under conditions that allow them to show what they have learned.

Quizzes and Tests

Another common assessment strategy is the use of quizzes during and at the end of a unit of study to test how well students have mastered the content. This approach allows students to show what they have learned after they have had opportunities to study the material. Research suggests that student learning may be better served by frequent short tests than by infrequent long ones (Boston 2002, 3), and by providing quality feedback and not simply assigning a mark (Black and Williams 1998, 144). The most significant factor in determining the value of a test is the quality of the questions.

For ease of student completion and teacher marking, quizzes tend to consist of two kinds of short-answer questions: either *closed-ended* questions such as multiple choice, true or false, labelling, and matching columns, or *open-ended* questions that can be answered in a few words or sentences. Although there is much that could be said about developing quality test items, we want to make two points only:

- use short-answer questions to assess beyond mere recall of information;
- ensure the validity of questions in quizzes and tests.

ASSESSING BEYOND RECALL

A common criticism of test questions is that they are often used to assess recall of information. This need not be so. Short-answer questions can be used to assess depth of understanding, critical thinking, social responsibility, and other important goals in social studies. As illustrated by the examples from the Begbie History Contest (2008) presented in Figure 34.2, we can frame multiple-choice questions around a variety of interesting visual and textual sources to assess conceptual understanding and interpretative abilities.

Despite their potential to go beyond mere recall, there are limits to what short-answer test questions can assess. For example, because of their format, multiple-choice questions can only measure students' abilities to select correctly from a set of supplied answers. In addition, multiple-choice ques-

tions reduce complex learning outcomes to individual test items, whereas we may be concerned with students' abilities to integrate what they know in realistic situations. While these limitations provide powerful reasons for using "alternative" strategies, there is a role for tests beyond measuring information recall. For instance, open-ended short-answer questions can be used to assess student reflection by inviting students to revisit initial ideas or opinions after they have had a chance to study and think more about the matter. Figure 34.3 outlines students' pre- and post-unit reflections on democracy in Canada. Responses can be marked by assessing post-unit responses in terms of the accuracy of their answers, the insightfulness of their reflections, and their open-mindedness.

As the example in Figure 34.4 illustrates, closed-ended questions can also be used to gather information about student attitudes towards open-mindedness by inviting them to indicate their level of agreement or disagreement with various statements.

WATCHING FOR VALIDITY

In using short-answer questions, we may be misled into thinking we are measuring something that we are not. Consequently, it is important to check that we actually measure the outcomes we have targeted. A common oversight with short-answer questions is that of presuming to assess students' *understanding* of a concept by asking students to offer a definition of the word. Understanding a concept is a much broader notion than recalling the definition. Assessing conceptual understanding requires more than asking for a definition that students may have memorized. Students need to provide fresh examples of the concept or explain why certain situations are or are not examples of the concept. As illustrated in Figure 34.1, we might ask students to place various domestic and international scenarios along a "globalization" continuum and to explain in their own words the reasons for each event's assigned level of globalization.

In-Class Observations

Another assessment strategy is to observe students' classroom behaviour and listen to their talk. This approach, sometimes referred to as "naturalistic assessment," involves the teacher as a participant-observer—collecting information about student learning while engaged in the normal duties of teaching. In some respects, teachers are involved in naturalistic assessment every time they confirm that students have understood a lesson, or check to see whether students have done their work, or ask students to indicate any difficulties they are having. The difference between these ad hoc assessment

FIGURE 34.2   SAMPLE MULTIPLE CHOICE QUESTIONS

1. British colonial relations

BRITANNIA'S BODY GUARD
Britannia's Body Guard
Canadian Courier, *Toronto, April 3, 1909*

This illustration was drawn in support of

A. internationalism.
B. imperial defence.
C. imperial expansion.
D. colonial independence.

2. Policy towards aboriginal people

"I want to get rid of the Indian problem. . . .
Our objective is to continue until there is not
a single Indian in Canada that has not been
absorbed into the body politic and there is no
Indian Question and no Indian department."
Duncan Campbell Scott,
Deputy Superintendent of Indian Affairs
(1913–1932)

Scott's policy is called

A. assimilation.
B. accommodation.
C. extermination.
D. multiculturalism.

3. Canadian federal elections 1953, 1957, 1958

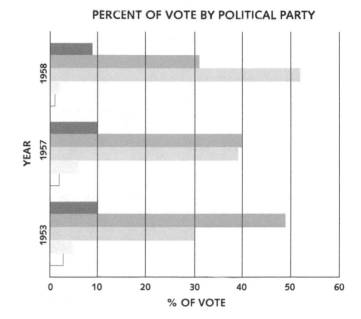

PERCENT OF VOTE BY POLITICAL PARTY

■ Co-operative Commonwealth Federation
(CCF)

■ Liberal

■ Progressive Conservative

■ Social Credit

☐ Other

A good subtitle for this graph would be
A. Canada's shift to the left.
B. Canada's shift to the right.
C. Canada's shift to the centre.
D. Canada's shift away from the centre.

FIGURE 34.3 DEMOCRACY—PRE- AND POST-UNIT REFLECTION

DEMOCRACY IN CANADA

Pre-unit questions

Before we begin our unit on democracy in Canada, consider the following questions:

1. If you were about to vote for a federal politician, what issues should you consider?
2. Make a list of the various ways that people can participate in the political decision-making process. Which one or two ways do you think are most effective? Why do you think they are more effective than other ways?
3. Do you think that you have a responsibility to participate actively in the political decision-making process? Explain the reasons for your answer.

End-of-unit reflections

At the start of the unit, you were asked about your opinions on three topics. Your answers to those questions are being returned to you. Please re-read each question and your response. Consider two things:

- Additional comments to further support or clarify your initial remarks;
- Changes in your initial opinions and the reasons for those changes.

Write any additions or changes to each of your initial responses in the spaces provided below—do NOT write anything on the pre-unit sheet.

1. _____
   _____
   _____

2. _____
   _____
   _____

3. _____
   _____
   _____

FIGURE 34.4 ASSESSING FOR OPEN-MINDEDNESS

Each of us should:	Strongly agree				Strongly disagree
1. Be open to changing our minds when new reasons are presented.	1	2	3	4	5
2. Have very clear, very firm opinions on most issues.	1	2	3	4	5
3. Believe that there is always one answer that is better than all of the other possible answers.	1	2	3	4	5
4. Believe that there may be more than one acceptable position on most issues.	1	2	3	4	5
5. Consider what those who disagree with us would say.	1	2	3	4	5
6. Often question matters that many people accept.	1	2	3	4	5
7. Often question our own reasons and motives.	1	2	3	4	5

strategies and naturalistic assessment lies in the extent of systematic collection of information and whether records are kept for use in student reporting.

In-class observations are particularly appropriate for assessing student abilities and attitudes not measured by traditional pen-and-paper assignments or by isolated assessment tasks. In addition, extended observation is more likely to provide rich accounts of student learning and insightful indications of factors that may influence learning, than are one-shot tests. Formal in-class observations make use of various information-gathering strategies:

- anecdotal "field notes" about significant comments or incidents—for example, by noting the strategies that a particular student uses to solve a problem, or by watching over several months for indications of students' growth in self-esteem or attitudes towards school work;
- student-teacher conferences as a means of gathering information about students while helping them learn;
- checklists or other devices to record the incidence of particular behaviour—such as completion of work, the number of books read, or students' co-operative participation in group assignments. The checklist in Figure 34.5 records how well students can use various aids to locating information.

Often, like an anthropologist, the teacher will seek to "triangulate" evidence, using several sources of information to corroborate judgments about students. For example, in drawing conclusions about students' critical-thinking abilities, a teacher may use information obtained from peer and self-assessment of students' willingness to entertain alternative opinions, analyses of selected products for the quality of reasoning, and suggestive anecdotal comments about attitudes towards "thinking things through."

In-class observation by students is a means of inviting them to reflect on their own learning as they work. Not only does peer observation and self-monitoring save teacher time, but it is an important learning opportunity for students. As well, students may have access to information that would not be readily available to the teacher. For example, the classroom observation device in Figure 34.6 can be used by students (or by teachers) to peer assess co-operative group work.

Identify one or two outcomes from the curriculum that would usefully be assessed by the three assessment strategies discussed thus far in this chapter (regular written assignments, quizzes, and in-class observations). Briefly outline what each strategy might look like if you were to use them to assess the selected outcome(s).

FIGURE 34.5 LOCATING INFORMATION CHECKLIST

				STUDENTS			
Uses information-locating aids: 0 = not at all / = somewhat ✓ = adeptly	SAUL	PAM	CHAN	NIAM			
locate section in table of contents	/	0	✓	✓			
locate page in index	✓	0	✓	✓			
find word in glossary	✓	/	✓	✓			
find word in dictionary	✓	/	✓	✓			
skim paragraph to locate information							
use headings to locate information	0	/	✓	✓			
. . .							

FIGURE 34.6   CO-OPERATIVE DECISION MAKING

Your name: _____   Group member's name: _____

1. For each criterion listed below, circle the number that most accurately reflects each person's behaviour while carrying out the project.
2. Wherever possible, describe an actual situation or identify a typical behaviour that is supporting evidence for your assessment.
3. Use a separate sheet for each person. Do not show your assessment to, or discuss it with, anyone else.

	Rarely or never in evidence		In evidence about half the time		Consistently in evidence	Not enough information to decide
1. Willingness to reconsider position	1	2	3	4	5	no information
Supporting evidence:						
2. Willingness to defend personal opinion	1	2	3	4	5	no information
Supporting evidence:						
3. Respectful of persons who disagree	1	2	3	4	5	no information
Supporting evidence:						
4. Challenges in responsible ways	1	2	3	4	5	no information
Supporting evidence:						
5. Works towards establishing consensus	1	2	3	4	5	no information
Supporting evidence:						

Essays and Research Reports

The use of extended-answer questions such as essays, reports, and position papers is a common assessment strategy with middle school and secondary students. These are generally a more holistic measure of learning than short-answer questions. There are, however, several limitations:

- essays are heavily dependent on students' writing fluency;
- students may be overwhelmed by the demands of large writing projects, particularly if used in earlier grades; and
- essays are time-consuming to mark.

For these reasons, it is worth considering whether the traditional research report merits the prominence it has in some social studies classes.

Many students dislike writing reports and often do little more than transcribe ideas drawn directly from reference books. The suggestions contained in chapter 12, "Escaping the Typical Report Trap," will help greatly in reducing the impediments to extended written reports. Even then, students might learn more effectively from smaller, less daunting assignments that place greater emphasis on multiple revisions of their ideas. Certainly we should expect students to think for themselves and not simply assemble ideas from other sources.

The merits of any given extended-answer assignment depend on the quality of the question or task. At the very least, this requires providing students with explicit, unambiguous directions. We think it also helps to provide (or to help students generate) a structure for organizing their report. For example, the question "Research and defend your personal position on establishing a world government" could be made to focus more clearly on thinking critically about the ideas (rather than rehashing undigested arguments found in books). To do this, the assignment might be described as follows:

Present and defend your personal position on establishing a world government using the following structure:

1. explain in your own words what this would involve;
2. identify and explain the major reasons to support your position;
3. identify and explain the major reasons that opponents might offer against your position; and
4. justify your position by arguing why the supporting reasons are more convincing than the reasons against your position.

When framing essay questions, we should not assume that there are generic formats that invite critical thinking. For example, asking students to evaluate the justification for Canada's immigration policy may not necessarily assess critical thinking. The validity of this question as a measure of critical thinking depends on what students were taught during the unit. If students studied the pros and cons of immigration, then the question may be largely one of regurgitation of previously presented material. Alternatively, if students have not had any instruction and practice in identifying appropriate criteria for evaluating legal policies and had no way of knowing the reasons that might be offered for or against immigration, it is questionable whether they are engaging seriously in critical thinking. Without some grounding in the appropriate considerations, student answers are more likely to be instances of guesswork or naive reactions. A more valid examination question that assesses students' ability to think critically about an issue is suggested in Figure 34.7.

Projects or Culminating Tasks

A relatively recent alternative approach to assessment, often referred to as performance assessment, focusses on students completing realistic tasks that a person would typically face as a citizen, writer, businessperson, scientist, community leader, historian, and so on. These tasks may involve performing a feat or producing a product.

Performing a feat
- perform a dramatic scene depicting a historical event
- hold a formal parliamentary debate on a controversial piece of legislation
- teach fellow students about cultural traditions
- organize and run a school fundraising event
- conduct a trial around a historical incident
- adjudicate between nominees for an award
- make a presentation to city council on a proposed change to local laws

Producing a product
- build a model demonstrating a geological phenomenon or daily life in a medieval village
- make a film about promoting racial harmony
- create a set of exam questions and sample answers for an end-of-unit test
- prepare a "consultant's report" on a local pollution problem
- develop a foreign-language script for a radio play
- create "museum" displays depicting local history
- create a web page on a famous battle in history

FIGURE 34.7 DEFEND YOUR POSITION

The following are four arguments commonly offered in support of increasing immigration levels and four arguments commonly offered in opposition to this policy.

Pro	Con
• many immigrants may be in desperate economic need; • many immigrants may need protection from war and political persecution; • many immigrants bring talents and human resources that benefit Canada; • immigrants provide a pool of workers to fill low-paid jobs that may otherwise go unfilled;	• increased immigration will put too great a burden on our health, welfare, and education systems; • increased immigration discourages the integration of ethnic groups into mainstream society; • increased immigration fuels racial/ethnic tensions in Canada; • immigrants take jobs that people who are already here need and want.

All things considered, what is the most defensible position regarding increased immigration to Canada? Defend your answer with specific references and a critical analysis of the arguments above. Justify why your position is more defensible than opposing positions.

- publish a (contemporary or historical) class newspaper or journal

Because they typically involve realistic tasks, performance assessments are more likely than traditional methods to measure students' ability to apply a complex set of "real-life" abilities and understandings. The emphasis in performance tasks is on knowledge-in-use, rather than regurgitation of "school" knowledge. Also important is their potential as a learning opportunity and not exclusively as an assessment tool: the working-through of the tasks should enhance—not simply measure—student understanding. A performance task to plan a summer vacation (described in Heckley Kon and Martin-Kniep 1992) illustrates these features. In this assessment, pairs of students are given a map of California and a list of state parks with camping facilities, and asked to plan the details of a family camping trip from the San Francisco area to any state camping facility in northern California. Students must measure distances, calculate travelling time, describe particulars of the travel route, and develop a contingency plan in the event of a strike by workers on the Golden Gate and Bay bridges. As well, they have to negotiate with a partner the destination and route that best accommodates the interests of family members.

As this example suggests, performance assessments can be engaging. It is suspected that some students do poorly on evaluations because they are unmotivated. The perceived irrelevance and drudgery of, for example, an extended written report may discourage some students from trying to do well. If we want to assess what students are *capable* of doing, it is only fair that we provide opportunities where students are likely to want to do well.

Because performance tasks are complex, they provide opportunities to assess a variety of outcomes using many methods, including:

- interviewing students about their experiences during the project and about their conclusions;
- analyzing students' preparatory materials for quality of research;
- analyzing group discussions for evidence of thoughtfulness in preparing reports/products and in justifying group decisions;
- assessing students' written or oral reports for quality of language use and presentation, and for content knowledge;
- scoring classroom discussions or debates for evidence of students' ability to engage in thoughtful dialogue.

Key features in developing performance assessments are choosing the task, setting the context, providing appropriate direction, and, when possible, creating an audience for students to present their work. A performance task should allow students to integrate what they have been studying into a culminating performance or product. It would be unfair to assess students on matters they have not been working with; the novel dimension of performance assessment is the drawing together of the various elements they have studied in order to solve a realistic problem. Setting a realistic context for the task provides a rich opportunity for students to think through their options. Students also require appropriate direction about the nature and requirements of the task. An example of the requirements for a culminating task is found in Figure 34.8. This outline, developed by Garfield and Laura Gini-Newman, directs students to prepare a written or audiovisual critique of the historical accuracy and realism of a feature film situated in the period they have just studied. More general advice on developing culminating assessment projects is suggested in the highlighted text.

SUGGESTIONS FOR DEVELOPING CULMINATING PROJECTS

- Identify the important outcomes for a unit.
- Think of "real-life" feats or products that, if completed successfully, would represent exemplary achievement of several key outcomes.
- Determine more precisely the details of the performance assessment, including:
  - the realistic nature and the context of each task;
  - the amount of direction to provide students regarding what they need to consider to complete the task and how they might proceed.
- Orally or in writing, provide students with a clear articulation of the requirements and parameters of the task.
- Consider what students must know in order to successfully complete the task. Ensure sufficient prior instruction to allow students a reasonable chance of competently undertaking the task. Assessment tasks can be made easier by providing detailed direction or additional instruction.
- For each of the desired outcomes, determine the criteria to be used in assessing students' feats or products. Share the criteria with students prior to their completing the task.
- Determine how information about the criteria will be collected (for example, through observation, conferencing, analysis of written products). Where appropriate, devise rubrics, checklists, or other marking sheets.
- After using the performance assessment, consider how it may be improved for next time. Asking students for their comments may be helpful in this regard.

FIGURE 34.8 HISTORICAL MOVIE REVIEW

Hollywood has created countless motion pictures following historical themes. While many, such as *Ben Hur,* have won Oscars for their costumes and stunning settings, others have been criticized for inaccuracies and perpetuation of unfounded myths. Your challenge is to work with two or three colleagues to review a movie critically from the assigned list to assess its historical accuracy and realism. Focus your critique on two areas (choose between four and six per group) selected from the following list:

- weapons and military strategy
- technological innovations
- values and beliefs
- clothing
- daily life
- historical events
- modes of transportation
- historical figures
- cultural and class interactions
- government structure and politics
- architecture
- geographical features
- social roles of men, women, and children

Based on an examination of the film and your research of relevant topics from the historical period, undertake *one* of the following tasks:

- individually, write a 500–750 word historical review assessing the film's historical value in your two focus areas

- with your group, present a 25-minute visual and oral report involving not more than 10 minutes of movie clips assessing the film's historical value in the selected areas of focus.

Individually, each of you must undertake the following:

- briefly outline their individual areas of responsibilities and explain the due dates established by their group;
- prepare an annotated bibliography of between five and seven sources;
- assemble three to six pages of research notes drawing upon approximately five sources;
- present an outline matching the historical research with depictions in the film;
- actively prepare the group presentation or the individual written review.

Collectively, each group must reach a consensus regarding the following:

- deadlines and a clear action plan for group members to complete the project by the required date;
- four to six areas to be examined in detail by the group;
- assigned individual responsibilities relating to the research and presentation;
- mechanisms for effectively sharing information for the purposes of preparing the group presentation or individual written review.

Portfolios

The final assessment strategy we consider involves students in compiling a collection or portfolio of work they have completed over a period of time. Portfolio assessment draws heavily on the practices of artists and designers, who carefully assemble samples that represent key characteristics of their work for use in demonstrating particular competencies to others. Assessment portfolios are characterized in a similar vein, as "a selective collection of student work and records of progress gathered across diverse contexts over time, framed by reflection and enriched through collaboration that has as its aim the advancement of student learning" (Wolf and Siu-Runyan 1996, 30).

Because portfolios are based on cross-sections of student work completed over time, they offer a richer portrait of a wider range of student achievements than, say, a single end-of-unit test. Also, unlike traditional forms of assessment, where assignments are marked and then forgotten, portfolios encourage both teacher and students to monitor growth over time. Typically, students are involved to varying degrees in selecting, analyzing, assessing, and reporting on the products that make up their portfolio. This involvement often results in significantly greater personal ownership of their learning. These benefits are particularly likely when portfolios are used as the focus for conferences where students explain to their parents or teacher what the portfolios show about their progress and levels of achievement. In fact, it has been suggested that portfolios be seen primarily as "a reason for talking" (Murphy and Smith 1990, 1)—that is, the collection of products is essentially a means to engage students, teachers, and parents in informed dialogue about learning.

Portfolios may be general in focus, covering many subjects, be subject-specific (for example, a social studies portfolio), or even topic-specific (for example, A Sustainable Environment Portfolio). Asking students to focus on one area can help them see that learning can be represented in different ways within the one area. When collecting samples of learning in social studies, students could web, list, write, videotape, draw, or brainstorm their understanding of specific concepts. Portfolio assessment has five phases.

- **Accumulation of products.** At the beginning of the unit when portfolios are to be used, establish procedures for collecting and storing all student work. The date when work is completed should be indicated on every assignment. If a specific set of outcomes has been identified as the theme for the portfolio, then ensure that students have varied opportunities during the term to produce work in these areas. The range of student materials produced during a unit, term, or year may include the following:
  - annotated bibliographies of books or documents read
  - artwork (preliminary sketches and final products)
  - audiotapes
  - book reports
  - charts and graphs
  - drawings
  - essays (drafts and final copies)
  - evaluations of self and peers
  - group reports
  - interview results
  - journals or diaries
  - maps
  - notes (classroom, laboratory, or field)
  - peer evaluations
  - photographs of projects, models, displays, or murals
  - reading inventories
  - tests and quizzes
  - videotapes of presentations, debates, interviews, or simulations
  - worksheets
- **Selection of portfolio pieces.** From the total array of products, direct students to select a sampling for inclusion in a portfolio. Near the end of a unit, discuss with students how they are to select those work samples. Students should have some discretion in selecting portfolio contents. The selected products may represent the student's best efforts, or be indicative of typical performance. They may focus on a particular theme such as growth as a critical thinker, development of a global perspective, or the importance of human rights. It may be important to limit the *number* of pieces to include in a portfolio, since thoughtful analysis becomes unwieldy if many pieces are examined. A summary or checklist (possibly a table of contents) may be helpful.
- **Reflection.** Alone or in collaboration with peers, each student reviews the portfolio contents as a vehicle for assessing achievement or progress over the term. These re-

flections might involve identifying criteria and standards, analyzing patterns or key features, diagnosing strengths and problem areas, and setting personal plans and targets. Providing samples of other students' work at various performance levels may assist students in assessing their own work.

- **Reporting.** Students should be expected to report (orally or in writing) on what they observe about their learning and to recommend a plan of action. Student-led conferences with the teacher, and often with parents, are common ways of student reporting. Alternatively, students might prepare audiotaped analyses of their portfolios. It may be helpful for students to prepare and practise their oral reports with fellow students.
- **Feedback.** Feedback from the teacher (and parents) may occur on two fronts: (1) on student achievement or progress over the term, as evidenced in the portfolio; and (2) on the quality of student analysis and reporting since the portfolio is itself a product representing students' capacity for critical self-assessment and personal accountability.

The Sample Portfolio Assignment described in Figure 34.9 and the rubric in Figure 34.10 were used in an integrated Grade 11 Humanities Co-op class (Social Studies, English, Career Planning) in British Columbia. The purpose was for students to create a big picture of their co-op experience. In different contexts it may make more sense to include specific learning outcomes in respect to which students should show evidence of growth. Because most of the evidence used by students had already been assessed, the emphasis in the assessment was on student use of the evidence and thoughtful reflection. Students assessed their completed portfolio using the rubric provided. They presented the portfolio to their parents who assessed it using the same rubric. The next day, students presented the portfolio in round table format to two peers who jointly assessed it using the rubric. All of this was submitted to the teacher, who completed a final assessment. All the assessments were used in arriving at a grade, although the teacher's evaluation counted for 85% of the mark.

The teacher's experience with this portfolio assessment was overwhelmingly positive. Although students complained about the scope of the project, the vast majority were very proud when it was completed. They could see how much they had accomplished over the semester and, although they claimed to do it reluctantly, they liked showing it to their parents. For most students, sharing it with their parents increased their level of ownership and helped them to get to know themselves better as learners and as people. The portfolio process motivated them to learn more in the future.

FIGURE 34.9   A SAMPLE PORTFOLIO ASSIGNMENT

HUMANITIES CO-OP 11—FINAL PORTFOLIO

What are we doing?

You are creating a portfolio to show where you are in your lifelong journey of learning. A portfolio is a collection of evidence (assignments, learning log entries, pictures, videos, projects, tests) to demonstrate your learning.

Why are we doing this?

Co-op can be a blur. Between guest speakers, field trips, job interviews, CPR training, work placements, social studies, English, career planning and Camp Jubilee, there are lots of learning opportunities, but it all happens so fast. We think that once you pull it all together, you'll be amazed at how much you've learned this semester. Your well-made portfolio is the proof of this learning and something to be proud of as you leave co-op.

What does the portfolio include?

1. *Title Page* includes a gripping title that sums up your co-op experience. You could also include drawings, photographs, quotes, and other documents.

2. *Table of Contents* organizes your portfolio so it is easy for others to peruse.

3. *Summation* offers a reflective summary of where you are now in your development as a person and a citizen. Reflect on Your Journey: the guiding questions for this portfolio are:

- What have I learned in co-op?
- What do I know now that I didn't know before?
- What can I do now that I couldn't do before?
- How am I different as a person?
- How have I grown?
- What has led to that growth?
- Where do I go from here?
- How do the things I have learned connect to each other?

Answer these questions in approximately 1,000 words.

Standards for your summation:
- Include and comment on at least 10 and no more than 15 pieces of evidence.
- Address a combination of content, skills, and attributes.
- Clearly and fully explain your evidence and its relevance.

- Clearly explain your progress (learning).
- Show deep, probing thought.
- Be genuine.
- Show deep thought about future growth.

Possible approaches for your summation:
- Brainstorm before looking at any material.
- Organize your comments around your own 4–8 themes.
- Organize your comments around the co-op goals.
- Include a final paragraph that brings it all together.
- Look through your binder to remind you of what you learned.
- Don't get hung up on just typical "school" accomplishments.
- Remember this is about the highlights, not a regurgitation of everything you learned.

Or...negotiate your own version of this assignment with your teacher

4. *Evidence* (10–15 pieces) includes projects, assignments, photographs, drawings, videos, tests, learning log entries, journals, self or peer evaluations, and anything else that shows your learning. Most of the evidence will already have been created; however, you will want to improve your work to demonstrate your learning more effectively.

For whom am I creating this?

If you see genuine value in what you've learned in co-op, you may consider that there is merit in creating this portfolio for yourself. However, it is also a way to involve others in your journey of personal growth and citizenship development.

Your portfolio will be reviewed and assessed according to the following rubric by five people: you, two of your peers, a parent, and your teacher.

FIGURE 34.10 PORTFOLIO ASSESSMENT RUBRIC

	EXCEEDS EXPECTATIONS 4	MEETS EXPECTATIONS 3	APPROACHES EXPECTATIONS 2	NEEDS MORE 1
Reflections	• shows deep understanding of the goals and deep thought about them • clearly and fully explains the evidence and its relevance • clearly and fully explains the progress (learning) and how the evidence shows growth • shows deep, probing thought about future growth	• shows good understanding of the goals and thought about them • explains the evidence and its relevance • explains the progress and how the evidence shows growth • shows considerable thought about future growth	• shows understanding of the goals and basic thinking about them • partially explains the evidence and its relevance • partially explains the progress and how the evidence shows growth • shows some thought about future growth	• shows little or no understanding of the goals and thinking about them • does not explain the evidence and its relevance • does not explain the progress or evidence of growth • shows little or no thought about future growth
Evidence	• all pieces are relevant • work is of superb quality, showing deep thought and superior understanding. • evaluated work is of excellent quality • sum total of evidence shows substantial growth	• approximately 80 per cent of pieces are relevant • work is of high quality, showing thought and understanding • evaluated work is of good quality • sum total of evidence shows growth	• approximately 60 per cent of pieces are relevant • work is of mediocre quality, showing some thought and understanding • evaluated work is of satisfactory quality • sum total of evidence shows some growth	• less than 40 per cent of pieces are relevant • work is of poor quality showing little or no thought and understanding • evaluated work is of poor quality • sum total of evidence shows little or no growth
Conclusion	• connects all goals to each other meaningfully • shows extremely deep thought about the overall goals of the program and progress towards them (better person/happier person/better citizen)	• connects four goals to each other meaningfully • shows deep thought about the overall goals and progress towards them (better person/happier person/better citizen)	• connects three goals to each other meaningfully • shows some deep thought about the overall goals and progress towards them (better person/happier person/better citizen)	• connects fewer than three goals to each other meaningfully • shows little or no deep thought about the overall goals and progress towards them (better person/happier person/better citizen)
Presentation and writing	• looks great (wow factor) • very easy to find relevant information • lively, interesting use of language and vocabulary • grammar, spelling, and punctuation are nearly flawless	• looks good • easy to find relevant information • interesting use of language and vocabulary • some minor grammar, spelling, and punctuation errors	• looks presentable • some relevant information is hard to find • some interesting use of language and vocabulary • some significant grammar, spelling, and punctuation errors	• looks messy • difficult to find relevant information • language and vocabulary is monotonous and repetitive • grammar, spelling, and punctuation errors interfere with understanding

The success of portfolios as an effective assessment tool is heavily dependent on the instruction and planning that precedes their creation. Teachers need to consider a variety of issues before implementing portfolio assessment:

- **Student engagement.** Unless students see a purpose in their learning and are engaged, the process of portfolio creation is unlikely to have much benefit. While the portfolio process can enhance engagement, it is unable to create it out of thin air. Unengaged students are likely to go through the motions when creating their portfolios, writing reflections that parrot what teachers want to hear and, in so doing, render the process meaningless, if not counterproductive.
- **Requisite skills.** Students need tools to complete a quality portfolio. These skills may vary depending on the type of portfolio but some general foundational skills for portfolio creation include writing, organization, reading comprehension, and reflection. It may be helpful to teach mini-lessons on these skills during the portfolio creation process.
- **Time management.** Students must be encouraged to manage their time effectively, particularly when portfolios bring together large amounts of material. Students who are delinquent in their assignments or in assembling the portfolio may become overwhelmed and discouraged. It is advisable to set numerous due dates along the way to ensure that all students stay on track.
- **Freedom.** It is essential, but challenging, to create a portfolio assignment that is sufficiently clear for students to meet expectations, but not overly rigid and prescribed.
- **Clear assessment.** Teachers and students must be clear on what is being assessed. Portfolios in social studies are especially well suited to assessing students' understanding of the big picture, their process of thinking, their growth over time, and their ability to reflect. Portfolios can also be used to assess specific content knowledge or progress with respect to a specific learning outcome.

Conclusion

In this discussion, we have explored various issues and techniques that deserve consideration when developing assessment strategies consistent with the principles of authentic assessment. Our overarching objective in presenting the six strategies described here is to encourage assessment practices that are valid, fair, and that richly support student learning.

ACKNOWLEDGMENT

We wish to thank Robert Hogg of the Alberta Assessment Consortium for his helpful suggestions when revising this chapter.

REFERENCES

The Begbie Contest Society. 2008. *The Begbie Canadian History Contest: Years eleven to fifteen.* Vancouver: author.

Black, P. and D. Williams. 1998. Inside the black box: Raising standards though classroom assessment. *Phi Delta Kappan* 80 (2): 139–148. Available online at http://www.pdkintl.org/kappan/kbla9810.htm.

Boston, C. 2002. The concept of formative assessment. *Practical Assessment, Research and Evaluation* 8 (9): 1–5. Available online at http://PAREonline.net/getvn.asp?v=8&n=9.

Heckley Kon, J. and G. Martin-Kniep. 1992. Students' geographic knowledge and skills in different kinds of tests: Multiple-choice versus performance assessment. *Social Education* 56 (2): 95–98.

Murphy, S. and M.A. Smith. 1990. Talking about portfolios. *The Quarterly* 12 (2): 1–3, 24–27.

Wolf, K. and Y. Sui-Runyan. 1996. Portfolio purposes and possibilities. *Journal of Adolescent and Adult Literacy* 40 (1): 30–38.

Identify four or five complementary outcomes from the curriculum. Using the three strategies discussed in the second half of this chapter (essays, culminating projects, and portfolios), briefly outline what each might look like if you were to assess the selected curriculum outcomes.

Acknowledgments

CHAPTER 4   "The 'Suburb of Happy Homes'" illustration by Fraser Wilson. First published in 1942 in the *Vancouver Sun* on the occasion of the fiftieth anniversary of Burnaby's incorporation.

CHAPTER 6   "The Road Less Travelled" cartoon is by Erica Ball, a librarian at Hazelton Secondary School, Hazelton, BC. Used by permission.

CHAPTER 7   Figure 7.1, "Promoting Critical Thinking," is adapted by permission of the publisher from Mike Denos and Roland Case, *Teaching about Historical Thinking* (Vancouver, BC: The Critical Thinking Consortium, 2006), 75. © 2006 by The Critical Thinking Consortium.
   Table 7.1, "Thinking Critically About Logging Old-Growth Forests," is used by permission of the authors from Sharon Bailin, Roland Case, Jerrold R. Coombs, and LeRoi Daniels, "Conceptualizing Critical Thinking," *Journal of Curriculum Studies* 31 (3): 285–302.

CHAPTER 9   World War II recruiting poster, "Well done son—RCAF," WP2.R15.F3 courtesy McGill University Digital Collections; available online at http://digital.library.mcgill.ca/warposters/search/searchdetail.php?ID=8736&version=e. World War II poster, "The walls have ears: propaganda for the security of Canada's army," #2846820 courtesy Library and Archives Canada; available online at http://collectionscanada.gc.ca/pam_archives/index.php?fuseaction=genitem.displayItem&lang=en&rec_nbr=2846820&rec_nbr_list=2959195,2846820,2846817,3930788,3919720.

CHAPTER 10   Map 1, "The town of Smithers," from Tourism Smithers; available online at http://www.tourismsmithers.com/about/maps-trail-guides/.
   Map 2, used courtesy of Sandra Smith, designer and project manager for Spark Design, formerly BC Design Works (www.SparkDesignCo.com); available online at http://www.tourismsmithers.com/images/map.gif.
   Map 3, "Trails of the Smithers Community Forest," from Tourism Smithers; available online at http://www.tourismsmithers.com/about/maps-trail-guides/. Used under a Creative Commons licence.
   Map 4, courtesy of Bill Tipton, chief cartographer, Compart Maps; available online at http://www.idcurrent.com/images/bourque_steel_map.jpg.
   "Imagining a Sense of Place": Photos are used courtesy of Susan Duncan.

CHAPTER 12   Figure 12.2, "Evaluating Resources on Canadian Explorers," is adapted by permission of the publisher from John Harrison, Neil Smith, and Ian Wright, eds., *Selected Critical Challenges in Social Studies—Intermediate/Middle School* (Richmond, BC: The Critical Thinking Consortium, 2004), 81. © 2004 The Critical Thinking Consortium.
   Figure 12.3, "Assessing Students' Notes," is adapted by permission of the publisher from Jan Nicol and Roland Case, eds., *The Resourcefulness of the Inuit* (Richmond, BC: The Critical Thinking Consortium), 116. © 2002 Ministry of Education, Province of British Columbia.

CHAPTER 16   "The Eporuvians Come to Call": The Eporuvian role play was developed by Anne Hill, an elementary teacher in Terrace, BC. Used by permission.

CHAPTER 17   "Believe it or Not" is reprinted by permission of the publisher from Jan Nicol and Roland Case, eds., *The Resourcefulness of the Inuit* (Richmond, BC: The Critical Thinking Consortium), 95. © 2002 Ministry of Education, Province of British Columbia.

CHAPTER 18   This chapter is reprinted by permission of the author from Robert Fowler and Ian Wright, eds., *Thinking Globally about Social Studies Education* (Vancouver, BC: Research and Development in Global Studies, University of British Columbia), 51–60. © 1995.

CHAPTER 19   Figure 19.1, "Drawing the Line on Our Right to Food," is adapted by permission of the publisher from Jan Nicol and Dan Kirk, *Caring for Young People's Rights* (Richmond, BC: The Critical Thinking Consortium), 79. © 2004 The Critical Thinking Consortium.

CHAPTER 21   Figure 21.1, "Consequences for Stakeholders," is adapted by permission of the publisher from Roland Case, Cliff Falk, Neil Smith, and Walt Werner, *Active Citizenship: Student Action Projects* (Richmond, BC: The Critical Thinking Consortium), 55. © 2004 The Critical Thinking Consortium.
   Figure 21.2, "Action Plan," is adapted by permission of the publisher from Roland Case et al., *Active Citizenship: Student Action Projects* (Richmond, BC: The Critical Thinking Consortium), 57. © 2004 The Critical Thinking Consortium.
   Figure 21.3, "Reflecting on Our Project," is adapted by permission of the publisher from Roland Case et al., *Active Citizenship: Student Action Projects* (Richmond, BC: The Critical Thinking Consortium), 69. © 2004 The Critical Thinking Consortium.

CHAPTER 23 Figure 23.6, "Sample Unit Plan," is adapted from Atul Bahl and Roland Case, eds., Recognizing an Historical Injustice: Canada's First National Internment Operations, 1914–1920 (Vancouver: The Critical Thinking Consortium, 2015). ©2015 The Critical Thinking Consortium and the Canadian First World War Internment Recognition Fund.

"The Descent of the Fraser River" is a shortened version of "The Descent of the Fraser River" in M.G. Parks and C.W. Jefferys, illus. *Discoverers and Explorers in Canada—1763–1911* Portfolio II #4 (Imperial Oil Ltd., n.d.). Reprinted by permission.

CHAPTER 24 This chapter is used by permission of the author. An earlier edition appeared online in *Canadian Social Studies* 39 (2). © 2005 *Canadian Social Studies,* www.quasar.ualberta.ca/css.

CHAPTER 25 Blackline Master 25.5, "Living Conditions of the Nlaka'pamux by 1878," is adapted by permission of the author from "The Fraser Canyon encountered," in Cole Harris, *The Resettlement of British Columbia: Essays on Colonialism and Geographical Change* (Vancouver: UBC Press) 103–136. © 1997 Cole Harris.

CHAPTER 26 Alan Sears' account of his experiences using local experts is used by permission of the author from "Using interviews in social studies" in Roland Case and Penney Clark, eds., *The Canadian Anthology of Social Studies* (Vancouver: Pacific Educational Press), 221–225. © 1999 Roland Case and Penney Clark.

CHAPTER 27 Figure 27.1, "Identifying Perspectives," is adapted from Catriona Misfeldt and Roland Case, eds., *Immigration in 20th century Canada* (Richmond, BC: The Critical Thinking Consortium), 87. © 2007 Ministry of Education, Province of British Columbia.

"Personalizing the Past" is used by permission from *Open Hearts—Closed Doors: The War Orphans Project.* © 2002, Vancouver Holocaust Education Centre, wwwkvhec.org. *Open Hearts—Closed Doors* website: http://www.virtualmuseum.ca/Exhibitions/orphans/english. Learning resources developed by Frieda Miller. The Vancouver Holocaust Education Centre gratefully acknowledges the financial investment by the Department of Canadian Heritage in the creation of this online presentation for the Virtual Museum of Canada.

Figure 27.2, "Using Multiple Sources": This task and the accompanying documents are used by permission from the 2003 Begbie Canadian History Contest. Used by permission from Charles Hou, ed., *The Begbie Canadian History Contest: The First Ten Years* (Vancouver: The Begbie Contest Society), 275–279. © 2004, The Begbie Contest Society.

CHAPTER 28 The photo "The shame of the city: Can we give our children no better playing space?" is reprinted courtesy Library and Archives Canada (C-030947).

The photo "Indians shamming to be at prayer for the sake of photography. Fraser River" is reprinted courtesy British Columbia Archives (E-04419). Used by permission.

The photo "Hon. Donald A. Smith driving the last spike to complete the Canadian Pacific Railway" by Alexander Ross is reprinted courtesy Library and Archives Canada (C-003693).

The photo "Hon. Donald A. Smith driving the last spike to complete the Canadian Pacific Railway" by Alexander Ross is reprinted courtesy Library and Archives Canada (C-014115).

The photo "Canoe manned by voyageurs passing a waterfall" is reprinted courtesy Library and Archives Canada (C-002771).

The illustration "A Jesuit Preaching to the Indians" by C.W. Jefferys is reprinted courtesy Library and Archives Canada (ICON113250).

CHAPTER 33 Figure 33.1, "Sample Notes," is adapted from Jan Nicol and Roland Case, eds., *The Resourcefulness of the Inuit* (Richmond: The Critical Thinking Consortium), 110. © 2002 Ministry of Education, Province of British Columbia.

Figure 33.3, "Self-Assessment of Role Play," is adapted by permission from Don Northey, Jan Nicol, and Roland Case, eds., *Brazilian Rain Forest* (Richmond, BC: The Critical Thinking Consortium), 106. © 2003 Ministry of Education, Province of British Columbia.

Figure 33.4, "Assessing Students' Self-Assessment of their Role Play Performance," is adapted with permission from Don Northey et al., eds., *Brazilian Rain Forest* (Richmond, BC: The Critical Thinking Consortium), 113. © 2003 Ministry of Education, Province of British Columbia.

CHAPTER 34 Figure 34.1, "Recognizing Levels of Globalization," is adapted by permission from Jan Nicol and Roland Case, eds., *Globalizing Connections: Canada and the Developing World* (Vancouver: The Critical Thinking Consortium), 32. © 2008 The Critical Thinking Consortium.

Figure 34.2, "Sample Multiple Choice Questions," is used by permission from *The Begbie Canadian History Contest: Years Eleven to Fifteen* (Vancouver: The Begbie Contest Society), 89, 96, 94. © 2008 The Begbie Contest Sociery.

Contributors

EDITORS

ROLAND CASE is the co-founder and executive director of The Critical Thinking Consortium. Prior to this he was a professor of social studies education at Simon Fraser University. Roland has edited or authored over one hundred published works. In addition to teaching elementary school and at four Canadian universities as a professor, Roland has worked with eighteen thousand classroom teachers across Canada, and in the United States, England, Israel, Russia, India, Finland, and Hong Kong to support the infusion of critical thinking into classrooms. Roland is the 2006 recipient of the Distinguished Academics Career Achievement Award sponsored by the Confederation of University Faculty Associations of British Columbia.

PENNEY CLARK is a professor in the Department of Curriculum & Pedagogy at the University of British Columbia and director of The History Education Network/Histoire et éducation en réseau (THEN/HiER) (www.thenhier.ca). She is co-editor of the journal *Historical Studies in Education/ Revue d'histoire de l'éducation*. She is the author of numerous educational boooks and has contributed articles to *The History of the Book in Canada*, Volumes II and III, *Canadian Journal of Education, American Journal of Education, Journal of Canadian Studies, Theory and Research in Social Education, History of Education* (UK), *Revue Internationale*, and *History of Education Quarterly*. She is editor of *New Possibilities for the Past: Shaping History Education in Canada* (Vancouver: UBC Press, 2011). Her awards include the Faculty of Education Killam Teaching Prize (2006), the BC Social Studies Teachers' Association Innovator of the Year Award (2008), and the Education 100 Award (2015). She has received publication awards from the Canadian History of Education Association (2012) and the Canadian Association for Foundations in Education (2013).

AUTHORS

WAYNE ANDREW was the Ontario representative to the Canadian Council for Geographic Education and the author of textbooks such as the InfoCanada Geographical Regions series, which he co-authored with Andrew Griffin. He taught geography for a long time and then became a teacher-librarian in the Ontario school system.

MARY-WYNNE ASHFORD is a retired physician and an adjunct professor at the University of Victoria who has been writing and speaking on peace and disarmament internationally for the past thirty years. She was president of the International Physicians for the Prevention of Nuclear War and of the Canadian Physicians for Global Survival. She has received many awards for her work on peace and disarmament, including the Queen's Medal from the Governor General of Canada.

KAMILLA BAHBAHANI has taught at the post-secondary level in education and geography, and has written for The Critical Thinking Consortium. She is involved in a range of research and writing projects on citizenship education, the former Soviet Union, and social networking and relationships. She started Beyond Diversity Consulting with the goal of facilitating individual and social transformation.

PHILIP BALCAEN is an associate professor at the University of British Columbia–Okanagan in Kelowna, where he teaches methods courses in mathematics and science education and graduate courses in curriculum studies. Previously, he taught at Simon Fraser University and in the public secondary school system in British Columbia. His research interests include school-university collaboration, critical thinking, and e-learning communities.

WANDA CASSIDY is an associate professor of social studies education and director of the Centre for Education, Law, and Society at Simon Fraser University. The latter is an endowed centre established to improve the legal literacy of children and youth through a program of research, teaching, curriculum development, and community-based initiatives. Her research focusses on: law-related, citizenship, human rights, and social justice education; cyber-bullying, cyber-civility, and social media issues at the K–12 and post-secondary levels; and the ethics of care, marginalized youth, and school culture. She received the Isidore Starr Award for Excellence in Law-Related Education from the American Bar Association Public Education Division in 2011.

LEROI DANIELS was a professor emeritus in the Faculty of Education at the University of British Columbia at the time of his death in 2011. He was a founding member of The Critical Thinking Consortium and an author of the model of critical thinking that forms the conceptual foundation of the consortium's work. Roi wrote various articles on critical thinking and was co-editor of Critical Challenges Across the Curriculum, a series of teaching resources for critical thinking.

MIKE DENOS taught high school in Vancouver for over thirty years, serving also as a social studies department head. He has been a faculty associate and consultant in education at Simon Fraser University, and he was a lecturer and faculty advisor in the Faculty of Education at the University of British Columbia.

CHRISTINE EIDE emigrated from Holland to northern British Columbia when she twelve years old. At age fifteen she found a job working in a Hudson's Bay trading post. After university, Christine taught in a number of communities spanning a range of grade levels. She was a faculty associate in Simon Fraser's teacher education program in northwestern British Columbia and, before retiring, she was the practicum placement coordinator with the University of Northern British Columbia.

MARGARET FERGUSON is a teacher in northern British Columbia. She has a law degree from the University of Alberta. She was school reorganizing coordinator for the Legal Resource Centre, Faculty of Extension, University of Alberta for thirteen years, and has published numerous articles on law-related education.

JOHN FIELDING has retired from teaching Canadian and World History Curriculum at the Faculty of Education of Queen's University after thirteen years. Prior to Queen's, John taught secondary school history for twenty-four years. John was the project manager for Ontario's Canadian and World Studies Curriculum. He has written several textbooks, designed numerous learning resources, and consulted widely on the teaching of Canadian history and global issues.

SUSAN GIBSON is a professor emeritus in elementary social studies in the Faculty of Education at the University of Alberta. Her major research interest involved examining how technology can be used effectively to enhance learning and how best to prepare pre-service teachers for the integration of technology into the teaching of social studies.

GARFIELD GINI-NEWMAN is an associate professor at OISE/University of Toronto. Previously he was a curriculum consultant with the York Region District School Board. During that time, he led teams in the development of history and philosophy curriculum for at-risk learners in grades 10, 11, and 12. He has spoken widely at conferences on critical thinking, brain research, curriculum design, and assessment. Garfield has also authored six textbooks and has taught in the faculties of education at York University and the University of British Columbia. Garfield taught high school history for many years.

LAURA GINI-NEWMAN is a facilitator and consultant with The Critical Thinking Consortium. Previously she was the instructional coordinator for Canada and World Studies and the social sciences with the Peel District School Board. Prior to entering education, she did doctoral studies in economics, attended law school, and was employed as a chartered accountant. She taught for eleven years in the public education system and was an instructor for advanced qualification history courses at OISE/University of Toronto. Laura is a senior author of *Philosophy: Questions and Theories*.

ANDREW GRIFFIN is a geography teacher at Thomas A. Stewart Secondary School in Peterborough. He has worked on curriculum implementation with students of all ability levels and co-authored the InfoCanada Geographical Regions series with Wayne Andrews.

SUSAN HARGRAVES is a secondary school teacher in Victoria, British Columbia. She has been involved in the design and development of a number of curriculum projects dealing with social justice issues.

MICHAEL LING is a senior lecturer in the Faculty of Education at Simon Fraser University. He works primarily with in-service teachers in graduate diploma and degree programs. He is interested in what occurs at the intersection of culture, education, and the arts, in the ways they contribute to our collective and individual pursuit of meaning in the world, and to a meaningful life.

CATHY MORGAN began teaching primary grades in a small northern community in British Columbia in 1971. She has taught at the elementary and secondary levels. For several years, Cathy was a faculty associate in Simon Fraser University's professional development program, where she worked with aboriginal and non-aboriginal student teachers.

TOM MORTON is one of the founders of the British Columbia Co-operative Learning Association and is the author of *Co-operative Learning and Social Studies: Towards Excellence and Equity* (Kagan Cooperative Learning). During his teaching career he received the BC Social Studies Teachers' Association Teacher of the Year award, the Kron Award for Excellence in Holocaust Education, and the Governor General's Award for Excellence in Teaching Canadian History.

JOHN MYERS is a curriculum instructor in elementary and secondary pre-service programs at OISE/University of Toronto. He has taught in elementary, secondary, and university classes in three provinces and three countries. His teaching and research interests include assessment and teaching strategies in differentiated instruction, as well as work in social and emotional learning. In the past five years John has contributed to three national projects dealing with immigration history and policy and their place in the development of anti-racist curricula.

PAUL NEUFELD is the director of professional programs and an associate professor of reading and learning disabilities at Simon Fraser University. His research interests are in the areas of reading development and instruction for students who struggle with learning to read, and more generally on addressing the needs of students who have historically not been supported well in schools.

LYNN NEWBERY graduated from the University of Toronto in the mid-1960s. She moved to a coastal community in British Columbia where she first discovered the excitement of teaching about First Nations history and culture. She has held teaching or administrative positions in secondary and elementary schools and been active in the communities in which she has lived. After retiring from the public school system, Lynn became a faculty associate at Simon Fraser University, working with student teachers.

KEN OSBORNE is professor emeritus, University of Manitoba. He is a prolific writer of school textbooks and academic publications. Ken is the recipient of the Prix Manitoba Award for Heritage Education. His books include *Education: A Guide to the Canadian School Debate* (Penguin) and *In Defense of History: Teaching the Past and the Meaning of Democratic Citizenship* (Our Schools/Our Selves).

STUART POYNTZ is an associate professor in the School of Communication at Simon Fraser University. His research addresses children's media cultures, theories of public life, and urban youth media production. He has recently completed a nationally funded research project, Youth Digital Media Ecologies in Canada, and will begin a new research program on Youthsites: Informal Learning, the State, and Networks of Culture. His two most recent books are *Media Literacies: A Critical Introduction* (Wiley-Blackwell, 2012) and *Phenomenology of Youth Cultures and Globalization* (Routledge, 2015). He has published widely in national and international peer-reviewed journals, including the *Journal of Children and Media*, *Cultural Studies*, the *Journal of Youth Studies*, the *Review of Education, Pedagogy and Cultural Studies*, and the *Canadian Journal of Education*, as well as various edited collections.

RUTH SANDWELL is an associate professor in the Department of Curriculum, Teaching and Learning at the Ontario Institute for Studies in Education at the University of Toronto. She is a Canadian rural, educational, and energy historian who has also written articles and book chapters about history teaching from elementary to post-secondary levels. Her recent books include *Canada's Rural Majority, 1870–1940: Households, Environments, Economies* (Toronto: University of Toronto Press, 2016) and Ruth Sandwell and Amy von Heyking, eds., *Becoming a History Teacher: Sustaining Practices in Historical Thinking and Knowing* (Toronto: University of Toronto Press, 2014). She is founding co-director and educational director of the award-winning Great Unsolved Mysteries in Canadian History project.

AVNER SEGALL is a professor of teacher education at Michigan State University. He is interested in how particular versions and visions of education, teaching, and learning are made possible during pre-service teacher education as well as what they make possible for students learning to teach. His research interests focus on secondary social studies education, critical theory and pedagogy, cultural studies, media education, and qualitative research methods.

ÖZLEM SENSOY is an associate professor in the Faculty of Education at Simon Fraser University, where she teaches courses in social justice education, critical media literacy, and anti-racism education. She is the co-author of the award-winning books *Is Everyone Really Equal? An Introduction to Key Concepts in Social Justice Education* and *Rethinking Popular Culture and Media*.

STEFAN STIPP has taught secondary humanities in Surrey, British Columbia, for eighteen years. He is an occasional instructor of social studies at the University of the Fraser Valley and has been a faculty associate in Simon Fraser University's teacher education program. Additional background about his work with portfolio assessment can be found in his master's thesis, "Tilling the Soil: Making Portfolio Assessment Work in an Integrated High School Humanities Setting."

KENDALL TAYLOR was for many years Geography Head at Thomas A. Stewart Secondary School in Peterborough, Ontario. Kendall has served as an executive member of the Ontario Association for Geographic and Environmental Education as well as providing leadership through newsletters and workshops at his school.

WALT WERNER is a retired associate professor in the Faculty of Education, University of British Columbia and a former social studies teacher. His research interests have included visual literacy across the curriculum, global education, and subject area integration.

SERINA YOUNG received her training as a social studies teacher from the Faculty of Education at Simon Fraser University. She has taught for many years in the Vancouver School Board.

Index

Italicized page numbers indicate figures and tables. Endnotes are indicated by "n" after the page number.

critical thinking *(continued)*
    as general goal of curriculum, 19, *251,* 252
    in geography, 109–15, *353–54*
    intellectual tools for, 77–81, 85
    and internet, 152, *153*
    investigation strategies, 145–47
    with limited background knowledge, 51–52
    as part of intellectual development, 32–33
    and primary sources, 302–3, 304–5
    questions for, 43–46, 82–83, *142,* 142–45
    rationale for, *34*
    and reflection, 145
    in research papers, 390–91
    and role play, 48, 273
    in sample First Nations lesson, 275, 279–82
    and seeing history as process, 304–5
    and social initiation, 29–30
    as societal goal, 78
    and student engagement, 141–42, *143*
    and studying law, 199–200
    teaching activities for, 45–46, 47–48
    teaching strategies for, 46–49, 91–95, 145–46, 313
    thinking strategies for, 75–76, 79, 81, 95
    in unit plan, *257*
    and values, 176–79, 180–81
    and visual materials, 271, 309, 312, 313, 315, *316*–18
The Critical Thinking Consortium, 53n3, 53n4
critiquing, 47, 94
cross-cultural awareness, 177, 184. *See also* multiculturalism
culminating tasks, 391–93
cultural history, 6
culture
    global view of, 185–86, 187
    and stereotyping, 188–89
current affairs, 185, 193–94
curricula
    based on inquiry questions, 143–44
    and big ideas, 18
    breadth vs. depth, 10
    and course planning, 249–52
    and defining purpose of social studies, 16
    and general goals, 19–20
    of historical thinking course, 103–6
    as huge puzzle, 15, *16*
    and new history, 8
    organizing themes, 21
    and priority goals, 252
    and program rationale, 21, 23, 250–52
    for student-centred classes, 31
    underlying themes, 20–21
    and unit development, 253–60
    and use of specific learning outcomes, 16–18
    See also covering the curriculum
curriculum goals
    and course planning, 250

and educational philosophy, 25
need for clear direction in, 33, 35
rationale for, 25–29, *34*
and research papers, 129–30

D
data charts
    in First Nations sample lesson, *276, 281*
    in geography, 350, *351*
    and lesson plans, 264, *266*
    for research papers, 134, *135*
    for visual materials, *319*
databases, 152, 154
debates, 90, 148, 270
debriefing
    after peer review, 381
    after role play/tableaux, 216, 273
    in lesson plans, 263, *265*
decision making
    assessment of, *390*
    in classroom as community, 89
    and computers, 156
    and role play, 272
    in teacher-directed classes, 87
    teaching activities for, 353
democracy
    and citizenship, 3–4, 9–10, 12–13, 199
    in the classroom, 12–13, 207
    and computers, 158
    and historical thinking, 11
Denos, Mike (teaching story), 97
Dewey, John, 42, 50, 233
dialogue approach, 11–12
differentiated assessment, 148
disabled students, 152, 158, 233
discipline, 87
disciplines approach, 32
discrepant event, 259
discussion
    in co-operative learning, 235
    in history class, 271
    of global problems, 194, 195, 196
    teaching strategies for, 93
    u-shape forum, 270–71
    whole class, 93–94
displays, 259
distance education, 92
diversity, 23, 189, 249
drama, 174
dualisms and stereotyping, 189
Duke, Daniel, 170–71
Duplass, James, 18
Durkin, Delores, 161

development of, 4–6, 119–22
and factual knowledge, 8, 9, 10
and field trips, 270
fragmentation of, 6–7
great man theory of, 4, 8, 30
ignorance of, 41
importance of primary sources to, 295–96, *296–97,* 298, 304–5
and literature, 121–22, 323–29
military, 5, 69
from mock trials, 202
and naming power, 124–25
and nation states, 4–5
and new history, 7–9, 10
of peace education, 210–11
primary sources in, 298, 300–303
resources of historical literature, 330–35
revisionist, 119–20
sample lesson on First Nations, 275–82
and science, 120–21
seen as interpretation not fact, 304–5
and social action, 226
and stories, 5, 6–7, 323–29
and student engagement, 269–74
taught separately, 32–33
teaching strategies for, 125–26, 271–74
from visual materials, 270, 309–15, *317,* 336–45
See also historical thinking; narrative history
Hodgetts, A.B., 5
holistic scales, 375–76, *377*
hope and sense of global chaos, 193–96, 210
How We Think (Dewey), 42

I

identity, 7, 9, 61
If This Is Social Studies, Why Isn't It Boring? (Steffay and Hood), 16
imagination, student engagement of, 269, 271–74
importance in geographical thinking, 111–*12,* 117
in-class observations, 386, 389
individual accountability in co-operative learning, 235, 237, 241
industry groups, 291, 292
inert knowledge, 42
informal curriculum, 207
information gathering
    compared to understanding, 42–43, 97
    and computers, 152–54, 157
    as general goal of curriculum, 19, *251,* 252
    geography exercises for, *110*
    questions for, 144
    and rationale for, *34*
    and recording information, 130, 134–36, 288
    for research papers, 133–36
    skills for, 152
    and social action, 222, 226–28
    teaching strategies for, 134–36
    in unit plan, *257*
    See also note-taking; recording information
information sources
    and computers, 152–54, 157
    on global issues, 194–95
    for research papers, 130, 131–33, 146
    students as, 52
    See also teaching resources
inquiry
    compared to research, 98–99, *99*
    geography taught as, 109, *110*
    reflective, 35n2
    and unit planning, 143–44
    See also critical thinking; historical thinking
Inspiration (website), 154
integration of subjects, 8, 69, 288, 357–58
intellectual development
    and curriculum goals, *34*
    in general planning, 248
    as underlying rationale of social studies, 26–28, 32–33
interactions
    in critical thinking classroom, 94
    interdisciplinary studies, 8, 69, 288, 357–58
    role in geographical thinking, 113–14, 117
internet
    benefits and uses of, 151–52
    and communication, 156–58, 159
    and film inaccuracies, 341
    and geography sources, *352,* 353
    and information gathering, 152–54, 157
    and primary sources, 298, 306–7
    and problem solving, 155–56, 157, 158
    and research papers, 132
    and visual resources, 321
    website publishing, 154–55
interpretation
    developments in, 119–22
    in film, 340
    role in geographical thinking, 111, 113, 117
    role in historical thinking, 100, 101, 106, 304–5
    See also perspective; point of view
interviews, 289, *290,* 291

J

Jackdaws series, 298
journals, 289, 298, 363
judging in critical thinking, 47
justice circle, 205, 206
Justice Denied (film), 214

K

Kindred, Hugh, 199
knowledge, 19, 20, 50, 55, 126. *See also* background information; content knowledge
Knowledge Forum (KF) software, 92

and brainstorming, 258, 259
and critical thinking, *257*
deciding on focus for, 253–56
historical thinking course, 103–6
introducing units, 258–60
and objectives, 256, *257*, 259, 260, *261–62*
outlining, 258–60
sample units, *257, 261*
and teaching activities, 256, 258–60, *261–62*
teaching resources for, 258, *261–62*
and teaching techniques, 258, *261–62*
types of organizers for, 255–56
u-shape forum for discussion, 270–71

V

validity in assessment, 361–63, *366*, 386
value judgments, 115, 117
values, 170–81
    analysis, 176–79
    clarification of, 176, 177
    coat of arms project, 177–78
    controversy over teaching, 170–71, 173
    deciding which to teach, 172–73
    influence of teachers on, 172–73
    teaching activities for, 176, 177–78
    teaching strategies for, 173–79
    See also personal values; social values
values clarification movement, 32
Venn diagrams, 64n1, 146, *147,* 164
victimology, 8, 9
video technology
    and computers, 155, 158, 159
    and co-operative learning, 241
    on field trips, 288–89
See also visual materials
video-conferencing, 158
violence, 210–11, 212
virtual experiences, 153, 292, 293
virtual learning communities, 92
virtual websites, 153–54
vision for better future, 195
visual materials
    assessment of, in reports, 138, 139
    and background information, 52, 318

and computers, 151, 153–54, 155–59
and co-operative learning, 238, 241
and critical thinking, 271, 309, 312, 313, 315, 316–18, *316, 317*
on field trips, 288–89
First Nations, 70, 174, 214, 310–12, *317*
follow-up activities, 319
in geography activities, 115, *116*
for history, 270, 309–15, *317,* 336–45
to introduce unit, 259
in oral reports, 137
paintings and photographs, 308–15
and perspective, 309–13, 317
preparation for using, 318–19, *320*
for research papers, 132, 146
Suburb of Happy Homes illustration, 45–46
for teaching about racism, 67
teaching activities with, 309, 312, *317, 320*
teaching resources for, 321–22
teaching strategies for, 318–19
and understanding concepts, 62
visual organizers, 164
visual summaries, 164
visualization, 195

W

Wasserman, Selma, 18
webbing, 130, *131,* 240
webcams, 159
WebQuest, 156, 157, 159, 293
website publishing, 154–55, 157
Werner, Walter, 30, 111, 123–24
What Culture? What Heritage? (Hodgetts), 5
What is History? (Carr), 296
Where the Spirit Lives (film), 174
Whitehead, Alfred N., 42
Wiggins, Grant, 18
Wilson, Marie, 68
Windschuttle, Keith, 6
women in history, 4, 6
writing
    assessment of, 138–40, 363, 383–86
    research papers, 136–37
    summaries, 164
Wrong, George, 41